Travellers **S**urvival **K**it

Australia & New Zealand

SUSAN GRIFFITH &
SIMON CALDER

REVISED BY
TIM RYDER

Published by
VACATION WORK, 9 PARK END STREET, OXFORD

TRAVELLERS SURVIVAL KIT
AUSTRALIA & NEW ZEALAND
by Susan Griffith and Simon Calder

First published 1988
Second edition 1992
Third edition 1996
Reprinted 1997

ISBN 1 85458 145 7

Publicity: Roger Musker

Cover Design:
Mel Calman
Miller Craig & Cocking Design Partnership

Maps of Australia and Sydney by Andrea Pullen

Chapter headings, logos and all other maps by William Swan

Cartoons by Patrick Ayoub

Printed by **Unwin Brothers Ltd,** Old Woking, Surrey, England

Contents

AUSTRALIA

Regions of Australia

Each city is dealt with as follows: City Layout — Arrival and Departure — City Transport — Accommodation — Eating and Drinking — Exploring — Shopping — Entertainment — Sport — Crime and Safety — Help and Information — Work

NEW ZEALAND

Preface

The Antipodes have bred a new type of traveller who might loosely be described as the 'yuppie backpacker'. Travelling independently on a low budget has acquired a new image. A person staying at hostels and travelling on a bus pass is as likely to be a German lawyer or Canadian environmentalist as a student. The range of facilities that has been developed in recent years to cater to this discerning traveller-on-a-budget is a sign of how well the tourist establishment in Australia and New Zealand understands and is in sympathy with the travelling style of the 1990s. Crude mass tourism is barely in evidence. The abundant opportunities to experience the flora and fauna and the amazing landscapes both marine and terrestrial often incorporate an admirable level of respect for the natural environment.

This book has become progressively less about 'survival' and more a kit to help you enjoy Australia and New Zealand to the full. Certainly there is no shortage of nasties to avoid, from spiders to crocodiles, riptides to rip-offs. But the great majority of local people will try to ensure that you find your way around their marvellous countries not only in safety but in the most interesting ways. Visitors encounter a phenomenal degree of generosity and hospitality from the locals, whether from a bus driver who directs you on your way, a farmer who gives you a temporary job or a friend-of-a-friend who lets you borrow the family car. Word is getting around: with far more than their fair share of colourful characters and natural wonders, these familiar yet delightfully alien and unpredictable countries can offer a uniquely enjoyable and satisfying holiday.

Whether you intend merely to dip a toe in the Pacific Ocean or to immerse yourself in the culture by finding a job (perhaps with a view to starting a new life down under), the *Travellers Survival Kit: Australia and New Zealand* will help you to locate real bargains in travel, accommodation and entertainment, and the best ways to explore the Great Outdoors. It tries to encourage you to step off the conveyor belt and put yourself in the way of chance meetings that might lead to a lift on a prawn trawler, a wool train or a flying doctor's light aircraft. Go for it.

Simon Calder and Susan Griffith

Acknowledgements

Many individuals and organisations have co-operated with the revision of this book. Substantial contributions, for which we are very grateful, were made by:

Carolyn Ackers, Graeme Beavis, Dianne Chester, Jennifer Gillan, Carole Knight, Thomas Konieczny, Matt Maurer, Prue Richard, Anne Robertson, Nina Rodsjo, Jon Rouse, Jan Simpson, Roger Stanton, Cecilia Sterk, Anne Weddle, Kathy Williams.

While every effort has been made to ensure that the information contained in this book is as up-to-date as possible, some details are bound to change within the lifetime of this edition, and readers are strongly advised to check facts and credentials themselves.

The *Travellers Survival Kit: Australia and New Zealand* is revised regularly. We are keen to hear comments, criticisms and suggestions from both natives and travellers. Please write to Susan Griffith and Simon Calder at Vacation Work, 9 Park End Street, Oxford OX1 1HJ. Those whose contributions are used will be sent a complimentary copy of the next edition.

BEFORE YOU GO

RED TAPE

Passports. A full ten-year passport is required for travel to both Australia and New Zealand. Application forms are available from post offices and should be sent with the appropriate fee, photographs and supporting documents to your regional passport office. Allow at least one month for processing by mail. If you're in a tearing hurry or realise your existing passport is soon to expire, you can obtain one more quickly in person if you're prepared to queue all day at a passport office. The London Passport Office (Clive House, 70 Petty France, London SW1) is for personal callers only.

For visits to both countries, your passport should have a minimum of six months to run and have two blank facing pages for the visa and entry/departure stamps.

If your passport is lost or stolen while travelling, first contact the police and then your nearest consulate. Obtaining replacement travel documents is easier if you have kept a separate record of the passport number and its date and place of issue.

Visas for Australia. Holders of New Zealand passports, and members of the British Royal Family, need no visas. All other intending visitors require one. It must be obtained in advance, which you can do through the High Commission, a consulate or even the Qantas office in Birmingham. Addresses are as follows:

Visa Section, Australian High Commission, Strand, London WC2B 4LA (0171-887 5107); Australian Consulate, Chatsworth House, Lever St, Manchester M1 2DL (0161-228 1344); Australian Consulate, 80 Hanover St, Edinburgh EH2 2DL (0131-226 6271); Qantas, 36 Union St, Birmingham B2 4SR (0121-643 4946).

Irish Republic: Australian Embassy, Wilton Terrace, Dublin 2 (761517).

United States: Australian Embassy, 1601 Massachusetts Ave, Washington, DC 20036-2273 (202-797-3000); or Consulates in Chicago, Honolulu, Houston, Los Angeles, New York and San Francisco.

Canada: Australian High Commission, 50 O'Connor St, Ottawa K1P 6L2 (613-236-0841); or consulates in Toronto and Vancouver.

New Zealand: Australian High Commission, 72–78 Hobson St, Thorndon (PO Box 4036), Wellington (04-473 6411).

Those seeking a Working Holiday Visa should see page 46. Prospective migrants are dealt with below. Most people, however, need just a visitor visa.

Visitor Visas: a separate form is required for each traveller. Two application forms are incorporated in the Australian Tourist Commission brochure, *A Travellers Guide.* Alternatively, British residents can get forms by sending a 9x12 stamped addressed envelope to Australian Outlook, 3 Buckhurst Road, Bexhill-on-Sea, TN40 1QF. Otherwise request a form from an Australian diplomatic mission (see addresses above).

Complete the visa application form as truthfully as possible, including the questions on criminal convictions and contagious diseases. The Australian authorities sometimes go to great lengths to check the veracity of your replies. They may, for example, phone your employer for confirmation of your story.

Fees: there are no charges for visas for single visits of less than three months for either tourists or business travellers if they are obtained direct from an Australian consulate. However, you may find it more convenient under new arrangements to pay £14 to obtain one from one of the list of approved travel operators, which includes Austravel, STA Travel, Trailfinders, Travelbag and Travelmood. For details of charges for multiple-entry visas etc. and other visa information in the UK call the premium-rate recorded message service on 0891-600 333.

Visa Issue: submit the form with your passport and a photograph. Processing time for postal applications is about two weeks assuming your documents are in order. Visitor visas can be obtained on-the-spot at High Commissions and Consulates, which also allows any problems to be sorted out on-the-spot. Visa office hours vary: in London and Edinburgh they are 10am–4pm, in Manchester 9.30am–3.30pm.

In general a visitor visa is valid for a year from the date of issue, but allows a stay of only six months. Young people under 25 who state on the form that they intend to spend several months may well be asked for documentary proof that they have sufficient funds.

Visas for New Zealand. Holders of British, Irish, Canadian or US passports need no visa for short tourist or business visits to New Zealand, providing they carry proof of onward or return travel and have sufficient funds to support themselves for their period of stay (NZ$1000 per month, unless they have a sponsorship form signed by a New Zealand resident, in which case the monthly sum required is $400). British passport holders are generally allowed to stay 6 months, other nationalities 3 months. If you enter the country on a return ticket and decide for some reason not to leave on the ticket you presented at immigration (e.g. perhaps you want to crew on a yacht across the Pacific), you will have problems cashing in the return half of your ticket. Airlines are not permitted to do this unless you can prove that you have resident's status.

Information about work visas and work permits is contained in the section *Work* in the New Zealand introductory chapter. Travellers intending to stay longer than 3 or 6 months, or who are considering emigration should consult a New Zealand High Commission or Consulate such as:

United Kingdom: Immigration Service, New Zealand House, Haymarket, London SW1Y 4TE (0171-973 0368/9)
United States: New Zealand Embassy, 37 Observatory Circle NW, Washington, DC 20008 (202-328-4848)
Canada: New Zealand High Commission, Suite 801, Metropolitan House, 99 Bank St, Ottawa, K1P 6G3 (613-238-5991)
Australia: New Zealand High Commission, Commonwealth Avenue, Canberra, ACT 2600 (06-273 3611); Immigration Service, New Zealand Consulate General, Level 14, 1 Alfred St, Sydney, NSW 2000 (02-9247 1999).

Migration. If you enter either country as a tourist (or Australia on a working holiday visa), you will not be able to apply for permanent residence unless you get married to a citizen of the country you choose, and furthermore can provide to the satisfaction of the authorities that it is not a marriage of convenience.

Failing that, if you wish to migrate you must approach the authorities well in advance of your intended departure.

For nearly 200 years, almost any British subject could obtain the right of residence in Australia and New Zealand. Many enjoyed free or cheap travel to Australia whether as convicts or as beneficiaries of the 'assisted passage' scheme under which you could travel to Australia for just £10. Now things are much tougher. The governments set quotas (e.g. 126,000 in Australia in 1991) and establish rigorous requirements. To be chosen from the million-plus who apply to live in Australia each year, you need to score a high number of points gained by such attributes as age, higher education and a skill such as computer programming or occupational therapy. It is also of considerable benefit if you have family in Australia willing to sponsor you, even more so if they live in less-popular areas (i.e. *outside* New South Wales, Victoria and urbanised parts of Western Australia and Queensland). The first step is to acquire form 802 from the High Commission *Preliminary Enquiry about Migration to Australia.* British people seeking to move permanently to Australia should write in the first instance to Migration Enquiries, PO Box 1114, Eastbourne, East Sussex BN21 3YU. The cost of application is £169, non-refundable if you fail or your circumstances change.

Similarly, people hoping to be among the 20,000 successful applicants to migrate to New Zealand must jump through a number of hoops before they are accepted. The government has recently switched over to a points system as in Australia, and done away with the old Occupations Priority List. The leaflet *Applying for Residence* is available from New Zealand House. Despite high unemployment, New Zealand is still considered to be underpopulated and the government has just started a dubious immigration campaign to attract more Europeans to apply.

INSURANCE

It is quite possible to survive a trip to Australia and New Zealand without insurance. The most important reason for travel insurance elsewhere in the world is for emergency health care, but emergency treatment in Australia is free for all visitors, and both countries have a reciprocal agreement with the UK whereby free hospital treatment is provided for British citizens. Further details on medical treatment may be found under *Health* in the introductions to both countries.

Crime levels in the Antipodes are relatively low, so insurance against theft might be an expensive luxury. If you have the misfortune to be involved in an accident in New Zealand, you can benefit from the government's Accident Compensation Scheme, which compensates every victim, regardless of the cause or nationality (it does not, however, cover sickness). All in all, it is unlikely that travelling uninsured will bring about financial ruin. Even so, insuring yourself and your possessions can prove beneficial, as only a minimum of care and compensation is provided free of charge. For visitors from North America, who do not benefit from the reciprocal medical agreements, insurance is strongly recommended.

The cover provided varies but the minimum is normally as follows: delay and cancellation insurance of up to £2500; around £250,000 for medical expenses and emergency repatriation; the same amount for personal liability; £20,000 for permanent disablement cover; lost or stolen baggage up to £1000 (sometimes valuable single items are excluded); and cash to a maximum of £250. Every airline, tour operator and travel agent is delighted to sell you insurance because of the high level of commission it earns them (sometimes over 40%).

Shopping around can save money or get you better cover for the same

premium. For example, Columbus Travel Insurance (17 Devonshire Square, London EC2M 4YP; 0171-375 0011) specialises in policies for Australia and New Zealand. Its policies are valid worldwide as long as those two countries are included. The cost is £30 for 31 days, increasing up to £199 for 12 months. Cover includes scuba diving (if you are qualified or under the supervision of a qualified instructor) and white-water rafting. The Travel Insurance Club Ltd (01702-423399) offers insurance packages aimed at the young traveller starting at £18 for 30 days, going up to £165 for a year. This includes access to a 24-hour medical emergency helpline. It is also worth getting a quote from Worldwide

Travel Insurance (PO Box 99, Elm Lane Office, Tonbridge, Kent TN10 3XS; 0173-277 3366).

Americans who purchase an ISIC card (International Student Identity Card) for $14 are automatically covered by a basic accident/sickness insurance package. Contact any Council Travel office.

If you stay longer than expected, you can buy a new policy from any insurance broker in Australia or New Zealand, but note that these policies do not cover the cost of flying you home for medical treatment. You can also insure yourself locally for risky activities such as skiing and scuba diving, for which a more expensive policy covering dangerous sports is required.

For any insurance claim, the golden rule is to amass as much documentation as possible to support your application. In particular, compensation is unlikely to be paid for lost baggage or cash unless your claim is accompanied by a police report of the loss.

GETTING THERE ... AND BACK

For most people, the cost of reaching Australia or New Zealand is the biggest obstacle to going there. Certainly a full-fare return ticket from London to Australia is beyond the budget of most. However price wars mean that fares per mile to the Antipodes are the lowest in the world. A score of airlines will fly you from London to Australasia for between £600 and £1000 return, depending on the time of year. Fares do not differ hugely except around Christmas when shopping around (and shopping early) is especially worthwhile. Your choice of airline will determine the stopovers you may take, from Houston to Honolulu and Bangkok to Bali.

From Britain. *Seasons:* The price is determined by the date of your outward flight. Not surprisingly, everyone seems to want to escape from the Northern Hemisphere to Australasia as soon as temperatures start falling. For flights through Asia, the peak season for outward travel is September plus the two weeks before Christmas. For the lowest price, you should travel out between April and June, the season classed as 'basic'. The next cheapest is 'off-peak', comprising February, March and July. The remaining times are 'shoulder' season, costing a little less than peak. At times you may find it difficult getting a seat: the worst periods are peak season (when it seems everyone wants to travel, regardless of cost) and the first few days after a drop in fares, e.g. early February, April and October. For flights through North America, the basic season is the same but off-peak runs from January to March plus July and

August, shoulder includes October and November, and peak covers all of December as well as September. It is wise to book a seat as early as possible, bearing in mind that you can usually change the date without penalty.

Agencies: To start narrowing down the many permutations of season, route and airline, find a travel agency that specialises in flights to Australia and New Zealand. Consult the advertisements in the quality press or free Antipodean newspapers in London such as *TNT* and *New Zealand News UK*. The following agencies are particularly recommended:

Bridge the World, 1–3 Ferdinand St, Camden Town, London NW1 8ES (0171-911 0900). Very good for cut-price flights and organising individual itineraries. Fast and efficient service.

Flightbookers, 177 Tottenham Court Road, London W1P 0LX (0171-757 2468). Specialises in pre-booking independent travel.

REHO Travel, 15–17 New Oxford St, London WC1A 1BH (0171-242 5555). Also has offices in Melbourne and Sydney.

STA Travel, 74 Old Brompton Road, London SW7 3LH (0171-361 6262). STA has offices throughout Australia and New Zealand, which can be useful if your travel plans change.

Trailfinders, 42–50 Earls Court Road, London W8 6EJ (0171-938 3366). Well respected agency specialising in tailor-made itineraries for independent travellers.

Travel Warehouse, 33 Maddox St, London W1R 9LD (0171-414 8808; fax 0171-414 8848). Specialists in low-cost flights to the Far East, Australasia and around the world; hotels, transfers and group reservations also arranged.

Travelmood, 246 Edgware Road, London W2 1DS (0171-258 0280). An established specialist in travel to Australia and New Zealand.

Scheduled Fares: Many British travellers opt for the fares offered on British Airways, Qantas and Air New Zealand, and sold by these airlines or any travel agent. None of these tickets has any advanced booking requirement.

The cheapest is a Pex ticket allowing one stopover either on the outward or return journey. The lowest fare, a return to Perth from 1 April to 30 June, is £761, while the most expensive (high-season to Auckland and back) is £1365. The Excursion fare, starting at £1010, allows four stopovers in Asia or North America. British Airways and Qantas give away four internal flights, so for no extra cost you can fly Perth–Adelaide–Melbourne–Sydney–Brisbane. Qantas throws in 31 days' free insurance. You can change flight timings (but not routes) at will; the ticket is valid for a year and if you decide to cancel before setting off you can get a full refund. You can also fly in to one city and back from another, and take advantage of free stopovers in Asia or North America.

In response to the intense competition from other carriers, these three airlines feature some excellent promotions to fill up their flights.

Discounted Tickets: London is the cheap fare capital of the world. The choice of route is enormous and most airlines allow stopovers on their route free of charge. For example Lauda Air, which has low fares to Sydney and Melbourne, flies via Vienna and Bangkok and you can break your journey in either city at no extra cost. Good deals are also available on Asian airlines such as Garuda Indonesia, Thai International and Malaysian Airlines, and on the American carriers Continental and United. Most of these services take 28 hours or more from London and require a change of aircraft *en route*, although they also allow some interesting stopovers.

Travelling via the USA on any service other than Air New Zealand's direct London—Auckland flights via Los Angeles, you must hold a valid US visa and pay a range of taxes even if you are only in transit. These will be incorporated into the cost of the ticket and will amount to £34 if you travel to the Antipodes via the States in both directions (£7 arrival tax, £4 departure tax, and £6 security tax, each way). If you don't want a stopover in the USA, bear this extra expense in mind when comparing flight costs.

A good way to visit both Australia and New Zealand is on a round-the-world (RTW) ticket. The lowest fares from discount travel agents (such as those listed above) at the time of going to press were less than £600. For about £900 you can get a RTW discount ticket combining the services of Thai International and Continental that permits stopovers in any or all of the following: Delhi, Bangkok, Sydney, Melbourne, Auckland, Honolulu, Los Angeles or San Francisco and New York. It is much more expensive to fly to the Antipodes via Africa or South America.

Charter Flights: Britannia Airways has a range of charter flights from Manchester or London Gatwick to Cairns, the Gold Coast (Queensland), Canberra, Adelaide, Melbourne, Perth and Auckland. Unfortunately they are available only from August to March. Contact Austravel, 50–51 Conduit St, London W1X 2AN (0171-734 7755). Lowest fares are £619 to Perth, and £719 to Sydney, Adelaide, Brisbane or Melbourne. Various restrictions apply, depending on the length of stay, and the lowest prices generally have the most restrictions attached to them. The only stopovers available are in Hong Kong or Singapore.

Acting as an Air Courier: Casual air couriers who carry the paperwork for air cargo documents are sometimes needed on flights to Sydney or Auckland. However the extra hassle is rarely worthwhile. A return trip to Sydney will cost a maximum of £925 at Christmas and a minimum of £650 during the low season, actually more than the cheapest charter flight. Book 3 months in advance if you want to fly on a specific date. Flights for Christmas are usually full by August each year. Try phoning the first few days of each month as this is when companies begin booking for the following months. A disadvantage of round-trip courier flights is that the length of stay is limited, usually between 7 and 28 days. Couriers are allowed a maximum of 23 kilos of luggage plus hand baggage. The main agencies with courier flights to Sydney or Auckland are:

Courier Travel Services (CTS): 346 Fulham Road, London SW10 9UH (0171-351 0300)
Jupiter Air: Unit 4, Pier Road, North Feltham Trading Estate, Feltham, Middlesex TW14 0TN (0181-751 3323)
Shades International Travel: Unit 6, Drumhill Works, Clayton Lane, Clayton, West Yorkshire BD14 6RF (01274 814727).

From North America. Cities with direct air services to Australia and New Zealand include Vancouver, San Francisco, Los Angeles and Honolulu. The main gateways are Auckland, Christchurch, Cairns, Brisbane, Sydney and Melbourne. Most services are operated by Air New Zealand, Canadian Airlines, Continental, Qantas and United Airlines. The cheapest way to reach Australia or New Zealand is with an advance purchase ticket, which must be bought 3 weeks before travel and has heavy cancellation penalties. From North America, peak season operates during May, August and September, with the lowest fares in March, October and November. Not surprisingly, the cheapest ticket is from Honolulu (about US$500 low season, $750 peak to Auckland); for a return flight between Los Angeles and Sydney, expect to pay at least US$1100. From the East Coast it may be cheapest to go the long way round via Europe, travelling on British Airways or Virgin from Miami, New York or Boston and connecting in London to their Australian services.

Air Passes. For those who have bought a return ticket to a destination in Australasia, several air pass options become available for getting around. One of the best-known is the Ansett *G'Day Pass*, which allows flights within Australia and New Zealand for £90–115 per flight, depending on the distance covered. You must buy between two and eight flights, and complete all your travel during the validity of your international ticket. Qantas offer similar passes, but for travel within Australia only. Air New Zealand's *Explore New Zealand Pass* covers just New Zealand, but may be more economic than the Ansett pass, depending on the flights you make, and easily provides more extensive coverage of the country. With this pass three flights cost NZ$465.

Getting Back. Australia and New Zealand have lively discount air travel markets, and fares to Europe and back can be even cheaper than tickets bought in Europe. Prices quoted for low-season travel to London start at about A$850 one way and a little less to Los Angeles. Fares from New Zealand can be real bargains. For example a one-way ticket Auckland–Honolulu–San Francisco–London might be had for NZ$1200 (less than £400).

To get the best deal, consult one of the discount travel agencies listed under *Arrival and Departure* in each regional chapter or keep a close eye on newspaper advertisements. Don't be tempted to buy an unused ticket from another traveller, as the details on your passport will be checked against the name on the ticket or boarding pass and you will be prevented from travelling (and probably arrested) if there is a discrepancy.

If your plans change and you wish to get a refund for the return part of your ticket, you must prove that you have residency. This is true in both Australia and New Zealand.

Sea. CTC Lines sells tickets for an annual sailing in October/November from Southampton to Sydney that takes about 5 weeks aboard the cruise ship *Byelorussia*. Fares start at around £3000, which includes a free air ticket back to London. The London office of CTC is at 1 Regent St, SW1Y 4NN (0171-930 5833).

Another way to fly/cruise from Britain to Australasia is to fly to Philadelphia or Charleston, then board a vessel that sails through the Panama Canal and across the South Pacific. Contact Weider Travel, Charing Cross Shopping Concourse, London WC2N 4HZ (tel 0171-836 6363).

Crewing on yachts is a slow but pleasurable way to travel to or from Australasia. Skippers of private yachts often need casual crew for voyages between Singapore or Bali and the north and west of Australia, notably Darwin and Fremantle. There are also plenty of boats sailing between South Pacific islands and New Zealand. Be prepared to share expenses unless you are an experienced sailor.

MONEY
Take your funds in a mixture of cash and travellers cheques, though credit cards or a cash machine card will do just as well if you have sufficient in your account at home.

Cash. Australian or New Zealand currency can be ordered through your bank or Thomas Cook, but it is easier to wait until you arrive at the destination airport where exchange facilities are open for every flight arriving from abroad. Foreign currency (including Australian dollars in New Zealand and vice versa) will need to be changed at a bank or *bureau de change* before you can spend anything. While this is no problem in big cities or in tourist towns such as Cairns and Rotorua, it might be difficult to persuade a small country bank to change foreign notes or travellers cheques. If you anticipate having to have money sent to you from home, see the introductory section *Australia: Money*.

Travellers Cheques. The added safety of carrying travellers cheques instead of cash costs an extra 1%. But this outlay is partly offset because you normally get a slightly higher rate of exchange for travellers cheques than cash. Australian dollar travellers cheques, from the main Australian banks such as Westpac, can be obtained through UK banks and travel agencies (particularly American Express and Thomas Cook) and are changed for face value by banks in Australia. Most visitors, however, buy their travellers cheques in sterling or US dollars.

The most easily negotiable travellers cheques are American Express, Thomas Cook and Visa. Using American Express travellers cheques has the added advantage of entitling you to use their customer mail service (the addresses for mail collection are given in the regional chapters).

Carry your passport as ID when changing travellers cheques, although you might not always be asked to show it if the bank has the appropriate computer information on lost or stolen cheques. Keep a separate record of the cheques you have, and where and when the last was cashed. The emergency phone numbers to report a loss and get a refund are as follows:

American Express: Australia (outside Sydney) — 008-251 902; Sydney — 9886 1921; New Zealand — call collect to the Sydney office, i.e. 61 2 9886 1921.

Thomas Cook: call collect to the Melbourne office, 9696 2952; the code from elsewhere in Australia is 03; from New Zealand the code is 61 3.

No charge is made for replacing lost or stolen travellers cheques.

Credit and Charge Cards. Credit cards are popular in Australasia. Almost every enterprise — from Australian taxi drivers to New Zealand youth hostels — accepts them. A card is also an accepted guarantee of your financial reliability when hiring cars, booking hotel rooms or even clearing immigration.

Fewer establishments accept American Express and Diners Club cards than Access/MasterCard and Visa cards. The latter two are accepted in most places that take the Australasian credit card Bankcard. You can also use these cards to draw cash at banks displaying the Visa or Access/MasterCard symbol, though cash advances incur a charge immediately unless your account is in credit. An excellent way to transfer funds abroad is to top up your credit card account at home and then withdraw cash on your credit card at any bank without incurring interest (as you are not borrowing).

As plastic cards can prove so useful, it would be unfortunate to run up against your credit limit or to fail to pay the sum required each month. So if you're going to be away from home for more than a few weeks, arrange for a friend or relation at home to make the appropriate payments, or pay by standing order from your home account, or send in regular cheques by post.

Keep a record of the numbers of your cards and the emergency telephone line in case of loss or theft. Report any loss to the local police and call the card company collect; the UK and USA Direct telephone numbers (see pages 58 and 389) are ideal for this purpose.

When you use a credit card in Australasia, don't be alarmed if you have to wait while the number is cleared with the issuing company; checks for stolen or abused cards are more frequent than in Britain.

ATM Cards. Cash cards linked to the Plus system (as many British building society cards, and North American bank cards are) can draw cash from a large number of Automatic Teller Machines. This is certainly the cheapest way to obtain local currency.

Opening a Bank Account. It is easy to open an account once you are in Australia or New Zealand. But you may want the security of knowing that a certain sum is waiting in your own bank account on arrival, especially if you are planning a long trip through North America or Asia en route.

The Commonwealth Bank of Australia has the most branches in Australia. It has an office for migrants at 3rd Floor, 1 Kingsway, London WC2B 6DU (0171-379 0955). You can open an account in person or by post by sending a photocopy of your passport and the application form. The Streamline Account pays interest and allows you to use Automatic Teller Machines throughout Australia. Another big Australasian bank, Westpac, has a London branch at 75 King William St, EC4N 7HA (0171-621 7000).

PLANNING AHEAD

YHA Membership. Joining the Youth Hostels Association is highly recommended even if you do not imagine yourself the type. Membership for people over 21 costs £9.30. Many enterprises in Australia and New Zealand, from bus companies to cafés, give good discounts to YHA members, which makes the price of membership well worthwhile. Furthermore Antipodean YHA hostels attract a different clientele from the ones in Europe and have excellent facilities such as double rooms for couples. See *Australia: Accommodation* for details. A YHA membership card is in fact more generally recognised than an international student (ISIC) card. The ISIC booklet *The Student Traveller* contains a selection of places that give discounts to card-holders.

The YHA for England and Wales is based at Trevelyan House, St Stephen's Hill, St Albans AL1 2DY (01727-855215).

Motoring Clubs. Members of motoring organisations should ask for free information on driving and services provided by affiliated organisations in Australasia. A Commonwealth Motoring Conference card (free to AA and RAC members) may smooth your way when requesting free maps or when you need to be rescued after a hired car breaks down. Unless you intend to stay longer than three months in Australia or a year in New Zealand, don't waste money on an International Driving Permit. Although plenty of sources (especially the motoring organisations that sell them) recommend an IDP, your national licence is sufficient for short stays in both Australia and New Zealand.

Booking Domestic Travel. If you are sure of your itinerary and like the security of having everything booked in advance, buy flights, train and bus tickets before you go. Several British travel agencies specialise in travel to and around Australia and New Zealand. The big airlines also act as agents for the established travel companies in the Antipodes; for example, Air New Zealand is the agent for the Mount Cook Line. It may be worth getting the bumph from one or two of these agencies, though try not to succumb to the pressure of pre-booking if you are not sure of your plans.

Some specialists act as agents for selected bus companies, car rental firms, motel chains, etc. They advertise in *A Travellers Guide* published annually by the Australian Tourist Commission. Among the major ones are:

Australia Destination Centre: 27/28 High St, Windsor, Berkshire SL4 1LH (01753-855457)
Australia & New Zealand Centre: Sun Blessed Travel, 9 High St, Wimborne, Dorset BH21 1HR (01202-842626)
Rainbow Holidays: Ryedale Building, Piccadilly, York YO1 1PN (01904-628080)
Southern Cross Travel: 2 The Square, Riverhead, Sevenoaks, Kent TN13 2AA (01732-740421).

Unlimited Travel Passes. If you want an air, bus or train pass, you may want to buy it before arrival. In most cases, however, even those unlimited travel deals available only to international travellers can be bought in Australia and New Zealand as long as you can show an international air ticket. Look under *Getting Around* for each country to see the offers available and details of how to book.

The *Downunder Coach Pass* is the only one valid in both Australia and New Zealand. It is valid on all Greyhound Pioneer Australia services in Australia and Mount Cook/Newman coaches in New Zealand. Prices range from NZ$448 for 9 days to NZ$1410 for 45 days. Greyhound Pioneer offers about two dozen regional Explorer Passes within Australia only. The company's nationwide *Aussie Pass* ranges from £143 for 7 days to £943 for 120 days (see *Getting Around: Bus*). You can buy these in Britain from Greyhound Reservations, Sussex House, London Road, East Grinstead, West Sussex RH19 1LD (01342-317317) or from specialist agencies.

For information on rail passes and combination road and rail passes in each country, see the respective introductory chapters. For information on Rail

Australia and Austrail Passes contact Leisurail, PO Box 113, Peterborough PE3 8HY (01733-335599).

You can get information on air passes and discounted fares by contacting the overseas offices of the main airlines, which are as follows:

Air New Zealand: New Zealand House, Haymarket, London SW1 4TE (0181-741 2299)
Ansett: 4th Floor, 20 Savile Row, London W1X 2AN (0171-434 4071). Information is also available on Ansett's associates like East-West.
Australian Airlines: 4th Floor, 7 Swallow St, London W1R 8DU (0171-434 3864)
Qantas: 182 Strand, London WC2 (0345 747767).

You can rent a car in advance through big companies that have central reservations numbers in Britain such as Budget (0800-181181) or Hertz (0181-679 1799). If you are planning a trip by campervan in the southern summer you might want to pre-book it. The specialist agencies can recommend a company such as Apollo Motorhomes in Australia (represented by Sun Blessed Travel) or Newmans Motor Homes for both countries (contact Newmans Tours, 8 Castle St, Farnham, Surrey GU9 7NY; 01252-734644). Maui Rentals in New Zealand is represented by Caravan Abroad, 56 Middle St, Brockham, Surrey RH3 7HW (01737-842735).

Cultural Preparation. London has thriving communities of Australians and New Zealanders who want to keep in touch with what is happening at home. Free weekly magazines and newspapers like *TNT, New Zealand News* and *Southern Cross* contain a wealth of information on Antipodean politics, culture and travel. They are well worth picking up to get a flavour of what is topical, corruption in

Queensland or unemployment in Western Australia. The magazines are full of advertisements for travel agencies. If you live outside London, you can subscribe to the following addresses:

TNT: 52 Earls Court Road, London W8 6EJ. £10 for 3 months.
New Zealand News: PO Box 10, Berwick-upon-Tweed TD15 1BW. £8.40 for 3 months.
Southern Cross: 121 Warwick Road, London SW5 9EZ. £8 for 3 months.

To consult Australian newspapers abroad, visit the library at any High Commission or Consulate. The London offices of individual states carry a selection of the local state press. The Australian specialist bookshop in the UK is Flinders Bookshop at 10 Woburn Walk, London WC1H 0JL (0171-388 6080). The Australian Gift Shop is at 66 Strand, London, WC2R 0AA (0171-836-2292).

To become acquainted with Australian radio before you go, listen to *Radio Australia* (the overseas service of the ABC). Its short-wave English language broadcasts can usually be heard in Britain between 6 and 9.30am GMT on 15240kHz and between 8 and 10am on 21775kHz. For details of programmes like *This Australia* and *Jazz Notes*, write to Radio Australia, PO Box 755, Glen Waverley, Vic 3150 (03-881 2222).

TOURIST INFORMATION

This book should give you some good ideas about where to go, how to travel and so on. But you can supplement this with information on specific interests — from Aboriginal culture to zoology — by contacting Australian or New Zealand tourist offices before you go. They can also help with comprehensive lists of accommodation, details of available tours, etc., allowing you to plan some or all of your itinerary.

Australia. For a country of just over 16 million inhabitants, Australia produces a remarkably wide range of information for tourists. Its international publicity organisation, the Australian Tourist Commission. produces *A Travellers Guide* each autumn. The British edition can be obtained by ringing 0181-780 1424. North Americans can obtain a copy from the addresses below. As well as the statutory glossy pictures and glowing text, *A Travellers Guide* contains a great deal of hard information: from the telephone numbers of National Parks to Tasmanian ferry timetables. It also has coupons for requesting specific information from airlines, motel chains, tourist offices, tour operators and so on.

If you ask for information on a specific city or state, the Commission will send you the relevant one from the series *Your Gateway*, which are reasonably useful. They have sections on how to get around the cities, as well as the usual sights to see. Other information can be obtained from one of the ATC's offices around the world, including the following:

United Kingdom: Gemini House, 10–18 Putney Hill, London SW15 6AA (0181-780 2227)
United States: 31st Floor, 489 Fifth Avenue, New York, NY 10022 (212-687-6368)
Canada: 2 Bloor St W, Suite 1730, Toronto, Ontario M4W 3E2 (416-925 9312).

In addition, each individual state has a government office in London. They are intended to increase trade and investment, but those mentioned below also supply a small amount of tourist information. It helps if you can be as specific as possible about what you need, otherwise you can expect only a glossy brochure full of pictures:

New South Wales: telephone enquiries only — 0171-283 2166.
Northern Territory: 4th Floor, 393 Strand, London WC2R 0LT (0171-836 3344).
Queensland: 392/3 Strand, London WC2R 0LZ (0171-836 7242).
South Australia: 50 Strand, London WC2N 5LW (0171-930 7471).
Victoria: Melbourne Place, Aldwych, London WC2B 4LS (0171-836 2656).

Tasmania and Victoria are jointly represented by the new Southern Tourism Promotion at the ATC.

Tourist offices abroad hold only a small selection of the available travel literature. Most travel promotion is done at state level, so if you know in advance which states you'll be visiting, contact the headquarters of the tourist organisations in Australia:

Australian Capital Territory: ACT Tourism Commission, Jolimont Centre, Northbourne Avenue, Canberra City, ACT 2601 (06-245 6464).
New South Wales: Travel Centre of NSW, 19 Castlereagh St, Sydney, NSW 2000 (02-9231 4444).
South Australia: Tourism South Australia, 18 King William St, Adelaide, SA 5000 (08-8212 1505).
Northern Territory: Government Tourist Bureau, 31 Smith St Mall, Darwin, NT 0800 (08-8981 6611).
Queensland: Tourist & Travel Corporation, GPO Box 328, Brisbane, Qld 4001 (07-3833 5400).
Tasmania: Tourism Tasmania, PO Box 3991, Hobart 7001 (03-6230 0211).
Victoria: Tourism Commission, PO Box 279, World Trade Centre, Melbourne Vic 3005 (03-9619 9444).
Western Australia: Tourist Commission, Forrest Place, Perth, WA 6000 (09-483 1111).

New Zealand. Publicity is handled nationally by the New Zealand Tourism Department in various countries around the world, including:

United Kingdom: New Zealand House, Haymarket, London SW1Y 4TQ (0171-973 0363).
United States: 501 Santa Monica Boulevard, 300, Los Angeles, CA 90401 (1-800-388-5494).
Canada: Suite 1260 IBM Tower, 701 West Georgia St, Vancouver, BC V7Y 1B6 (604-684-2117).

For specific information on a particular area, write to the local tourist offices listed under *Help and Information* for each region of New Zealand.

Phoning Ahead. You can find most numbers in Australia and New Zealand from Britain by dialling international directory enquiries on 153. To call a number in Australasia from Britain, first dial the international access code (00) followed by the country code for Australia (61) or New Zealand (64). Next dial the area code without the initial zero (for Sydney dial 2, for Auckland 9, etc.) and then the number. So to call the British High Commission in Canberra (area code 06) from the UK, dial 00-61-6-270 6666.

From the USA and Canada the international access code is 011, and so to call the US Embassy in Wellington (code 04) dial 011-64-4-722068.

To make a collect (reverse-charge) call to Australasia from the UK, dial straight through to an Australian operator on 0800-890061, or a New Zealand one on 0800-890064. These calls are free (for you).

Before ringing relations to announce your arrival, or calling a hotel to make a booking, estimate the time at your destination; see *Time*, below. Your conversation will cost 70p per minute between 2.30pm–7.30pm and from midnight to 7am, and 84p per minute at other times.

Travellers' Clubs. If you lack friends and relations in Australasia, you might consider joining an organisation that arranges hospitality exchanges. For example members of the Globetrotters Club (BCM/Roving, London WC1N 3XX) can request a list of members in Australia, New Zealand and other countries who have expressed a willingness to provide hospitality to other globetrotters. Membership costs £7; the list of members is a further £1.

Servas International was founded by an American Quaker. The organisation runs a worldwide programme of free hospitality exchanges for travellers, to help the cause of peace and international understanding. To become a Servas traveller, you must join the organisation for £25 and pay a refundable deposit of £15 for the relevant list of members. Contact Servas at Bankside Cottage, Walton le Wold, near Louth, Lincolnshire LN11 0QT, or in the USA at Room 706, 11 John St, New York, NY 10038-4009.

The World Travellers Club mentioned in the *Sydney* chapter has a UK office at Concorde House, 18 Margaret St, Brighton, East Sussex BN2 1TS (01273-672262). For a membership fee of £52 you get reassuring advice and three nights in a hostel (worth about £18) plus a few other facilities.

Disabled Travellers. Before your flight to Australia you may wish to consult *Care in the Air*, a useful free booklet from the Air Transport Users' Committee (103 Kingsway, London WC1X 9LP; 0171-242 3882). *Access to the Skies*, a guide to airport facilities for the disabled, is available from RADAR, 25 Mortimer St, London W1N 8AB (0171-637 5400). RADAR has a holidays officer who can provide specialist advice. Every airline gives free assistance to handicapped travellers, and will provide a wheelchair at 24 hours notice. Some airlines, including British Airways, Qantas and Air New Zealand, require a medical certificate of fitness to travel.

Mobility International exists to promote international activities and conferences of interest to both disabled and able-bodied people; its UK office is at 228 Borough High St, London SE1 1JX (0171-403 5688). North Americans can consult the Society for the Advancement of Travel for the Handicapped (SATH) at 26 Court St, Brooklyn, NY 11242 (718-858-5483). See page 124 for details of similar organisations in Australia.

WHAT TO TAKE

Maps. Free maps are issued by the national and state tourist offices listed above. Most visitors are satisfied with these hand-outs, but you might want to buy a larger scale map such as a government topographical map. For government maps of New Zealand, write to the Infomap Centre (Private Bag, Upper Hutt, New Zealand) for its catalogue.

To see what is available at home, visit a specialist travel bookshop. The best in Britain for maps are Stanfords, 12–14 Long Acre, London WC2E 9LP (0171-836 1321) and The Map Shop, 15 High St, Upton-upon-Severn, Worcestershire WR8 0HJ (01684-593146). In addition, Roger Lascelles (47 York Road, Brentford, Middlesex TW8 0QP; 0181-847 0935) distributes Australian and New Zealand maps.

In North America contact the Travelers Bookstore (113 Corporation Road, Hyannis, MA 02601) or the Travel Bug (2667 W Broadway, Vancouver, BC, Canada V6K 2G2).

Electrical Items. Power in Australia and New Zealand is the same voltage (240) and frequency (50Hz) as the UK and Europe. But if you're taking a travel iron, hair dryer or anything else electrical you'll need an adaptor. The standard Australasian mains plug has three pins but is unlike other plugs elsewhere in the world. As convertors that accept British three-pin plugs are difficult to find in Australia and New Zealand, buy a suitable adaptor before leaving or simply buy a new plug locally. Equipment made for use in North America needs a transformer if the appliance does not have a voltage selector, and mechanical equipment will run at the wrong speed due to the difference in frequency.

Medications. Prescribed drugs (except contraceptives) that you take with you should be accompanied by a doctor's letter explaining why you need them. Do not carry non-prescribed drugs stronger than aspirin, and then only in the original packs. Customs officers are highly sensitive about drugs of all kinds, and can be suspicious of some available over the counter in Britain but that are available only on prescription in Australia and New Zealand.

If you are planning a long trip, take a prescription from your doctor. It can be endorsed by a doctor in Australasia and used to obtain drugs.

Gifts. Choosing what to take to impress friends or relations, or to ingratiate yourself with friends-of-friends on whom you wish to impose, is an art. If your beneficiaries are migrants from the UK, then virtually anything British — from newspapers to Scotch whisky — is appreciated. Otherwise, take the kinds of things that are more expensive in Australasia, such as foreign books.

What Not to Take. Because of the stringent quarantine laws in both Australia and New Zealand, take no food even if your Australian friends are Stilton-lovers. And don't splash out on a new wardrobe of clothes for your trip; you can find equally fashionable garments more cheaply in Australasia, or pick them up for next to nothing in Asian countries *en route*.

TIME

Travelling to and around Australia and New Zealand can be chronologically confusing. Australasia straddles several time zones. At noon in Perth it is already 4 or 5pm in Auckland (depending on whether New Zealand Daylight Saving Time is in effect). New Zealand is covered by a single time zone, but Australia is divided into three during the winter and five in summer. (All Australian states except Western Australia and the Northern Territory use Daylight Saving Time.) Eastern Standard Time is observed in New South Wales, ACT, Victoria, Tasmania and Queensland; Central Standard Time, half an hour earlier, is used in South Australia and the Northern Territory; and Western Australia's Western Standard Time is two hours behind EST.

	Winter (Oct-Mar)	Summer (Mar-Oct)
Western Australia	5.00 pm	5.00 pm
Northern Territory	6.30 pm	6.30 pm
South Australia	6.30 pm	7.30 pm
New South Wales	7.00 pm	8.00 pm
Australian Capital Territory	7.00 pm	8.00 pm
Victoria	7.00 pm	8.00 pm
Tasmania	7.00 pm	8.00 pm
Queensland	7.00 pm	7.00 pm
New Zealand	9.00 pm	10.00 pm

It is always later in the Antipodes than it is in Europe and North America. The time in each state is indicated in the table above compared with 9am Greenwich Mean Time (4am Eastern Standard Time in North America).

Australian Daylight Saving Time usually begins on the last Sunday in October and ends on the first Sunday in March.

New Zealand summer time lasts from the first Sunday in October until the third Sunday in March. This is contrary to Daylight Saving Time in the Northern Hemisphere.

As a guide, you can assume that Western Australia is eight hours ahead of British time and 13 hours ahead of Eastern Time in North America, and the other Australian states are about 10 hours ahead of Britain, 18 ahead of eastern North America. Converting 'am' to 'pm' or vice-versa gives a rough idea of the time in New Zealand compared with Britain.

Australasia has not fully adjusted to the 24-hour clock. In many timetables times are given in local time using the 12-hour clock. The convention is that times printed in light type are before noon, those in **bold** after noon.

On business cards, classified advertisements and so on, you'll sometimes see 'AH' and 'BH', meaning 'after (working) hours' and 'business hours'.

USEFUL CONVERSIONS

Shaking off their Imperial measures, Australia and New Zealand have gone thoroughly metric. Although you may still hear people talking about 'gallons', 'miles' and 'ounces', everything from speed limit signs to packs of butter are in metric units. Some of the trickier conversions are given below.

Capacity and Volume. The standard unit for liquids is the litre (l), about 1.8 Imperial pints or 2.2 US pints. There are about 4½ litres to an Imperial gallon, 5½ to a US gallon. In a pub, most measures are in millilitres: 585ml is an Imperial pint (20fl oz). See page 96 for the most common measures.

CONVERSION CHARTS

Fuel Consumption. Australasians reckon in terms of the number of litres they use to travel 100 kilometres (litres/100km). To convert fuel consumption between miles per gallon (mpg) and litres used per 100km (litres/100km):

mpg (UK)	20	25	30	35	40	45	50
mpg (US)	16	20	24	28	32	36	40
litres/100km	14	11½	9½	8	7	6	5½

Tyre Pressure. The unit used in Australia and New Zealand is kilograms per square centimetre (kg/cm²), sometimes known as the *kilopascal*. To convert from pounds per square inch (psi):

psi	16	18	20	22	24	26	28
kg/cm²	1.1	1.3	1.4	1.5	1.7	1.8	2.0

AUSTRALIA

Australia is like nowhere else on earth, yet it is also strangely familiar. Images of the country are extraordinarily strong: the Sydney Opera House has been voted the greatest wonder of the modern world; Ayers Rock could be sketched by many people who have never been nearer than 10,000 miles; and the beach-beer-barbecue axis gives many foreigners the impression that life in Australia is a perpetual party held by sun-bronzed surfers in an endless summer.

Two things happen when you reach Australia. First, many visitors are struck (and some mightily alarmed) by the humdrum ordinariness of some of it; Australian cities float amid a sea of suburbia, the like of which is all too familiar to those brought up in Croydon or Cleveland, Ohio. Second, this sensation is (with luck) quickly replaced by astonishment at the physical and cultural uniqueness of the country. Geographic isolation followed by massive and diverse immigration have produced flora, fauna and folklore way beyond any European or American experience. The way that the people interact with such an alien environment is fascinating, not least in coping with weather that is often far from perfect.

CLIMATE

The seasons in the Southern Hemisphere are opposite those north of the equator. But it can be difficult getting used to schools adjourning for their summer holidays around Christmas and the ski season beginning in June. The terminology can become quite confusing when you are making plans to meet up with an Australian friend: 'See you next summer' always has to be clarified by naming the months intended. But while you are in Australia, spring means September to November, summer is December to February, autumn is March to early June and winter is the rest.

The Australian sun needs no elaboration. Even the state capital nearest the South Pole, Hobart in Tasmania gets over 5 hours of sunshine a day on average, while Perth gets nearly 8 hours. People say that even when you have no money in Australia, the weather keeps your spirits high. Furthermore the water temperatures are wonderfully warm in most places, and Poms trained at Scarborough and Southend will have no trouble diving into the sea. (Meanwhile the more mollycoddled Aussies close down their open-air swimming pools when the water temperature falls below about 20°C.)

To judge from the weight of media coverage, Australians have an obsession for information about the weather. Many newspapers devote a full colour page to forecasts, and news programmes on radio and television are usually followed by extremely detailed weather analysis and forecasts. Since the weather patterns in Australia are usually more stable than they are in Britain, the meteorologists have a higher success rate, though they are often overconfidently precise.

Australia's vastness means that there are tremendous variations from zone to zone, encompassing Alpine zones (like Tasmania) and sub-Equatorial Monsoonal regions (like Darwin). July in Canberra is decidedly cold, with minimum temperatures approaching freezing, while Cairns is 15–20°C. The main coastal cities of Sydney, Brisbane, Melbourne, Adelaide and Perth all have temperate winters and hot summers. Naturally the direction you must travel to reach warmer climes is opposite to the one to which Europeans and North Americans are accustomed, which gives rise to such expressions as the 'Deep North' usually applied to northern Queensland. For the really scorching heat that can make railway lines buckle and lakes evaporate you will have to penetrate into the interior of the country, which often suffers a series of 'snorters' (i.e. exceedingly hot days).

Darwin and Cairns are true tropical cities, and are therefore subject to rainy and dry seasons, invariably referred to in Australia as the Wet and the Dry. These areas are best avoided in the wet season, which lasts from about December to April, not only is it less enjoyable travelling in rain, but the downpours are so severe that roads become flooded or impassably muddy, possessions go mouldy and, even when it isn't raining, it is unbearably humid. Travellers in the dry Outback should beware of the flash floods that can follow rainstorms. In particular, you should never pitch a tent on the bed of a dried-up river or stream in case an overnight flood washes you away.

Sydney and Brisbane can become unpleasantly humid in summer, though refreshing sea breezes and the occasional 'cool change' bring relief. On the other hand, the heat of the west coast, though intense, is very dry, and Perth's wet season falls in winter.

If you are in Australia for a long period, it is possible to follow the seasons around, ideally seeing Queensland and the interior deserts between June and September, before arriving in Western Australia in time to see the wild flowers bloom in spring, and crossing back to the southeast for the long balmy evenings and sunny days of summer. Each regional chapter provides a more detailed description of the kind of weather you can expect.

THE PEOPLE

back of Bourke	remote place, like 'the back of beyond'
banana bender (or banana eater)	person from Queensland
bitumen blonde	an Aboriginal girl or woman
blow-in	a newcomer to any place; a person who has not yet been accepted by local inhabitants as one of themselves
bumjumper	male homosexual
Cockie	gentleman farmer
Corroboree	Aboriginal ceremonial dance; or any social gathering especially if rowdy
Croweater	person from South Australia
Dad and Dave	two fictional characters from the 1890s who typify outback humour and tenacity
dag	a loser with yobbish qualities
de facto (noun)	a common law husband or wife
derro	a tramp or derelict person
drongo	a stupid person
fringe-dweller	Aboriginal who sets up camp near a white-owned property and lives on handouts
gin	Aboriginal woman
God-botherer	one who touts religion

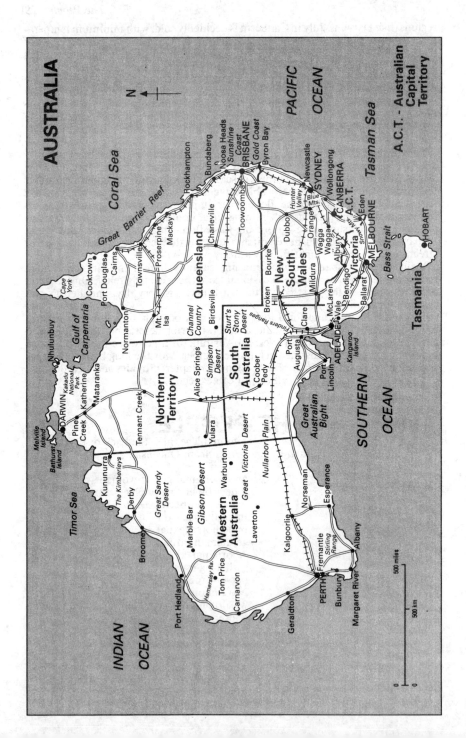

hoon	lout, stupid youth, layabout
Koories	name Aboriginals call themselves
Larrikin or lair	unruly youth, rogue, someone who doesn't take things too seriously
Lezzo	lesbian; or any woman who rebuffs an advance from a male
Mexican	person from Victoria (due to location south of the border, i.e. of New South Wales)
Ocker	a typical yobbo-like Australian
pongo	variation on Pom for English person with reference to their reputation for infrequent washing
poon	lonely, somewhat crazy, outback dweller; also a simpleton or fool
ratbag	rude or eccentric person
root	sexual intercourse
sandgroper	person from Western Australia
septic (or seppo)	an American (from rhyming slang tank/Yank)
sticky beak	nosey person
Taswegian (or Tazzie/Tassie)	person from Tasmania
Topender	person from the far north, especially the Northern Territory
wog	foreigner (including new Australians)
woodheap	white man who has been ostracised by white Australians for associating with Aboriginal women
wowser	straight-laced killjoy (origin unknown)

At last count there were over 16,000,000 Australians, half of them less than 30 years old. You may be disappointed to learn that not many of them spend their time wrestling with crocodiles, mesmerising savage beasts by outstaring them or attending Aboriginal corroborees. The mythical swagman, who wandered the country living on his wits and precious little else, a law unto himself, is a dying breed.

In fact Australia is an overwhelmingly urban culture, though it treasures its bush lore. While the people cling to the edges of their vast island continent — 80% live within 20 miles of the sea — they glorify their untamed interior. They regale you with stories of the dangers or rewards that lurk in the Outback, but they are most unlikely to have eaten a kangaroo steak themselves, seen a crocodile except in a zoo or met an Aboriginal.

Even if your average Australian would not know where to begin to shear a sheep or fight a bushfire, they have some unique characteristics that set them apart from their North American and European counterparts. One of their most endearing qualities is that they place a higher value on leisure than on work, preferring relaxation to money. People visiting on business are often taken aback by the seemingly slack hours kept by their Australian colleagues. At weekends it seems everyone is at the beach, a barbecue or a sporting event.

Of course these generalisations need to be qualified. In Sydney and Melbourne and maybe even Darwin there are executives suffering from stress, while in Perth and Adelaide you find a few individuals more intent on making money than on having fun. But the majority maintain their traditional priorities; perhaps as a remnant of their convict past, they value their freedom from external constraints above most other things. Australia's trading partners, especially Japan and the US, find these laissez-faire attitudes bewildering and are exerting pressure on Australian managers to increase productivity. These pressures are apparently having some impact judging from reports that American motivation schemes have started to catch on. Furthermore Australia is becoming more Americanised in its language, eating habits and outlook.

The recession has caused genuine alarm, though not much actual hardship so far, and there is a suspicion growing in some quarters that the 'no worries' attitude that has always prevailed is no longer sufficient. 'She'll be right' may yet turn out to be an over-optimistic forecast. But such habits of mind and expectations are slow to change in a workforce, especially one that is as heavily unionised as Australia's. The people are by nature dismissive of authority, which makes it all the more difficult for bosses to try to alter traditional loyalty to leisure. Where else in the world would a national song glorify the theft of a sheep as *Waltzing Matilda* does?

If the world is divided between debunkers and dreamers, Australians would almost without exception fall into the first category. Since the Great Aussie Dream has often been identified as owning a house and since the vast majority of working Australians already own a home, there is little point in being a dreamer. At best, Australians can be gifted and colourful when they decide to take the mickey, and as long as you do not find yourself on the receiving end, their conversation is often very amusing.

Although the word Ocker is sometimes translated as down-to-earth basic Aussie, it carries with it in most circles pejorative connotations. The image of the beer-swilling, gambling Ocker has been glorified as constituting the Australian identity, which is now lamented as having been lost. People who used to swill beer now drink Semillon wines at streetside cafés, slobs wear designer T-shirts, and instead of playing the 'pokies' (slot machines) or watching the footy (football) on TV, they now catch the latest Australian film or go jogging. The satiric force of Barry Humphries' Cultural Attaché Sir Les Patterson is now somewhat diminished since Australia is fast losing its boorishness. The ever-increasing number of Aussies coming to Europe for extended stays has contributed to the de-Ockerisation of Australia.

A sociological analysis might claim that this transformation is inevitable when a predominantly working class culture becomes middle class — due to increased affluence and improved education — and not everyone bemoans this shift. This school of thought expresses unmitigated relief that Australiana is no longer considered synonymous with hard-drinking Philistinism and rampant male chauvinism. The visitor will have to decide for him or herself just how far Australians have left that image behind. Certainly you will encounter a fair degree of male chauvinism and racism. Away from the cities you are quite likely to meet the so-called 'dinkum' (i.e. authentic) Aussies who wear old pairs of stubbies (shorts) and seem to be happy as long as they have a good supply of the other kind of stubbies (bottles of beer) and a few mates with whom to discuss the coming football match.

ETHNIC BACKGROUND

Three-quarters of the Australian population have British origins, and one million were born in the United Kingdom. Furthermore Britons continue to flock to the land of opportunity and the UK continues as the largest source of migrants, providing about 17% of the total, well ahead of the next most numerous sources in 1991 — Hong Kong and Vietnam. This makes it all the more remarkable that Australia has such a separate identity. But it also accounts for the large number of similarities with Britain, from driving on the left side of the road to the prevalence of fish and chip shops.

The word 'Pom' or 'Pommie' is in widespread use to refer to English people. Although it is often used neutrally, it can also convey a hint of disdain. Poms are caricatured as stuffy and snobbish, complaining and inflexible. (The classic 'whinging Pom' joke runs: 'Q: What is the difference between a Pom and a 747? A: A 747 stops whining when it gets to Sydney.') The origin of the word Pom is not certain, but it has been suggested that it was an abbreviation for 'Prisoners of Motherland' used of the early convicts. A more pleasing derivation is given by D H Lawrence in his (otherwise unpleasing) novel set in Australia *Kangaroo*. He claimed Pommie is short for pomegranate which is rhyming slang for immigrant, and furthermore recently arrived Brits turn red in the sun like pomegranates.

In some quarters hostility towards Poms appears to be fading as Australians grow more secure in their independence from the mother country. But there is also a strong and influential Australian Republican Movement. ARM wanted to see all links with Britain severed by the year 2001 and is supported by many important figures such as Thomas Keneally, Gough Whitlam, John Pilger and the historian Manning Clarke. ARM bumper stickers abound.

Anti-American feelings also run high. The post-war generation in Australia embraced everything American from junk food to foreign policy, and American language and customs continue to colonise Australian culture. The blows that have been dealt by the USA to Australia in international trade (such as on the wheat market) are bitterly resented. The power of American-owned multinationals, not to mention American military involvement in nuclear defence stations like Pine Gap near Alice Springs, has soured Australian feeling towards the United States and bred distrust, at least at the level of pub politics. But most Australians have had little contact with Americans except through television and the movies — only one in 500 of the Australian population is American in origin — and individually, Americans rarely arouse animosity.

The cultural diversity of Australia is one of the country's most appealing features. To take just two examples, the Germans who settled the Barossa Valley near Adelaide in the 19th century and the descendants of Chinese pearl divers who live in Broome, Western Australia have maintained cultural traditions that add immeasurably to the colour and variety of the social spectrum. More significant has been the influx of Europeans since the Second World War, especially from Greece and Italy. These waves of immigration were encouraged by the government to provide manpower for expanding industries, but had the fringe benefits of introducing many aspects of Mediterranean civilisation such as good food and (possibly) a Latin temperament.

Although Southern Europeans continue to arrive, fully half of the most recent waves of 'new Australians' (as migrants are known) are from Southeast Asia. These newcomers are having the same beneficial effect on the economy and on the cultural-cum-culinary life of Australia as their European predecessors did but are bitterly resented by a proportion of the Anglo-Celtic population.

Most new arrivals encounter difficulties in adjustment, though they are given free accommodation in migrant hostels and, if necessary, free English lessons for three months. But white Australians are not known for their broad-minded tolerance of different cultures, and new Australians have certainly suffered and continue to suffer discrimination, the least harmful being a range of derogatory names used to describe them, such as reffos (refugees), dagos, wogs, ikeys, ities, balts, spags, slopeheads, choongs, etc. A nation whose first Minister for Immigration was capable of saying, 'Two Wongs don't make a white' is bound to make life difficult for newcomers. Understandably national groups cling together and as a result many immigrants never adapt to Australian life, in fact some never learn English. The suburbs of many cities, especially Sydney, are delineated along ethnic lines, and the newest migrants tend to occupy the poorer areas. Despite all this, patriotic feeling runs high among migrants, just as it does in the USA, and most new Australians will claim to be Australian rather than Italian, Yugoslav or Malaysian.

ABORIGINAL PEOPLE

Some visitors are almost as eager to see Aboriginal culture as they are to see the Sydney Opera House, the Great Barrier Reef or Ayers Rock. Many are disappointed. Not only do they fail to see Aboriginals playing the didjeridu, hunting with boomerangs or feasting on witchetty grubs, but they see hardly any at all. The estimated total population of Aboriginal people (including many of mixed race who are now more inclined to claim their Aboriginal ancestry than previously) is between 200,000 and 300,000. This is less than 2% of the Australian population and only double the number of migrants that Australia accepts in any one year.

Overall their numbers are sadly depleted. It is conjectured that as many as 600,000 were wiped out in the first couple of generations after European settlement. Just as in North America white man's diseases, to which the indigenous people had no immunity, were at least as destructive to the Aborigines as the great plague was to 14th-century Europe. Furthermore there was wholesale slaughter of the natives who were considered troublesome by the settlers, though on the whole the Aborigines were far more pacific than their North American Indian counterparts. Even the former Prime Minister Bob Hawke admitted that the treatment of Aboriginal people had been 'a long and tragic history of demoralisation and despair'.

People often contrast the appalling conditions of Aboriginal life today — the nation's highest infant mortality, lowest life expectancy and poorest standard of living — with the much happier situation of the Maori in New Zealand. But Aboriginal culture, especially in the desert, was less advanced than the seafaring Pacific Island Maori culture and the clash with the alien invaders was much more extreme. Anthropologists studying some of the remote tribes in the Great Australian Desert who had had very little contact with whites until the 1950s, maintain that these were the last living stone age people on earth, with the possible exception of the Bushmen of the Kalahari Desert in Africa. Their social organisation and means of survival were incomprehensible to Europeans and vice versa.

In earliest British legal documents, Australia is described as 'Terra Nullius', that is, uninhabited land. This was not because the first arrivals did not encounter the native people — Captain Cook describes his meeting with them in 1770 — but because they seem to have been considered sub-human. This is a cause of bitter grievance today. Aboriginals had been in Australia, having crossed from Southeast Asia, for at least 40,000 years by the time the first fleet sailed into Sydney Harbour in 1788 carrying its cargo of convicts. The whole razzmatazz of the Australian Bicentenary was resented by the majority of Aborigines who deemed 1988 a year of mourning, since it celebrated something that brought nothing but misery to them. Among the most radical Aboriginals, there is a feeling that the whites should return to the places from whence they came, though most concentrate on regaining lost land or receiving compensation for it.

Aboriginal people have suffered enormous spiritual losses and terrible damage to their self esteem. Their religion revolves around the Dreamtime, an oral tradition relating to an ancient time when spirits roamed over the land creating all animate and inanimate objects, tree and stone, rivers and people. According to some interpretations, the land itself is sacred, not just specific features. So white man with his fences and animals and railway lines inevitably interfered with this network of significance, as the indigenous people watched helplessly and without comprehending. (For an unsentimental but fascinating account of this see Bruce Chatwin's book *Songlines*).

This attitude to the land, which is completely at odds with European notions of ownership, is at the root of the land claims that dominate discussion of Aboriginal affairs nowadays. Large chunks of Australia were set aside as reserves from the beginning of this century. But just like the so-called homelands of South Africa, they were usually established on barren and remote land, and the occupants were not allowed to govern themselves. They were administered by missionaries, police or government officials, and many communities still rely on white leadership. Furthermore, their rights to the land were overridden if a mining company found some new source of wealth on a reserve. Attitudes are now changing to some extent, as in the highly controversial decision to return Ayers Rock to the Pitjantjatjara tribe to whom it is sacred. But there are still bitter disputes to be fought. To learn more about land rights in Australia, contact Survival International (310 Edgware Road, London W2 1DY, tel 0171-242 1441).

This subject is a very delicate one for any government. Unlike the Maori people, Aboriginals signed no treaties with the colonisers and so have no legal basis from which to start proceedings. It would be difficult to draft a document to which both sides could agree, though a treaty of some kind might prevent the native peoples from being at the whim and mercy of changing political opinion.

Few Aboriginals are to be seen in the capital cities. They do congregate in certain suburbs (such as Redfern in Sydney) but these are usually well away from tourist areas. Most live in or near country towns, mostly in Queensland and the Northern Territory. In the Territory, Aborigines represent a quarter of the total population and have won land rights to over a third of the state. It is illegal to visit most Aboriginal reserves without permission from the community. If you have some special reason for wishing to visit a reserve you must write to the relevant Land Council four to six weeks in advance. Addresses are given in the appropriate chapters of this book and further advice is available from Aboriginal support groups in all the major cities. Roadhouses on main outback highways, a few of which are actually owned by Aboriginal communities, will also be able to advise. In the northwest of Australia quite a few Aboriginals live in missions rather than on reserves and some of these are quite welcoming.

After regretting the scarcity of Aborigines, it can be distressing when you do eventually see these people whose mystique has been widely publicised. Travelling on a train to Alice Springs, you may notice a group of Aborigines (or 'black fellows' as they sometimes refer to themselves) sitting next to the track at a small Northern Territory station. As you get closer and as other tourists on the train are reaching for their cameras, you notice that they are staring straight ahead with seemingly unseeing eyes, oblivious to trains and cameras and dust. They seem utterly demoralised.

Not all exposure to Aborigines is so depressing. Many who have adopted European attitudes display the same friendliness as white Australians. Hitchhikers, particularly in the north of the country, frequently get lifts with them. Conversely, you might encounter some on a bus through the Outback and attempt to strike up a conversation as you have done with so many other Australians, only to find that your conversational gambits fall flat, leaving you feeling rebuffed. Pure Aboriginal culture does not have much place for small talk with strangers. Again a typical exposure might be a group sitting in a park in northern Queensland, sharing a few bottles of wine and listening to Country music on a cheap radio, until a policeman comes along and the Aboriginals meekly disperse.

The sad fact is that the Aboriginal 'problem' is complex, and namby-pamby liberal criticisms of past atrocities do not achieve very much. It is crucial for white Australia to acknowledge that the 200 years of their occupation has resulted in the extermination, slavery and economic oppression of Aboriginals. Although a handful of Australians with Aboriginal blood have gained positions of authority, the majority remain silent and powerless. Even when Aboriginals seem to have adapted to the modern age, they are subject to the old ways such as 'going walkabout', which Europeans find inexplicable. Even the few blacks who have achieved fame as painters or actors, have proved depressingly liable to fall foul of the law.

The statistics for alcoholism and crime among Aborigines are horrific. Their life expectancy is 20 years less than for white Australians, and their health and housing are abysmal. Their plight is often compared to that of South African blacks and indeed there are some similarities. But the comparison is not a fair one: the essential difference is that racial discrimination is not now legislated in Australia. Belatedly, Aboriginals were granted full rights of citizenship in 1967, and officially have equal (and some special) rights. Over 70% of Aboriginal income derives from the government, which funds a multiplicity of worthy projects such as setting up an Aboriginal television station, recording Aboriginal music, making a computerised dictionary of Aboriginal languages (of which there were about 500), etc. Many white support groups are struggling to improve the standards of health, housing and education, and specifically trying to teach them how to assume control of their lives.

But reforms of the law can accomplish only so much. Racial discrimination is still widespread among the white population, especially in the south. Many were taught at school that Aboriginals are savages who refuse to adapt to the higher culture introduced by Europeans. In otherwise reasonable urban white settings, derogatory words like 'boong', 'coon' and 'Abo' are used quite unselfconsciously. Even more disconcerting for the visitor is the way city folk (who have probably never talked to an Aboriginal in their lives) advise foreigners not to talk to blacks, not to park by the roadside in Outback areas and to carry a shotgun for self-defence. This is nonsense. There have been virtually no unprovoked assaults on whites; any such attacks would have made unforgettable headlines. What is making headlines is the ill-treatment of Aboriginals by whites, especially police in remote areas. There has been a scandalous number of deaths in custody which few believe are suicides as the police claim.

Aboriginal life is not an unmitigated tale of woe. Aspects of Aboriginal art and culture are on display in many museums and cultural centres around the country, one of the best is the new Tandanya Aboriginal Centre in Adelaide. Various Aboriginal-inspired tours are mentioned in this book such as the 3-day trip to a Victorian Aboriginal community to learn about tracking, etc. sponsored by the YHA of Victoria, and the tour of sites of significance located in Metropolitan Perth by an Aboriginal guide.

Plenty of books have been written about Aboriginals, many of them with names like *The Passing of the Aboriginals* or *The Aborigines the Way they Were*. One that has become quite a standard work is A P Elkin's *The Australian Aborigines* which has been revised many times since it was written in 1938.

In the past few years Aboriginal writers like Ooodgeroo Noonuccal (Kath Walker) have achieved some recognition. The Western Australian writer Sally Morgan provides a moving account of coming to value her Aboriginality in her autobiography *My Place*. She describes the barbaric practice, common until a few decades ago, of removing Aboriginal children from their families and forcing them to live with white families in order to 'civilise' them.

You may be lucky enough to get some first-hand tastes of contemporary

Aboriginal culture. There are a few good Aboriginal bands, though they generally receive scant attention from the disc jockeys and club owners on the east coast. In 1990 the first Aboriginal musical *Bran Nu Dae* was premiered to great acclaim. Occasionally Aboriginal festivals of dance are held, for example at the annual women's festival in Adelaide or by the Bararroga Mimi Dancers from Arnhemland. Inevitably you will also find some commercialisation of Aboriginal culture, particularly the handicrafts in tourist shops. But at least now some of the profits are finding their way to the communities that make the souvenirs.

MAKING FRIENDS

Australians are no-nonsense folk who do not suffer fools gladly. Just as Eskimos have a large vocabulary for the concept of snow, so Australians have an impressive range of descriptions for a fool: nong, dill, drongo, galah, peanut, boofhead, someone with kangaroos in his top paddock, three bangers short of a barbie, a shingle short, like a stunned mullet, silly as a cut snake, off his kadoova, silly as a two-bob watch, mad as a goanna, and so on. Despite this flair for abuse, you are unlikely to be victimised (unless of course you happen to be a dill, a drongo, etc.). Normally their disrespect is underpinned by a strong sense of fair play, though it has to be said that there is a certain cruel streak in their sense of humour.

Australians are the first to poke fun at pomposity, and are themselves the most unpretentious of people. This leads to the frequent characterisation of openness, i.e. they will tell you their opinions straight. This in turn can result in a certain abruptness, coarseness and insensitivity. For example visitors may be shocked to hear racist sentiments or extreme political views expressed, before any attempt has been made to discover the likelihood of a favourable hearing.

Their openness falls well short of unburdening their hearts, as Americans are prone to do. Analysis of the emotions is not a very popular pastime. (Woody Allen would make few friends were he to emigrate.) Even when people are good mates, in this land where 'mateship' is venerated, they are liable to demonstrate their attachment not through words but actions (archetypally risking their lives in a crisis). In keeping with their penchant for irony and lack of sentimentality, an exchange of verbal abuse can be one way of expressing affection. It might also explain why the family dog in Australia is more often than not referred to as 'the mutt,' which in other countries would be a pejorative expression and why males might refer to their friends as 'bastards'.

They may take a similar line on their country and be reluctant (compared to Americans at any rate) to express nationalistic fervour. For example it would not be impossible for a highbrow radio announcer to compare a new piece of Australian music he was about to play to a 'man struggling with a roll of wire fence'. Nevertheless most natives harbour few doubts that Australia is the best country in the world, the 'lucky country'. Just as in the States, it is unwise (not to mention discourteous) to speak critically of Australian habits and assumptions. The romantic view of the convict heritage, of bushrangers (i.e. bandits), explorers and outback characters has taken on the mythic quality of America's Wild West, sometimes with as much papering over of the truth. But it is not your role as guest to disillusion them.

Outside the cities and especially in the Outback, the natives are eager to help a visitor. If you fall into friendly conversation on a campsite or in a milk bar, you are likely to be offered a meal or even a bed. Advice and offers of assistance are often most welcome in areas prone to drought, flood and widely scattered fuel supplies. If for example your boat or bus was delayed causing you to miss a connection, it would not be unusual for the staff to help with alternative transport or accommodation arrangements. But even in the cities most people are struck by how friendly the cab drivers are, how helpful the shop assistants and how courteous the man-in-the-street.

Your fellow travellers are also a valuable source of information and company. A surprisingly large proportion of people travelling in campervans in remote areas are older Australian couples who undertake major expeditions as soon as they retire. In a spirit of camaraderie, they are always willing to share information about road conditions, etc; you may even find some who go to the trouble of preparing lists of recommended campsites and attractions to exchange with people travelling in the opposite direction.

The Australian love of leisure is a boon to visitors who often find that new acquaintances are generous with their time. And of course it is much easier to meet people if they are frolicking on a beach or drinking in a pub rather than buried away in an office block.

An attempt to identify 'typically Australian' characteristics and pin down the national character as generous, gregarious, egalitarian and so on, must always be frustrated by the enormous differences between city and country, recent and long established migrant, European and Asian, not to mention the differences from state to state. A pub encounter in Tasmania is bound to be very different from one in Queensland, and the citizens of Melbourne are more difficult to get to know than the people of Alice Springs. But given the native open-heartedness of the majority and the common language (with occasional exceptions), you will find it easy to make new friends.

Visiting Friends and Relations. Eight million Britons have relations living in Australia. Even if you are not in this category, you are quite likely to have some addresses pressed upon you by friends, neighbours, colleagues or bank managers. Do not refuse these. Even if you feel inhibited about making contact with strangers, give it a chance. After all, Australians visiting Britain have been doing so in good conscience for years.

Two scenarios to which you might give some thought are visiting your own relations (whom you may or may not have met previously) and looking up distant contacts who will feel no particular obligation towards you. Always make it clear that you are a traveller on the move, rather than a freeloader (known as 'bludger' in Australia). Unless you are very obtuse (a dill, a drongo. . .) you should be able to tell whether it is appropriate to visit. When you unfold your plans for the rest of your stay in Australia, you may find that your current host immediately calls his or her mate on the other side of the country, tells them what a 'ripper' person you are, and insists that they pick you up from the airport or bus station and look after you.

Sex. The Australian male is the source of much discontent on the part of the Australian female. Many theories, such as the dire shortage of women in the early days of the colony, have been put forward to account for the unshakeable male chauvinism and egotism of so many Australian men. Although equal opportunities legislation is now in force, gross discrepancies between men and women persist in earnings and promotions, and sexism is rampant.

Women may notice that travelling in Australia, especially in country areas, is a little like being in a Moslem country: men either treat you as though you do not exist (swapping dubious jokes over your head with their mates) or else pay unwanted attention. Most advances can be repelled with a straightforward rebuff, which means you revert to being treated as though invisible. Obviously there are countless exceptions to this and the women's movement is making it more difficult for this kind of passé behaviour to go unnoticed or unchallenged. But it may take a long time before men and women can strike up friendships as equals.

In spite of the prevailing image of the Australian male as aggressor, many people are struck by the frankness of overtures made by Australian women towards men. Foreign men may find themselves approached at parties or on beaches (but not usually in pubs). If the opportunity for casual sex presents itself, you should be aware that the whole range of venereal diseases flourishes in this land of sexual freedom. AIDS is a serious problem, especially in Sydney which has Australia's largest gay community. The macho elements of Australian society are intolerant of gayness, and in the state of Queensland male homosexuality is still technically illegal.

Language. Australians subject the English language to some hideous indignities. Not content with recklessly abbreviating words, Australians insist on adding the suffix 'o' to the result, as in 'garbo' (dustman), 'derro' (down-and-out, from derelict) and male names such as Geoffo, Robbo, etc. Such formations inevitably strike the visitor's ear as childish.

Australian slang at its best is full of humour and vitality. An expression like 'ankle-biters' or 'rug rats' is much more vivid that 'kids' or 'infants', and 'flat out like a lizard drinking' is infinitely preferable to 'overworked'. Another favourite way of giving emphasis is to use absurd comparisons as in 'busier than a brickie in Beirut' or suggesting that a car is so economical that it 'runs on the smell of an oily rag' or 'he felt as inconspicuous as Liberace at a wharfies' (i.e. dockworkers') picnic'. They are of course famous for their line in crude expressions, such as describing anything that protrudes as 'sticking out like a dog's balls'.

Pronunciation (or lack of enunciation) can present problems for the visitor. The excuse often given for the Australian habit of barely moving the lips while talking is that it keeps out the flies and conserves energy in the heat. Predictably accents are broadest in isolated rural areas and weaker among people representing 'Old Money' who have tended, until the present rise of nationalism, to pride themselves on their 'Britishness'. Just remember that short vowels are often swallowed out of existence and a long 'a' becomes a long 'i' (and so Australia becomes (Au)strilya and mate becomes mite); 'i' becomes 'oi' (so pie-eyed meaning drunk becomes poyoyed). Meanwhile other vowel sounds, like 'ai' and 'ou', are pronounced so as to turn fairy tales into 'furry tiles' and down south into 'den seth'. Furthermore Australians have adopted an unusual interrogative inflection, so that statements can sound like questions. Try to avoid the temptation of supplying answers to these non-questions.

Most British speakers of English will encounter few real problems of misunderstanding, though there are some borrowings from Aboriginal languages that may be unfamiliar such as 'corroboree' for social gathering and 'bombara' for submerged reef. Americans can expect the same problems that they would encounter in Britain with words like 'boot' (trunk) and 'bonnet' (hood), and expressions like 'Would you like to be knocked up in the morning?' An Australian habit more familiar to Americans than to Poms is to transmute nouns into verbs such as 'to suicide' and 'to headquarter'.

The term 'bastard' is widely used when addressing males and is often a sign of familiarity and affection. Foreigners should probably avoid aping this expression since they might get the nuance wrong.

Literature. Marcus Clarke's novel *For The Term of his Natural Life* (1874), a sensational tale of convict life, documenting all the horrors of the penal system, is a good starting point. Another 19th century writer who should not be missed is Henry Lawson, whose short stories about life in the Australian Bush and male 'mateship' are most entertaining.

Miles Franklin rose to fame in 1901 with *My Brilliant Career*, a novel of pioneering life that has become familiar through the film version. Whereas Lawson's focus is on the poor bush battlers, Franklin describes the well off lives of established landowners (the 'squattocracy'). Katherine Susannah Prichard did something new by venturing into the harsh and arid outback in her novel about an Aboriginal woman, *Coonardoo* (1929); if this kind of subject matter appeals to you, then you will also enjoy Xavier Herbert's massive *Capricornia* (1938), a story of race conflict set in the Northern Territory.

Contemporary Australian literature is very much alive, with such internationally acclaimed writers as Peter Carey, Thomas Keneally (both Booker Prize winners), Christina Stead and the Nobel Prize winner, Patrick White. Olga Masters writes seemingly simple tales of narrow-minded rural towns in the 20s and 30s revealing unpalatable truths about domestic and family life. Helen Garner is another well known author whose novel about drug addiction, *Monkey Grip*, has also been made into a film. David Malouf will appeal to those who like poetic prose (try *Imaginary Life*).

In recent years a number of fine Aboriginal poets have emerged, such as Kath Walker, Kevin Gilbert and Colin Johnson, and Jack Davis is an Aboriginal playwright who wrote *Barungin*. Amongst white Australian playwrights, David Williamson is probably the best known for *Don's Party*, a bitingly satiric look at middle-class Australian life.

The vast majority of travellers to Australia arrive by air. After a long flight they are subject to a series of official controls. Most flights from abroad land early in the morning, and the queues for immigration and customs can add a couple of hours to the ordeal. It is easy to develop an instantly unfavourable (and undeserved) image of Australian society.

Before you touch down, you will be handed an *Incoming Passenger Card* and a *Customs, Quarantine and Wildlife Statement* to complete. As well as the predictable questions about name, age and length of stay, the Card asks you about how you intend to spend your visit. The authorities are quick to point out that this is not a sinister erosion of civil liberties but merely a means of identifying tourism trends. The Statement asks yes/no questions about the goods you are carrying and whether you have visited a farm or abattoir in the last 3 months.

Upon touchdown, you won't be allowed off until the interior has been sprayed with insecticide. Once the spray is deemed to have killed off foreign bodies, the doors are opened and the passengers may then leave the aircraft. On the way to immigration you can pause to buy duty-free drinks and cigarettes at the airport shops.

IMMIGRATION

Australian immigration officials can be harsh; if you anticipate an unfriendly welcome and close questioning then at least you may be pleasantly surprised if your encounter with them turns out to be less than stressful. Australia has an estimated 50,000 illegal immigrants (nearly a quarter of them British) and the authorities are not keen for this number to increase. So you can expect to be quizzed about your motives for visiting the country, and how you intend to support yourself during your stay. Young people are particular targets, and it seems that officials assume anyone under 30 plans to work illegally.

Bear in mind that your visa merely confers permission to apply for entry into Australia rather than the right of automatic admission; 'subject to entry permit on arrival' is the wording used. To pass this hurdle successfully, ensure that you have as much in your favour as possible.

When you signed your visa application form, you undertook to have an onward or return ticket. You will probably be asked to produce it. You also promised that you have 'sufficient funds' to support yourself during your stay, and the immigration officer may ask you to verify this with a display of your wealth. Although travellers on working holiday visas carrying less than £10 have been allowed in, try to have at least a couple of hundred dollars in cash or travellers cheques backed up by a credit card or two. This is particularly important if you are travelling on a visitor visa, which specifically prohibits taking up employment. If you are not flush with funds, the authorities will be keen to see the address of a person (preferably a relation) who you claim will look after you during your stay. And even though it may be 6am, the officer won't hesitate to call and check your story.

Assuming you persuade the officer that you are a suitable candidate for entry into Australia, he or she will stamp your passport and write in the maximum length of stay. If all is in order, this should be 6 months for British citizens and 3 months for North American visitors.

You can apply for an extension from the Immigration Department, but you need a convincing story and plenty of money. It is easier to fly out (e.g. to New Zealand or Indonesia) and reapply. You can never change a visitor's visa to a working visa inside Australia, so don't try.

Overstaying. Many people stay beyond the maximum permitted duration and by no means all are caught before leaving. You will certainly be found out upon departure, as the normal passport check catches offenders. You may be blacklisted for a year.

Occasionally overstayers are detected before they attempt to leave. Prosecution and subsequent deportation are not automatic if you are caught overstaying. Although the maximum penalty is $1000 plus 6 months imprisonment, most illegal immigrants are simply asked to leave. If they are discovered by the Immigration Service but leave of their own accord, they are barred for 3 years. Those who are actually deported are prohibited for 5 years, or longer if they owe their fare to the government.

QUARANTINE

The immigration officer who deals with you will also carry out a preliminary quarantine check. The zeal with which the authorities try to keep out plants and animals and their derivatives may seem excessive. However, the nation is free of most of the world's serious agricultural diseases and the Australians intend to keep it that way. On your Statement you are asked if you are carrying any plants or animals (alive or dead) or items derived from them: from dogs to dairy products, and salami to snakes. Even the straw hat you might have picked up in Singapore is prohibited.

Be prepared for the official to look you straight in the eye and ask you to verify your claims verbally. To avoid this grilling, bins are placed strategically in which you can dump suspect items. This is also where you should throw away the biscuits that you forgetfully lifted from the airline meal tray. As well as these prohibited items, you are supposed to declare all wooden articles (including matches), flower seeds and baby food. The immigration officer will ask a customs official to inspect them (so don't wrap the teak salad bowl you've brought as a gift for an aunt), but you will normally be allowed to take them through. If you admit to visiting a farm in the last 3 months, you can expect closer questioning and inspection of your shoes.

Avoid any temptation to evade the quarantine laws. In keeping with the authorities' concern for keeping out alien diseases, the penalties for failing to declare all dubious items can be stiff; the maximum is a $50,000 fine and 10 years' imprisonment. Frequent travellers to Australia report that by declaring a harmless little item or saying you have recently visited a farm, your honesty rating is considerably enhanced and you may get through the customs formalities more quickly. On the other hand declaring something you believe to be harmless (say a small packet of homeopathic dried crocodile meat bought as a joke in Malaysia) may well result in its confiscation. Such items can be reclaimed on your way out of the country but only within 2 months; otherwise you have to ask for permission to post it out of the country from the airport post office, under the surveillance of a customs official.

CUSTOMS

The last thing the immigration officer does is mark your *Customs, Quarantine and Wildlife Statement* with a single letter. The meaning of these is mystifying to outsiders, but it is a code that indicates whether your belongings should be checked by customs. You pick up your (freshly sprayed) luggage from the baggage carousel and proceed to the customs area. At the entrance, an official will direct you either to the least crowded customs desk or — if you have the right letter — straight through the exit to the outside world. In any event you'll be handed a *Health Warning Card*, which you are supposed to keep for 6 weeks and show to a doctor if you fall ill.

Alcohol and Tobacco. Australian duty-free allowances are not over-generous. Travellers aged 18 or over may import one litre of alcoholic liquor (beer, wine or spirits) plus 250 cigarettes or 250 grams of tobacco. As mentioned above, you can buy your allowance upon arrival. This useful facility means you need not lug drink and tobacco from one side of the world to the other, but note that the prices in Australia are much higher than at duty-free shops such as those in Singapore.

Prohibited and Restricted Goods. In addition to the articles forbidden under the quarantine laws, many goods are either prohibited or need a permit. For specific information, contact the Australian Customs Service, Customs House, 5 Constitution Avenue, Canberra, ACT 2601 (06-275 6666).

The restrictions are divided into two categories: animal products that do not carry a health risk but are derived from endangered species, including ivory and rare furs; and items thought likely to endanger Australian society such as weapons, obscene publications and non-prescription drugs. As in many countries, the Australian authorities make stringent checks to keep out illegal narcotics. The penalties for trying to import even a small amount of cannabis, cocaine or opiate are severe. Anyone caught bringing in a 'commercial' quantity of any illegal drug may be locked up for life.

Despite Australia's stringent quarantine regulations you can bring in a cat or dog from the UK or Ireland subject to getting the required certificates and leaving Rover or Tiddles in quarantine kennels for 3 months after arrival. Get the relevant forms from the Commonwealth Veterinary Officer, Australia House, London WC2B 4LA.

Other Goods. You are allowed to import a 'reasonable amount' of personal effects free of duty, plus gifts up to a value of $400 ($200 for travellers under 18). The next $160-worth is taxed at a concessionary rate of 20%. Duty on higher amounts can be much steeper. Television sets and fur products do not qualify for exemption.

Currency. There is no limit to the amount of money that you can take out of Britain or into Australia, but you may not export more than $5000 in Australian notes and coins. Americans wishing to import or export sums of US$10,000 or more must declare the fact to US Customs.

DEPARTURE

For a country that is otherwise fairly civilised, Australia imposes an improperly high charge on anyone who wants to leave the country. Departure tax of $27 is payable by every international traveller aged 12 or over. You have the option of paying it at any post office or the Department of Immigration, Local Government and Ethnic Affairs in advance. While this is worthwhile for people who can't trust themselves to preserve $27 to pay the tax upon departure, most travellers simply pay at the airport.

After checking in for your flight, you must go to a special counter to hand over your $27 and have a stamp affixed to your ticket. The tax cannot be paid by credit card; only Australian dollars in travellers cheques or cash will do. If you are utterly penniless, you will be permitted to leave the country after filling out a form explaining your plight. You will not be readmitted until you pay the Australian government the money owed.

Two classes of travellers are exempt from departure tax (but it is still necessary to go to the departure tax counter to get an 'exempt' stamp). The first group is those who have been in Australia for less than two calendar days: i.e. if you arrive on one day and depart at any time the next day, you are exempt. Note that you are allowed to leave the airport (for example, to stay in a hotel overnight before an onward flight to New Zealand), as long as you have a valid Australian visa. The other exception is for those who take a side trip overseas during their visit to Australia. Exemption is granted after you have paid the tax once, until you return to your 'point of origin' (your home country). So if you visit New Zealand or anywhere else as a side trip during the course of your stay, subsequent departures are tax-exempt. The process of claiming exemption is easier if you can produce a return ticket for the side trip.

Customs and Migration. You have to pass through customs and migration checks on your way out of Australia, which is where they discover if you've overstayed. You are required to fill out an *Outgoing Passenger Card* explaining when you arrived and where you're heading. In addition, your luggage may be searched, and any goods made from endangered species will be confiscated. In view of the number of crocodiles and goannas that appear to be thriving in Australia, you may be surprised to learn that they are on the list of threatened animals, and any items made from their skins will be seized. You need a permit to export 'items of heritage significance to Australia', such as Aboriginal objects, opals worth more than $100,000 and ancient fossils. If you think you might require a permit, contact the Cultural Heritage Section of the Department of Communications and the Arts, GPO Box 2154, Canberra, ACT 2601 (06-279 1610).

Duty-Free Goods. As well as the usual airport duty-free shops, many Australian cities have downtown shops where you can buy goods free of duty within the 10 days before you leave the country. Prices at these places are lower than at the airport duty-free shops, and you can take the goods out of the shop (rather than just ordering them and then picking them up at the airport as in most countries). A label indicating the fact that you have bought duty-free goods will be firmly attached to your flight ticket and is inspected at the airport of departure. The contents of your bags will be checked against the paperwork to make sure you have resisted the temptation of consuming any of your purchases before leaving the country.

Returning to Britain. Apart from the culture shock induced by returning from the coast of Queensland to a wet Monday morning at Heathrow Airport, your biggest problem is likely to be bringing in expensive purchases (some of which you may have picked up *en route* at bargain prices in the Far East). You are allowed only £31 of goods free of duty; on the remainder, you have to pay Value Added Tax plus additional duty on some items.

The duty-free allowance for alcohol is one litre of spirits or sparkling wine plus 2 litres of still wine. The standard size for wine bottles in Australia is 750ml: if you bring in three bottles you'll be marginally over the limit but are unlikely to be charged duty. You may also bring in 200 cigarettes or 50 cigars or 250g of tobacco.

Returning to (or through) the USA. American customs laws apply equally to returning US residents and other travellers passing through the States *en route* to Canada, Europe or elsewhere. The alcohol and tobacco limits of 1 quart (just under 1 litre) plus 200 cigarettes or equivalent are available only to travellers above the minimum drinking age of the state you first arrive in; in the case of California, this is 21 years. Gifts to the value of US$100 are allowed duty-free. The booklet *Know Before You Go* (free from the US Customs Service, PO Box 7407, Washington, DC 20044) contains full details of duty rates and restricted goods.

TRAVEL RESTRICTIONS WITHIN AUSTRALIA

Numerous quarantine regulations govern the movement of agricultural produce across state borders to prevent the spread of pests such as the aphid phylloxera (which attacks vines), Queensland fruit fly and boil smut (which affects corn). Tasmania and South Australia are the only two states to be free of fruit fly. The rules are enforced by occasional agricultural checkpoints. The best advice is not to take fruit and vegetables across any state border. There are also some local restrictions within states, such as the rule that prohibits bananas being taken into an area within 40km of the post office at Carnarvon, Western Australia.

It is illegal to visit certain areas of Australia without first obtaining a permit to do so. Most restricted areas are those on Aboriginal land or around Aboriginal communities. Information concerning how to apply for a permit is given in the relevant state chapters. There are also restrictions on visiting military zones, such as the areas of South Australia around Woomera rocket station, and Maralinga where the British tested atomic bombs in the 1950s.

arvi	afternoon
award rate	union agreed wage
blockie	vegetable or fruit farmer
CES	Commonwealth Employment Service (job centres)
compo	workers' compensation
dole bludger	one who lives off social security
jackaroo	station hand (female version is a jillaroo)
penalty	extra pay for working unsocial hours
sickie	a day off due to sickness (normally feigned)
smoko	coffee break
yakka	hard work

When it comes to finding a job, people have started to say that Australia is no longer the lucky country. In 1996 unemployment stood at 9%, and jobs for foreign travellers are more scarce than they were a few years ago. But people still pour in with working holiday visas and expect to step into a job. There is still work available but it may take time to find it, and pay and conditions may not be what you had been hoping for.

Early in 1996 the Australian government set a worldwide cap on working holiday visas in a belated attempt to get the unemployment rate down, and the British quota of visas was fully allocated 4 months before the July deadline was reached. This left many young Britons who were counting on getting a working holiday visa in order to travel to Australia during their 'year out' with no option but to wait for the following year's allocation. However, following the conservative coalition's election victory later in the year the allocation was almost immediately bumped up from 16,500 to 21,000, apparently as a result of pressure from Australian farmers. Check with the High Commission to confirm the current situation.

Travellers who have working holiday visas in their passports will be allowed into the country even if their funds have been depleted by a long trans-Asia trip, and many have found it possible, even in the midst of recession, to save enough in a couple of months to fund a voyage around Australia and perhaps on to New Zealand. This is not so surprising in a country where the average male wage is over $550 per week, though many travellers find themselves earning about half this in take-home wages. On the other hand, fast word-processors (men and women) can earn $15 an hour in the big cities.

Trades unions are strong in Australia and in many fields of employment have negotiated high wages and some interesting benefits. Weekend work is usually paid at 'penalty' rates, often twice the hourly wage. The building unions have considerable clout: among other perks, all workers on buildings over eight storeys high earn a height allowance, even if their work keeps them firmly on the ground. There are many other such perks, such as holiday pay at a level 17½% above the basic wage, but these are unlikely to benefit temporary employees.

Working Holiday Visas. British, Irish, Canadian, Dutch and Japanese people between the ages of 18 and 25 are eligible to apply for a working holiday visa. New Zealanders can work in Australia without any formalities. UK citizens over 25 and under 30 are occasionally given a visa if they plead their case especially well at an interview. The visa is valid for 12 months and is not renewable either in Australia or at home. Normally the visa expires 13 months from the date of issue. If you are travelling to Australia slowly and want to maximise your time downunder, ask for the visa to be dated from entry rather than from the time it is issued. It is meant for people intending to use any money they earn in Australia to supplement their holiday funds. Working full-time for more than 3 months is considered contrary to the spirit of the visa, and doing so for one employer is illegal.

The first step is to get the working holiday application information sheet and application form M418 from Australian Outlook, 1 Buckhurst Road, Bexhill-on-Sea, East Sussex TN40 1QS, enclosing a 9x12 stamped addressed envelope (47p stamp). The completed form, passport and fee are then returned to one of the addresses indicated on the information sheet. The non-refundable processing fee in the UK is currently a steep £71. Travellers have reported that it is easier and faster to get visas outside London: San Francisco, Bangkok, Kuala Lumpur and Beijing have all been praised for their speed and efficiency.

The second step is to get as much money in the bank as possible. Each application is assessed on its own merits, but the most important requirement is a healthy bank balance. The amount recommended at present is £2000, from which the cost of travel may come. Exceptions are sometimes made if you can supplement your more meagre savings with an official letter of guarantee from a bank manager who has been persuaded a large sum will be coming your way. The more money you can scrape together the better, especially if you can't supply the authorities with a list of friends and relatives in Australia willing to bail you out financially if necessary. If you have borrowed a large sum to bump up your balance, rather than saved steadily over a period of time, be prepared to provide a plausible explanation for this. Sometimes the visa will be processed by return of post, but at other times of the year (particularly autumn) it can take weeks. Whatever you do, don't make a firm flight booking until your visa comes through.

Some people worry that if their application for a working holiday visa is turned down for some reason, they won't be granted a visitor's visa. But the High Commission maintains that this is not the case.

Official Work Schemes. BUNAC, in association with STA Travel, has set up a working holiday package for British young people who hope to work in Australia. This includes flights to Australia, advice on working visas, orientation on arrival and a back-up service from STA offices throughout Australia or from the allied organisation SSA (Student Services Australia, PO Box 399, Carlton South, Vic 3053). Departures are in July and September. For details contact BUNAC, 16 Bowling Green Lane, London EC1R 0BD (0171-251 3472).

SWAP in Canada has a similar programme for students and recent graduates aged 18–25. Departures take place in May and September. The registration fee is $250 and you must have funds of $1800. Ask at any Travel CUTS office across Canada.

The organisation GAP Activity Projects (44 Queen's Road, Reading, Berkshire RG1 4BB; 01734-594914) arranges work overseas for school-leavers during their 'gap' year before starting college. There are several projects in Australia starting at various times of the year, lasting between 4 and 9 months and usually involving work on farms or in private schools.

Unofficial Work. It is well known that many people who do not qualify for a working visa still manage to find work. The majority get jobs in fruit harvests where farmers are so desperate to have their crops picked that they will hire almost anyone. The problem is that these massive harvests become targets for immigration investigators. Tales of large-scale deportation have emerged from, for example, Mildura in Victoria, Donnybrook and Carnarvon in Western Australia, and Mundubberra in Queensland. Some make it a rule never to work with Swedes as it always seems to be Swedes who get caught. If you work on small family farms or in the city, detection is less likely.

Bureaucracy and Tax. All people in employment in Australia are obliged to apply for a nine-digit tax file number. If you refuse to divulge it to an employer within 28 days (which is your legal right), you are automatically taxed at the top rate of 49% and furthermore will arouse suspicion about your entitlement to work. If you plan to work for less than 28 days, it should be enough to say that you have applied for a tax file number.

Foreigners are eligible to apply for a tax file number at a post office or tax office, but normally will have to show a passport with a valid entry permit (e.g. a working holiday visa). It is also possible to obtain a tax file number with weaker documents, such as vehicle registration, an Australian driving licence, a bank book or evidence of payment of a gas, electricity or telephone bill. Travellers have been known to be given a tax file number even when they show their passport stamped 'Employment prohibited'. Others who lack the appropriate visa have invented a number and have got away with it; others have been discovered and deported.

The ultimate tax liability for non-residents of Australia is 29% of all income earned up to $20,600. Residents are taxed at a lower rate and only on earnings over the personal allowance of $5200 in the tax year. There are also concessionary tax rates, for example residents who work north of the 26th parallel and those who work in the fruit and vegetable industries have only 15% tax deducted; non-residents are technically not eligible.

Despite a tightening-up of the tax situation, many working holidaymakers still successfully apply for tax rebates. Always tick 'resident' on any official forms (officially you are a resident, for the purposes of the tax man, if you intend to be in Australia for at least 183 days). Your application is more likely to succeed if you use a tax agent; many have found that a brief visit (costing about $80) to a tax professional will gain them hundreds of dollars. The best time to apply is in July just after the end of the tax year on June 30th. You will also need a leaving certificate called a 'group certificate' from your employer. With luck your rebate will come within ten days though you may have to wait for a month. A recommended tax agent in Sydney is Income Tax Professionals, Lower Level, 60 Pitt St.

THE JOB HUNT

Many British travellers have been greeted very positively by prospective employers, despite the Australian propensity for 'Pommy-bashing' (as illustrated in a popular joke: 'Q: What is the difference between a Pom and a computer? A: You have to punch information into both of them, but with a computer you only have to do it once.' Naturally employers do not want to hire a mere tourist who might take off on a whim, so it is a good idea at interviews to say that you are in Australia for an 'indefinite period'. A little experience goes a long way with Australian employers, so it is also wise to exaggerate your experience. Anyone who does have a trade, skill or profession should bring references from home. British nurses should register in the UK before departure — this will make the job hunt easier and the salary higher. Similarly tradesmen (of which there is a dire shortage in Sydney and elsewhere) should bring their papers and tools.

Most people agree that the best way to find work is to walk in and ask, especially at bars, restaurants and stores in the cities and at farms in the country. This is the method used by about one third of all successful job-seekers in Australia. There are four other main ways of finding work: the Commonwealth Employment Service (CES), private employment agencies, newspaper advertisements and notice boards.

The CES. The Commonwealth Employment Service is not solely for the benefit of Commonwealth visitors; it happens to be the name for Australian job centres ('Commonwealth' here refers to the Commonwealth of Australia, not the British Commonwealth). In almost all cases, any foreigner who uses a CES will have to present a working holiday visa.

Like job centres anywhere the CES posts details of vacancies that have been registered with them. The card should give the name and address of the employer, the number of helpers required, the approximate duration of employment, accommodation (if any), pay and conditions. In some offices free phones are provided for contacting prospective employers. If you are short of money they might even supply a bus ticket to your work destination.

Some CES offices have separate departments that specialise in casual work or in jobs in the hospitality industry; look for branches called Temp-Line or CasHire. Often the work is for only a few hours, perhaps unloading a ship or moving office furniture. Competition for short-term jobs varies from place to place, but there will always be a hard core of travellers attracted by the prospect of instant cash (usually $50–$90 a day). To be in the running for such day jobs, you usually have to turn up very early (between 5 and 6am). Even then you might have to put in an appearance on two or three consecutive mornings before you get sent to a building site, factory, restaurant, warehouse, or whatever. Normally doggedness is rewarded.

Reports vary about how useful the CES is. Obviously it depends on the individual office and the time of year. Some users have said that smaller suburban offices tend to be more helpful than big city branches, though with less choice of work. The addresses of the main offices in the state capitals are given in the regional chapters, together with other suggestions for finding work. Further addresses can be found in any Australian telephone directory; look under 'Employment Agencies' in the *Yellow Pages*. In smaller towns, the CES may be represented by an agent in a post office or shop, and it may open only for a limited season, for example for the duration of a local harvest or busy resort season.

Private Employment Agencies. Although not as widespread as in Britain, private agencies are a good potential source of jobs for travellers, especially those who have some office skills, computer or financial experience. Some agencies have even been known to visit hostels to recruit casual staff (e.g. Bligh in Sydney). Big agencies include Bligh, Centacom, Drake, Ecco and the Staffing Centre. Most won't let you sign up unless there is a fair chance of work; November is a quiet time but things pick up in December and January. The standards expected by the temp agencies are often much higher than in Britain and most will subject you to a stringent typing test.

It is worth comparing terms and wages among these agencies; some pay your wages directly and these can be higher than those paid by individual firms for similar work. Some agencies specialise in rural, station and farm placements or in offshore tourist resort placements. It may take some time before you get continuous assignments, but it is worth sticking with a good agency for a reasonable length of time, as placements will become more frequent and more interesting once they realise you are reliable and hardworking.

An agency called Involvement Volunteers acts as a consultancy and keeps a register of voluntary positions and some paid work on farms for individuals from abroad. Among recent placements have been research assistants in Queensland and at a bird observatory in Western Australia and a cataloguer at a historic house. In exchange for the registration fee participants will be met at Melbourne Airport and given an orientation and back-up service. Details from the Director Tim Cox (PO Box 218, Port Melbourne, Vic 3207; or in the US Involvement Corps Inc, 15515 Sunset Boulevard, 108 Pacific Palisades, CA 90272). An organisation called World Travellers Network provides help with job placements, accommodation and discount travel, and also helps arrange voluntary conservation work with the Australian Trust for Conservation Volunteers (see below). Further details from their Head Office, 14 Wentworth Avenue, Sydney, NSW 2010 (02-9264 2477).

Newspaper Advertisements. The 'Casual Work Available' columns of the daily press carry a tempting-looking range of opportunities from 'promoting art' (selling prints) to working as a film extra (where you will be required to pay a registration fee with little immediate prospect of work). Although you may occasionally find worthwhile employment this way, many travellers find more fruitful opportunities under specific headings such as 'Positions Vacant — Hospitality Industry'. If you think you might make a successful door-to-door salesman, the newspaper is the place to look, and some Poms have said that their accents went over surprisingly well on Australian doorsteps. There is so much competition for the jobs listed in papers like the *Sydney Morning Herald*, the Melbourne *Age* and the Perth *West Australian* that you should try to buy the paper the preceding evening (anytime after 9.30pm from the newspaper offices) so you can start your job search first thing in the morning. Sometimes labouring jobs are advertised, giving only an address and the first person to arrive at the site (usually by 8am) gets the job. Specialist magazines might also be worth checking for station work, such as *Land* and *Queensland Country Life*.

Notice Boards. Check notice boards at YHA and other hostels (particularly those that are the most popular with backpackers) or at universities, especially as summer approaches (October/November). If you are settled in one place and are looking for work, ask around for suitable notice boards and post a notice indicating your availability.

WORKING IN THE COUNTRY

There is no doubt that work is much more readily available in the cities, especially Sydney, Canberra and Melbourne. However to discover the exotic features of Australia, it is necessary to leave the comforts of city life behind. One of the best ways is to get a job as a seasonal farm worker on a fruit farm or in the Outback. You may well make good money, but even if you don't you can save most of what you earn, while working in uninterrupted sunshine. But bear in mind that the hours will be long, the work hard, the heat debilitating, the flies infuriating and the spiders and snakes a constant worry.

Fruit Picking. The country CES offices should be able to help, if only by giving you the *Harvest Table* that they publish; this is a good starting place, though it is by no means comprehensive. Asking in local pubs and hostels might also turn up a lead. Try the local fruit-growers' association (if there is one), some of which are so eager to attract foreign pickers that they advertise in the cities.

Harvest seasons vary from state to state: crops ripen first in Queensland and finish in Tasmania as you move further away from the equator. Even the two major grape harvests of New South Wales and South Australia do not necessarily take place simultaneously during the harvest months of February, March and April. Mechanisation has reduced opportunities for itinerant grapepickers but there is a growing trend to market 'hand picked' wines that guarantees a certain amount of work.

Just as in Europe and North America, there are professional pickers who follow the harvests around the continent, so if you find yourself falling behind your fellow-workers during the first few days of the harvest, you should console yourself with the knowledge that you are competing with years of experience. The standard hours for a fruit picker working in hot conditions are 6am–6pm with two or three hours off in the middle of the day. Most picking is paid at piece rates though in some cases you will be paid an hourly wage of $8–10. Not many fruit farmers can supply accommodation, so serious fruit-pickers carry a tent. It also helps to have your own transport, first to find a vacancy and then for shopping, banking, socialising, etc. Failing that, you will have to rely on hitch-hiking. Details of various fruit and other harvests (including tobacco in Queensland and Victoria, hops in Tasmania, etc.) are given in each of the regional chapters.

Conservation Volunteers. Several organisations give visitors a chance to experience the Australian countryside or bush. The Australian Trust for Conservation Volunteers (PO Box 423, Ballarat, Victoria 3353; 03-5333 1483) welcomes overseas participants on projects, which are mostly in the state of Victoria. The work may include fencing off areas where the soil has been eroded or where birds and flowers need to be protected, controlling noxious weeds and vermin, planting trees, restoring historic buildings or constructing trails or bird hides in National Parks. Accommodation might be in shearers' cottages, village halls, ski lodges or under canvas. Overseas volunteers are welcome if they can make a minimum commitment of six weeks and a daily contribution of A$20 to the Trust. Food, accommodation and transport during the project are provided.

There is also an active organisation called Willing Workers on Organic Farms (WWOOF) in Australia, which has its headquarters at Mount Murrindal Co-op, Buchan, Vic 3885 (03-5155 0218). Its Australian list includes over 400 organic farms, which are concentrated in New South Wales, Victoria and Queensland. All of these farms are looking for short or long-term voluntary help, and in exchange for 4–6 hours' labour per day volunteers receive food, accommodation and tuition/practice in organic farming methods. The farm list comes automatically with membership, which costs £10/US$25 from abroad or A$25 in Australia.

Interesting research projects take place throughout Australia and some may be willing to include volunteers. Check university department notice boards, especially biology, zoology and marine science.

The Outback. Working on a station or ranch is one of the most authentic experiences of Australia you can have. Some properties are so big and so remote that flying is the only practical means of access. Despite the vast areas and enormous flocks, it is usually possible for one or two experienced stockmen to look after the property, though they may need an assistant (a jackaroo or jillaroo) at busy times, which vary between states and according to the specialisation of the property. If you can't ride, you might get taken on as a cook or home-help to amuse and teach the children. Station work is easiest to find in the Northern

Territory, western Queensland and northern Western Australia, especially in February/March when station managers tend to do their seasonal hiring.

Shearing is out of the question for the uninitiated but the post of roustabout is open to the inexperienced. Roustabouts fetch, carry, sweep and trim stained bits from the fleeces. Check adverts in the agricultural press under the heading 'Stock and Land' for shearing team recruitment. One particularly unpleasant job assigned to roustabouts is catching and holding lambs for 'mulesing' (i.e. having the fleshy area around their sacrums removed to prevent blowfly) and castration.

As more and more working stations are also being opened to tourists, you may also find work as a Jack (or Sheila)-of-all-trades on a ranch, looking after the guests. There is no special season for this, so check newspaper adverts. Before answering such an advert, you should remind yourself of all the hazards and drawbacks of outback life (see *Health*) and bear in mind that it is often a rough, male-dominated world, so not for fragile types of either sex.

TOURISM AND CATERING

As in the hospitality industry anywhere, most employment demands in Australian tourism are seasonal and therefore ideally suited to the traveller. Working for a few months at any of the hundreds of coastal resorts, particularly in Queensland, can be one of the most enjoyable ways of saving money. In remote areas, the employee turnover is often brisk and there is a good demand for waitresses and barmaids (though be sure to distinguish between these and 'hostess' jobs that require altogether less savoury skills). Australian bars and hotels are not renowned for their sexist-free attitudes though topless waitressing is increasingly being banned.

Casual catering wages are high compared to the equivalent British wage: typically $8.50-$9 an hour, time and a half for Saturday work and weekday overtime (anything over eight hours) and double time on Sundays and public holidays. Since many pubs and restaurants are shut on Sundays jobs that require you to work on Sundays are rare and, because of the high pay, much in demand. You can't expect to earn much extra in tips. Anyone with experience as a cook or chef will probably find themselves in great demand.

In addition to the multitude of resorts along the Great Barrier Reef (see *Queensland: Work*), another holiday area to consider is the Australian Alps where ski resorts are expanding and gaining in popularity. Mount Buller, Falls Creek and Mount Hotham on the Victorian side and Thredbo and Perisher on the New South Wales side are ski centres where you might find work. Ask at the CES offices in Cooma or Wangaratta, preferably four to six weeks before the season begins in June.

A company that advertises heavily for working travellers to join its itinerant sales team is the World Information Network (9 Belmore St, Surry Hills, Sydney, NSW 2010) with positions in Cairns, Brisbane, Sydney, Melbourne, Adelaide and Perth and offices in all those cities except Cairns.

Fishing. It is sometimes possible to get work on prawn fishing vessels out of Darwin, Cairns, Townsville, Broome or even Karumba on the Gulf of Carpentaria, work that can be idyllic outside the rush periods when there is spare time for snorkelling, island-hopping, etc. Catches are much less lucrative than they used to be and most deckhands now prefer to be paid a wage rather than take a percentage of the profits. The work of sorting and loading prawns is tedious but not too unpleasant except when the spines stick into your hands.

Women are often taken on as cooks. They should make it quite clear before leaving harbour whether or not they wish to be counted among the recreational facilities of the boat, since numerous stories are told of the unfair pressures placed on women crew members at sea. There are even worse potential dangers; a few years ago a prawn trawler was capsized by a whale and the two deckhands were eaten by sharks.

Naturally, skippers prefer to recruit experienced deckhands. If after enquiring at all the fishing offices and after making yourself a familiar sight at the wharfs you still have had no luck, you might consider going along to a net shed and volunteering to work unpaid for a few days, learning how to mend nets. Then if an opening on a boat does arise, you will be the first to be considered for the job.

The CES harvesting booklet includes prawning and scalloping on the coast of Western Australia around Carnarvon. The season lasts from March to October and accommodation is available in caravan parks. Sometimes you see advertisements for 'oyster openers', a skill worth cultivating if only for your own consumption. Scallop-splitting is another favourite among casual workers, e.g. around Bicheno on the east coast of Tasmania.

At the time of writing the exchange rate was about A$2.06 = £1 and A$1.35 = US$1.

Exchange rates are listed in the Australian daily press, but are quoted in terms of what the local dollar is worth (typically £0.46 or US$0.80); to convert to what your £ or US$ will buy, divide one by the rate quoted.

See *Before You Go* for advice on how to carry your travel fund.

Coins. 5c, 10c, 50c, $1 and $2. British visitors will be familiar with the feel of the 10c and 20c coins as these are identical in size and weight to 5p and 10 pence pieces at home, but should remember that the Australian versions are double the units of their British counterparts. Most visitors quickly learn to hoard 20c and 50c coins for use in all sorts of machines from parking meters to chocolate bar dispensers.

In addition to these coins in general circulation, there are gold 'Australian Nuggets' whose face value is between $15 and $100 but whose actual value is many times this. Watch out for New Zealand coins in your change; they are worth less than their Australian counterparts.

Notes. $5 (orange/mauve), $10 (turquoise/yellow), $20 (red/khaki), $50 (gold/green), $100 (blue/grey). As with high-value notes anywhere, $50 and $100 bills may be treated with some suspicion and are not welcomed by taxi drivers.

BANKS

There are four big banks in Australia: ANZ, National Australia Bank, Westpac and the partly government-owned Commonwealth Bank, which has 1800 branches. In addition there are numerous smaller banks (notably the Advance Bank in New South Wales and the State Banks of Victoria and New South Wales), plus many savings institutions such as building societies and credit unions. Since financial deregulation in Australia, a number of foreign banks such as Barclays and Citibank have appeared. Note that the ANZ Bank is no relation of the ANZ Bank in New Zealand and neither is Westpac directly affiliated with Westpac New Zealand, so do not give them your custom in the hope of easing money transfers to New Zealand.

Exchange Transactions. You get a better rate for travellers cheques than for cash, but commissions vary dramatically. For example the Commonwealth Bank charges $2 per cheque whereas Westpac charges a flat $10 for an exchange transaction. If you are carrying American Express or Thomas Cook travellers cheques try to encash them at one of their branches (addresses given in the regional chapters) since then you pay only the stamp duty (of 20c per cheque).

Banking hours are usually 9.30am to 3.30 or 4pm, Monday-Thursday, with late opening until 5pm on Fridays. Some city-centre branches open 8am to 6pm, Monday-Thursday and to 8pm on Fridays. In rural areas, you may find that the only bank for miles around opens on only one or two days each week and charges high commission on changing travellers cheques.

Except at international airports, it is difficult to change foreign currency or travellers cheques outside banking hours. Travel agencies and luxury hotels are worth trying, but you will get an unfavourable rate. If a small town bank won't change your cash, try to draw funds on an ATM card or Credit Card. Better still, organise a bank account in Australia.

Opening a Bank Account. It is surprisingly quick and easy to open an account in Australia. Although you need to have a mailing address in Australia, you are unlikely to be asked for references and can open an account with just a few dollars. You will be asked to provide proof of identity which for most travellers would simply be their passports. Personal cheques are used less frequently in Australia than in Britain (partly because automatic banking is so efficient) so a cheque account is of little use. It is more profitable to open an interest-bearing savings account with a passbook or an automatic banking card. Another advantage of an Australian account is that you can lodge important papers with your branch, either free or for a nominal fee.

As the Commonwealth Bank has more branches than the others, and has links with most post offices allowing withdrawals to be made by passbook holders, you would be advised to open an account with them. If you intend to travel in rural areas, a passbook account is best since you can then withdraw cash at most post offices; but if you want rapid access to your money in cities at any time, opt for the Keycard account.

One irritating feature of Australian bank accounts is that state and federal taxes are levied on transactions, making it difficult to keep precise track of your finances; it is worth allowing 10c or 20c for taxes on each transaction. If you wish to open a bank account before you leave home, see the section in *Before You Go.*

Bank charges are generally high in Australia. For example if you let the balance in certain accounts slip below $500 there may be a charge of $2 or $3 in addition to the state tax. You are unlikely to be granted an overdraft facility unless you are (according to Westpac) 'a resident customer with a stable, long-term job', but there's no harm in trying. You could also apply in Australia for a credit card, although again evidence of secure employment will probably be necessary.

Automatic Teller Machines (ATMs). As mentioned in *Before You Go* the Link and Plus Systems to which many UK building societies and North American banks belong, has outlets in Australia. You can withdraw money from your UK current account in Australian dollars. But a locally issued ATM card is even more useful. Australian banks are well advanced in terms of their 'hole-in-the-wall' ATMs. As well as drawing cash you can shift funds from one account to another, check your balance and even pay the electricity bill.

The four main banks have brand names for their money machines: ANZ — Night & Day; Commonwealth — Autobank; National Australia — Flexiteller; Westpac — Handybank. They are gradually becoming linked together, so that any customer can use the machine of any bank. You can also use your card to pay for goods and services through retailers equipped with electronic shopping facilities. A very high percentage of shops, petrol stations and other outlets have installed EFTPOS machines, Electronic Funds Transfer — Point of Sale, comparable to 'Switch' in the UK.

Credit Cards. Australians, it seems, like nothing better than to use a credit card. They collectively owe $2,500 million to the Australasian organisation Bankcard, equivalent to over $150 for each Australian woman, man and child. While many shops are unwilling to accept cheques, they gladly take credit cards. In general, any establishment that accepts Bankcard also takes Access/MasterCard and Visa. In keeping with the electronic revolution in Australian finance, an increasing number of establishments wipe your card through a machine to check its validity and solvency. This also means that the amount is charged to your account much more quickly than used to be the case. You can also draw money on a foreign credit card when the banks are open. They will advance cash up to your credit limit without undue formality, and may not even want to see your passport.

TIPPING
You are probably unlikely to find yourself in a situation where you feel obliged to tip. Restaurant staff in particular are paid (by law) a fair hourly wage and good overtime. But even in occupations like taxi-driving where there is no guaranteed wage, tips are not expected. While a number of tourist guides recommend a 10% gratuity for restaurants, hotels, etc., in reality this is practised in only the more upmarket establishments favoured by American and Japanese customers. And since these places are also frequented by some Australians who would rather die than leave a tip, you can cheerfully fail to tip without giving offence. You might feel inclined to round up a $4.75 taxi fare to $5, but you're equally likely to find a driver rounding down a fare of $10.25.

EMERGENCY CASH
You may find yourself 'boracic' (short of money) for a number of reasons: the banks being closed, non-arrival of promised funds from abroad or dropping your wallet into the South Pacific. If you have just a little, there is virtually no limit to the ways in which you can gamble your last $5 to make $1000, but the odds are stacked against you. When this strategy fails to pay off, being penniless need not spell total disaster. If you have a refundable airline ticket you could try to cash it in to sustain yourself until help (or a job) arrives. British Consulates can cash a personal cheque drawn on a British bank and backed with a cheque card for up to £50 in an emergency, though they do so reluctantly. You can do this only once.

Alternatively, you can get a relative or friend to send you an International Money Order in sterling or dollars. After paying a commission of around £7, your benefactor then sends the Order through the post. Most banks will not encash these immediately and may take as long as a month to clear them.

If you have money in your own bank account, you can cable the bank to telegraph funds to a specified Australian bank. It helps to nominate a bank linked with your own bank at home, such as the National Australia Bank (which owns the Clydesdale and Northern Banks in the UK). Even so you should allow at least 48 hours for your funds to reach a branch in major cities and longer in the depths of the Northern Territory or Tasmania. Should weekends or public holidays intervene, you may have to wait up to a week.

Provided you have an interesting story to tell about the cause of your financial embarrassment, you might approach the local (small town) newspaper. If they publish your tale, they may slant it in the form of a request for assistance, and with luck soft-hearted Antipodeans will respond with cash and offers of help. The information given in the chapter *Work* could suggest a more reliable solution to a cashflow crisis.

If you are really desperate and can find no one at home or among your fellow travellers willing to lend you some money, you can ask your consulate to repatriate you by putting you on a plane home. Your passport will be removed upon your arrival in your home country and will not be returned until you have paid the government for the flight plus a 'handling charge'. In fact permission to repatriate is very rarely granted these days because of the thousands of unpaid debts incurred by indigent travellers.

TELEPHONE

Australia's efficient national telephone system is operated by Telecom. In common with networks in Europe and North America, it is taking new innovations on board at a feverish rate while retaining long-established features such as manual exchanges and radio telephones in outlying areas, and antiquated payphones. A high proportion of phones are now card phones. Phone cards can now be bought in denominations of $2, $5, $10, $20 or $50 and are handy for international calls.

One great benefit of the Australian phone system is that you can, at present, make local calls of unlimited duration for the price of a single unit (21c from private telephones and 30c from payphones). And considering the distances involved, charges for trunk calls are reasonable (e.g. across the country for $1.75 for 3 minutes at night). A feature that you may enjoy less is the propensity of many businesses to play schmaltzy music while you hang on.

Tones. The tones used are the same as in Britain, which may be a little confusing for visitors from other countries. The dial tone is a constant buzz or continuous note. The ringing tone is two short rings in quick succession, followed by a longish pause. The engaged tone — a single repeated note — sounds similar to the American ringing tone, except faster. Dial 1100 (a free call) to hear the entire repertoire.

Numbers. Every Australian number has a two or three-digit area code, although at the time of writing area codes and numbers were undergoing a major nationwide overhaul that will standardise all codes at two digits and all numbers at eight digits by the end of 1997. Many numbers are already in this format, but be aware that the others will change during the lifetime of this book; keep an eye on local directories for up-to-the-minute information. The codes for the capital cities are:

Adelaide 08	Hobart 03
Brisbane 07	Melbourne 03
Canberra 06	Perth 09
Darwin 08	Sydney 02

Calls within the same area code are by no means all classed (and charged) as local calls: for example the Northern Territory is counted as all one area (code 08) but calls from Alice Springs to Darwin are charged at long-distance rates.

Directories. You may be pleasantly surprised to find that most phone booths in Australia have intact directories. The introductory pages of the phone book contain a wealth of useful information, from what to do in the event of a cyclone (Darwin) to a map of the suburban railway network (Melbourne). Directories are made up of 'white pages' (the regular alphabetical listing, sometimes divided into separate areas), the classified 'yellow pages' listing everything from abattoirs to zoos, and 'blue pages' containing community information and government organisations. In large cities, directories are split into separate volumes, and there may be a separate commercial directory such as the Melbourne *BIG* (Business Information Guide).

Numbers for directory enquiries (information) vary from place to place, but in most cities you should dial 013 for local numbers, 0175 for other destinations within Australia and 0103 for international assistance. All these calls are free. An ex-directory private line is called a 'silent number'.

Dial-a-Service. Every city has a wide range of numbers to call for various types of information or advice, many of which are shown at the beginning of the telephone directory (a list that invariably includes a number for the latest cricket scores). Unlike many of the similar services offered in other countries, all these calls are charged at local rates.

Payphones. You need not go far to find a public telephone in Australian cities, though many of the street booths are vandalised or otherwise out-of-order. But a great many pubs, restaurants, shops, etc. have a version of the payphone called 'Red' or 'Gold' phones (differentiated below) which are only slightly larger than domestic phones and usually in working order. As mentioned above, a local call can last as long as you like for 30c. You may find it difficult to adjust to the idea that you can talk for as long as you wish for a single payment, rather than having to rush breathlessly through your conversation before the pips sound, but once you acquire the habit don't ignore the queue forming to use the phone (some payphones bear a sign saying 'three minutes maximum, please').

The telephone found in most street booths, and at post offices, airports, bus and rail stations, is the 'Green' phone. It is a large, metallic instrument that looks fairly archaic. All green phones accept 10c, 20c, 50c and $1 coins.

A fairly high proportion of phones are marked ISD (International Subscriber

Dialling). These permit direct dialling worldwide, though they are sufficiently scarce for hostels to advertise their proximity. A notice tells you how many coins can be inserted at any one time. The warning for time expiry is both audible (a short burst of pips) and visible (a flashing red light). If you don't insert more coins, you have about 10 seconds from when the warning starts until you are cut off. Any unused coins are returned at the end of the call. Note that this does not mean you will get change from a $1 coin if you make only a 30c call. Only wholly unused coins can be refunded, so as you are nearing the end of your conversation, it is better to insert plenty of 10c and 20c pieces rather than 50c or $1 coins.

Second-rate Green phones are known as STD (Subscriber Trunk Dialling) phones and can be used to call anywhere in Australia plus New Zealand and some South Pacific islands. For long-distance calls, you may insert up to seven coins initially, then replenish supplies gradually as the money drops through. To call elsewhere in the world from an STD phone, you must go through the operator.

Red phones, commonly found in shops, restaurants and bars, etc., are only for local calls and accept only 10c and 20c coins. Gold phones are a modern derivative (located in similar establishments) that can cope with the full range of telephonic possibilities, from local calls to international direct dialling. These push-button phones take 10c, 20c, 50c and $1 coins and give a display showing how much money you have left. As with green phones, any unused coins are returned at the end of the call.

For those without pocketsful of loose change, there is an increasing number of 'creditphones' which are ideal for long-distance and international calls. Most accept Visa, American Express and Diners Club, and a few accept Access/MasterCard. If you have opened an Australian bank account and have an EFTPOS card (explained above), you will probably be able to use that as well. You can find them at Overseas Telecommunications offices, airports and other key locations; there are about 50 in Sydney for example, a few of which are open 24 hours. You 'wipe' the magnetic strip on your card through the slot, key in your personal identification number, then dial and talk. There is a fairly high minimum charge, so try not to use them for local calls.

Long-Distance Calls. There are five separate rates increasing according to distance, combined with the different charges depending on the time of day. The cheapest calls can be made at the 'economy' rate from 10pm to 8am daily and all day on Sundays. Next up is the 'night' rate from 6pm to 10pm, Monday-Saturday. The 'intermediate' rate covers weekday lunchtimes (12.30pm to 1.30pm). At all other times you pay the peak 'day' rate. A peak-rate call from a private phone in Sydney to Perth costs $0.75 per minute, from Adelaide to Melbourne $0.50 per minute. Savings at other times are 10% (intermediate), 33% (night) and 50% (economy). Payphone tariffs are 50–100% higher.

International Calls. The international service is operated by Overseas Telecommunications (OTC), a separate organisation from Telecom. It has telephone centres in the major cities where making an international call is straightforward. You can also place calls from booths in major post offices.

Not all telephones in Australia are connected to the international network. Payphones that have this facility are clearly marked 'ISD' or 'IDD' (International Direct Dial) and include all gold phones. To determine if a telephone is equipped for ISD, dial 00 11 00 (a free call). If it is, you'll hear a message of confirmation ('congratulations: you're connected to ISD...'); if not, there will be no answer. Once you find a suitable phone, insert at least $3 in coins or a phone card, dial the international access code (0011), the country code (1 for North America, 44 for the UK), the area code without the initial zero, and finally the number. So, to call Vacation Work Publications in Oxford from Australia, dial:

International Access Code	Country Code	Area	Code Number
0011	44	1865	241978

For calls to New Zealand and the South Pacific, the access code is 0014. The cheap times for overseas calls are 11pm-6am and all day Saturday.

The following are the standard rates per minute from private telephones. Charges from payphones are approximately double.

New Zealand and the South Pacific:	$1.50
UK, Asia, North America, Western Europe:	$2

To make an international call in areas where direct dialling is impossible, go through the international operator on 0107. You will be asked whether you want a particular person (called, accurately, the 'Particular Person' service) or merely a number ('Call-A-Number'). Charges for the latter are roughly half those for personal calls. On all operator-assisted calls, the minimum duration is three minutes.

For reverse-charge (collect) international calls, you can be put straight through to an operator in your country by using the service Country Direct. The service is available to the UK (access code 0014 881440), to the USA on 0014 881011 plus 17 other countries. The overseas operator will place the call for you and the recipient will be charged the current international reverse-charge rate.

Calls from Hotels. Free phones for local calls can often be found in the lobbies of the most expensive hotels. The instructions will tell you to dial the access digit (usually 9 or 0) followed by the local number. Your chances of using these phones undisturbed are enhanced if you look like you could be a guest, or at least as if you could be visiting a guest. Beware of making non-local calls from a hotel room: rates for long-distance and international calls are high.

Manual Exchanges. To contact the operator for calls within Australia dial 0176. A surprising number of rural areas still have a manual telephone exchange. To get through, you should call the appropriate operator (listed under 'area codes' at the start of the *White Pages*).

Radio Telephones. Some outlying settlements (particularly in Western Australia and the Northern Territory) are served only by radio telephone; numbers are shown as, for example, 'Alice Springs R/T 1234'. It is possible to make calls between the national network and these places via the Radio Telephone Exchanges, but charges are expensive. Only one person can speak at a time. It helps if you say 'over' when you finish speaking, and don't try to interrupt the other person.

POST

Australia Post does a reasonable job considering the vastness of its territory. Even in areas a thousand kilometres from the nearest city, mail is flown in at least once a week. Although there is no mail delivery at weekends, service is fairly quick and reliable; ordinary letters are despatched by air mail to distant destinations within Australia, for which there is no extra charge.

Unless you use aerogrammes (currently 65c to anywhere in the world), sending letters abroad is expensive, i.e. $1.20 and 90c for post cards. (If you want to be a real cheapskate and will be stopping off in Singapore on your journey, buy your stamps and post your cards at the airport there, to take advantage of low air mail rates.)

Mail boxes are red with a white stripe. The modern ones resemble litter bins, but there are still some elegant Victorian 'receiving pillars' dotted around.

Post Offices. Every town and village has a post office, although in outlying areas it may double as a petrol station, restaurant, bank and general store. The range of services is impressive: as well as buying stamps or collecting poste restante mail (see below) you can consult telephone directories for the whole country, buy lightweight Postpak envelopes of various sizes, send telegrams, pick up application forms for driving licences or naturalisation, etc. At main offices, credit cards can be used to pay for purchases totalling $10 or more; but when the office is crowded you won't be popular if you use your Visa card to buy a dozen postcard stamps. Opening hours are normally 9am to 5pm, Monday-Friday. However, the main office in each state capital has extended hours for a restricted range of services. In addition, there are sub-post offices attached to shops (and sometimes even restaurants) that often open on Saturday mornings and late on some evenings.

Outside post office hours, stamps can be bought from some postcard retailers and newsagents, or from machines. Most issue stamps of fixed values but the more sophisticated electronic machines print out gummed 'postage labels' of the denominations you require.

Addresses. One confusing feature of Australian addresses is that they give no clue if a locality is close to, or part of, a larger city. Postal addresses bear only the name of the suburb without indicating that it is part of the state capital. For example, it is not obvious that Northbridge WA and Glebe NSW are neighbourhoods close to the centre of Perth and Sydney respectively. You can to some extent deduce the promiximity to the main city from the last three digits of the postcode; numbers close to -000 tend to be near the centre of the state capital. The correct place to put the post code, whether after the suburb or state, is also a matter of personal preference.

Other quirks in Australian addresses include the way that 'care of' is written: c/- rather than c/o. For small settlements, you should write 'via' instead of 'near' as in 'Amoonguna via Alice Springs'. The phrase 'locked bag' in an address means roughly the same as a Post Office box number. In cities, don't expect always to see a street number; if an address is given as 'Cnr George and Oxford Sts', copy it out faithfully and your letter will get to the appropriate street corner.

All addresses should contain the name of the state, which is normally abbreviated to ACT, NSW, NT, Qld, SA, Tas, Vic or WA. To speed your mail (and to distinguish between towns with the same name such as the two Breakfast Creeks in New South Wales, 200km apart), add the four-digit post code. These codes are listed at the back of any Australian *White Pages* and follow a fairly logical system, with the first digit indicating the state: 2 New South Wales and the Australian Capital Territory; 3 Victoria; 4 Queensland; 5 South Australia and the Northern Territory; 6 Western Australia; 7 Tasmania. The post code for the central area of each state capital ends 000, so the code for downtown Adelaide is 5000. (For Canberra, the code is 2600 and for Darwin 5790.)

Poste Restante. It is easy for people to write to you in Australia if you have an idea of where you will be going and when. They should address mail to you 'c/- Poste Restante, Chief Post Office' at a city you plan to visit, and should include the state and postcode (2000 for Sydney, 3000 for Melbourne, etc.). You then take your passport to the main post office in the city and collect your mail. No charge is made for this service. At popular places such as Cairns, the scramble around the Poste Restante desk can be chaotic and there are often signs begging people to arrange for Poste Restante mail to be sent to suburban post offices. At the Martin Place office in central Sydney, you have to consult a computer list of mail to check if you have any.

If you prefer to avoid the queues and are an American Express customer (by virtue of carrying their travellers cheques, for example), you can have mail (but not parcels) sent to their offices in Australia; addresses are given under *Help and Information* for each city.

Overseas Mail. Air mail service to countries with direct flights can be impressively fast, taking only three or four days between Australia and the UK or USA. To minimise delivery time, try to catch the latest posting times for international mail which are displayed at post offices and printed in the daily press. A cheaper and slower alternative to air mail, yet one that is much faster than surface, is 'Surface Air Lifted' or 'SAL'. Your despatch travels overland to an airport, whereupon it is consigned by air cargo. Typical time to the UK or North America is two weeks. Surface mail takes up to four months.

If, on the other hand, you are desperate for fast delivery of your letter, you can send it *International Express* which costs an extra $4.20. With *International Priority Paid*, you can take a document to the main post office in Sydney by 10am, and be guaranteed delivery in central London the next day. Such speed, however, costs an extra $25, and you cannot use the service for anything other than paper.

Parcels. All parcels must be securely wrapped and clearly addressed. Counter clerks will not hesitate to send you away to re-wrap a parcel (or even take over the job themselves) if they consider it not to meet Australia Post regulations. Charges increase according to distance: parcels to neighbouring towns or cities cost less than those of the same weight being sent across the country. All parcels are sent overland unless you pay an extra amount for air mail. When sending parcels abroad you must complete a customs declaration form, available at all post offices. Take note of Australian postal and customs regulations before you send a parcel: a few years ago two Germans were jailed for attempting to post 135 live reptiles out of the country.

Fax. Most post offices offer a facsimile transfer service across Australia. A single A4 sheet sent to a private fax machine costs around $5. If the recipient has no fax machine, then use the Imagegram service — your communication is faxed to the nearest post office, and delivered by hand.

THE MEDIA

Australians support an extraordinary range of newspapers, radio and television. Collectively they buy 27 million newspapers each week, making them among the world's most prolific readers (twice as many as Canada and France, for example). They can tune into radio broadcasts in 52 different languages, and — in the bigger cities — watch five regular television stations plus two satellite TV networks. Equally surprising is the way that ownership of much of the media is concentrated in the hands of a few proprietors. Interference in editorial decisions is not unknown; one former television tycoon was known for his habit of ordering movies to be cancelled so that races featuring his horses could be screened. The federal government has strong links with these media barons, and also effectively controls two national TV networks. Some pundits argue that Australia has the least independent media in the world. Nevertheless, the reader, viewer or listener has a great deal of choice.

Newspapers. Standards of journalism in the Australian press are variable. The leading quality dailies are excellent newspapers (although some may find them a little conservative). The tabloid press have suffered over the last few years and in most cities the *Sun* equivalents have been forced either to amalgamate or close. One criticism among British visitors and migrants of all Australian papers is that they are too parochial, with foreign news being poorly covered, and that only bad news from the UK is published.

The recommended retail price of most newspapers is around 60c (but up to $1 for the bulky weekend editions, generally published on Saturdays). This cover price applies only within the area close to where it is printed; in isolated locations newspapers cost about 20c more than the cover price, and prices are higher still in other states or distant cities.

The Australian is the main national daily. The national Sunday paper (and one of the few newspapers to be published at all on Sundays) is the excellent *Times on Sunday*. The best Australian dailies, however, are regional publications. The *Sydney Morning Herald* and Melbourne *Age* are among the finest papers in the English-speaking world. These and other leading broadsheets (such as Adelaide's *Advertiser* and the Brisbane *Courier-Mail* manage to maintain high circulations as well as decent standards. Most towns of any size support a weekly paper, although in the smallest settlements the only print medium may be a notice board.

Weekly journals enjoy more independence than much of the daily press. Recently a disillusioned journalist began publishing *The Eye*, a monthly journal featuring satire, comment and 'the stories the Big Boys won't print' (price $2.50). The weekly *Bulletin* (which incorporates part of *Newsweek* magazine) has good coverage of international events.

As in North America, newspapers carry a great deal of advertising, and you may soon tire of wading through endless advertisements in search of real news. On the other hand, you may find the classified sections useful when looking for work or a secondhand car. When confronted by this mass of advertising, don't overlook the highly useful entertainment sections that most quality newspapers include once a week.

To keep in touch with life at home while in Australia, a good but slightly outdated selection of foreign newspapers is available from city-centre kiosks, and in the libraries of High Commissions and Consulates. Daily newspapers from Europe and North America cost around $5 (Sunday editions $9), and the excellent *Guardian Weekly* only $2. *USA Today* is widely available for $2.50. Many specialist publications are produced in Australia for homesick Poms, such as *British Soccer Week*.

Radio. A sweep along the tuning dial of your radio in any Australian city will reveal a surprisingly large number of radio stations. The nationwide network is operated by the Australian Broadcasting Corporation (ABC), widely known as 'Aunty'. Licence fees were abolished in 1974, and ABC radio and television are now funded entirely by the government. *Daybreak* is the equivalent of BBC Radio 4's *Today* programme and is broadcast from 6am on the ABC AM network. It includes regional slots for local news, World Round-Up (international news sent by satellite from the BBC in London) and plenty of soothing classical music to fill in the gaps.

Few Australians wake up to ABC, however. Most tune in to one of the many local commercial stations, a far cry from the well modulated tones and high technical standards of the ABC network. There seems an insatiable appetite for pop music blended with constant news updates, traffic and weather reports. In the cities, this is catered for by dozens of competing stations, many operating on a shoestring. (It is not unknown for a city station to play a recording of helicopter sound effects behind a presenter who pretends to be flying above the city's traffic while instead he or she is sitting in a studio reading reports from the highway police.) The location of a radio station can be deduced from its call sign, the first number of which corresponds with the first digit of the state's postal code: thus 2UE is a Sydney station, 3CR a Melbourne one, etc.

As well as mainstream pop and rock, there are stations to cater for almost every taste in music. A number of AM music stations broadcast in stereo but the quality is inferior to FM stereo. There are also a large number of 'talkback' stations that fill transmissions largely with phone-ins. Many have star presenters who try to outdo each other in their outrageous behaviour, rudeness to listeners who phone in, etc. Community radio stations are considerably more restrained, but often make interesting listening with a varied diet of ethnic programmes, broadcasts for women and local information. At the other extreme, you should try to hear a sports programme or two, since their entertainment rating can be high even if you know nothing about the sport at issue. The major stations (such as 2GB in Sydney) employ over-the-top commentators who don't mince their words, and are appallingly rude about players' performances.

In each chapter you will find some indication of the format of local stations in the area, but this should be taken as a guide only. Australian commercial radio is notoriously volatile, and adverse audience figures can change the format of a station from middle-brow talk to rock music overnight.

Television. Although the larger cities have a wide choice of viewing, the programmes on offer are mostly unimaginative: soap operas ('soapies'), chat shows, sensationalised news coverage and large doses of sport are the norm. The government-financed ABC goes after high ratings as energetically as any of the privately owned networks, but can still be counted on to provide a higher proportion of documentaries, especially on Australian flora and fauna. It is often known as 'Two' from its usual place on the dial. The name changes from state to state: in Sydney it's called ABN (N stands for New South Wales), in Melbourne ABV and so on. The other networks are known as 'Seven', 'Nine' and 'Ten'.

SBS (Special Broadcasting Service) is the other government-sponsored station; it caters for minority groups and interests, and is not available in all areas of Australia. The standard fare of SBS is similar to Channel 4 in Britain or PBS in the USA. It has, unkindly, been described as 'Egyptian soap operas, Iraqi sitcoms and wacky zero-rating Herzegovinian folk-dancing shows'. This is, of course, a ludicrous exaggeration: SBS shows many English-language programmes and has the best international news coverage.

All stations except ABC and SBS carry large amounts of advertising. The number and frequency of commercials exceeds even American television. They take up more than one-fifth of airtime and include continual self-promotions of the stations (and sometimes their proprietors). Many pubs and clubs subscribe to one of the satellite stations on offer. Superstation and Skychannel broadcast a mix of major sporting events and rock music videos. Schedules for these channels are normally published in the daily press along with terrestrial TV network information. The magazine *TV Week* contains details of all programmes, with separate editions for each state. Note that time differences between the states means that nationwide programmes are transmitted earlier in the western half of the country.

It will be no surprise that soap operas are extremely popular in the country that brought the world *Neighbours* and *Home and Away*. Australian television is crammed with soap operas both home-grown and imported, though visitors from the UK may be disappointed to learn that *EastEnders* was dropped by the ABC in 1991. Of the many indigenous soaps, most revolve around the themes of surf, unrequited love and terminal illness. The newest one (on Kerry Packer's Nine) is *Chances* which has the usual execrable acting and an atmosphere of soft porn.

There are also some good original Australian programmes. *Sunday* on Channel Nine (9am-11am), which has been on air for over ten years, is a mix of news, current affairs and arts. If you want to acquire an understanding of the intricacies of Australian politics, watch a few editions of *A Current Affair*, daily at 6.30pm on Nine. For an idiosyncratic and characteristically Australian (i.e. irreverent) version of the news, tune into Clive Robertson at 10.30pm on Nine.

Films on TV are rated just as they are for cinema performances. Although the networks are less paranoid about nudity than in America, you're unlikely to see anything terribly explicit on Australian television. Serious current affairs programmes and documentaries are most likely to be found on ABC, while the best international news is on SBS at 6.30pm (eastern time).

Although sport features heavily on all the networks, purists would regard the coverage it receives as contemptible. Cricket is probably worst affected: commercials are shown after every over or dismissal and sometimes advertisements are shown at the foot of the screen during play. The networks are even prepared to interrupt crucial points in the game with commercial breaks in order to maintain their maximum allowance of 13 minutes of advertising per hour.

Getting Around

Never underestimate the size of Australia when planning your itinerary. It is a massive country, as big as the USA or Europe. It is also a continent where the harshness of the terrain has made it difficult for land links to be built or maintained. The last stretches of Highway 1, the road encircling the country, were sealed only a few years ago and even now some of it is more like a pot-holed track than a main road. Away from the state capitals, the volume of traffic using both road and rail is low, and investment in modernising links to allow for higher speeds is small.

Time is not a problem if you fly across the vast empty interior. Deregulation of airlines in 1990 brought in several new domestic carriers and fierce competition has kept fares down. On land, bus companies compete aggressively, so shop around before investing in a ticket.

Many long-stay visitors insist that the flexibility of having their own vehicle is extremely valuable; see below for advice on renting or buying a car or campervan. Hitch-hiking is fine for short trips, and even over long distances is faster and less problematic than you might expect. Cycling is not always pleasurable in the largest cities, but is perfect for touring country areas; if you have the time and stamina, you can pedal right across Australia.

AIR

Easily the most efficient way to travel around Australia is by air. But even with increased competition the luxury of travelling thousands of miles in a few hours does not come cheap. Until October 1990, the federal government protected the monopoly of the two big airlines: Australian Airlines and Ansett. They charged the same fares as each other and operated near-identical services. The arrival of new airlines forced the big two to cut fares.

East-West Airlines, owned by Ansett but operated as a separate company, offers a 'no-frills' service, but not necessarily the cheapest fares. Its route network is restricted to the east coast and Tasmania. Good local services are operated within each state by local and regional carriers, but most use small aircraft that are often booked up well in advance, and they do not normally offer bargain fares.

Daily flights link the state capitals although, some journeys, like Melbourne to Darwin, require several stops. But demand is insufficient on many other routes to justify more than one or two services each week.

The Australian aviation industry is in a state of flux and these deals are bound to change during the lifetime of this book. It is always worth asking agents and other travellers, or checking newspaper advertisements, to get the best available deals. Note that some agencies have close links with the two big airlines, and that discount travel agents generally deal only with international flights. So research is needed to find the best deal.

In the UK you can contact the two leading airlines in London: Australian Airlines on 0171-434 3864, and Ansett on 0171-434 4071. Within Australia each airline has a toll-free reservation number. For Ansett call 008-131353 (or 008-131355 for its discount fare information hotline), East-West 008-366 1300 and Australian Airlines 008-922 5122.

Fares. Full-fare tickets are expensive but allow considerable flexibility: dates, times and airlines can be changed at will, and if you decide not to travel you can obtain a full refund. A good trick with these tickets is to include a stopover free-of-charge: for example, if you're travelling from Brisbane to Cairns, take the first flight out as far as Townsville. You can spend the day there and continue your journey to Cairns on the last flight of the day. As long as you make the journey in one day, you pay only the through fare.

If you're feeling flush, you can pay extra for business class or first. This buys separate, more comfortable seating, better food and free drinks. The following special deals, which start with the cheapest, are available only in economy and often only to international visitors.

Discounts for Visitors. The big airlines offer a confusing number of cut-price deals for foreigners. The best, however, is marketed as 'Blue Roo' fares by Australian Airlines and 'Down-Under Discount Deals' by Ansett. It works in units costing $60 each. Provided you purchase at least $300 worth, you get up to 55% off the normal economy fare. For example Brisbane–Gold Coast costs one unit ($60), Perth–Melbourne costs five ($300) and Sydney–Cairns four ($240). These fares must be bought outside Australia or at airline offices within 30 days of arrival in Australia. You can change dates of flights at will, but if you change route a charge of $50 is made.

Qantas Domestic Flights. Foreign visitors — but not Australians — can travel on the internal sectors of international Qantas flights. Because the carrier flies thousands of empty seats around Australia on domestic legs of international services (e.g. Melbourne to Sydney before going on to Singapore), it is keen to offload them — often at 50% off normal fares.

Note, however, that Qantas does not have a comprehensive network around Australia and that flights are prone to departure at unsocial hours. Furthermore, travelling on the domestic sector of an international journey is more bothersome than flying on a regular domestic flight. The first difference is that you should go to the international terminal. Check-in will be considerably earlier, due to the formalities you will have to undergo. The authorities are paranoid about the opportunities for smuggling afforded by the intermingling of passengers and their belongings, so you are subject to the same controls as international passengers. The boarding pass you receive will bear a 'D' sticker to indicate you are a domestic passenger. You must queue up for the passport and customs check; your boarding pass will be stamped and must be retained for collection upon arrival at your destination. You will, of course, arrive at the international terminal. Follow the signs for 'Aircrew and Domestic Pass Holders' to make a quick getaway through Customs.

Advance Purchase (Apex) Fares. To save 35% on round trips with guaranteed flights, you need to book and pay 21–30 days in advance (depending on the airline). You must stay away for at least a Saturday night and a maximum of a year. If you cancel within the 30 days before your flight, you get a refund of half the cost of the ticket.

See Australia Fares. These allow tourists to benefit from a 25% discount and are almost as flexible as full-fare tickets. *See Australia* fares are available only to visitors from overseas, though they need not be bought outside Australia. Travel must be completed within 60 days of arrival in Australia, and does not have to bear any relation to your international flight (for example, if you arrive at Perth and depart from Sydney, you can still buy a *See Australia* ticket from Brisbane to Darwin). The rules are the same as for full-fare tickets, e.g. you can change times of flights or get a refund without penalty.

Student Discounts. Overseas students under 26 years of age can claim a 25% reduction on normal economy fares by producing an ISIC card or an international airline ticket issued at a student discount.

Standby. Travelling standby is fraught with anxiety, but saves 20% on normal economy fares. Get to the airport as early as possible before the flight, to buy your ticket and register at the standby desk. If the flight is lightly booked, you may be issued with a boarding pass immediately. More likely, however, you will be told to report back 10 minutes before the flight departs. After giving full-fare passengers every possible chance to turn up, the staff will eventually call out the names of the lucky standby passengers. If you are not among them, you can try for the next flight or obtain a full refund. Standby tickets on Ansett and Australian are interchangeable, so if the staff of one airline tell you there's no chance of a seat, try the other. Note, however, that once you begin your journey you must stick to the same airline.

For any standby flight it is worth calling the airlines in advance and asking how heavily loaded they are. This is particularly recommended for multi-sector flights such as Brisbane–Sydney–Melbourne, on which you must standby for each individual sector. If you don't succeed in getting back on the same flight, costs for overnight accommodation and meals are your responsibility.

Airports. Travellers who are used to busy European or North American airports may be surprised when arriving at Australian airports. For most of the time they are deadly quiet, bursting into life only for a few hours each day when a number of flights arrive and depart in a flurry. International terminals at smaller airports are locked up and deserted most of the time. They open 2 hours before arrivals or departures and close shortly after the last flight has arrived or left.

In most cases the international terminal is separate from the domestic building, ranging from next door (e.g. Melbourne) to 10km away (Perth). Consult the *Arrival and Departure* section of each regional chapter for details of links from the airport to the city and between terminals.

Smoking. All scheduled domestic flights are non-smoking, with a maximum $500 fine for offenders. This ban does not apply to charter flights, nor to the Prime Minister's private jet.

Safety. Australian carriers are fastidious about safety. This can be irritating (e.g. you might be instructed to move your handbag from behind your feet to in front of them) but their attitude is to be commended and has made Australia the safest place in the world to fly. Be careful of what you consume beforehand; an Air Navigation Order makes it illegal to 'board an aircraft whilst intoxicated'.

Baggage. Economy class travellers are allowed one piece of checked baggage, the weight of which must not exceed 30kg. In keeping with the concern for safety, carry-on luggage rules are enforced strictly. These allow two small bags — which must fit inside the metal frames measuring 34cm by 48cm by 23cm dotted around all airports — plus, for women, a handbag. As you'll be warned repeatedly, if you conceal the true extent of your luggage and try to take it all aboard as hand baggage, it may be confiscated at the aircraft door and travel on a later flight.

Left Luggage. Most airports have lockers where you can leave your belongings. After the 24 hours that $1 buys, the locker may be sealed to force you to pay the excess due. To save the small change, it's worth asking the airline baggage enquiry office if you can leave your bags. Ansett permits this for up to 24 hours if you are travelling with them.

BUS

Buses cover almost every stretch of tarmacked highway in Australia. Bargains are available on the main routes like Sydney–Melbourne and Sydney–Brisbane. The biggest operator is Greyhound Pioneer Australia, which is made up of what used to be three separate companies: Greyhound, Pioneer and Bus Australia. Their services cover the whole country.

Australian buses are relatively luxurious, equipped with air-conditioning, loos, reclining seats and video screens. But bus travel is not everyone's idea of fun: journeys can be long and arduous, lacking the freedom of movement offered on trains. Away from the main inter-city routes, services tend to be infrequent and fares high. But for those unwilling to risk the vagaries of hitch-hiking and unable to meet the cost of flying or buying their own vehicle, it provides a reasonable means of seeing a great deal of the country.

Reservations. See *Before You Go* for specialist travel agencies in the UK that can book Australian bus passes and tickets for you in advance. However it is usually better to wait until you arrive in Australia and see where the best deals are.

Within Australia, you can book direct with the bus company in person or by telephone. For bookings or information on Greyhound Pioneer Australia ring 132030. Most travellers now avail themselves of the plethora of bus booking agencies, many of them based in popular backpackers' hostels. YHA Travel offices in the major cities, for example, will be able to inform you of all the options. VIP Backpackers Resorts of Australia runs Backpackers Travel Centres in Sydney, Brisbane, Melbourne and Adelaide, which provide a 'Dial-a-Coach' service. You can book a bus ticket over the phone with a credit card.

The ticket you receive bears more than a passing resemblance to an airline ticket. Each destination has a three-letter code like an airport code, and indeed cities that have an airport use the same code: thus ADL–Adelaide, BNE–Brisbane, CNS–Cairns, etc. These codes are quoted in timetables and on luggage tags. If checking baggage, ensure that the code matches that of your destination.

Fares. Bus prices work out at about one-third of the corresponding air fare. In view of how long most journeys take by road, more people are choosing to fly and the bus companies may have to work even harder to compete. In general, the more popular the route among travellers, the greater the competition and the lower the fares.

Fares offered by the smaller companies often fluctuate wildly. For example the current price from Sydney to Melbourne (with discount as explained below) is $40, but can drop to $25 if a certain departure is relatively empty (compared to the lowest possible $120 by air). Fares with Greyhound Pioneer Australia are not discretionary to the same extent, but special deals do crop up from time to time and there may be substantial savings if you book at the last minute. Otherwise you should expect to pay a minimum of $40 Melbourne–Adelaide, $85 Canberra–Adelaide, $104 Melbourne–Brisbane, $160 Adelaide–Perth and $120 Brisbane–Cairns.

Cancellations. Most operators charge cancellation fees of about $10 providing you cancel at least 24 hours before the journey; thereafter you lose the lot.

Stopovers. It is much cheaper to buy one ticket for a long trip rather than separate ones for shorter journeys. You can normally stop off *en route* at state capitals for no extra charge.

Discounts. So many companies offer discounts for so many reasons that it is always worth asking for one. All the main bus companies give a 10% discount to YHA members, students and holders of various other backpacker passes. The most widely known of these is the VIP Backpacker card sold for $10 by Backpackers Resorts of Australia. It gives discounts with a range of bus operators, as well as on accommodation, tours, etc.

Travel Passes. Each of the major companies has a selection of bus passes, which may be cheaper when bought abroad than in Australia. But before investing hundreds of pounds or dollars in a bus pass, you should consider whether a bus pass is ideal for your travel plans. Just as Inter-railers complain that they soon succumb to a compulsion to travel as fast and furiously as they can, so too people who have bought an Australian bus pass have regretted the loss of flexibility. For example, if you find a job or fall in love with a place (or in a place) and still have months of your expensive bus pass to run, you may be disinclined to stop.

But if you want to see a lot of Australia and have no intention of finding a job or falling in love, one of the many bus passes on the market may suit you. Greyhound Pioneer Australia, for example, offers a range of discount passes, including the Aussie Pass, which provides a certain number of days' travel; 7 days cost $380, 15 days $635 and 30 days $1080. Days can be used up individually, so that the '30 days' ticket, for example, doesn't have to be used up within one calendar month. Another option is the Aussie Kilometre Pass, which allows you to purchase kilometres of travel in blocks of a thousand; 5000km costs $379, and 10,000km $704. Once you've bought the pass, you are free to travel as you like on the extensive Greyhound Pioneer Australia network. The pass is valid for 12 months from the start of travel. Alternatively a range of set route tickets is also available, under the name of Aussie Explorer Pass. Discounts of 15% apply on all of these tickets for YHA members, VIP Backpackers and ISIC cardholders.

Rules. Surprisingly many regulations affect bus travellers. On some services, travel between two points in the same state is prohibited by licensing regulations. And travellers' behaviour is carefully controlled. For example, you may be instructed not to drink from cartons and not to put rubbish in the ashtray, and told of the precise location of the flushing mechanism in the toilet. What you ingest in transit may have to be confined to odourless foods and drinking to non-spill cartons. You may also get a stern lecture about alcohol and non-prescription drugs; these must be deposited with the driver (no questions asked). If you are caught drinking alcohol on a bus, you will be put off at the nearest police station (maximum fine $500) and your ticket will be ripped up. Smoking is prohibited on all coach services.

Backpacker Buses. In keeping with the explosion in facilities for 'yuppie backpackers', a number of new bus-cum-tour companies connect the main cities (Sydney–Brisbane, Adelaide–Melbourne) going at a leisurely pace on off-the-beaten-track routes and stopping overnight at campsites. You can expect to pay about $40 a day or thereabouts, plus extras for food, accommodation and tours.

Sydney-based Oz Experience (3 Orwell St, Kings Cross; 02-9368 1766) is an 'alternative transport network'; it covers the route Sydney–Melbourne in 3 days for $105, Melbourne–Adelaide at the same rate, and Sydney–Cairns in 9 days for $280.

TRAIN
Rail travellers have less choice of routes and services than bus passengers. The network consists of a route across the south from Perth to Sydney, a spur from this line up to Alice Springs, a loop from Adelaide through Melbourne to Sydney, and the line north along the east coast through Brisbane as far as Cairns. Most journeys are long, slow runs at speeds around 100 km/h, with a few high speed trains in the south-east and networks of suburban services around the main cities. For a colourful yet informative account of Australian rail journeys, see Colin Taylor's *Australia by Rail*, distributed by Bradt Publications.

A train journey can be a fascinating and not excessively expensive way to see the country with a fair degree of comfort. All trains have buffet cars and bars (with substantial leg room and the ability to move around). Another benefit of train travel over buses is that it is possible to break your journey. When planning an itinerary, bear in mind that the main tourist rail routes can be booked out months in advance in the busy tourist season or school holidays, so you should reserve a seat or berth well in advance.

Railways still form an essential part of rural Australian life, great expresses draw to a halt in the middle of nowhere to deliver passengers and sustenance to an outback cattle station. Train treks across the country appeal to many, although the romance (and scenery) may begin to pall a little after the 478km arrow straight run across the Nullarbor — the longest straight stretch of railway in the world — that forms part of the journey from Perth to Adelaide. The other

GREAT RAIL PASSES
OF AUSTRALIA

AUSTRAIL PASS

Unlimited travel anywhere on the rail network in
Australia with some metropolitan trains included,
from 14 to 30 consecutive days.

AUSTRAIL FLEXIPASS PASS

Enjoy economical rail travel in Australia for 8, 15, 22
or 29 days, within a 6 month period.

DISCOVERY PASS

Travel from Sydney to Surfers Paradise and Brisbane
or Sydney to Cairns within a 6 month period.

RAIL AUSTRALIA

Leisurail, PO Box 113, Peterborough, PE3 8HY
Reservation: 01733 335599
Brochureline: 01733 335556

Limelight RA065

famous rail journey is The Ghan which operates from Adelaide to Alice Springs and return. This is a great way to visit the centre or 'heart' of Australia.

Each state government (except Tasmania and the Northern Territory) has its own railway company. These are subsumed in Rail Australia (1 Richmond Road, Keswick, Adelaide, South Australia 5035). Interstate trains have glamorous names such as *Indian Pacific*, the rolling stock of this particular service was once in a poor condition, but a two year $12,000,000 refurbishment programme has just been completed which has rejuvenated every part of the train, from the carriages and facilities through to an intensive training programme for staff. Other services include the XPTs (Express Passenger Trains), which link Melbourne, Sydney and Brisbane, the Gold Coast (Murwillumbah), Tamworth, Dubbo and Albury

Plans to introduce a 350km/h Very Fast Train (VFT) service between Melbourne and Sydney have met with financial and environmental hitches that still seem a long way from being solved. Genuinely fast trains also travel between Perth and Kalgoorlie (the Prospector) and Perth and Bunbury (the Australind).

Minimum journey times are: Sydney–Perth 64 hours, Adelaide–Perth 37 hours, Adelaide–Alice Springs 20 hours, Adelaide–Melbourne and Melbourne–Sydney both 11^1/$_2$ hours, Sydney–Brisbane 14 hours and Brisbane–Cairns 31 hours.

Reservations. Local services do not require reservations — you just buy a ticket and board the train. Long distance trains are a different matter; on some routes there are only one or two services each week, so advance booking is advisable in peak times. You can get this at stations, city ticket offices or travel agents. If you're unable to call in personally, you can make or change reservations by telephone. For reservations and enquiries in Sydney, Adelaide, Canberra and Melbourne dial 132232, in Brisbane dial 07 235 2222 and in Perth dial 09 326 2222.

You can book from abroad through appointed agents such as LEISURAIL in the UK (PO Box 113, Peterborough PE3 8HY; 01733-335599) or the Australian Travel Service in the US (100 N First St, Burbank CA 91502, 800-423-2880). Write and ask for the brochure, *Rail Australia*, which contains information on on-board services and facilities; up-to-date timetables and fare schedules are also available.

Fares. Basic economy class fares on most journeys (e.g. Sydney–Surfers Paradise, Brisbane–Cairns, Melbourne–Canberra) work out at about $10 for 100km. Short journeys (e.g. Sydney–Canberra) are more expensive ($16 per 100km), while the long trips are cheaper. Sample one-way economy ('coach class') fares include Sydney–Melbourne $98, Melbourne–Adelaide $50, Adelaide–Perth $220 and Brisbane–Cairns $129. First class fares are 40-50% higher. With ordinary tickets, you may break your journey anywhere en route provided you have onward reservations. Children aged 4-15 years and Australian pensioners are entitled to substantial discounts.

Supplements. Sleeper berths cost extra, but you may think the added expense worthwhile for long journeys. The rate for an economy berth in Queensland is $30 and elsewhere ranges from $33–$99 depending on the length of the journey. Sleeping accommodation on some services is confined to first class; on others, such as the *Prospector* between Perth and Kalgoorlie, a meal is included in the fare.

Unlimited Travel Passes. The Austrail Pass is sold only outside Australia to foreign passport holders; it is available in the UK from LEISURAIL (PO Box 113, Peterborough PE3 8HY; reservations 01733-335599; brochure requests

01733-335556). It allows unlimited travel anywhere on the rail network, including some metropolitan trains, for periods of 14 days ($460), 21 days ($595) and 30 days ($720); all of these prices are economy class. Supplements for meals and sleeper berths are not included. To ensure maximum benefit from the Austrail Pass, reservations should be made as far in advance as possible; these can be changed subsequently at no charge if your plans change and if there is still availability.

Those who do not plan to be travelling continuously may find it more economical to buy the Austrail Flexipass Pass, which allows travel on a set number of days within a six month period. The current cost of these passes in economy class are $380 for any 8 days; $550 for any 15 days; $770 for any 22 days, and $995 for any 29 days. The 8 Day Pass cannot be used for travel Adelaide–Alice Springs or Adelaide–Perth.

There are also a number of regional rail passes available. These include the Victoria Pass, which costs $75 for 7 days or $130 for 14 days; others include the Westrail Premier, Westrail Southern and NSW Discovery Passes. There are also several East Coast Discovery Passes, which allow a journey to be made over a six month period; the Sydney to Surfers Paradise and Brisbane pass costs $76 and the Sydney to Cairns ticket costs $199.

Some states such as Victoria offer rail passes covering their network; details are given in the regional chapters.

Baggage. Passengers are permitted two items of luggage not exceeding 25 kilos each, and within 180 lineal cm. In addition, passengers are allowed one piece of hand luggage. All items of luggage may be either carried as unchecked luggage on board the train, or checked in and carried in the baggage car. It is recommended when travelling on an overnight service that luggage is checked in and only an overnight bag is taken on board.

DRIVING

bowser	petrol pump
brown bomber	traffic warden in some cities
canary	yellow sticker attached by traffic police to parked vehicles that they wish to inspect for mechanical soundness
clicks	kilometres
drop (or chuck) a U-ey	make a U-turn
late model	new (ish) car
long paddock	the open road
Moke	small open-topped jeep available for hire in seaside resorts
muffler	silencer
nature strip	grass verge in suburban street
prime mover	tractor unit of articulated lorry
rego (pronounced 'redgo')	registration (road tax)
RWC	Road-Worthiness Certificate
run-out	new car made obsolete by new stock, hence

	sold off cheaply
semi	articulated lorry
traffic area	zone with parking restrictions
traffic officer	traffic warden
ute	utility vehicle, i.e. pick-up truck

If your first journey is by road from Sydney Airport to the city centre, you may quickly become convinced that driving in Australia is a battle fought on inadequate roads by badly behaved motorists. If your driving is confined to the metropolitan areas, you might not find any cause to alter this opinion. Australia retains the British convention of driving on the left. Australian roads have been greatly improved over the last decade. Still it would be unreasonable to expect them to be maintained to the standards found in Europe and North America due to the low density of cars (only 9 million in a country the size of the USA). Only one-third of the total of 850,000km is sealed, and you can't rely upon finding a properly tarmacked road. Even main highways, such as the Western Australian coastal road, have stretches that consist of one paved lane with broad dirt shoulders. This means you must move onto the shoulder when you meet a 'road train' (see below) or perhaps even drop your nearside wheels into the dirt or gravel whenever you meet oncoming traffic. Freeways are rare, usually restricted to short stretches out of the major cities. Some highways have an unnerving habit of degenerating from a fast dual carriageway into the main street of a small town. Signposting is dismal.

Even when a real freeway is built around a town, the locals steadfastly refuse to acknowledge it as such. Don't be surprised to find people and animals crossing a freeway as though it were an ordinary road. Most regular highways have only two lanes, though there is sometimes one paved shoulder on to which slower moving vehicles move when they notice a vehicle coming up behind. Quite a few rural roads and tracks can be negotiated only by four-wheel-drive vehicles (often written 4WD or 4x4).

Until recently Australia had an appalling road death record. Tighter safety and drink-driving regulations have markedly improved the situation. Even so, with an average of six road deaths each day, this rate is still significantly higher (in terms of population) than Britain's. Most daily newspapers publish a Road Toll Chart, showing harrowing statistics for the city or state, such as 'total deaths this month' and 'best death-free run' (i.e. the most consecutive days without a fatal accident — often a distressingly low figure).

Of course, driving in Australia can have its compensations. Motoring in a country where most road users regard a queue of five cars as a traffic jam can't be all bad. Outside the cities, traffic is light and driving is often a real pleasure.

Licences. Carry your licence at all times while driving. Your national driving licence is valid for 3 months, an International Driving Permit (issued by a motoring organisation in your home country) for a year. If you stay longer or take up residence, you must apply for a state licence. Holders of full British or North American licences need not take a driving test to obtain one, but must undergo a physical examination and an oral or written test based on the appropriate state traffic code.

Fuel. Petrol costs 60c–70c per litre in cities, about 15% more in rural areas. This corresponds to about £1.25 per Imperial gallon. Visitors from densely populated nations may be perturbed to discover that outside the major cities, most service stations keep limited opening hours, typically 7am–6pm Monday to Friday and 7am–noon on Saturday. Details of fuel outlets that keep longer hours are given in the local press, or you can ask at a police station. In rural areas there is normally a rota, while in the smaller cities one or two stations on main routes out of town open 24 hours. Some that advertise '24-hour petrol' merely provide an automatic dispenser that takes $5 or $10 bills, so ensure you have a good selection of notes. City petrol stations normally accept credit cards or ATM cards, but don't rely on paying with plastic outside built-up areas.

Australia is rapidly converting to unleaded petrol ('ULP'), perhaps in mitigation of its pollution record (a third of one percent of the world's population produces 1.6% of the world's carbon monoxide). Petrol is sold in one leaded grade (super — around 97 octane), and two grades of unleaded. The nozzles of unleaded fuel pumps are smaller, to prevent drivers of unleaded-only vehicles filling up with leaded fuel. However, it is quite possible to fill up a vehicle intended to use leaded fuel with unleaded petrol. This won't necessarily be a disaster as many cars can run happily for a time on unleaded fuel, but you should top up with the leaded variety as soon as possible. Diesel pumps are also often located next to the petrol pumps adding to the possible confusion. For further advice consult one of the motoring organisations in Australia.

Fuel consumption is measured in litres used per 100km. Confusingly for visitors, this means that the higher the figure the less economical the vehicle. To convert to miles per gallon, see page 26.

Motoring Organisations. Each state has its own organisation, under the umbrella of the Australian Automobile Association (AAA, 212 Northbourne Avenue, Canberra, ACT 2601; 06-247 7311). Members of the AA, RAC or any other foreign motoring organisation can ask for a free copy of the *Motoring in Australia* booklet.

The state motoring organisations have reciprocal arrangements with each other and with British and North American associations, so foreign members can take advantage of their free route information and breakdown services. Their acronyms are not always obvious: for example, New South Wales' NRMA stands for National Roads & Motorists Association. Details are given under for each regional chapter.

If you are not a member in your home country but want to join in Australia it will cost $60–70 for a year. As in the UK you can pay an extra $30 for a premium service that will, for example, provide additional services in remote areas, such as free accommodation and a replacement vehicle if a repair will take more than 3 days.

Routes and Maps. Before embarking on any long distance jaunt, acquire a good map. The motoring organisations produce good ones (free or at cut rates to members of overseas associations), or you can buy the excellent George Philip and O'Neil *Australian Road Atlas* (published also in London and Boston by Faber & Faber).

When choosing a route or asking directions, remember that road numbers are rarely used: highways are known by names instead, such as the Princes Highway along the south-east coast from Adelaide via Melbourne to Sydney, and the Great Northern Highway in Western Australia, which links Perth with Broome.

When you are navigating, remember that the sun spends most of its time in the north, not the south. Thus when deciding whether to go left or right, don't go by the sun. Europeans and North Americans are so accustomed to judging direction by reference to the sun that it takes a while to get reoriented.

Road Signs. The quality of direction signposting varies from good to less than adequate. Keep your eyes peeled for signposts concealed behind trees. On main roads, there are small shields every 5km bearing the initial letter of the last or next major town above the distance in kilometres: thus S25 indicates 25km from Sydney. Direction signs for tourist drives (popular around the cities) can be identified by their brown five-sided signs. City streets are full of 'road furniture', and identifying direction signs among the plethora of instructions, warnings and hoardings can be a problem.

Australia is gradually moving towards the use of internationally recognised symbols on warning signs, and most of those used will be familiar (or obvious) to European and North American motorists. When artistic inspiration fails the signwriters, instructions are spelt out in clear English, such as 'Wrong Way — Go Back'. Signs are often reinforced by painted warnings on the road surface. Until you get used to it, this can be confusing, as from the driver's point of view they are written in reverse; thus you see CLEAR first followed by KEEP.

Some junctions controlled by traffic signals have a sign saying 'turn left at any time with care', which means there is a filter lane to allow turning traffic to avoid the lights. Don't however, ignore pedestrians crossing the filter lane or traffic on the road you wish to join. School crossings are clearly indicated by flashing yellow lights, often indicating a reduced speed limit for that stretch of road.

RULES OF THE ROAD

Each state has its own set of motoring regulations, and quirks are pointed out under *Getting Around* in the appropriate chapter. On the open road, the usual rules apply; on freeways stopping is prohibited except in an emergency, U-turns are not permitted and cyclists and pedestrians (including hitch-hikers) are banned. Australian drivers do not scrupulously stay in the nearside lane unless overtaking, so be wary of cars passing on the inside.

City driving has a number of rules that seem designed to confound the uncertain visitor. It is almost invariably illegal to make a U-turn at traffic signals, or anywhere in a 'Central Business District' (CBD; i.e. town centre); you are expected to drive around the block instead. At some crossroads, particularly in suburbia where priority is not assigned, the rule is to give way to traffic from the right. This often means that cars travelling along a main thoroughfare must stop for vehicles turning out of minor side streets.

At some sets of traffic lights curved dotted lines indicate the route a vehicle should take when turning right, which can be confusing to the uninitiated; you should turn keeping your offside wheels inside the appropriate dotted line. Visiting drivers often find it difficult to decide which is the correct line to follow, and prefer to steer a sensible course without any reference to the line.

It is compulsory to wear seat belts if they are fitted, as they certainly will be (to both front and back seats) on modern vehicles.

Speed Limits. The maximum permitted speed varies from one state to another, but is generally 100 or 110km/h; the exact limit is shown inside standard red circular signs. Lower limits are posted as appropriate; on city and town streets the maximum is usually 60km/h. A double arrow above a speed limit sign indicates that the limit is a continuation of one imposed earlier on the road. Limits are widely flouted, particularly on highways through open country.

Alcohol. A high proportion of road fatalities are caused by drunken driving. In the wake of appalling accident statistics, the police have built up a considerable repertoire of deterrents. Breath tests are not so much random as mandatory, as traffic police regularly set up road blocks and test every driver who comes along. In some cities, 'booze buses' fitted with testing equipment are on hand to give an instant and definitive reading. The blood/alcohol limit varies between states and sometimes depends on age (with those under 21 subject to a lower limit). The legal maximum in New South Wales, Queensland, Tasmania and Victoria is 0.05, while in South Australia, Western Australia and the Northern Territory it is 0.08 (the same as in Britain).

Some pubs have breath-testing machines on hand, on which you can check your approximate blood/alcohol level. Be warned, however, that these machines are not foolproof; and even if you are below the legal limit, the police can still charge you with 'driving under the influence' if they believe your driving to be impaired.

Penalties. Traffic police in Australia are more vigilant than their counterparts in Europe, and the fines for motoring offences are stiff. Police aircraft patrol some highways looking for speeding vehicles. Illegal manoeuvres of the kind that might earn a caution abroad are treated more seriously: a safely executed U-turn at an otherwise deserted set of traffic lights could cost you $100, and a fine of $250 for jumping a red light is commonplace. Don't assume you're safe if you run a red light at an otherwise deserted junction: some traffic signals are equipped with cameras that photograph vehicles that jump the lights. Fines for speeding tend to increase exponentially: exceeding the limit by 10km/h typically costs $20; by 20km/h, $80; and by 30km/h, $150. The fines for these misdemeanours are accompanied by the award of 'demerit points'; if you accumulate too many you are banned. Penalties for exceeding the alcohol limit are very severe, usually comprising a ban (notified to your home country), a large fine and possible confiscation of the vehicle.

HIGHWAY HAZARDS

Animals. Even in the crowded south-east the number of creatures roving across and along the roads at night is alarming. Kangaroos are the worst 'offenders'; a collision with one at speed can cause considerable vehicle damage, not to mention the harm done to the animal. 'Roo bars' are fitted to the fronts of many vehicles used for long-distance journeys. Some buses are equipped with a 'Shu-Roo', which emits a high-pitched noise that frightens kangaroos. Buffaloes are a menace in the northern part of the country and grazing cattle pose problems everywhere. Drive slowly enough, especially at dusk, to avoid any wildlife or farm animals that cross your path. Pay particular heed to signs warning of animals in the vicinity. On some stretches of remote highway, the only remarkable feature will be the number of dead kangaroos, which in summer create a terrible stench.

Outback Driving. Some motorists choose to ignore the warnings put out by the road authorities and set out ill-equipped for journeys across inhospitable terrain — modern folklore is laced with stories of skeletons being discovered still inside their broken-down cars. The first essential when planning a journey off the beaten track is to ensure your vehicle is fit for the task. It should be mechanically sound, and suitable for the roads you intend to use. Always seek advice from a motoring organisation, the police or locals on whether your vehicle is fit for the journey you plan to make. Some tourist boards issue brochures specifically on Outback driving and routes. On some roads through the Outback, you are required to fill in a destination card, giving the police your expected time of arrival in the next town.

Secondly, at least two spare wheels are advisable; the heat on desert roads can melt the bitumen, which then sticks to tyres. Punctures are commonplace on unsealed roads and so make sure you know how to change a tyre (and that the wheel nuts are not jammed) before you leave civilisation. Petrol stations are thin on the ground and sometimes out of fuel, as deliveries are occasionally held up. Substantial supplies of fuel and water should be carried, not least in case you need to help out a less well prepared motorist. The standard calculation of the amount of water needed is 10 litres per person per day. A selection of spare parts such as a fan belt and electrical fittings is also advisable, as well as shovel, axe and tow rope. Should you break down, stay with your vehicle until help arrives. In an emergency. crawl under the vehicle for shade and drink the radiator water, provided it has no chemical additives.

Many roads and tracks in the Outback are deeply rutted. There is said to be a certain skill in 'riding the ruts', which involves travelling at the appropriate speed to match your vehicle's suspension rhythm to the undulations. In Outback Australia, roads can be washed out by flash floods, and can remain impassable for days or weeks.

One of the hazards on unsealed (or newly surfaced) roads is of flying stones hitting the windscreen. Some drivers take the precaution of placing their fingers on the windscreen whenever they meet an oncoming vehicle, which absorbs the shock of the impact and reduces the risk of shattering. If the windscreen breaks, however, use gloves or a cloth to punch out a hole to see through. It is a good idea to carry a plastic windscreen for emergency use. Otherwise, drive to a service station with the other windows closed, to reduce the strain on what remains of the windscreen. Note that most rental agreements for hired vehicles specify that windscreen replacement is not covered by the insurance.

Road Trains. These fearsome beasts terrify other motorists, hitch-hikers and kangaroos alike. A road train consists of a powerful tractor unit pulling three or four full-sized trailers. It can weigh over 100 tonnes and be 50m long. This massive brute can attain high speeds, making its momentum such that stopping or swerving is a tortuous process. Therefore other road users are obliged to yield to road trains, even if this means driving off the main carriageway.

To ease the boredom of the long distances, truckies often play games such as 'tig', touching bumpers and then accelerating, or driving for miles alongside each other passing drinks between cabs. Truck drivers can be intolerant of other road-users and have even been known to run caravans off the road. Although the use of road trains is restricted to certain roads (notably across the Nullarbor, and up the Stuart Highway through Alice Springs to Darwin), their journeys usually begin and end in towns. So think twice before attempting to overtake one on the suburban approaches to Darwin.

CAR RENTAL
The minimum age for hiring a car is usually 20 or 21, and drivers under 25 may have to pay extra for insurance. Most rental agreements apply only to a single state, and many restrict you to a radius of 150 or 200km from the rental outlet or to sealed roads. To breach these regulations invalidates the insurance cover. Among the major companies it is usual for different rates to be quoted for 'metro' travel, 'country areas' and 'remote areas' (Alice Springs and Darwin count as 'remote'). If the basic daily rate in, say, Sydney or Perth is $45 per day unlimited distance, you might be charged 20c per kilometre after 100km in country areas, and the same in remote areas plus a surcharge of $10 per day.

Collision damage waiver insurance is not always available and so if you are responsible for an accident you will have to pay the excess of between $200 and $800 (normally $500 to people under 25). Personal accident insurance adds a further S2.50 a day. The final extra is state government stamp duty of 1% or

1.5%. Some smaller operators boast fully inclusive rates (often with a full tank of petrol), which are worth considering if you want to be certain of the final cost.

It is standard practice for rental companies to keep a bond of about $200. Most companies allow this to be left on a credit card slip. On returning the vehicle check what deductions have been made from the bond.

The multinational car rental corporations — Avis, Budget, Hertz and Thrifty — charge high prices, over $80 a day unlimited mileage. However they often offer special rates locally that are substantially less. Rates for one-way rentals are uniformly high, comprising the full daily rate plus a distance charge plus a fee for dropping off the vehicle elsewhere (known as 'repositioning'). When you see the final bill, you'd be forgiven for believing you've bought the car. Reservation numbers are:

Avis: 02-9516 2877
Hertz: 02-9669 2444

Budget: 008-331331
Thrifty: 02-9360 4055

If you make a booking through a central reservation service you will pay the published rate. But by approaching an outlet directly, it is quite possible to negotiate a discount. One researcher for this book went to a branch of Budget in a Melbourne suburb to hire a cheap hatchback for $30 a day, and drove away in a Mazda MX-5 convertible for just $20 more, saving $100 on the official rate. Individual managers can exercise considerable discretion.

In general, though, cheaper deals are available from local operators or from cut-rate nationwide chains such as Half Price (toll-free 008-221888). Suggested companies are given under *Driving* in each city section. Companies with names like 'Rent-a-Rocket' and 'Hire-a-Heap' are usually cheapest of all (about $40 per day, unlimited distance, for a rental of 7 days or more), but their vehicles are not the fastest, quietest nor most economical on fuel.

Campervans. Renting a campervan for the family holiday is less popular in Australia than New Zealand. Nevertheless it may be attractive to visitors looking for a fairly economical way to travel and sleep. Rates start at about $120 a day for a two-person campervan and are nearly $200 for a six-berth travel home. You will be told which roads are closed to you because of their poor surface; for example, rented campervans may not be used north of Mossman, Queensland or north of Geraldton in Western Australia. Most companies impose a minimum hire period of at least 3 days or, more commonly, a week.

Hertz and Avis (numbers above) rent out campervans; so too do Newmans Holidays (c/o Southern World Vacations, Level 12, 25 Bligh St, Sydney 2000; 02-9237 0360) and Apollo Motorhome Holidays (698 Nudgee Road, Northgate, Queensland; 07-3260 5466; toll-free within Australia 008-777779), which has depots in most key eastern cities. If you plan a tour of the country, you may want to consider buying a van (see below).

Car Delivery. Partly because of the hassles involved in re-registering vehicles in another state (see below), car delivery is rare in Australia. In addition, rental cars that need to be returned to base are few and far between, because the cost to the hirer of repositioning is so high.

BUYING A CAR

For longer stays it can be worthwhile to buy a cheap second-hand vehicle and sell it at the end of your stay. Most of the cars on Australian roads will be familiar to visitors: many Japanese models (some assembled in Australia) and plenty of locally produced Fords: the Falcon is equivalent to a Granada, and the Telstar broadly similar to an Orion. But the leading marque is Holden, one of the many car companies gobbled up by the American giant General Motors, and its products are similar to GM models elsewhere in the world; the Holden Camira is the same as a Cavalier, while the Gemini approximates to a Chevette. The Holden Barina is a small hatchback.

However, if you have less than $2000 to spend, you can forget about owning one of these models. You might find a 1976 Holden Premier or a 1970 Volkswagen Beetle instead. The amount you will need to spend on maintaining your vehicle is more difficult to predict, but if you cover long distances then your tyres will wear out at a fearsome rate; you can replace them most cheaply by buying retreads.

The best source for buying or selling a vehicle is the notice board at hostels, where travellers about to leave Australia advertise their cars. Otherwise, try the Saturday car sales held in car parks. Sellers pay a nominal $5 to park their cars so that potential buyers can inspect them. The classified columns of the main newspapers, especially the Wednesday and Saturday editions, are also recommended. If you are mechanically minded, the car auctions that are held regularly in the cities are worth attending. Whenever you are buying a vehicle privately be wary of shifty deals and make sure it comes with a two-part pink slip, which is the registration document.

If you want to be sure of the vehicle's condition, you can pay the state motoring organisation (assuming you are a member or have affiliated membership in your home country) to carry out a mechanical test on it; this costs about $100. If the vehicle is completely roadworthy they will affix a sticker, thus enhancing the resale value. Vehicles bought from second-hand car dealers are more expensive but usually come with all the right paperwork. Some dealers specialise in cars for overseas travellers and are prepared to quote a guaranteed buy-back price.

Once you buy a vehicle you take on the responsibility for the annual 'rego check', the compulsory annual mechanical check that results in a Road-Worthiness Certificate. When registering your vehicle, you must take the RWC to the local road licensing authority. Here you pay a transfer tax and stamp duty, which comes to about 8% of the stated value of the car; therefore buyers routinely undervalue the vehicle on the form.

If you want to sell a vehicle outside the state in which it was initially registered, you must submit it for a new mechanical check before re-registering it in the state. Even if you have a valid 'rego', the police may still take an interest in the health of your car. They can attach a yellow sticker (known as a 'canary'), which tells you they wish to inspect the vehicle; if they attach a red sticker, it means you may not move it because they consider it unroadworthy.

The fee for registration includes the cost of compulsory third-party insurance cover. Charges for a typical four-cylinder car vary considerably, from around $220 in Western Australia to nearly $400 in the ACT. Once you take over the registration of a car you also assume the responsibility for any outstanding fines; call the Registry of Encumbered Vehicles before you buy.

Insurance. Compulsory Third Party (CTP) insurance is the minimum required by law. It covers people, not property. Insurance against damage is wise — 'bomb' insurance, which covers damage to other vehicles, costs about $80 a year. If you have motor insurance with a no-claims bonus in the UK, the discount may well be transferable to your Australian insurance. Take a letter from your insurers. Some companies sell 6-month policies, but if you have to buy a full year's worth of insurance, a rebate may be possible if you don't keep the vehicle that long.

Buying a Campervan. The advice above on buying a car applies equally to campervans. One of the most popular vehicles is a Volkswagen Kombi van, and there is normally a fairly active second-hand market among travellers in Australia, especially in Cairns and Darwin where many travellers end their tours. With a little bargaining, you should be able to pick one up for less than $3000.

HITCH-HIKING
Despite rumours to the contrary, hitching in Australia is generally safe and fast. The proportion of drivers prepared to pick you up is lower than in New Zealand, partly because of the bad experiences some motorists have had after picking up hitch-hikers. But there are enough friendly drivers to make most journeys pleasantly straightforward. Even bus drivers have been known to pick up hitch-hikers. Considering the length of most trips (which are often measured in days instead of hours), it is surprising how many drivers are willing to gamble on your acceptability. The risk of attacks from malevolent drivers is low but real, and single women should think carefully before accepting a long-distance ride through the Outback. On the other hand ingrained male chauvinism means that most drivers will be reluctant to leave women hitchers by the side of the road.

One big difference compared with hitching elsewhere is that Australians hitch with a finger pointing down at the road, since an up-raised thumb can be construed as an offensive gesture. Even hitching 'correctly', be prepared for a surprisingly large number of knockbacks and yelled insults, perhaps due to the national contempt for 'bludgers', i.e. spongers. Still, lorry drivers can usually be relied on to stop. Life on the road with a truckie allows you a glimpse into their culture. They drive for 2 or 3 days at a time, only stopping for meals and keeping awake by taking speed. You will undoubtedly meet many interesting and unusual Australians who will go out of their way to show you local sights.

The key to fast travel is, as anywhere, a question of picking the time and place. But even if you do get dropped on the Nullarbor, there are enough roadhouses for you to wait for your next lift in comfort. Waits at places like Coober Pedy in the South Australian desert and Three Ways in the Northern Territory (where the roads from Townsville, Darwin and Alice Springs meet) may be long but eventually a bored truck driver will come along. Most experienced hitchers claim that you rarely wait more than 5 hours though it is not impossible to be left waiting for a couple of days. If you find this prospect terrifying, you're probably better off on a bus.

Bear in mind that the terrain is much harsher and settlements far fewer than in Europe. Be prepared for any eventuality, and carry tent and cooking equipment in case you are stranded. Try to avoid hitching in the far north during the summer, but if you have to, be sure to carry plenty of water.

Many visitors find hitching fine for short- and medium-distance travel, but for long distances prefer the predictability of the bus or train. Hitching on Australian freeways is not so much life in the fast lane as life on the hard shoulder. The access roads are the only places where hitching is technically legal, but are mostly lightly travelled. You are much better off on an ordinary highway where all the traffic is channelled past your waiting thumb and, except in Queensland, the police never bother you.

Advice for hitching out of the state capitals is given in the appropriate *Arrival and Departure* sections. A destination sign, with 'please' added, and a rucksack are useful adjuncts. You might wish to draw attention to your foreignness by composing a jokey sign, such as 'London to Wagga Wagga' or 'Canada to Canberra'. It is useful to be able to recognise the number plates of each state at a distance:

ACT: blue on white   Queensland: green on white

New South Wales: black on yellow   South Australia: green on yellow
Northern Territory: red on white   Tasmania: blue on white
Victoria: green on white (new); white on black (old)
Western Australia: black on yellow (new); black on white (old)

You will see many other varieties in addition to those listed above; these are for commercial, official or diplomatic vehicles, or personalised registrations.

Lift Sharing. Sharing driving and fuel costs on long trips is popular among young travellers in Australia. Advertisements for lifts offered and wanted are posted on notice boards at hostels and university Students' Unions. Some lift-sharing agencies have been set up; see the regional chapters.

A variant of lift-sharing is to visit the depots of long-distance trucking firms on the outskirts of the major cities — you can always ring the despatcher ahead of time, but a personal visit is usually more successful. You may also hear of truckies' favourite pubs where a long-distance lift can be arranged.

Airborne Hitching. The notion of hitching a ride on a light aircraft or helicopter is not too far-fetched in Outback areas. Many people in the Outback use helicopters like cars, and even fly them like cars, dropping down to read road signs. Light aircraft do not have quite this versatility, but are still a popular means of getting around. If you spend any time in an isolated community, you will get to hear about who flies where, and need feel no embarrassment in asking for a ride.

MOTORCYCLING
There is a buoyant market in Japanese bikes, and hostel notice boards are a good source. Bikes are the preferred mode of transport for a high proportion of affluent Scandinavians, many of whom are keener on selling their machines in a hurry than at a good price. You might pick up a five-year-old Honda or Yamaha 250cc machine for around $700. Buyers who choose carefully should have no trouble reselling at the end of their stay. One Sydney specialist is Cyclecraft (107 Bondi Road, Bondi; 02-9387 3366), which sells used bikes and will buy back the bike at the end of your trip.

The information above regarding buying and registering a car is true also for motorcycles. You can hire motorcycles from around $35 per day from dealers in most cities. For further information, contact the local branch of the Motorcycle Riders' Association (MRA), listed in the *Yellow Pages* under the heading 'Clubs: Motorcycle'.

Bikers should take great care in the big cities, where motorcycle couriers are as unpopular as elsewhere, and car drivers react accordingly. Because of the custom among bank robbers of using motorcycling helmets as a form of disguise and protection, most banks now have signs directed at motorcyclists asking 'Please remove your helmet before entering this bank'.

The largest operator of motorcycle tours in Australia is Outback Motorbike Safaris, Factory 3, 59 Jersey Road, Bayswater, Vic 3153 (03-9720 4400). The Motorcycle Racing Club of New South Wales (67 Dora St, Hurstville, NSW 2320; 02-9605 9174) can advise on road conditions off the beaten track and on the availability of petrol in rural areas.

CYCLING
The Australian climate — and much of its terrain — lends itself to cycling. Only the keenest cyclists will attempt to cover the long distances between capital cities, but many interesting areas are ideal for inexperienced cyclists. For

example, a bike is a very pleasant way to explore the hills of Victoria, the east coast of Tasmania or the South Australian wineries (though the Barossa Valley is long and boring to cycle). If you stick to these areas you can enjoy the delights of the typical small town (i.e. six people, 12 dogs and two million sheep). Cycling also enables you to take a much closer look at Australian wildlife. Due to your speed and relative quietness you have a much better chance than other road users of seeing animals and birds. Don't be surprised if a kangaroo hops along beside you.

Helmets are compulsory for cyclists in Victoria and New South Wales, and can be uncomfortable in hot weather. But wearing one protects you against injuries and on-the-spot fines.

You can hire a bicycle by the hour for $3 upwards, with a day costing $12–20. Hostels often have bikes for hire. Most commercial rental outfits require a deposit of around $25, or a passport as security.

It soon becomes worthwhile buying a bike. Expect to spend between $350 and $400 on a new Taiwanese ten-speed mountain bike, helmet, water bottle, tools and panniers. You should be able to recoup half of this at the end of your trip. Good second-hand bikes are advertised in hostels or in papers like the weekly *Trading Post*. You could get a good mountain bike for $175.

Thefts are common, so buy a good lock and try to insure your bike. One way to do this is to enrol with Australian Bikefile, a nationwide bicycle registration and insurance scheme. You pay an annual fee of $10 plus $20 if your bicycle is worth less than $300, up to $45 if your bicycle is worth less than $1000. You can get details of the scheme from cycle dealers, or contact Bikefile direct at PO Box 137, Caloundra, Qld 4551 (07-5491 9011).

Riding a bike is a serious undertaking in a land where food and water supplies can be hundreds of kilometres apart. (At least cyclists don't have to worry about the next petrol station.) The condition of the roads in Australia varies and your route will determine the type of bicycle you use. A mountain bike is recommended if you want to get off the beaten track to some otherwise inaccessible but very worthwhile places. Beware of plank bridges in the country; the gaps are sometimes wide enough to trap a wheel and cause a nasty accident. Beware also of dogs, especially unleashed blue cattle dogs, a common and vicious breed. A couple of thwacks around the nose with a bicycle pump is enough to deter most brutes. Much more likely to interfere with your pleasure are the aggressive driving techniques favoured by the locals (much more dangerous than dogs, country bridges and venomous snakes put together).

Climbing over the Great Dividing Range, which separates the coast between Melbourne and Sydney from the interior, is an exhilarating experience, though a gruelling one. Due to the way the continental shelves are formed it is easier to cycle from west to east; in the opposite direction one is faced with almost a brick wall, though with a 10 or 12 speed touring bike with a mountain block it is possible. Mountains in Australia like the Snowy Mountains are no more difficult than their North American or European alpine counterparts. Some roads are blocked by snow in the winter, so check weather forecasts with police and tourist organisations before setting off. Being stranded in cold, wet conditions can be just as dangerous as being stranded in the desert. Cycling up the Queensland coast is less strenuous, principally due to the helpful tailwind that will blow you all the way to Cairns, Daintree and beyond (though the bitumen stops at Daintree).

Detailed information on cycle routes and touring can be obtained from the following organisations:

Bicycle New South Wales: GPO Box 272, Sydney 2001; street address Level 2, 209 Castlereagh St.

Bicycle Victoria: GPO Box 1961R, Melbourne 3001; street address is Somerset Place.
Freewheeling: PO Box K26, Haymarket, Sydney, NSW 2000 — the Australian equivalent of the Cyclists Touring Club in Britain with its own magazine and a range of cycle information.

It is possible to transport your bicycle on buses and trains, although some suburban trains impose restrictions. The cost is usually lower if the bike is dismantled and boxed. One drawback using bus services is that the operators do not guarantee that the bicycle travels with you, so you may have to wait around for it at your destination. You can also take your bike by air, so long as you box it and deflate the tyres to avoid high-altitude explosions. Your bicycle box may well be weighed, so don't overload it.

CITY TRANSPORT

All the state capitals have cheap and efficient public transport systems. One of the more pleasing features of city transport networks in Australia is the flexibility of tickets. In most areas, tickets for buses, trams and suburban trains are valid for free transfers to any other mode of transport within a certain time limit. Specific details are provided under *City Transport* in the regional sections.

Taxis. Cabs are usually large, brightly coloured saloon cars. They can be hailed in the street or found at ranks in busy locations. Availability is indicated by a light on the roof. Some cabs announce themselves to be 'Share Ride' taxis, so it is always worth hailing cabs that are already occupied. Even if you're on your own, taxis are not prohibitively expensive. There are generally two rates: one for weekdays, and a higher rate for night and weekend use.

It is customary to sit in the front seat. Those who don't will quickly be branded as stuck-up Poms. Don't neglect the chance to chat to drivers, as they are often good sources of information and opinion assuming their knowledge of English is sufficiently advanced. Visitors are often pleasantly surprised by the apparent absence of avarice among Australian taxi drivers. While few reject a tip, none will expect one and some will switch off the meter while tracking down a precise location.

demountable	portable prefabricated motel units
dunny	outdoor loo (of which there are not many left these days)
flatting	sharing an apartment
garbo	dustman/refuse collector
hotel	any establishment that sells alcohol, which may or may not have rooms
humpy	crude hut shelter
on-site	common abbreviation for on-site caravan
private hotel	unlicensed accommodation
pub	any hotel
Salvos	Salvation Army

snib	door latch
unit	flat/apartment/condominium

Places where travellers tend to congregate usually have a good selection of reasonably priced accommodation. Hostelling is popular among a broader spectrum and age group than it is in Europe or North America. For many visitors, hostels are the key to an excellent holiday. Not only do they provide an affordable place to sleep (usually $10–12 per night) but they provide access to a valuable range of information about what to see, how to get there and who to go with. Because of fierce competition between individual hostels and hostel groups (including the YHA), a range of perks such as courtesy pick-up, tour agency facilities, etc. is offered. Many hostels, both private and YHA, are in prime sites and are often in beautifully restored old buildings.

Off the beaten track in Australia — and until fairly recently even Ayers Rock would have qualified — the low density of population, both resident and visiting, means that accommodation is fairly sparse, and not necessarily cheap. It is better in such circumstances to be self-sufficient for accommodation (see *Camping* below).

A wealth of tourist and accommodation information greets the new arrival in most Australian towns and cities, but if you are completely stuck, you could do worse than to check advertisements in the *Yellow Pages*; look up the headings 'Homes and Hostels', 'Hotels — Private' or 'Guest Houses'. One accommodation possibility that is not mentioned in the tourist literature is the network of Aboriginal hostels in outback areas that sometimes take in transients; ask at roadhouses and in pubs, or look up the Aboriginal Hostels Association in relevant phone directories.

YHA. The youth hostelling movement is thriving in Australia. Many hostels are in wonderful environments from Tasmanian rainforest to Northern Territory desert. One disadvantage is that many of the most beautiful ones are fairly inaccessible without private transport. If your image of a YHA hostel is of a spartan, puritanical place run on vaguely militaristic grounds, you will be surprised. YHA hostels are shedding their boy-scout image and creating more single and double rooms rather than dorms, and as a result many 'yuppie backpackers' choose to stay at them. In contrast to the more party-oriented private hostels (described below), YHA hostels in Australia are geared more to people who want peace and quiet and who enjoy studying their maps around a log fire.

Australia has 135 year-round hostels, offering beds costing between $7 and $19. Anyone hoping to travel extensively on a low budget should join their national YHA, which automatically gives membership of the International Youth Hostels Federation (IYHF). There is nothing to stop you from joining the Australian YHA after you have arrived, but it may be cheaper to join before your arrival: new members over 21 pay £9.30 in Britain compared to $26 in Australia. As in Europe and North America, you should carry a sheet sleeping bag — otherwise you will often need to hire one for a dollar or two.

The Australian *YHA Accommodation Guide* is a mine of travel information. It describes in detail all YHA hostels and affiliated hostels, with instructions on how to find them, lists of available facilities (such as laundry, bicycle hire, barbecues, etc.). It also includes some private accommodation such as campsites and Alpine Club huts in the hostellers' price range. The guide is free to all YHA members, and is available from the Australian Tourist Commission at Gemini House, 10–18 Putney Hill, Putney, London SW15 6AA (0181-780 2227; fax 0181-780 1496), from YHA Adventure Shops and from national YHA offices.

The YHA headquarters in Australia (Level 3, 10 Mallet St, Camperdown, NSW 2050; 02-565 1699; fax 02-565 1325) does not encourage mail-order requests. If you can't get hold of the *Accommodation Guide* you will have to rely on the much sketchier information given in Volume II of the *IYHF International Handbook*, which includes Australia and is widely available in all hostelling countries, and wait until you arrive in Australia to pick up the *Guide*. Upon arrival you can also pick up the free *Australia Visitors Map* showing the location and addresses of all Australian hostels.

YHA
AUSTRALIA
OFFERS

YHA AUSTRALIA

HOSTELLING INTERNATIONAL

YHA Australia have complete travel packages which include accommodation, 12 month valid coach travel, entrance tickets to Australia's favourite tourist places & more plus the Sydney Discovery Package @ AUD $230.00.

Packages are from as little as AUD$25 a day - e.g. Aussie Explorer 'Best of East' bus pass with Greyhound Pioneer with 60 nights' accommodation for AUD$1,380.

Stay in over 140 Australian YHA Hostels. There are also over 5,500 Hostels world wide, all with friendly, helpful hostel staff.

No age limits in any Australian YHA Hostels.

A centralised booking system where YHA Hostels can be booked for your next destination.

Access to over 600 discounts throughout Australia - a saving of thousands of dollars to YHA members only. The discounts are listed in the 1995-96 YHA Accommodation Guide.

YHA Hostels that feature clean and comfortable accommodation at all of Australia's favourite tourist destinations.

Self-catering facilities to help you save money.

Travel Agencies in every State capital city as well as Alice Springs, Cairns, Airlie Beach and Canberra. Each Travel Office offers special discounts to YHA members on a wide range of travel products from international airline tickets, coach passes, travel insurance and local tours.

Please send further information on the excellent travel packages available from YHA Australia

Name

Address

Postcode

Country

Send to: Australian YHA, Level 3, 10 Mallett Street, Camperdown, NSW 2050 Australia   VW 95-96

Hostelling is so popular, especially in the major cities, that it is often difficult to find a bed. You might want to pre-book your first couple of nights in Australia by following the instructions provided in the *International Handbook*. Reservations can be made for the 'gateway' and larger hostels through the International Booking Network (IBN), and this service is available from most of the YHA Travel Centres and hostels around the world. Once in Australia you can also make reservations throughout the country at Membership and Travel Centres, or hostel staff can arrange bookings for you (note that a fee of $2 may apply for this service).

The notice boards in popular hostels are excellent sources of information, especially if you are looking for some people with whom to share expenses on a long car journey. Another advantage of joining the YHA is that your card entitles you to an impressive range of discounts from buses to ferries, travel books to camping equipment. Many of these discounts are indicated throughout this book, but you should pick up the free *YHA Discounts* booklet for the full list (the 1996 edition included 800 discounts available to YHA members throughout Australia).

For further information about hostels in a specific state, you might want to contact the regional offices whose addresses are as follows:

New South Wales: 422 Kent St, Sydney 2001 (02-9261 1111; fax 02-9261 1969).
Northern Territory: 69a Mitchell St, Darwin 0801 (08-8981 6344; fax 08-8981 6674).
Queensland: 154 Roma St, Brisbane 4001 (07-3236 1680; fax 07-3236 1702).
South Australia: 38 Sturt St, Adelaide 5000 (08-8231 5583; fax 08-8231 4219).
Tasmania: 28 Criterion St, Hobart 7001 (03-6234 9617; fax 03-6234 7422).
Victoria: 205 King St, Melbourne 3000 (03-9670 9611; fax 03-9670 9840).
Western Australia: 236 William St, Northbridge 6003 (09-227 5122; fax 09-227 5123).

Backpackers' Hostels. In 1983 the first so-called backpackers' hostel started in Cairns. It became an instant success, and such has been the growth in this sector of tourism that many conventional hotels and motels are either opening a backpackers' section or converting to hostels. Backpacker accommodation means hostels and lodges that cater mainly for non-Australians. They appeal to travellers who find the restrictions at 'proper' YHA hostels irksome. Therefore emphasis on the social life is strong and people who want to turn in early may not only feel out-of-place but may find it too noisy to sleep. Many hostels have regular social events like barbecues or video evenings for about $5. Don't stay in a private hostel if you are determined to meet Australians, as most are foreigners' ghettoes full of people following a set route. Privately run hostels often have a more nakedly commercial feel about them, but the standard of the facilities that they provide is generally high.

VIP Backpackers Resorts of Australia is one group that has been especially successful and provides stiff competition for the YHA, especially in Queensland and New South Wales. You can get an up-to-date booklet listing the 100 or so hostels from its headquarters in Queensland (PO Box 600, Cannon Hill, Brisbane, Qld 4170; 018-666 888); this is free within Australia but costs $5 if ordered by post from abroad. Backpackers' prices rival those of YHA hostels, starting at $12 a night in a dorm and $16 in a double. One hostel will book others in the chain for about $1.50. The group markets a VIP Backpacker Kit (partly to finance the free hostel directory), which sells for $20. It includes discounts that can be used at any member hostels, plus 10% discounts on bus lines and many other outlets; many of these overlap with YHA discounts.

There are several other backpacker hostel groups. One source of hostel addresses that is not tied to a backpacker organisation is the *Aussie Backpacker Accommodation Guide* (published by North Australian Publishing, PO Box 1264, Townsville, Queensland 4810; 077-723244). Another source of information on backpacker accommodation is the *Independent Travellers Guide to Australia* published by STA Travel and available from any STA office (addresses in regional chapters).

Ys. Several city YMCAs and YWCAs offer casual accommodation to both men and women, though prices are well above hostel levels. Write to the national office of the YWCA (139 Hoddle St, Richmond, Vic 3121; 03-9417 2131) for a pamphlet listing available accommodation possibilities. Some are listed in the regional chapters of this book.

Student Residences. Out of term-time (mid-November to mid-February) University halls of residence (known as colleges) are let out to travellers. Priority and discounts are given to those who can produce student identification. A student might pay $12–15 per night for a single room, while the cost for others is typically 50% higher. Often part of the college will be taken over for a convention, so you could find yourself sharing a corridor with ophthalmologists, jugglers or born-again Christians.

Some suggestions of colleges worth trying are given in the regional chapters; for others, call the Accommodation Officer whose number should be listed in the *White Pages* under the main University heading.

Camping. The cheapest accommodation of all is a tent, an attractive option if you're travelling into remote areas where accommodation is in short supply. Bear in mind that when it rains, it rains hard, and when insects bite, they do so in earnest. Caravan camping is popular among holidaying Australians, and so there are plenty of campgrounds, which are good places to meet Aussies. Most campgrounds have tent pitches for $8–$12 which, if you're on your own is not significantly cheaper than hostels. The best deal is staying at a council-run campsite with which a few towns are blessed; here it should cost no more than $5 to pitch a tent. Campsites in national parks are often open only to those with tents. They cost between $3 and $8 depending on facilities. Motoring organisations such as the NRMA publish caravan and camping directories and state tourism authorities normally includes campgrounds in their brochures about accommodation.

Australia is so empty a country that it is usually possible to find a free place to pitch a tent. Camping by the side of the road and in rest areas can be done, though discretion is recommended. In outback areas the roadsigns are often peppered with bulletholes, so it is advisable to camp in a place hidden from the highway. Most rest areas offer water, toilets, tables and barbecue stands. Away from rest areas, finding a supply of water may present problems. Never be tempted to camp in a dried-up river bed, since a flash flood can wash you away. If you are travelling by car, an axe can be a useful addition for building campfires, provided there is not a fire ban in force.

Caravanning is extremely popular both among locals and overseas holiday-makers, especially in campervans (see *Getting Around: Driving*). These permit a degree of luxury unknown in tents, especially if you stop at campgrounds where you can plug into a power supply (usually at a cost of $12 a night) to run a fridge and/or a TV.

Even travellers who do not have a tent or campervan should not discount the possibility of staying at campsites. On-site caravans can be found at most campgrounds around Australia, and are especially worthwhile if you are travelling with a group of friends (or if you are a tent-camper who has hit a patch of bad weather). The price will be in the neighbourhood of $25 for two people or $35 for four people, which includes the use of all cooking equipment, but not bedding.

Hotels. It is puzzling to hear how often the word 'hotel' crops up in the conversation of the locals, and not in the context of where to house their mothers-in-law on their annual visits. Usually they are referring to the local pub, since the licensing laws of Australia require drinking establishments to offer accommodation as well. Although some pubs do have rooms available for travellers — and it is always worth asking, especially in country areas — the majority of pubs are not set up to offer overnight tourist accommodation. Some hotels emphasise their ability to provide accommodation by calling themselves 'hotel/motels'.

To distinguish hotels that have accommodation but no bar, the term 'private hotel' is used. These are a little thin on the ground though you can find them in the cities with prices starting at $20 for a single. But in many places there is an uncomfortable gap between hostels and campsites on the one hand and pricey motels on the other. The equivalent of the British bed and breakfast or the European one-star hotel is scarce, though the number of bed and breakfasts is increasing.

Licensed hotels in the country are more likely than city ones to have accommodation. All settlements, however remote, have a pub and therefore a hotel, often called the 'Commercial' since its main customers were travelling sales reps. Some are classics, with crumbling verandahs, chatty proprietors and colourful histories. They tend to have more character, less luxury and lower prices than the purpose-built tourist hotels in resort areas. If you drink in the hotel bar, you are bound to meet locals and may be offered good inside advice or even offered a ride.

One disadvantage is that the bar may make it too noisy to sleep — ask about noise levels in the room you are assigned and what time the bar closes. Women on their own can sometimes feel uncomfortable when they ask about accommodation at the bar (since there will be no reception desk). Sometimes the breweries issue details of their tied houses that offer accommodation as in the case of the Tooth brewery's list of country inns in New South Wales. Prices vary greatly, but some are remarkably cheap, say $15–$20 per person.

Motels. Just as in North America, motels are the favourite style of accommodation for Australian families. And like their American counterparts motels in Australia are usually comfortable but indistinguishable from one another and unlicensed. Predictably they are to be found on the approach roads to cities and towns. Look for the chains like Flag Inns (toll-free 008 011 177) and Quality Inns (008 090600) or the slightly cheaper ones like A1. A full colour directory of all 450 motels in the Flag Inn chain is widely available. Top-class motels charge about $70 single and $80 double, moderate motels $45/$60 and budget motels $30/$35. The state motoring organisations issue their own lists of accommodation.

Airlines and tour operators are keen to sell you vouchers for use at motels in the major chains, each of which entitles you to a night's accommodation at a reduced rate compared with normal tariffs. If you intend to stay in motels anyway, this is a good deal, but you may tire of identical decor in indistinguishable buildings away from the centre of town.

If you are travelling by car in remote areas, you will probably travel between road stations, which normally comprise a petrol pump, snack bar, pub and perhaps a few motel-type units, sometimes in prefabricated portable constructions called 'demountables'. Some road stations also provide a shady place for campers as well as showers.

In contrast to the Outback, resort areas offer an abundance of accommodation. Often motels in these popular areas will offer self-contained fully equipped 'units' for people who want to cater for themselves.

Homestays and Farmstays. More and more Australians are opening their houses to overseas visitors, and the tourism authorities are only too delighted to encourage this trend and to exploit the Australian reputation for friendliness and hospitality. 'Home-hosted holidays' are big business. Although the system is not developed to the same extent as in New Zealand, it is gaining in popularity, especially the farm stays, which are taking advantage of the growing interest in Outback tourism.

A typical listing for a station (large farm) offering hospitality would include farm and district tours, transfers, accommodation and meals. Farms normally provide dinner, bed and breakfast, which is why they are more expensive than city homes. Prices start at about $70 per adult per day. Out-buildings on some farm properties have been converted into backpacker accommodation starting at $7.

Several organisations act as agents for homes, farms and ranches. Although it is not necessary to book before you arrive in Australia, you might like to request the literature from one or more of the following:

Bed & Breakfast Australia: PO Box 408, Gordon, NSW 2072 (02-9498 5344; fax 02-9498 6438).

Farm Holidays: 98 Fletcher St, Woollahra, NSW 2025 (02-9387 6681).

Host Farms Association: 6th Floor, 230 Collins St, Melbourne, Vic 3000 (03-9650 2922). Specialises in Victoria but has links with other state organisations.

Town & Country Hosts, 110 Alfred St, Milsons Point, NSW 2061 (02-9955 0536; fax 02-9957 3108). An umbrella organisation of hosting organisations (to which Farm Holidays belongs). It represents about 200 properties in all the states.

The 1992 prices quoted by Town & Country Hosts for self-catering cottages start at $250 per week and for standard homestead accommodation with all meals and activities from $85 a day. Other organisations specify a price range from $40 in a double (bed & breakfast) at a beach suburb of Sydney to $115 per night at a ranch. The agency brochures often contain a resumé of the hosts' hobbies, such as 'ex-grazier interested in horses; wife interested in spinning and weaving'. You may be able to choose from amongst a homestay in central Sydney run by a ballet-loving Hungarian-speaking retired couple and one on a Queensland cattle station with Arab horses and peacocks.

The average bed and breakfast place charges $50 double. An excellent source of addresses is the *Australian Bed & Breakfast Book* published in New Zealand by Moonshine Press (PO Box 41022, Eastbourne). It includes 140 addresses throughout Australia with a paragraph written by the proprietors singing the praises of their establishments. To order a copy send £9.95/US$16.95 to the above address which includes air mail postage. This is much better than the book *Homestay Australia* which costs $22, whose listings are almost wholly confined to New South Wales.

Travellers who belong to certain clubs may be able to stay in Australian homes without money changing hands. For example Bicycle New South Wales (Level 2, 209 Castlereagh St, Sydney) can give you a list of their members who may be willing to put up touring cyclists.

Longer Term Accommodation. If you are planning to stay put, possibly in order to work, check hostel notice boards for flat-shares, which is less hassle than relying on newspaper adverts. Modest one-bedroom flats vary from about $80 a week in Adelaide to $135 in Sydney. The normal minimum leasing period for a 'unit' or flat is three months. Most are let on term leases for 6 or 12 months. Usually bonds of several hundred dollars are required not only to cover any damage to the property but also in case you leave before the lease expires. When flat-hunting, it helps if you can show a reference from a previous landlord. For traditional digs where the landlady provides meals and does your laundry, look under 'Board Vacant' in the classified columns.

| brekkies | breakfast |
| bug | small crab tasting rather like crayfish or |

	prawn
Cherry Ripe	chocolate-covered bar of coconut and cherry jelly
Chiko rolls (pronounced chicko)	Australian fast food faintly resembling a spring roll
Chook (pronounced as in book)	chicken
Coon	brand of Australian cheddar cheese
counter meal	food served at a pub
cut lunch	sandwiches
damper	unleavened bush bread, often sold at country fairs
dead horse	tomato sauce
dim sims	Australasian corruption of Chinese Dim Sum or Yum Cha, consisting of bland meat and vegetables wrapped in pastry then steamed or fried
dog's eye	meat pie
entree	starter or hors d'oeuvre
flake	shark meat
hoggett	sheep meat killed at between one and two years
hot bread shop	bakery
jaffle	toasted sandwich
jatz	cracker/biscuit especially popular in Queensland
lamingtons (lammies)	classic Australian cake: cubes of sponge covered with chocolate and coconut
lollies	sweets/candies
milk bar	small (and usually dowdy) snack bar
pavlova (pav)	classic Australian meringue, cream and fruit dessert
Pavlova Magic	freeze-dried egg whites, sold in a plastic egg and used to make inferior versions of the above
paw paw	papaya (tropical fruit)
sanny/sammy	sandwich
savouries	canapés, finger food
show bag	bags of sweets and other items sold at country fairs for about $5
slices	cakes or baked goods
snags or snaggers (also known as *mystery bags*)	sausages
spicy tucker	food at an ethnic restaurant
Twisties	cheesy corn snack to which most Australians are extremely partial
Vegemite	yeast spread, which Australians claim is far superior to Marmite
veggies	universally used abbreviation for vegetables
Violet Crumble bars	chocolate-covered honeycomb bars (like Crunchies) in purple wrappers
witchetty grubs	one-time Aboriginal delicacy: the white larvae of certain beetles

yabbies	freshwater crayfish
yiros (pronounced year-oss)	doner kebab
yum cha	alternative name for Dim Sum

Eating is one of the great pleasures in Australia. Whether you dine at the fanciest restaurant, grab lunch at a pub or buy the ingredients for a picnic from market stalls, you can rely upon good, fresh food at reasonable prices. It is easy to put on weight in Australia. But it is also easy to eat healthily and (in cities, at least) diversely. Most of the raw ingredients will be familiar to the visitor: Australians enjoy good beef, lamb and poultry, tasty seafood and fresh fish, plus excellent fruit and vegetables.

You can also enjoy uniquely Australian food: it is no longer illegal for butchers to sell kangaroo meat and, although you are unlikely to be served a kangaroo roast at a family Sunday lunch, many upmarket restaurants feature it. Most visitors find it tasty and tender, even though the idea of chewing such a cute creature may be worrying. Kangaroo testicles — on the menu of at least one South Australian restaurant as 'Flinders Ranges Fancies' — are less popular. And even the humble meat pie in the Northern Territory is sometimes made with kangaroo or buffalo. You are more likely to encounter unusual crustaceans like bugs and yabbies than crocodile steaks (expensive, and resembling a chewy cross between pork and chicken) and emu (which French importers maintain tastes like duck, though others have compared it to old goat). The Aboriginal delicacy of witchetty grubs is available in a handful of restaurants specialising in 'bush tucker', and is made into a sauce in some Northern Territory outlets (said to taste like peanut butter).

Whereas American cuisine has arguably been homogenised into one huge hamburger, Australian food is still developing and assimilating a number of influences. Successive waves of immigrants have adapted their native cuisines to the plentiful and excellent produce of Australia. And meals can be washed down with some of the best beers and wines in the world.

Mealtimes. One unfortunate habit that Australia has retained from its British colonial past is inflexible eating habits. Most restaurants keep limited hours and you may well have to adjust your evening eating pattern to fit in. 'Tea' is not a late afternoon snack, but the main evening meal which is ideally taken no later than 6 or 7pm. By 10pm most diners will have left the average restaurant and the staff will be clearing up around the stragglers. In small towns, it is difficult to find anywhere except the local fish-and-chip shop prepared to serve you after 8pm. The fancier restaurants in cities stay open until late, incidentally allowing diners to circumvent licensing laws.

The Barbecue. In keeping with their love of the outdoors, Australians are great ones for barbecues — in the back garden, in the grounds of a YHA hostel, on the beach or in a National Park. Steaks, chops, 'snags' and vegetables wrapped in foil can be grilled over glowing charcoal or firewood, electric bars or gas (with adjacent meters taking 20c coins). The resulting feast is served with bread, salad and copious quantities of beer. If you are invited along to one, take drink and ask whether guests are expected to bring a piece of meat. You don't need to ask whether to take insect repellent.

Barbecues are an essential ingredient of Australiana and you should attend or initiate at least one during your stay. Do not expect the occasion to demonstrate any social advances that Australia has made. Men normally hover round the fire, while women are permitted only to assist with preparing the side dishes, yelling advice and clearing up afterwards.

Picnics. It is easy to prepare a cheap and tasty picnic. Bread costs $1.50 a loaf, cheeses and cold meats $6–$9 per kilogram and fruit from market stalls is generally cheap in season. If you have the use of a car, you might want to invest in an 'Esky' (insulated cold box) to keep your food fresh and your drinks chilled. Ice cream is a widely available treat. One of the best kinds is Norgen Vaaz, a name that echoes the American Haagen Daz, itself an invented Scandinavian name.

Pub Food. Many pubs, especially those with large courtyards or gardens, operate a splendid system whereby you select a piece of meat and cook it over the pub's barbecue yourself. The price (usually around $8–10) in most cases includes unlimited bread and salads to which you help yourself.

Otherwise, pub food can be disappointing. Your average 'counter meal' at a country town hotel might consist of a slice of ham with white bread and an undressed salad. But at least it won't be overpriced. You can usually find a good steak or chop with potato and salad for about $10 at many pubs, in large cities as well as smaller towns (where the pub may be the only place to eat out). The hours during which food is served in pubs are even more restrictive than those of restaurants: unless you order between 12.30 and 1.30pm or 5.30 and 7.30pm, you may be out of luck.

Cheap Deals. The Scandinavian term *Smorgasbord* can refer to any buffet. If you're hungry, a lunchtime eat-what-you-can deal can fill you up for the day. A surprising number of employees' canteens, particularly of public service organisations, are open to the public and can be relied upon for cheap (if not necessarily tasty) food.

RESTAURANTS

The range of style and ethnic cuisine in Australian restaurants is remarkable: from small Greek, Italian and Vietnamese cafés where the proprietor is likely to cook, serve, wash up and take the money, to impeccable French restaurants with elaborate hierarchies of waiting staff.

Prices are lower than you would pay for similar food and surroundings in Britain or North America. For as little as $8 you can gorge yourself at a cheap café while a good evening out in a mid-range restaurant with three courses and coffee will probably cost $18–$25 per person. All the big cities have enjoyed an explosion of restaurants serving imaginative food, sometimes referred to as '*nouvelle* Australian' cuisine. At these places you pay $3–$5 for soup, $5–$8 for an 'entree', $13–$16 for a main course and about $5 for a sweet.

The bill should arrive without any additions for tax and service, although at weekends and public holidays you may have to pay a 10% surcharge to meet the higher cost of staff. In cheaper places, few people leave a tip. At mid-range restaurants the habit is growing to leave 5–10%, but no one will mind if you don't. If the restaurant is busy, it is common practice to leave the correct money (plus a tip if you wish) in the saucer and walk out.

In the state capitals you can choose from dozens of price brackets and cuisines. Sydney, Melbourne and Perth each have a wonderful guide to good eating in the form of an annually revised book *Cheap Eats*. Invest in it if you intend to spend any time in these places. Outside the big cities, however, the choice of places to eat narrows dramatically. Often the only alternatives will be the local pub and possibly a chip shop. But there are always surprises to be found; one of the most innovative restaurants in New South Wales — La Petite Malice — is hidden in a shopping arcade in Thirroul, an anonymous suburb of Wollongong south of Sydney.

At any restaurant more fancy than a cheap café, you may well encounter rules governing dress. Despite the highly casual attire to be found on the streets of Australia, many pubs and restaurants — including those that could hardly be described as the ultimate in sophistication — have strict rules about their clients' clothing. In particular, thongs (flip-flops) are unpopular, which usually means shorts are banned (unless you are prepared to abandon all sartorial pride and wear shorts with shoes and socks).

Foreign Cuisines. Melbourne and Sydney are the premier eating cities. Each has at least as wide a range of cuisines as London or New York. While most visitors are familiar with French, Greek and Italian food, there are plenty of more exotic options. In particular, every Asian country from Turkey to Japan is represented and you may well try your first Kampuchean or Burmese meal in Australia. Until recently, there were few good Indian restaurants, but that is changing, at least in Sydney. Thai food continues to be (justly) popular. It is well worth being adventurous, since you are unlikely to have a bad experience: spicy dishes are usually taken down a step or two in hotness, and alarming dishes such as roast dog from Korea, raw monkey brains from Singapore or pickled jellyfish from Japan have not survived the transition to Australia. One ingredient that was used in abundance in many Chinese restaurants was the chemical tastebud stimulant monosodium glutamate (MSG). It received so much bad publicity, however, that many places now advertise an MSG-free menu.

The Southeast Asian concept of 'food market' has been imported into some of the cities. The idea is that a central eating area of tables and chairs (sometimes out-of-doors, sometimes incorporated into a shopping arcade) is surrounded by kiosks offering all manner of interesting foods. Thus you can buy a Lebanese starter from one vendor, a Japanese main course from another and an Italian ice cream and cappuccino from a third.

Fast Food. The predictable multinational chains such as Kentucky Fried Chicken and McDonalds crop up repeatedly, but some chains display more flair and imagination. For example Fast Eddy's in Perth and Melbourne, open 24 hours a day, is American in style and good in quality. Also the Hungry Jack chain sells excellent hamburgers (not called beefburgers in Australia).

Milk Bars serve the closest that Australia has to a national cuisine, which does a great deal to explain why foreign food is so popular. Their staple is the meat pie (usually costing $1.50), topped with tomato ketchup. Australians munch their way through two million pies each day. A recent study revealed that the average pie contained a surprising amount of textured vegetable protein and blood plasma.

Bring Your Own (BYO) Restaurants. Only a small proportion of Australia's restaurants is licensed to serve alcohol, which is a great advantage to those on a tight budget. Most restaurants are 'BYO', inviting you to bring in beer, wine or stronger liquor. Usually corkage of $2 per bottle or $1 per person will be charged, but some places advertise 'no corkage'. Many licensed restaurants also allow customers to bring their own wines, but most charge a stiffer corkage fee of about $5. Even so, you can usually reckon on saving considerably by bringing your own wine, thereby avoiding paying $8–10 or more for a bottle of house wine. The exceptions are restaurants that advertise 'wine at bottle shop prices'; in fact the prices are likely to be more expensive than the Liquorland store down the road, but still lower than in most licensed restaurants. In wine-growing areas, the restaurant wine list is supplanted by a wine selection room where you choose from the wines made on the property.

DRINKING

amber nectar	beer
billy	a tin pot in which water is boiled for tea
bombo	cheap wine
bottle shop	liquor store/off-licence
Bundy	rum from Bundaberg, Queensland
chunder	vomit, usually after excessive drinking (also *technicolour yawn*, *pavement pizza* and many other expressions)
DD	drunk driving
echo	returnable bottle
Esky	insulated cold box to keep food or (more usually) drink cool; also *chilly-bin*
grog	any drink containing alcohol
grog-on	to keep on drinking
heart-starter	first drink of the day
hotel	the more formal name for pub
jamberoo	a party at which excessive drinking is the norm
LA	low-alcohol beer
lunatic soup	cheap wine
neck oil	alcohol
nobbler	small measure of spirits
package beer	beer sold in bottles or cans, rather than on draught
PCA (palate-cleansing ale)	a late-night beer consumed to round off a binge of wine or stronger liquor
session	a long spell of afternoon drinking at a pub, usually on Sundays and with free entertainment
shout	to buy a round (it is said about stingy types that they 'wouldn't shout if a shark bit them')
slab	carton (of beer, especially in Queensland)
sly grog	after-hours drink; the act of obtaining sly grog is known as 'running the rabbit'
steam	cheap wine
stubby	bottle of beer
throat-charmer	beer
tinny	can of beer
two-pot screamer	one who gets drunk easily
waterbag	teetotaller
yankee shout	paying only for one's own drinks in a pub

Australia has numerous expressions for being drunk, including *drunk as Chloe*, *drunk as a fowl*, *full as a tick*, *full as a goog*, *off your face*, *inked*, *on the slops*, *on the tiger*, *schicked* and *stinko*. There are few idioms for refusing a drink, though you may sometimes hear someone say they'll 'sit on this'. A great deal of time, money and energy is spent on drinking in Australia, not merely as a social activity but — by some — for its own sake, trying to get as legless as possible. A common expression for 'would you like a drink?' is 'could you hold one down?', and much of the male population seem determined to reinforce the stereotype of Australians as a nation of heavy drinking slobs. But the demand for wine is rising at the same rate as consumption of beer is falling.

Pubs. In Australia, all pubs are officially 'hotels'. However, the main function of most of these places is to supply drink. In many hotels, such overnight accommodation as there is exists only to satisfy licensing regulations. If you ask for a room at most city hotels, you probably won't get one (although in country areas you often can). Many hotels also sell drink for consumption off the premises; see *Bottle Shops*, below.

While an Australian town does not have the same range of pubs as a British one would have, there are places to suit most tastes: raucous, barn-like drinking palaces, lazy tropical bars, and country hotels with spacious verandahs ornamented with fretwork. The interior furnishings are determined by the clientele (or vice-versa). The public bar of the roughest dives will certainly not be carpeted (except possibly with sawdust or a plastic sheet to facilitate cleaning) and is often the venue for regular fights. Women, while not actively prohibited from such places, will be made to feel most unwelcome and might receive unwarranted attention from the drunker customers; most women feel more comfortable in the lounge bar. It is relatively easy to avoid this type of pub in cities (where they tend to be in deprived inner-city areas) but in the Outback they may constitute the only social centre for 100km in any direction.

Most city and town pubs, however, are pleasant and friendly. They tend to be larger than pubs or bars in Europe or North America, and are often equipped with noisy juke boxes but friendly staff. Always go to the bar to order and pay, before taking your drinks (almost always beer) to a table. The most popular pubs are those with built-in breweries (see *Real Ale*, below); while not typical of Australian pubs, they are probably the busiest, trendiest and most enjoyable for a good night out. For a country that produces so much excellent wine, Australia has surprisingly few wine bars, though trendy pubs have a small but select wine list for about $10 a bottle, $2.50 a glass.

Returned and Services League (RSL) clubs and other private clubs for certain trades or ethnic groups are popular drinking places, particularly in southeastern Australia. As the number of returned servicemen dwindles, clubs are being opened up to all-comers. In many country towns they constitute the main social centre (with 'pokies' for gambling and satellite TV transmissions of sporting events), while the city clubs are often venues for rock bands. Admittance is officially only for 'members and bona-fide guests in the company of a member', but in practice most admit strangers, especially if from overseas.

Licensing Laws. Hours vary from state to state, pub to pub and even season to season. As a rough guide, weekday opening is 10am–10pm or 11am–11pm; on Sundays between noon and 8 or 10pm. There are numerous exceptions; some pubs serving the market trade open at 6am, and the landlord of any pub is not obliged to open for the maximum hours permitted by law. Needless to say, a great deal of drinking takes place after 10 or 11pm: at pubs with late licences, in nightclubs and discos (some of which remain open until 6am) and at restaurants. To drink legally after hours at a restaurant, you must have an 'intention to dine'; in one or two places this rule is satisfied at closing time by every customer being given a free and unsolicited plate of spaghetti. If you want to find out where to get 'sly grog', ask a taxi driver.

The minimum drinking age is 18. No one younger than this is allowed into bars. Anyone who appears under age is likely to be asked to produce ID with evidence of age before being served.

Prohibition. Partly as a response to increasing alcoholism among native Australians, the government has restricted alcohol in and around some Aboriginal settlements. Notices on the approaches to these areas warn that 'possession or consumption of liquor without a permit can lead to a $1,000 fine or six months, plus the confiscation of your vehicle'.

Bottle Shops. You can save money by buying liquor from bottle shops, which can be found in any town centre or suburban mall. Many are part of hotels, and some are drive-in shops, sometimes with two lanes marked 'browse' and 'express'. The lowest prices are found at branches of chains such as Liquorland and Liquor Mart. The maximum permitted hours are the same as for pubs but most close at 10pm at the latest.

BEER

'Knock off work? Crack a couple of stubbies. Going to a barbie? Bring a carton. Going fishing? Fill up the Esky'. So goes the Australian attitude to beer. Despite the rise of wine, Australia still ranks as one of the heaviest beer drinking nations in the world.

From the widespread advertising of certain Australian beers abroad you'd be forgiven for thinking that the natives drink only Foster's or Castlemaine XXXX. This is not true. South Australians swear by West End, Western Australians by Swan, and Tasmanians by Boag's or Cascade. One of the most popular beers in the southeast is VB (Victoria Bitter) and smaller regional varieties such as Coopers in South Australia and Emu in Western Australia have devoted followings.

Some excellent beers are produced by boutique breweries or in-house pub breweries. The brewery whose products are most widely available is the Matilda Bay Brewing Company in Perth. If you find a pub featuring their range of beers, it's sure to be congenial and yuppified. The other famous Perth name in beers is Redback which is available in cans, bottles and on draught throughout the country. Its nearest European equivalent is a German *weiss* beer, though the habit of serving it with lemon is distinctively Australian.

Most drinkers are content with Australian lagers which are sweet (made with a base of 25% sugar), bland and fairly strong (5% alcohol). About 95% is produced by the beer conglomerates that own Foster's/VB, Castlemaine and Swan. Not only is most beer sold almost ice-cold (usually 2°C) but the glasses are often chilled in a cold cabinet and bottles and cans insulated in a 'stubby holder' made of polystyrene. Fresh glasses are always given, so the British habit of taking glasses back for refills is not understood.

Measures. Apart from the 2.25 litre Darwin stubby, most beer is sold in small measures in Australia. This does not signify any restraint on the part of native

ml	NSW & ACT	NT	Queensland	SA	Tasmania	Victoria	WA
115					small beer		
140			small beer				
170					beer six	small beer	
200	seven	seven		butcher			glass
225	glass	glass	glass	glass	glass	glass	
285	middy	handle	pot	schooner		pot	middy
425	schooner	schooner		kite			schooner
575	pint						pint

drinkers, but reflects the fear of beer warming up to anything approaching room temperature. Even without a drink or two, it is easy to get confused by the variety of measures, especially when one name can mean different sizes in different states. To muddle things further, some of the new 'real ale' pubs have reverted to the Imperial measures of half-pint (285ml/10fl oz), and pints (575ml/ 20fl oz). The table on p. 95 shows the most common quantities and names used in each state.

Prices. In view of how cheap food and wine are in Australia, you may be surprised to find that beer in pubs is no cheaper than in Europe or North America. A 285ml glass starts at around $1.50 in an ordinary pub. Posher places cost much more, and may not sell draught beer at all. Bottled beer is usually sold in 375 or 750ml bottles. It is a little cheaper to buy beer in a jug and a lot cheaper to drink it at home after buying in bulk (unchilled) from a bottle shop. The cost of a dozen 750ml bottles varies from about $20 to $25 ($1.65–$2 a bottle), while a single chilled bottle from a bottle shop will cost around $2.25 and the same quantity of beer drunk in a pub at least $3.30. The standard 375ml can at a bottle shop works out at around $1.35 for single cans, reducing to $24 for a case of 24. As part of the 'Keep Australia Beautiful Campaign', you can get a few cents refund on empty aluminium cans.

Some 'generic' (i.e. unbranded) beers on the market, with names like 'No Name', can be found. They do not taste significantly different from branded varieties and cost about 20% less, since they do not bear the cost of advertising, sponsoring cricket matches, etc.

Light Beer. The trend towards healthy living and away from drunk driving has had a significant impact on the Australian consciousness. For example all Swan products carry a warning to men not to exceed four standard measures a day and women two. Although few Australians spend their evenings drinking mineral water, the change in attitude has led to a huge increase in the consumption of various brands of light or low-alcohol (LA) beer, such as Swan Light and Foster's LA. The strength of these varies from 0.9% to 3.4% alcohol and the taste does not suffer greatly in comparison with regular beer. Low-alcohol beers are also cheaper.

Real Ale. For many years it was virtually impossible to find cask-conditioned beer in Australia, but now aficionados can taste dozens of 'real' ales. Coopers, a South Australian brewery, has always made beer traditionally. It is still the largest purveyor of real beers in the form of its naturally conditioned bottled ale and stout, which can be found throughout Australia. But each of the southern mainland capitals has a number of boutique breweries, usually built into pubs and making a range of beers that are as enjoyable as their names are imaginative, like Brass Monkey Stout and Dogbolter. They are served warmer than other Australian beers, but still much cooler than British bitters. As well as drinking at the pubs, you can take away bottles and casks of the beer. Prices for these premium brews are higher than for other beers, typically $4–$5.50 per pint. The best real ale houses are listed under *Eating and Drinking* in the regional chapters.

Numerous foreign beers are available in Australia, from Guinness (brewed under licence in Melbourne) to Sol and Dos Equis from Mexico. But the diverse range of native brews should keep your thirst pleasantly quenched and save you paying premium prices for imported beers.

WINE

Australian wine no longer needs to be pleaded for. Its quality is admired from France to California and it is bought prolifically in Britain. Although it is not quite the bargain in its country of origin that it was a few years ago — before the world discovered it and decided to import it in bulk — good Australian wines are still very affordable. Cheap Australian wine compares very favourably with the *vins ordinaires* of Europe and America, while a good Australian wine is excellent by any standards. The three largest producers are Penfolds, Lindemans and Orlando (known collectively as 'PLO'), but there are over 500 other wineries making as diverse a range of wines as any country could wish for. Many of these wineries produce only small quantities of wine for local consumption, and are well worth seeking out.

The main grape varieties used in Australia are Cabernet Sauvignon (the main grape in claret), Merlot (the grape of St Emilion), Shiraz (also known as Syrah and the grape used in Cote du Rhone), Riesling (drier than European Rieslings), Chardonnay (the white grape of Burgundy). A bottle of wine is either a varietal, i.e. made from only one grape variety, or a blend. These are often excellent, such as the Semillon/Chardonnay blend which is peculiar to Australia. Winemakers in Australia are not bound by narrow geographical constraints governing viticulture in Europe: a winemaker in the Hunter Valley looking for a match for his Chardonnay grapes will think nothing of ordering a truckload of Semillon grapes from his mate in South Australia. Due to the imaginative attitudes to blending wines, there is no national wine appellation and quality control scheme.

Making sense of labels can be difficult for the uninitiated. At first sight some appear to be a jumble of English, Aboriginal and French or German names. A South Australian bottle described as 'Watervale/Coonawarra Shiraz/Cabernet Sauvignon' contains a blend of Shiraz grapes from Watervale in the Clare Valley, and Cabernet Sauvignon ('Cab Sauv') grapes from Coonawarra near the Victorian border.

Most labels on casks and bottles admit to the addition of preservatives such as sulphur dioxide. Don't be unduly alarmed; such additives are present in most wines worldwide, but Australia is among the few nations that insist that their presence is recorded. One additive — ascorbic acid — is positively beneficial, being better known as vitamin C.

The cheapest wine comes in three-litre boxes, costing $5–10. More upmarket wines are sold in two-litre casks from about $7. Although sophisticated Australians turn their noses up at them, these 'cask' wines account for two-thirds of sales and anyone used to French or Italian plonk will find them perfectly acceptable. They are also subjected to discriminating assessment by experts and some are pronounced decidedly good, such as Renmano Chardonnay or McWilliam's Shiraz Cabernet.

The cost of a 750ml bottle of wine starts at $4 but you would need to spend twice that to get anything better than just adequate. For less than $10 you can drink some superb wines. A few examples: Wynns Coonawarra Cabernet Sauvignon and the same maker's Estate Hermitage; Tyrell's Old Winery Cabernet Merlot 1989 and its Long Flat Chardonnay Semillon; Normans Fine Hermitage 1990; Seaview Cabernet Sauvignon 1989; Penfolds Koonunga Hill 1989; Wolf Blass Yellow Label Rhine Riesling; Seppelt Gold Label Chardonnay; and Houghton White Burgundy.

Perfectly drinkable Australian 'Champagne' costs as little as $5 a bottle, but for this price the drink has very little in common with its illustrious French namesake. However for $10 you can get an excellent *Methode Champenoise* wine, fermented in the bottle like proper Champagne. European (particularly French) wines are available but very expensive.

Free Wine. Every Australian state grows grapes; even the Northern Territory has Chateau Hornsby near Alice Springs. The associated wineries almost always welcome visitors. In the most important wine-making areas — around Adelaide, on the Margaret River in Western Australia, and in the Hunter Valley of New South Wales — wine-tasting is a major industry and it is possible to drive, cycle or even travel by balloon around neighbouring wineries. The most popular areas are described in the regional chapters.

Every winery encourages 'cellar door' sales of their product. Prices, however, are not always as low as you might expect: you might even find the same bottle sold a little more cheaply at a liquor store in another state.

Coolers. These are blends of cheap white wine with sugar and fruit juice or fruit flavour, and have misleading names like Bliss. Their alcoholic strength is around 5% (about the same as beer) although the taste is similar to drinking a non-alcoholic punch. Indeed, the packaging may also be almost indistinguishable from fruit drink containers. Beware of the effects of coolers (particularly if you plan to drive) and be warned that some people suffer an almighty hangover which they attribute to excessive amounts of sugar and flavouring, and the poor quality of the wine used to make them. To quench thirst, an ice cold light beer is far more effective.

Other Drinks. Consumption of whisky and other hard liquor is fairly low (only one litre per person per year on average), but this is not because of prohibitively high prices. For a litre of imported whisky you could expect to pay no more than you would in Scotland or Ireland and sometimes less, while home-produced spirits such as brandy and Bundaberg rum are pretty cheap. A 30ml nip in a pub costs about $2. The usual range of liqueurs is available, but the most popular after dinner drink is port. Australia produces some excellent varieties, and even at the cheapest end of the market you are unlikely to be disappointed by a $7 bottle of the stuff.

As a sign of the continuing Americanisation of Australia, it was reported at the end of 1991 that Coke was set to surpass milk, tea and beer as Australia's favourite drink.

Entertainment

For a long period in Australia's recent history the arts were afflicted by Cultural Cringe. This was supposedly a massive inferiority complex that led Australians to believe that Australia was in fact the cultural desert depicted by Monty Python, Dame Edna Everage and Sir Les Patterson. Talented Australians fled to Europe leaving a cultural vacuum that made everybody back home cringe the more. There is a strong streak of anti-intellectualism in Australian society that has made it difficult for writers and thinkers to find an appreciative audience: perhaps it is no accident, as the noted Melbourne journalist Phillip Adams has observed, that the Australian coat-of-arms comprises two of the smallest-brained beings around, the kangaroo and the emu.

Cultural self-assurance started to develop in the early 70s partly as a result of the investment in the arts made by the Labor Government under Prime Minister Gough Whitlam. Not only were more plays written and films made, but they began receiving international recognition. And, as appreciation of Australian artists, musicians, film-makers and writers has grown both at home and abroad, the arts have continued to flourish.

As well as the so-called high culture that Australia has to offer, there are many other popular indigenous entertainments to satisfy the deeply felt Australian need for a good time. These include the spectacle of Surf Carnivals (see *Sport* below) and a whole range of bizarre contests such as dwarf-tossing, melon-seed spitting, throwing-a-Barbara-Cartland-novel (for female competitors only) and various races for everything from cows to cane toads.

Tickets. You can buy a ticket for most big entertainment and sporting events anywhere in the country from BASS, Ticketek or the other main agencies listed in the regional chapters. Tickets to the big name performances like a Broadway musical or the Grand Prix range from $25 to $40. BASS normally adds a processing fee of $5. You are unlikely to be able to take advantage of student and other discounts if booking through a ticket agency. If an event is sold out, you'll have to try your luck with the touts (called 'scalpers' in the US).

MUSIC

Rock Music. You may be relieved to learn that the pinnacle of Australian popular music is *not* represented by Kylie Minogue, her sister Dannii or Jason Donovan. On the other hand, few serious Australian musicians ('musos') have become household names. Still groups like AC/DC, Mental As Anything and INXS, and singers like John Farnham have had a global impact.

The acclaim given to Archie Roach, a talented songwriter whose single *Took the Children Away* recently won a human rights award, confirms that there is a strong strain of political awareness in Australian music-lovers.

Aboriginal Music. To the Western ear, the traditional music of Australia's original inhabitants can sound inharmonious, but the more you hear the more you are likely to appreciate the constantly changing rhythms. Ancient instruments such as the didjeridu (a tube of wood producing a strange, haunting sound) are used to accompany ceremonial dances. The biggest problem is hearing an authentic performance; while many places in northern Australia stage 'corroborees' (like Papua New Guinean 'sing sings') these are normally diluted and sanitised for easy consumption (and admission is charged). Unless you become friendly with an Aboriginal group or attend a special cultural festival, your chances of catching an authentic performance are low.

Few contemporary Aboriginal bands have had commercial success. Yothu Yindi from Arnhemland in the Northern Territory are the first Aboriginal band to have a mainstream hit (*Treaty*) which, along with the name of their most recent album *Tribal Voice*, indicates their main themes.

Other kinds of music in which there is some Aboriginal input is 'Koori' music, an unusual cross between traditional Aboriginal and Country music. You may also hear of 'gumleaf bands' which are usually (but not exclusively) composed of Aboriginals who create music by blowing on gum leaves.

Folk Music. The music that derives from the early European settlers consists largely of songs of the Outback, of which *Waltzing Matilda* is by far the best known. As in Britain and North America there is a loyal following, and you can find folk clubs in every city. As part of a 'new roots revival', folk/rock is making advances with bands like Weddings, Parties, Anything. More traditional bands are also successful like Redgum and 'bush bands' such as Bloodwood while bands like the Bushwackers are famous throughout Australia. A popular percussion instrument among such bands is the 'lagerphone' (also known as a zob stick), a wooden cross covered in metal bottle tops and alternately hit with a stick or thumped on the ground.

Australia's closest equivalent to Nashville is Tamworth, New South Wales. Every January, the town is invaded by around 30,000 Country music enthusiasts who drink, sing and listen to songs about the hazards of life and love.

CINEMA

Australian cinema has a noble history. Long before the renaissance of the 1970s and 80s, Australians were making copious and impressive newsreels, an era of film-making captured in the film *Newsfront*. The Australian Film Commission has been supporting film-makers since 1972, much to the envy of struggling cinema industries in other countries. Classic films like *Picnic at Hanging Rock, Breaker Morant, Gallipoli* and *My Brilliant Career* are good not just as movies, but as comments on aspects of the Australian character and situation, so are especially worth trying to see if you have a chance. The current generation of film-makers is moving beyond the pretty costume dramas that have been so successful abroad. Watch for films of the award-winning Aboriginal director Tracey Moffatt.

A trip to the cinema normally costs about $10, though tickets are usually half-price for matinees and on Tuesday evenings. Most cinema seats are bookable in advance and in some places students get a discount. Smoking is generally banned.

The censorship classifications are as follow: G (general release), PG (parental guidance for children under 15; not recommended for children under 12); M (approved for mature audiences over 15) and R (restricted to those who are not between 2 and 18).

The great American tradition of the drive-in movie ('drives') has flourished in the benevolent Australian climate. Saturday evenings spent watching the big screen from a motor car are favourite social occasions.

MUSEUMS AND GALLERIES

Australians are especially keen on the visual arts. Seven million people visit a public art gallery every year. (Exhibitions are sometimes referred to as 'ekkas'). Although Australia's famous painters such as Arthur Streeton, Tom Roberts and Sidney Nolan are perhaps not as widely known abroad as are Australian writers, they are well worth investigating. One of the most interesting contemporary schools of art is the Brushmen of the Bush based at the remote mining town of Broken Hill. Here painters like Jack Absolom, Pro Hart and John Pickup display their naif paintings of shearing scenes and other outback subjects, and give art classes (in case you want to learn how to capture the essence of a gum tree).

Canberra houses the national collection of paintings, but all the state capitals have interesting galleries and worthwhile museums. Australia has more than its fair share of eccentric private collections of objects as various as old umbrellas and salt and pepper shakers. Each state has its own National Trust that cooperates with the federal Heritage Commission to preserve buildings of historical interest.

SPORT

Most Australians are sports mad. The climate is ideal for almost every outdoor sport, facilities for watching and participating are excellent and the leading sports are given massive coverage by the media. This is unfortunate for people who have no great interest in sport, but visitors have to accept its high profile and resign themselves to sport as a constant topic of conversation.

Australian nationalism manifests itself more visibly in sport than in any other activity. After their Rugby Union World Cup triumph in 1991 there was a positive orgy of self-congratulation. If their chauvinism becomes unbearable, try mentioning the time an Australian cricketer bowled underarm at New Zealand in order to prevent the opposing team from hitting a six and winning the game.

The main team games are cricket in summer (October–March) and 'footy' in winter (March–October). Tread warily when talking football as there are several codes and so 'footy' means different things in different places. The one thing you can be sure it doesn't mean is soccer or American football (though the latter sport has made inroads into Australian sporting life in the past few years). In Melbourne, Adelaide, Perth and Tasmania footy refers to Australian Rules football; in these states the rugby codes are regarded as slow, unskilled and boring. Queensland and New South Wales favour Rugby League. Violence among spectators is rare. While football clubs in the UK are installing seating at their grounds, there is a trend in Australia to take out the colourful plastic seats and revert to gravel-and-dirt terraces to encourage old-style barracking.

Australian Rules Football. To form an accurate picture of Australian society you should try to see at least one game of this extraordinarily aggressive sport, which some have described as a poor excuse for a punch-up. The game originated among Irish gold miners in Victoria as a loose interpretation of Gaelic football, where any part of the body can be used to propel the ball. Today Rules footy is a kind of organised mayhem, remarkable for its lack of obvious rules. Each side has 18 players (plus two substitutes), and violent bodily contact is widespread as each team strives to get the oval ball past the opposition's back line for a 'behind' (which scores one point) or to kick a goal between the uprights (six points). The game requires a much larger playing area than most other ball games, and is usually played at cricket grounds ('ovals').

There are four quarters of 25 minutes each, but the overall length of the game can be extended to three hours or more with the addition of intervals between quarters and 'time on' added for stoppages due to treatment of injured players, disputes with the 'field umpire' (referee), etc. The score is given for each quarter with goals and behinds listed separately followed by the final score, in the style:

| Fitzroy | 4.2 | 4.4 | 6.8 | 8.10 | (58) |
| Carlton | 2.1 | 4.3 | 7.5 | 8.9 | (57) |

Match reports include lurid details of injuries suffered, and players reported by the field umpires for foul play which usually verges on grievous bodily harm.

For a good history of the game, read *Up Where, Cazaly? The Story of Australian Rules Football* by Leonie Sandercock and Ian Turner (Granada Books). You can see Australian Rules on television most weekend afternoons in winter, and usually hear commentator Lou 'The Lip' Richards giving his outspoken interpretation of events on the field.

Rugby. Compared to Australian Rules, Rugby football seems almost genteel. Most Sydneysiders are passionate about League footy. The media star John Singleton (now employed by Bob Hawke to run his advertising campaign) is noted for having said, 'Anyone who doesn't watch Rugby League is not a real person; he's a cow's hoof, an ethnic, senile or comes from Melbourne'. The State of Origin series is the premier competition played between New South Wales and Queensland. Rugby Union, played by amateurs (15 a side) is less popular than Rugby League (13 a side, professional). Nevertheless Australia were until 1995 the world champions in the sport, which is undergoing a resurgence.

Soccer. In Britain Australian soccer results are used for summer pools coupons. So it may come as a shock to see how minor a sport it is in Australia. As in

North America it is mainly a game for immigrants as evidenced by the names of the teams like Sydney Croatians and Wollongong Macedonia. Soccer is often referred to as 'wogball'. The leading teams are Sydney Olympic (predominantly Greek) and the Italian-led teams of Melbourne. Although it is widely played, especially at the junior level, the standards are fairly primitive, comparable with Third Division teams in England. The best players are attracted to European teams, further diminishing the domestic game. The national team is the Socceroos, who repeatedly fail to qualify for the finals of the World Cup.

Cricket. Everyone should try to sample the atmosphere of an Australian cricket match, particularly an international game. The (usually) good-natured banter of the crowd adds enjoyment to a sport that, once comprehended, is strangely addictive. Beginners should try a one-day match, as these are usually fast-moving and exciting. Each state fields a team for the national championship, the Sheffield Shield, in which matches lasting three or four days are played at fortnightly intervals. Once you acquire a taste for the game, you may wish to see a full five-day Test Match between Australia and a visiting side from overseas. These take place at intervals from the beginning of November until the end of January.

Horseracing. The Turf creates a fervour that rivals that of 'footy' or cricket. Most of the state capitals have several race courses ('tracks'). While few Australian horses are in the same class as the top thoroughbreds from the USA or Britain, the best Australian jockeys (such as the former champion Scobie Breasley) are outstanding. Major events can attract crowds of tens of thousands. One big attraction is the chance to gamble. If you are prepared to lose a few dollars it can be great fun to embroil yourself in the excitement of a race meeting. The biggest annual event is the Melbourne Cup, held each November at the Flemington track; the whole of Australia grinds to a halt to watch the race. All races are listed in the press, together with a guide to form that is impenetrably complicated for the uninitiated. See *Gambling*, below, for off-track opportunities for betting on the nags.

In small country towns you might find a picnic race meeting, usually the biggest annual get-together and well worth attending. Farmers from hundreds of miles around join the local population on a monumental betting spree fuelled by huge quantities of liquor. A certain amount of audience participation is encouraged, and not merely in the form of gambling. Prizes may be awarded to the best-dressed couple, to the winner of an egg-tossing competition and so on. The event often ends with a bush dance. The most notable such race meeting is held each year at Birdsville in remotest Queensland.

Trotting. Most race courses have days or evenings set aside for 'the trots', where jockeys (known as reinsmen) drive around the track in a cart attached to a horse. Recently the sport has been trying to improve its image by changing the name to 'harness-racing', the name used in North America. The day's races are shown under this title in newspapers, but the sport is still widely known as trotting.

Motor Sport. You may gather from their sometimes over-exuberant style of driving that Australians enjoy motor racing. Indeed, two of the best Formula One drivers ever — Jack Brabham and Alan Jones — are Australian. The main attraction is the Australian Grand Prix (now held in Melbourne in March), which attracts a massive following. It is the last and often decisive race in the Formula One calendar and therefore usually exciting. There are many smaller races held each year, including rally driving, speedway and moto-cross. The

Bathurst 1000 is the leading domestic event, an endurance race for production cars held each year at the town of Bathurst, 150km inland from Sydney.

Participation. When the federal government became concerned at the number of Australians watching (usually with a beer to hand) rather than joining in with sport, it instigated a campaign to persuade all unfit armchair sportsmen to become active. Whatever your chosen sport, you will be able to practise it in Australia (with the possible exception of dog-sledding). Tennis, golf and competitive cycling are popular and well provided for, and the climate usually cooperates. Jogging has many devotees, and many city parks and riversides have suitable tracks. There are plenty of events for amateurs to join, whether a 5km fun-run or a full Marathon. If you want to take part in the world's longest point-to-point athletic race, join the 1060km Ultrathon run from Melbourne to Sydney held each spring over at least 50 days. Winners of this event tend to be farmers who have trained by running around their properties in Wellington boots.

"WINNERS TEND TO BE FARMERS WHO HAVE TRAINED IN WELLIES."

A popular event amongst obese males in the Outback is 'whammying', in which two pot-bellied contestants attempt to knock each other down using only their stomachs. Other less demanding activities include bowls (which enjoys surprisingly strong support) and kite-flying, especially popular in blustery Tasmania.

As most of the population lives close to the sea, watersports attract the greatest participation. Swimmers and surfers argue constantly about the best beaches, anglers about the finest reaches and sub-aqua divers about the most beautiful coral. Windsurfing (also known as boardsailing) is popular; beginners will make much faster progress on inland water than on the ocean.

Surf Carnivals. There are 55,000 volunteer lifesavers who patrol the beaches of Australia every weekend. Surf lifesaving is a combination of a sport and a service. Each summer Lifesaving Clubs organise surf carnivals which make a very colourful spectator sport. When the surf is up, it is unlikely that you can find as exciting a sporting competition anywhere. The carnivals begin with a precision march of hundreds of be-capped lifesavers who proceed to demonstrate their team skills in surfboat races and their individual skills in endurance swimming and surfski riding in their bid to win the highest accolade of 'iron man'.

GAMBLING

Australians are inveterate gamblers and will bet on virtually anything, so it will come as no surprise to find that there are limitless ways to make a fortune or lose your shirt. The non-specialist masses are entertained by poker machines or 'pokies' (slot machines/one-armed bandits), housie (bingo), state lotteries and football pools, while on- and off-course betting and casinos cater for those who prefer to put a little study into the art of losing money.

Try to observe Australians as they gamble away a fortune (about three times the annual defence budget). The easiest way is probably to go to a social club where dozens of 'pokies' are in constant use (legal in all states except Western Australia). Many advertise that they can be played for small change (i.e. 20c) or boast of massive jackpots (up to $25,000). The most common clubs are the Returned and Services League (RSL) clubs where there is an occasional brief intermission from the pokies, snooker and fish and chips for a minute's silence and a rendition of God Save the Queen.

You might also visit a betting shop or casino, or stumble upon the national game of chance known as 'two-up'. If you intend to indulge in a little risk-taking yourself, do so where the odds are least stacked against you: casino games like roulette and blackjack are a better bet than lotteries or poker machines. Set aside a certain amount that you can afford to lose, and try to have some fun losing it.

Casinos. To satisfy some of this phenomenal appetite for gambling, most states have a casino or two. Although Las Vegas has nothing to fear, Australian casinos are big and ritzy, and enforce strict dress rules: no T-shirts, running shoes, thongs or shorts. Even government ministers have been turned away for failing to comply. If you can get in, casinos are great places to see the sleazy side of

society, where gamblers become frighteningly involved with the business of winning or losing money. As anywhere the odds are against the punter: the casino has the edge by 2.7% in roulette (with one zero), 5.8% in blackjack (played mathematically correctly) and up to 25% for Keno. If you decide to take part, you can maximise the length of time it takes to lose your money by betting small amounts on red/black or odd/even chances at roulette.

At most casinos visitors are encouraged to play 'keno'. This game is related to bingo in that numbers are drawn, but the difference is that you mark your own card. The keno ticket carries 80 numbers. You cross between one and 15 numbers, and if your numbers are among the 20 that are drawn, you win. If you mark more than three, then you win even if some of your numbers fail to come up. The usual minimum stake is $1, and payouts generally correspond to three-quarters of the mathematical

"EVEN MINISTERS ARE NOT EXEMPT FROM THE CASINO'S DRESS REQUIREMENTS."

odds; in the simplest case, if you mark only one number, the chances of it coming up are four to one, and if it does you win.

Two-up. This game, sometimes known as 'swy', is the purest form of gambling in Australia, and is an integral part of Anzac Day festivities on April 25. Yet it is illegal outside casinos. Bets are placed on two coins that are tossed together. If one is heads and the other tails, there is no result. If both show the same, you win or lose depending on whether you bet on two heads or two tails. Further sophistications include betting on a run of heads or tails. If one coin fails to spin when tossed, it is known as a 'butterfly' or 'floater' and the spin is usually declared void by the 'boxer', a person who arbitrates tosses and bets. Casinos take their cut of around 3% by keeping the stakes on a sequence of five identical events (unless you also bet on this possibility).

Lotto. This game is basically large scale bingo where the participants select six or more numbers from one to 40. Six numbers are drawn once or twice each week, and anyone selecting three or more correct numbers wins a prize. The average payout is around 60% of the total money staked. The minimum stake is $1, and the maximum win decided by the number of participants but is likely to be in the thousands. Results are published in the press (even by the conservative *Australian*) and may be heard on special 'hotline' telephone numbers.

Soccer Pools. British visitors will be familiar with the idea of picking games to end in draws, and will also know the names of Australian teams whose fixtures are used when British clubs are not playing. In fact the coupons used by Australian Soccerpools (the national organisation) do not even mention teams, but just use numbers that can be correlated with the matches by looking in the daily press. The minimum stake is about $1 and if you use any of the many complex permutation systems the cost of your entry goes up at about the same rate as your chances of winning.

Horses and Dogs. You can bet on horse races, harness-races and greyhounds either at the track, or at betting shops run by State Totalisator Agency Boards (TABs). State governments take a cut of around 15% on bets placed, i.e. about 85% of stakes are returned in winnings. The times that TAB outlets operate are given in daily newspapers. In general, the hours are around 10am to 8pm on Saturdays, with later opening and earlier closing on other days.

To place a simple bet on a horse, write the beast's number and that of the race on one of the slips provided and hand it in with your payment. If the horse wins, you can usually collect your payout soon after the race so long as no enquiry is announced. (To create an impression of familiarity with the sport if it loses, mutter about the animal having 'run like a hairy goat'. If you hear someone says it's 'in the bag' this means a particular horse won't be running.)

Bets are totalled and payouts made according to the proportion staked on the winner, thus not necessarily providing the same keen starting prices to be found at racecourse bookmakers. There is an illegal betting fraternity that quotes starting prices off-course and also operates on events not covered by the TABs, dealing only in large amounts. Although you may get better odds from these characters, you have no recourse to the law if you are cheated.

daks	trousers
dancing shorts	men's baggy shorts ('plenty of ballroom')
deli	corner store
durex	brand of sticky tape
lay by	putting a deposit of about 20% on an article to be paid for and collected at a later date
op shop	charity shop (like Salvation Army or *Salvos*)
lollies	roll-up cigarettes
shonky or *bodgy*	dubious, fake
strides	trousers
stubbies	shorts (also beer measure)
thongs	rubber flip-flops

Australian society is not yet as consumer-oriented as American society. But one indication that consumerism is on the increase is that shopping hours are gradually being extended. Traditionally the vast majority of shops closed at 5pm on weekdays and noon on Saturdays with one late-night shopping night on Thursday or Friday. In the cities, however, many shops remain open all day Saturday and moves are afoot to introduce Sunday trading in several states. In small-town Australia though, do not expect anything to be open in the evenings or weekends after Saturday lunchtime. In well populated areas, you can always find a corner shop ('deli') open later. Convenience store chains like 7–11 and Food Plus, often open 24 hours and with a petrol station attached, are increasing in number at the expense of neighbourhood businesses and 'strip shops', i.e. the suburban rows of shops that traditionally supplied essentials to the local community.

Outside the city centres, shops are surprisingly shabby and old-fashioned looking, though the service is usually excellent without being obtrusive. (The garish signs on the other hand are anything but unobtrusive.) The main department stores are the smart Sydney-based David Jones, Coles and Melbourne-based Myers while the discount chain K-Mart (comparable to Woolworths) is also widespread. Many Australian shops carry notices to the effect that by entering you consent to having your bags searched upon leaving. In addition, in many supermarkets you are obliged to take a trolley even if you only want to buy a carton of milk.

Students with ISIC cards can get a free copy of the Australian Studentsaver Guide which lists over 2,000 outlets that give ISIC holders a discount. Enquire at Student Services Australia (PO Box 399, Carlton South, Melbourne, Victoria 3053) or pick up a copy at any office of STA Travel. YHA members are often eligible for discounts in outdoor gear shops.

Duty Free. As mentioned under *Red Tape*, each capital city has a tempting range of duty-free shops downtown. Upon presentation of a valid international air ticket, you can buy these things and take them away, though the fact that you have them will be indelibly marked on your ticket and the bag itself will be sealed with a large red sticker saying 'Important — duty-free goods in possession'.

Australia has no sales tax. However the introduction of one is under serious discussion.

Tobacco. Cigarettes are sold in a bewildering range of quantities: 10, 15, 20, 25, 30 or 35 cigarettes to a pack. The price for 25 or 30 usually starts at $3 except in Queensland where taxes are lower and prices about 50c less. You can save money on bulk purchases of 200. Hand-rolling and pipe tobacco costs about $7 for 50 grams (2oz).

Photography. The cost of developing and printing your holiday snaps is high. The price for 24 colour prints is about $13 and $17 for 36, although the cost of film (about $6 for a roll) is about the same as in Britain and North America. Another good reason for waiting until you get home to get your pictures developed is the extra weight and bulk of prints or slides. Beware of the adverse effects that dust and extreme heat can have. Keep your films in their plastic or foil containers and, if necessary, inside a plastic bag for protection.

Books. The Australian appetite for the printed word is voracious and their publishing industry is thriving. Bibliophiles will be delighted by the prevalence of seven-day-a-week (and sometimes night) bookshops in the cities. One of the best gifts or souvenirs you can buy is a well produced book on Australia of which there are a great many, from collections of realistic photographs of modern Aboriginal life to cartoon books. Try to confine yourself to books published in Australia since there is a 25%–50% mark-up on imported books. Many Australian bookshops routinely sell their stock at 10% less than the recommended price.

GIFTS AND SOUVENIRS

Australian items like Akubra hats (the bush hat worn by Crocodile Dundee) and Vegemite have almost become cultural artefacts and might make suitable presents for your loved ones. There is an astonishing number of shops specialising in Australiana. It is easy to find kitsch, such as a wind-up koala that plays Waltzing Matilda, a set of pink koala salt and pepper shakers, a koala tea cosy (so life-like that guests will think there is a marsupial sitting on your table) or a triple life-size sew-it-yourself kookaburra. If you have a taste for the bizarre, look out for goanna oil, said to be good for arthritic pains, though you probably won't want to invest in a tin of dehydrated convict sweat. There are a few tasteful gifts too such as opals and sheepskin products. You might not want to buy native hardwood souvenirs and thereby contribute to the destruction of forests. Because of Australia's proximity to the Far East imported goods, some of good quality like leather handbags and jewellery, are much cheaper than in Europe.

Clothing. T-shirts can be high fashion in Australia (as a result of the climate). Shops stock an amazing range, from hand-printed designer numbers to ones with mildly obscene cartoons demonstrating the Australian sense of humour. One of the most famous names in Australian clothing is R M Williams, a firm that started in Adelaide as a mail-order supplier of riding apparel for agricultural workers mainly elasticated leather boots (like English jodphur boots) and 'strides' made from moleskin, a superior quality cotton twill. R M Williams has now achieved boutique status and has spread across Australia and the world.

Aboriginal Artefacts. It is easy to tell from the price, and usually from the appearance, which are the fakes made in Taiwan and which are the real thing.

Boomerangs are the most obvious choice and will appeal to the kite-flying and frisbee-playing set. Most come with a leaflet explaining how they should be thrown. Although most boomerangs used by Aboriginals are weapons that are not designed to return, those sold by gift shops usually come back when thrown expertly. Didjeridus, an Aboriginal wind instrument, might appeal to those who play the bagpipes; other people find their lungs are not equal to the task of producing a sound. Woomeras (spears), bark paintings, basketware and carvings are also tempting, though prices for all authentic Aboriginal artefacts are high. Aboriginal Arts Australia was established by the government to market Aboriginal and Torres Strait Islander arts and crafts. They have galleries in Sydney, Perth, Darwin and Alice Springs (addresses in regional chapters).

billabong	waterhole left by retreating river
bogey hole	any swimmable water hole
bombora	submerged rocks or reef that creates disturbed water dangerous to swimmers
bore	a well in the Outback, sometimes containing brackish water
brumby	wild horse
bush (to go)	to go into the country
bushwalking	hiking (like New Zealand tramping)
cossie (also *bathers, togs*)	swimming costume
dumper	large wave that breaks unexpectedly and scrapes swimmers and surfers along the bottom
free beach	nude beach
iceberg	dedicated surfer who surfs in all weathers
langlauf	cross country skiing
rip	strong undersea current
roly-poly	wind-blown ball of brush
spinifex	outback grass with sharp spikes that have an irritant chemical
sun-baking	sun-bathing
wedgie	wedge-tailed eagle (Australia's largest bird of prey)

Attractive as Australian cities are, few people cross oceans to see only the townscapes of Australia. The endless beaches, primeval deserts, hills and reefs with their unique and abundant wildlife are a tremendous attraction to most tourists, as are the activities that can be enjoyed such as diving, ballooning, hiking and rafting. There has been a great surge of interest on the part of both Australian and foreign city-dwellers to visit the Outback, and an accompanying increase in the number of tour operators specialising in eco-tourism.

THE OUTBACK

Merely seeing the Outback from a bus or train window can be a disappointment; it is far better to experience it, canoe on its rivers, walk amidst its ancient geological formations, meet the people who live there, etc. For all the glamour that attaches itself to windswept sand dunes and the frisson of excitement associated with crocodile-infested waters, it must never be forgotten that outback landscapes can be unimaginably dull. Although there are points of interest such as Aboriginal rock drawings and opal mines, there can be a lot of nothingness between them. Dreaming of endless horizons where, some say, you can actually see the curvature of the earth, is quite different from the reality of a marathon train or coach journey across the Nullarbor where the only variation in scenery is determined by the intensity of the heat haze. In the Kimberleys of northern Western Australia, cattle properties are limited by law to one million acres, larger than Suffolk or Shropshire. Your chances of seeing the desert at its most blooming and least scorched are best between September and November.

Outback Australia is among the most hostile environments in the world, a place of suffering and tragedy. It has been thus from the time of the hunter-gatherer Aboriginal tribes who had to devote every waking moment to the business of wresting a living from the desert, to the present day when every year people become lost and die of dehydration or from contact with the wildlife.

The early explorers and settlers were often defeated by the land, as a quick perusal of a map of Sturt's Stony Desert will convey: 'Cadelga Station (uninhabited)', 'Miranda (ruins)', 'Coongie (abandoned)' and so on. Other places marked on the road atlas in the same area include the Ephemeral Lakes, Lake Yamma Yamma ('full only twice this century') and nearby a vast area of outback Queensland labelled 'subject to inundation'. When there isn't a drought there's a flood, and the rainy season, which usually lasts from January to March in northern Australia, can cut homesteads off for weeks.

All of which can sound more than a little daunting to visitors. Any independent trip into the remote Outback cannot be undertaken lightly: four-wheel-drive vehicles fitted with spare parts, water tanks and extra fuel are essential for any trips off the principal long distance routes. Secondary tracks often peter out and it is easy to become lost in the featureless scrub and spinifex (spiky grass). The earth can get so hot that it burns through rubber-soled shoes.

A large water bottle and sun hat are essential pieces of equipment. Water is a precious commodity in places where the time between rainfalls is measured in years rather than days. It should never be squandered. On drought-stricken properties, bath water is recycled for laundry and showers are rationed. One of the worst crimes that city slickers commit is to pollute bores of drinking water with soap powder. The red dust of northern Australia seems to get everywhere necessitating daily dousing of vehicles (including the interiors) and of clothes. Visitors to the Outback must be prepared for a certain amount of discomfort from the heat and dust if nothing else.

To reach remote attractions, it is worth considering an outback adventure tour. It is best to choose one operated by an established organisation, such as those offered by the Youth Hostels Association. These range from two-day trips into the Kakadu National Park for $140 to 29-day camping safaris around the Red Centre of Australia for $1,750 (details of the latter from 61 Leonard Avenue, Melbourne; 03-9306 5805). Expect to pay at least $70 a day for the most basic outback tours.

More upmarket outback adventures are also widely available. The longest-established of the operators is Australian Pacific Tours (475 Hampton St, Hampton, Vic 3188; 03-9277 8510), which is represented in the UK at 14 Worple Road, Wimbledon, London SW19 4DD (0181-879 7444). Their coach and camping trips cost roughly $100 a day. An alternative is AAT King's Tours, which has a large range of coach holidays and touring options, including camping safaris and 4WD adventure tours. In Australia contact 29–33 Palmerston Crescent, South Melbourne, Vic 3205 (03-9274 7422), or in the UK Bishops Palace House, Bishops Hall, Kingston-upon-Thames KT1 1QN (0181-974 9922). Another operator with tours along the same lines is the Austour & Travel Company (12 Liddesdale Avenue, Frankston, Vic 3199; 03-9770 2145).

THE WILDLIFE

No matter how slim your grasp of Australian geography may be, everyone knows something of its wildlife. Because the continent of Australia became an island eons ago, animals developed in forms quite different from anywhere else in the world. Marsupials (whose partially developed young are carried in pouches) are peculiar to Australia, with one minor exception in South America. Koalas, kangaroos, possums, wallabies and wombats are all marsupials, and can be seen at wildlife parks throughout the country.

Provided you get far enough from the cities, you are likely to see kangaroos, especially at dusk or dawn, grazing in paddocks or woods or trying to cross the road. Sadly you will also see a number lying dead by the roadside. Despite the threat from motor vehicles, they are so numerous that they are constantly being culled (about 1.3 million a year in Queensland alone) by farmers who view them as competing with sheep and cattle for a share of the sparse grazing. There have been one or two cases of kangaroos attacking humans without provocation but the vast majority are too shy to approach even when food is offered.

Koalas. You are unlikely to see koalas in the wild, since their numbers have been severely depleted. Initially man was responsible — two million koala skins were exported in a single year in the first half of this century, the fine for killing one now is $3000. More recently a sexually transmitted disease called chlamydia is seriously disrupting their reproduction patterns. It has been suggested that the species is headed for extinction. The word koala is thought to come from an Aboriginal word meaning 'does not drink water', which accurately describes them. The average koala is quite happy to spend his or her life in the branches of a single eucalyptus tree, munching on gum leaves (which are mildly intoxicating) and sleeping. One of the best places to see them is Magnetic Island in Queensland where 2000 koalas live in the wild. To be sure of seeing one, head for a zoo or wildlife reserve where you may be encouraged to cuddle one. When the Minister of Tourism referred to koalas a few years ago as smelly little creatures (after one had reportedly relieved itself on him) there was a huge public outcry and the number of people eager to cuddle-a-koala did not seem to be affected. Remember that it causes distress in some quarters to hear the animals inaccurately referred to as bears.

Kookaburras. The kookaburra's distinctive laugh (and its mirth, unlike the koala's disease, can be contagious for humans) is heard in urban areas as well as in the bush where it fulfils the same function as the rooster and so is sometimes called the 'bushman's clock'. There are many other memorable birds such as galahs, parrots and the pink and grey rosellas which enliven dry, brown landscapes wonderfully. You may be struck by the preponderance of screeching or calling birds instead of songbirds. The Royal Australian Ornithologists Union (03-9370 1272) operates bird identification courses.

Dingoes. Not all Australian wildlife is so charming. Dingoes are wild dogs whose howling at nightfall and cheekiness at campsites can be alarming to the uninitiated. They also pose a real threat to stock animals. A Dingo Fence has been erected to contain the threat, stretching nearly 8000km (5000 miles). It roughly follows the borders of Queensland and New South Wales and continues through South Australia and Western Australia. It must be constantly maintained to protect the sheep on the eastern side from the dingoes on the other.

"*THE LONGEST FENCE IN THE WORLD SEPARATES THE SHEEP FROM THE DINGOES*"

Crocodiles are a serious menace. Although they occasionally turn up in town drains or culverts, you can be fairly confident of avoiding an encounter by refraining from swimming in crocodile habitats, which are usually signposted. Of the 24 deaths from crocodile attacks in the past 100 years, a third have been in the past two years. The increase illustrates that more tourists are entering crocodile territory rather than that the crocodiles are becoming more fierce. Legislation to prosecute people who venture too close to crocodiles is on the agenda in a bid to reduce the death toll. For more information about crocodiles and other dangerous wildlife, see *Health*.

NATIONAL PARKS
Over the past century, nearly 500 areas of land have been designated by the Government as worthy of protection. National Parks cover every possible habitat from bleak desert to mangrove swamp. For a complete list contact the Australian National Parks and Wildlife Service, 217 Northbourne Avenue, Turner, ACT 2601 (06-250 0250). Park information centres and rangers are normally very helpful.

Park rules are taken seriously. They prohibit the lighting of fires during fire ban periods, taking in pets, leaving rubbish, desecrating Aboriginal sites and tampering with the flora and fauna (including crocodiles). Some charge a modest entrance fee. It is usually possible to camp in National Parks. There is often a supply of chopped firewood to which you are welcome to help yourself assuming there is no fire ban in force.

ACTIVITIES
Most of the states are associated with a particular activity: in Queensland, it's scuba diving; in Tasmania, bushwalking; in Western Australia, sailing; in Victoria, skiing. But you can find most sports and outdoor activities being taught, practised and enjoyed in every state. Having a go in Australia is more important than mastering an activity. If for example you decide to go riding on an Outback property there is unlikely to be much preamble before setting off. Similarly the ski resorts have little emphasis on formal instruction. Beginners learn by doing

and by watching others. Remember that you may need special insurance if you undertake dangerous activities.

Bushwalking. Being ill-prepared for bushwalking is dangerous. For example long-distance walks in Tasmania require careful provisioning and waterproof equipment. Hikers are also encouraged to practise 'minimal impact bushwalking' whereby the land is not desecrated by rubbish. If you intend to do a lot of hiking in one state look for the series of books *100 Walks in Tasmania, 120 Walks in Victoria*, and so on, published by Hill of Content in Melbourne. High achievers might be interested to learn that a 5000km National Trail stretches from Cooktown (north of Cairns) to Melbourne, following the old stock routes, bush tracks and fire trails.

Water Sports. Frolicking in ocean waves seems harmless enough sport until a freak wave or rip current occurs. Rips fluctuate in their intensity and location and often come close in to shore. If you are caught in one, do not tire yourself out by swimming against it, but swim with it, even out to sea if necessary. Once you are out of the current, alert the lifesavers by lifting one arm above your head. If you want to swim rather than frolic, many beaches are provided with an ocean swimming pool, which is filled with sea water at high tide but protected from the waves.

Anyone who decides to have a go on a surfboard should, after attaining a certain level of confidence in the waves, be accompanied by an experienced surfer. Body surfing is universally enjoyed and requires only a modicum of skill. There are numerous variations on the surfboard that do not require the skill and balance, such as the surf mat, surfoplane and boogie board. This latter is a lightweight body mat with wrist strap that costs about $150, but can sometimes be hired from surf shops, or even for free from backpacker hostels. Another way of enjoying the balmy ocean is to go 'boom-netting' as described in *Queensland*. The zoological risks of which swimmers should be aware are set out in the chapter *Health*. Bear in mind that swimmers who go out beyond the line of breakers are known as 'sharkbait'.

Many visitors to Australia — especially Queensland — are inspired to take up scuba diving. It is a dangerous activity and there have been accidents involving beginners signed up with cowboy operators who provide a 20m dive after a few minutes' pep talk.

Skiing. Australia, despite its warm climate, has good skiing from June to September in two alpine regions: one in the Snowy Mountains on the New South Wales/Victoria border, the other in Tasmania. The former region boasts a larger area of ski mountains than Switzerland. The relatively high altitude of the Snowy Mountains means that the snow is more reliable than in Tasmania, though it tends to become slushy more readily than in the Alps of Europe or New Zealand. Cross-country skiing is particularly popular (and is usually referred to in Australia by its German name *Langlauf*), though the main resorts are equipped with plenty of lifts and pistes for downhill skiers.

Australian travel companies have realised for a long time that many visitors want to be introduced to the water, air or earth in a gentle and supervised way. So you will soon be faced with a plethora of choice, from small local firms that will take you ballooning, camel riding, snorkelling or river rafting to national organisations such as the YHA or adventure tour companies like Outdoor Travel (55 Hardware St, Melbourne 3000; 03-9670 7252) that arrange all these and others. Each regional chapter includes sections on *Sport* and, at the end of the chapter, *The Great Outdoors*.

blow	cyclone
blowie	blowfly
bung-eye	a painful eye inflammation caused by flies
crook	ill (when used about a person)
going for a sixer	stumbling/falling over
mozzie	mosquito
Noah	shark (rhyming slang with ark)
oprist	optician
podiotrist	chiropodist
quack	any doctor
troppo	affected by the heat
wetcheck	condom (Durex is a brand of adhesive tape)
wog	illness, particularly flu or diarrhoea

Health care in Australia is sophisticated and reaches the remotest parts of the country. Food and drink are normally prepared and served in hygienic conditions. Tap water, despite often being unpleasant in taste and colour, is safe to drink everywhere. However there have been many reports of 'gastro' (gastroenteritis) from people who have gone walking in the bush, probably caused by the failure of other trampers to dispose of fecal waste; if you are walking in a heavily used wilderness area where cases of gastro have been reported, it is advisable to boil your water for three minutes.

Because so much of Australia is in the tropics it is subject in small measure to tropical diseases. Although malaria was largely eradicated 50 years ago, there are occasional outbreaks in Queensland. Also insects have been discovered in Darwin capable of spreading both yellow fever and the debilitating dengue fever, and there have been dozens of reported cases of dengue fever in Queensland in recent years.

Other dangers come from Australian fauna, discussed at length below. Unfortunately there is more to Australian wildlife than cuddly koalas, kangaroos and wallabies, and the range of lethal species in Australia — both in the water and on dry land — is extraordinary. And there is a host of other natural phenomena that threaten both natives and visitors. But to keep the risks in perspective, bear in mind that statistically the biggest threat to your health in Australia is a road accident.

MEDICAL TREATMENT

The Australian version of a National Health Service is the Medicare system. UK residents on short-term visits are entitled to treatment under the same terms as Australians for any 'episode of ill-health that occurs during the visit'. This specifically excludes treatment for pre-existing conditions. In order to qualify for Medicare you need to register with any Medicare office, producing your passport and visa. This can be done retrospectively, so if you need treatment urgently go direct to a hospital or doctor. If you prefer to be well prepared, obtain a Medicare card shortly after arrival. Medicare has offices in all the main towns, or you can apply by post to PO Box 9822 in any capital city. In either case you will need a mailing address in Australia. The card takes two to three weeks to come through, though you will be assigned a number straightaway. People staying longer than six months are expected to pay contributions towards Medicare.

Under Medicare, all in- and out-patient treatment at a public hospital is free, apart from drugs and dressings for which a nominal charge is made. If you have to consult a GP, make sure you find a practice or health centre that 'bulk bills' which means the only charge to patients is a nominal $2.50 fee. If you go to a GP who does not practise bulk-billing, he or she may charge whatever they like while Medicare will refund only 85% of the scheduled charge for a consultation. Note that ambulance charges are not covered and must be paid for in full. If you are covered by travel insurance, you can claim back any shortfall from your insurer. Anyone who is working legally is automatically covered by a compulsory workers' compensation insurance scheme to which employers contribute. The insurance guarantees full wages in the event of an accident during the course of your employment or while travelling to and from your place of employment, plus all related medical costs.

Visitors from North America receive free health care only for emergency treatment; for subsequent convalescence or non-urgent treatment they must pay in full. Insurance is therefore a wise investment for US and Canadian citizens.

The major hospital in each state capital is listed under *Help and Information* in the regional chapters; elsewhere, ask the police or any local for the nearest hospital.

Royal Flying Doctor Service. The scheme to fly doctors to patients in the Outback, and patients to hospitals was set up in 1927 by the Reverend John Flynn. Nowadays this non-profit aerial medical organisation provides primary health care to 80% of the Australian Outback by means of a network of bases and aircraft staffed by medical personnel. Medical evacuations are provided free of charge and in emergency situations local residents will give advice on how to call the Flying Doctor.

Dental Treatment. Dentistry is not covered by Medicare. It can be very expensive (typically over $50 for a simple filling), so ensure that your teeth are in good order before travelling to Australia or take out insurance that covers emergency dental treatment. To ease the pain a little, most dentists accept credit cards. If you are uninsured, dental teaching hospitals can treat you for less than the usual cost of a private dentist.

Blood. There are no opportunities for selling blood, but you may donate it through Red Cross centres in return for a hot drink, a sandwich and a Mars bar. All donors are screened for antibodies to the Aids virus HIV. According to some reports, the Acquired Immune Deficiency Syndrome was spreading faster in Australia than in any other developed country except the United States. There are estimated to be well over 50,000 carriers of the HIV virus. The majority of cases at present are in New South Wales, attributed to the large numbers of homosexuals and drug abusers in Sydney. Significant numbers of cases of the disease have also been reported in Victoria, Queensland and Western Australia. The Federal Government funds a massive health education campaign, in the face of opposition from the National Party. Apparently Outback health workers encountered a problem when they urged the local people to use condoms. Their puzzled looks were due to the fact that a favourite Aboriginal tree fruit is called the condom.

Inoculations. If you are travelling on to a tropical country you can obtain the necessary advice, jobs and pills at a Traveller's Medical and Vaccination Centre (TMVC) in any big city.

CLIMATIC HAZARDS

Heatstroke and Sunburn. Most visitors from the cooler reaches of the Northern Hemisphere are unused to the high temperatures encountered in Australia, particularly in the central deserts and tropical north. To avoid 'going troppo' and collapsing from heat exhaustion, you should wear suitable clothing and a hat to keep as much of the sun off as possible. Drink plenty of non-alcoholic fluid, and avoid over-exertion until you acclimatise. In extreme conditions you need to drink a litre of water every hour to prevent dehydration.

Of course many people visit Australia to bask in the sun, a practice shared by the natives. Perhaps because of their Pommie origins, many Australians are careless about protecting themselves, and as a result Australia has the highest incidence of skin cancer in the world. Although a temporary visitor is unlikely to succumb to a melanoma, it is easy to become badly burnt. As a reaction to the cold European winter (or summer) they have just left, many British visitors ignore their better judgment and spend a whole day on the beach resulting in severe sunburn. The advice adopted by cancer campaigners sounds childish, but bears repeating for temporary visitors: 'Slip, Slop, Slap'. The idea is to slip on a shirt, slop on some sun lotion and slap on a hat. The sun's rays are at their most severe between 10am and 3pm. Start off with a lotion of a high protection factor (at least 6 or 7, or even 15 is not too high for sensitive skin), and re-apply the cream at frequent intervals, particularly after swimming. Try to ration your sunbathing (known by Australians as 'sun-baking') so you don't literally become sun-baked.

One notable sunscreen favoured by Australians is zinc cream. This mixture of zinc, lanolin and oil is sold in various lurid colours (e.g. fluorescent green) and is usually applied to the nose and surrounding exposed flesh to prevent burning. Its effectiveness in preventing sunburn over long periods gives rise to the cricketing joke 'What's the definition of an optimist? A Pommie batsman wearing zinc cream.' Other precautions used include Arab-style neck flaps attached to sun hats.

If you ignore these precautions and become severely burnt, seek medical advice. Treat a mild dose of sunburn with a lotion such as Caladryl (calamine lotion — cheaper in Britain than Australia). Coconut oil is widely available but has been found to cause blotches on the skin after persistent use. Try natural yoghourt instead.

Another nuisance you might encounter when the conditions are tropical is skin fungi. Every chemist sells a range of preparations to combat them.

Acts of God. Australia is not nearly so seismologically active as New Zealand, and you are most unlikely to encounter one of the infrequent earth tremors which are usually confined to the south of Victoria. But to keep you on your toes, particularly in the far north, there are plenty of meteorological threats. The worst are cyclones ('blows'), one of which devastated Darwin in 1974. During the risk season from November to April you may hear news of one or more degrees of alert for cyclones from blue (little risk) to red (severe danger). The standard advice is to take shelter in the nearest secure building, fill the bath (to ensure a supply of water if the mains supply is cut off) and keep tuned to the radio. If you are out of doors and the winds pick up (they can reach over 250km/h), try to find a ditch to lie in and keep well away from anything that might be blown on top of you.

Fire. The long, hot, dry summers that much of Australia enjoys create just the right conditions for bush fires to start, whether naturally or triggered by man. Bush fires can affect any area of Australia with forest (especially eucalyptus), scrubland or the desert weed spinifex. By reading the local press and (particularly) listening to the radio, you can learn where the danger areas to avoid are.

During 'total fire bans' when trees and scrub are tinder-dry, no fires may be lit in the open and you should not throw cigarette butts from your vehicle; the penalties for transgression are severe. It is sensible to avoid such areas, but if you do go into them you should look for places such as pools and clearings where you could take refuge. If you find yourself in an area where a fire has broken out, there are several steps you should take to maximise the chance of survival. In buildings, you should close all doors and windows, clear the gutters of leaves then block them and fill them with water and stay inside until the fire passes. If you are driving, but unable to get away from the fire, park as far away from vegetation as possible. Close all the windows and air vents, turn your headlights on (so rescuers can find you), lie on the floor and wait for the fire to pass. Don't attempt to empty your petrol tank, since this would merely fuel the fire around you, and if the temperature gets high enough to ignite the tank it is likely you would perish anyway. Walkers should try to find an open space and clear combustible material away from it. Water is better still, but don't try to take refuge in a raised water tank since you may be boiled alive.

PERILS OF THE DEEP

One of the more staggering facets of Australia is the number of aquatic nasties that will not hesitate to deliver a fatal sting, bite or snap. The chief menaces are sharks, crocodiles and an unpleasant little creature known as a marine stinger. One beast can even kill you when it's dead: the ugly-looking toad fish has deadly poisonous flesh.

Sharks. Man-eating sharks can be found at many places around the coast of Australia, in the south during the southern summer and mainly in the north from May to October. Some Australians may try to unnerve you with grisly stories, but it is most unusual for sharks to attack near the shoreline. In addition, most popular bathing spots (particularly around Sydney) are protected by netting, and the incidence of attacks by sharks is very low. These nets do not provide a continuous barrier against sharks, but manipulate their migration patterns sufficiently well to keep them away from beaches.

If you find yourself in shark-infested waters, it is better to do the breast-stroke, which creates an impression of calm strength, than the crawl, which can make it look as though you are flailing helplessly. It also helps if you are wearing a wet suit, so that if you are bumped by a shark you will not lose blood into the water. If you are feeling confident, a sharp tap on the shark's nose is sometimes sufficient to send it packing.

Marine Stingers. These potentially lethal creatures are also known as sea wasps and box jellyfish, and are common on the coast of Queensland and the Northern Territory from October to May. Don't rely upon seeing them before they see you, since they are almost transparent. They have tentacles over a metre long that attach themselves to you and inject a sometimes-fatal sting. The venom is contained in stinging capsules, and can cause violent shivering, nausea, a fall in blood pressure and paralysis of breathing muscles. Apart from these symptoms, the pain can be so excruciating that victims die of shock. Applying vinegar to the affected area within a minute or two counteracts the sting. A tight tourniquet should be applied and you must get to hospital as quickly as possible for a dose of antivenom. The only sensible way to escape the threat is to stay out of the sea during the marine stinger season. If, despite the constant warnings, you insist on swimming, wear long-sleeved clothing, women's tights or a wet suit.

Crocodiles. Saltwater crocodiles ('salties') are the world's largest living reptile. In recent years they have killed far more people than have sharks, due partly to their status as a protected species. They are found on or near the coast of the northern half of Australia. Despite their name, they can and do live in fresh water as numerous unfortunate victims have discovered. Never swim in an area that you're not sure about: if there are no warning notices, check with locals anyway as many of the signs are vandalised or taken home as souvenirs. It is likely that swimming in an area inhabited by crocodiles will soon become an offence. Don't camp next to a river bank in the Outback, and don't leave food or remains around from your fishing expedition. Most recorded fatalities have occurred when people were swimming at night in areas known to contain salties and where caution had been dampened by the effects of alcohol.

Freshwater or Johnston's crocodiles ('freshies') are smaller and are considered harmless. In the wild, nesting freshie females do not attend or defend their nests. In captivity however they will actively defend their nests. Female salties vigorously defend their nests, and at no time should a saltie nest be approached or tampered with, as the female is usually nearby.

Crocodiles are basically aquatic animals, and do not chase prey on land. There are some recent reports from around Kununurra (northern Western Australia) of salties attacking canoes or dinghies. One couple were dumped into the Chamberlain Gorge but managed to swim to safety when the their assailant was distracted by their rucksacks. The accepted wisdom about what to do if confronted by a crocodile in the water is to swim in a zig-zag fashion though this is not wholly reliable. If you are caught, chances of survival are slim, though there are survivors of attacks by crocodiles who have escaped when the animal has momentarily opened its jaws to get a better grip. Victims are not always eaten immediately. Some crocodiles prefer to drown their prey first, using the notorious 'death-roll' technique where victims can expect to be brought up for air several times before drowning. Then the body is hidden away on an underground ledge for future consumption.

Further information about crocodiles and their habits is available from the Conservation Commission of the Northern Territory, PO Box 496, Palmerston, NT 0831 (08-8989 5511).

Reefs and Rockpools. It is a bad idea to go walking barefoot on a coral reef, or to investigate a rockpool too closely. Various types of coral can inject a nasty poison if you tread on them in bare feet, and the crown of thorns starfish (which is currently attacking the Great Barrier Reef) has a painful sting. Stonefish like nothing better than to imitate a rock in shallow water, waiting for an unfortunate victim to step on them and be mortally stung. They are indistinguishable from ordinary small, grey rocks until their jaws open, revealing a vile yellow mouth complete with poison glands. Similarly, the tiny and pretty blue-ringed octopus which lives in shallow rockpools can give you a fatal venomous bite if you poke around too much. (The blue rings appear only when the creature is angry.) As with marine stingers, you should apply a tight tourniquet and get to hospital as quickly as possible.

Other marine hazards include venomous sea-snakes (found in the same places at the same times as marine stingers), and catfish that can sting so savagely that you die of shock caused by the pain. Flatworm larvae are also known to penetrate the bodies of swimmers, especially in lagoons or coastal inlets favoured by large numbers of sea birds. The symptoms are an itchy rash accompanied by red lumps which (unless infected) disappear within a couple of weeks since humans are resistant, leaving a brown spot behind.

INSECTS

You will have to contend with the danger, not to mention the annoyance, of Australia's famous insect life. An anonymous poem called *The Bushman's Farewell to Queensland* could just as easily have been written about the other states:

> *Queensland thou art a land of pests,*
> *For flies and fleas one never rests*
> *E'en now mosquitoes round me revel –*
> *In fact they are the very devil.*
> *Sandflies and hornets, just as bad,*
> *They nearly drive a fellow mad;*
> *With scorpion and centipede*
> *And stinging ants of every breed...*
> *To stay in thee, O land of mutton,*
> *I wouldn't give a single button,*
> *But bid thee now a long farewell,*
> *Thou scorching, sunburnt land of hell!*

The standard advice offered by the natives regarding insect bites is 'don't scratch.' People from parts of the world where being devoured by all manner of insect life is not a normal daily occurrence will find this difficult advice to follow. Always carry a powerful repellent and, if camping, make sure the door is secured before turning on a light inside your tent or van.

Spiders. Arachnids in Australia can be alarmingly large: most have a body length of 25mm or over. The majority are relatively harmless, such as the enormous Huntsman spider which commonly lurks behind picture frames, emerging in the evening. Another favourite haunt of spiders is on top of sun visors in cars; try to check before setting off since there can be few more disconcerting surprises than to have a huge spider land in your lap on the freeway. Another classic place for spiders to appear is in a suburban garden as the first barbecue of the season is lit. After a peaceful winter of nesting in rotten wood the heat of the fire drives them out, in a none-too-friendly mood. Although a bite from a spider can be painful or induce nausea, it is not usually dangerous.

However, there are two species that are potentially lethal. One is the Funnel Web (*Atrax robustus*), found mainly in gardens in the Sydney region. This vicious creature is very aggressive and rears up on its hind legs to attack. The male version (very dark and shiny, with a spur on each of its second front legs) is the most deadly, although an antivenom does exist. The bite of the Redback (*Latrodectus hasselti*; black or brown with sometimes — but not always — a red flash) can also prove fatal, but there have been no deaths from its bite since an antivenom was discovered in 1956. However every year about 200 people are treated for extremely painful bites. The Redback is infamous for its habit of lurking under toilet seats and biting the bottoms of the unwary. One other particularly nasty creature is the Wolf Spider (found mainly in Victoria), whose bites can cause gangrene and paralysis.

You should seek medical attention for all spider bites, and if you have any reason to suspect the offending beast of being lethal, immediately apply a tourniquet between the bite and the rest of the body, and wash the affected area. Try to kill the spider and take it to the hospital or doctor, so they can give you appropriate treatment. The Flick Pest Control company produces a useful guide to identifying spiders, which can be picked up from any of the company's offices in Australia. However, if you're close enough to distinguish between a male Funnel Web and the painful but non-lethal male Trapdoor, you're probably too close.

Mosquitoes. These creatures are a pest anywhere in the world. Imported malarial mosquitoes have caused several outbreaks of malaria in Queensland. Mosquitoes in the southern half of the country spread two serious, though rare, diseases. The more common is epidemic polyarthritis, a virus whose effect is similar to influenza but causes considerable pain in wrist and ankle joints. It can last for several weeks, but after you have suffered once from the disease you should be immune for life. A more serious (but very rare) threat is a bite from a mosquito carrying Australian encephalitis, a virus that attacks the brain and can cause brain damage or death. To protect yourself against mosquitoes keep the screens on doors and windows closed, wear long sleeves and trousers (particularly in the evenings) and use a repellent. The best repellents contain diethyl toluamide (commonly known as 'deet') and should be applied to your skin every few hours or, for longer effectiveness, used to impregnate cotton clothes. The most widely used repellents are 'Aerogard' spray and 'Rid' cream.

Flies. The corks around the stereotyped Australian hat are not there for decoration. They serve a useful purpose in keeping away flies, of which Australia has far more than it has rabbits, sheep or kangaroos. Buffalo flies are found mainly in the northern half of Australia. They are huge blue-green flying insects (reputedly growing as big as matchboxes) with a long sucker that is plunged into your skin. The resulting bite is more painful and itchy than a mosquito bite. You are much more likely to encounter the sandfly, a small but vicious brute that can cause painful and itchy bites. Sandflies usually live in sand near fresh water, and respond to the same repellents as do mosquitoes. If you are sleeping outside, try if possible to find somewhere raised above ground (e.g. on a roof), since sandflies are land-based and cannot jump more than 60cm.

Ticks, Fleas and Lice. The bites from these irritants can, in northern Australia, pass on typhus, whose early stages are like flu and can develop into nausea, skin rashes and even pneumonia.

OTHER HAZARDS

Snakes. Australia is the only country in the world to have more venomous than non-venomous snakes, and most of the 74 species of poisonous snake are unknown in the rest of the world. They include the Western Taipan (the world's deadliest snake), the unassumingly named Brown Snake and Black Snake, the Yellow Whip, the Tiger Snake and the Death Adder. You will only be bitten if you provoke a snake (by treading on it, or rolling over it in your sleep), and since snakes' jaws are not designed to bite humans many people survive attacks by venomous reptiles. When walking in the bush or the Outback wear sturdy footwear and keep an eye out for them, especially in spring when they are rousing and early summer when they are mating and at their most aggressive.

But the old adage 'for every snake you see, a hundred see you and slide away' is quite true. If you are unlucky enough to get bitten, try to fix in your mind a description of the offending snake or, better still, kill it and take it with you. (This is unnecessary in Tasmania where the same antivenene is used to treat the bites of all three poisonous snakes.) Do not wash or cut the affected area, apply a bandage firmly above and below the bite, and try to remain calm. All hospitals carry serums against the venom of local species, so get help as quickly as possible.

Malevolent Creatures. Australia has no man-eating mammals, nor any cases of rabies, but plenty of beasts can cause you damage. The native wild dog — the dingo — may or may not devour babies, but does on occasion bite tourists. More commonly, they boldly approach campsites and steal belongings (and not necessarily food) so be cautious if you notice a dingo lurking. Bites from dingoes or domestic dogs, whether 'bitsers' (mongrels) or pedigree breeds, should be cleaned and dressed and you should get a jab against tetanus if you haven't had a recent booster.

Other animals that boldly take food from campsites are possums and bandicoots, so keep food inside your zipped up tent. You are advised not to feed these animals to prevent them from becoming dependent and a nuisance to future campers. In more remote areas, you may find water buffaloes and wild pigs: leave them well alone.

An unexpected menace in urban areas from Canberra to Perth is the common magpie. These large birds are territorial and during the spring will defend their patch by divebombing any intruders. In badly affected areas children ride bicycles with tall flags and some adults hold umbrellas aloft to deflect a swooping magpie away from their heads.

barrow	Black Maria
bashed	beaten up
blue	fight
bong	opium pipe with bowl, often used for smoking marijuana
bongover	the morning-after effect of smoking too much marijuana
crim	criminal (noun)
demon	policeman, detective
dob in	to turn someone in, grass on them
donnybrook	bar fight
early release licence	parole
ginger	a prostitute who works with an accomplice to rob a client
hop	policeman
hop-head	heavy smoker of marijuana

Most Australians are refreshingly trusting and trustworthy. This does not mean that they are all law-abiding: there is less personal crime than in most parts of the western world, but conversely Australia has plenty of scandals involving corrupt politicians and crooked police, and there are vast underground networks of criminals. The visitor is unlikely to be affected by this except as a topic of discussion in pubs. Indeed you may feel so safe that you could be lulled into a sense of false security. Sneak thieves do, of course, exist, and relaxed tourists rank among their favourite targets. Don't leave your possessions on full view in a car. Pickpocketing is a threat in crowded areas, especially at major sporting events.

Dangerous neighbourhoods are rare in Australia. Even the sleazy inner suburbs associated with red lights and drug dealing are relatively benign, though plenty of women would not feel comfortable walking around Kings Cross in Sydney at night. Although some tourist literature maintains that 'mugging is a crime that does not exist in Australia, either by day or by night', it is a marginal danger in the cities. The number of serious assaults has increased overall in Australia five-fold in the past 16 years. A more likely threat, however, is that you will be the victim of theft by other travellers, particularly in hostels in popular areas.

Violent Crime. Gun laws are formulated and enforced by individual states. While most states have strict controls, weapons are on open sale in Queensland and Tasmania. As a result any Australian can buy a gun by mail order from a dealer in Brisbane or Hobart. There are over 3,500,000 privately owned guns, around one for every four inhabitants. Most are used for sport or farming, but some find their way into the hands of criminals and the mentally unstable. In recent years there have been several massacres where psychopaths have indulged in random murder. The free availability of weapons means that their use cannot be ruled out in mugging attempts.

Most women visitors feel much safer in Australian cities than in, say, London or New York although walking alone late at night in badly lit areas is not advisable. Although it is not necessary to be alarmist, there have been four murders of women backpackers travelling alone in the past few years. The accepted wisdom is that there is safety in numbers especially in the Outback. A hazard for both women and men is the fighting that can break out in and around the rougher sorts of pub at closing time.

THE LAW

Most Australian police are armed but not necessarily dangerous. You are likely to encounter them if driving around late at night, and are required to provide a sample of breath or blood if they suspect you of drinking.

Australia has its own version of MI5 or the CIA, known as ASIO (the Australian Security and Intelligence Organisation), which is popularly thought of as incompetent in the extreme.

Arrests and Charges. The police in Australia have wide powers of arrest, and may arrest you if they have 'reasonable grounds' for suspecting you of having committed an offence. If you are arrested, you are not obliged to give your name and address and are entitled to contact a friend or lawyer before answering any questions. (The police supply a duty lawyer if necessary.) In several states, your interrogation will be recorded on video. If you are subsequently charged with an offence, you may be remanded in custody or released on a surety. Foreign visitors are likely to have their passports confiscated to stop them leaving the country.

Before a court appearance, seek legal advice. Each state has a Legal Aid

Commission that should fund the cost of a lawyer to represent you. These are admirably even-handed bodies, and can be relied upon to do their best to get you off the hook. Most prosecutions are made by the Crown (technically representing the Queen but in reality a branch of law enforcement). If your sentence is considered too lenient, the Crown may appeal for a tougher one just as you can ask for clemency if you feel you have been too harshly treated.

Drugs. Marijuana grows extremely well in most parts of Australia, including a large number of back yards. Among young middle-class Australians smoking marijuana at a private gathering is considered as natural as drinking beer (and almost as cheap), and joints are offered around as casually as cigarettes. But the laws on drugs are complicated and can be harsh. Each state fixes its own penalties which are generally more severe than in Britain or liberal states of the USA. In New South Wales and Western Australia possession of a small amount of cannabis is liable to a fine of $2000 and/or two years in prison. In Queensland the penalties are even more severe, but at least life imprisonment is no longer mandatory for certain drug offences. In South Australia, the possession of a small amount of cannabis for personal use has been virtually decriminalised; it incurs only a small on-the-spot fine like a parking ticket. Penalties for possessing harder drugs, including the increasingly popular cocaine, are severe as are those for dealing of any kind.

The most bizarre way of getting stoned is perfectly legal. Apparently if you lick the secretions of the cane toad, which proliferates in Queensland, you can simulate the hallucinogenic state induced by LSD or magic mushrooms.

Other Laws. One vestige of Australia's convict past is the number of seemingly trivial rules and regulations that each state concocts. Controls on drinking alcohol may seem ludicrous — like the time restrictions on drinking on certain trains — but are taken very seriously by the authorities. Taking alcohol onto Aboriginal lands is also a serious offence.

There are also many pieces of progressive legislation, in particular those outlawing discrimination on grounds of race or gender. If you feel you have been unfairly discriminated against, get in touch with the state's Equal Opportunity office.

As the laws on marijuana become more liberal, controls on smoking tobacco increase. Smoking is banned on virtually all public transport, in cinemas and theatres, in lifts, museums and galleries, in public buildings such as post offices and all federal government offices. Melbourne has gone one stage further and is banning smoking even in some outdoor areas. Finally, you should note that every state, city, town and national park has strict laws against littering, with stiff fines for transgressions.

Sources of Help. If you do get into trouble with the law, inform your nearest Consulate. Although they will not be able to secure your release, they can help to ensure that you are treated in accordance with Australian law and can supply a list of local lawyers. In the case of longer-term incarceration, British residents should contact the National Council for the Welfare of Prisoners Abroad, 82 Rosebery Avenue, London EC1R 4RR. American citizens can get in touch with the International Legal Defense Council, 111 South 15th St, 24th Floor, Philadelphia, Pennsylvania 19102.

TOURIST INFORMATION

Each state spends a great deal on extolling its virtues to other Australians as well as to foreign tourists. Consequently plenty of good information is available for travellers. See *Before You Go* for sources that you can contact from abroad. But when you arrive in Australia it's well worth calling in at the travel bureaux of the states you intend to visit. You can get information about a particular state from its tourist office in the capital of other states: thus there is a Western Australian Tourist Office in Melbourne, a Queensland Government Tourist Bureau in Adelaide, etc. A couple of hours spent at the tourist offices for each state in, say, Sydney can equip you with more than enough information for a nationwide tour. The addresses of each state's tourist bureaux are listed under *Help and Information* in the regional chapters. These organisations act both as information sources and as booking agencies, so that a Tasmanian Travel Centre for example can tell you about accommodation on the island and book a ferry crossing to Tasmania.

When you call or write to a state tourist office, mention any special interests such as theatre, cycling or ornithology, since the offices have leaflets on all sorts of subjects. But don't expect a discriminating tone in the bumph; be prepared for the hard sell. It is a worthwhile exercise for the free maps and the list of forthcoming events.

As well as these official organisations you will encounter a number of other 'information bureaux'. These fall broadly into two categories: the first type are local or regional tourist offices, such as those run by City Councils or Regional Tourism Associations, which supplement the state's promotional activities with a stronger emphasis on local attractions; the second are privately run enterprises that make money by charging organisations for the privilege of recommending them to tourists.

Each city or region has at least one free magazine or newspaper. The giveaways *This Week In...* and *What's On In...* can be found in all major cities, at hotel and hostel receptions, transport terminals and information bureaux. They are good sources of information on coming events and normally have a map or two. The expansion in backpacker travel has led to a wealth of information about hostels, discounted bus tickets and airfares, adventure trips, etc. being widely distributed in mainstream locations like airports and state tourist offices.

TNT for Backpackers is an admirable series of free magazines produced by TNT in Sydney (5th Floor, 55 Clarence St, Sydney 2000; 02-9299 4811) covering where to stay, jobs, things to do and ideas for travelling on. The Sydney/NSW/ACT edition is A4-sized and monthly; the other editions have a chunkier format and are quarterly — they cover Queensland and Byron Bay; Melbourne, Victoria and Tasmania; and the Outback (the Northern Territory, South Australia and Western Australia). All of these are recommended for up-to-the-minute information.

Emergencies. In state capitals and larger towns, dial 000 for the police, fire or ambulance service. Different numbers may apply elsewhere, but will be shown in the front of directories and in telephone booths. If you need emergency medical assistance see the chapter *Health* and the hospitals/health centres listed under *Help and Information* for each city. For dealing with a financial crisis see *Money*. The addresses of the post office, American Express and Thomas Cook appear under *Help and Information* for each of the major cities.

There are British diplomatic representatives in Adelaide, Brisbane, Canberra, Melbourne, Perth and Sydney; addresses are given in the relevant chapters in the *Help and Information* sections. Unless you lose your passport, get arrested, become destitute and want to be repatriated or war breaks out in the South Pacific, you won't need to consult these addresses. If your passport is lost or stolen, notify the police immediately, and go to the nearest consulate where you will be issued with travel documents that will allow you to complete your stay and return to Britain. It is also worth notifying the local office of the Department of Immigration, Local Government and Ethnic Affairs of the loss, to avoid suspicion of overstaying.

The Australian equivalent of the Samaritans is known as Life Line. The number of the nearest branch can be found at the front of the telephone directory. In smaller towns the line may operate only at night. For more specific crises (such as those experienced by women, alcoholics, drug abusers and gay people) most big cities have additional agencies, listed under *Helplines* in each chapter.

Handicapped Travellers. In general, provision for travellers with disabilities is good. All new building projects provide special facilities, with the gradient and length of ramps shown on signs. Facilities for people with a vision disability are good, in particular to help cope with city traffic. The audible signals from pedestrian crossings are helpful, and some cities even provide ridged pavements to indicate crossing points. Further information from the National Federation of Blind Citizens of Australia (45 Waverley Road, East Malvern, Vic 3145; 008-033660).

ACROD (the Australian Council for Rehabilitation of the Disabled) is the umbrella organisation in the disability field and is able to provide a list of specialist travel agents and tour operators, as well as a list of access guides available from various organisations around Australia. Contact ACROD at PO Box 60, Curtin, ACT 2605 (06-282 4333). The Australian travel industry is highly aware of the problems facing handicapped travellers and makes careful provision for ease of access. Accommodation presents few problems as long as you book well in advance.

PUBLIC HOLIDAYS
As well as the eight days noted below, each state has two or more extra holidays which are listed in the *Calendar of Events* at the end of each chapter. For example most states celebrate Labour Day but at various times of the year.

January 1	New Year's Day
January 26	Australia Day (NSW, ACT and NT)
January 28	Australia Day (all the other states)
March/April	Good Friday
March/April	Easter Monday
April 25	Anzac Day
June (second Monday)	Queen's Birthday
December 25	Christmas Day
December 26	Boxing Day

If a fixed Bank Holiday falls on a weekend, it is normally taken on the following

Monday. The one exception is Anzac Day, which is moved only when it falls on a Sunday.

Finally, you should be aware of school holidays in Australia: accommodation can be in short supply, and trains, buses and aircraft fully booked. There are three main holiday periods each year; dates vary from one state to another; Tasmanian school holidays, for example, tend to be a month earlier. All states except Tasmania close their schools for a week over or near Easter. School children have two weeks off in the autumn/winter usually starting late June/early July, two weeks off in the spring, starting in late September and finally a long summer break from before Christmas to late January or early February.

Sydney and New South Wales

Population of Sydney: 3,600,000   **Population of NSW: 5,761,000**

In the imaginations of many, Australia has just two places: Sydney and the Bush. Some say that Sydney has overtaken Paris, Rome and San Francisco as the city of style and romance. Nearly all tourists to Australia include Sydney on their itineraries and find that the reality of the city comes close to matching the dream. Few visitors can fail to be impressed by its rich variety, from the elegance of the Opera House to the seemingly countless Thai restaurants, from the Harbour Bridge to the renowned golden beaches.

In recent years an enormous amount of money has been spent on redevelopment projects in the city, much of which has greatly modernised its visual appeal. A lot of work is still going on — stroll around central Sydney for a while and you will soon come across a construction site of one sort or another. The Rocks — where the original settlement in Sydney was built — has been tidied up and reinvented as a visitor-friendly glimpse into the past, and the redevelopment of Darling Harbour has transformed an area of tumble-down warehouses, derelict docks and a railway goods yard into a futuristic extravaganza of boutiques, museums, restaurants and tourist attractions. Circular Quay, where the many harbour ferries dock, has been thoroughly 'uptarted', with ambitious arcades, more chic shops and restaurants, and a two-kilometre promenade along the waterfront that leads right up to the Opera House.

Much of Sydney's life is focused on its magnificent harbour and coastline. Each little indentation in the coast has its own name and atmosphere, from the celebrated Bondi Beach to the bizarrely named Dee Why Beach north of the harbour. Outdoor theatre venues, restaurants, tower blocks and a zoo have all been placed so as to capitalise on views of the harbour. The Harbour Bridge — opened in April 1932 — provides an important landmark: as long as you can see it you can get your bearings. The harbour's beauty is not best captured in a photograph, as much of its interest and charm stems from the activity that it generates: private speed boat taxis, dinghies, ferries and hydrofoils, supertankers and 18ft skiffs. These fast little sailboats race at weekends between September and April, and it is possible to join spectator ferries. But most of the harbour spectacle can be appreciated free of charge from any number of vantage points on, beside or above the harbour. If you happen to be in Sydney on Australia Day (January 26th), try to take in the 'ferrython', when Sydney's ferries race around the harbour.

Added to all these physical delights are the social and cultural pleasures of a city that has achieved new levels of sophistication in the past couple of decades. Some would say that there is now as much diversity in the suburbs of Sydney as there is in the boroughs of London or the *arrondisements* of Paris. All of them — from conservative Vaucluse to trendy Balmain — have their own bookshops, art galleries, cafés and nightlife.

With over 60% of the New South Wales' population concentrated in the capital, it is easy to deduce that the rest of the state (which is six times the size of England) is very sparsely populated. There are other cities, though — such as Wagga Wagga, Wollongong and Dubbo — and also over 30 National Parks, and for those interested in taking a break from the glamour of Sydney it is easy to get away (indeed, the bush is just beyond the city limits). The most rewarding parts of the state, however, are probably the coastal resorts stretching both north and south from Sydney, the Blue Mountains, Mount Kosciusko National Park (where Australia's highest peak can be found) and the famed vineyards of the Hunter Valley, about 170km north-west of Sydney.

CLIMATE

In an area as vast as New South Wales there are great differences in climate, from the drought-prone Outback to the bushfire-prone forests all around Sydney, from the balmy coasts near the Queensland border to the winter snows in the Snowy Mountains. Snow and ice are unknown in Sydney itself but inland roads through the Blue Mountains occasionally become impassable in winter.

But it is Sydney's climate that is of most interest to prospective visitors. Sydney's sparkling sunshine and opaque blue skies are justly renowned. Of course there are grey and wet days — and occasionally even weeks — when the city is not at its best, especially around Easter, and you should be prepared for the occasional downpour; surprisingly there is at least some rain on an average of 150 days each year. But most visitors are treated to the weather that makes the harbour and outdoor activities around Sydney so memorable, and which partly accounts for Sydneysiders' smug assumption of superiority over Melbourne.

There is no season one needs to avoid. The summers are whole-hearted summers when the heat and humidity sometimes become intense. But, unlike other cities in a heat wave, tempers in Sydney do not seem to soar. Sydneysiders simply flock to their favourite city beach, where the water and breezes of the Pacific Ocean deflect any bad temper. One famous breeze is known as the 'Southerly Buster', a wind that blows at the end of a scorching day bringing the temperature down as much as 15°C and upsetting dinghies. Much more common are the cooling breezes called north-easters and the gusty southerlies that accompany a cool change. This latter phenomenon takes place frequently and results in fairly dramatic drops in temperature for a few days.

The most humid time is from January to March while the wettest months are

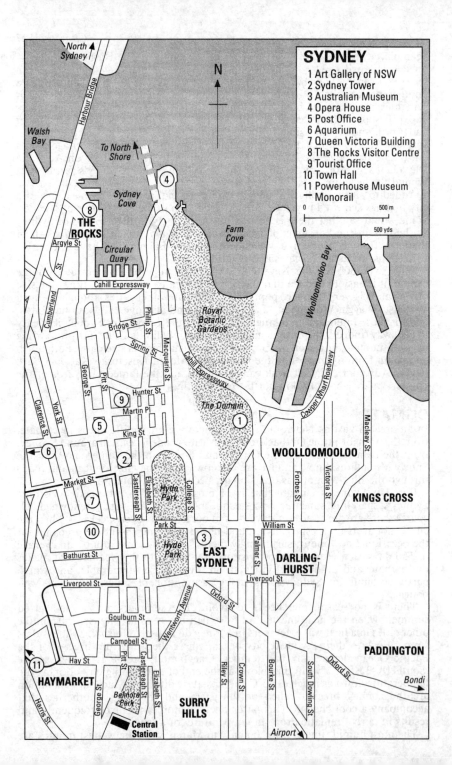

April to June. The driest months are September to November with less than 2cm of rain falling in September. The air in winter is crisp though the temperatures remain mild, usually averaging about 13°C/55°F in July and August.

THE LOCALS

Sydneysiders, as the natives are known, share with New Yorkers the easy confidence that their city is the 'Big Smoke'. One rhyming slang name for it — Steak and Kidney — is a term of affection rather than a slur, though the same could not be said of Melbourne's favourite nickname for its rival, 'Sinney', which successfully conveys something of the sensuous enjoyment and ostentation that the natives go in for. The inhabitants, like the tourists, seem to have fallen under the spell of their city, and the great Australian pastime of belittling one's circumstances is less in evidence in Sydney than in other cities.

But they do demonstrate many other Australian characteristics to perfection, such as a penchant for shrugging off anxiety. The fact that their city is invariably linked with political and financial scandal does not worry them unduly. Sydneysiders are even less prudish and puritanical than their fellow Australians. They are on the whole tolerant, worldly and pleasure-loving. This is a society that is descended from petty criminals rather than one (like North America) that is largely derived from people escaping religious persecution.

The range of races and nationalities that has congregated in Sydney contributes to the interest and complexity of the city. Although Smith and Jones are still the most numerous names in the 2000-page telephone directory, Chan and Nguyen are in the top 20. This is not only a recent phenomenon: even in the 1880s, 15% of the population of New South Wales was Chinese.

From the New Zealanders who favour Bondi to the Aboriginals of whom there are a total of 11,000 in Sydney, mainly in the inner city suburb of Redfern, from the Greeks in South Sydney to the Italians in the inner west, Sydney is a city though has a place (though not necessarily a job) for everyone. There is a small Chinatown on one side of Central Station and a pronounced Middle Eastern influence in Surry Hills on the other side. There are mosques and Japanese grocers, Highland gatherings and German folk festivals, and over 10,000 citizens who were born in what was the Soviet Union. Among the sprawling suburbs there are unexpected and remarkable concentrations of different nationalities — Lebanese people dominate Bankstown, for example, while Cabramatta is largely Vietnamese. Before the Vietnamese refugees began arriving in such numbers, Cabramatta was predominantly Hungarian. But as the older immigrants have improved their economic status they have moved to more desirable parts of town, closer to the city centre. Spanking new neon signs in Asian characters for textile importers and Vietnamese restaurants have been erected alongside the fading obsolete signs of Middle European watch repairers, demonstrating the state of flux to which many residential areas of Sydney are subject and the degree of social mobility that still exists in Australia.

While the new migrants join in the scramble towards affluence, Sydneysiders downtown lead relatively indulged lives, spending a lot of time and money eating out, drinking, surfing and listening to music — whether pricey productions inside the Opera House or free jazz outside on the terrace. By outback Australian standards, Sydney is full of posers; but despite frequently being compared with California, Sydney is no Los Angeles. Apart from the sprinkling of picturesque weirdos, trendies and snobs, Sydneysiders are sane, happy-go-lucky people with whom you can share a drink and a joke without much ado.

Making Friends. It is never as easy to meet people in big cities as it is elsewhere and it may take some time to make friends among the locals. Many travellers, even those who get a job in the city and stay for several months, find that their social lives often revolve around other foreigners, probably because they live in a hostel, frequent the same bars and restaurants as other travellers, and so on. But Sydneysiders are even more informal than their compatriots and friendly overtures are seldom rebuffed. So much of Sydney's life is lived outdoors that it is easy to meet people, whether families swimming at Manly Beach, office workers eating lunch in Martin Place while listening to free entertainment or odd bods promenading around Kings Cross late at night.

Despite its sleazy and increasingly dangerous aspect, Kings Cross has a thriving and eccentric nightlife, where it is easy to meet both young locals and travellers. Many establishments 'up the Cross' are open until 6 or 7am and women may find that they are treated to drinks by men whose intentions are not necessarily suspect. Darlinghurst, near Kings Cross, is also full of friendly trendies; see the section on *Nightlife* for some suggestions.

But you don't have to be in Kings Cross to meet people. The pubs and restaurants in Newtown and Glebe are favoured by students from the nearby 'uni' (Sydney University) as well as travellers. Two of the best Glebe pubs are the Excelsior in Bridge St — there is another (also lively) in Foveaux St in Surry Hills — and the Nag's Head in St John's Road. There are two other universities in Sydney, the University of New South Wales next to the Randwick Racecourse and Macquarie University in the northern suburbs, though the density of student haunts is lighter than around Sydney University. In Randwick try the Royal Hotel (corner of Perouse Road and Cuthill St), which is a popular meeting place.

There is such a high concentration of travellers in Sydney that you can't help but run across them — in fact, you may sometimes feel that you can't get away from them. The New South Wales YHA organises occasional get-togethers and excursions attended by local YHA members as well as tourists; contact 422 Kent St (9261 1111) for a programme of events. Another possibility is to contact the Champion Worldwide Pen Pal Club whose director arranges social events in Sydney too (ring 9281 6935).

If you are the type to answer friend-seeking adverts, read (or write in to) the regular 'Meeting Place' column in the *Sydney Morning Herald*. Scanning the forthcoming events in the same newspaper is bound to introduce you to some form of social entertainment, from guided walks around Aboriginal cave drawings in North Sydney's bushland to BYO sailing trips.

Getting Around

ARRIVAL AND DEPARTURE

Air. Sydney's airport is called Kingsford-Smith, after a famous aviator, but is more commonly referred to as 'Mascot' after the suburb in which it is located. It juts out into Botany Bay only 12km south of the city centre. But the price to be paid for this proximity is serious overcrowding and the resultant delays and confusion. The problems are worst in the early morning when numerous international flights arrive at once (due to the restriction on night landings to placate Mascot's residents). A new airport is planned about 50km west of the city at Badgery's Creek. In the meantime, be prepared for an unholy scramble. To freshen up, use the free shower adjacent to gate 6 in the international terminal or, for men only, on the ground floor of the Australian Airlines domestic terminal.

The Travellers Information Service on the ground floor of the international terminal is open from 6am. Although they advise on accommodation (as well as travel), they consider a $40 bed cheap, so are not very useful for backpackers' accommodation. They do however display hostel leaflets on a side table.

The international and domestic terminals are 5km and a $2.50 bus ride apart.

It is not possible to walk from one to the other due to the no-pedestrian rule on the link roads.

Do not be discouraged by your first impressions formed on the drive from the airport; things quickly improve. For travel to the city, take the green and yellow Airport Express 300 bus service, which stops outside both terminals. It charges a flat fare of $5 into town ($8 return) and is scheduled to take 15 minutes to get to Central Station, then stops several times on George St before arriving at Circular Quay another 15 minutes later. In heavy traffic these times can be nearly doubled, so allow for this if travelling to the airport during a rush hour. The Eddy Avenue stop near the Railway Station is very convenient: lots of hostel courtesy buses stop there and many local buses go from around the corner in Railway Square. The 300 service begins from downtown at 6am and from the airport at 6.25am, and runs every 20 minutes during the day and then every 30 minutes after 6.30pm. The last bus leaves Circular Quay at 9pm and the airport at 10.15pm.

If you are heading for Kings Cross, take bus 350, which costs $6. For Bondi take bus 400. There is a new service to Glebe and Chippendale — a cooperative of taxi drivers called the Kingsford Smith Airport Bus (9667 3221/9667 0663). They run a half-hourly service between various Glebe hostels, hotels and the airport that costs $5. You should ring to reserve a seat.

The cheapest journey into town is on city bus 302, which departs from the eastern perimeter of the airport and runs to Circular Quay via a suburban route. The most expensive is by taxi, which costs about $18.

If you are in the market for an air ticket out of Australia, check the Travel Review in the Saturday *Sydney Morning Herald* where a large selection of Sydney's hundreds of discount travel agencies advertise cheap flights to anywhere. Ringing round will not guarantee the cheapest flight, since some refuse to discuss fares over the telephone for fear of giving away information to competitors; you may have to call in personally. The Sydney Flight Centre is recommended for offering efficient service and consistently low prices (especially for flights to Asia and New Zealand). The agency is in the underground Shopping Circle at Martin Place between Castlereagh and Elizabeth Sts (9221 2666). As several agencies use the name Flight Centre it can be confusing. Try also the Jetset Flight Centre around the corner from Martin Place on Castlereagh St in the first arcade on the left. Reho Travel is at Tower Square, 155 Miller St, North Sydney (9957 6969), while STA is at 732 Harris St, 1st Floor (9212 1255). The World Travellers Centre at 185 Victoria St in Kings Cross (9357 4477) is a budget travellers' agency offering discounted coach as well as air tickets.

Qantas passengers may want to take advantage of the facility for checking their luggage in downtown between 2 and 12 hours before departure at the Regent Hotel on George St. This facility operates only between 8am and 5pm. There are mail boxes after the Customs and Immigration controls, which are handy for last-minute postcards.

Air NSW (corner of Oxford and Riley Sts; 9268 1242) has a comprehensive network within the state. Its 'Network 30' discount is available only to overseas visitors who buy in advance. East-West is at 54 Carrington St (9299 6676). Hazelton Air Services, which serves Queensland and Victoria as well as New South Wales, may be contacted on 9235 1411.

Bus. All the coach companies use the Eddy Avenue coach terminal, next to Central Station (9281 9366; open 6am–10pm daily). Service is fast and efficient, and the facilities are excellent, including a waiting room, information desk, ticket sales, showers, lockers and snack machines. There is an information area for backpackers, which can also provide help with accommodation.

When you want to buy a ticket out of Sydney, plenty of competing agencies specialise in selling discounted bus tickets to YHA members, VIP Backpackers and students (see *Accommodation* in the introductory section). Ones to try include World Travellers Network (14 Wentworth Avenue, Darlinghurst; 9264 2477); Dial-a-Coach in the Imperial Arcade (Shop P33, Pitt St Level; 9231 3699); Lets Travel (165 Victoria St, Kings Cross; 9358 2295); YHA Travel (422 Kent St; 9261 1111) and Travellers Contact Point (7th Floor, 428 George St; 9221 8744).

Here is a selection of the principal operators:

Greyhound Pioneer Australia: Eddy Avenue coach terminal (9212 1500).
McCafferty's: 179 Darlinghurst Road, Kings Cross (9361 5125).
Firefly: 482 Pitt St (9211 1644).
Kirklands: 486 Pitt St (9281 2233).
Casino: 9749 2400.
Murrays Coaches: 9319 1266.

If you want to travel between Sydney and somewhere nearby in New South Wales, such as Wollongong or Katoomba, you must take the train. In order to protect State Rail, the government imposes restrictions on coach companies; for example, private bus companies cannot carry passengers on journeys of less than 160km within the state. Of course bus tours are not bound by this rule and many travellers choose to join a day-long or weekend tour of the Blue Mountains with an operator like Wonderbus (contact YHA Travel: 9261 1111), which charges $48 for a day trip, or Oz Trek (9369 7055).

Those heading north might want to try the excellent Mountain Coach Company (toll-free 008-077 423), which takes 2½ days to make the 1000km trip to Brisbane. The coach travels via back roads, National Parks and seaside resorts and costs $99, plus an optional food kitty charge of $15. Oz Express is a backpackers service to Cairns, and is also worth considering.

Train. As is the way these days, New South Wales State Rail has been divided into separate 'business units'. Cityrail operates commuter rail services in the Sydney Metropolitan area plus services to the Hunter Valley to the north and Nowra on the south coast. Countrylink operates the long-distance trains and coordinated coach services. It takes public relations very seriously, with brochures that look as though they have been designed by Saatchi and Saatchi, and not necessarily for ordinary timetable users. However it is not difficult to find out about the services you require, most of which are efficiently run and relatively cheap and frequent. If you are making enquiries in the Central Station, remember that Countrylink and Cityrail have separate ticket offices. The long-distance travel office in the station is known as 'the man in blue'.

Second class one-way fares on long-distance services are generally about 8c per kilometre, with first class costing about 40% more. Savings of up to 30% are available to those who book in advance, and there are 25% discounts for YHA members. Both commuter and long-distance ('country') trains share Central Station, which is referred to as 'Sydney Terminal' on country train timetables. Countrylink trains depart from platforms 1 to 5, Cityrail's intercity services to Muswellbrook, Nowra, etc. from platforms 6 to 15 and metropolitan Sydney services from platforms 16 to 25; a 10-minute walk divides the sets of platforms.

Countrylink is very proud of its XPT services (express passenger trains), which are replicas of British Rail's Intercity 125 trains. They run north to Brisbane, inland to Tamworth, west to Dubbo, and south to Albury on the Victorian border. The fastest overland route between Sydney and Adelaide is known as 'Speedlink', which uses the XPT train to Albury (departing Sydney at midday) and a connecting coach service on V/Line to Adelaide taking a total of less than

20 hours. There are two services daily to Melbourne: the *Intercapital Daylight Express* operating Monday to Saturday and the overnight *Melbourne Express* operating daily. The journey takes about 10½ hours and costs $93.

Overseas visitors can also avail themselves to some special deals, such as the East Coast Discovery Pass, which offers unlimited stops to Brisbane and the Gold Coast for $199, and one-way tickets to Surfers Paradise or Brisbane for $76.

All Countrylink enquiries can be made by telephoning 132232, or by visiting a Countrylink Travel Centre — at the station, at Transport House, 11–31 York St, at Wynyard Station or at Alfred St, Circular Quay.

The pleasant and spacious Central Station has facilities such as a setting-down area labelled 'Kiss and Drop' and a luggage-checking office at one end of the concourse. The cost is $1.50 per bag per day, but if you fail to collect it by 11pm, a charge of $4.50 per day extra is made.

Driving. The main approaches to Sydney are via the scenic (and usually empty) Princes Highway along the south coast and the busier Pacific Highway from the north, which seems to get held up at every suburban junction until expanding into a glorious six lanes. Otherwise you may be on the Hume Highway from Canberra or the Great Western Highway from the Blue Mountains and beyond (Lithgow and Bathurst). Whichever route you choose be prepared for what seems like a never-ending sea of suburbs, which stretch 55km east–west and 90km north–south. Central Sydney is fairly well signposted from all directions, though drivers should try to arrange to have a passenger with a good road atlas, since it will take all their concentration to dodge Sydney's aggressive drivers.

The rules of the road do not differ very much from other states. If you are planning to drive extensively around the state you might like to acquire the state Roads and Traffic Authority's free *Road Users Handbook* (PO Box K198, Haymarket, Sydney 2000; 9218 6888). The alcohol limit is a stiff 0.05% and there are frequent random checks carried out by 'booze buses' in towns throughout the state. The speed limit is generally 100km/h on the open road but 60km/h where there are street lights. It is an offence to pass on the inside or to drive slowly in the passing lane, so Poms may find driving around the state more familiar than in some of the other states.

As usual, car hire firms impose restrictions on your destinations, or impose surcharges if you want to visit remote parts. Try Getabout Oz at 85a William St (toll-free 1800-656899), who rent cars from $25 per day; No Worries at 483 King St, Newtown (9519 7149); Rent-a-Ruffy, 33 Pittwater Road, Manly (9977 5777) and Pegasus (9267 3088). Try also the cut-price Kings Cross firms like Bayswater Car Rental, 120 Darlinghurst Road (9360 3622); Kings Cross Rent-a-Car at 169 William St (9361 0637) and Reliable Rent-a-Car, 124 Bourke St (9358 6011). Prices are advertised from $25 a day (unlimited kilometres), but with insurance and New South Wales stamp duty you shouldn't count on renting a car for less than $40 a day. You can of course spend much more with the big-name firms like Thrifty (75 William St; 9380 5399).

If you want to buy a second-hand vehicle, Kings Cross is the best area to check noticeboards and adverts. This is also a good way to pick up a second-hand motorcycle (affluent Scandinavian travellers often sell off their bikes for relatively low prices when they're just about to leave the country). The Kings Cross International Backpackers Car Market is on Level 2 of the car park on the corner of Ward Avenue and Elizabeth Bay Road — you pay $5 a day (weekly rate) to park your car, but nothing to inspect. Several car dealers specialise in cars for backpackers and guarantee to buy back the vehicle at the end of your stay; try Auto Becker at 16–20 Oxford St (9360 7211) and Travellers Auto Barn at 177 William St (9360 1500). Scotts Motorcycles (609 Harris St; 9212 6044/6033) do the same for motorbikes.

The National Roads and Motorists Association (NRMA) in Sydney is at 151 Clarence St (corner of Barrack St; 9292 9222). A recorded message about road conditions can be heard by ringing 11571. If you want to join, it costs $80 for 1 year; reciprocal arrangements exist for members of overseas motoring organisations, such as the AA and the RAC in the UK. If you want the NRMA to inspect a car you are considering buying, it will cost $105. You can have this done much more cheaply by travelling mechanics who often advertise on hostel notice boards their willingness to do mechanical checks for about $25.

Hitch-hiking. In a city of 3.6 million inhabitants, the majority of whom seem to be on the roads at any one time, you must get past the suburbs before attempting to hitch any distance. If you want to clear the city completely, take the train to Gosford in the north, Waterfall in the south (a small station on the edge of the Royal National Park where the freeway that runs parallel to the Princes Highway begins) or to Mittagong (90 minutes from Central Station) for the Hume Highway to Canberra. Nearer recommended hitching spots are the expressway near Wahroonga train station for those heading north or near Liverpool train station for the Hume Highway. To pre-arrange a shared lift, try OK Car Pools on 9281 6741.

It is worth bearing in mind that there are real risks involved with hitching — especially for women — and even couples hitching together in New South Wales have been murdered in recent years. Give it serious thought before you decide to travel this way.

CITY TRANSPORT

State Transit runs an integrated service that includes buses, ferries and Cityrail's underground system and suburban trains. Although Sydney's public transport is more expensive than that of any other Australian city, it is still quite reasonable — for example, $2.50 pays for some journeys as long as 13km. Combination tickets on bus and train are sold, so state your final destination when boarding either bus or train. All times and prices are available by ringing the Public Transport Infoline on 131500, or call in at the State Transit kiosk in Carrington St behind Wynyard Station. They distribute timetables for specific routes and larger brochures for the regions, e.g. Eastern and South & West. Newsagents sell a State Transit directory for $2.45.

There are separate day passes for the buses and trains. Unlimited bus travel is available on the Bus Tripper ticket, which costs $7.80, while the City Hopper for $2.20 allows unlimited travel after 9am on the rail system between Kings Cross and North Sydney only (if you are travelling into Sydney by train, you can add on a City Hopper ticket for just $1). If you are planning to use the buses occasionally over a period of time, buy ten tickets in advance (from stations and some newsagents). These strips of tickets are called Travelten and cost between $8 (covering journeys of about 3km) and $15.40 (up to 13km), although tickets covering longer journeys are available. These tickets save you about 40% on single fares.

If you are staying in Sydney for some time and intend to do a lot of travelling, you should investigate the range of Travelpasses available. One of the most attractive is the weekly ticket known as a 'red pass' (Monday to Sunday), which covers travel on trains, buses and ferries in the central zone, a large area on both sides of the harbour; this costs about $16. If you are staying further out investigate travel passes that cover your zone. If you are going to be in the city a short time and want to compress a lot of sightseeing into 3 days, the tourist Sydney Pass may be of interest. The cost of $60 allows you to use all public transport, plus the Sydney Explorer, harbour cruises operated by Sydney Harbour Ferries and the Airport Bus (even if you need the latter after the Pass has expired).

Bus. Sydney is well served by buses, from free downtown shuttles (rare as unicorns) to long suburban runs. There is a bus information desk in the inspectors' offices on Loftus St at Circular Quay (open 8am–10pm) and in the Queen Victoria Building on York St (shorter hours); ring 131500 for specific bus information. Bus stops are painted yellow. Buses beginning 100 and 200 leave from Wynyard Park and head north, buses in the 300 series leave from Circular Quay and head east, while 400 and 500 buses also leave from Circular Quay but head south and west.

Suburban routes are usually served every half hour between early morning and early evening but there are severe curtailments at weekends. Night services have improved recently and one of the most useful is route 150, which runs at infrequent intervals through the night between Wynyard Station and Manly Wharf.

Fares are calculated according to the number of zones crossed starting at $1.20 for one zone (about 3km), $2.50 (3–13km), $3.30 (up to 23km) and $4 to the furthest outskirts. Remember that smoking is banned on all buses.

There are two free bus services. The first is route 666, which runs between Wynyard Station and the Art Gallery of New South Wales in the Domain, making several stops on its outgoing route along Macquarie St and back via Market St. This runs every half hour daily from 10.10am until 4.40pm (except Sunday mornings).

The other free bus covers roughly the same ground. Route 777 is principally meant as a park-and-ride service across town between the Domain Parking Station and Wynyard Station. It runs only on weekdays between 9.30am and 4pm.

The Rocks–Darling Harbour Shuttle is another service worth knowing about. It covers this short distance every 20 minutes via the Opera House, the Queen Victoria Building and the Botanic Gardens. It was launched in 1991 on an experimental basis but looks set to continue.

Visitors are urged on all sides to take the Sydney Explorer bus, which costs $20 for the day. It runs continuously around 26 points of interest, and you can get off and on as often as you like. However as many of the attractions on its route are clumped together around The Rocks or Kings Cross, it is cheaper to take a couple of public buses and then explore on foot. By the time you locate the bus stop and wait a potential 17 minutes for the next bus, you could have walked to the next attraction. A further disadvantage is that it stops running about 7pm and few people want to visit Kings Cross in the daytime.

Train. The Cityrail network provides what amounts to an underground system for the city centre as well as serving the suburbs. Because of Sydney's heavy traffic, especially at rush hour, trains are often much faster than buses. The principal downtown stations are Central, Town Hall, Wynyard, St James, Museum and Circular Quay. Fares range according to distance from $1.20 upwards. There are special off-peak fares (e.g. after 9am) that permit savings of up to 60% on return journeys. Sometimes the ticket you buy bears the name of a different destination from the one you asked for, but trust the booking clerk: the frequency of fare increases means that ticket stocks are often out-of-date and are used up by selling to the 'wrong' destination at the correct price.

Sydney's 'red rattlers', which were in service as long ago as 1927, are being replaced by ultra-modern Tangara trains (Tangara is an Aboriginal word meaning 'to go'). The old trains consist mainly of double-decker carriages on which the doors are rarely closed during warm weather, so hold on tight if you are standing near an entrance. Many have the nifty feature of seats that can be reversed so that passengers may face forwards, or face their friends if they are in a group. Some trains are composed of four rather than eight cars; the signs on each platform bear a red and yellow stripe, with the yellow section indicating the end of the platform at which these half-length trains will stop. On certain suburban lines, train travellers have been plagued by violence, causing Cityrail to cancel services after midnight on some routes.

Monorail. The privately owned TNT Monorail opened for the Bicentennial. It runs in a loop from Market and Pitt Sts in the city centre, along Liverpool St and around the Sydney Entertainment Centre and Darling Harbour complex, returning over Pyrmont Bridge to the planned Casino. The project was widely condemned by conservationists and others as the mirror-clad pylons fail abysmally to blend in with the surroundings and even after building was well advanced, there was talk of rerouting it away from Pitt St. However it is now in place and a favourite way for tourists to reach Darling Harbour. However it is probably easier to walk to Darling Harbour from George St or Glebe now that the pedestrian bridge is in use. The most useful aspect of the Monorail is that it allows you to get good views of the huge building projects scattered around central Sydney, and also of the large number of derelict areas that the gloss of Darling Harbour hasn't touched. The Monorail operates from 7.30am until 9pm (11pm on weekends) and there is a flat fare of $2.50. Call 9552 2288 for information.

Car. Unless you have nerves of steel it is probably not sensible to drive in Sydney. According to some Sydney makes Rome seem like a Dorset village. (At least Romans don't kill tourists for sport.) Although the locals complain loudly about the number of traffic lights in Sydney, some of which they swear stay red for as much as three minutes, these provide a much needed respite for harassed drivers from out-of-town.

The toll on the Sydney Harbour Bridge is charged heading south only, at the booths on the north side of the Bridge. Some of the booths have automatic coin-collecting baskets into which you hurl your $1.50, but there is always at least one manned booth for those without change. All of this causes serious delays on the bridge at busy times. There is now also the cross-harbour tunnel between Milson's Point and the Opera House, which connects the Cahill Expressway and the Warringah Expressway. If you consider the toll on the Sydney Harbour Bridge too steep, you can cross the harbour free of charge further inland, for example over Gadesville or Ryde bridges. There is now talk of building a second tunnel for trains, which would connect Sydney airport with the north shore.

The 'tidal flow' system of traffic management where lanes are switched between inbound and outbound traffic according to the hour of day has reached an art form on the Bridge and its approach roads, so keep your eye on the lane markers.

Parking downtown can be a serious problem especially in the vicinity of Circular Quay. There are several privately run 'parking stations' as they are called on the west side of Harrington St leading down to the Rocks and in other prime locations but their charges are astronomical on weekdays ($3.50 for half an hour is typical). Metered parking is more reasonable; before 8am and after 6.30pm street parking is free. In prime locations, however, there may be a maximum of one hour or even less. The council-run Domain Parking Station (entrance on Cathedral Road) is one of the most useful since free bus 777 runs nearby, as does a park and ride bus to the Opera House in the evenings (5.30pm to 11.45pm) for a total cost of $9.

Taxis. With such a discouraging situation for drivers, it is welcome news that Sydney taxis are relatively cheap. There is a standing charge of $1.70 on top of which you pay 90c per kilometre. An extra 90c is charged for a telephone summons and an extra $1.50 is charged if a bridge toll is involved in your journey, but there is no surcharge late at night. A large proportion of cabs accept credit cards for fares of over $5. An even larger proportion of cabs are driven by Asian migrants, so you might ask your driver for advice on restaurants. The main ranks are at Central Station, Circular Quay and St James Station. To request a cab in the Sydney area by telephone, dial Legion (9289 9000), RSL (9581 1111), Taxis Combined (9332 8888) or Premier (9897 4000). It is not usually difficult to get a taxi late at night, as lots of taxis have 'night licences'. There is now a range of water taxis from Circular Quay.

Ferry. A ferry ride in the harbour, especially the trip to Manly, is among Sydney's foremost delights and is even more enjoyable than the famous trip to Staten Island. Even if you are not particularly interested in what's on the other side of the harbour, it is worth going out to admire the view of downtown Sydney from the water.

Fortunately the opening of the Harbour Bridge in 1932 did not entirely remove the ferry trade and there is a network of ferries running between Circular Quay (which is in fact square) and numerous points around the harbour. The principal destinations are Balmain, Taronga Zoo, Kirribilli, Neutral Bay, Mosman, Cremorne and Manly. The 30-minute trip to Manly is a bargain at $3.60 compared with the scant 10-minute trip to the Darling St Wharf in Balmain, though this shorter trip has the advantage of taking passengers under the Bridge. There is also a high-speed jetcat to Manly, which costs $4.80 and is nowhere near as much fun.

Services operate frequently during rush hours but otherwise are half-hourly. Tickets are sold at Circular Quay from lots of automatic machines so have some change. Sydney Harbour Ferries publishes a comprehensive timetable of all ferry services and connecting buses. Most services run between about 6am and 11.30pm. For information phone 131500.

A destination in the harbour not often visited by tourists is Goat Island, which is where many of the original convicts were incarcerated. Ferries leave at 11am and 1pm (Wednesday to Saturday). Fort Denison is another island fortress, now a museum.

The Sydney Flying Squadron (9955 8350) puts on special ferries on Saturdays to follow sailing races; the cost is $6 and the ferries leave from Milsons Point (near the northern end of the Harbour Bridge).

Sydney Harbour Ferries operates several sightseeing cruises on the harbour, namely the History Cruise and the Harbour Sights Cruise, which last 2½ hours and depart respectively at 10am and 1 or 1.30pm; both cost $12. The evening cruise, which is just an hour and a half, departs at 8pm and costs $10. More expensive and gimmicky cruises are available from Captain Cook Cruises and Vagabond Cruises (9660 0388), both of whom incidentally hire travellers as ticket salespeople in the busy season.

Cycling. The wearing of helmets is compulsory in New South Wales. Offenders are liable to be given a $32 on-the-spot fine. Given the general discourtesy of the drivers (not to say homicidal tendencies) it is no fun cycling in Sydney. Even if you are used to London cycling, it is much more enjoyable to rely on public transport.

Although there is a cycle path across the Harbour Bridge, it is difficult to find when approaching from the east. However there is a pleasant cycle track through parkland between Cleveland St east of South Dowling St and the University of New South Wales (inland from Coogee).

Bicycles including tandems may be hired from Centennial Park Cycles, 50 Clovelly Road, Randwick (9398 5027) and from City Cycles at the beginning of Glebe Point Road. For advice on cycle touring or equipment, visit Cranks Bike Shop, 92 Pacific Highway, Roseville (9411 5466). Second-hand touring bikes often change hands in the hostels of Kings Cross. Bicycle New South Wales (formerly the Bicycle Institute of New South Wales) is at Level 2, 209 Castlereagh St (9283 5200).

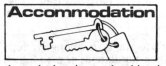

As most people spend more than a few days in Sydney, it is worth being more particular about your lodgings than usual. The choice is enormous but there are not always enough beds for the huge numbers of people passing through the city, so booking in advance makes sense. A number of hotels and hostels offer special rates for long stays, though if you intend to work in Sydney for 6 months it is usually cheaper to rent a unit (flat) with a few friends, provided you are prepared to scrounge around for furniture, since almost all rented accommodation is unfurnished.

YHA Hostels. There are three YHA hostels in Sydney, as well as an extra summer hostel in a Sydney University college. A leaflet containing details of the hostels and information on how to get to them from the city centre is widely available. The Kingsford Smith airport bus mentioned above serves all the hostels. There is no time limit at any of the hostels. The YHA of New South Wales has its travel information and membership office at 422 Kent St (9261 1111).

Two of the hostels are in the congenial area of Glebe, between Sydney University and the harbour; both are accessible by buses 431 and 433 from George St and Railway Square. The main one is Hereford YHA Lodge at 51 Hereford St (9660 5577), which has 260 beds, starting at $17 per night. Twins and doubles start at $24 per person. The hostel has modern rooms with private bathrooms and balconies, a roof-top pool, a sauna and a cafeteria. It also gives all guests an orientation leaflet on Glebe. Not far away is the excellent Glebe Point YHA Hostel (262–4 Glebe Point Road; 9692 8418), which is slightly cheaper than the Lodge. The Summer Hostel is at St Andrews College on Carillon Avenue in Newtown, which is part of Sydney University — it operates as a hostel from December to mid-February, and beds start at $16. Buses 422, 423, 426 and 428 will take you there from the city. Contact the Glebe Point YHA for more information.

If you want to escape from city life completely, the Pittwater YHA, 28km to the north of Sydney, is an excellent place to stay (9999 2196). It has the further charm of being on the edge of the Kuringai National Park, and accessible only by ferry, which makes commuting into Sydney impossible (the whole trip takes over 2 hours, 4 hours on a bad day) — contact the hostel directly for journey details. Beds start at $14, and telephone booking is essential.

Private Hostels. There is plenty of budget accommodation in the lively, seedy area of Kings Cross, which can be reached on foot from Central Station in about 45 minutes. Before committing yourself to staying here for any length of time, though, consider some of the alternatives, as described below. The price of a dorm bed in a Sydney hostel averages about $14–15 per night, although you can pay $17–20 for smaller, more comfortable dorms. Most hostels also have single and double/twin rooms, which unsurprisingly cost more. Some hostels have quite elaborate pricing structures, and you should phone around to check prices. Booking ahead is also a good idea, as competition for beds can be quite tough.

Most hostels offer such facilities as kitchen, lounge, TV room and café, but they vary enormously in their level of congeniality. As usual the hostels are good sources of travel information and many will book bus tickets or alternative tours for you. Many can also provide advice on finding work locally. One of the most comprehensive lists of backpacker accommodation is contained in the monthly free magazine *TNT for Backpackers* (published by TNT: 5th Floor, 55 Clarence St; 9299 4811), which at last count listed over 80 hostels.

In some people's view, Kings Cross is no longer the backpackers' paradise it once was, and quite a few travellers are choosing other areas instead, such as Glebe and some of the beach suburbs. Although the travelling time to these parts of the city is longer, the atmosphere is more relaxing, and consequently several of the hostels in these areas are thriving. Nonetheless Kings Cross has cleaned up its act a lot in recent years, and doesn't have too much trouble attracting travellers.

Of the 15 Sydney hostels in the VIP Backpackers Resorts chain, five are in Kings Cross. The Backpackers Headquarters Hostel is at 79–81 Bayswater Road (9331 6180) and has dorm beds from $11. The Jolly Swagman Central Backpackers at 144 Victoria St (free pick-up on 9368 1332) has a roof garden with city views and also offers a range of free bus tours; beds start at $15. The hostels at 14 Springfield Mall (9358 6400) and 16 Orwell St (9358 6600) are part of the same set-up, and have cheap beds at similar prices. The Pink House at 6–8 Barncleuth Square (9358 1689) is a converted Victorian mansion with dorm beds from $12.

Also in the Kings Cross area are the highly rated Eva's Backpackers (6–8 Orwell St; 9358 2185), with dorm beds from $17; Original Backpackers at 162 Victoria St (9356 3232), which has beds from $16; and the Astoria at 9 Darlinghurst Road (9356 3666), with beds from $15. There are many more; see *TNT for Backpackers* for up-to-the-minute details.

The neighbouring suburbs of Darlinghurst, Potts Point and Surry Hills also offer a range of accommodation possibilities. For example, Rucksack Rest at 9 McDonald St, Potts Point (9358 2348) specialises in rooms for couples and is generally thought to be one of the best. Alfred Park Lodge (207 Cleveland St; 9319 4031) has its cheapest beds at $17. City-side Backpackers at the Excelsior (64 Foveaux St; 9211 4945) is handy for Central Station and has a recommended (cheap) restaurant; it has dorm beds from $12. The YWCA at 5 Wentworth Avenue (the 'Y on the Park') has bunk-beds for $22.

West of the city is the spankingly clean Wattle House at 44 Hereford St, Glebe (9552 4997); there are just 28 beds, ensuring a quiet and friendly atmosphere, and prices start at $17. Facilities include tennis courts and a library. Another VIP Backpackers Resort is Glebe Village Backpackers at 254–258 Glebe Point Road (9660 8133). A small, quiet place for those wanting to work in Sydney and save up their money for further travels is Carole's Accommodation at 209 Bridge Road, Glebe (9660 0998). Various rooms and flats are available; double rooms are $80 per person per week. There is also a four-bed dorm for girls only — this is $70 per person per week. The minimum stay is one week, and due to the place's popularity booking ahead is advisable. Carole is well versed in work possibilities in Sydney, and is a good source of advice.

Of the beach suburbs one of the most popular is Coogee, which has a lovely beach south of Bondi. There are also plenty of drugs around, according to recent reports. Try Coogee Beach Backpackers at 94 Beach St (9315 8000/9665 7735), which has beds for $16. Surfside Backpackers is at 186 Arden St (9315 7888), and is a bit more expensive. Aegean Backpackers at 40 Coogee Bay Road (9314 5324) has a good reputation.

Bondi now has fewer drugs than a few years ago, and is on the up as a backpacker area. One possibility is the Lamrock Hostel at 7 Lamrock Avenue (9365 0221), right on the beach. Manly is even better provided with budget accommodation, such as Manly Astra Backpackers at 68 Pittwater Road (9977 2092). Manly Backpackers Beachside at 28 Raglan St (9977 3411) is even closer to Manly Wharf, and has dorm beds from $14. Another option is Manly Beach Resort at 6 Carlton St (9977 4188).

One of the most attractively located hostels is the Harbourside Hotel at 41 Cremorne Road, just a short walk from Cremorne Wharf on the north side of the harbour. It has excellent views towards the Harbour Bridge and Opera House, and dorm beds from $12, which includes tea, coffee and breakfast.

Hotels and Guest Houses. Just because something in Sydney is called a hotel does not mean that it will be significantly more lavish and expensive than the accommodation described above, though it will probably be more noisy due to the presence of a bar. For example, the CB Hotel downtown (412 Pitt St; 9211 5115) has shared accommodation available starting at $15, with doubles costing $49; the cockroaches are free. The Sydney Central Private Hotel (75 Wentworth Avenue; 9212 1005) has single rooms from $28 per night and twin/double rooms from $45; the St George Private Hotel (9211 1800), in the murkier depths of George St at No 700A, charges similar prices. The Wynyard Hotel (corner Clarence and Erskine Sts, near Wynyard Station; 9299 1330) is a 'traditional Australian pub', with singles for $50 and doubles for $60; meals are also available.

There are lots of other more sedate addresses in Sydney, such as Neutral Bay Lodge on the North Shore near Kirribilli (45 Kurraba Road; 9953 4199) where accommodation starts at $110 per week and single rooms with TV, fridge, etc. from $160 a week. Pension Albergo in Italian-dominated Leichhardt (5 Day St; 9560 0179/9810 8906) charges $38 per night for a single room, or $60 for a double; the price includes an Australian-style breakfast consisting of fruit salad and croissant. Back in Kings Cross, Carnarvon Lodge (16 Ward St; 9358 6611) has self-catering apartments for $70 and a helpful management.

Longer Term. Compared to rents in London and Manhattan, units in Sydney are relatively affordable and many people soon move out of their hostel. Kings Cross/Darlinghurst and Bondi are the main areas for such accommodation. A two-bedroom unfurnished unit in a central but unfashionable area like Kings Cross will cost about $340 a week. Often these small flats house up to eight backpackers, which is uncomfortable but comparatively cheap (compared with, say, a typical backpacker hostel, which might charge $90 per week per person). This category of accommodation proliferates along Victoria St in the Cross, as do fleas and cockroaches, which are almost as serious a problem in Sydney as they are in New York.

One of the main drawbacks of renting is that you will be expected to sign a lease, typically for 6 months. Then you will be required to pay a sizable bond, usually 4 weeks rent or 6 weeks in the case of furnished accommodation, which will be held back if you leave before the lease expires or if you leave the property in poor condition. As long as you stay for 6 months, there is normally no problem getting your money back. Some flat-letting agents will give shorter leases for higher rents, but this is uncommon. Furthermore you may be asked to provide evidence that you are in employment. Bondi landlords seem to post the highest bonds, possibly because Bondi attracts such a large itinerant population (especially Poms) who are suspected of planning to do a bunk. If you have any queries about the tenancy rules, consult the NSW Department of Fair Trading's Tenancy Service (Level 4, 234 Sussex St; 9377 9100); if you have a query concerning a rental bond, ring 9377 9000.

If you are following up adverts in the paper (the Wednesday and Saturday editions of the *Sydney Morning Herald* are best) you must move quickly. On Saturdays, for example, the best places will disappear during the afternoon. Most people find long-stay accommodation by word of mouth in their hostel. Try to avoid using an agency if possible: they charge a hefty fee and often give out scant details about houses advertised in the newspaper anyway. One possible exception is Northshore Flatshare (9953 2636); ring afternoons and evenings during the week. They mainly deal with rentals exceeding 3 months, and rents average $110–130 per week.

Rooms or bed-sits in divided houses are usually a little cheaper and you can usually find space in a house by reading the notices posted by other travellers at budget hostels or by Sydney students on university notice boards. The atmosphere in rooming houses is often less pleasant than in hostels, and they often have permanent low-life rather than casual residents. You may also be able to rent a room above a pub (though in Kings Cross be prepared for lots of coming and going into the wee small hours).

Camping. Not many people choose to camp in Sydney, but if you do, there is a campsite on the Lane Cove River in North Sydney — East's Van Village (Plassey Road, North Ryde; 9805 0500). This tourist park also has on-site vans and cabins for rent.

Eating and Drinking

Recommending places to eat in 'Steak & Kidney' is both fraught with difficulties and perhaps superfluous, since there are so many good places scattered all over the city. Even an unpromising suburban row of shops is quite likely to contain a good Thai restaurant, Italian pizzeria or vegetarian café. And nearly all are affordable. Sydney has the ideal combination of access to superb ingredients (including tropical fruit from Queensland, fresh fish and shell fish and regional cheeses) and a cosmopolitan population to prepare them in interesting ways. To admire the high quality of produce visit Paddy's Saturday market (see *Shopping* below) or the early morning fish markets at Blackwattle Bay, Pyrmont. For a display of gourmet food to rival Harrods in London, visit the food hall downstairs at David Jones Department Store on Market St which also has several fast food counters (where a half-dozen oysters can be bought for $9).

Anyone who intends to eat out more than a handful of times should buy *Cheap Eats in Sydney*, an up-to-date and discerning guide to over 500 restaurants almost all of which are described in such loving detail that you are prompted to add each one to your list of possibilities; the book costs $6.95 and is on sale everywhere. Where to eat is just as popular a topic of conversation among Sydneysiders as defending their favourite beach, so you'll soon be directed to a few undiscovered hideaways.

RESTAURANTS

Neighbourhoods with the highest concentration of good eating establishments are Glebe, Balmain, Kings Cross, Surry Hills, Paddington, Bondi and Crows Nest as well as The Rocks and the city centre. Crown St stretching from Surry Hills to the large downtown park known as The Domain has scores of interesting restaurants and cafés. If you haven't chosen a place by the time you reach Oxford St, turn east towards Paddington and you will soon pass dozens of other possibilities. *Cheap Eats* includes a convenient index by suburb as well as by type of cuisine from Cajun to crepes, Vietnamese to vegetarian. One of the few complaints which can be levied against the eating scene in Sydney is the surprising shortage of pavement or garden tables.

As usual BYO restaurants are generally cheaper than licensed ones, especially those which charge nothing for corkage. There is an increasing trend for restaurants to have both a licence and to allow you to bring your own liquor, which is useful if you have not remembered to stock up.

Before venturing into Sydney's many ethnic cuisines, you might find yourself in The Rocks looking for lunch. Try one of the innovative salads served at the Gumnut Tea Garden (where despite the name you can drink wine as long as you have remembered to bring some) at 28 Harrington St or the nearby Sorrento's Seafood at 13–17 Playfair St. The Red Onion (formerly the Spaghetti Factory) serves TexMex food, or you can try the generous hamburgers with salad and chips at the Cove Café in the Old Sydney Park Royal Hotel for about $7. To cook your own steak, go to Phillip's Foote in The Rocks (101 George St), which has an outdoor dining area open 7 days a week; the charge is $13 for your choice of steak plus six salads and bread. If you don't mind the idea of eating at a chain restaurant, try the pancakes at Pancakes on The Rocks at 10 Hickson Road in The Rocks, or at its newest branch at 636 George St; the original is open 24 hours a day around the calendar. BYO creperies are usually excellent value and can be found all over Sydney.

Excellent take-aways can be found almost everywhere, but especially in Kings Cross, and it is possible to survive cheaply and pleasurably on pizza and ice cream. Other bargains worth investigating include the $4 bowls of soup at Soup Plus (383 George St) which gives a 10% discount to ISIC holders and is also a jazz venue (see below), Cabrini's at 150 Victoria St, Potts Point where pasta meals cost a fiver, The Piccolo Bar at 6 Roslyn St in the Cross which serves cheap food from 11am to 6am, the adjacent Bagdad Café at 7 Roslyn St which serves breakfast for $6 from 7.30am, and the Hare Krishna café called Govinda's at 112 Darlinghurst Road where a good vegetarian meal costs $5 at lunch or $7.50 a dinner; at one time you could expect a free meal on the takeaway side if you were prepared to discuss life, the universe, etc., but nowadays prices are the same as in the café. Also on Darlinghurst Road is the very cheap Astoria at number 7 (in the backpackers' hotel) which serves straightforward roast meals for $5. Of the other Kings Cross hostels and hotels that run their own cafés, the Pink Pig at 6 Barncleuth Square is one of the cheapest with two-course vegetarian meals for $4.

If you are at all interested in food and don't mind splashing out occasionally, Sydney is paradise. Apart from the wealth of ethnic restaurants treated separately below, there is an increasing number of places serving what can best be described as modern Australian cuisine. Among the best are Dean's Verandah (13–15 Kellett St, Kings Cross), Bayswater Brasserie (32 Bayswater Road, Kings Cross) and Nelson's Brasserie upstairs at the recently renovated Lord Nelson Hotel, Sydney's oldest, at the corner of Kent and Argyle Sts in The Rocks. You would expect to pay around $7 for a starter, $18 for a main course and $7 for a sweet at any of these places. Most have well chosen and fairly expensive wine lists.

For a most unusual variation on the theme of Australian cuisine, you could try Rowntrees Australian Restaurant (188 Pacific Highway, Hornsby) which incorporates Aboriginal and bush ingredients (including witchetty grubs) into its original menus; a meal here will cost over $40.

The most famous restaurant in Sydney is remarkable for being unpretentious and not astronomically expensive. Nor is it despised by the locals who willingly queue alongside tourists. Doyles Restaurant on the beach at Watsons Bay specialises in serving unadorned fresh fish; you can travel there by water taxi from Circular Quay or bus 324. A second Doyles on the pier does take bookings. An even more famous venue is the Opera House which has a decent self-serve cafeteria and a not-overcrowded terrace from which the view is unbeatable. Try not to let your attention wander too far, however, in view of the management's policy as stated on their sign: 'No refunds will be given to customers whose meals are taken by seagulls'.

Pub Food. Pub eating in Sydney is more sophisticated than anywhere in Australia, so that you are just as likely to find spiced fish (at the Albury Hotel in Paddington) or spicy fried chicken wings (at the trendy new Pumphouse Brewery Tavern at 17 Little Pier in Darling Harbour) as steak and chips. Most hotels which serve meals tend to separate the two functions, so you will hardly be aware of being in a pub, such as the Nelson Brasserie or the Cove Café mentioned above. The popular Woolloomooloo Bay Hotel at 2 Bourke St serves excellent seafood ($10–12) and filled bagels ($9); it even operates a courtesy bus from the city (ring 9357 1376).

Perhaps the most famous pub restaurant is No Names in the Friend in Hand pub (58 Cowper St, Glebe) which serves plain Italian food at great speed. Eat all the pasta you can for $6. There is another branch at 2 Chapel St, East Sydney where the accompaniments like bread and fruit cordial are free.

Of course there are plenty of places serving standard pub fare, such as the East Sydney Hotel at 111 Cathedral St or the Dolphin Hotel at 412 Crown St in Surry Hills. Even the deluxe hotels may be worth a visit: the Old Sydney Bar of the Sheraton-Wentworth Hotel (61–101 Phillip St) serves fish and chips, curries and roast meals for about $10 and is very popular with downtown workers at lunchtimes. The 5-star Regent at 199 Regent St in The Rocks (Australia's premier 'pub') has ordinary counter meals in the George St Bar as well as serving $15 cream teas to homesick Brits.

Other travellers will probably alert you to pubs which offer real promotional bargains from time to time. Recently for example the Royal Hotel in Randwick was offering steak and unlimited salad meals for an incred-

"NO REFUNDS TO CUSTOMERS WHOSE MEALS ARE EATEN BY SEAGULLS"

ible $3, as was the Bondi Hotel if you were prepared to cook it yourself. Both are listed in the section *Drinking* below.

Ethnic Restaurants. If you have been travelling around Australia long enough to have grown tired of steaks, the range of authentic ethnic cuisines at which Sydney excels may hold more appeal than the pubs.

Although Sydney's Chinatown might lack the colour and bustle of Hong Kong or even San Francisco, the streets around Dixon and Hay, where many Chinese people gather to shop and dine, are lined with good Chinese restaurants many with book-length menus. You can choose between the proletarian style of Chinese diners like Dixon Foods (41 Dixon St) where a whole barbecued duck costs less than $10 to China Sea at 94 Hay St where a single serving of duck with plum sauce costs about the same. On average a main dish will cost $8.50 — with fish dishes costing a little more — and a bowl of soup $5. Don't miss the Chinatown Centre at 25 Dixon St with its underground supermarket of exotica, a series of food stalls all serving their own specialities and a huge upstairs restaurant called Chinatown Garden which serves yum cha (the Australian equivalent of dim sum) daily and is usually packed out. Outside Chinatown try the Lantern Family Restaurant at 515 Kent St where a Chinese all-you-can-eat smorgasbord costs a mere $6. The food at the Mekong Restaurant (711a George St) is better and even cheaper.

Asian cuisines are also superbly represented in Sydney. After many years of lagging behind the others, Indian cuisine has finally taken off in Sydney and a number of excellent new restaurants have opened which put the basic British curry restaurant to shame. One of the best remains the informal Curry Bazaar across the Bridge in Crows Nest (334 Pacific Highway), a suburb with a surprisingly high concentration of good ethnic restaurants. (If you're too lazy to travel there, they'll deliver within a reasonable range; ring 9438 2966). The best Indian restaurant in Glebe is the Flavour of India on the corner of Bridge Road and Glebe Point Road. If you want to have a choice of a dozen or so Vietnamese restaurants in one area, you will have to take the train to the distant anti-yuppie suburb of Cabramatta where you can eat interesting noodle dishes all costing less than $6 at Far East (11/117 Hill St) or Buddhist vegetarian food at An Lac (94b John St); both restaurants are dry. Otherwise try Chu Bay (312A Bourke St, Darlinghurst) or Kim-Van (147 Glebe Point Road, Glebe); both are BYO.

The choice of other East Asian cuisines is also bountiful. Indonesian and Thai cuisine are both at the forefront of Sydney trends so try Effa's Indonesian at 453 Parramatta Road in Leichhardt (with very good satay) or the Thai Silverspoon at 203 Oxford St in Darlinghurst. Thai food has even penetrated to unfashionable suburbs such as Erskineville where Prasit's Imperial Thai (above a pub at 35 Erskineville Road) has excellent first courses for $6 and main courses for under $10. Unusual combinations of cuisines engender interesting restaurants such as the Mosquito Bar (Shop 5, Lane M13, 142 Spit Road, Mosman) which features Sri Lankan and African cuisine, and Rengaya (22 Glebe Point Road) which is a Japanese curry house.

Lebanese food is less trendy and in many places the prices are rock bottom. The best plan is to go to the corner of Elizabeth and Cleveland Sts in Surry Hills, a comparatively unprepossessing area were it not for the choice of excellent value Lebanese restaurants within 50m of the junction. These include Emads at 298 Cleveland St and Abdul's at 563 Elizabeth St, where a set meal of six main dishes plus a few side dishes will cost about $13. These are great places to go with a group of friends.

European cuisines are just as well represented as Eastern ones and are almost as cheap. Even good Italian restaurants in prime downtown locations such as

Rossini at Circular Quay (between Wharves 5 and 6) serve delicious bowls of pasta for $7. Other recommended Italian restaurants are Forbes (155 Forbes St, Woolloomooloo) which is understandably crowded since it offers three-course meals for $10, Piccola Italia (481 Crown St, Surry Hills), John's Pizzas (199 Bondi Road) where no pizza costs more than $10 and Sorrentino (266 Darling St, Balmain) which has an appealing blackboard menu.

The selection of Greek restaurants in Sydney is not as great as it is in Melbourne, however Diethnes at 336 Pitt St in the City has an inexpensive range of classic Greek dishes as well as Retsina. At the time of writing they had a special offer of meal (main course, dessert and coffee or wine) plus a ticket to a film at the Greater Union Cinema at 525 George St for $21.

Snacks. Since your finances are unlikely to allow constant eating out, you will have to rely on snacks, fast food and picnics to some extent. Sydney has a number of food halls, for example the massive international Food Hall at Darling Harbour which sells everything from soul to kosher food. If in Manly visit the food hall above the amusement arcade in the Manly Wharf Complex, a brand new mini-Darling Harbour. Try also the basement of the MLC Building where a variety of ethnic dishes plus superb fruit salads are on offer all served in convenient take-away containers for outdoor consumption. Similarly in Australia Square downtown and at Tower Square just off Miller St in North Sydney, you can choose a different dish from neighbouring kiosks before sitting at communal tables. Downtown there are numerous sandwich bars and doner kebab stalls where you should be able to find something appetising to munch during a lunchtime concert in Martin Place.

If you find yourself rebelling against all the nouveau and imaginative food around you, buy a meat pie and sachet of tomato sauce down at one of the milkbars at Circular Quay and watch the ferries and the buskers come and go. Pie carts also purvey hot dogs and mushy peas for between $1 and $3. The most famous pies in Sydney are available from Harry's Café de Wheels a pie cart parked in the Woolloomooloo Docks (immortalised in a Billy Joel song). If you're too hard up even to buy a pie, you can give blood at the clinic at number 153 Clarence St in the city and get a free lunch.

Sydney must have some of the most elegant branches of McDonalds anywhere, for example the tasteful Victorian conversion in North Sydney or the hi-tech branch built into the Entertainment Centre. The one in Kings Cross stays open 24 hours a day. Less predictable fast food may be found in the form of burgers with unusual toppings at the Green Park Diner, 219 Oxford St, Darlinghurst.

Pastry and coffee shops abound, many of which will be open when you emerge after a play or film. Try the cappuccinos and ice cream at Caffé Troppo at 175 Glebe Point Road and on the same road (at number 144a) the wonderful sweets at the Pudding Shop which, despite its name, also serves savoury snacks as well. Another place with a misleading name is the Gelato Bar at 140 Campbell Parade in Bondi Beach which is not an ice cream emporium but a Hungarian pastry shop.

The beach suburbs are well supplied with takeaway places; try the excellent fish and chips for sale at Manly or Bondi. Zio Nino's is a humble Bondi café with wonderful scampi.

DRINKING

Despite claims that Sydneysiders are becoming less enthusiastic drinkers as a result of the new health-consciousness and the 'booze buses', few could complain about the density of hotels in Sydney. Furthermore many of these hotels have character, such as the comfortable old hotels in the beach suburbs and the attractively renovated Victorian pubs in Paddington and elsewhere. A great many hotels have live music (see *Entertainment*) and some have happy hours as well, usually from 5pm; at a really good one you can get middies (10oz) of beer for 80c and schooners (15oz) for $1. In an attempt to go upmarket many hotels now offer special deals to attract 'ladies' into what was once a male domain.

Most hotels are licensed from 11am to 11pm in summer and 10am–10pm in winter, with a few staying open until midnight or beyond on Fridays and Saturdays especially in tourist areas, and a few others having a 6.30am–6.30pm licence to serve the market trade. Hours are restricted on Sundays to noon to 10pm. Cocktail bars and discos of course stay open much later than hotels, and Kings Cross is full of them.

The most popular sizes of beer glass in New South Wales are the 10oz/285ml 'middy' and the 15oz/425ml 'schooner'. Otherwise you may ask for a 'pint' (20oz/585ml) or a 'seven' (200ml) or even a 'lady's waist' which is New South Wales slang for a 5oz glass. The two New South Wales breweries which traditionally vied for Sydney's custom had very similar names — Tooth's and Tooheys. Although these have both been taken over by huge conglomerates (Carlton and Swan respectively) they continue to use the same names for the same brews such as KB lager (which stands for Kent Brewery) and the highly recommended Toohey's Old (called Hunter Old when packaged). The most popular take-home beers in Sydney are probably Toohey's Draught and the ubiquitous Fosters. Try Reschs (in cans or on tap) which is slightly more bitter than the average Australian drop.

Sydney's luxury hotels are surprisingly popular drinking holes for ordinary people. Try the ornately fitted-out Marble Bar in the Hilton at 259 Pitt St which is one of four bars in the hotel. The management even publish a guide to the various happy hours which can be followed in a circuit to provide half price drinking from 5–9pm Monday to Saturday. Meanwhile the Terrace Bar at the Sheraton in Potts Point (40 Macleay St) has a relatively late weekend happy hour of 9–10pm and gives free Champagne to women on Thursdays.

There are a few boutique breweries in Sydney including the Pumphouse Brewery in the Darling Harbour complex (Little Pier St) which can be visited between 11am and 2pm (no free samples) and the Lord Nelson in The Rocks brews its own for on-the-spot consumption. The Hahn Brewery in Camperdown has been in business for about five years and its brews are very popular. Draft Guinness is more widely available than it used to be with homesick Celts seeking out places like the Mercantile in The Rocks (the travellers' favourite hotel in The Rocks) and the Henry the 9th bar of the Hilton which has the Irish Drovers as its resident band. The British Lion at 182 St Johns Road in Glebe is popular among beer enthuasiasts since it has 13 varieties on tap and 115 kinds of bottled beer as well as good food. Not far away on St Johns Rd is the friendly Nags Head. The Rose and Crown on Glenmore Avenue off Oxford St in Paddington carries British beers and is normally not as packed to the gills as other English-clones. Bondi is a favourite night-out destination at weekends: from the Cock and Bull where beer is served in pints and there is a good disco, good atmosphere and sing-alongs, people migrate to the Bondi Hotel which stays open 24 hours. As each of the four bars and a disco closes, hangers-on move to the next one.

If you are particular about the architecture when you go drinking, try the National Trust-listed Rag and Famish (at 199 Miller Road, North Sydney), the Royal Hotel in Randwick (corner of Cuthill St and Perouse Road) and the Bellevue in Paddington (at 159 Hargrave St), all of which serve excellent food as well as being in attractive buildings. One of Sydney's most famous gay pubs, the Albury Hotel at 6 Oxford St, Paddington, also serves good food (in huge quantities) in its upstairs restaurant called Hog Heaven. There is no shortage of atmosphere at the many old hotels in The Rocks, such as the Hero of Waterloo, the Orient or the Fortune of War, all of which tend to fill up inside but you can usually find a spot on the pavement or in the beer garden if they have one.

If the gardens in The Rocks are too cramped for you, cross the bridge or take a ferry to Neutral Bay and have a drink in the spacious garden of the Oaks (118 Military Road). On a different Military Road in the beach suburb of Watsons Bay the hotel next to Doyles has a picturesque outdoor drinking area. Away from The Rocks, there are few decent pubs in the city centre. Two busy friendly and reasonably priced places are Jacksons on George St opposite the Regent Hotel and the George St Bar in the Regent itself. Two very popular hotels in areas where you might find yourself are the Harold Park Hotel in Glebe (115 Wigram Road) and the Woolloomooloo Bay Hotel at 2 Bourke St which is right on the waterfront. If you are looking for a typical and unpretentious drink, call into any neighbourhood hotel.

For stocking up before eating at a BYO restaurant, visit one of the discount wine stores such as Liquorland which can be found downtown as well as in suburban shopping plazas. There is even an Oddbins at 110 Brougham St in Kings Cross. Wines are usually organised according to state of origin, so if you want to sample the local wines, head for the Hunter Valley shelves. Wine tastings at the Australian Wine Centre in The Rocks are widely publicised but don't seem to be readily available to visitors who are not in the market for cases of premium Australian wines.

For a restful drink to accompany the harbour view, invest in an only slightly over-priced glass of wine or can of Fosters on the Opera House terrace. These are guaranteed not to interest the seagulls.

Walking. For the first day or so, you will probably confine yourself to the harbour area, many of the attractions of which are within easy and pleasant walking distance of one another. Although Sydney is crowded by Australian standards, most of its streets will seem blissfully spacious to anyone who has lived in London. One of the best routes with which to begin is to walk from the picturesque El Alamein Fountain in Kings Cross along the harbour all the way to The Rocks via Potts Point, Woolloomooloo Bay, Mrs Macquarie's Point, through the Botanic Gardens to the Opera House and along Circular Quay, a distance of about 5km. The walk between the Bridge and the Opera House along a four-million-brick promenade is full of street-life and entertainment, and plaques along the walkway quote literary extracts pertaining to Sydney.

But even without this ready-made scenic route along the waterfront, it is possible to enjoy walking around the city. For example, you can walk from Central Station to the Opera House (a distance of about 3km) almost entirely through parks. This route will not appeal to shoppers who will prefer to walk along George St, a busy shopping thoroughfare, which is so crowded with pedestrians that in a few places the authorities have painted lanes on the pavements. It is also about a half-hour walk from Glebe to Darling Harbour.

Buildings and Venues. Whereas in New York you admire the buildings from the water, in Sydney it is the other way round. The city's skyline is not its strong point, especially as it is increasingly dominated by anonymous tower blocks and the cranes involved in all manner of construction projects. Walking around central Sydney it is hard not to be struck by the extent to which old buildings — and sometimes entire blocks — are being torn down to be replaced by new developments, usually offices and shopping centres. While all this concrete and glass undoubtedly gives the city a dynamic, modern (or post-modern) feel, it also ensures that downtown Sydney is losing much of its historic character.

Nowhere has the redevelopment been more total than at Darling Harbour, which most people want to see even if they can't bring themselves to love it. It is still extremely popular with the locals, and is certainly worth a walk round, even if only to decide what you think of it. Many find the overall effect rather superficial and tacky. The Harbour includes hotels, restaurants, shops, parks, pedestrian areas and monorail stations, all densely packed around the water's edge.

Sydney's arts centre is the famous Opera House. This ingenious and beautiful building is often described as a symbol of modern Australia, although it was designed by a Dane (just as the Harbour Bridge of which Sydney is so proud was built by a firm from Newcastle in England). It is also sometimes referred to locally as the Nun's Scrum. Unfortunately when you get up close to the building the first thing that strikes you is that it looks as if it's falling apart; although less than 20 years old, the timbers have suffered badly in the drenching sunlight and the building is in urgent need of repairs, which are expected to cost not much less than the original construction.

The Opera House contains four theatres, which feature opera, drama, concerts, dance and ballet. Unfortunately the acoustics are widely regarded as poor, and various (largely unsuccessful) attempts have been made to improve them since it opened. There is also a large performing arts library and three restaurants: the fancy Bennelong, the brasserie-style Forecourt, and the Harbour, which has a cafeteria-style take-away section. Note that the whole complex is now non-smoking apart from some designated areas in the restaurants. Hour-long guided tours are available for $8 daily between 9am and 4pm from the Lower Forecourt; special $12 tours take place on Sundays and include backstage.

Especially on a clear day, few visitors can resist joining the queues at the 305m-high Sydney Tower and paying $6 to take in the view, which is indisputably excellent, though the development has a self-congratulatory American-style big-business atmosphere that does not perhaps show Sydney at its most original. Although the tower can be easily spotted from a distance, it is possible to lose track of it at close range among the other skyscrapers, so head for the corner of Market and Pitt Sts, enter the shopping centre and follow signs to the lifts. The Observation level is open 9.30am to 9.30pm (on Saturdays to 11.30pm).

The Rocks. There are other eminences from which to enjoy a view. For example, you can pay $1 to climb the 200 steps inside the southern

"PEDESTRIAN LANES HAVE BEEN INTRODUCED IN PARTS OF SYDNEY"

tower of the Harbour Bridge (open daily). The tower is located at the northern extremity of The Rocks, an area full of buildings of historic interest. The best plan for exploring The Rocks is to go to the Visitors Centre at 106 George St (9255 1788) and pick up the leaflet on self-guided walking tours. This will direct you to one of Sydney's oldest buildings, Cadman's Cottage, which was built in 1816, the old Police Station (now a craft centre), some old restored pubs, and so on. Nearby Susannah Place is a small terrace of houses from 1844, including a corner shop set up in the style of 1910–1920. It is open Saturday and Sunday, 10am–5pm (9241 1893). The glitzy Story of Sydney at 100 George St is a high-tech multi-media entertainment that dramatises the history of the city from the arrival of the convicts to the present day. The entrance fee is $10.

The Rocks may not be to everyone's taste (for example, the satirical writer Howard Jacobson says you go to The Rocks 'for tourist gewgaws, opals, Ken Done tea towels, duty-free electronics and Devonshire teas') but it is undeniably pleasant and interesting to spend an afternoon there.

Museums and Galleries. One of Sydney's most striking buildings is the Power-house Museum (9217 0111), which opened at 500 Harris St (near Darling Harbour) for the Bicentennial celebrations. The Powerhouse combines a science centre with displays on decorative arts and social history; admission is $5 and the hours are 10am–5pm daily. There are plenty of hands-on gadgets for kids (and plenty of kids). Although there is a wealth of material here, it is confusingly organised and can seem more of a mish-mash than a coherent collection. Stage One is another vast space nearby to which some exhibitions are moved from the Powerhouse.

The Australian Museum on College St (along the east side of Hyde Park) is among Australia's best museums and specialises in natural history. It has regular high-profile (and very popular) exhibitions, and its Aboriginal displays are especially recommended. The Museum is open daily 10am–5pm, with free admission (9339 8111). There are also some Aboriginal exhibits at the Art Gallery of New South Wales (9225 1744; same opening times) in the Domain, along with representative paintings of some of Australia's foremost artists and frequent touring exhibitions; one of the most recent was a blockbuster Renoir show that drew huge crowds. The Museum of Contemporary Art on Circular Quay West (9252 4033) is an innovative centre that is well worth a visit for anyone interested in modern art; it also has a good bookshop. One of its most recent exhibitions was an interactive extravaganza on animation that was named simply *Kaboom!*

Sydney also has some other good specialist museums and exhibitions. These include the small collection of ancient artefacts in the Nicholson Museum at Sydney University; the Environment Centre at 39 George St; the National Maritime Museum in Darling Harbour; and the renovated Earth Exchange in The Rocks, which is especially recommended for people planning to visit New Zealand, as there is an exhibit that simulates an earthquake and a volcanic eruption.

The National Trust has its headquarters on Observatory Hill in Millers Point, housed in an early 19th century military hospital. It publishes a selection of leaflets on Sydney's historic buildings. The Historic Houses Trust of New South Wales manages a number of fascinating buildings that provide glimpses into Australia's history. Vaucluse House (Wentworth Road, Vaucluse; 9388 7922) was the home of William Charles Wentworth, the 'father' of the Australian Constitution. It is open Tuesday to Sunday from 10am to 4.30pm; admission is $2. Bus 325 will take you there from Circular Quay. Elizabeth Bay House (7 Onslow Avenue, Elizabeth Bay; 9356 3022) is another beautiful house from the colonial era, although its once-extensive grounds have been gobbled up by suburban sprawl since its heyday in the mid-1800s. It has the same opening times as Vaucluse House; take the Sydney Explorer Bus or bus 311 from Circular Quay.

Parks and Zoos. The beautifully maintained Royal Botanic Gardens (9231 8125) are so centrally located that you can't help but find yourself strolling through them at some point. Open daily from 8am to sunset, they feature palm groves, a cactus collection, huge Moreton Bay fig trees and temporary exhibits on topics as various as Japanese grasses and rainforest flora. There is also a pair of glasshouses known as the Tropical Centre (10am–4pm daily; entrance $5), which are certainly worth a look.

There are pleasant parks dotted all over Sydney. Some are in unlikely places, such as the delightful park in Potts Point that is on top of an appalling multi-storey car park. Just one of the many harbourside parks that few people go to is the amphitheatre-shaped park at Blues Point on the North Shore, which affords as good a view of the harbour as any and, like so many of the city's parks, is a great place for a picnic.

Taronga Zoo on the North Shore (9969 2777) is an easy place to be introduced to some of Australia's native wildlife. Colourful native parrots and kookaburras fly overhead wild. There is a koala park (where the koalas seem to be a little more lively than at other zoos), kangaroos, and so on, as well as gorillas, tigers and elephants, whose enclosure is said to be on one of the most valuable pieces of real estate in the city. Unfortunately, though, years of monotony seem to have had their toll on the elephants, who look rather sad. There are regular shows and feeding sessions involving various animals throughout the day; check times at the entrance. It is nice to see that animals formerly kept in what closely resembled prison cells now have bright, spacious living quarters; the lifestyle of the orang-utans, for example, has dramatically improved following sponsorship by a well known chain of hamburger restaurants. Admission to the Zoo is $12.50 (less $2 if you show your YHA card). An inclusive ticket including the return ferry and a shuttle bus to the entrance (a short distance but up a steep hill) can be bought at Circular Quay for $14.

Another popular attraction featuring wildlife is the Sydney Aquarium in Darling Harbour (9262 2300) in which sharks and other legendary Australian sea creatures swim around in an enclosure while awe-struck visitors watch from underwater tunnels. The effect can be amazing, and having a shark swim directly over you as it shreds a hapless fish to bits with its teeth is an electrifying experience. The Aquarium also features less dramatic but nonethless interesting collections of other marine animals. Admission is $12.50 and opening hours are from 9.30am to 9pm daily. Manly Oceanarium (9949 2644) on West Esplanade in Manly is not dissimilar and costs $10 ($7 with special backpackers' coupon).

The interesting Sydney Observatory on Watson Road in Millers Point is primarily a museum of astronomy but is sometimes open to the public for star-gazing sessions. Ring 9241 2478 for information.

Beaches. Not only are there miles and miles of ocean beaches, but there are beaches along the harbour as well and these are less affected by the pollution which has scandalised Sydney in recent years. Daily Beachwatch reports are published in the *Sydney Morning Herald* and might typically report the where-abouts of 'sewage grease', 'stormwater rubbish' or 'algal froth'. The famous swimmer Dawn Fraser was recently quoted as saying that she was considering refusing to swim in the ocean pool named after her in Balmain for this reason. (Many beaches have sea water swimming pools on the high tide line.) But the authorities are working very hard to cure this problem. They have spent $350 million on cleaning up Bondi and these days you are much less likely to see a 'Bondi cigar' (floating faeces).

Compared to British beaches, Sydney's beaches and the quality of water will seem pristine, even on beaches where warnings are posted. Few residents and fewer visitors are put off by the situation and continue to enjoy choosing from one of Sydney's 70 beaches. You can choose famous crowded beaches like Manly or Bondi or virtually empty ones, for example some of the northern beaches like Shelley Beach. If you prefer to visit a beach full of typical bronzed Australians flaunting their bodies, try Camp Cove near Watsons Bay. Parsley Bay and Neilson Park are also recommended on the south side of the harbour. These beaches are accessible from bus routes 324/5.

At the main beaches there is no need to worry about sharks, since the marine authorities have strung an underwater net which stretches 80km along the coast to prevent sharks from coming in to shore. Unfortunately harmless creatures such as sea turtles become entangled, and so the nets are patrolled daily and rescues carried out where necessary. But nets cannot protect swimmers from other dangers such as rips; there is a particularly dangerous one at Rilgola, 36km north of the city. Always be sure to swim between the flags.

Fame has not spoiled Bondi Beach. Its pleasing curve of perfect sand with a backdrop of painted wooden houses covering the surrounding green hillsides is scenically at its best on a clear winter's day. Dodging all the body-surfers can be tiresome on a summer weekend, but that is when it is fun to watch the surfies and their admirers. There are plenty of cafés, gelaterias and pubs to choose from for your post-beach refreshments. Bondi has a perpetual carnival atmosphere. There is an easy and delightful coastal walk south from Bondi to Bronte, though you'll have to dodge the power walkers (who have replaced joggers). To get to Bondi Beach by public transport take bus 380, 382 or 389 either from Circular Quay or from the train station at Bondi Junction.

The next beach along is Tamarama (usually called Glamarama) which is also pleasant, but Coogee Beach a kilometre or so further south is extremely congenial, despite its unpromising Aboriginal meaning of 'stinking fish'. Take bus 372/3/4.

After Bondi, the most famous beach is Manly, whose motto is 'Seven Miles from Sydney and a Thousand Miles from Care'. Riding the ferry is far more carefree than taking the long road round, though this will mean you'll miss the sign directing you to the 'Manly Women's Rowing Club'. Manly Beach is a classic city beach, crowded with sun lovers, surfers, families and life-savers. It is lined with Norfolk pines and excellent fish and chip shops (as well as plenty of more ambitious eateries).

In recent years new legislation has been proposed to make nude bathing illegal in New South Wales. Pending the outcome, there are several official nude beaches though the city fathers have chosen ones that are difficult to get at. Try Obelisk Bay and Reef Beach on the north shore or Lady Bay past Watsons Bay, which is a mostly male preserve.

If the pollution report is too discouraging, head for the open-air swimming pool at Victoria Park on the Parramatta Road across from the end of Glebe Point Road; admission is $2. The pool is open only October to April due to the lower tolerance of Australians to cold temperatures. If you have proof of being a university student at home, you can ask to swim at the University of Sydney's heated pool.

SHOPPING

The basic shopping hours in Sydney are from 9am to 5.30pm, Monday–Friday, with some shops opening on Saturday till noon or 4pm. Late-night shopping is available on Thursday till 9pm and on Fridays till 7pm. The Harbourside shopping complex at Darling Harbour is open 10am–9pm Monday to Saturday and 10am–6pm on Sundays. The Queen Victoria Building (described below) is also open on Sundays, as are a few of the 80 speciality shops in the tourist-zone of The Rocks.

Downtown Sydney is packed full of swanky shopping centres and arcades, such as the Strand Arcade between George and Pitt Sts, which comes complete with wrought-iron balconies and catwalks, and the Centrepoint Shopping Complex. But the prize for elegant downtown shopping must go to the restored Queen Victoria Building at the corner of Market and George Sts, which was built in 1893 as a produce market. The building is usually referred to simply as the QVB. It looks like a giant department store from the outside, but inside are several levels of shops and cafés linked by ornate staircases and footbridges — the overall effect is similar to that of the famous GUM store in Moscow. Many of the 193 shops and boutiques will be familiar to British visitors, such as The Body Shop and Monsoon.

The largest department stores in Sydney are Grace Brothers (near the Town Hall Station) and David Jones (near St James Station), both connected to the Centrepoint Complex by underground passages. If you want to shop in ultra-glamorous surroundings, go out to Double Bay, where many Jews from central Europe have settled; the atmosphere is somewhat reminscent of New York's Fifth Avenue or Bond St in London.

At the other extreme there is the Salvation Army Warehouse ('Salvos'), which is one of the biggest, best-stocked charity shops ('op shop') in the world. It is on Bellevue St in St Peters; take bus 422. This is the place to buy your 'black and whites' for that unexpected waiting job, the old clothes for a farm job or furniture for an unfurnished flat (they even deliver).

Otherwise try Vincent de Paul charity shops, which are everywhere, or the jumble sales on Thursday and Friday mornings at the Hornsby Salvation Army Centre (corner of Hunter and Burdett Sts). There are also plenty of discount stores along the unfashionable parts of George St between the pinball arcades and the taco joints. Smokers should pay a visit to Sol Levy ('Tobacconist Extraordinaire') at 713 George St, just down from Central Station, to see the largest range of pipes, Zippo lighters and smokers' accessories in Australia.

Serious shoppers might like to browse (though not necessarily purchase) *The Bargain Shopper's Guide to Sydney* (published by the same publisher as *Cheap Eats in Sydney*) at $6.95. Also check the 'Browsing and Buying' section of the Friday *Sydney Morning Herald* for information on sales of everything from roses to antiques.

Over 100 shops in Sydney offer discounts to YHA members, and these can provide significant savings on the cost of travel, tours, museums, restaurants, car rental, and outdoor and leisure equipment. Pick up the YHA discounts leaflet from any of their hostels. Second-hand equipment can be picked up at army disposal stores.

Duty Free. Duty-free stores proliferate in downtown Sydney, all offering similar ranges of goods (cameras, opals, perfume, etc.) at similar prices. These are much cheaper than duty-free shops in Britain and North America, but are not necessarily cheaper than those in Hong Kong and Singapore. Anyone with an outgoing ticket can buy duty-free goods 10 days or less before departure, to a maximum value of $400. It makes sense to use the downtown shops, as these are much cheaper than the one at the airport; for some items, such as film, the difference can be as much as 30%.

If you are in the market for opals and are planning to travel in an opal-mining area (such as Lightning Ridge in northern New South Wales — see *Further Afield*), then it is better to buy on location, and cut out the middlemen. But if you aren't, there are plenty of shops in Sydney desperate to give you a lesson in the kinds of opal available.

Souvenirs. In Sydney there is no escaping the full range of Australiana gifts and souvenirs, and after a morning of browsing in The Rocks, you may never want to see another stuffed koala or plastic boomerang again. Australian Craftworks, housed in a former police station at 127 George St, is worth visiting even if you don't intend to buy, in order to see a large range of good-quality handicrafts from all over the country. At the Sidewalk Gallery in The Rocks you can see craftsmen and women at work on Sundays. Most downtown shopping complexes have at least one shop specialising in Australian-made handicrafts, everything from designer mohair jumpers to handprinted greeting cards. Typical of the genre are the five branches of Everything Australian, including one near the Strand Arcade. Away from the town try the new Manly Wharf shopping centre or the shop Shark Attack on Manly's Corso, which specialises in bizarre T-shirts.

Aboriginal handicrafts may be viewed (and purchased) at a number of outlets, including:

Dreamtime Aboriginal Art Centre, Level One, Argyle Centre, Playfair St, The Rocks (also on Walker Lane, Paddington);
Bush Church Aid Society, 135 Bathurst St;
Aboriginal Artists Galleries, 477 Kent St, behind the Town Hall (9261 2929) and in the Opera House (Upper Concourse).

There is a good shop above Dymocks Bookstore on George St that sells interesting and reasonably priced crafts from Papua New Guinea.

Books. If Pitjanjatjara bark paintings, hand-printed silk shirts and hand-turned Tasmanian pine bowls are out of your price range, you might prefer to shop for souvenirs in one of Sydney's hundreds of bookshops. One of the most interesting and accessible is the Australia's Heritage Bookshop at 39 Argyle St in The Rocks, which is the retail outlet for the Library of Australian History at 17 Mitchell St. The Heritage Bookshop carries a range of guides, books and maps relating to Australia, as well as a good selection of postcards and greeting cards. Another bookshop specialising in Australiana is Grahame's Australian Bookshop between Pitt and George Sts. The State Government's map shop is at 33 Bridge St.

Dymocks at 424 George St is the largest bookstore in Sydney and has an excellent travel section. You might be unnerved, however, by the assistants' habit of approaching customers and asking them what they're looking for, which doesn't exactly lend itself to casual browsing. The specialist Travel Bookshop (9241 3554) can be found at 20 Bridge St and also in the Old Scots Church (dating from 1824) at 1 Jamison St, on the corner of York St; it offers a 10% discount to YHA members.

An interesting places to browse (as well as stop for a cup of coffee) is the New Edition Tea Rooms at 328 Oxford St in Paddington. Gleebooks at 191 Glebe Point Road is a good source of second-hand books and will also buy your unwanted books; it sells cards and calendars too, as well as being a good source of information about what's going on in the neighbourhood. Many other second-hand book and record shops are clustered around the junction of Goulburn and Pitt Sts; one of the most popular is Ashwoods (376 Pitt St). Try also the Sydney Book Exchange at 16 Goulburn St.

Markets. Among the excellent markets in Sydney, the two you should try not to miss are the Paddington Market on Saturdays and Paddy's Market in Haymarket (between Chinatown and the University of Technology) on Saturdays and Sundays. Paddy's is where you go for cheap and cheerful goods of all kinds as well as a fantastic choice of fruit and vegetables, while Paddington Market, which is held in the grounds of the Uniting Village Church on the corner of Newcombe and Oxford Sts, is more trendy and expensive. It is a colourful affair where Sydney's counter-culture tends to congregate to buy old jewellery, rag rugs, screen-printed clothes and leather goods.

There are also many other interesting markets, such as the craft market in Balmain on Saturdays; take bus 433 from Circular Quay to get there. The Saturday market in Glebe — in the schoolyard at the beginning of the Glebe Point Road — has become popular as a Sydney equivalent of Camden Market in London. As well as lots of interesting bric-a-brac (at much cheaper prices than at Paddington), there are also lots of stalls with crafts, new and second-hand clothes, food and music. The Kings Cross Arts and Crafts Market is held on Sundays near the El Alamein Fountain on MacLeay St. The Kirribilli Market in the lovely harbourside suburb of the same name (5 minutes by ferry from Circular Quay) is held on the last Saturday of the month from 7am. Over 160 stalls offer toys, clothes, handicrafts, exotic foods, homemade chocolates, stained glass and many other interesting items. It is held in the gardens of the Kirribilli Neighbourhood Centre at 16 Fitzroy St.

There is never a dull moment in Sydney. Whether it is one of the surf carnivals outdoors or a jazz concert indoors, whether a trip up the tallest building in Australia or down below the harbour waters in a scuba diving class, there is always something to watch or listen to in Sydney at any time of the year.

One of the best times to visit Sydney is during the Sydney Festival, which starts on New Year's Eve and continues into February. In some ways it resembles a mini-version of the Edinburgh Festival, and there is a 'fringe' of sorts, featuring a range of 'umbrella' shows. There are plenty of free events, such as Opera in the Park and lots of other jazz, folk, rock and classical concerts in the Domain. Arrive early with a picnic and an esky. Although sultry summer evenings are the norm, an alternative 'rain date' (usually a day or two later) is sometimes provided. There is a pronounced carnival atmosphere, especially in Hyde Park where rides, puppets, minstrels, stalls and street theatre amuse visitors.

Even if you miss the Festival, there is usually plenty of free entertainment, from the regular outdoor entertainment on Sunday afternoons in Clocktower Square in The Rocks and at Circular Quay West (normally bands but occasionally dance groups or street theatre) to the Council-sponsored concerts at 12pm and 1pm in the small open-air amphitheatre in Martin Place, outside the MLC Centre skyscraper. Sydney's pale imitation of 'Speaker's Corner' (on Sundays) is in The Domain and sometimes bands accompany 'Art in the Gardens' at the Botanic Gardens.

The *Sydney Morning Herald* is a good source of information on entertainment at any time of the year. Its *Metro* supplement appears each Friday and is essential reading. The YHA distributes a free 'What's on in Sydney'. There is also a fairly comprehensive diary of what's on in the free magazine *TNT for Backpackers*, which is widely available from outlets serving the backpacker/independent traveller community (hostels, travel centres, coach terminals, etc.). The 'Halftix' kiosk in Martin Place sells half-price tickets on the day of performance from 12–6pm (plus service charge). All tickets must be bought in person and with cash.

Also check with the Visitor Information Centre for details of special events, some of which are listed at the end of this chapter. One which is not normally promoted in the official 'Coming Events' list is the Gay Mardi Gras held each February. As befits one of the world's gay epicentres, a colourful, imaginative, outrageous fancy dress parade is followed by a series of parties throughout the city's pubs.

If you're in Sydney at Eastertime, join the throngs of country folk who attend the Royal Easter Show in Paddington, which is a carnival as well as an agricultural fair and a fleamarket. The most popular exhibit is in the District Exhibits Pavilion where five regions compete to display the most lavish fruit and vegetables.

Most mainstream cultural events can be booked through the Ticketek Booking Service, either over the phone with a credit card (9266 4800) or by visiting one of their many outlets. The recorded number for what's on is 11688.

Predictably, entertainments at the Opera House are expensive, though tickets do start at $15 for some concerts (and rise to $110). Be prepared to mingle with Sydney's 'Kangaglam' (the glitterati). The box office number is 9250 7777 (there is a $4 surcharge for all telephone bookings). Tickets may be booked in advance from abroad through any Qantas office or by post through PO Box R239, Royal Exchange, Sydney, NSW 2000.

A less elitist venue is the Sydney Entertainment Centre near Darling Harbour, which seats up to 12,500 people for major-league rock concerts, sporting events (such as wrestling and basketball) and various other spectacles. The bookings number is 9266 4800.

Theatre. The *Herald*'s Friday Metro Guide includes a full-page theatre directory which will point you to half-price previews, pub theatres, outdoor performances and experimental plays as well as the mainstream theatre venues like the Opera House, the Belvoir St Theatre in Surry Hills (9699 3273) and the York Theatre in the Seymour Centre on the corner of Cleveland St and City Road (9692 3511). The Seymour Theatre in Sydney University hosts avant garde dance companies and similar. The Sydney Theatre Company can be seen at their home, the picturesque Wharf Theatre on Pier 4, Hickson Road in Walsh Bay (9250 1777). The Bondi Pavilion is an unusual and attractive venue where plays as well as art exhibitions are put on (9130 7211). The Griffin Theatre at 10 Nimrod St, Kings Cross (9361 3817) occasionally puts on free shows for students, pensioners and the unemployed. The licensed Pilgrim Theatre next to the Pitt St Church at 264 Pitt St sometimes puts on lunchtime performances.

Tickets for most productions in the city cost $20–$30 while fringe theatres charge from $10. Some late-night coffee shops in Darlinghurst double as alternative theatres. For comedy try the Gap (in the Trade Union Club of Surry Hills), the Excelsior at 64 Foveaux St, also in Surry Hills (9211 4945) or the Monday night sessions in Glebe's Harold Park Hotel.

For impromptu theatre you can sit in the gallery of the New South Wales Parliament on Macquarie St next to the Domain when it is in session (9230 2111 for details).

Cinema. The highest concentration of cinemas is along George St near Town Hall. Expect to pay $11 for a ticket except on Tuesdays (and also Mondays in winter) at Hoyts and Village when tickets are half-price. The Stanmore Twin Cinema at 200 Parramatta Road shows all the latest movies for $9.50 ($5.50 on Mondays and Tuesdays). The Academy Twin Cinema in Paddington (3a Oxford St; 9361 4453) and the Valhalla in Glebe Point Road (9660 8050) usually show alternative or cult films. The once-famous experimental cinema called the

New Mandarin on Elizabeth St closed a few years ago and now shows only Chinese films.

Music. The established venues for serious music are the Opera House, the Town Hall (where tickets usually cost $40, $25 for students; 9265 9333) and the Pitt St Uniting Church at 264 Pitt St (9267 3614). The University puts on concerts in the Old Darlington School (9818 1329) which are generally much cheaper, while the Conservatorium of Music in the Botanic Gardens puts on free lunchtime concerts at 1pm on Wednesdays.

The principal rock venue is the Sydney Entertainment Centre though other big concerts are held elsewhere such as at Cronulla's Endeavour Field, otherwise known as Ronson Park. A shuttle bus usually operates from Woolooware station whenever there's a concert. There is a no-alcohol rule at most events and bags will be inspected as you enter.

Sydney has a very lively pub and club circuit. Check free newspapers like *OTS* (On the Street) or *Drum Media*, which can be picked up in most bottle stores. The best areas are Kings Cross (try the Kardomah Café at 22 Bayswater Road, Magnums at 155 Victoria St and Springfields at 15 Springfield Avenue which gives students free admission except Friday and Saturday) and Darlinghurst (for instance the Hard Rock Café at 121 Crown St and the Exchange Hotel at 34 Oxford St). The Observer in The Rocks, the Cat and Fiddle at the corner of Elliot and Darling Sts in Balmain (mainly rhythm and blues) and Sheila's Tavern at 77 Berry St in North Sydney can also usually be relied on to feature good bands. The Woolloomooloo Bay Hotel on Cowper Wharf Road features a popular sixties night on Sundays from 6.30–9.30pm. A surprising number of gigs in Sydney takes place in RSL clubs, which will usually admit non-members, especially those from overseas. It is best to ring ahead to check. Diggers above the RSL Club in Bondi (cheap admission and drinks) is especially recommended while the RSL at 226 Oxford St in Paddington features good local bands. Admission to see live bands is usually between $5 and $10. Meals are often available for $5 which makes a cheap evening out.

Jazz and folk are also well represented at pubs scattered throughout the city. If you want to find out what folk events are forthcoming, contact Folkways Music at 282 Oxford St, Paddington (9361 3980) where you can also buy tickets for some events. If you don't mind the touristy trappings, the Argyle Tavern in The Rocks often has foik bands. Also popular is the Rose, Shamrock and Thistle (known as 'The Three Weeds') in Rozelle.

For jazz, try Round Midnight on Roslyn Avenue in Kings Cross, the Basement at 29 Reibry Place at Circular Quay, the Orient Hotel in the Rocks, Soup Plus Restaurant at 383 George St or the Real Ale Café at 66 King St both in the City or the Unity Hall Hotel on the corner of Beattie and Darling Sts in Balmain. Check the Friday Metro supplement to the *Sydney Morning Herald* which provides exhaustive listings.

Nightlife. Again the back page of the Metro tells you the line-ups at Sydney's nightspots. Among the most popular are Selina's in the Coogee Bay Hotel and the exclusive Cauldron at 207 Darlinghurst Road which has a $12 cover charge and attracts all the beautiful people who come to hear the house music. Many such establishments are open until at least 3am and a few are open till dawn such as the Colosseum in Kings Cross (54 Darlinghurst Road) which has lots of promotional offers such as free entry for women on Wednesdays and half-price drinks till 9pm on Fridays. A few hotels advertise 'bop till you drop' evenings which can mean a closing time of anything from midnight onwards.

The tourist copywriter's description of Kings Cross as 'bohemian' is somewhat euphemistic since it continues to slide even further from the quaintly sleazy to the downright nasty. It is repeatedly at the centre of scandals involving sex and drugs and police corruption, and if you spend much time there you may soon tire of seeing cast-off syringes, sad derelict people and massage parlours. Prostitutes may be seen along William St, usually recognisable by their favourite apparel, swimming costumes, and you will see plenty of red lights along Kellett St and neighbouring streets. Though depressing by day, Kings Cross is still the place to which many turn for their nightlife.

Gambling. New South Wales' first casino is scheduled to open in 1992. The City Casino will be housed in an historic government building on Bridge St in the city. A slightly more downmarket casino will open later at Darling Harbour. Otherwise gamblers will have to make do with poker machines (especially at RSL clubs) and horse races. Residents of New South Wales are among the heaviest gamblers in the world; they spend over $12 million each day on lotteries alone. The TAB agency has nearly 1000 outlets in the state. Their betting shops are usually open from 11am to 6pm.

SPORT

Sydney's successful bid to host the Olympic Games in the year 2000 will inevitably result in sport assuming an increasingly high profile as the event approaches.

Spectator Sports. As elsewhere, horse racing is a major preoccupation in Sydney. There are four courses, viz. Randwick, Rosehill, Canterbury and Warwick Farm. Flat racing usually takes place on Wednesdays and Saturdays, while harness racing events are held at Harold Park, Glebe on Friday evenings. Also in Glebe, the Wentworth Park Trots is not a left-wing political group but another trotting venue.

Anyone who is keen (or merely lukewarm) about cricket should try to visit the Sydney Cricket Ground (SCG) during the season (October to March). The 'Hill', where the riff-raff recline on the grass, is a famous Sydney landmark. The atmosphere is reputed to be a lot tamer since they banned eskies and limited spectators to buying their beer in small, easily spilled styrofoam cups. Beware of the stampede when the giant video screen above the Hill shows replays. Admission is usually about $10 to the Hill, $20 plus to the stands. Take bus 378 from Railway Square or 380 from Circular Quay to Centennial Park.

Rugby League is the favoured version of football in Sydney and is played at various venues including the newly renovated Sydney Sports Ground adjacent to the SCG. There are matches on most Friday and Saturday evenings and Sunday afternoons between April and September. Aussie Rules is not so popular in Sydney as in Melbourne and Adelaide, though the Sydney Swans do their best. The home of Rugby Union is the Concord Oval near the Parramatta Road in the suburb of Concord. It is here that the Grand Final is held in late September. The best place to see soccer is at the new Sydney Football Stadium, home of the predominantly Greek side Sydney Olympic.

Although most visitors go to Sydney's beaches not to observe but to participate, you might try to take in one of the Saturday surf carnivals held at various beaches in the summer, for example the Sun Pentathlon at Fresh Water Beach or the rough water swim in early February at Bondi Beach. These events are uniquely Australian and are threatened with declining interest among young people. Further information is available from the State Centre for Surf Life Saving (9663 4298). Locations of surfing competitions are apt to be chosen at the last minute to take advantage of the best surf conditions.

Participation. If you are intent on keeping fit and want to participate in a sport, contact Sports House (formerly the Hall of Champions museum) at 157 Gloucester St (9241 2311) for courses and centres. Fitness to Perfection in the Westpac Plaza gives a $2 discount to students on a $10 day membership. Classes of all kinds are also available at the YWCA on Wentworth Avenue and at the Sydney University Sports Centre. Gyms that can be used by non-members include the Broadway Gym (160 Broadway; 9211 5068) and the City Gym (107 Crown St; 9360 6247); both are open daily.

If you are in Sydney in August, you might be tempted to join the 25,000 runners who participate in the 14km City to Surf marathon between Hyde Park and Bondi Beach. For more leisurely exercise there are plenty of bushwalks within easy range of the city (see *Great Outdoors* below). There is a North Shore Trail which you might like to follow either north from Manly to Palm Beach (30km) or south along the harbour to Spit Bridge (9km). If you want to join a group, Libby Buhrich (9810 4518) organises bush picnics. Small parties go from Circular Quay to Spit Bridge (via the Blackwattle Bay Fish Market) and then follow the trail past Dobroyd Head (with its Aboriginal rock drawings) and Forty Baskets Bay to Manly.

You can ride a horse through Centennial Park; ring 9332 2770. If you would like to take up scuba diving contact the Fun Dive Centre (225 Stanmore Road, Stanmore; 9569 5588) which conducts free introductory sessions in a pool. If you take to the sport, the fee for an introductory course in the sea is $50.

The Northside Sailing School at Spit Bridge in Mosman (9969 3972) offers introductory sailing courses and also hires out sailboards. If you don't want to do the sailing yourself, they also operate day sailing trips.

THE MEDIA

If you are staying in Sydney long enough to want an occasional evening indoors, buy the Monday *Sydney Morning Herald* which has a media supplement called *The Guide* printed on pink newsprint, carrying complete listings for radio and television for the coming week with previews, reviews and recommendations. Other newspapers include a television guide as a Sunday supplement.

Newspapers. The *Sydney Morning Herald*, which has been recommended throughout this chapter, is an excellent newspaper and has wreaked havoc with the competition in New South Wales. The two prinicipal rivals have merged to form the *Telegraph Mirror* and the sensationalist *Sun* folded. Some cafés and brasseries stock newspapers for the benefit of customers, for example the New Edition Tea Rooms in Paddington (328 Oxford St), though you'll have to arrive early to beat Sydney's celebrities who favour this café-cum-bookstore.

If you want to buy a paper from home go to the World News Centre newsagent in the Harbourside building at Darling Harbour or visit the TNT Skypak office at 33 Pitt St. Naturally the main public library (at 321 Pitt St) stocks a range of foreign papers. The best expatriate paper for Brits is arguably the excellent *Guardian* weekly, which is widely available from newsagents.

Radio. The choice of many listeners is determined by the character of the anchormen who become prima donnas in Sydney. For example John Laws who hosts the morning programme on Sydney's leading talk-back station 2GB (873AM) commands one of the highest salaries in Australia. The second most popular talk station is 2UE on 954AM. 2MMM (105FM) is another top-rating station which plays mainstream rock, pop and heavy metal. The leading adult-oriented rock station is 2DAY on 104FM. One station which disdains the rivalry and has announcers in the Radio 3 mould is 2MBS on 101.5FM, specialising in classical music and run by enthusiastic amateurs.

ABC National Radio broadcasts on 576AM and 92.9FM. Triple J (part of the ABC) plays indie and alternative music and is free of commercials. For solid stereo middle-of-the-road music, try 2CH on 1170AM. At the other extreme 2CBA (103FM) offers only religious devotions. The foreign language station 2EA on 1386 offers programmes in everything from Macedonian to Mandarin.

Television. Sydney viewers have a choice of five channels, including three commercial stations ATN7, TCN9 and Ten. The ABC (called ABN in New South Wales since all stations in the state have call signs ending in N) on Channel 2 and SBS (on channel 28 on the UHF band requiring a special aerial) have the most adventurous programming, but even these offer an overdose of sport at weekends. If you would like to become part of the audience of a television programme, contact Channel 9's Midday Show with Ray Martin (9958 9999), which is recorded live weekdays at the Channel 9 Studios in Willoughby on the North Shore.

Crime and Safety

Sydney has been described as a 'wholesome Manhattan', a huge and energetic metropolis without much crime. This is perhaps a result of the relative absence of poverty and deprivation in much of the city compared with New York, although an hour or so spent wandering around the suburb of Redfern will provide the visitor with a salutary alternative view of what Sydney life can mean. Furthermore New South Wales has a lower crime rate even than the other states of Australia, possibly because it has a higher police-to-population ratio. So there are few areas in which the visitor needs to feel at all anxious. If you are out late at night it is likely to be in a place like Kings Cross where there will be plenty of other pedestrians into the small hours, though you probably wouldn't want to be there by yourself much after midnight. Kings Cross is not of course free of illegal activities — however these are unlikely to affect the visitor unless he or she chooses to get involved. Whereas massage parlours are illegal, brothels aren't, at least on specified streets. Avoid empty train compartments late at night as there is a significant risk of being mugged, especially if you look the part of an out-of-town 'high roller'.

Drugs are used as widely in Sydney as elsewhere in Australia, but possession is against the law. Stiff on-the-spot fines have been proposed for people caught in possession of soft drugs. On-the-spot infringement notices (normally $32) are issued for a number of offences such as riding a skateboard on the road, failing to pay for public transport, littering (especially aimed at refugee smokers from office buildings who invariably drop their butts on the street; Sydney really has smokers on the run) and drinking liquor when it is forbidden at sporting or musical events. It takes just three middies of beer in a short time to put someone over the limit of 0.05%, and the fine for those caught is $1000.

Safety. As has been explained already, the chances of being eaten by a shark are fairly remote, and the blue-ringed octopus is rare. However, both redback and funnel web spiders are commonly found throughout the Sydney area, and these are a genuine cause for concern, even if the statistics are not overly alarming (17 redback deaths in recent years, mostly children, and 13 funnel web deaths in 60 years). These spiders usually live underground, but can occasionally be seen appearing from suburban drain pipes or even in swimming pools. The funnel web has an ugly brown body and evil-looking mandibles. Do not stick your hand into piles of rotting leaves, and be sure to shake out shoes that have been left outside before putting them on. An anti-venom has been developed so if you are bitten seek medical help immediately.

A confrontation with New South Wales' version of the Abominable Snowman, the 8-foot-tall Yowie, is far less likely, though there have been occasional reports of sightings.

The area code for Sydney is 02. For emergency fire, police and ambulance dial 000.

NSW Travel Centre: Countrylink Travel Centre, 11–31 York St (9224 4442; within Australia only: 132 077). Open Monday–Friday 8.30am–5pm. There are branches in only three Australian cities outside the state:

Adelaide: 45 King William St (08-8231 3167).
Brisbane: 40 Queen St (07-3229 8833).
Melbourne: 388 Little Bourke St (03-9670 7461).

The Rocks Visitors Centre: 106 George St (9255 1788). Open 9am–5pm daily.

Tourist Newsfront: 22 Playfair St (9247 7197). Non-government information centre that holds a large number of brochures, and offers advice only about participating tour operators, etc.

Travellers Aid Society: Assembly Platform, Central Station (9211 2275). Open 7am–5pm Monday–Friday and 7am–noon on Saturdays. A charitable organisation that aims to help the travelling public, especially the handicapped or others with special needs.

NRMA: 151 Clarence St (9260 9222).

British Consulate-General: Gold Fields House, 1 Alfred St, Circular Quay (9127 7521).

US Consulate: T & G Tower, corner Elizabeth and Park Sts (9261 9200).

American Express: 388 George St, corner of Pitt St (9239 0666).

Thomas Cook: 175 Pitt St, corner of King St (9234 4000). Currency Exchange Centre in Shop 509, Hyatt Kingsgate Shopping Centre, corner of Darlinghurst and Kings Cross Roads (9356 2211).

Hospitals: Sydney Hospital — 9228 2111. There are now lots of 24-hour emergency medical centres.

Dental Emergency Service: 9332 3092.

Chemist: 9438 3333

General Post Office: Pitt St between King St and Martin Place. Open 8.15am–5.30pm Monday to Friday, 8.30am–noon on Saturdays. The Poste Restante counter is overburdened, so if possible use a suburban post office (all of which offer poste restante services).

Telecom Phone Centre: 100 King St (corner of George St). Open 24 hours.

Overseas Telecommunications Commission (OTC): Phone Room, 231 Elizabeth St.

Helplines: Weather 1196; Rape Crisis 9819 6565; Drug & Alcohol Counselling 9331 2111; Lifeline 9264 2222; Wayside Chapel Crisis Centre in Kings Cross 9358 6577.

Sydney. Sydney seems to be able to absorb a great many working travellers into its employment scene, and there continues to be plenty of work for travellers that want it. Some jobs are advertised in the daily papers, especially the Saturday employment section in the *Sydney Morning Herald*, which has a 'Casual Work' column and a 'Hospitality Industry — Positions Vacant' section. But most people find work by word of mouth (especially in certain key hostels like The Pink House, Carole's Accommodation in Glebe and Coogee Beach Backpackers) and by simply asking in shops, fast-food restaurants and bars. Check all noticeboards regularly. Your chances are better away from the city and Kings Cross; try the North Shore, especially the tourist shops in Manly.

There always seem to be jobs handing out leaflets (which pays $10 an hour, cash-in-hand) though few seem to stick at this for long. Other jobs you may hear of are probably best avoided, such as selling uninspiring prints or pens (on behalf of the Australian Quadraplegic Association) door-to-door. On the other hand, if you are a natural salesperson, you can do well selling roses in restaurants.

Many job-seekers (provided they have working holiday visas) join the crush at City Casuals CES at 10 Quay St, Haymarket (9201 1166). By getting there before 6am (it opens at 6.30am), it is sometimes possible to pick up work gardening, moving furniture, working in a kitchen, making sandwiches, helping with mailouts or carrying out general office work. The minimum pay is usually $10 per hour, and work is normally offered for 1 day only. Other Commonwealth Employment Service addresses are Haymarket CES at 699 George St (9201 1111) and City South CES (13–15 Wentworth Avenue, Surry Hills; 9261 5655).

People with office experience should contact one of the many temping agencies, many of which seem to be hidden away in large office blocks and require some effort to locate. One that makes a concerted effort to encourage backpackers to register is Bligh (9th Floor, 428 George St; 9235 3699), which concentrates on secretarial, accountancy and clerical vacancies. Other recommended agencies are Ecco Personnel (9221 5955) and Forbes Consulting (9252 2344). Remember that smart working clothes will be needed for many office jobs. *TNT for Backpackers* has a section on finding work and many recruitment agencies advertise in its pages. If you have experience in quick data entry, are a nurse, a tradesman or a chef, you should be able to find work immediately. Tradesmen should bring their papers and tools while British nurses should register before leaving home. Anyone with a background in environmental science should do well with the Water Board or other government bodies, as the state is pouring millions into combating pollution.

The best way to find work in Sydney is the direct approach. In a city with literally thousands of restaurants, hotels and stores, vacancies are constantly occurring and being filled before the procedures of advertising or registration at the CES need to be set in motion. In particular, try the usual places like McDonalds and the hotels frequented by foreigners.

Outside Sydney. Plenty of opportunities exist outside the state capital. Some you may find out about in Sydney — for example, the *Herald* carries advertisements for job openings in remote parts of New South Wales. Also, some hostels may be able to put you in touch with farmers in the Sydney area who need assistance.

Fruit-growing areas are dotted around the state. The Hunter Valley is a leading wine-producing area. Asparagus is grown around Dubbo and Cowra, and cherries blossom in the town of Young. Orange, despite its name, is not a citrus town but a soft-fruit and apple centre. Jobs can also be found around Wentworth, near the Murray River in the south-west corner of the state. The towns of Griffith and Leeton are in the successful Murrumbidgee Irrigation Area; peaches and apples are picked in the late summer and autumn while onions are picked throughout the summer. One little-known area for casual work is around WeeWaa on the Queensland border, where travellers have been known to earn $600 a week on the cotton crop. Work is available year-round though the cotton gins are mainly operated in October/November.

Even if the local CES office is discouraging, talk to farmers and publicans about possibilities. Other harvests take place nearer Sydney such as the strawberry harvest in Campbelltown and Glenorie from September to December and the apricot harvest in Kurrajong (on the northern edge of the Blue Mountains) in November. If you get taken on for the peak of the harvest you should be able to save $500 in a fortnight.

Another possibility is to work in some of the state's ski resorts, though competition is stiff. The CES office in Cooma should be able to advise on prospects; alternatively travel straight to Perisher and Thredbo before the season begins in June and ask around.

No other state is so dominated by its capital as New South Wales. Whereas no one goes to Queensland specifically to visit Brisbane or to the Northern Territory to see Darwin, the situation is reversed in New South Wales — everyone wants to see Sydney, and few visitors care much about the rest of the state. Yet there are good arguments for exploring the state further before heading elsewhere. Anyone travelling by rail or coach to another capital city can easily arrange a stopover or two, not only to break those interminable journeys, but to see some of the remarkable scenery and equally remarkable animal and human life that is so different from anything Sydney can offer.

DAY TRIPS FROM SYDNEY

The *Weekend Sydney Map*, available from petrol stations, etc. for a couple of dollars, shows various routes and points of interest and covers the following suggested day trips. Apart from the enjoyable day excursions that can be made to either of the National Parks just north and south of Sydney (see *Great Outdoors*), the best day trip is probably to the Blue Mountains, about 2 hours by road or rail from the city.

The Blue Mountains. This beautiful range gets its name from a blue haze that hangs exquisitely over the hills and valleys. Although it would be pleasing to think that the cause is evaporating eucalyptus oil, in fact it is the same phenomenon as occurs over any expanse of wooded, sun-drenched mountains, such as the Blue Ridge in Virginia. Although the Blue Mountains are really just steep-sided hills, they presented an impenetrable barrier to the early settlers, many of whom believed China was on the other side. Summer temperatures in the Blue Mountains are cooler than in Sydney and so in summer the towns have a bustling yet quaint hill-station atmosphere.

The Blue Mountains are easily accessible by a delightful railway service to Katoomba and beyond, which operates hourly from Central Station. A day return (departing after 9am) costs $10.50, only $2 more than the one-way fare (if you are travelling as a couple enquire about a family ticket, which may work out cheaper). Otherwise join a day tour: the Wonderbus runs a day trip taking in a good selection of the Blue Mountains sights for $48; bookings can be made with a number of Sydney agents, including YHA Travel (9261 1111). Another one to consider is Oz Trek (9369 7055), which has similar day trips for the same price, and also 3-day camping trips for $165, which includes meals and all camping gear.

The main centre for tourists is Katoomba, with fine views over the mountains and valleys of eucalyptus trees. It is possible to descend to the valley floor either by foot on the 1000-step Giant Stairway or by the funicular, which is not recommended for the fainthearted; just watching the bright yellow train descending the seemingly vertical wall and disappearing into the dense bush before arriving at the bottom is sufficient excitement for some, who thereby save the $2 fare. An alternative heart-stopper is the scenic skyway, which costs a little more.

The well appointed Visitor Information Centre at Echo Point in Katoomba (047-396266) is open every day, complete with bird feeders that attract some of the colourful parrots and other tropical birds that favour this mountain habitat. At the Centre you can find out more about the various walking tracks, some of which have been designed around certain themes such as vegetation, geology or the history of mining in the area, with points of interest well signposted. The NSW National Parks and Wildlife Service booklet *Bushwalking in the Katoomba and Leura Area* is recommended. Riding and cycling are also popular; plenty of local outfits will hire you the vehicle of your choice.

Other Blue Mountain towns along the railway line such as Leura and Mount Victoria are also pleasant and picturesque. The Jenolan Caves southwest of Katoomba are worth a visit; you can choose a guided walk in any of eight caves open to the public. The region abounds with tea rooms, craft shops and graciously restored hotels such as the delightful Victoria and Albert Guest House in Mount Victoria. Some are less expensive than they look, especially if you take advantage of off-season mid-week packages.

There is a YHA hostel in Katoomba (66 Waratah St; 047-821416), which has its cheapest beds at $12 and a pleasant, laid-back atmosphere. There are also VIP Backpackers Resorts at 190 Bathurst Road (047-824226) and 31 Lurline St (047-823933); dorm beds start at $10 in both, although the prices vary according to the time of year. The Nomads Gearin's Hotel is part of the Nomads Backpackers chain and is at 273 Great Western Highway (047-826028); dorm beds are $12. All of these hostels offer a range of discounts with local businesses, although the YHA hostel is hard to beat in this respect. There is also a primitive hostel (no hot water, etc.) on the edge of the Blue Mountains National Park at Hawkesbury Heights (047-543056).

The Hawkesbury River. Unlike so many of Australia's rivers, the Hawkesbury runs abundantly year round, debouching into the sea north of Sydney between the Kuringai National Park to the south and the Brisbane Waters National Park to the north. The Pacific Highway provides ready access (though with frequent traffic delays) to these parks. If you want to avoid paying a toll, leave the highway before it turns into a tollway at Berowra; this happens to be the turn-off to the Berowra Waters Inn, widely regarded as the best restaurant in Australia.

The Hawkesbury River is both scenic and ideal for water sports of all kinds. Cruisers may be hired from the bustling little marina at Akuna Bay, though they are very expensive. A more affordable option is to join a cruise such as the one on the old wooden ferry-cum-mail boat that departs Monday to Friday at 9.30am from Brooklyn near the freeway, or on the *MV Bataan*, an ex-World War II navy launch. It is even cheaper to hire a canoe and paddle yourself from Bobbin Head, where the headquarters of Kuringai National Park are situated. The nearby YHA hostel at Pittwater (see *Sydney: Accommodation*) hires out boats and will direct you to the Aboriginal engravings in the Park. One of the highlights of any visit to this area is dining on the fresh fish, and especially on the oysters from the dozens of oyster leases on the river. One final possibility is the Waratah Park Wildlife Reserve; if you were ever a fan of Skippy the Kangaroo, you will be interested to see his home.

NORTH OF SYDNEY

The Hunter Valley. This is Australia's oldest wine-making region. It makes some distinctive wines as well as a range of highly quaffable table plonk. One of the centres is Cessnock, also a mining town, 170km north of Sydney. Most of the wineries that spread up the valley to Muswellbrook (94km from Cessnock) are open to the public for tastings and buying, and often dining as well. Visit the information centre on Wollombi Road in Cessnock (049-904477) to pick up a leaflet on the 'Wine Trail'. One of the most venerable and attractive wineries is Tyrrells near the village of Pokolbin, which has tried to retain its old wooden presses and picturesque vats while keeping the new-fangled stainless steel machinery out of view as much as possible. Another good one is Rothbury Estate, Pokolbin, which has the advantage of being open on Sunday afternoons. Without your own car, you will have to join a tour or hire a bicycle – for example, from the Pokolbin Village, Broke Road, Pokolbin. The nearest hostel is in the old Black Opal Hotel in Cessnock (049-901070). It is worth asking here, at local pubs and at the Cessnock CES about the possibility of picking grapes in February/March.

The North Coast. Travelling along the Pacific Highway is not as enjoyable as it may sound, as the road is often very busy and rarely goes along the coast. Many prefer the inland New England Highway, which passes through rich agricultural country, and the town of Tamworth, the self-proclaimed (and undisputed) Country & Western capital of Australia. But despite the advantages of the New England route, many will not want to miss the coast, as some of the coastal places — such as the Myall Lakes near Forster, Nambucca Heads, Byron Bay and Lennox Head — are real gems and preferable in many ways to the more brassy resorts further north over the Queensland border.

There are a few stretches of coast in northern New South Wales that have been over-developed, such as Port Macquarie (known for its nightlife), Port Stephens near Newcastle (which features Australia's first nudist resort) and Coffs Harbour (which is fun to visit, especially if you have a tractor ride through a banana plantation, admire the giant concrete banana in town and visit the pet porpoise pool). But it is not difficult to find solitude on perfect beaches. Since this is a favourite area for backpackers, there are lots of hostels competing for your business by offering the free use of bicycles or canoes, heated swimming pools, etc.

BYRON BAY

Many thousands of backpackers make this highly popular resort their base for gentle, indulgent relaxation in delightful surroundings. Despite its poetic beauty, the town was not named after Alfred Lord Byron, but after his grandfather Vice-Admiral John Byron. Australia's Land's End (the most easterly point in the country) is close to the town. It also has New South Wales' only north-facing beach, which increases its appeal for sun-worshippers. Despite its popularity, the place has remained more-or-less untarnished by big tourism development, but this could change, so the sooner you can get to visit Byron the better.

Arrival and Departure. Regular buses from both Brisbane and Sydney serve the town, and drop you off on Jonson St, Byron's north–south axis. Greyhound Pioneer Australia charge $71 for Sydney to Byron, and $33 for the journey from Brisbane. Cheaper deals are available with other operators, such as Kirklands; it will pay to shop around.

The alternative is to arrive and leave by train. Byron Bay is connected to Sydney by XPT train, with a fare of around $72 for the 12-hour journey.

Brisbane costs $40. The station is right in the middle of town, next to the Railway Friendly Hotel where you can drink while you wait for the evening departure.

Accommodation. There are a large number of hostels in Byron to cope with the ever increasing numbers of backpackers that flood into the place. As a rule the hostels are weighed under with free bikes, surfboards, boogie boards and all manner of other bonuses, so phone around for the best deal. Pick-ups from the bus stop or train station are other fairly standard freebies, even though they're scarcely necessary in a town of Byron's size.

There are two YHA hostels; one on the corner of Middleton and Byron Sts (066-858788), which has beds from $13, and a new one on the corner of Carlyle and Middleton Sts (freecall 1800-678195), which has similar rates. Of the VIP Backpackers Resorts, Belongil Beach House (Childe St; 066-857868) is one of the best; others are the Arts Factory Lodge (Skinners Shoot Road; 066-857276) and Backpackers Holiday Village (066-858888), which is away from the beach at 116 Jonson St, but closer to the town's amenities.

Eating and Drinking. Prices are high but the quality is excellent at most of the town's restaurants. For breakfast, go to the Beach Café at the top end of Massinger St; your bacon and eggs is served with melon, kiwifruit and grapes. For a vegetarian lunch, try Suppertime Blues just up from the roundabout. The choice for dinner is wide, and includes excellent saté at Patto's (opposite Woolworth) or chilli at Mexican Mick's on Jonson St (corner of Kingsley St). Finish off with dessert at Afters, around the block at Carlyle and Middleton Sts, which serves only cheese, chocolate and coffee. Or go back to enjoy the stars with cappuccino at the Beach Café.

Exploring. You can spend a wonderful day going out to the most easterly point and back. A trail leads around the headland passing Clarkes Beach, the Captain Cook Lookout and Wategos Beach on the way to the easternmost lookout point. On a clear day you can see Surfers Paradise, which is not much of a blessing. With luck you might also see turtles and dolphins in the waves below you. Cape Byron Lighthouse has a postbox with a special 'Most Easterly Point' postmark. Your round-trip also takes in a hang-glider launch pad and the site of the town's first settlement.

The 30km return journey by bicycle from Byron Bay along Seven Mile Beach to Lennox Head is highly recommended; there is a nudist beach *en route* at Broken Head. Better still, hire a horse and explore the lovely hills south of the town, and ride along the seashore. Call 858000 to book a ride.

Help and Information. The Tourist Information Office, next to the Post Office at 69 Jonson St (066-858050), has lots of information about everything from ceramics galleries to whale-watching (June/July and September/October). It opens 9am–4pm from Monday to Saturday.

Lennox Head is a picturesque oceanside village between Byron Bay and Ballina. If anything it is even more of a town for indolent travellers and pleasure-seekers than Byron Bay. As well as trendy restaurants and good surfing at The Point, Lennox Head has excellent fishing. The Beach House Backpackers Hostel is a kilometre from the village centre at 1–3 Ross St (066-877636) and provides free windsurfing lessons.

About 75km inland from Byron Bay is the interesting community of Nimbin, which you may have heard referred to in Sydney in the sneering expression, 'gone to grow muesli in Nimbin'. Hippies and their successors have settled in this lush area on a number of communes to grow organic vegetables and herbs, keep goats, bake bread and practise handicrafts — what they make can be admired and purchased at any number of shops and at the weekend craft markets. The largest commune in Australia at Turntable Falls may be visited. The Nimbin YHA hostel (066-891333) — which has the charming address of Granny's Farm on the Creek — has 40 beds, the cheapest of which are $12.

THE SOUTH COAST

Unlike the Pacific Highway north of Sydney the Princes Highway allows frequent and spectacular views of the south coast. The seaside towns south of Sydney have a less glamorous reputation than those further north. There are so many fine beaches all along the Pacific coast of Australia that it is inevitable that many will be known only to the locals. Places like Austinmer, Bombo and Ulladulla are hardly household names, even in Sydney; and yet these little towns have splendid beaches which in less generously endowed nations would have been turned into prize resorts long ago. Although Bombo's railway station has the distinction of being as close to the sea as it is possible to be, comparatively few people get off the train here. Only the occasional caravan park indicates that holidaymakers have discovered this coast.

Any visitors considering exploring this part of New South Wales should not allow themselves to be put off by the surprise tinged with contempt which Sydneysiders who have never visited properly are bound to express at the idea. Wollongong, the major city on this coast is invariably described as ugly, since it is associated with the enormous steel works at Port Kembla a few kilometres further south. Yet it is an attractive city in a lovely setting between excellent safe surf beaches and the dramatic Illawarra Escarpment. The region is full of surprises, such as the unexceptional little town of Thirroul just north of Wollongong which turns out to have an extremely good restaurant called La Petite Malice (042-474774) and a beachside house where D H Lawrence lived for most of his stay in Australia in 1923. The restaurant is in an unprepossessing side street, while the Lawrence house gets no mention in the tourist literature let alone a blue plaque (or Australian equivalent thereof). It is this understated quality which makes the whole region so attractive to those who may have tired of following a prescribed tourist trail. There are of course a few well-known attractions such as the blowhole at Kiama (just beyond the Blowhole Caravan Park and a shop with what must be the biggest display of souvenir teaspoons in the world) which blows to a spectacular height in rough seas (but not otherwise).

Further south, historic places like Eden and big game fishing ports like Bermagui are better known, but are still unspoiled. Eden's whaling past is particularly colourful if somewhat improbable even by Moby Dick standards: the local museum proudly displays the skeleton of a killer whale which is said to have cooperatively towed the whalers' boats out to the herds of lesser whales, where it attacked them and then shared the spoils with the fishermen. Bermagui also has its share of legends, mostly on the theme of giant marlin being caught from the shore. Game fishing here is more like its counterpart in New Zealand than, say, some ritzy Queensland resorts, i.e. it is not just the preserve of the wealthy. It is possible to join a boat party for about $70 or hire small tackle for $18. In some pools you can collect prawns without any equipment at all.

INLAND

Like the other states, New South Wales covers a vast area traversed by several routes. Except for the much improved Hume Highway between Sydney and Melbourne, driving any of the highways is a major undertaking, especially the route to Adelaide via Broken Hill, on which you have to be sure to carry emergency supplies of petrol. Although in the same state as Sydney, Broken Hill is 1161km from the capital and for most purposes behaves as part of South Australia; most importantly the city observes South Australian time (30 minutes behind the rest of New South Wales). The huge deposits of zinc, lead and silver that spawned Australia's most powerful corporation, Broken Hill Proprietary (BHP), guarantee a high standard of prosperity not normally associated with the Outback. But despite its financial and industrial importance it clings to its outback culture and is an interesting place to stop over if you have the chance.

But there are plenty of places of interest before you get to Broken Hill and other remote places in New South Wales. One is Cameron's Corner where three states meet in the middle of emptiness. More picturesquely named places include Wilson's Downfall and the Risk, or even Bourke where the railway ends (from whence derives the expression 'Back o' Bourke', which refers to any godforsaken place) and Wagga Wagga, the name of which (pronounced 'Wogga') is probably more memorable than its attractions. The Willandra Lakes Region is a World Heritage-listed area because of its Aboriginal remains. There are many small wayside towns like Berrima and Carcoar that were settled early and have retained their colonial atmosphere; the Surveyor-General Hotel in Berrima is said to be the oldest continuously licensed pub in Australia. Dubbo, 415km from Sydney, has an excellent zoo that is so extensive the best way to explore it is by bicycle.

There are more of the inevitable large follies such as the ridiculous turd-like potato in Robertson, the centre of a potato-growing area near the scenic Kangaroo Valley and Fitzroy Falls, inland from Wollongong. There are opal mines at far-flung Lightning Ridge in the central-northern part of the state, and in White Cliffs, which is even further from civilisation, it is possible, with a permit, to do some fossicking for opals.

The NSW Tourism Commission in Sydney and any of the numerous local tourist offices will eagerly supply you with literature on any of these country attractions. They will also be able to tell you about forthcoming special events, such as the Festival of the Falling Leaves each May in Tumut, the Great Goat Race in Lightning Ridge in April, or the balloon races in Canowindra, which are always worth trying to take in. The NSW Tourism Commission publishes a comprehensive listing called *Coming Events*. Another worthwhile experience is a farmstay. For example, ten farms scattered over a fairly large area northwest of Sydney belong to the Quirindi Host Farm Group (c/- 'Karanilla', Quirindi, NSW 2343; 067-465660) where kangaroo-spottings are virtually guaranteed and you can pay as little as $65 for dinner, bed and breakfast.

New South Wales offers great environmental contrasts from the highest snow-capped peaks in Australia to the unrelenting desert which covers the whole of the country's interior and therefore much of New South Wales. Furthermore water-based activities of all kinds can be enjoyed along the 1120km coastline.

The state boasts 68 National Parks which come in all shapes and sizes, some massive like Kosciusko (pronounced cozy-*oss*-coe), incorporating part of the Snowy Mountain range, others tiny with just one feature, such as Cathedral Rock National Park near the amiable university town of Armidale; some within easy range of Sydney (see below), others extremely remote like the Mallee Cliffs National Park near the Victorian border to which there is no road access; some are coastal such as the lovely Ben Boyd National Park around Eden, others are in desert locations like the Sturt National Park in the north-western corner of the state 360km north of Broken Hill. The National Parks and Wildlife Service in Sydney (189 Kent St, Sydney 2000) can provide further information if you have a specific interest in certain habitats, wildlife, zoology, etc. Most National Parks charge admission of about $4 per car. The Australian School of Bushcraft and Survival in Nowra (165km south of Sydney) runs one-day and weekend activities in a range of sports (ring 044-221379 to find out their very reasonable prices).

Near Sydney. Many Sydney-based organisations can help you explore the bushland near the city. For example, the Wilderness Society (1st Floor, 263 Broadway, Glebe, Sydney; 02-9552 2355) organises weekend bushwalks — the programme is available from the Society's shop on the Castlereagh St level of the Centrepoint Tower (9233 4674). The Australian Museum organises occasional weekends away for (non-serious) bushwalkers. Those who prefer something more challenging might join a day-trip rafting, abseiling, etc. with Wild Escapes (9482 2881).

As mentioned above, the Blue Mountains are criss-crossed with walking tracks of varying degrees of difficulty. Bush camping can be arranged through the National Parks and Wildlife Service, which is constantly upgrading facilities. Riding is another popular way of seeing the Blue Mountains, especially in the Megalong Valley not far west of Katoomba. The Australian School of Mountaineering, based at the Rockcraft Outdoor Shop, 182 Katoomba St (047-822014), runs daily abseiling, climbing and canyoning trips and courses; enquire about YHA discounts for members.

The Royal National Park is a short train ride south of Sydney. It has the distinction of being Australia's oldest National Park (and the second oldest in the world after Yellowstone in the United States). The highlight here is the chance to walk along sea cliffs. The hardier breed of youth hosteller will be interested in the primitive hostel at Garie Beach which is accessible only on foot either a kilometre from the car park, 10km from the railway station at Waterfall or 20km along the coastal track from Bundeena where the ferry from the Sydney suburb of Cronulla docks. This Hostel is unmanned so you must pre-pay at the YHA headquarters in Sydney (422 Kent St; 02-9261 1111) before you can obtain the key. Stanwell Park just south of the Royal National Park is a favourite spot for hang-gliders.

The two National Parks which straddle the Hawkesbury River north of Sydney are not so well suited to bushwalkers since much of their area is covered by mangrove swamp. Ku-ring-gai Chase National Park is especially attractive in spring when the wild flowers bloom in profusion. The park rangers organise activities during the school holidays, for example tours of Aboriginal drawings and nocturnal nature walks; ring 02-9457 9322 for details. Similarly in the summer you can join a walk for $1 with a park guide to the rock engravings at Kamaregal and to the now defunct quarantine station at North Head (02-9977 3292/9337 5511 for details). It is possible to cross Broken Bay at the mouth of the Hawkesbury by ferry, from the exclusive suburb of Palm Beach to Ettalong; cyclists are also allowed to use this service.

At all these ocean-side parks, there is good surfing, canoeing, fishing and also bush camping if you have permission from the park authorities.

Bushwalking. There are opportunities for good walking throughout the state from the Kangaroo Valley (inland from Wollongong) to the memorably named Warrumbungle National Park, where you are more likely to see a field of kangaroos than in the Kangaroo Valley since it is so much further from the big cities. (If you do get as far as the Warrumbungle Range north of Dubbo try to visit the Siding Spring Observatory, a NASA space centre with powerful stargazing telescopes.)

The 6200 square kilometre area of Kosciusko National Park, which is so well known to skiers, is also a fine walking area in the summer. A superb view of the Snowy Mountains can be had from any of the peaks in the park; the walk up Mount Stilwell from the Chalet at Charlotte's Pass on the eastern slopes of Mount Kosciusko is especially recommended. Mount Kosciusko itself (2230m) is a rounded hill which can also be climbed without difficulty in summer.

If walking in the rainforests in the northern part of the state, beware of giant leeches. Big Scrub Rainforest Tours (856554) in Byron Bay even advertises 'creepy crawly tours', though for the most part they take travellers in groups of less than 12 on day adventures to climb hills, swim in waterfalls and generally explore the outdoors. If you want to do some bushwalking on your own obtain the brochures *Broken Head Nature Reserve* which describes the popular rainforest walk to King's Beach and the *Cape Byron Walking Track* from the Byron Bay tourist office.

Skiing. Kosciusko National Park which contains a large area of the Snowy Mountains and is 450km from Sydney is the place everyone heads to in winter, since the Blue Mountains are not high enough to be skiable. There are six ski areas in the state, all of them in the Snowy Mountains. Although there is a large choice of downhill runs, cross-country skiing or 'langlauf' is especially popular in this area. The ski season lasts from July to September, though the snow stays on the upper slopes until November or even December.

The main resorts like Thredbo (which specialises in teaching beginners), Guthega (mainly for families), Perisher, etc. are not cheap. For example, the Thredbo YHA hostel (064-576376) charges from $36 in the ski season instead of the summer price of $14. If you want to economise, stay in one of the sub-alpine towns such as Berridale or Jindabyne and commute to the slopes on one of the regular buses. Jindabyne Accommodation Reservation Centre has a toll-free number: 008-026331. If you're hardy enough you can camp at Sawpit Creek 10km away. Getting around the area is not a problem because of the Skitube, an underground railway that covers 3km between the Thredbo Road and Perisher, which has been extended a further 3km to the new Mount Blue Cow Ski Area.

Watersports. There is year-round surfing off the north coast of the state at places like Ballina and Byron Bay. Other well known places are Port Macquarie and Redhead Beach near Newcastle. But the sport is equally popular on the south coast. Watch for aquatic carnivals throughout the summer, for example the Australia Day celebrations held near Taree about half way up the coast. Windsurfing, diving and snorkelling are widely available. Hostels can usually advise or even hire out equipment themselves as at the Beachhouse Backpackers Hostel at Lennox Heads, while the Dive Centre at 9 Lawson St in Byron Bay arranges scuba and snorkelling trips and courses. Although the south coast is not quite so balmy, contact the Shoalhaven Tourist Centre (Princes Highway, Bomaderry; 044-210778) for information about adventure holidays in the region.

Whitewater rafting has come to New South Wales and takes place mainly on the Nymboida River inland from Grafton. The company Rapid Action (018-759427) charges less than $100 for a 5-hour raft trip over 22 rapids. The Backpackers Resort (065-686360) in Nambucca Heads (a pleasant resort about halfway between Sydney and Brisbane) can also book rafting trips. Coffs Harbour is another gateway for rafters; try Whitewater Rafting Professional (066-514066) or Wildwater Adventures (066-534469).

Other Activities. Many species of wildlife thrive in corners of the state. The Tollgate Islands, offshore from Batemans Bay, are a penguin reserve. Birdwatching is a rewarding pastime at any of the vast coastal lakes north of Sydney such as Lake Macquarie and the Myall Lakes (part of a National Park of the same name). If you are travelling the Hume Highway, stop at the Mount Gibraltar Reserve near Bowral and listen for lyre birds, the amazing bird which can imitate sounds it hears frequently, and not just the sounds of other species but man-made sound such as that of a chainsaw. Koalas can also be seen there in the wild, though the largest numbers inhabit a few North Coast localities. Closer to Sydney, you might want to visit the koalas and kangaroos at Koala Park, Castle Hill Road, West Pennant Hills.

Those who prefer the pursuit of inanimate Australiana, i.e. minerals and fossils, might try their hand at fossicking, which originally referred to hunting for gold but is used more generally now to cover opals and other minerals. Contact the Department of Mineral Resources in the State Office Block in Sydney for further details and also for a fossicking licence.

Opportunities to mount a horse abound in the state. One of the best places is at Byron Beach where the Beach Resort (066-858000) charges $15 for an hour or $25 for two hours of riding in sub-tropical rainforest or through bushland near Seven Mile Beach.

Calendar of Events

January (all month)	Festival of Sydney
January 26th (Australia Day)	Celebrity Thong-throwing Contest at Dee Why Beach
January/February	Chinese New Year (Chinatown festivities)
February	Gay and Lesbian Mardi Gras
March/April (Easter)	Royal Easter Show (Sydney)
June (second Monday)	**Queen's Birthday**
June (second and third weeks)	Sydney Film Festival
August (first Monday)	**Bank Holiday**
August (first week)	Turf to Surf Fun Race, Coffs Harbour
August	Moon Festival (Chinatown)
September/October	Sleaze Ball
October (first Monday)	**Labour Day**
early October	Manly Jazz Carnival
October	Kings Cross Carnival
November	Queen St Fair, Woollahra
December 26	Sydney to Hobart Yacht Race begins

Public holidays are shown in **bold**.

Canberra

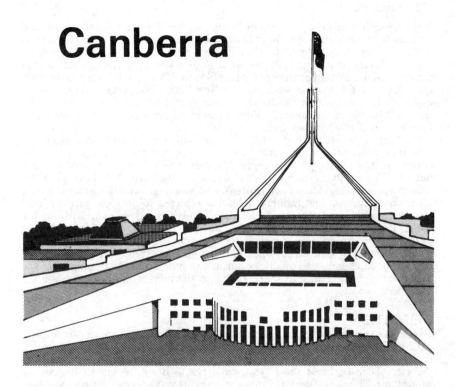

Population of Canberra: 280,000   **Population of the ACT: 290,000**

Canberra is one of those places that evokes an instant and often hostile response. Jokes comparing the nation's capital to a cemetery with lights on are commonplace. Someone has suggested that the old cliché should be revised in the case of Canberra to read 'nice place to live, but you wouldn't want to visit'. But these are cheap jibes. Of course the nightlife is not as varied as in Sydney nor the choice of restaurants as great as in Melbourne, but this does not prevent a very high proportion of visitors to the nation's capital from thoroughly enjoying a stopover of a couple of days.

No one would deny that Canberra is in a lovely setting. The large man-made lake at the city's centre is named after the American architect Walter Burley Griffin, whose progressive thinking won him the chance to plan Canberra in 1911. There is a saying in Canberra that you can't call yourself a native unless you can remember the city before the lake was created in 1963. Burley Griffin's plans have been very slowly implemented (and adapted) over this century and in fact the process continues. Anyone remotely interested in town planning should make an effort to visit, as Canberra is one of the most pleasing examples of planning in the world, especially when compared to such places as Brasilia, Milton Keynes or Chandigarh, the bleak city in Northern India designed by Le Corbusier.

Canberra's *raison d'être* is as the seat of federal government. A site was chosen in the middle of nowhere from a long list of contenders as a way of placating Sydney and Melbourne, each of which was bitterly opposed to its rival being chosen. Canberra is often thought to be roughly half way between Sydney and

Melbourne, but this is a convenient fiction, as it is 3½ hours from Sydney and 8 hours from Melbourne. Another little fabrication favoured by the city fathers is that Canberra means 'meeting place' in an Aboriginal language; however some experts contend that it actually means 'a woman's breast'. The city lies within the Australian Capital Territory (ACT), a 60km by 95km chunk of land gracelessly carved out of the south-eastern part of New South Wales. One very peculiar quirk of the ACT is that its charter stipulates that it must have access to the sea; so it has an ocean annexe 230km due east at Jervis Bay, which is a naval base as well as a recreation area.

Canberra is a strange and artificial place, self-consciously a showpiece. To maintain high aesthetic standards in this planned environment, residents must comply with a number of restrictions, such as their not being allowed to have outside TV aerials or to use motor boats on the lake. Not only does the municipality lovingly tend its gardens and streetside floral displays, but it gives away trees to new residents who are expected to do their part for local beautification. Flowering trees, including some exotic species, transform the streets in spring, and deciduous trees do likewise in autumn. Canberra deserves to call itself a garden city, as well as the more commonly heard soubriquet the 'bush capital'. But Canberrans like to have it both ways; they are proud of their city's sophistication but equally proud of the bushland that impinges on the urban setting sufficiently to make kangaroo sightings within the city limits a daily occurrence.

CLIMATE

Canberra experiences four distinct seasons, with baking dry summers (complete with an invasion of flies), crisp cold winters and proper transitions between them. Although temperatures in winter drop below freezing, it rarely snows in the city. To experience snow, you will have to drive 200km to the Snowy Mountains. The ACT Tourism Commission posts two telexes a day on mountain snow conditions or you can ring 11544 for the snow report. Winter days are not unpleasant as they are usually bright and sunny. In fact Canberra receives an average of 7 hours of sunshine around the calendar. There is almost no industry in or near the city, so the air is always pristine. Rainfall is very low (an average of 64cm per year) and is fairly evenly distributed.

THE LOCALS

It is perhaps more difficult to meet the locals in Canberra than elsewhere. Some would say that the place is crowded out with fat cats not worth meeting anyway, and of course Canberra has its share of besuited career bureaucrats with whom the average traveller would have little in common. But there is also a large and important university, the Australian National University (ANU), which attracts a large proportion of overseas students as well as Australians from all over the country.

Although a high proportion of Canberrans are involved with government in some way, this does not mean that it is a dull place. There are Aboriginal activists, lobbyists, journalists and people from many different ethnic backgrounds. The range of clubs is enormous, from Lithuanian to Croatian, Dutch to Welsh. Locals who are involved in government often have a sharp eye for both the positive and negative aspects of Australian culture and politics, and are well worth meeting. Like the city itself, the population is comparatively young — it is said there are no grandparents in Canberra and hence a huge demand for childminders — and the vast majority of residents were not born in Canberra.

The average Canberran spends a lot of time in the great outdoors, partly because populations with a high proportion of yuppies tend to be concerned

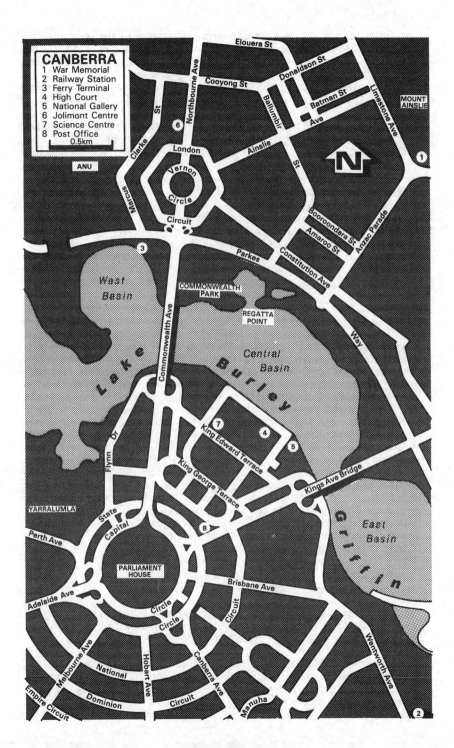

CANBERRA
1 War Memorial
2 Railway Station
3 Ferry Terminal
4 High Court
5 National Gallery
6 Jolimont Centre
7 Science Centre
8 Post Office
0.5km

about fitness and partly because Canberra offers more to the sportsman and sportswoman than to those with disco mania. The Canberra YHA arranges regular outings, weekend trips and social events; so check their notice board even if you are staying elsewhere.

If you are arranging to meet someone, a good meeting place is the old merry-go-round in the city centre at the corner of City Walk and Petrie Plaza.

It is surprising that a national capital does not have a large airport, and that it is about 70km off the major train routes and the main Hume Highway.

ARRIVAL AND DEPARTURE

Air. Flying from Sydney or Melbourne is easy, as there are dozens of flights a day on the two main domestic carriers Ansett (245 1111) and Australian Airlines (268 3333). Cheapest is Air New South Wales (a subsidiary of Ansett), which flies propeller aircraft between Sydney and Melbourne calling at Canberra.

The airport is 10km south-east of the city centre and there is no public bus service into town. The taxi fare is about $12.

Bus. Services between Sydney and Canberra are frequent: Greyhound Pioneer run five or six services each throughout the day. The local company Murrays (295 3611) runs three services daily and gives a discount to backpackers. The trip takes between 4 and 5 hours, and the cost is $24. The bus station is in the Jolimont Centre on Northbourne Avenue.

There are direct services to other cities in New South Wales, for example to Wollongong and Eden on the coast south of Sydney and to Cooma and the Snowy Mountains. New South Wales licence restrictions mean that only travellers coming from or going to another state can travel between Canberra and certain towns in New South Wales such as Newcastle and Lismore by bus. Because competition is less intense on non-Sydney routes, prices are higher, for example the fare for the 3-hour journey to Wollongong is $24 with Canberra Cruises (Mundaring Drive, Kingston; 95 3544), and the trip to Perisher Ski Resort in the Snowy Mountains (also 3 hours) is $42 on Pioneer. Unfortunately the mountain bus services are timed to suit Sydney skiers and hikers rather than Canberra ones, so you might have to depart Canberra at 4am or arrive in Perisher or Thredbo at 1.45am. The only reasonable time is the 12.30pm departure from Canberra. The YHA hostel arranges its own excursions to the Snowy Mountains, which you might prefer to join.

Canberra is also connected with the other eastern capitals: the 16-hour trip to Adelaide costs $75 and the 9-hour trip to Melbourne costs $35. The V/Line coach/rail service takes just over eight hours and costs $39 (476355). All Queensland services go via Sydney.

Train. The main Sydney–Melbourne line passes through the city of Goulburn (famed for its giant replica ram) about an hour north-east of Canberra. You must disembark here if you are trying to get from Melbourne to Canberra. There are no connecting bus services and the only possibility is to get off the *Sydney Express* (departing Melbourne at 8pm, arriving Goulburn 5.49am) and wait around for the bus to Canberra that leaves over 3 hours later. Another possibility is to get off at the nearer town of Yass Junction and hitch along the Barton Highway into Canberra.

Services to Sydney are more convenient but remarkably slow. The faster of the two services (i.e. the *Canberra Express*, which departs Sydney at 7.10am) makes nine stops and takes 5 hours while the *Southern Highlands Express* (which departs at 5.05pm) makes 24 stops and takes about half an hour longer. In the opposite direction the *Canberra Express* departs at 12.45pm and the *Southern Highlands Express* at 6.05am. The cost is $30 economy. For timetable and fare information contact the Travel Centre on 239 0133. The station is 6km south of the city centre just off Wentworth Avenue.

Driving. Four highways converge on Canberra: the Monaro Highway from Cooma and the south, the Kings Highway from the New South Wales coast, and the Federal and Barton Highways, which both join the Hume Highway north of Canberra. The approach roads to the city are so wide that there is never any traffic congestion.

The majority of car hire firms in Canberra are not of the rent-a-heap ilk as rusting Volkswagens are not the preferred vehicle of visiting delegates and dignitaries. Many companies are located along Lonsdale St in Braddon, for example Discount, Budget and Thrifty. You may be able to get a better deal away from the city centre; try Rumbles Rent-a-Car in Fyshwick (Shop 17, 157 Gladstone St; 280 7444) where Holdens start at $35 a day plus 20c per km over 100 or $130 a weekend including 700km free, or Rick's, 162 Melrose Drive, Phillip.

The National Roads and Motorists Association (NRMA) is at 92 Northbourne Avenue on the corner of Elouera St (243 8988). The emergency road service number is 243 8888.

Hitch-hiking. You tend to get a better class of lift when hitching out of Canberra. One of the authors was picked up by a Canberran (a former Australian trade commissioner to Bahrain) who carried in his car taped lectures on Australian history for the edification of hitch-hikers on long journeys.

If you want to get on to the Monaro or Kings Highway, take a bus or train 12km to the New South Wales town of Queanbeyan (not pronounced Queenbean, but *Queen*-bee-un). To join the Hume Highway take any of the buses heading north: for the Barton Highway take bus 906 to Hall; for the Federal Highway take bus 383 (or on weekends 362).

CITY TRANSPORT

Bus. The public transport system of Canberra is confined to buses called ACTION (ACT Internal Omnibus Network) which serve all suburbs, though at infrequent intervals. The single fare within Canberra is $1.40. ACTION also has several sightseeing routes out of the city, some of which operate only on certain days. These cost either $4.60 or $9.20 depending on distance. Ask for timetables 904 to 909. Timetable and fare information is available from the Bus Interchange office at the top of City Walk (251 6566) open 6am to 11.30pm except Sundays when it opens 8.30am to 6.30pm. If you plan to do a lot of travelling around Canberra it is worth buying a *Bus Book* for $1.95 from the ACTION office or newsagents. A loop service (route 777) travels from bay 13 of the city centre to the main sights on the south side of Lake Burley Griffin between 9am and 4.30pm. Route 202/3 takes in the War Memorial. The daytripper ticket for $4.60, which allows unlimited bus travel, is good value.

Canberra has an Explorer bus (operated by Murrays; 295 3611); tickets are available at the Tourist Office for $9. Explorer buses leave the Jolimont Centre hourly between 10.15am and 4.15pm. This is probably an unnecessary extravagance unless you want to hear the driver's commentary.

Car. Many newcomers to Canberra encounter difficulties in navigation, partly because the planners wanted to avoid a boring grid system and partly because they seem to have been very sparing in their use of street signs. Careful study of a good map is essential before trying to get from A to B. A further difficulty is the seeming invisibility of petrol stations. Ugly as the approach roads to most cities are, lined with garages, motels, etc., at least you can easily find petrol. Not so in Canberra, where you must look for the discreet blue signs pointing you towards a fuel supply. There is a 24-hour petrol station on Lonsdale St in Braddon.

One problem you won't encounter is heavy traffic. The main thoroughfare, Northbourne Avenue, is usually empty and you could wheel a television across it at midday with no difficulty. Avoid using bus lanes and watch out for cycleways across streets. Red lines on the kerb mean that you can't park. Just as in New South Wales, random breath testing is commonplace, though in the ACT a limit of .08% applies rather than .05% as in New South Wales.

As befits a city planned with the motor car in mind, there are few parking problems. Vast car parks surround the city centre both inside London Circuit and west of Ballumbir St. 'Voucher' parking means 'pay and display'. Increasingly, parking meters are being installed on city streets.

If you do have a car, you might like to follow one or more of the five tourist drives, all of which start at the City Hill Lookout on Vernon Circle and radiate in various directions towards various attractions.

Taxi. Flagging a taxi on the streets of Canberra is an almost impossible task, principally because there is only one taxi firm. Ring Aerial Taxis (285 9222) for a cab.

Boat. Although there is a designated ferry terminal on Lake Burley Griffin, there are in fact no ferries. However you can get good views of the civic buildings from the lake, so you might want to join a two-hour cruise at 1pm ($12) or an economy one-hour tour at 11.45am ($8) from the Acton Ferry Terminal (295 3544). Otherwise you can paddle yourself out into the lake (see *Sport* below).

Cycling. Canberra is very proud of its cycleways, many of which cut through parks and across open spaces rather than go alongside roads. There are over 100km of cycle paths, which are marked on most maps, as well as on the tourist office's free brochure *Canberra Cycleways*. The term cycleways is a partial misnomer as the paths are also used by pedestrians; this is only fair as cyclists may legally ride on the footpaths of Canberra.

Bicycles may be hired from the Canberra YHA (see below), from Mr Spokes Bike Hire (Acton Ferry Terminal), from near the Glebe Park kiosk or from Canberra Bicycle Hire (Woolley St, Dickson, near the corner of Northbourne Avenue and Antill St). Dial-a-Bicycle (4 Harcourt St, Weetangera; 254 0550) has mostly geared mountain bikes which can be delivered to you. The inclusive hire fees are $18 a day, $40 for 4 days, $50 a week and $68 a month.

Accommodation

A selection of Canberra's motels, caravan parks and few hostels and guest houses may be found in the tourist office leaflet *Canberra Accommodation*.

Canberra YHA is at 191 Dryandra St in O'Connor (248 9155), 5km from the centre of town near bus route 380. Although not many overseas travellers go to Canberra, the hostel is often booked out with groups of Australian school children, so it might be an idea to book ahead for one of the 124 beds; the nightly fee for a bed in a dormitory room is $15.

Canberra lacks the usual range of backpacker accommodation. There is one hostel in the VIP Backpackers Resorts chain: Victor Lodge Bed & Breakfast at 29 Dawes St in Kingston (295 7777), for which bookings are advised; ring ahead for pick-up information. The most inexpensive places are the bed and breakfasts on Northbourne Avenue in the suburb of Downer. All three of the following charge $18 each in a twin including a full breakfast: Chelsea Lodge at 526 Northbourne Avenue (248 0655), Blue Sky Lodge at number 524 (248 8277) and Northbourne Lodge at number 522 (257 2599). Another place where backpackers stay is the Kingston Hotel at 73 Canberra Avenue in Kingston (295 0123) which charges $15 single, $30 double.

Several colleges at ANU offer cheap rooms out of term; the best deals are at Burton and Garran Hall (267 4700) where single rooms start at $16 per person, and at Fenner Hall (279 9000) where the rate is from $18 per night or $85 per week. Institutional accommodation is also available at government-affiliated private hotels such as the Macquarie in Barton (273 2325) and the Gowrie at 210 Northbourne Avenue, Braddon (249 6033). Both charge about $55 double bed and breakfast with substantial weekly discounts.

Canberra has plenty of anonymous motels and hotels that are outside the price range of budget travellers. For people looking for more upmarket accommodation, the secluded Tall Trees Lodge Motel at 21 Stephen St in Ainslie (247 9200) costs $73 for a double.

Many Australian families on holiday stay at one of the camping and caravanning parks that are signposted on the approach roads. The Federal Highway Tourist Park in Sutton (241 6411) just north of Canberra has cabins as well as tent pitches. The Motor Village (247 5466) is the most central, just a stone's throw from the YHA and north of the Black Mountain Nature Reserve. It has on-site caravans at the standard rates but no tent sites. The South Side Motor Park in Fyshwick (280 6176) is further from town but larger, with 650 sites including some for tents, plus cabins and on-site vans.

Eating and Drinking

Seeking local advice on eating places is always a good idea, but in Canberra it is especially worthwhile, as many good restaurants are not in obvious locations. Authentic Sri Lankan, Japanese, Turkish and Thai restaurants are often concealed in suburban shopping malls. For example the small row of shops in the suburb of Lyneham contains not only the Phuket Thai Restaurant (247 8524) where you can eat good Thai food for $12, but also Tilley's, a feminist-run cafe where a good range of beers and coffees is available and where men must be accompanied by women except Fridays when men are banned completely. Other good eating places are inauspiciously attached to clubs and motels, such as the Pinocchio Italian Restaurant in the Kythera Motel at 100 Northbourne Avenue.

But it is also possible to find worthwhile places on spec by walking around the Civic Centre, comparing menus and prices. East Row and nearby Garema Place are worth strolling along. A few spots have entertainment such as Dorette's Bistro, upstairs at 17 Garema Place, which offers live jazz, classical or folk music every night of the week, as well as an original menu with dishes like kangaroo with brandy and blackcurrant for about $15. Vegetarian food is available at much lower prices at the Parakeet Cafe in Ainslie (6 Wakefield Gardens; 248 5018).

Many of Canberra's restaurants do special business lunches at reasonable prices (compared with the cost of similar meals served in the evening). The majority of restaurants open Monday to Saturday. If you are hungry on a Sunday, ethnic restaurants are most likely to be open, such as the Vietnamese restaurants at 21 and 27 East Row. The Pancake Parlour on the corner of Alinga St and East Row is open 24 hours a day every day, and provides a good late-night alternative to the mobile food vans that appear each night, especially near the university campus. The crepes served at the French Kitchen in the Boulevard Centre on Akuna St are less mass-produced, and are popular after the nearby theatres and cinemas adjourn.

If you want to sample a specific ethnic cuisine you might contact the relevant club, most of which allow visitors to dine in their restaurant but not to use the bars. Many of them are family places and may stop serving food at 9pm. Try the Trevi Restaurant in the Italo-Australian Club (78 Franklin St, Forrest; 295 1015) or the dining room at the Austrian-Australian Club (Southlands Shopping Centre, Mawson; 286 5793). One of the best known and reasonably priced club restaurants is the Tramway Eatery at the Tradesmen's Union Club in Dickson (Badham St; 248 0999) where seating is in one of ten old city trams from all over Australia.

There are plenty of conveniently located cafés and take-aways for quick snacks, such as the cafeteria-style café in the High Court, the outdoor café at the National Gallery and the Bistro in the Jolimont Centre. You might also try the ANU Student Union cafeteria.

Picnics are also highly recommended at any of the 60 parks and lakeside reserves, many of which have coin-operated barbecue facilities. Surprisingly, food in the shops and markets is substantially cheaper in Canberra than in other Australian cities; in fact the cost of living is one of the lowest for capital cities in the developed world.

DRINKING

There are no licensing restrictions in Canberra so hotels can stay open as long as they like, and the occasional nightclub like the long-established Private Bin at 50 Northbourne Avenue (near Alinga St) stays open for drinking and dancing until dawn. Even if you are not feeling particularly homesick for British beer, you might enjoy an evening at the Oaks and the Attic near the station (Green Square, Jardine St); it has nightly rock music, except Fridays which are devoted to jazz. The beer is imported from Britain but the menu is Australian (mostly steaks).

The Downer Club in Hawdon St, Dickson is associated with the Tradesmen's Union Club and has bar and bistro facilities as well as a display of beer from over 100 countries and what is reputed to be the world's largest bottle of beer, over 2m high.

A larger proportion of Canberra restaurants are licensed compared to other Australian cities, though there are some BYO establishments. Although Canberra is hardly famous for its wines, there are a couple of wineries within range of the ACT. Advertisements urge Canberrans to support their local wine with the rather unappealing name Lake George, named for the intermittent lake 40km north of the city. But vineyards in Australia can change character and improve rapidly, so you might like to make an expedition to the Murrumbateman Winery, 30 minutes by car along the Barton Highway. The winery is set in pleasant grounds with picnic facilities and wine tastings seven days a week.

During the Canberra Festival in March, the Food and Wine Frolic (sponsored by American Express) attracts thousands of people who either buy sampling tickets ahead of time or on the spot, and then trade them for a selection of the many snacks prepared by some of Canberra's 200 restaurants and for tastes of wine representing wineries from all over the country. The annual event is held in Commonwealth Park.

The main commercial centre is around London Circuit, north of the lake. The area south is largely devoted to administrative and diplomatic life. Try to obtain a copy of the tourist office free map *Canberra and District*, though for a street and suburbs index, you'll need the excellent *UBD Tourist Map* which has insets of the city, the university and the whole ACT. Walking between points of interest is not really feasible. As throughout Australia, people refer to suburbs rather than streets, some of which are only a stone's throw from the city centre.

All cities are changing all the time but in Canberra the process is more in evidence and more self-consciously promoted as entertainment in itself. The new Parliament Building, the new National Museum (which will open later in the 1990s) and the new science centre all have an exhibition centre with sophisticated models, detailed plans and films pitched at the general public. Anyone with a glimmer of interest in modern architecture or town planning will enjoy these displays, which are free as they are part of the government's public relations. The one that gives the best general picture of Canberra and its development is the Canberra Planning Exhibition at Regatta Point (246 8797).

Before you strike off to see specific buildings, you should admire the city as a whole. As the site of Canberra was chosen partly for its pleasing situation, there are several hills from which to admire the city's lake and buildings. Mount Ainslie is the highest hill at 842m, though the highest viewpoint is from the top of the Telecom Tower (195m) on the top of Black Mountain (812m). Admission to the viewing platforms is from 9am to 10pm and the cost is $2.

Buildings and Venues. The new Parliament Building was opened for the Bicentennial in 1988. It is a stunning (and very expensive) showcase for Australian handiwork, paintings, sculptures, etc. The building's architectural uniqueness derives from the fact that its low profile in the shape of two back-to-back boomerangs follows the contours of the hill rather than towering above it. It is possible to walk up the outside of the building on grass-covered slopes, which affords a wonderful view over the lake and surrounding buildings.

If Parliament is in session, you may want to attend a session of Question Time in the House of Representatives in the hope of seeing some of the fiery and colourful exchanges that are the hallmark of Australian politics. Question Time starts at 2pm and lasts between 45 minutes and an hour. You can book a ticket by telephone (277 4890) which can be collected from the Ticket and Cloaking office on the day. Free guided tours of the public areas of Parliament House are available on non-sitting days. These tours begin on the hour and the half hour and last just under an hour. On sitting days you can wander around and listen to a commentary that the guides provide regularly in the Great Hall. Just as the House of Lords in London is much less appealing to tourists than the House of Commons, so the Senate of Australia (the upper house) is less popular than the House of Representatives. Therefore you can visit the Senate without any problem, including the 2pm Question Time. For further information about tours, etc. ring the Guides Desk on 277 5399.

Two other striking modern buildings occupy the Parliamentary Triangle, an area bordered by Commonwealth Avenue, Kings Avenue and the lake, i.e. the National Gallery and the Law Courts. Not everyone likes them and some even think that they clash with each other; others find them splendid buildings, especially when considered in their lakeside setting. In any case they are worth a visit.

The campus of the Australian National University (ANU) is north of the lake between the city centre and Black Mountain. In addition to attending concerts and plays at the Arts Centre, you may want to visit some of the university institutes that have specialist exhibitions open to the public. Enquire at the ANU Information Centre at 28 Balmain Crescent (249 2229). For recorded information about what's on at ANU, ring 249 0742.

Most of the more exotic embassies (of the 70 in Canberra) are located in Yarralumla just west of Capital Hill along Empire Circuit, Arkana St and Turrana St. During the Fiesta Capitale around the new year, many of the embassies open to the public and host special national events. Elements of the vernacular architecture are reflected in some of the buildings, such as those of Thailand and Papua New Guinea, though not in sufficient measure to permit you to imagine yourself in Bangkok or Wewak rather than Canberra suburbia. The Papua New Guinean High Commission and Indonesian Embassy both have exhibitions of art and artefacts open to the public. If you are pining for Asia, it is a better idea to visit the newly opened Nomura Court in the National Gallery which houses a collection of Asian art.

The Australian Capital Territory incorporates some old colonial mansions and farmhouses, some of which are still in use as in the case of Duntroon House built in 1833 which is now part of the Royal Military College, while most others have been restored as tourist attractions with tea shops, gardens, and craft centres, such as the Ginninderra School House off the Barton Highway. The Lanyon Homestead and the nearby Cuppacumbalong Homestead, both set on the Murrumbidgee River less than an hour south of Canberra, are in delightful settings and their grounds are occasionally used for outdoor concerts.

Museums and Galleries. The Australian War Memorial claims to be the second most heavily visited attraction in all of Australia after the Sydney Opera House. This museum of war is housed in a suitably dignified building at the top of Anzac Parade and was the largest war memorial in the world when it was built in 1941 (at a time when the Australian population was just four million). Most Australians take great pride in their country's military history, particularly the heroism of Gallipoli, and all of the theatres of war in which they were involved, including Vietnam, are dealt with in the museum displays, which are open every day from 9am-4.45pm (243 4211; admission is now $3). Voluntary guides conduct free tours at 10.30am and 1.30pm on weekdays.

The Australian National Gallery (271 2502) has 11 spacious galleries in which to show off its excellent permanent collection of Australian painting and its other holdings. The National is also the Australian gallery that is most likely to attract major international touring exhibitions from Europe or America, and mounts an impressive array of supporting events such as films, lectures and concerts. The normal admission fee of $3 is usually increased for one of these prestigious visiting exhibitions. Like most of Canberra's important sights, it is open seven days a week.

The new National Museum of Australia is not due to open until the mid-1990s but can be visited at its site at the end of Lake Burley Griffin. It has been acquiring many objects of national importance, for example a stunning collection of 40 ceremonial Aboriginal paintings in 1991 so it will be worth visiting when it does open.

A small selection of the work of one of Australia's most important contemporary artists, Sidney Nolan, is on display at the Lanyon Homestead property (237 5136; combined entrance fee with Lanyon Homestead of $2.50). Closer to the city centre you might prefer to inspect the collection of unusual and antique bicycles at the Canberra Tradesmen's Union Club on Badham St in Dickson (free admission). The National Film and Sound Archive on the university campus (McCoy Circuit; 267 1711) chronicles the development of the Australian media with interesting visual and audio exhibits (free admission).

Visitors with a scientific bent will want to visit Questacon the National Science and Technology Centre on King Edward Terrace (270 2800). Like other state-of-the-art science centres, it specialises in hands-on exhibits (admission $5). The National Aquarium on Lady Denman Drive (at the western end of Lake Burley Griffin) allows visitors to view aquatic life from various Australian habitats, including the Barrier Reef (admission $10).

There are also opportunities to examine the southern skies in the unlikely context of a social club. Apart from serving food and drink, the Downer Club in Dickson mentioned above has an observatory that is open every night of the week between nightfall and midnight, with an astronomer on duty to assist with the outdoor telescopes. You can also go on an excursion to the Tidbinbilla Deep Space Tracking Station (38km south-west of the city) which has photographs and models of the galaxy.

Parks and Zoos. Canberra is famed as a garden city and green spaces virtually surround the lake. Furthermore the streets have been carefully planted with many species of flowering tree, so that September is especially lovely when the Japanese apricots flower followed by the cherry plums and wattles. This is also the time of year that sees Commonwealth Park covered in spring flowers for the Floriade Festival, which lasts until mid-October and features outdoor entertainment as well. High summer is probably the worst time to visit, as the lack of rain turns the city drab and brown, especially the central strip of Anzac Parade.

The National Botanic Gardens are interesting at any time of the year. They are unique in that they contain primarily native Australian flora. The gardens occupy the eastern slopes of Black Mountain, itself a very large nature reserve. Guided tours leave from the Visitor Information Centre (267 1805) every Sunday at 10am and 2pm, though it is not necessary to have a guide to enjoy the trails, such as the one-kilometre Aboriginal Trail (where labels indicate the uses to which the Aboriginal people put the species available to them) and the simulated rainforest in a normally parched gully. There is also a selection of eucalpytus species that might persuade you that gum trees are not as boring as most people think. Admission is free to the Gardens and there is a pleasant outdoor café.

If you want to hear music free of charge, go to Aspen Island in Kings Park (on the north side of Kings Avenue Bridge) on Sunday afternoons or Wednesday lunchtimes to hear a recital of the carillon, a set of 53 bells, which was a gift to Canberra from Britain in 1963.

One of the most enjoyable excursions from Canberra is to the Tidbinbilla Fauna Reserve, a 40-minute scenic drive away. Kangaroos, emus and a confused wombat, who has forgotten that he is a nocturnal creature, freely roam the grounds. If you bring a picnic (and there are no refreshments for sale at Tidbinbilla) be prepared to defend it from the emus. Rangers provide free guided tours of the koala enclosure and will even lend visitors binoculars. The exotic bird section is especially worthwhile visiting at feeding times (2pm, April to September).

If you haven't the time nor the transport to get to Tidbinbilla, you can sometimes see kangaroos at dawn or dusk on Mount Ainslie or Black Mountain. The range of habitats near Canberra includes wetlands at the eastern end of Lake Burley Griffin which attract many exotic birds especially pelicans. Only 6km south of the lake you can visit the Mugga Lane Zoo (admission $4.50, discount for YHA members) where 100 species of animals and birds live in relatively natural surroundings.

SHOPPING

Most shops are open the usual Australian hours with late night shopping on Fridays and morning-only shopping (sometimes until 2 or 3pm) on Saturdays. Outside these hours you can go to the Eight Till Late Supermarket at 10 Lonsdale St, Braddon, where food and drink can be purchased until midnight every day of the week.

Buying something at the corner store is not usually a simple matter in Canberra, and automobiles are usually involved in the simplest shopping expedition. Although most suburbs have their own shopping centres, these are not always easy to find as they are tucked out of sight and away from the main thoroughfares. A proper map of Canberra, such as the UBD map, will highlight shopping centres in colour. The main city centre shopping mall is the Monaro Mall though the suburban Belconnen Westfield Shopping Town and Woden Plaza are much larger. The Belconnen Mall has all the main stores such as Grace Brothers and Woolworths and offers free parking, babysitting services, etc.

For more unusual items, visit the 14 stalls of the Fyshwick Antique Centre in the unlikely suburb of Fyshwick, an industrial estate. There is a boomerang factory in Fyshwick at 1/42 Wollongong St where there are hourly demonstrations between 2pm and 5pm. The Canberra Arts & Crafts Market is held every Saturday from 10am to 4pm at the Gorman House Community Arts Centre on Ainslie Avenue in Braddon.

Fyshwick is where Canberra's best weekend fruit and vegetable market is held and also where several of Canberra's many bookshops are located, such as Clouston and Hall Academic Remainders at 28 Kembla St (open seven days a week) and Winchbooks (secondhand and rare books) at 68 Wollongong St. The Alternative Bookshop is at 46 Northbourne Avenue, City (not a very alternative address), while there is a women's bookshop called the Glass Bell.

For a city of its size, Canberra has plenty going on, and not just for the benefit of diplomats and plutocrats. It has a wealth of museums many of which are government-funded and free to visitors. A casino is on the drawing board, mainly to encourage visiting business people to extend their stay.

Canberra's entertainment weekly is called *Pulse* which may be picked up free of charge at the tourist office or various pubs and entertainment centres around town. Most gigs are listed in *Pulse* with articles about local and visiting bands, theatre companies, etc. This supplements the more conventional listings published daily on the 'I Page' of the *Canberra Times*, which is a guide to events, tours, exhibitions and performances. The student newspaper, called *Woroni*, will keep you informed of events on the campus.

Canberra can be seen at its most lively during the Canberra Festival which lasts ten days each March. Many of the events take place outdoors and are free, such as the Birdman Rally (in which contestants attempt to propel themselves 50m through the air without motorised aids), lunchtime jazz and other outdoor concerts, flower and art shows, raft races and processions. To get a complete calendar of festival events, contact the tourist office or ring the Festival Information service on 249 1277.

Theatre and Music. The BASS ticket agency sells tickets to most Canberra events; phone 247 4144 or visit their downtown outlet in the Jolimont Tourist Centre.

Canberra has its own symphony orchestra and opera company, as well as a choice of local theatre companies including several fringe groups. The Canberra Theatre Centre in Civic Square (257 1077) has several auditoria of varying size and is the principal venue. Canberra also has more cinemas than most cities with a similar population. The main cinemas downtown are the Electric Shadows at the Boulevard Twin Cinemas off Akuna St (247 5060) which shows late night films at weekends, and the Civic Twin Cinemas at 6 Mort St (247 5522). There are also a couple of drive-in cinemas on the outskirts of Canberra. For example the Starlight Double Drive-in on the Federal Highway in Watson screens two films at 7.30pm on weekends and hires out in-car heaters in winter.

The main rock venue is the Canberra National Indoor Stadium in Bruce. Most other popular music can be heard in pubs or clubs with which Canberra is generously supplied. Clubs of all kinds — for working men, for school teachers, for Finns, etc. — all have regular evenings of entertainment; check for details in *Pulse*. Among the pubs that have music are the Ainslie Hotel in Braddon (upmarket but pleasant) which has free jazz on Sunday afternoons, the Kingston Hotel and its popular nightclub Maddies and the Stockade at 17 Lonsdale St in Braddon which is mainly a do-it-yourself barbecue restaurant.

SPORT

Lake Burley Griffin is very handy for lovers of water sports who find themselves in Canberra, although surprisingly few people venture in for a swim. Swimmers and others trying to escape the summer heat head to one of the city's many sports complexes and swimming pools or else to a recreation area out of town such as the Cotter Reserve 22km west of the city where swimming is popular. If you have driven in from Sydney, you might have noticed inviting-looking Lake George, 40km northeast of Canberra. However, don't bother to plan a swim here, as its vast surface is never more than a few inches deep, and in dry summers the water disappears completely.

Windsurfers, canoes and rowboats may be hired from Dobell's Boat Hire at the Acton Ferry Terminal for frolicking on Lake Burley Griffin. You might even catch a fish from the lake; no fishing licences are required in the ACT. The lake hosts special events such as the raft race held during the Canberra Festival in March.

Cycling is probably the most enjoyable way of combining sport and sightseeing. The 35km circumference of the lake could be cycled in three hours, though you will probably want to stop along the way or make detours away from the lake to see buildings or areas of interest.

Bushwalks of various standards are accessible within and near Canberra. A booklet *25 Family Bushwalks in and around Canberra* is widely available though it is stronger on autobiographical anecdote than clear instructions. The Tidbinbilla Fauna Reserve has five nature trails that can be walked in between 30 and 60 minutes. Another very scenic area for walkers is Ginnindera Falls, 12km north of Canberra. A local residents' association charges $5 to park near the reserve but admission is free and the surroundings are lovely.

Skiers and mountaineers will probably head for the Kosciusko National Park about three hours drive south of Canberra (see *New South Wales: Great Outdoors*) though some people head for the artificial snow slopes much nearer town at Corin Forest just past Tidbinbilla, 30 minutes drive from the city.

Spectator Sports. Just because Canberra is full of bureaucrats and intellectuals does not mean that there isn't much interest in sport. In fact former Prime

Minister Bob Hawke had a huge television screen in his office, rumoured to be mainly for watching horse races and rugby matches. There are a great many sports clubs and the Sports Results telephone number (1187) is dialled just as frequently as elsewhere in Australia.

The Canberra Rugby League team is up with the best in the New South Wales league, and can be seen in action at the Seiffert Oval (which also stages cricket in summer). Soccer is played at the National Stadium in Bruce.

The premier horse race of the year is the Black Opal Stakes which takes place at the Canberra Race Course during the Festival. The course, which is located where the Barton Highway meets Northbourne Avenue, has the distinction of having introduced Sunday racing to the nation. Harness-racing takes place at the National Exhibition Centre.

Canberra at night is as safe and peaceful as it looks during the day. Poverty and crime are virtually non-existent and the newspaper is hard-pressed to find any sensational local news (outside the arena of politics). Even with the large political and diplomatic contingents, security is very low-key.

There is one unexpected source of danger — magpies. These raucous common-place birds become quite aggressive during the nesting season in the late winter and will divebomb intruders. Children's bicycles are often equipped with a tall rod to deflect magpie attacks, and nervous adults have been known to carry an umbrella in fine weather.

The area code for Canberra is 06. For emergency fire, police and ambulance, dial 000.

ACT Tourism Commission: Jolimont Centre, Northbourne Avenue, Canberra City 2601 (245 6464; toll-free 008-026 166). Also has an information centre at the north end of Northbourne Avenue for arriving motorists. Both open 7 days a week. There are also ACTTC branches in Sydney: 14 Martin Place (02-9233 3666) and in Melbourne: 102 Elizabeth St (03-9654 5088).

British High Commission: Commonwealth Avenue (270 6666).
US Embassy: Moonah Place, Yarralumla (270 5000).
Hospitals: Royal Canberra, Acton Peninsula (243 2111); Royal Canberra South, Yamba Drive, Garran (244 2222).
General Post Office: Jolimont Centre, corner of Moore and Alinga Sts (248 5211). Open Monday to Friday 9am–5pm.

The ACT is somewhat insulated from the recession that hit Australia in the early 1990s and there are jobs available especially for anyone with office skills. The CES's Templine office is at 33 Ainslie Avenue (274 4000).

Calendar of Events

December/January	Fiesta Capitale
January	Sports Carnival (10 days)
February	Royal Canberra Show
March (third Monday)	**Canberra Day**
March (starts second	Canberra Festival (10 days)

Saturday)

March	Black Opal Stakes
March/April	National Sheepdog Trials
April	Hot Air Balloon Gathering
April	Nike Marathon
April/June	National Eisteddfod
June	Festival of Australian Drama
August (first Monday)	**Bank Holiday**
mid-September/mid-October	Floriade Spring Festival
October	*Canberra Times* Fun Run
November	National Wine Show

Public holidays are shown in **bold**.

Melbourne and Victoria

Population of Melbourne: 3,050,000   **Population of Victoria: 4,500,700**

Victoria is the same size as Great Britain, and is easily Australia's smallest mainland state. Yet it contains as great a variety of terrain as any other state, encapsulating almost the entire range of Australian landscapes and climates in microcosm: from the Little Desert to the Snowy Mountains, rich pastures to rainforest, and tumbling vineyards to dramatic coastline. Together with Tasmania, Victoria is promoted as 'Australia Naturally', to draw to the world's attention the fact that Victoria has a wealth of little-known natural attractions.

From the urban point of view, Victoria comprises big-city style and small-town country life, laced with a fascinating colonial history. Victoria is the most densely populated state in Australia, and mightier than New South Wales in its economic power: mineral reserves and fertile farmland, commerce and hi-tech industries. Underpinning its financial strength is the sprawling city of Melbourne, the only rival to Sydney in terms of sophistication.

Melbourne has received a relatively bad press as a destination for travellers, not least from other Australians; for a start, its skies are noticeably greyer than elsewhere on the mainland, and compared with the spectacular setting of Sydney, Victoria's capital can strike the newcomer as a trifle drab. Set around the sluggish Yarra River, Melbourne has little appeal to the eye and the solid Victorian buildings convey an air of dourness. But an international survey in 1990 proclaimed Melbourne to be the most desirable city to live in in the world. Everyone will tell you what a mess the Victorian economy and politics are in, but you wouldn't guess it to see the place. An accelerated building programme has seen the cityscape shoot skywards, old buildings renovated and the Yarra

River cleaned up to become a popular location for boating and barbecues. Melbourne is even more cosmopolitan than other Australian cities, and boasts the best sporting venues, the liveliest arts and indisputably the finest food.

If you stick to the city centre of Melbourne you'll be disappointed as it is an ungraceful business and shopping area. Like London or Manhattan, picturesque cosmopolitan neighbourhoods are dotted around the heart of Melbourne and are far more interesting and satisfying than the commercial centre: St Kilda, once a seaside resort for the wealthy, now a down-at-heel yet attractive beachside suburb; Port Melbourne, a refurbished waterfront area; Carlton, Fitzroy and Richmond, paradise for cut-price gourmets.

The rivalry between Sydney and Melbourne is intense, each vying to be the most dynamic and exciting state capital (even Melburnians admit that Sydney is more beautiful). Sydneysiders abuse Melbourne for its weather, its staidness and its social snobbery, most prominent among those with 'old money' inherited from the pioneering days. The people of Melbourne roundly condemn Sydney for what they see as a lack of real values and concern, and an insatiable quest for wealth. Melbourne itself is comfortably rich, with sturdy Victorian banks dating from a time when Melbourne was the largest financial centre in Australia. It has been overtaken by Sydney, whose location on the Pacific Rim is so much more popular with foreign investors.

One of the strongest images in urban parts of the state is wrought ironwork. Pig iron was used as ballast for ships sailing from Britain. It was unloaded in Melbourne, then wrought into ornate balconies on suburban villas or bigger structures such as the Ballarat Oval.

The state had inauspicious origins, as the colonial powers in Sydney had little interest in exploiting far-flung regions. The first attempted settlement in 1803 on Port Phillip Bay (on which Melbourne stands) was abandoned in May 1804, and the settlers moved to Van Diemen's Land (now Tasmania). The first overland crossing to the Great Southern Ocean was made in 1836 by Surveyor-General Thomas Mitchell, who travelled past Port Phillip Bay as far west as the present-day town of Portland. As permission had not been granted for settlement of the southern regions, he was startled to discover a European family, the Hentys. Disgruntled with life in Tasmania, they had sailed across the Bass Strait in 1834. Edward Henty had been followed in May 1835 by John Batman, who bought a million acres of land around Port Phillip Bay from the Aboriginals. Melbourne was founded three months later by John Fawkner, who built a house on the banks of the Yarra River. Two hundred more 'squatters' had arrived before the area was officially declared open for settlement in 1836.

The settlers resented being governed at a distance by Sydney. After mounting protests the new state of Victoria was established in 1851, named almost inevitably after the Monarch who dominated much of the world in the 19th century. In the same year, gold was discovered inland in the region around Ballarat and Bendigo. In the gold rush that followed, the population of Victoria increased seven-fold. Melbourne grew into a real city, as a port was needed to service the miners and their production. The government of Victoria was keen to take a share, and made licences compulsory for prospectors. The law was enforced by the Red Coats, a harsh militia. Resistance against the increasing demands of the state and poor treatment of 'diggers' culminated in the storming by troops of a makeshift stockade at the Eureka claim near Ballarat. Twenty-two miners were killed, and the public outcry that followed forced the government to capitulate to many of the demands for social reform.

No other state is so much a part of the development of an Australian consciousness, of the struggle for independence and individuality. The most significant figure was Edward 'Ned' Kelly. He came from a typically poor rural family and, through a series of skirmishes with the police, became an outlawed bushranger. Although eventually captured, convicted and hanged in Melbourne Gaol, Ned Kelly was regarded as a folk hero who epitomised the fight of the impoverished against injustices perpetrated by the authorities.

CLIMATE

You are sure to be told that Melbourne experiences all four seasons in a single day, or to be asked 'Don't like the weather? Don't worry, it'll change in a minute'. But while the weather rarely takes a grip for weeks on end as it does in other parts of Australia, the climate of Victoria is certainly more benign than that of Tasmania, Scotland or New England. The weather is quite English: though there can be unremitting cloud, cold and rain in winter and long, hot spells in summer, mostly it is blustery and changeable.

Melbourne lies in a climatic region classified as 'warm temperate'. The average maximum during the hottest months (January and February) is 25°C/78°F; with occasional summer heatwaves touching 40°C and (because of Melbourne's southerly location) long, balmy summer evenings. The beginning of the football season in April is asssociated with cold, wet, windy weather. The mean midwinter maximum in June and July is 14°C/57°F. While temperatures in the city rarely fall below 4°C/40°F, the mountainous areas of Victoria can be below freezing for long stretches in winter. Rainfall averages 66cm annually, slightly less than in London and New York and, surprisingly, half that of Sydney and Brisbane. Rainfall is highest in June and July but showers occur throughout the year: even the driest month, January, has only 15% less rain than the average.

THE LOCALS

In the past 150 years, two million people have migrated to Victoria, three quarters of them since 1945. One in four Victorians was born overseas; the state has immigrants from over 100 countries. Melbourne has the largest Greek population (115,000) of any city outside Greece, plus big Italian, Vietnamese, Lebanese, Chinese, German and Maltese communities.

Despite this rich, multicultural mix, most Melburnians are fairly conservative. The first settlers were pioneering 'squatters', opening up the land and rapidly becoming rich and powerful. The influence of the 'squattocracy' is still pervasive. Melbourne is the home of old money: while these establishment families have been financially dwarfed by the new tycoons, their conservative influence prevails.

Making Friends. A good way to remove the social barriers is to find work in the hospitality industry, as you are sure to meet some of Melbourne's more colourful characters. If time does not permit getting a job, or if your funds don't require topping up, you could visit some of the livelier pubs in the city such as the Lord Newry in North Fitzroy and the Flower in Port Melbourne. The city has a large student population, and it is easy to meet people on the University of Melbourne campus in Carlton; in particular, try Milligan's Café on the ground floor of the Union building, or the nearby Albion Arms on Lygon St. The *What's On* magazine mentioned below lists meetings that interested visitors could attend as various as the Melbourne atheist society and Chinese cookery classes.

Getting Around

City Layout. Metropolitan Melbourne covers an area spanning 80km from east to west and 100km from north to south, making it larger by half than New York City and three times the size of Greater London. The central business district lies alongside the Yarra River, which forms one of its boundaries. The other boundaries are Spencer, Victoria and Spring Sts. Within this area the roads form a grid pattern, making navigation fairly straightforward. If you're trying to find an address within the central area, remember that the low numbers are at the southern ends of north–south streets, and at the eastern ends of east–west streets.

The central parts of Bourke St and Swanston St are pedestrian malls, but trams run through them. A possible source of confusion with main east-west streets is that most have another street a block north prefixed 'Little', e.g. Little Bourke St runs a block north of Bourke St.

The *Melbourne Tourist Map* is free from the tourist information offices in the City Square and Bourke St Mall as well as the RACV at 227 Bourke St. It is adequate for short stays, but if you intend to stay awhile you should invest $29 in the *Melway Street Directory*. About the size of a telephone book, the *Melway* is an essential part of living in Melbourne: locations given on advertisements often quote the map reference for the directory. As well as street maps of the whole area, it lists almost everything you could possibly want to locate, from bicycle tracks, bus and tram depots, cinemas, libraries and markets to squash courts, swimming pools, parks and gardens, tennis courts and skating rinks. The *Melway* also includes detailed information on train and tram travel, with helpful diagrams of the various types of tickets available, and even has a double-page map of the Victorian Arts Centre complex. As mentioned below (*City Transport*) The Met Pass has recommendations for outings and excursions in and around the city. A phone service gives details of free (and almost free) activities in Melbourne: 0055-14946.

Plans are afoot to redevelop Flinders St Station on the river, which will include tearing down the ugly concrete Gas and Fuel Towers, two abominations left over from the 1960s. The project, in imitation of Sydney's Darling Harbour, will include two galleries of shops, restaurants, etc. built above the historic old station, and a new pedestrian bridge over the Yarra to the Arts Centre. On the south side of Spencer St bridge, the new Southbank site is being developed to house the Museum of Victoria.

Melbourne has many interesting suburbs (and many more dull ones). Close to the city centre, visit Toorak and Richmond to the east, and Carlton to the north. South-west, on Port Phillip Bay, is St Kilda. Many decades ago it was the seaside holiday destination for Melbourne's wealthy. It still has the grand old homes and hotels, wide streets and other once-beautiful buildings, though now they are a little the worse for wear. One unexpected feature is that fairy penguins have taken to nesting in the tunnels of the Breakwater so you may not need to go to Phillip Island (see page 212) for this wildlife experience. Finally, note that the suburb of Prahran is pronounced either as Pran or Pre'ran, but never as Prar-ran.

ARRIVAL AND DEPARTURE

Air. Melbourne's main airport is Tullamarine, 23km north-west of the city centre. It is the only airport in Australia open 24 hours a day. The international and domestic terminals are adjacent, making transfers easy. The airport bus into Melbourne is the Skybus (9335 2811). It operates half-hourly between 6am and 10pm to Spencer St Station. It stops by request anywhere along its route (including both main YHA hostels). The one-way fare is $9. If you have time to spare, you can travel from the airport to the city by public transport for $3; this involves taking the bus to the suburb of Essendon (which also has an airport) where you change to tram 59.

Other airport buses from Tullamarine serve various suburbs of Melbourne

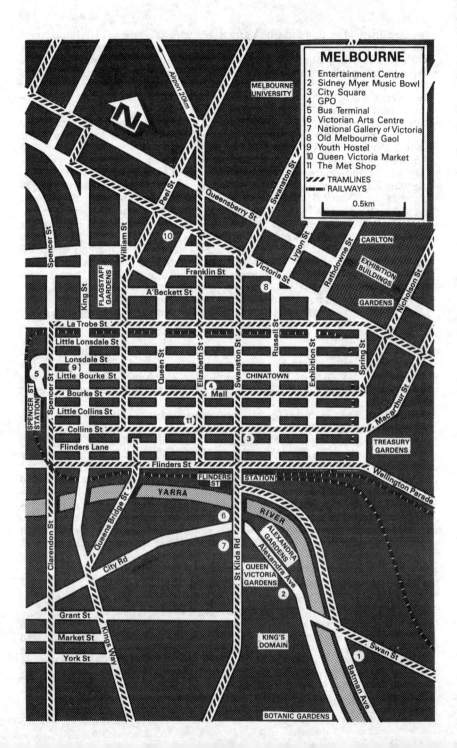

including Dandenong (9791 2848), Frankston (9786 6888) and Knox (9793 4298). Buses also run to the towns of Ballarat (5335 9770) and Geelong (5222 4966). If you land at a quiet time for arrivals (particularly in the evenings), you may find that the supply of taxis far outweighs demand. The normal fare is about $24–28, but you may be able to negotiate it down to the bus fare.

Melbourne's second airport is at Essendon, between the city and Tullamarine. Its airport code is MEB, distinguishing it from the international airport (MEL). The only services from Essendon are local flights to other Victorian towns and to Tasmania. There are also flights to Tasmania from the airport at Moorabbin (south-east of Melbourne) and from Cowes on Phillip Island.

Melbourne does not match Sydney in its range of cheap fares abroad but there are still many bargains to be found using Garuda Indonesia, Lufthansa or the Yugoslav airline JAT to Europe, or United and Air New Zealand to the USA. The main STA Travel office is at 222–4 Faraday St, Carlton (9347 6911); seven other branches are dotted around. The Melbourne Flight Centre (no relation to the Sydney Flight Centre) is at 317 Swanston St (200m from Museum Station; 9663 1304) and the associated Flight Shop is nearby at 287 Elizabeth St (9670 5565). REHO Travel has an office at 21 Toorak Road, South Yarra (9867 7822).

Passengers flying from Melbourne on Qantas can check in at the Hyatt Hotel on Collins St between 2 and 12 hours before their flight; this facility is available 8am–5pm daily, and saves you lugging your bags out to the airport.

Bus. Most country and interstate buslines use the Spencer St Coach Terminal at 205 Spencer St, near the railway station at the west of the city centre. There are several specialist bus booking agencies where you can find out about discounts and book tickets. Try Interstate & Country Bus Services' Dial-a-Coach section at Shop 14, 177 Flinders St (9654 8477) or 14 Spencer St (9629 3848). The YHA Travel Centre at 205 King St (9670 9611) offers a full booking service with discounts for YHA members. The main companies are:

Firefly Express: Spencer St Coach Terminal (9670 7500).
Greyhound Pioneer: 58 Franklin St (9663 3299).
McCafferty's Express Coaches: Spencer St Coach Terminal (9670 2533).

Competition is fiercest between Melbourne and Sydney, and fares can be less than $50 ($40 for YHA members). Fares to Adelaide are about the same. The Wayward Bus Company (see page 254) charges $110 for a 3-day backroad trip to Adelaide.

Train. The Victorian State Railway network V/Line operates all rail and associated coach routes within Victoria. Country and interstate trains use Spencer St railway station, on the western edge of the city centre. For rail information call 132232 or visit V/Line Travel at 589 Collins St.

There are both daytime and overnight daily XPT services between Melbourne and Sydney in both directions. The overnight *Sydney Express* departs daily from Spencer St Station at 8pm. The corresponding train from Sydney, the *Melbourne Express*, departs at the same time. It normally carries both first and second class passengers, although sleeping berths are only for first class. But at busy times a relief service leaves at 9.35pm (8.30pm from Sydney) and the *Sydney Express* is then first-class only. The trip takes 13 hours.

The *Overland* is a daily overnight service that runs in both directions between Melbourne and Adelaide. Departures are at 9pm daily, and the journey takes 12 hours. The *Daylink* service to Adelaide leaves Spencer St each morning at 7.55am: you take the train as far as Dimboola, then change to a connecting bus service. In the reverse direction, you leave Keswick rail station in Adelaide at 7.15am, arriving in Melbourne at 6.38pm.

There is also a range of combined train and coach interstate services to various destinations, including Canberra. The fastest surface link to Canberra is the daily *Canberra Link*, involving a train from Melbourne to Wodonga and a bus connection from there to Canberra. The journey time is just over 8 hours.

V/Line offers two passes valid on all V/Line trains and buses in Victoria. The one-week pass costs $69, and the two-week pass $120.

Ferry. Station Pier in Port Melbourne (4km south-west of the city centre) is the terminal for the *Spirit of Tasmania*, a three-times-weekly ferry to Devonport, Tasmania. The service departs from Port Melbourne on Mondays, Wednesdays and Fridays at 6pm, and from Devonport on Saturdays, Tuesdays and Thursdays at the same time. The trip takes 14½ hours. Ring 132010 for bookings and information.

The fast catamaran to Tasmania leaves from Port Welshpool 200km east of Melbourne. See page 227 for times and fares. There are also frequent services to Phillip and French Islands from Stony Point and across the heads of Port Phillip Bay from Sorrento and Portsea to Queenscliff.

Driving. The roads of Victoria are more crowded than those of other states. The overall maximum speed is 100km/h, with the usual 60km/h limit in towns. The maximum allowable blood/alcohol level is 0.05%, and there are many random breath test stations. Those who are caught are fined heavily and banned from driving for not less than two years. On main highways you might find a coffee station serving free coffee, intended to reduce the number of accidents caused by driver fatigue.

The most popular and shortest route from Sydney to Melbourne is via the Hume Highway (number 31). The longer and prettier Princes Highway (number 1) will take you along the southern New South Wales coast and through some interesting beachside towns. Between Adelaide and Melbourne the most direct route is the Western Highway (number 8), but the Princes Highway is more picturesque.

Melbourne has numerous car hire outfits and rates are highly competitive. Worth a try are Rent-a-Bomb (9429 4095), Delta (9387 7199) with a dozen locations, Ugly Duckling (9525 4010) and Dam Cheap Hire (9484 1364). Even with Avis, Budget and Hertz, it is worth asking (e.g. at the airport) for a discount. You can hire a motorbike from Norvin Australia (9555 7014). To buy or sell a car, try A & M Car Wreckers, 238 Coppin St, Richmond (9428 7655).

The state motoring organisation is the Royal Automobile Club of Victoria (RACV), whose main office is at 250 Collins St (9650 1522). It opens 9am–5pm from Monday to Friday, 9am–noon on Saturdays. The emergency road service number is 131111. The RACV publishes a good road map of the state (sold to members of foreign motoring organisations for 75c) and a free brochure *Motoring Holiday Planner*.

Hitch-hiking. Melbourne's sprawling suburbs make hitching difficult, but fortunately good hitching spots on the main routes to Sydney and Adelaide are fairly easy to reach. For the Hume Highway north to Canberra and Sydney, take a train on the Broadmeadows line to Craigieburn and walk a few hundred metres north to the junction with Craigieburn Road. To hitch north-west to Ballarat and Adelaide, get the Melton line train to Deer Park and walk north-west to the start of the Western Freeway.

CITY TRANSPORT

Melbourne's public transport system is cheap and efficient. The excellent free *Get around on The Met* public transport map is a comprehensive guide to the tram, bus and rail services, which are known collectively as 'The Met'. All public transport information is available from the City Met Shop at 103 Elizabeth St, open 7.30am–8.30pm daily except Sunday (9.15am–2pm). For information by telephone call 131638. Tickets can be purchased at train stations, on board trams and buses, at the Met Shop and from various retail outlets, including selected newsagents, chemists and milk bars. The Met also publishes a DIY tour guide of the city and environs called *The Met Pass* for $3.

As in London, fares are calculated by the number of zones travelled. Once you have mastered the basics of the system, it is easy to calculate how much your journey will cost. Zone 1 covers the city centre and a large area around it, with two further zones outside. Tickets are fully interchangeable from one mode of transport to another. A basic Zone 1 ticket costs $2.10 and allows 2 hours' travel within the central area; a daily ticket costs $4.10. Zone 1 'short trip' tickets are also available for $1.50, or ten for $12. A daily ticket for the whole of the network costs $9.20. If you plan to be doing a lot of travelling in Melbourne, a weekly ticket for Zone 1 costs $18.00 and a monthly one $68.

Passengers travelling without valid tickets are regularly caught and fined up to $200.

Trams. The best way to get around the city and inner suburbs is on Melbourne's efficient tram system, which has 700 trams on 325km of track. Some stretches are dedicated to trams only, providing an excellent light rail service — route 96 offers rapid transit between East Brunswick, Bourke St in the city centre and St Kilda on the bay.

How to track it down by tram on The Met is a free guide to the system, available at railway stations. If you don't already have a ticket when getting on a tram you should buy one from the conductor on board. On the older trams, he or she will approach you; on new ones you must enter at the front and pay the ticket collector. On Sundays some trams are replaced by bus services.

Suburban Trains. Areas beyond the reach of the tram system are served by electric trains. The city-centre part of this network forms an underground railway around the centre, known as the 'City Loop'. The stations on the Loop are Spencer St, Parliament, Museum, Flagstaff and Flinders St, the latter being the main station for the suburban network. All suburban lines converge on the City Loop, which means you can get out to any destination from one of these stations. Frequent trains run from Monday to Friday, but at weekends some services are reduced to one an hour. Timetables and tickets are available at the usual Met outlets.

Bus. Many Melbourne bus services are privately owned, but all operate within the Met system, charging standard fares and accepting Met transfer tickets. There are few routes in the central area; most run in the inner and outer suburbs, connecting with tram and train services.

The double-decker 'City Explorer' bus (9619 1111) operates every day from 10am to 4pm, and you can board and reboard as often as you like in a single day. Buses depart on the hour from Flinders St Station. Tickets cost $14.

Taxis. Partly because of the tough drink-driving laws, taxis can be in short supply after the pubs close. At other times you should have little trouble hailing one in the street or picking up a cab at one of the many ranks in the city suburbs.

To summon a taxi by telephone (for an extra fee of 60c), call one of the following companies:

Arrow — 9417 1111   Embassy — 9320 0320
Astoria — 9347 5511   Regal Combined — 9810 0222
Black Cabs — 9567 3333   Silver Top — 9345 3455
Dandenong Taxis — 9791 2111   North Suburban Taxis — 9480 2222

On top of the standing charge of $2.60, there is a kilometre charge that varies with the time of day. From 6am to 6pm the rate is 62c per kilometre; after 6pm the rate is 78c, and after midnight you pay a surcharge of $1.

Car. The most confusing thing about driving in Melbourne is the peculiar form of turning right at city-centre junctions that are crossed by a tram line. Drivers intending to turn right indicate so, then pull into the left lane, go across the lights and come to a halt in front of the cars waiting to go straight ahead. When the lights change they make their turn. These 'hook turns' are something of an acquired skill, so try to watch the natives in action before attempting the manoeuvre.

Trams must always be passed on the inside, never on the outside. Also, you must never pass a stationary tram unless directed by a tram driver, conductor or policeman. Passengers getting on or off have the right of way until they are safely on the footpath. Tram lines are delineated by yellow lines; the solid lines cannot be crossed, the broken ones can be so long as you do not obstruct a tram.

Parking anywhere in the centre during business hours is difficult, and illegal parking earns a fine of between $20 and $60 depending on the flagrancy of the offence. The City Parking Information service based at the Town Hall (9658 9800) can offer advice, but staff usually recommend that you leave your vehicle on the city fringes. The free *City Parker's Guide* shows all off-street car parks in the city centre. On-street parking in the evenings is fairly easy, but you should by law leave a gap of 1.2 metres between your vehicle and the next.

Outside the city, the grid system for roads disappears in a tangle of arterial roads and freeways, so a good map is essential.

Cycling. With its boulevards, parks and gardens, and the absence of steep gradients, Melbourne is a good city to cycle around. Furthermore Victoria has a positive attitude to cycling — the capital is laced with over 500km of cycle tracks. Bicycle Victoria (29 Somerset Place or PO Box 1961 GPO, Melbourne 3001; 9670 9911) has information and maps for cyclists including *Melbourne's Bikepath Book*. The guide has detailed maps of the tracks and surrounding areas, and covers such topics as train crossings and other danger areas, track surfaces and places of interest slightly off the track.

The most central and popular bikepath is the Yarra Path. Starting beneath the Victorian Arts Centre, it follows the Yarra River through parkland, past the Botanic Gardens, on through the wealthy suburbs of Toorak, Hawthorn and Kew. Other recommended bicycle tracks can be found in Fawkner Park, Alexandra Gardens and Gellibrand Hill. You can take your bicycle free on off-peak suburban trains.

To cope with the difficulty of turning right in city-centre traffic, most cyclists practise the box turn (like the hook turn described in *Car* above), where you cross in the left-hand lane to the corner of the street, wait for the lights to change and go across with the flow of traffic. Because of the high number of accidents involving bikes, helmets for cyclists are compulsory in Victoria.

Hire-a-Bicycle (9801 2156) operates in several locations: during school holidays and at weekends, a trailer is parked on Jeffreys Parade immediately south-east of Princes Bridge. Rates range from $6 per hour to $25 for a full day (double for tandems) with a discount for YHA members and students. The Melbourne Bicycle Centres at 179 High St, Prahran (9529 3752) and 37 Queens Parade, Clifton Hill (9489 5569) rent secondhand bikes for $10 per day; if you subsequently decide to buy, the rental paid is deducted from the cost.

Ferry. The *MV John Batman* sails between the World Trade Centre and Williamstown via St Kilda on Sundays and public holidays; call 9397 2255 for details. Tickets can be bought on board for $20, which allows unlimited travel. If you only want to hop from the port of Williamstown (10km west of the city centre) to St Kilda, the cost is $5. Another Sunday excursion on the water is the two-hour cruise on the Wattle Steam Tug (advance bookings on 9328 2737 are necessary.) For a short scenic cruise on the Yarra River, contact City River Cruises on 9650 2214 which charges about $8.

Hostels. The YHA Travel Centre in Victoria is at 205 King St, at the corner of Little Bourke St (9670 9611). It opens 9am–5.30pm from Monday to Friday, 9am–noon on Saturdays. Try to pick up a copy of the state YHA's free magazine, *The Hosteller*, issued three times a year. Of the 18 YHA hostels in the state, the huge purpose-built Queensberry Hill International Hostel is the most luxurious. It is located in the city fringe suburb of North Melbourne, at 79 Howard St (9329 8599). Access to the hostel is by tram 55 along William St, or by tram 19 or 59 along Elizabeth St. The hostel has 312 beds in a variety of room types, with a dorm bed costing about $17 a night. It has 24-hour access, security lockers, a roof-top sun deck, a full travel agency and licensed bistro meal service.

The other YHA hostel in Melbourne is Chapman Gardens, also in North Melbourne, at 76 Chapman St (9328 3595). It costs $15 for a bed in a shared room, or $17 per person in a twin room. Both hostels offer discounts for stays of four nights or longer and telephone bookings by credit card are accepted.

VIP Backpackers Resorts have several hostels in Melbourne. One of the best is in the appealing area of Carlton; it is called The Nunnery and is at 116 Nicholson St (9419 8637). Cheapest beds are $12. To get there take a number 96 East Brunswick tram from Bourke St, and get off at stop 11. Many hostels are in the popular backpacker area of St Kilda, including The Ritz for Backpackers (169 Fitzroy St; 9525 3863), which promises a non-stop party atmosphere; dorm beds start at $12. Take tram 15 or 16 from Franklin St or tram 96 from Spencer St. Many hostels offer advice on job-hunting, such as Enfield House Backpackers at 2 Enfield St (9534 8159) — again, beds start at $12 (there are also long-term flats available from $45 per week) — use the same tram numbers as for The Ritz. In the same area are the Coffee Palace (24 Grey St; 9534 5283) and Leopard House (27 Grey St; 9534 1200), which have dorm beds in the same price range; Leopard House also has free bike hire.

Other hostels include Toad Hall Guesthouse in the city centre (9441 Elizabeth St; 9600 9010) and The Richmond, in the inner city suburb of the same name (353 Church St; 9428 6501) — beds in shared rooms start at $15 in both. Also in Richmond is Central House, which is at 337 Highett St (9427 9826). Carlton Hotel (also known as the Backpackers City Inn) is right in the centre at 197 Bourke St (9650 2734). The northern suburbs also have some good budget hostels, including The Terrace at 418 Murray Road, Preston (9470 1006), which as well as offering a full range of backpacker facilities 'guarantees employment opportunities' for those looking for work, whether casual or long-term. Beds start at $12 in the last three hostels.

Hotels and Motels. Avoid the motels and private hotels opposite Spencer St Station unless you're completely stuck. These places are cheap but are also home to a weird selection of local transients. The motels and private hotels of St Kilda, the closest Melbourne has to a red light district, are a little better, but the higher quality motels in the area (e.g. the Diplomat at 12 Acland St; 9534 0422) are clean and safe enough. Cheap private hotels include the Hollywood at 348 Beaconsfield Parade (9534 3402) where compulsory full board costs $152 a week.

The Miami Motor Inn at 13 Hawke St, West Melbourne (9329 3003) is a pleasant bed and breakfast that caters to backpackers and students. It offers single and double rooms at $36/$52 per night; weekly rates are $189/$308. VIP Backpackers Resorts of Australia has an upmarket place in Melbourne called the Pension Melbourne in St Kilda (96 Barkly St; 9537 1412) where the rate is $23 bed and breakfast. The YWCA hostel and headquarters is in the city centre at 489 Elizabeth St (9329 5188). Rates are $45 for a single, decreasing to $15 per person for four people sharing. Weekly rates are about five times the corresponding daily rate.

Student Residences. The University of Melbourne has several colleges open to visitors during student vacations. Ring the Central Booking Office on 9347 9320 for information. Although more expensive than the cheapest hostels, the University is well situated north of the city centre and the quality of accommodation and breakfast is good. Student rates are around $30 for bed and breakfast and $38 for non-students. Try Ormond College (9348 1688 or 9347 7113), Queens College (9347 4837) or St Hilda's College (9347 2258 or 9347 1171).

Longer Term Accommodation. There are plenty of apartments to choose from in Melbourne, and they are less expensive than in Sydney. The notice boards in the hostels are the best starting place. Enfield House Backpackers, mentioned above, operates an informal flat-finding service for travellers. Otherwise, try the notice board at Readings Bookstore, 338 Lygon St, Carlton where many advertisements for shared accommodation are posted. The window is changed every Friday morning, but notices awaiting display may be viewed on request. The best days to look at advertisements in the *Age* are Saturday and Wednesday. Again St Kilda is the most likely neighbourhood for affordable rented accommodation. For example Esquire Apartments (65 Acland St; 9525 4547) advertises three-person apartments starting at $30 a night.

Camping. The closest site to the city centre is the Melbourne Big 4 Holiday Park, 10km north in Coburg at 265 Elizabeth St (9354 3533). It has on-site cabins and caravans for hire, as well as space for tents; rates for campers are $9 per person per night. There are also excellent facilities, including a swimming pool. The site is reached by tram 19 or 20 from Elizabeth St in the city to Bell St, and then bus 526 to the front door.

Eating and Drinking

In terms of value and variety, Melbourne is arguably the best city in the world for eating out. You can eat your way around the world and through the alphabet in Melbourne, from Afghan to Zulu. Melbourne has over 2,000 restaurants, four-fifths of them BYO. The *Yellow Pages* devotes 36 pages to restaurants. Dining out is one of the most popular forms of entertainment for Melburnians, and is taken very seriously. Food shopping is also a joy, for example at the glitzy new suburban Chadstone market where 'if you can eat it you can buy it'.

To assist with your choice of restaurant, the Melbourne *Age* produces an annual called *Cheap Eats in Melbourne*, a bible for budget gastronomes. It covers the Melbourne metropolitan area, country, hills and Yarra Valley areas. Another source is the free Restaurant Advisory Service on 9328 4442 or 9328 3800 (although this service is sponsored by certain restaurants and is not, therefore, altogether objective). Similarly there are information lines for seafood (9426 8152), international cuisine (9426 8158) and steakhouses (9426 8154).

Individual cuisines are concentrated in certain communities or streets. Lygon St, Carlton is famed for its Italian restaurants; Swan St, Richmond for Greek; Johnston St in Fitzroy for Spanish; Little Bourke St in the City for Chinese; Victoria St, North Richmond for Vietnamese and Brunswick St for vegetarian. The following selection is just the tip of the iceberg, but all are recommended as providing good value.

One of the best places for breakfast is Mittons (10 Murphy St, South Yarra, just around the corner from Toorak Road). Mittons is very popular on Sunday mornings and is famous for its home-cooked eggs benedict, brains and kidneys, at reasonable prices, with newspapers provided.

Melbourne's Chinatown is at the Spring St end of the city and extends three blocks into the city. Try to attend the Chinese food market held on Sundays. The area has many Asian cuisines besides the basic Chinese varieties of Cantonese, Szechuan and Mandarin. The cheapest tend to be the Malaysian restaurants, for example Rasa Selangor (at 7 Waratah Place, just off Little Bourke St) which offers cheap Malaysian meals in bright, clean surroundings. The curry laksa ($8 for a huge bowl) is great value and a meal in itself, but you have to like your food hot. Little Malaysia (9662 1678), on the corner of Little Bourke St and Liverpool St, is slightly more expensive but serves good food and is cheap if you stick to the many dishes that don't contain crab, prawns or lobster. Unless you book, be prepared to wait for a while during peak times; Sunday nights are particularly busy. 'Little Saigon' on Victoria St in North Richmond has lots of cheap and basic places with formica-topped tables, serving excellent Vietnamese food for next to nothing. There is also a Vietnamese community, and hence restaurants, in the suburb of Footscray.

Out at St Kilda, Mariners (9 Fitzroy St; 9534 5630) is an excellent seafood restaurant with leaded windows and stylish decor; the oysters are good value and the pasta dishes superb. Next door at number 7 is an unpretentious pizza place run by the same owners.

Several good Thai restaurants charge about $25 for a wonderfully tasty meal; try Ruan Thai, 91 Johnston St, Collingwood (9419 4814); Chiang Mai, on Chapel St at Grosvenor St in South Yarra (9826 1181) or Restaurant Thai 505 at 505 Chapel St (9241 8682); all are BYO. Sawasdee is more central at 139 Little Bourke St (9663 4052), but is licensed and hence a little more expensive. In St Kilda go to Ruan Phya, 290 St Kilda Road.

Most University of Melbourne students eat at the cafés and restaurants on Lygon St, though the canteen on the ground floor of the Union building (which outsiders are welcome to use) has filling daily specials for about $5. Lygon St probably has more pizza restaurants per kilometre than any street in Italy, and the smell of garlic and baking dough assails your nostrils as you walk along it. (For the very best pizzas, however, *Cheap Eats* recommends the takeaway-only Pizza Nova at 111 Hoddle St, Richmond, 9417 2791; and La Porchetta at 392 Rathdowne St, Carlton North, 9347 8906.) Signs in Lygon St café windows say 'never mind if you don't speak Italian — we speak a good broken English'. You can buy pizza by the metre from Da Salvatore at number 132. Toto's at 101 claims to be the first pizzeria in Australia, and its speciality is the 'Aussie' consisting of cheese, tomato, bacon and egg. Toto's also does a 'spaghetti' ice cream, a brilliant creation that looks like spaghetti bolognese; piped banana ice cream is topped with strawberry sauce and grated white chocolate. Unfortunately Toto's is huge and impersonal. At 141 Lygon St is Casa di Iorio, which is notable for the large proportion of Italian diners. And Ilios, at number 174, is an exceptional Greek restaurant.

Late at night go to Bobby McGee's at the corner of Exhibition and Little Bourke Sts, which does some interesting suppers. Stalactites, on the corner of Lonsdale and Russell Sts manages to provide good food in decent surroundings around the clock. Pasta around-the-clock can be had at Chapelli's, on the corner of Chapel and Oxford Sts. One of the most popular 24-hour fast food places is Fast Eddy's at 32 Bourke St (which often has jobs).

One restaurant with a difference is Dracula's Theatre Restaurant which offers an entertaining horror show as you eat (98 Victoria St, Carlton). The most unusual restaurant, however, is the Colonial Tramcar. Every evening except Mondays, this mobile tramcar-cum-restaurant makes a circuit of the city serving the diners on board with a five-course meal and excellent wines. The price (including drinks) is $50 before 7.15pm and $75 after. Advance reservations should be made at Level One, 319 Clarendon St, South Melbourne (9696 4000).

Just as in Sydney, lots of the trendier pubs serve good food. Try the Waterside Hotel, 508 Flinders St, the Golden Age Hotel, 287 King St, the Lemon Tree in Carlton at 10 Grattan St and the Met at 42 Courtney St, North Melbourne.

The up-and-coming area to eat is Fitzroy, notably the restaurants and cafés on Brunswick and Rathdowne Sts. On Brunswick, try Annick's Bistro (licensed/BYO) at the corner of King William St (9419 3117), Goldini is a good Italian place just north of the junction with Gertrude St. On Gertrude St itself are some interesting Yugoslav places, including the Yugoslavia at 193 Gertrude St (licensed and BYO, with a range of Dalmatian wines) which has excellent *burek*; meat, cheeses and fruit wrapped in pastry. (Incidentally, Gertrude St is where the Aboriginal community of Melbourne is concentrated.)

Cafés. Many people finish their meal by adjourning to one of the excellent cafés in the area. If you have eaten at one of the Fitzroy restaurants, a good place to finish up is at Mario's at 303 Brunswick St; this is also a fully fledged restaurant with an all-day breakfast for $7 and main meals including a glass of wine for $12. There are several other good places on Brunswick St between Johnston St and Alexander Parade. They include 25 varieties of 'the best ice-creams in the world' at Charmaine's ice cream parlour at 370 Brunswick St.

If you emerge from a film at the Carlton Moviehouse near the University, pop into Genevieve's next door on Faraday St for coffee and ice cream (or pasta if you are more peckish). Cake-fetishists should head for Acland St in St Kilda, which is lined with cake shops, most of which open daily, and are reminiscent of patisseries in Vienna or Budapest.

DRINKING

Melbourne's licensing hours are reasonably liberal, and with a little application it is possible to drink around the clock. Pub hours are usually 10am-midnight except Sundays (noon-8pm), but some clubs and discos remain open until 7am daily, around the time when the market pubs open. The Central Club Hotel at the junction of Victoria and Queen Sts opposite the Queen Victoria market is open 6am-6pm. In a feeble attempt to reduce the level of drunkenness, it is illegal to drink at the bar of pubs after 10pm; you have to sit at a table.

Most Melburnian males drink the local brew VB (Victoria Bitter). Other local beers worth trying include Wattle Lager (German-style), Abbotsford Invalid Stout (5.9% alcohol, dark and sweet) and Old Ballarat Brew (made by the Sovereign Brewery in Ballarat) which comes in at 4.9% but has far more taste and character than most bottled beers. Try also the Ballarat Gold Pure Malt Lager. For Bendigo lager, you need to go to the Rifle Brigade brewery-pub in Bendigo.

Pubs. The range of pubs in Melbourne is nearly as diverse as the range of restaurants. Many have courtyards that are perfect for whiling away the hours on a sunny afternoon with a few glasses of wine. Others provide live rock or jazz music. Bookshops stock a *Guide to Melbourne's Pubs* which includes those of Ballarat and Bendigo.

Among the most interesting are the brew-pubs which make their own beer on the premises. The Redback Brewery at 70 Flemington Road, North Melbourne is the Melbourne branch pub-brewery of Perth's Matilda Bay Brewing Company. It produces a wide range of real ales, lagers and stout, including Dogbolter, Brass Monkey Stout, Dark Lager and of course Redback. The pub serves good food and has live music every night until late. In the city centre, try Young and Jacksons, an elegant old Victorian place at the foot of Bourke St by Flinders St Station. It is a beautifully presented National Trust property, and the saloon bar has a celebrated portrait of Chloe. At the other end of the city centre, Mac's Hotel is ideally placed for Greyhound Pioneer bus passengers with time to spare. It is on Franklin St between Swanston and Elizabeth Sts, and is the city's last surviving coaching hotel — it even has a horse trough outside.

The answer to the old pub song 'Does anyone know of a better old place than Bourke St on a Saturday night?' is yes. Indisputably the best range of beers can be found at the Loaded Dog at 324 St Georges Road, North Fitzroy (9489 8222). This is a roomy and friendly pub-brewery, making five different beers and selling around a hundred others. The name of the pub comes from a Henry Lawson short story, set in the mining days in Victoria. It concerns a retriever named Tommy who finds a stick of gunpowder, a yellow mongrel that steals it from him and a pub that subsequently explodes (together with the mongrel); the full story is related on the pub's menu and on the wall of the dining room, and there is a large fibreglass sculpture of a beer-swilling dog. Beers available include Yellow Mongrel (light, cloudy and similar in taste to home-brewed beers), Cobrungra Bitter (golden, well hopped), Ruby Bitter (like a stout) and Thunder Ale (9% alcohol, the same as light wines). The Loaded Dog also has imported beers, ranging from Samuel Adams' Boston Lager to Tennant's Milk Stout from Scotland. The menu (snacks, steaks, seafood) includes recommendations for suitable beer accompaniments (discount for hostellers); there is also a good wine list and live music every night, sometimes performed by string quartets rather than loud electric bands.

The Limerick Arms at 364 Clarendon St in South Melbourne has over 30 imported beers for sale, including English, Irish and Scottish. Apart from the excellent meals and choice of beverages, the Limerick is Melbourne's top jazz pub with live bands seven nights a week playing everything from cool jazz to Dixieland.

The Old Homestead Inn at 170 Queen's Parade, North Fitzroy has a wide range of out-of-state beers including Coopers from Adelaide and overseas beers including some British beers on tap. It stocks board games and darts that can be borrowed for a small returnable deposit. Another pub that features five British beers is Dickens on Collins downstairs in Block Court at 290 Collins St.

The Flower Hotel in Bay St, Port Melbourne, is the current trendy place to spend a Sunday afternoon drinking and listening to a rock band. Its frontage is a complete glass wall which slides up to open out onto the street. The Botanical at 169 Domain Road, South Yarra and the Lord Newry on Brunswick St, North Fitzroy are other trendy places to go during the evenings. The cosy Alexandra in Powell St, South Yarra has a lovely courtyard where you can dine on good food. In winter, various roasts are served for Sunday lunch. The Lemon Tree at 10 Grattan St, Carlton is a popular pub which specialises in Saturday afternoon 'sessions' and which has an upstairs area whose roof is folded back in good weather so you can dine and drink in the sunshine. Travellers staying in St Kilda often congregate at the Esplanade Hotel which serves cheap drinks and has live entertainment seven nights a week. There is a shortage of pleasant, rather than merely functional, pubs in the city centre; one of the best is the Mitre on Bank Place off Collins St.

For civilised late-night drinking in the city centre, go to Mietta's on Alfred Place; this is a side street off the top end of Collins St, between Russell and Exhibition Sts. The main feature is a fancy restaurant upstairs, but there is also a lounge bar round to the right of the ground floor. Don't be put off by the rather grand facade and formality (they insist upon seating you, and serving you at your table). You can drink relatively cheaply (e.g. $4 for a bottle of beer) until 2 or 3am (midnight on Sundays) and study the fascinating clientele; sophisticates, illicit lovers and the morose and solitary drinkers. Mietta's also stages occasional poetry readings, including recitals by Benjamin Zefaniah.

Victoria is not the greatest wine-producing state in Australia, but there are good local wines including some splendidly full-bodied Cabernet Sauvignons. The area around Rutherglen, in Northern Victoria near the Murray River, produces fine fortified wines such as Muscat, Tokay and vintage port. When buying wine to take to a BYO restaurant, you might want to try Dan Murphy's Cellar at 280 Chapel St in Prahran (9510 8531) which reputedly has eight million bottles of wine and is the largest liquor store in Australia. Melbourne's few wine bars provide a pleasant alternative to pubs and restaurants. Try Jimmy Watson's at 333 Lygon St and the Alphington House wine bar at 2 Grattan St (both in Carlton), and McCoppins Wine Pub at 166 Johnston St, Fitzroy. One cocktail you might wish to avoid is the 'Keating Sour' named after the former Prime Minister Paul Keating. It is served at the Last Aussie Fishcaf (256 Park St, South Melbourne). It consists of a glass of water with a twist of lemon. On the other hand, the fresh fish served here is highly recommended.

For an overview of the city, go to the top of the 53-storey Rialto Building or up the Collins Tower, an office block at 33–45 Collins St. You're not officially supposed to go to the top, but some adventurous types have enjoyed the view before being turfed out by security guards.

It should not take you too long to see the main points of interest in Melbourne. Edward 'Ned' Kelly was hanged in Melbourne Gaol, aged 25, on 11 November 1880. The last relics of his body were stolen from there in 1978. The Gaol, at the top end of Russell St in the City (9663 7228), is a well preserved three-storey building. It is open daily (9.30am–4.30pm) and consists mainly of refurbished cells containing rather grisly death masks (plaster casts of heads) of former inmates. The theory was that phrenologists would measure the skulls to determine features common to criminals. The Gaol has a small souvenir shop. Admission costs $5.

The lawmakers reside at Parliament House, a grand but rather gloomy Victorian edifice. While Parliament is in session, you can visit the debating chamber every Tuesday, Wednesday and Thursday. Try to catch 'Questions Without Notice' at 10.30am each day, a rumbustious debate in which the Premier gets involved in slanging matches with the opposition.

The centre of Melbourne is busy and noisy, but the Cathedral Church of St Paul on the corner of Flinders and Swanston Sts is a charming oasis of calm. The residents of the street in which exterior scenes of the TV programme *Neighbours* are shot would no doubt prefer calm to gawking tourists, but curious visitors is what they get. 'Ramsey Street' is Pinoak Grove in Glen Waverley (*Melway Street Directory* p 62, reference E8).

Museums and Galleries. Melbourne's best is the National Gallery of Victoria, at 180 St Kilda Road (9208 0222), adjacent to the Arts Centre. The gallery houses 75,000 items, including some outstanding Aboriginal and other Australian art, and excellent collections of Asian, European and Pre-Columbian paintings, sculpture, photography, prints and drawings and decorative arts. It opens daily from 10am to 5pm. Admission is $6 (students $3), which entitles you to a free guided tour (on Monday–Friday at 11am, 2pm or 3pm, fewer tours at weekends). You can visit the downstairs galleries free of charge on Mondays.

Other galleries worth a visit include Ebes-Douwma (at the top of Bourke St) for antique prints and maps, and Heide Park and Gallery, home of several significant works of Australian art. The Performing Arts Museum (at the rear of the Melbourne Concert Hall at 100 St Kilda Road; 9281 8263) is one of the most unusual museums in Australia. It has exhibitions featuring a wide range of arts and artists from Dame Nellie Melba to Dame Edna Everage. They are presented in theatre form, making it an easy museum to enjoy. Entrance is normally $2.50 but is higher for some exhibitions. It opens at 11am, Monday–Friday, noon at weekends and closes daily at 5pm.

The Museum of Victoria (9669 9997) is a major museum featuring large displays on Australia's history, the natural environment and aboriginal culture. It is also the home of the Children's Museum, with its exhibition of the human body and water, the Melbourne Planetarium, and Phar Lap, Australia's most famous racehorse. The main entrance is at 328 Swanston St (near the corner of Little Lonsdale St) and it opens 10am–5pm daily, admission $3. Scienceworks was formerly part of the same museum, but it is now a separate hands-on science and technology centre; exhibits include an energy-efficient house and a science adventure playground. It is at 2 Booker St in Spotswood (9392 4800).

The Australian Gallery of Sport and Olympic Museum is located at the Melbourne Cricket Ground (MCG) in Jolimont Terrace, Jolimont. It covers the whole range of sport in addition to cricket. It opens 10am–4pm daily, and the admission charge of $8 includes a guided tour of the MCG Members' Pavilion (on non-event days). Outside is a plaque commemorating the first Australian team to tour England, composed entirely of Aboriginals.

Parks and Zoos. More than one-quarter of inner Melbourne is taken up by parkland. If you're planning to spend some time out of doors in Melbourne get the brochure *Parks and Gardens* from the city tourist office.

The nearest park to the centre is Treasury Gardens, south-east of Macarthur St. It includes Captain Cook's Cottage, the English childhood home of the explorer. This was dismantled in Great Ayton, Yorkshire and rebuilt in Australia in 1934. The cottage opens 9am-5.30pm daily, admission $2. In the centre of the gardens is a model Tudor village, presented to the people of Melbourne after World War II by Londoners in gratitude for food supplied to them. Finally, you might like to inspect the Conservatory (open 9.30am–5pm, admission $1).

Melbourne's biggest park is Kings Domain which includes the Alexandra and Queen Victoria Gardens, stretching a long way along St Kilda Road into South Yarra. Unfortunately the parkland is ruptured by busy roads, such as the five-lane Alexander Avenue. King's Domain is the home of the Floral Clock (opposite the National Gallery), the Women's Memorial Garden, the Sidney Myer Music Bowl and the Shrine of Remembrance. The Shrine is a spectacular memorial to the Anzac troops who died during the two World Wars. It was constructed so that at the 11th hour of November 11th (Armistice Hour) a shaft of sunlight strikes the Remembrance Stone. An eternal flame burns for the memory of the Australian dead. The Shrine opens 10am-5pm daily, and yields good views across the city.

The Royal Botanic Gardens (9650 9424) on the south bank of the Yarra River cover 36 hectares on the edge of Kings Domain. It has 10,000 plant species from most countries of the world. It is also the home of the National Herbarium. You can take a free guided walk around the Gardens from Plant Croft Cottage on Tuesday and Thursday at 10 and 11am, and from gate F on Sundays at the same times.

Albert Park Lake (between the city centre and South Yarra) is very popular with joggers and cyclists, and also with picnickers who make good use of the gas barbecues at the lake's edge on summer nights. The lake, which can be enjoyed in a hired canoe or paddle boat, is man-made and is surrounded by good roads which were originally designed as a motor racing circuit. At Yarra Bend Park in Kew, you can also hire a canoe from the boathouse to take out on the river. Flagstaff Gardens right in the City (Latrobe and William Sts) are the venue for free summer concerts on Sunday afternoons.

The Royal Melbourne Zoological Gardens opened in 1857 and comprise Australia's oldest (and the world's third-oldest) zoo. It is north of the city centre on Elliott Avenue in Parkville (9347 1522), on tram routes 18, 19, 20, 55 and 56. You can also reach it by suburban train to Royal Park station. It opens Monday-Saturday from 9am to 5pm, admission $7.50; the entrance by the railway station opens 30 minutes later and closes 30 minutes earlier.

The zoo is forward-looking, with a system of keeping animals by habitat rather than by species. The kangaroo, emu and wallaby section is a walk-through area where the animals roam freely amongst visitors. The zoo also features a gorilla rainforest area which is home to Mzuri, a baby lowland gorilla, the first surviving birth using artificial insemination.

Beaches. Sydneysiders may tell you that Melbourne cannot hope to have a decent beach as its location on Port Phillip Bay is 60km from the open sea of the Bass Strait. Indeed, if you are after huge breakers for surfing, Melbourne will be a disappointment. There are, however, pleasant and safe swimming beaches west and south-east of the city. The closest are Albert Park, St Kilda, Middle Park (recommended) and Half Moon Bay (even better). At the windsurfing school on the beach at Beaconsfield Parade you can hire windsurfers and/or have lessons.

The nearest ocean beaches are a long way from the city, at Torquay (96km south-west of Melbourne, beyond Geelong) and Portsea (96km south). The treacherous surf at Cheviot Beach, beyond Portsea at the mouth of Port Phillip Bay, has claimed the lives of many, including Prime Minister Harold Holt in 1967. The Mornington Peninsula south of the city (see *Day Trips*) has many beaches, including a nudist one at Somers.

SHOPPING

Melbourne is said to be the favourite destination in Australia for airline cabin crew, as it has the best shopping. The time for bargains is during the January sales. Most shops in the city centre are open 9am–5.45pm Monday to Wednesday, with late opening to 9pm on Thursdays and Fridays. On Saturdays most open all day though some still close at lunchtime. Shops along Barkly, Acland and Fitzroy Sts in St Kilda open on Sundays. The leading department store in Victoria is Myers whose downtown branch on Lonsdale St is one of the ten largest stores in the world. Georges, David Jones and the new Japanese store Daimaru, in the huge new Melbourne Centre in Lonsdale St are also popular.

The trendiest and most expensive boutiques are in Chapel St in South Yarra (south of Oxford St), and Toorak Road in Toorak. Some of the arcades are worth visiting simply for their architecture, such as the Italianate three-storey arcade at 280 Chapel St. Another recommended sight is the ultra-modern Chadstone Shopping Complex on the Dandenong Road in Chadstone. The High St of Armadale (between Toorak and Prahran) is famous for its antique shops. North of the city centre, Brunswick St north of Johnstone St has some fascinating New Age stores.

One of the several opal shops in the city centre is worth visiting even if you have no wish to buy gems. Andrew Cody Opals at 119 Swanston St has a room in which you can watch opal cutters at work plus the owner's private collection of valuable and unusual stones including an opalised dinosaur skeleton. Nearby in the Century Building at 125-133 Swanston St you can shop for Aboriginal art at Aboriginal Handcrafts on the ninth floor.

You can buy all your camping gear from tin pans to tents, overcoats and sleeping bags from one of Melbourne's many disposal stores. These stores specialise in army surplus but also stock a wide variety of non-military gear. In the city Mitchell's Army and Navy Store at 134 Russell St, and Bush and Mountain Sports at 360 Lonsdale St are among the best.

For cheap secondhand stuff, try the Salvation Army Thrift Shop at 144 Chapel St, South Yarra; further along at 350 is the Oriental Pearl pawnbroker (9241 5179), with yet another pawnbroker at 378 selling good deals with sad stories attached. For clothing bargains the 'sample and seconds' shops run by mainstream clothing retailers and manufacturers can be good. There is a large selection of these shops in the area surrounding the junction of Church and Swan Sts in Richmond (mostly women's clothing) and more in Bridge Road, Richmond (with a few men's stores).

Books. Perhaps because Melbourne prides itself on being a more intellectual city than Sydney the city has a stunning selection of bookshops. Among the best for second-hand and discounted books are Book Affair (1st Floor, 238 Flinders Lane) and Colourcode Book Discounts (391 Bourke St). The International Bookshop on the second floor at 17 Elizabeth St (9614 2859) is hard to find but has an interesting selection of feminist, Marxist and gay literature. Readings at 338 Lygon St (with three other branches) is also progressive. It has an excellent noticeboard for flat shares, etc. which is changed every Sunday. Readings stages poetry recitals upstairs at the nearby Lord Newry pub (corner of Brunswick and Newry Sts) most Wednesdays at 8pm. If you're based in Fitzroy try the Brunswick St Bookstore at 305 Brunswick St (north of Johnstone St). It opens 10am–11pm daily, and has a sister shop in Albert Park, the Avenue Bookstore at 25 Victoria Avenue.

Bonanza Books (at 191 Bourke St) is open daily until 10pm and has some good bargains. The interesting Whole Earth Bookstore at 83 Bourke St opens until at least 9pm daily except Sundays (1–6pm). The Paperback Bookshop at

60 Bourke St does even better, opening until 11.15pm every night except Sunday (1–4pm). The widest selection of books is at the Technical Book & Magazine Co at 289–299 Swanston St. Don't be put off by the name: it sells books of all types, including a comprehensive travel collection, and if you can't get it there it probably isn't available in Australia.

Records. Melbourne is saturated with record shops but the following are among the best in their field. For classical discs, Thomas's at the Southern Cross on the corner of Exhibition and Bourke Sts has long had the biggest selection. For pop/rock try the Mighty Music Machine in Chapel St, South Yarra. Hound Dog's Bop Shop at 313 Victoria St in West Melbourne specialises in re-issues and original 50s and 60s rock and roll, rockabilly, hillbilly blues and boogie (open Thursday to Saturday only). Discurio at 20 McKillop St in the city centre are stockists of obscure recordings, most notably of classical music but also of jazz, folk and pop. Readings (see *Books,* above) deals in secondhand discs at its 366 Lygon St branch. The Virgin Megastore at 152 Bourke St opens until midnight on Friday and Saturday, and noon-6pm on Sundays.

Markets. There are so many markets in the state of Victoria that 'Life. Be in it' (4 James St, Windsor 3181) publishes a guide to all of them (for $25). The Queen Victoria covered market (near the corner of Elizabeth and Victoria Sts on the north-west edge of the city) is a wonderful place. As well as fresh produce it has a huge selection with stalls selling bargain priced clothing, household goods, and hardware items. It opens 6am–2pm on Tuesday and Thursday, 6am–6pm on Friday, 6am-1pm on Saturday and 9am–4pm on Sunday. On Sundays most of the food vendors are replaced by merchants selling souvenirs; the other days tend to be less touristy.

Smaller but similar markets are held at Prahran and South Melbourne. The Prahran Market (on Commercial Road) is open on Tuesdays and Thursday to Saturday while the South Melbourne Market on Cecil St is best for flowers and produce on Wednesday, Friday, Saturday and Sunday. Another suburban market worth visiting at weekends is the Preston market (take train on Epping line to Preston or tram 10/11).

The Meat Market at 42 Courtney St in North Melbourne may not sound promising unless you need a side of beef, but this lovely renovated building has been converted into a craft centre with occasional demonstrations of pottery, spinning, etc. For souvenirs try the makeshift market on the Esplanade in St Kilda each Sunday morning. A larger market is held in the Fitzroy Town Hall on the second Sunday of the month.

Entertainment

For a city of over three million people, Melbourne has surprisingly few 'sights', but to compensate it has a lively arts scene and splendid sport. Details of forthcoming cultural events can be found in the *EG* (entertainment guide) section of Friday's *Age*, while the quarterly *What's On* magazine has entertainment and festival listings as well as ideas for excursions, etc. It is published as part of the 'Life. Be in it' campaign and costs $2 at newsstands or from 4 James St, Windsor 3181.

The main ticket agency is BASS whose enquiry number is 11566 and whose booking number is 11500 (Monday to Saturday 9am-9pm). At the Half-tix booth in the Bourke St Mall you can buy half-price tickets on the day of performance. The booth is open Tuesday to Friday 11am–6pm and Monday and Saturday 10am–2pm. Ring 9650 9420 for a recorded message on ticket availability.

'Fantastic Entertainment in Public Places' (FEIPP) is the city council's catch-phrase for free entertainment. Venues include the City Square, the Sidney Myer Music Bowl and various parks and gardens. Events cover a wide range of music and street theatre. Programmes are available from the Town Hall or by calling 9658 9800.

Festivals. Melbourne's rich culture and ethnic mix means there are plenty of festivals during the year. The Lygon St Festa is a weekend in early summer when the street is closed to traffic and becomes a street party. You can enjoy live entertainment, food from the many (mostly Italian) restaurants and street stalls, browse through craft displays and even take part in a spaghetti eating contest. Chapel St in South Yarra has a similar festival in early February each year.

Moomba is an annual festival running for ten days in late February/early March, with many activities in which most of Melbourne gets involved. Moomba is an Aboriginal word meaning roughly 'let's get together and have fun'. The beginning (and end) of Moomba is marked by a fireworks display which is visible all over Melbourne and is one of the best in the world. One good vantage point for the viewing of the fireworks is the 35th floor of the Regent Hotel; this floor is devoted to restaurants and a lounge area, and the best view is attainable from the large picture windows in the toilets, where you are high enough to be next to the exploding fireworks. Another highlight is the Moomba Masters Water Ski Championships on the Yarra River in the city, contested by the world's top water-skiers and well worth seeing. Other attractions include theatre and dance, exhibitions of art, photography, pottery, ceramics, and events like the Walk on Water Contest, for which young Melburnians invent some ingenious contraptions.

For the duration of the festival an amusement park takes over Alexandra Gardens. The closing highlight of the Festival is the Moomba Parade and fireworks, when thousands of people line the streets (and people outside Melbourne tune in on television). Many local organisations construct floats which participate in the procession down Swanston St. Despite the tacky aspects of this event (such as floats carrying bikini-clad aspirants to the crown of Queen of Moomba and many commercially sponsored floats), it is all great fun.

For those interested in higher-brow culture, a less commercialised yet thoroughly enjoyable festival is the Melbourne International Festival, held in the last three weeks of September. Performers from the US, Europe and Japan are joined by artists from Australasia. There is a lively fringe and good writers' workshops.

THE BEST VIEW OF THE FIREWORKS IS FROM THE TOILETS ON THE 35TH FLOOR."

For information call 9614 4484. A relatively recent addition to the calendar of festivals is the Comedy Festival held each year during the first three weeks of April (9417 7711).

Victorian Arts Centre. Compared with the setting of Sydney's Opera House, Melbourne's performing arts centre has a second-rate site on the western side of St Kilda Road, just south of the Yarra River. Nonetheless the Victorian Arts Centre (9617 8211) is a striking piece of architecture (particularly at night when its graceful 115m spire is illuminated), and its galleries and auditoria have sumptuous interiors. Performances are staged in the Concert Hall (2600 seats), the State Theatre (2000), the Playhouse (880) and the George Fairfax Studio (420). In addition there are often free foyer performances. Guided tours leave from the Concert Hall at noon and 2.30pm daily (except Saturday) at a cost of $4. Special backstage tours are conducted each Sunday at 12.15 and 2.15pm for $9.

Dial 11566 for specific enquiries. Tickets for all events can be booked through BASS on 11500 (008-338998 from outside Melbourne for the price of a local call).

Theatre. Apart from the theatres at the Arts Centre, Melbourne has a number of others offering a diverse range of entertainment. The major theatres are Her Majesty's at 219 Exhibition St; the Comedy Theatre at 240 Exhibition St; the Russell Theatre, 19 Russell St (home to the Melbourne Theatre Company); the 1854 renovated Princess Theatre at 163 Spring St; and the Athenaeum Theatre at 188 Collins St. Fringe theatres include the St Martin's in St Martin's Lane, South Yarra; TheatreWorks at 14 Acland St, St Kilda; and the Union Theatre on the University campus (where Dame Edna began her career in the revue *Return Fare* in the mid 1950s). A listing of independent theatre productions appears in the *Live Theatre Directory* each day in the *Age*. Although not quite as theatrical as the Sydney Stock Exchange (as the financial world in Melbourne goes in for blue chip stocks), you can visit the gallery of the Melbourne Stock Exchange 10am–12.15pm and 2–3.15pm.

Opera. The Victoria State Opera season at the State Theatre runs through July and August plus November and December. Ticket prices start at $25 ($20 for students) but cheap student standbys at $15 are sometimes available on the day of performance. The Australian Opera Booking Office can be contacted on 9629 3421.

Cinema. Melbourne has the usual chain cinemas such as Hoyts at 140 Bourke St (9663 3303) and Greater Union at 131 Russell St (9654 8133), but also has a lively independent circuit. These cinemas have their own listing in the *Age*. In particular, the Valhalla Cinema at 89 High St, Northcote (9482 2001), the Trak at 445 Toorak Road in Toorak (9827 9333) and the Longford at 59 Toorak Road in South Yarra (9867 2700) have good repertoires. The Carlton Moviehouse is at 235 Faraday St near the University campus (9347 8909). It also aims to show uncommercial films including many late-night or all-night shows. The State Film Centre is buried amid government offices at 1 Macarthur St. Despite its source of funding, it shows an extremely wide range of movies, including an annual season of gay and lesbian films.

Music. Melbourne is always on the itinerary of visiting rock performers. Most big concerts are held at the Sports and Entertainment Centre on the banks of the Yarra; others take place at Flinders Park, Batman Avenue (9655 1277). Concerts in summer are often held outdoors at the Sidney Myer Music Bowl in

Alexandra Gardens, Olympic Park and Kooyong Stadium. In addition the Youth Affairs office of the Department of Labour sponsors some free outdoor concerts (no alcohol allowed). For rock music on a smaller scale go to one of the many pubs around Melbourne which feature live bands.

For a selective recorded gig guide to Melbourne dial the Gig Guide on 0055 14747; more comprehensive listings can be found in the entertainment guide free with the *Age* on Fridays, or in the excellent music weeklies *Beat* and *In Press* free from clubs, pubs and restaurants. Some of the pubs mentioned above in *Drinking* have live entertainment such as the Redback Brewery, the Old Homestead Inn (weekends only, no cover charge).

Jazz can be heard at the Tankerville Arms at 230 Nicholson St in Fitzroy, the Bridge Hotel at 642 Bridge Road, Richmond and the Limerick Arms at 364 Clarendon St, South Melbourne. Most Friday and Saturday nights at 11pm, the Victorian Arts Centre stages Jazz After Dark. The Melbourne Folk Club (9489 2441) meets every Friday at the East Brunswick Club Hotel, 280 Lygon St, East Brunswick.

The Melbourne Concert Hall is the home of the respected Melbourne Symphony Orchestra. A Summer Music Festival is held each January at the Concert Hall; contact BASS for details and bookings.

Nightlife. Melbourne has more than twice as many nightclubs as Manhattan. Most are open until at least 3am daily, some until 7am. King St in the city is Melbourne's nightclub centre, and is very busy on Friday and Saturday nights. Starting from the bottom end of the street, popular discos are the Grainstore Tavern, Inflation at number 54, X — The Nightclub at 62 and Lazars. The largest nightclub is the Metro at the eastern end of Bourke St ($7 cover charge mid-week) while the Shout Rock Café at the northern end of King St is popular. Don't try to get into any of these clubs while drunk, and make sure you are reasonably dressed.

Other popular nightclubs outside the city centre are the Chevron on the corner of St Kilda and Commercial Roads, Bortolotto's Café at 16 Fitzroy St, St Kilda, Chasers at 386 Chapel St, South Yarra and Stringfellows in Lygon St, Carlton. The Last Aussie Fishcaf (256 Park St, South Melbourne) becomes a party venue late at night when diners dance to 50s rock and roll.

For comedy try the Comedy Café at 175 Brunswick St (9419 2869). For hoky nationalistic entertainment go to the Dinkum Oz show at 55 Cheywynd St, North Melbourne for an evening of comedy, music and food.

Gambling. In an effort to raise government revenue, poker machines have been legalised and 10,000 of them are to be installed in clubs and hotels over the next couple of years. (This has dented the economy of the New South Wales town of Albury, as it is no longer necessary for gambling Victorians to cross the border.) Victoria has no casino, but there is a state-run gambling palace at the Rialto Hotel on Collins St which is open 11am to 'late' every night. The Victorian TAB (which runs the new 'Tabaret') has restored the building to its original Edwardian splendour and offers betting on virtually any sport as well as high-class poker machines.

SPORT

Melbourne is the home of Australian Rules Football, the Australian Open Tennis Championship, the Melbourne Cricket Ground (known the world over simply as 'the MCG'), the Melbourne Cup horserace and many thousands of rabid sports fans. From 1996 it is also the location of the Australian Grand Prix. Tickets for most major events can be booked through BASS Victoria on 11522.

Most of the clubs in the Victorian Football League (VFL) are from around Melbourne. Throughout the winter you can see Sunday afternoon matches at various grounds, culminating with the Grand Final at the MCG in late September.

The Australian Open Tennis Championship takes place each January at the National Tennis Centre at Flinders Park. It is the first of the four international Grand Slam events each year and lasts for two weeks. Tickets are cheap (except for finals days, when the 'scalpers' make fortunes); book from late September onward. Anyone can play at the Centre for $10 an hour.

Australia's biggest horserace is the annual Melbourne Cup, held on the first Tuesday of November at Flemington racecourse. The 2.40pm race over 3200m is considered extremely important. The day is declared a public holiday in Victoria, the federal parliament is suspended for the duration of the race and millions of dollars are staked on the outcome. While racing during the rest of the year does not achieve quite the same level of excitement, there are still some good events. As well as the Flemington track, there is racing at Caulfield, Sandown and Moonee Valley (which also has harness-racing every Saturday evening). The dogs race at Olympic Park and Sandown.

While the MCG has no equivalent to Sydney's 'Hill', the excitement generated by 100,000 cricket fans during Test matches or one-day games can be electric. Tours of the ground ($8) depart on the hour from 10am to 3pm daily (9657 8879).

The coming of the Australian Grand Prix to Melbourne makes the city's list of major sporting attractions look even more impressive. The race is held in March over the 58 laps of the Albert Park circuit, 2km south of the city centre. As well as the main event and several other categories of motor racing, the four-day weekend includes displays of classic and exotic cars, a celebrity race, activities on the Park's lake and an after-race rock concert. Grandstand seating for the full 4 days starts at around $300, although you can pay a lot more for the best views; general admission on the day of the main race is $67.

Not all of the city's inhabitants are purely armchair sports fans. The city's parks abound in jogging tracks, especially Albert Park Lake and the Tan Track in the Botanic Gardens. Melbourne has plenty of places to keep fit, including the City Baths at the corner of Swanston and Franklin Sts (9663 5888); south of the city centre try the Ultimate Sporting Club at 88 Surrey Road, South Yarra (9826 8781) or Hunt's Total Fitness Centre at the corner of Spring and Johnston Sts (9419 3636).

There are numerous public tennis courts (e.g. the Exhibition Courts on Nicholson St, Carlton), golf courses and public swimming pools in the city. In winter, the stage of the Sidney Myer Music Bowl is laid with ice and you can hire skates and spend the afternoon or evening ice skating.

For the latest cricket scores, dial 1188. The racing results are on 1185, and boating weather on 11541.

MEDIA
A recorded news summary can be heard by dialling 1197.

Newspapers. The Melbourne *Age* is both an excellent newspaper and a highly useful information source for visitors. As well as the Friday entertainment supplement *EG* mentioned above, Thursday's edition has a *Green Guide* to radio and television programmes. As in Sydney the two competitors have amalgamated and so the only other Melbourne paper is the *Herald-Sun*.

Radio. Melbourne's ABC station is 3LO on 774AM. The best rock is on the Geelong station Bay FM (93.9), which can usually be heard in Melbourne; city rivals are Triple R (3RRR, 102.7), Fox (101.9) and ttFM (101.1). For bland soft rock tune to Southern FM (88.3), and for oldies try 88.6. The most outspoken and irritating 'talkback' presenters are on 3AW (1278AM). For good community radio and native Australian music, listen to 3CR (855AM). The AM station 3UZ (927AM) is owned by Victoria's racing industry and hence features the sport rather heavily.

The city and most of Melbourne's suburbs are safe to walk around at night. In some ways St Kilda is Melbourne's equivalent of Kings Cross with drugs and prostitution in evidence. Women on their own should avoid the darker streets behind Fitzroy St in St Kilda or risk being mistaken for a street-walker. Some of the parks and gardens around the city centre, which are beautiful by day, should be avoided by people of both sexes after dark.

On-the-spot fines are doled out for littering and for traffic offences (including boating infringements). A great deal of marijuana is grown and smoked in Melbourne. Possession or use of even a small quantity is an indictable offence and, if you are charged, will result in being placed on bail and a compulsory attendance at court which will usually result in a non-custodial sentence. Penalties for dealing are harsh. The Legal Aid Commission of Victoria is located at 179 Queen St (9607 0234), and has nine other regional offices in Victoria.

The area code for Melbourne is 03. Call 000 for the emergency services.

Tourism Victoria is located at 55 Swanston St (9653 9777). It distributes appealing brochures in the series *You'll Love Every Piece of Victoria* and has offices in three other state capitals:

Adelaide: 16 Grenfell St (08-8231 4581).
Brisbane: 221 Queen St (07-3221 5200).
Sydney: 403 George St (02-9299 2288).

There are information booths located in the Bourke St Mall, at the City Square, Rialto Towers, Melbourne Town Hall and 422 Little Collins St. The RAC of Victoria Visitor Information Centre at Melbourne Town Hall (9650 1522) can also provide information.

Free tourist hand-outs include the *Official Visitors' Guide to Melbourne & Surrounds* and the *Melbourne Visitors' Map & Guide to Local Attractions*. There is also a host of telephone information services, many of which are mentioned in this chapter. The FOX FM Community Switchboard provides information on what's on, the weather, and so on, between 10am and 6pm. For specific information on Melbourne, it may also be worth contacting the Melbourne Convention & Marketing Bureau at 114 Flinders St (9654 2288).

The Travellers Aid Society of Victoria is at 169 Swanston St (9654 2600), with a branch at Spencer St Station (9670 2873). Like their counterparts in North America, they provide help and advice for travellers in difficulty and have public showers ($4.50, including the hire of a towel).

British Consulate-General: 17th Floor, 90 Collins St (9650 4155). Open 9.30am–12.15pm and 1.45–4pm, Monday to Friday.
US Consulate-General: 553 St Kilda Road (9526 5900).
American Express: 105 Elizabeth St (9608 0333).

Thomas Cook: 261 Bourke St (9654 4222); plus branches throughout suburban
Melbourne.
Post Office: corner of Bourke and Elizabeth Sts (9660 1343); open 8am–6pm,
Monday to Friday; restricted service on Saturdays and public holidays,
9am–noon.
Telecom Payphone Centre: corner of Elizabeth and Collins Sts.
Medical Treatment: Royal Melbourne Hospital, Parkville — 9342 7000; Alfred
Hospital, Prahran — 9520 2811; St Vincent's Hospital, Fitzroy — 9418 2211;
Women's Hospital — 9344 2210. AIDS hotline — 9419 3166.
Dental Emergencies: 9341 0222.
Women's Information and Referral Exchange (WIRE): 3rd Floor, 238 Flinders
Lane (9654 6844).

Helplines. Melbourne has a wide selection of useful numbers: Gayline — 0055
14515; Lifeline — 9662 1000; Quitline (information for smokers) — 11538;
Poison Information — 9345 5678. To report a 'national disaster', dial 9823 1122.

The Victorian economy is in particularly bad
shape and unemployment is nearly 10%. But
opportunities still exist for the itinerant
worker in most of the familiar categories
such as fruit and tobacco picking, plus resort
and city work. The *Age* has a massive employment section on Saturdays, though
some visitors find it less stressful registering with one of the temporary work
agencies. Drake has been particularly recommended and is accustomed to dealing
with people on working holidays: Drake Overload is at 35 Collins St (9654 4855)
while Drake Industrial is at 9 Queen St (9629 3575). Other temp agencies include
Riddells (9654 8811), Ecco (9866 2466) and Denise Lock & Associates (9670
4244). The main Commonwealth Employment Service office is at 128 Bourke
St (9666 1222). It opens 8.45am–5pm, Monday to Friday.
    As usual hostels are the best way to find out about work and Melbourne has
more than its fair share of hostel managers willing to advise. (See *Accommodation* above.)

Tourism. With so many restaurants, opportunities in Melbourne's hospitality
industry are numerous. If you fail to find work through adverts in the newspaper
or in restaurant windows, door-to-door visits often succeed, especially if you are
neat, clean and eager.
    If you happen to be in Melbourne in late October or early November for the
Melbourne Cup, your chances of finding casual work escalate remarkably. Hotels,
restaurants and bars become frantically busy in the period leading up to the
Cup. Private catering firms are also often desperate for staff. An application to
one of these (such as Rowlands and O'Brien Catering) in September or October
is sure to turn up some casual work at the Flemington racecourse at Cup time.
In addition to caterers, an army of sweepers and cleaners is recruited to go
through the whole course clearing the huge piles of debris left by the 15,000 odd
spectators in time for the next day's races. At other times of the year try showing
up at the MCG by 7am where it is possible to get a day's work (at $11 an hour)
picking up litter from the cricket ground.
    Outside Melbourne, the highest concentration of tourist facilities is along the
East Gippsland Coast (see *Eastern Victoria*, below) and the resorts of the Great
Dividing Range which are particularly active during the ski season. There is a
strong demand for seasonal workers in the main ski resorts of Mount Hotham,
Mount Buller, Baw Baw and Falls Creek. The largest employer in Hotham is

the Arlberg Inn Resort (5759 3618). Watch for adverts in the *Age* in April/May or ask at the CES in Wangaratta (at the corner of Ovens and Faithful Sts; 5721 5411). Staff turnover is high so it is still worth asking around mid-season. Other places to try are the Jack Frost Restaurant & Bar, the General Store & Bistro Tavern, White Crystal, Crumbies Café, BJ's Restaurant and Herbie's Bar & Grill.

Fruit Picking. More than New Jersey, Victoria deserves the designation Garden State. The fertile river valleys are prime fruit-growing regions. The Goulburn River has its source just north of Melbourne and flows north to join eventually the mighty Murray River near Echuca on the New South Wales border, irrigating the land along the way. Soft fruit is especially prolific around Shepparton and Cobram. Grapes are grown in most corners of the state, though the harvest around Mildura in the north-west seems to attract the most itinerant pickers.

Grapes and other fruit are grown quite close to Melbourne. For example grapes are grown in Lilydale; cherries and berries are picked in the outer suburbs of Wonga Park, Silvan and Monbulk from November onwards; and apples and pears are picked on the Mornington Peninsula from March to May. To get a job on a market garden in the Dandenongs just east of Melbourne ring 5968 4086.

But for the mass harvesting of fruit you should travel to northern Victoria where the Northern Victoria Fruitgrowers' Association in Shepparton (23 Nixon St; 5821 5844) and the Victorian Peach & Apricot Growers' Association in Cobram (30a Bank St; 5872 1729) should be contacted before Christmas. These associations represent over 500 orchard owners in the Goulburn/Murray Valley and direct willing workers to farms where jobs are available between January and April. They are so eager to attract foreign fruitpickers that they have published a leaflet on working holidays for distribution abroad. A bin of pears earns around $20, apples only $18.

The tobacco harvest is another possible source of employment. The area surrounding Myrtleford on the Ovens River and the Kiewa Valley further east are the places to head in early February.

If you would like to get to know Victoria better, you might volunteer to work on a farm or on a conservation project. See the introductory chapter on *Work* for details.

Further Afield

The main attraction of Melbourne's hinterland is its accessibility. The distance from Melbourne to the scenic mountains of the north-east or to the vineyards of the north-west can be covered in a day, though there are exceptional landscapes and attractions much nearer Melbourne. The density of roads in the state is high by Australian standards except in the large mountainous area east of Melbourne.

Victoria is more intensively agricultural than the other states, which accounts for the high number of dairy and wool museums, wheat research institutes and soup factories, all of which are open to the public. Of more interest to tourists is the fact that you are never far from a winery. The highest concentrations are along the Yarra and Goulburn Valleys not too far from Melbourne, around Avoca north of Ballarat, and in the northern corners of the state around Mildura in the west and Rutherglen in the east. Many wineries have colonial architecture and features of interest such as the 130-year old cellars at Chateau Tahbilk.

Alternative tour operators run a range of interesting tours, most of which can be booked through Melbourne's hostels. Autopia Tours (contact YHA on 9670 9611) and Melbourne Backpackers Sightseeing (9670 9706) both run tours to most of the destinations mentioned below.

DAY TRIPS FROM MELBOURNE

Try to pick up a copy of the brochure *Melbourne's Best Day Trips and Accommodation Deals*.

Organ Pipes National Park. This is difficult to find on maps, but easy to reach if heading north-west from Melbourne on the Calder Highway. Just before the Calder racetrack is a turning to the right, a road which leads through scrubland — a most improbable location for a National Park. Suddenly the ground drops away to reveal a deep gorge, formed by the babbling brook at its foot. A simple network of trails takes you around the highlights — Rosette Rock, so-called because it resembles one, and the tessellated pavement.

The park would be a pleasant picnic spot were it not for the proximity of Melbourne's Tullamarine airport.

Phillip Island. No one is surprised to learn that Ayers Rock and the Great Barrier Reef are Australia's top attractions. But who would have supposed (according to a recent tourist survey) that the Phillip Island Penguin Parade is rated just as highly?

Within a two-hour drive from Melbourne is the island named after the first governor of the colony. Its residents include a troupe of fairy penguins, so-called because of their relative daintiness though they still stand a foot high. At dusk they waddle up onto Summerlands Beach to their nests among the sand dunes. Special viewing stations have been set up, partly so that the rangers can keep an eye on the hundreds of tourists who might succumb to the temptation of using flash photography — harmful to the penguins and against the rules. Meanwhile the beach is floodlit, though the penguins remain happily oblivious to their role as circus performers. The advantage of visiting in summer is that the number of penguins swells; the disadvantage is that the number of tourists does likewise (it is possible to make an advance booking). Outside summer it can get surprisingly chilly at night so take a blanket. Tickets to the Penguin Parade cost $3.50 and are sold at the Phillip Island Information Centre in Newhaven (5956 7447).

Phillip Island is worth visiting for other reasons. The attractions of a Wool Centre pale in comparison to those of the 'world's only Giant Earthworm Museum' (apparently some worms grow to be 3m long). It also has an excellent wildlife park (admission $5) where you can hand-feed kangaroos (some with joeys) and wombats. There is even a tame Tasmanian devil.

You might want more than a day to explore the island's beaches. You can enjoy surfing on the south coast, or sheltered swimming on the north. Seals congregate at the westernmost tip of the island and can be observed from the 'Nobbies' kiosk, where binoculars can be hired for a small fee. Boats operate from Cowes to Seal Rock which will interest only those who don't suffer from sea sickness. The resort town of Cowes has two affiliated YHA hostels as well as lots of holiday accommodation.

The island is accessible by road (135km via the Bass Highway and bridge to Newhaven), ferry ($10 between Stony Point on the Mornington Peninsula and Cowes) or air ($200 return on the daily Penguin Express out of Melbourne's Essendon Airport; ring Moloney Aviation on 9379 2122 for details). If you are driving, get on to Dandenong Road (which is the Princes Highway) then turn onto the South Gippsland Highway at Dandenong.

The Dandenongs. The attractive hills called the Dandenongs 40km east of Melbourne are an ideal destination for a day's motoring, cycling or bushwalking (do not confuse the hills with the south-eastern suburb of Dandenong, which is some distance away, and dismal). Mountain Bike Hire in Belgrave (9754 4059) charges $15 a day including helmet and maps.

The main attraction is the rainforest ecology and the slender pale gums that line most of the roads and tracks. The best known of the parks and forests are Ferntree Gully National Park and Sherbrooke Forest Park. The area is at its most beautiful in the autumn. The many galleries, nurseries and antique shops are open 7 days a week, and Sunday lunch in the Dandenongs is almost an institution. Another place of interest in the same direction is the William Ricketts Sanctuary at Mount Dandenong, a sculpture park which attempts to demonstrate the close relationship between Aboriginal people and nature (admission $4).

About 25km further east along the Maroondah Highway is the world renowned Healesville Wildlife Sanctuary, a walk-through park with hundreds of wallabies, platypus, koalas, etc., many of which have been bred at Healesville. If you take a picnic, watch out for the emus and ibises which deprive incautious picnickers of their sandwiches.

The other principal attraction of the area is the Puffing Billy steam train which travels 13km through lush mountain scenery between Belgrave and Emerald Lake every day (recorded timetable information on 9870 8411). The cost is $8 single, $12 return.

Geelong and Environs. Although Geelong (pronounced Jer-*long*) is Victoria's second city it is a miserable blot on an otherwise lovely landscape. The main street is Ryrie St, which has a fine Victorian Post Office and Telegraph Station, but precious little else of interest. The social hub is the Preston Hotel. Geelong also has the National Wool Museum & Centre (5226 4660), plus a couple of mid-19th century homes, both overlooking the Barwon River in the suburb of Newtown and both run by the National Trust. A worthwhile stopover may be made at Werribee Park, about halfway between Melbourne and Geelong, which is an Italianate mansion built in the 1850s set in lovely grounds. It has a free range zoo, managed by the Zoological Board of Victoria which runs a park safari minibus tour at weekends (9741 2444). Polo is played here in season.

From Geelong, it is worth travelling 31km to the end of the Bellarine Peninsula, which encloses the western half of the enormous bay on which Melbourne is situated. Queenscliff, at the end of the highway, has lovely parks and some beautiful Victorian hotels which offer good lunches on Sundays. The Queenscliff Hotel and Ozone Hotel, both on Gellibrand St, are delightful. The Royal Hotel has no sea view and is consequently cheaper, with doubles from $50 and good meals. A more minor road follows the south coast of the peninsula past the lighthouse at Point Lonsdale (which guides ships through The Rip, one of the world's most treacherous stretches of water) and on to the beachside towns of Ocean Grove and Barwon Heads. The latter has a good pub popular at mealtimes, and both have good surf beaches.

Mornington Peninsula. On the other side of The Rip is the Mornington Peninsula, the long Italy-shaped peninsula on the eastern side of Port Phillip Bay which is a popular spot for holidaying Melburnians who flock down to the excellent beaches and large developments of holiday homes; try to miss the weekend traffic jams. The song 'Morningtown Ride' by The Seekers is about the rail journey out along the peninsula, but now the line runs only as far as Frankston, where you take the Portsea bus to Sorrento; the two-hour trip costs $9 altogether.

If approaching from Queenscliff, take the car ferry across to Sorrento near the tip of the Mornington Peninsula trip which takes half an hour rather than the 3½-hour trip by road via Melbourne. The ferry ride costs $38 per carload of passengers. The car ferry is operated by Peninsula Sea-Road Transport (5252

3171). The journey on *Peninsula Princess* is splendid on a clear day. The towers of Melbourne, 35km away, are visible on the horizon. For information on the western side of the bay, see *Geelong and Environs*, above.

Sorrento is a quiet town with little in common with its counterpart on the Bay of Naples, except for Il Sorrentino restaurant which offers all the pasta you can eat for $10. The Hotel Continental is a fine place to stay, though much of its grandeur has faded. The YHA hostel is on Lander St, the town's main street.

Back Beach is the town's greatest attraction, a long walk south from the centre. The views are excellent, though the beach is rocky. A good one-hour trail from the car park takes you through the hills and back along the beach. An easier prospect is a quick five-minute scamper only as far as the first lookout, from where you can see both the bay and the Bass Strait. It gives a good view of the layout of the peninsula. A mile or so beyond Back Beach, accessible along the shore at low tide, is London Bridge — a rock with a hole — and some interesting caves.

The tip of the peninsula is Point Nepean, until recently an out-of-bounds military reserve. It now hosts the School of Army Health, and is part of a National Park. It is open to carefully controlled numbers of visitors — no more than 600 are allowed at any one time, so you need to book in advance on 5984 4276; admission is $6. Some people circumvent the restriction and the entry fee by going to the furthest car park on Back Beach and getting to the park that way.

One of the highlights of a stay in Sorrento is the chance to swim with dolphins (currently threatened by scallop fishing) and sea lions. Magenta Boats runs dolphin trips which can be booked through the YHA-affiliated Bells Hostel (5984 4323).

A couple of miles out of Sorrento is the Collins Settlement, site of the first official European occupation of Victoria in 1803, 40 years before Melbourne was founded. The 500 early settlers were led by Colonel David Collins, who chose a beautiful spot overlooking the bay. Unfortunately the lack of freshwater drove them out, to Hobart in Tasmania. The graves of those who died at Collins Settlement can be visited between 10am and 4.30pm; the adjacent display centre opens at 1pm.

The Melbourne area has a few modest wineries along the Yarra River in Greater Melbourne or further out such as the Yarra Burn Vineyards near Yarra Junction. Here you can attend a spit roast and hear bush music at weekends, provided you book in advance (5967 1428).

EASTERN VICTORIA

The Gippsland region of eastern Victoria is the home of Australia's largest inland waterway system. It combines wilderness, wildlife and welcoming towns. The Princes Highway is the main road through Gippsland, bisecting the area as it travels between Melbourne and Sydney along the eastern coast of Australia. Although there is a certain amount of tourist development around the oddly named town of Lakes Entrance, National Park status saves it from being too spoiled by commerce. Lakes Entrance is at the head of Ninety Mile Beach — a secluded and unspoiled ocean beach — and borders an interesting coastal lagoon system.

Heading east from Melbourne you soon hit the so-called 'Wildlife Coast' starting at Westernport Bay (100km from Melbourne) and running through Port Arthur which was the first major port in this area. The coast comprises both rocky scenery and sand dunes and has some picturesque down-at-heel resorts like Inverloch. In this coastal area and on the offshore islands are great numbers of Australia's native animals. Inland are the open cut coal mines of the Latrobe

Valley, providing most of Victoria's electricity. The Coal Creek Historical Park at Korumburra is a recreated town of the 1890s built around an old mine tunnel. In the rolling green hills around Warragul, a number of farms which make cheese, grow fruit, raise deer for venison, etc. are open to the public. Other National Parks throughout the area contain areas of dense rainforest, once widespread through the Strzelecki Ranges.

Travelling east, Lakes Entrance serves as a port for one of the biggest fishing fleets in the country, keeping Melbourne's wholesale market well supplied with fresh fish and scallops. This area has long nautical associations as can be seen at St Peter's Church in the resort of Paynesville near Bairnsdale whose spire is in the shape of a lighthouse tower with a cross and a light to guide boats on the Gippsland lakes. The Buchan Caves area, inland from Lakes Entrance, is recommended for camping because of the prevalence of kangaroos and birds, and also the towering trees in some of the oldest surviving forests in the state.

By turning off the Princes Highway along unsealed roads, you can find unspoiled coastline at places like Marlo, Cape Conran, Bemm River and Malla-coota (known for its abalone beds) near the New South Wales border. Turning north from the highway towards the mountains you can get some wonderful views, though mists are common in autumn and winter.

Wilsons Promontory. The 'Prom' is a mountainous and thickly forested peninsula about 200km east of Melbourne which is also known for its lovely white sandy beaches. It has been made into a National Park where wildlife and wildflowers abound. The park headquarters are at Tidal River, a small settlement at the end of the sealed road, where you can stay if you book in advance (5680 8538). In summer the rangers conduct wildlife-spotting tours at night and also give talks about the area. (If you are approached by an echidna, don't be frightened by his spines; he's tame and friendly.) A dirt track continues to the granite headland at the end of the peninsula which is the southernmost point on the Australian mainland. Walking tracks and nature trails invite further exploration. Both camping and cabin accommodation are available.

WEST OF MELBOURNE

Great Ocean Road. The most scenic (though by no means the quickest) route heading west from Geelong, is the classic coastline drive along the Great Ocean Road. The 200km stretch of road hugs the coastline for most of its distance between Torquay and Peterborough. It was built during the 1920s by hand and horse power. After passing through the picturesque coastal town of Lorne and the seaside resort of Apollo Bay, both of which attract thousands of visitors in the summer, the road cuts inland through the lush forested hills of the Otway Ranges and Otway National Park. Backpacker tours of the region are run by Kangavic Tours (contact the YHA hostel in Sorrento on 5984 4323 for details) and by the YHA, which charges $80 for a 2-day tour.

Port Campbell National Park comprises the long strip of land between the road and the sea west of Cape Otway, so that the natural beauty of cliffs and beaches remains unspoiled. The most spectacular features are the Twelve Apos-tles (huge multicoloured sandstone sea stacks), The Arch, London Bridge and The Blowhole, all formed over thousands of years by wind and sea erosion.

Although the Great Ocean Road peters out at this point, it is worth continuing west to Warrnambool (another overly popular resort in season) which is accessible from Melbourne on a twice-daily V/Line coach. The main attractions are Tower Hill, a dormant volcano, and Port Fairy, a harbour town of Irish origins which has changed little since the 1880s and is still an important crayfishing centre. It has an excellent YHA hostel in a National Trust listed building dating from 1864.

Mount Bunnenyong. Three-quarters of the way along the Midland Highway from Geelong to Ballarat is a turn-off to this viewpoint. This part of Victoria bears a strong resemblance to El Salvador, due to the parade of extinct volcanoes. Mount Bunnenyong is one of the tallest, and has excellent views over the surroundings. Although the shady trees at the 790m summit obscure the view, a tower on the peak allows you to see the lovely countryside.

Ballarat. The most direct route west from Melbourne along the Western Highway takes you through Victoria's largest inland city with a population of 85,000. Built on the riches of the 1850s gold rush, Ballarat prospers as a bustling market town and the home of Mars Australia, manufacturer of confectionery.

The main attraction is Sovereign Hill (5331 1944), a recreated goldmining township complete with costumed staff carrying out daily tasks of pioneer life such as baking bread, working in the post office and printing a newspaper. To cover the 3km from the train station to Sovereign Hill take bus 9 or 10. Note the statue to honour the eight-hour day, bearing the legend, 'Eight hours labour; eight hours recreation; eight hours rest'. The area was one of the first in the world to recognise the rights of workers, when resentment against the cost of mining licences led to the attack by British soldiers on the stockade at Eureka on 3 December 1854 in which 16 diggers and six soldiers died. Eureka St was then the Melbourne Road; a rough wooden stockade had been built by the diggers, but gave them little protection. A 1981 version now appears in the memorial-cum-playground, which backs on to a caravan park.

Interestingly Sovereign Hill is a non-profit-making enterprise, though the adult admission charge is steep at $16.50. Hostellers staying at the Government Camp YHA (5333 3409; dorm beds from $16) across the road from the tourist village are entitled to a discount on admission. Entry to Sovereign Hill also includes an underground mine tour and entry into the Gold Museum across the road from the historical park.

Ballarat is on a big scale, with a large lake — Wendouree — upon which the rowing events for the 1956 Melbourne Olympics were held. The Botanic Gardens are interesting, with an avenue featuring busts of all the Australian Prime Ministers up to and including Paul Keating.

The old cemetery is north-east of the town centre, at the corner of Macarthur St north of Lake Wendouree. It is a fascinating source of social history, with the diggers who died at the Eureka stockade buried on one side and the soldiers who perished on the other. The new cemetery north of the centre is similarly interesting.

Ballarat's Visitor Information Centres are at 39 Sturt St (5332 2694) and The Great Southern Woolshed, Melbourne Road, Warrenheip (5334 7933).

Heading north from Ballarat along the Sunraysia Highway you come to Avoca in a region well known for both sparkling and Cabernet wines. A V/Line coach leaves from the Ballarat train station in Lydiard St every Friday at 2pm; the one-way trip costs $10. There is also another route to Avoca via Maryborough: a coach departs from Ballarat for Maryborough at 12pm each weekday, and passengers change onto the service for Avoca at Maryborough railway station, for which a reservation is necessary.

Lovers of history will also want to take in the historic town of Castlemaine 120km north-west of Melbourne with its grand market building and museum. About halfway between Ballarat and Castlemaine you might like to stop over in Hepburn Springs to help yourself to the natural mineral waters discovered by the early settlers. In the recently redeveloped Mineral Springs Reserve, the springs are marked according to the main ions the water contains — sulphate, bicarbonate, and so on — all of which supposedly have their own health-giving properties.

NORTHERN VICTORIA

The Victorian Alps. The Great Dividing Range starts near the Queensland border and runs parallel to the coast of New South Wales. It reaches its highest elevations in the Australian Alps which straddle the New South Wales/Victoria border. The highest peak on the Victorian side is Mount Bogong which is just under 2000m high. The Alps of Victoria are wonderfully scenic, and worth visiting even if you are not a skier or a bushwalker. Typical of the high country are lush alpine meadows and poor roads. On clear days you can sometimes see across to the Snowy Mountains of New South Wales. From the lookout near Omeo, Mount Kosciusko (Australia's highest peak) is sometimes visible. Facilities at the main resorts of Hotham, Falls Creek and Mount Buller are described in *Skiing* below.

The Great Dividing Range comes surprisingly close to Melbourne. The Calder Highway which runs north from the airport leads to Mount Macedon, a pictur-esque hill which suffered devastation during the 1983 bush fires but which affords sweeping views over Melbourne. The cross at its summit, in memory of World War I soldiers, takes its height to over 1000m. From its summit you can see Hanging Rock, sticking up like a bad tooth from the plains.

Hanging Rock. The ancient rock formation on which the book and Peter Weir's film *Picnic at Hanging Rock* are based is one of the most awesome sights in Australia. Hanging Rock is about 70km north of Melbourne past Mount Macedon and stands starkly 120m above the rolling hills surrounding it. Unfortunately it is almost impossible to reach without a car, but hiring one for the day is strongly recommended. Admission is $5 per car. A huge car park is at the foot of the Rock, complete with ghetto-blasters belching out AC/DC at full volume.

The climb itself is no picnic; the upper reaches are steep rocks ground smooth by a million pairs of feet, and it is easy to see how picnickers could get lost. The rock formations are a catastrophic jumble, as though a deity had hurled a pile of boulders in the air and let them land randomly. Koalas sit in the eucalyptus trees, unperturbed by the shrieking and panting of visitors.

The tea shop at the bottom sells copies of the fascinating book (and its abysmal sequel) plus Hanging Rock handkerchiefs, teaspoons and tea towels. The nearest town where you can buy provisions for your picnic is Woodend about 9km away. From Woodend, head towards the rock but turn right at Straw Lane for another remarkable place — Anti-Gravity Hill, where the lie of the land creates the illusion of going uphill when in fact you are rolling downhill. The best way to experience this is to release the handbrake on a car, which makes this one of the most dangerous stretches of road in Australia.

One final mystical treat in this area is on the back road to Melbourne. The village of Clarkefield has an excellent pub, the Coach and Horses, haunted by the ghost of a seven-year-old girl who fell into a nearby well. The human inhabitants serve excellent fish and chips, which you can wash down with Abbotsford Invalid Stout. Clarkefield has something of a ghost station, but in fact four trains serve it from Melbourne each day except Sunday.

The Gold Towns. When gold was discovered in the 1850s, many settlements sprang up and developed into flourishing towns. Some, like Bendigo, have survived, while others like Walhalla are almost ghost towns. Many have superb railway stations, town halls and rambling old hotels, all lovingly restored with an eye to the tourist dollar. Bendigo's principal boast is that it has a talking tram, i.e. a vintage tram which has been rehabilitated and provided with a taped commentary on the points of interest in town. One of these places is the Joss House, a Chinese temple which served the large influx of Chinese miners in the 1800s. Bendigo Art Gallery has the usual second-division British and European art, plus some interesting Australian paintings. It is at 42 View St (around the corner from the Information Centre), and opens 10am–5pm during the week, 2–5pm at weekends.

Beechworth and Yackandandah, east of Wangaratta, are in more scenic countryside and have a large number of National Trust listed buildings from the gold era. Beechworth has many well preserved sites. These include the old powder magazine (where explosives were stored), the school and the Chinese cemetery with Burning Towers. Even the YHA hostel is in a 125-year old converted pub, with a new (and recommended) pub across the road.

From Beechworth turn south towards the mountains rather than north to the border town of Wodonga, immortalised in the opening lines of a song: 'Who would linger longer in Wodonga?' It is a new planned city without a single gracious building to temper its ugliness. Another place you might choose to avoid is Glenrowan (much easier now that the Hume Highway bypasses the town, to the chagrin of local entrepreneurs) which is stuffed full of Ned Kelly kitsch (demonstrating the Australian penchant for turning criminals into heroes). One of the most remarkable is the computerised theatre show and giant replica of the man at Ned Kelly's Last Stand.

The Murray River. The second longest river in Australia starts in the Snowy Mountains. Before irrigating the vineyards of South Australia, it forms Victoria's northern border, providing opportunities for a spot of relaxing river cruising or camping. Remote free camping spots can be found with the help of locals where you will not be troubled by noisy speed boats. Sleepily attractive river towns such as Kerang and Swan Hill are dotted along its banks.

Echuca, at the confluence of the Goulburn and Murray Rivers, was once a busy inland port. Many relics have been preserved, amongst them paddlesteamers and gracious old hotels. The Port of Echuca Historic Area on Murray Esplanade charges admission of $4 (YHA discount available). Upstream is Rutherglen, a scenic wine-making area; ring 060-329249 for information on free wine tasting. Mildura, several hundred kilometres downstream, has paddlesteamers offering two-hour cruises twice a day. The Murray River supports an enormous amount of agriculture, primarily vegetables, citrus and grapes; some wineries such as Mildara Wines near Mildura are accessible by riverboat. The river is particularly worth seeing when in flood from July to September.

Bushwalking, skiing and water sports are especially accessible in Victoria. An agency that specialises in wilderness trips on foot, skis, bicycles and hang-gliders is Outdoor Travel at 55 Hardware St in Melbourne (9670 7252). It operates weekend introduction courses for groups of six in activities such as rock climbing. Prices vary according to activity but are usually between $65 and $120 a day, including transport from Melbourne and accommodation. Another adventure tour operator in Melbourne is Peregrine Adventures, 258 Lonsdale St (9663 8611). In north-eastern Victoria, you can join a fully outfitted bicycle tour, alpine bushwalk or cross-country ski trip with Bogong Jack Adventures (8 King St, Oxley 3678; 5727 3382).

Gear can be hired from plenty of Melbourne outfitters — for example, from Outsports Wilderness Centres (340B Hawthorn Road, Caulfield South and 36

Young St, Frankston), which offer 10% rental discounts to YHA members. Further information about the National Parks in the state, such as the Little Desert National Park in the west (where more than 200 species of birds have been sighted) and Wilsons Promontory National Park, can be obtained from the Department of Conservation and Natural Resources, 240 Victoria Parade, East Melbourne 3002 (9412 4795). Their Outdoors Information Centre has maps and leaflets on everything from camping in the Alps to rock-climbing on Mount Arapiles.

The YHA of Victoria organises reasonably priced weekend outings incorporating various outdoor activities. Ask at the YHA Travel Centre (205 King St, Melbourne; 9670 9611) about trip schedules for groups involving such activities as bushwalking, canoeing, sailing and waterskiing. There is also a large variety of sightseeing and adventure day-trips available from the Centre and the Melbourne YHA hostels, usually with member discounts.

Bushwalking. If walking along the Yarra River in Melbourne's suburbs is a little tame, you need only travel a short distance to the bushland with its lush ferns and lyrebirds. Mount Donna Buang (1250m) is not much more than an hour's drive from Melbourne and can be easily climbed in a day. If you want to leave the big city behind, a tent is a valuable asset as there are excellent campsites near a host of tracks and nature trails from the 'Prom' in the east to the Grampians National Park in the west.

Most of the bush near Melbourne, such as the fern gullies that are so popular among hikers, are lush and damp and so you should beware of leeches. Mosquitoes are also a nuisance in summer. If you want to evade all insect life (as well as plant life), it is possible to walk for several kilometres by torch-light through the Byaduck Caves near Hamilton (300km due west of Melbourne). Other recommended walks include the strenuous two-day walk through the Lederderg Gorge between Melbourne and Ballarat, and the Coastal Walking Track from Sorrento on the Mornington Peninsula.

Cycling. Melbourne is sprawling and surrounded by fairly daunting hills. Therefore take a local train to places like Stawell, Geelong or Lilydale before embarking on a cycling trip. It is usually possible to put your bicycle in the guard's van for a small extra charge. Otherwise you can hire a bicycle in places like Port Fairy Township, Geelong and Echuca. If you undertake any long trips you must consider your route carefully as many scenic back roads deteriorate into gravel or rutted mud, while traffic on the main arteries can be unpleasantly and dangerously heavy. The Bicycle Victoria organisation publishes a bi-monthly newletter called the *Australian Cyclist*.

To join an organised cycling trip near Melbourne, try the optimistically named Downhill Mountain Bike Rides (5962 3632), which charges about $55 a day for trips around Mount Donna Buang and the Southern Ranges.

Water Sports. Downtown Melbourne is 60km from the open sea, so surfing is not as handy as it is in Sydney. Surf beaches are concentrated west of Melbourne, for example at Torquay, Bells Beach (where championships are often held), Anglesea, Lorne and so on. Swimming is mostly safe, though be careful at Ninety Mile Beach in Gippsland which has dangerous rips and sharks.

To be sure of avoiding the dangers of the ocean, you might prefer to enjoy your aquatic recreations at any of the many inland lakes, such as the enormous man-made Lake Eildon or the Crater Lakes around Camperdown. For white water rafting on the Snowy River go to the small town of Buchan, which is also well known for its caves. For details of rafting in the Victorian Alps, contact

Snowy River Expeditions (5155 9353). Peregrine Adventures' 2-day rafting trip on the Mitchell River north-west of Bairnsdale costs $200 inclusive (9663 8611). For gentler river descents, you can hire canoes on the Murray; contact Upper Murray Canoe Hire in Walwa or Jack O'Mullane (5480 6208) for three-person canoe hire and camping equipment. The tranquil Gippsland Lakes are a premier boating and watersport area; to hire a leisure craft, head for such lakeside townships as Metung, Paynesville and Nungurner.

Skiing. The high plains of north-east Victoria become a skiers' playground from June onwards, and you may find yourself competing with many out-of-state visitors as well as Melburnians. The nearest snow recreation area to the state capital is Mount Donna Buang near Warburton, though it is not high enough to offer reliable snow cover. Similarly Mount Baw Baw, which is the nearest resort to the capital (180km due east), is subject to rain-bearing winds from the south. Yet it can provide some fine skiing, especially to novices and cross country skiers, and is surprisingly uncrowded considering its proximity to the city.

Helpful information on all ski resorts can be found in *Alpine News*, a free monthly newspaper available at tourist offices and ski shops in the state. It includes the latest developments in the resorts, alpine and nordic trail maps, a ski event calendar and advertisements for accommodation. The national weather reports in the eastern states always include a snow report from the major resorts. Alternatively you can dial the 'ski info line' on 11545. Skis and equipment can be hired from Melbourne outfitters such as Outsports for $22 a day or $45 a week.

The main ski resorts are in the Victorian Alps, outside the range of most daytrippers, although Melburnians sometimes go 250km north to Mount Buller for a day's skiing. Day trips are organised by the Alzburg Inn Resort (5775 2367) every day except Tuesday and Thursday; the fee of $85 includes bus transport (normally $45), lift ticket (normally about the same) and a beginner's lesson. Buller is Australia's largest and most popular resort with 80km of runs for advanced skiers and beginners, and an extensive and expanding system of ski lifts. Useful information on the resort can be gleaned from the giveaway newspaper *This Week in Mount Hotham*. Ring 5759 3550 or 008-32061 for tourist information. If you want to stay in the resort, don't count on a bed in the YHA hostel (5777 6181). Bookings for the winter season close in mid-April.

Hotham and Falls Creek on the Bogong High Plains are a scenic 5-hour drive from Melbourne. Despite the distance from the state capital, they still can be exceedingly crowded especially on the beginners' slopes. Both get plenty of snow because of the elevation (up to 1828m at Mount Hotham), though runs are longer in the mountains of New South Wales. 'Falls' is the most picturesque of the Victorian alpine villages, set in a natural bowl. Mount Buffalo (about 70km away) is one of the oldest ski resorts in Australia and is best known for its beginner and cross country facilities. For information on Falls Creek, call 5758 3224.

All the resorts are well provided with ski hire shops, restaurants, shops, post offices, etc. There is an abundance of commercial lodges, but by far the cheapest are those run by private ski clubs. For bookings and information ring the Victorian Ski Association (9699 4655) and the Victorian Alpine Accommodation Centre (9826 8966). As in Kosciusko across the state border, it is much cheaper to stay some distance from the slopes. Try Harrietville (31km from Mount Hotham) or Mount Beauty and Tawonga at the foot of Mount Bogong.

Much of Victoria's terrain is most suitable for cross-country skiing. Marysville, an old-fashioned resort town not too far from Melbourne, has some excellent *langlauf* possibilities at Lake Mountain. You can get here on McKenzies Coachlines (9861 6264) from Spencer St Station in Melbourne for $7.50. Bogong Jack

Adventures, mentioned above, specialises in cross country ski courses and holidays; a weekend break costs $250.

Calendar of Events

January	Australian Open Tennis Championships, Melbourne
January	Melbourne Summer Music Festival
February	St Kilda Festival
February	Chinese New Year Festival
late February/early March	Moomba Festival
March (second Monday)	**Labour Day**
March/April	**Easter Tuesday**
March/April	Bendigo Easter Fair
April	International Comedy Festival
June (second Monday)	**Queen's Birthday**
June	Winery Walkabout, Rutherglen
late June	Melbourne International Film Festival
September	Melbourne International Festival of the Arts
September (last Thursday)	**Royal Melbourne Show Day** (ending ten-day event)
September	Australian Football League Grand Final
mid-October	Avoca Wool and Wine Festival
November (first Tuesday)	**Melbourne Cup Day**
November	Lygon St Festa, Melbourne

Public holidays are shown in **bold**.

Tasmania

Population: 450,000   **Capital: Hobart (population 180,000)**

If Tasmania was an independent nation rather than just an island off Australia's massive whole, many more people might be tempted to go there. It has an area of 68,300 square kilometres (slightly smaller than Scotland) and is distinctly dissimilar to the rest of Australia, softer and damper than the dry environment of the mainland. In terms of pace of life, people, terrain and climate, Tasmania is more like the South Island of New Zealand than Victoria or New South Wales. It is a popular destination for vacationing Australians, for whom the trip across the Bass Strait is something of an overseas adventure.

But it is difficult for Tasmania to make its uniqueness recognised abroad. Other islands of about the same size, such as Sri Lanka and Ireland, have a national identity, while Tasmania languishes as a low-profile state dangling from the coast of Victoria. Its reputation for dismal weather and the expense of getting to the island deter many would-be visitors, thus indirectly preserving the unspoiled character of the island. Few visitors who include Tasmania in their Antipodean itinerary are disappointed.

The chief attractions are outdoor ones, such as the wilderness of the south-west, the mountains of the north and the pretty east coast. The south-east has the historic capital of Hobart and some fascinating remnants of the island's past as an island of penal servitude. Tasmania is a relatively poor state, dependent largely on agriculture, forestry and hydro-electric power. The latter two industries have aroused opposition from conservationists. Tasmania has been the scene of notable battles about the commercial exploitation of the natural wilderness, but vast tracts remain untouched. Although it is strongly tourist-oriented, the brand of tourist development is mainly charming and inoffensive rather than aggressive and commercial. Tourism is responsible for the tasteful conservation of numerous old buildings and the preservation of the island's historic past.

As well as numerous scenic delights and some interesting towns, Tasmania has had a rich modern history. The Dutch explorer Abel Tasman first sighted the peninsula that bears his name in 1642. He called the whole island Van Diemen's Land after the then governor of the Dutch East Indies. The British subsequently settled at Sullivan's Cove (now part of Hobart) in 1804, and the island was subsumed into the colony of New South Wales. Because of its cool climate and isolation, the island was considered good territory for establishing penal settlements. Tasmania, as it became, gained a separate identity in 1825 under the notorious Governor George Arthur. He was convinced that mankind was 'born and saturated in wickedness', and treated his charges accordingly. The island had the smallest proportion of free settlers of any Australian colony, and for years was regarded as the worst spot in the English-speaking world. Governor Arthur gave free licence to his soldiers to kill the island's Aboriginals on sight, and 2 years later launched a military operation called the Black Line, intended to corner the Aboriginals on the Tasman Peninsula and eliminate them from settled areas.

Transportation ended in 1853 and freedom was eventually granted to those convicts who had survived the evils of hunger, disease and vicious treatment. The Aboriginals fared much worse: survivors of Governor Arthur's genocide were rounded up by a missionary and taken to remote Flinders Island off the north-eastern coast. This misguided attempt to rehabilitate them failed and the last pure-blood Tasmanian Aboriginal died in misery in 1876.

During the next half century, Tasmania evolved into a harmonious state where man enjoyed a fairly peaceful co-existence with nature in what came to be regarded as Australia's backwater. Economic realism forced Tasmania to take the 20th century seriously. With barely adequate agriculture and no significant industry, Tasmania slipped well behind the other Australian states in terms of wealth. Entrepreneurs eyed the island's natural resources, particularly the opportunities for supplying timber and cheap hydro-electric power. Tasmania's extensive scope for water-driven energy was first harnessed over 70 years ago, and the construction of hydro-electric schemes continues. A few notorious ideas such as the proposed damming of the Franklin River have attracted considerable attention, with conservationists from around the world converging on Tasmania to defend the environment. The ecologists eventually won that particular argument — without wholehearted support from the locals — but other large-scale projects are under way.

CLIMATE

Tasmania's climate is far removed from the hot and predominantly dry weather of Adelaide, Perth and Sydney. Mainlanders are often rather rude about the island's climate, assuming that it is always wet and cold.

In fact Tasmania has a temperate climate with definite seasons but few extremes. Hobart is no colder than Madrid and receives half as much rainfall each year as Sydney, only 62.5cm (30 inches). However it rains on average on half the days of the year; the heaviest rainfalls occur from July to October and the lowest in February. Launceston is considerably drier and a few degrees warmer on average.

The wild and scarcely inhabited west of the country is very different from the more populous east coast including Hobart. In the west the average rainfall is four times as high as Hobart and the average summer high only 16°C/61°F. Hobart receives a quarter of that amount of rain and the temperatures usually climb above 20°C/68°F on most summer days. In fact the average winter minimum on the east coast of Tasmania is higher than that of Alice Springs, Kalgoorlie and Canberra.

Hot dry spells do occur and bush fires are a sufficient risk for campfires to be banned in many National Parks. During 'Fire Permit Periods' in summer picnic fires can be lit only in designated places, and dropping matches or cigarette ends is an offence. During total fire bans, announced in the media, lighting any fire out-of-doors is prohibited.

All that being said, be sure to take a rain jacket and waterproof footwear whatever time of year you visit. Water temperatures are uniformly chilly, so don't plan on too much sea bathing, even on the east coast, which is the warmest and sunniest part of the state.

THE LOCALS

For about 40,000 years Tasmania was inhabited by Aboriginals. When ocean levels rose after the last Ice Age about 20,000 years ago, it became an island and the inhabitants grew racially distinct from mainland Aboriginals. They followed a semi-nomadic life, had primitive tools and spoke more than one language. The destruction of the race began when the white colonists arrived. While there are still people claiming descendancy from Tasmanian Aboriginals, they encounter great difficulty gaining recognition and claiming rights.

Modern Tasmanians (Tassies, or — if you wish to risk offending them — Taswegians) are almost a race apart from other Australians. The islanders tend to dissociate themselves from the mainland, and display an odd blend of Australian and New Zealand characteristics. If you arrive direct from Queensland or the Northern Territory, be prepared for a culture shock. Most come from the same European stock that holds sway over the rest of Australia, but Tasmanians show a sensitivity that is less prevalent on the mainland. This quality of gentleness is often misinterpreted as a sign of dullness by other Australians, and jokes about Tasmanians roughly correspond to Irish jokes made in Britain or Polish jokes in the USA. There is a streak of puritanism, akin to the stoic Presbyterianism in the south of New Zealand.

Making Friends. You will find even more openness and hospitality than in other states. Indeed, Tasmanians in other parts of Australia often remark that they realised how friendly their fellow-islanders are only after moving to the mainland. And a visit to Tasmania can be as much of an antidote to the sometimes strident mainlanders as the lush scenery can be to the parched terrain elsewhere. While it is easy to avoid the phenomenon of the travellers' ghettoes as found in the big mainland cities and resorts, there is an easy-going camaraderie among travellers attracted to the great outdoors.

Meeting the locals is easy. Most are interested in visitors and will bend over backwards to help you. Be discreet, however, in your conversation: while many Tasmanians are firmly committed to the preservation of their natural environment, others resent what they see as federal interference in the island's affairs (e.g. conservation laws restricting logging and the woodchip industry). If you voice opinions agreeing with the government on preserving Tasmanian wilderness, or associate yourself with what some call 'those bloody greenie mongrels' you could be in for a lot of arguments. Sound out the Tasmanian concerned — before you suggest, for example, that the halfwits logging the lemon thyme forest should be shot. If you do feel strongly about conservation and want to let off steam, go to one of the shops run by the Wilderness Society, where you're certain to find a receptive ear.

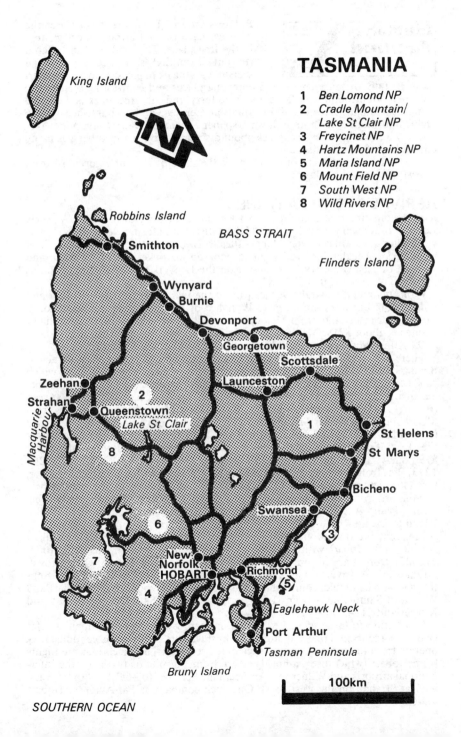

TASMANIA

1 *Ben Lomond NP*
2 *Cradle Mountain/*
  Lake St Clair NP
3 *Freycinet NP*
4 *Hartz Mountains NP*
5 *Maria Island NP*
6 *Mount Field NP*
7 *South West NP*
8 *Wild Rivers NP*

King Island

Robbins Island

BASS STRAIT

Flinders Island

Smithton

Wynyard

Burnie

Devonport

Georgetown

Scottsdale

Launceston

Zeehan

Strahan

Macquarie Harbour

Queenstown

Lake St Clair

St Helens

St Marys

Bicheno

Swansea

New Norfolk

HOBART

Richmond

Eaglehawk Neck

Port Arthur

Tasman Peninsula

Bruny Island

100km

SOUTHERN OCEAN

Getting Around

Progress around Tasmania is slow. But the leisurely pace is what attracts most visitors in the first place. The roads are uncluttered (to put it mildly) and meander through scenery varying from pleasant to spectacular. As in Britain, distances between interesting places and contrasting scenery are not great. Information on fares and bus, ferry and air timetables is available from Tasmanian Travel and Information Centres, and is published in the highly informative free bi-monthly newspaper *Tasmanian Travelways*. Whenever booking a ticket or hiring a car, ask about discounts for YHA members, as many enterprises offer 10% discounts.

A good booklet of maps of the island is the *Atlas of Tasmania*, price $4 from tourist offices and bookshops.

ARRIVAL AND DEPARTURE

Air. The only international flights to Tasmania are from New Zealand. Air New Zealand flies from Christchurch to Hobart direct, and from Auckland to Hobart via Melbourne. Alternatively Qantas flies to Hobart via Melbourne from Christchurch or Auckland. If you want to book an air ticket out of Australia and you are in Tasmania, try STA Travel on the University of Tasmania campus (Sandy Bay, Hobart; 03-6223 4825).

From mainland Australia you can fly to the two largest cities of Hobart and Launceston, but fares are lower to Wynyard or Devonport on the north coast. The regular return fare from Melbourne to Hobart on either Ansett Australia or Qantas is about $219. Melbourne to Launceston with Ansett Australia is about $199 return, and Sydney to Hobart with Qantas about $309 return.

There are several cheaper alternative airlines. Some of the smallest fly across the Bass Strait in propeller aircraft (sometimes as small as an eight-seater), which can result in lower prices. For example, Kendell Airlines (008-338894 toll-free) has flights from Melbourne to Devonport (one-way Apex fare $87) and Wynyard (Burnie) ($83). Aus-Air (008-331256 or 03-9580 6166 in Melbourne) flies from Moorabbin airport near Melbourne to Devonport (from $199 return), Wynyard (from $186 return) and Launceston (from $215 return). Airlines of Tasmania flies from Traralgon or Sale (Victoria) to Launceston (via Flinders Island) for $190 one-way (standbys from $126). Geelong Air Services in Victoria (03-5264 1273) flies from Geelong to Wynyard via King Island, with unlimited stop-over, for $405 return. East-West (03-6238 0800) has services to the capital and Devonport from Melbourne and Sydney, and to Wynyard from Melbourne. Phillip Island Airlines (03-9882 9355) runs services from Melbourne to Phillip Island to Burnie.

Frequent internal services on Airlines of Tasmania, Ansett and Australian Airlines link Hobart with Launceston. Flights on Airlines of Tasmania (003-918422) from Launceston serve Flinders Island, King Island, Queenstown, Strahan and Wynyard. The same destinations — plus Devonport and Smithton — are available from Hobart. Eastwest links Devonport with Hobart and Wynyard. Sample fares from Hobart are Launceston $40, Devonport $85 and King Island $154.

In addition to these scheduled flights, numerous air charter companies offer sightseeing tours and one-way flights for bushwalkers. With two exceptions, they operate from the same airports as scheduled services. The exceptions are flights from Hobart (which use Cambridge Aerodrome, a mile or two from the international airport) and Wilderness Air Seaplane Services (03-6471 7280) from the jetty at Strahan on the west coast. One such company is Par-Avion in Hobart (03-6248 5390).

Sea. The main ferry operating to Tasmania is the *Spirit of Tasmania*, which is owned by the TT Line and sails three times weekly in each direction between Melbourne and Devonport on the north coast. Departures in each direction are at 6pm, with arrivals at 8.30am the next morning. Both hostel-style and cabin accommodation are available. Services from Station Pier in Melbourne operate on Monday, Wednesday and Friday, and from Devonport on Tuesday, Thursday and Saturday, with slight seasonal variations. (Skybus in Melbourne serves Station Pier for $3.50.) To book or for more information ring 132010.

Fares are calculated according to season and the quality of accommodation booked: paying for a berth is compulsory. The seasons are 'bargain' (late April to mid-September), 'holiday' (before Christmas to March) and 'shoulder' (the rest of the year). The cheapest one-way rate is for a berth in hostel-style accommodation with shared facilities on D Deck. Students are often eligible for a 25% discount and there may also be mid-week discounts. Vehicles are carried on the ferry; the cost for a typical car varies from $90 to $150 one-way, depending on the season. Motorbikes and bicycles are carried much more cheaply.

A Seacat service connects George Town, east of Devonport, with Port Welshpool, nearly 200km from downtown Melbourne. It runs daily in the summer and daily except Tuesdays and Thursdays from May to September. The 4½-hour journey departs George Town at 8.30am and Port Welshpool at 2pm. Port Welshpool is served by a connecting 'Roadcat' bus. The one-way Seacat fare is $89 off-peak and $99 high season. For further details ring 008-030131 toll-free. The Bass Strait is a notoriously choppy stretch of water and there are frequent complaints of seasickness on the fast service. The operators claim that the risks are no greater on the Seacat; it is simply that affected passengers are more visible than on the ferry where they can escape to their cabins. Many passengers refute this.

Bus. Most destinations in Tasmania can be reached by bus, but some journeys require careful planning because of the infrequency of services; buses to country centres are scarce on Sundays, for example. Furthermore several companies cover different routes, and their respective timetables do not always complement one another. Note that Greyhound Pioneer bus passes are not accepted on Tasmanian carriers.

The leading operator is Tasmanian Redline Coaches (TRC) with its head office in Launceston (Launceston Transit Centre, 18 Charles St; 1300-360000). Its buses meet the *Spirit of Tasmania* ferry at Devonport, and also flights arriving at Launceston and Hobart airports. Shuttle buses into the city cost $6.60. TRC runs services mainly along the Midland, Lyell and Bass Highways, and has five or six journeys Monday—Friday along the Midland Highway between Hobart and Launceston (down to three at weekends). This trip takes 2½–3 hours and costs $17.80 each way. Most services on this route are extended to Devonport, Burnie, Wynyard and Smithton. TRC buses also deviate from the Midland Highway to serve east coast towns such as Bicheno, St Marys and St Helens. But there is no east coast service on Sunday. Other sample TRC fares are Hobart–Devonport $30.30, Launceston–Devonport $12.50, Hobart–Queenstown $33.30 and Queenstown–Strahan $5.20. Note that there are no services from the west coast on Sunday or Monday.

Coastliner Express (a subsidiary of TRC) is a luxury express coach that operates along the state's main highway (weekdays only) between Smithton, Launceston and Hobart. It departs Smithton at 7am and Launceston at 11am, arriving in Hobart at 1.20pm. The Hobart departure is at 2.15pm.

TRC's main rival is Hobart & Intercity Coaches (41 Liverpool St, Hobart; 03-6234 4077). It connects Hobart with Launceston, Devonport and Burnie, plus

Port Arthur and the east coast towns of Triabunna, Swansea and Bicheno. On routes that overlap with TRC's, fares are identical. Other operators' fares may be lower. For example, the single fare from Hobart to Port Arthur is $10 on Hobart & Intercity Coaches but $9 on the Peninsula Coach Service.

Smaller local bus companies operate on stretches of the east coast, for example Peakes Coaches (between Swansea, Bicheno and St Marys) and Haley's Coaches (between St Marys, St Helens and Derby). This can make some journeys complicated, although some services now connect more conveniently than they did just a few years ago. Fares are higher on these local services than on the main routes, but they are still reasonable; the 90km trip between Swansea and St Marys costs $8.

If you are going to explore Tasmania seriously, you might want to consider one of the bus passes on the market. TRC offers the Tassie Pass costing $98 for 7 days, $138 for 15 days and $178 for 30 days of unlimited travel on the TRC network. For comparison, a Hobart–Queenstown–Burnie–Launceston–Hobart circuit would ordinarily cost about $95.50. Note that if you plan to use the Tassie Pass on the Midland or Bass Highways services, you must book in advance by phoning the nearest TRC office.

Hobart & Intercity Coaches has a $100 Explorer Travel Pass in addition to a more flexible 14-day Wilderness Rover for $159 which is offered in conjunction with Invicta's Wilderness Transport (008-030388 toll-free). Several other companies specialise in charter transport for bushwalkers, such as Mountain Stageline (003-314240) and Cradle Mountain Coaches (Backpacker's Barn, 12 Edward St, Devonport; 03-6424 3628).

Train. In the 19th century, Tasmania had a network of brilliantly engineered railways used mainly to support the mining industry. Sadly, the only remaining passenger line in Tasmania is a tourist run, from Ida Bay to Deep Hole in the far south. The train from Ida Bay takes a pretty route along the banks of Line River and out to Deep Hole beach, but departure times seem to depend on the driver's mood.

Driving. Tasmania's roads suffer little from traffic. In the cities, a five-car queue is regarded as a jam, and the main highways are well surfaced and almost empty. Beware, however, of dangers not normally experienced elsewhere in Australia: a sudden blizzard in the central highlands can make surfaces treacherous, many roads are icy in winter, and the massive slow-moving logging trucks can pose problems. The *Visitors Road Safety Guide* (free from Thrifty Rent-a-Car offices) warns that they are most common on the Tasman Highway in the east, in the Huon region (south-west of Hobart) and in the north-east. Bear in mind also that random breath tests are common: the blood/alcohol limit is 0.05%. The penalty for those over 0.15% is up to 18 months in prison plus a fine. The speed limit in towns is 60km/h and 100km/h outside unless otherwise posted. Radar checks and speed cameras are used to catch offenders.

With distances of only 200km from Hobart to Launceston, and 100km from there to Devonport, most journey times are short. Road conditions, however, can vary alarmingly. While cross-country distances may look small on a map (and they are, by Australian standards), many roads are narrow and twisting and must be driven carefully; take these factors into account when planning your mountain or coastal jaunt.

The road numbering system is better organised than elsewhere in Australia. National Highway 1 runs down the middle of the island, from Devonport to Hobart via Launceston. Other primary routes are prefixed A, secondary roads B and minor roads C. However most people refer to highways by their names rather than by their numbers. There is no exact correlation between the names and numbers, for example the A10 has three different names (Lyell, Zeehan and Murchison) for separate sections, and the Bass Highway has two different numbers during its course (A2 and State Highway 1). Good signposting overcomes most confusion, though the list that follows might be useful when planning a trip:

HIGHWAY CHART		
Hobart – Launceston (direct)	Midland Highway	Highway 1
Launceston – Burnie	Bass Highway	Highway 1
Burnie – Smithton (and beyond)	Bass Highway	A2
Hobart – Launceston (via East Coast)	Tasman Highway	A3
Melton Mowbray – Deloraine	Lake Highway	A5
Hobart – Southport	Huon Highway	A6
Sorell – Port Arthur	Arthur Highway	A9
Hobart – Queenstown	Lyell Highway	A10
Queenstown – Zeehan	Zeehan Highway	A10
Zeehan – Burnie	Murchison Highway	A10

Fuel prices are higher than in cities on the mainland. Most stations open around 6.30am and close around 9pm. There are also a few 24-hour or late-opening stations in Hobart and Launceston. Emergency road services are provided by the Royal Automobile Club of Tasmania (RACT), which has its head office at the corner of Patrick and Murray Sts in Hobart (03-6238 2200). For roadside service anywhere in the state ring 131111.

Vehicle Rental Tasmania has a good range of low-cost alternatives to the multinational car hire companies. The lowest daily rate is $15, which is increased to $25 by compulsory insurance, available from several Hobart companies such as Bargain (03-6234 6696), Lo Cost (03-6231 0550), Boss (03-6273 1260), Range/Rent-a-Bug (03-6272 1137) and Ulli's VW Hire (03-6272 1137). The choice of cheap car rental firms is even greater in Launceston and the north of the island. Try Bargain (003-441401), Apple (003-311399), Discount in Devonport (03-6424 8222) and Price-Less (003-267744). The latter company promises a $5-a-day discount to YHA members.

Hiring a campervan is particularly popular in Tasmania; with the amount of spectacular scenery in National Parks and the lack of cheap accommodation in out-of-the-way places, the advantages of having a home on wheels are considerable. The two cheapest are Tourist Economy Rentals, 189A Harrington St, Hobart (03-6234 8848) and Motor Holidays (03-6249 4880). Both charge less than $500 a week.

Hitch-hiking. The short distances, friendly motorists and pleasing landscapes make hitching in Tasmania a more enjoyable experience than elsewhere in Australia. In summer you should have little trouble getting around. Winter hitching is less predictable: the second car will stop if the first one doesn't, but you may have to wait hours for the first one. Try to stick to 'A' roads. Don't expect to be picked up by the innumerable logging trucks: not only do they run to tight schedules but the drivers tend to see all backpackers as 'greenie ratbags', and prefer not to be accused of helping destroy Tasmania's wilderness in the course of their work. Some hitch-hikers have even been ejected from vehicles after expressing sympathy for the conservationist cause.

The only other warning concerns the hitchers' congestion in Devonport after the arrival of the *Spirit of Tasmania*. To avoid this problem, try to fix up a lift over breakfast on board the ship, or invest $11 in the bus fare from the quayside to Launceston.

Cycling. The distances are more manageable than on the mainland but the terrain and weather can be as gruelling as in the South Island of New Zealand. Settlements are often a long way apart though the YHA has a few strategically placed hostels, such as the one in historic Oatlands between Hobart and Launceston. The YHA is also the best source of bicycles to rent; the main Hobart hostel hires out touring bicycles; ring 03-6231 0977. Otherwise try Backpackers Barn (12 Edward St, Launceston; 03-6424 3628). If you want to join a cycling day trip from Hobart for $20 or a longer trip, contact Brake Out Cycling Tours on 03-6229 1999.

Even away from the larger towns and developed resort areas, there is usually a range of options, from campsites to colonial mansions, plus 21 YHA hostels (see below) and a number of guest houses and bed and breakfasts whose prices are not inflated. Again the free newspaper *Tasmanian Travelways* has comprehensive listings of the commercial accommodation available throughout the state including prices and facilities. To test the claim that Tasmanians are among the friendliest people in the world, try a home stay. HomeHost Tasmania (PO Box 550, Rosny Park, Tasmania 7018; 03-6244 5442) has about 60 host families which charge $42 single, $64 double for bed and breakfast.

Another scheme is the Tassie Bed and Breakfast Pass whereby you buy vouchers and a directory of 44 hotels around Tasmania, and spend one voucher on each night's stay. Prices range from $78 per person for three nights sharing to $735 for 21 nights single accommodation. Call 003-341787, or book through any Tasmanian Travel and Information Centre. The advantage is that you pay less for the accommodation than you otherwise would do; the drawbacks are the inaccessibility of some of the hostelries to those without transport, and the need to book ahead in busy seasons.

A similar but more expensive option is available from Country Accommodation (03-6297 8155), which organises bed and breakfast and farm stays throughout Tasmania. Tasmanian Colonial Accommodation offers 15 cottages and houses ranging from an old sea captain's cottage to country mansions. They are predominantly located in the south-east of Tasmania, with four in Hobart. Tasmania Bed & Breakfast (03-6295 1582) has a more comprehensive coverage (part of Town & Country Hosts in Sydney, listed in introductory chapter *Accommodation*).

Hostels. The YHA of Tasmania is based at 28 Criterion St in Hobart (03-6234 9617). Its 21 hostels are extremely good value and offer high standards of comfort — most charge $10–12 per night. Many hostels provide additional services such as bicycle hire, canoeing trips and bushwalking tours. Demand in summer is high, so book in advance if you possibly can. Postal bookings should be sent to YHA Tasmania, GPO Box 174B, Hobart 7001, enclosing full payment plus a $2 booking fee.

Eating and Drinking

Dining out in Tasmania holds more surprises than it did a few years ago when reef 'n' beef (equivalent to the American surf 'n' turf) was the order of the day. Choice is still limited in many country areas but the cities and especially Hobart now offer a range of ethnic restaurants, brasseries, and cafés serving interesting food at low prices.

In rural areas, often the best you can hope for is a pub serving decent-but-plain counter meals, mainly seafood and steak. Generally the steaks are fine, while much of the seafood is exceptional. In particular, try the Tasmanian delicacy of smoked trout. Another speciality not to miss is the range of Tasmanian cheeses. King Island Brie is famous throughout Australia (and is vastly superior to imported French brie) but there are lots of other farm-produced cheeses which are not available on the mainland.

DRINKING

Licensing hours in Tasmania are liberal. Publicans can virtually choose their own hours though, in practice, few hotels open beyond midnight. The only restriction is on Sundays when opening hours are restricted to an 8-hour stretch, which varies between establishments. Boag's in Launceston claims to be the oldest brewery in Australia. Since it was established in 1881, it has failed to grab the world's attention as effectively as its mainland rivals even if it is now exported in modest amounts. Yet it has more taste and character than some of its more celebrated competitors. Boag's is owned by the same company that runs the Cascade brewery in Hobart. But there are fierce differences between the north and south of the island about which is best; you can usually tell where a beer-drinker comes from by the beer he or she drinks: Boag's in the north, Cascade in the south. Pub prices are noticeably lower than on the mainland; beer is some 10% cheaper than in most other states.

Winemakers take advantage of the fact that the Tasmanian climate is the most typically European of anywhere in Australia, and thus ideal for growing premium cool-climate grapes such as the red Cabernet Sauvignon and white Chardonnay. Traditionally, most grapes have been sold to mainland winemakers, but the growing popularity of Tasmanian wines has led to the development of new wineries, particularly along the banks of the Tamar and Piper Rivers northwest of Launceston. The winery-visit industry is not nearly as developed as in South Australia, but a handful are open to the public and are worthwhile visiting. Among the best known are the Rochecome Vineyard at Pipers Brook north of Launceston, St Matthias (in Rosevears, 15km north-west of Launceston) and Moorilla Estate at 655 Main Road, Berriedale on the outskirts of Hobart, which has excellent lunches. Tasmania is the first state in Australia to have adopted a legally enforceable wine appellation system.

Exploring

Parks and Zoos. As throughout Australia a visit to a wildlife park is a staple activity. About half-a-dozen centres are dotted around the island; most are difficult to reach without a car. Admission charges vary from $2.50 at the Talune Wildlife Park (60km southwest of Hobart) to $6 at the East Coast Birdlife & Animal Park on the Highway near Bicheno. One of the main attractions is the Tasmanian devil, a carnivorous marsupial about the size of a small dog with horn-like ears, which derives its name either from the havoc it wreaked on the stock of early settlers or from the bloodcurdling cry it makes when cornered. Displays of viciousness are unlikely to occur, especially at the wildlife parks where you can cuddle Tasmania's state symbol.

SHOPPING

Tasmania is renowned for its contemporary handicrafts, especially woodcarving. Shops of the Wilderness Society can be found in all the main towns and offer the highest souvenir-credibility rating. In particular, posters are excellent. The Hobart headquarters are at 130 Davey St (6234 9366). There are good though expensive souvenirs made from Huon pine and other native hardwoods (if your conscience permits). Tourist trivia can be found though generally visitors to Tasmania are surprised by the degree to which commercialism has been kept at bay.

Despite being the birthplace of actors such as Errol Flynn, Tasmania is off the beaten track for leading theatre companies, rock bands and orchestras. Don't expect to catch too many big-name acts on the island. Formal entertainment is distinctly low-brow, with farces being the theatrical staple and up-and-coming, or ageing-and-declining musicians the best you can hope for. The Derwent Entertainment Centre in Hobart is the closest Tasmania has to a big-league venue. Check the Friday edition of the *Mercury* for details of forthcoming events. *Press Press* is the Tasmanian quarterly magazine on music, theatre and dance.

Tasmania has its own symphony orchestra and chamber orchestra which perform mainly in Hobart. The island used to be considered the Australian centre for folk music, though interest is on the decline and folk festivals like the one at Longford have been dropped. Country music fans should head for Richmond just north of Hobart in late February for an annual festival.

SPORT

The island has never figured highly on the sporting map of the world, although the occasional local boy makes it into the Australian national cricket team or Australian Football League. Mainland teams are loathe to cross the Bass Strait, so Tasmanian sportsmen and women encounter little high-class competition. Cricket's Sheffield Shield, fortunately, obliges the other states' teams to visit the island, so you can expect to see some good players. There is some trotting and horseracing, but with little of the fervour felt on the mainland. The main races are the Hobart Cup and the Launceston Cup, both held in February.

In terms of participation, it is difficult to define where travelling ends and sport begins. By hiking, cycling or canoeing around the island, you are doing what most Tasmanians regard as exercise enough. The larger towns have their share of gasping joggers, but there is little organised activity apart from Hobart's 'Run For Fun' each May. Tennis and golf are well catered for, and the cool climate means facilities for indoor sports such as squash and badminton are good. For details of beaches, and the opportunities for skiing and scuba diving, see *The Great Outdoors*.

THE MEDIA

Newspapers. The Hobart *Mercury*, the Launceston *Examiner* and the Burnie *Advocate* are Tasmania's leading dailies. The first two contain useful information for the traveller, such as air and bus departure times. The Sunday *Tasmanian* and Sunday *Examiner* are regarded as better newspapers. You can read *The*

Times and *Guardian* of London and the *New York Times* at the State Library at 91 Murray St, Hobart.

The *Treasure Islander* is a free monthly aimed, like the bi-monthly *Tasmanian Travelways*, at tourists, though it has less practical information.

Radio. The small audiences of Tasmania support a surprising range of stations. ABC-FM is on 93.9MHz, easy listening on 92FM, sport and farming on 7NT (630 AM), and minority programmes on 7RPH (1620 AM). Some stations on the Australian mainland can be picked up, especially those broadcasting on the AM band.

Television. Options for the viewer are similarly limited. TasTV is the local commercial station, transmitting on channels 1, 6, 8 and 10. ABC occupies channels 2 and 3, and SBS is available on UHF channel 28 in some parts of the island. The Southern Cross Network is the commercial station on channel 9 for the north of the state. As with radio, transmissions from some mainland stations reach the north of the island.

Theft was rife during the early years of settlement: Ikey Solomon, upon whom Dickens based Fagin, picked plenty of pockets when he moved to Hobart from London. Nowadays, however, you would be most unlucky to be robbed, and violent crime is almost unknown.

Drugs. The average bluff Tasmanian has little to do with illicit drugs, preferring the legitimate attraction of beer. Tasmania is, however, a popular destination for people seeking an 'alternative' way of life; some marijuana is cultivated, and finds its way to the cities, but the penalties for possession are higher than in more liberal states. If you are arrested for narcotic offences or any other crime, the subsequent interrogation is likely to be recorded on video.

The area code for Tasmania is 03, with the exception of Launceston and the Midlands, which will use the code 003 until August 1997, at which time they will switch to the same code as the rest of the island, and insert '63' at the start of all their numbers. In an emergency dial 000.

The Department of Tourism, Sport and Recreation's mailing address is GPO Box 399, Hobart 7001. There are Tasmanian Travel and Information Centres at 20 Davey St, Hobart (03-6230 8233) and in three other Tasmanian towns: Launceston (corner of Paterson and St John Sts; 003-363133), Devonport (5 Best St; 03-6424 4466) and Burnie (Pioneer Village Museum Complex, Little Alexander St; 03-6434 6111). The Department of Tourism, Sport and Recreation also has representatives in several mainland capitals:

Adelaide: 32 King William St (08-8400 5522).
Brisbane: 40 Queen St (07-3405 4122).
Canberra: 165–167 City Walk (06-209 2122).
Melbourne: 256 Collins St (03-9206 7922).
Sydney: 149 King St (02-9202 2022).

American Express: 74A Liverpool St, Hobart (03-6234 3711).
Thomas Cook: 40 Murray St, Hobart (03-6234 2699).

Unemployment in Tasmania is the highest in Australia, above 10%. Much of the available casual work is strictly seasonal, and most of it is taken up by the locals. Even so, there are casual jobs in agriculture, and occasionally in industry and tourism for those with the energy to look for them.

Tasmania is not known as the 'Apple Island' for its shape alone. The island produces 70% of Australia's apples. Although picking apples is slow going and not ideal for beginners, many working-holiday makers travel to the Huon Valley (around Franklin and Geeveston) for the harvest from late February to late April or June at the latest when snow begins to fall. In 1991 the statutory rate per bin was $15.62 and on good days it is possible even for relative beginners to earn up to $70. Another area where apples are grown is the Tasman Peninsula. There is also some limited grape picking work in the Huon Valley from March to May, with more along the Tamar River north of Launceston. Willing Workers on Organic Farms (mentioned on page 50) has several members in Tasmania where you can earn good farm accommodation and meals by working for as few as three days a week.

If you can bear the irritation of hop-itch, most of Australia's hops are picked in Tasmania from mid-March to the end of April. The main growing areas are around New Norfolk (inland from Hobart) and Scottsdale in the northeast, on the road from Launceston to St Helens. Men usually do the picking and tractor driving, women work in the sheds on hop-stripping machines. Although the work is arduous, it is well-paid (you might earn $1000 in three weeks) and some locals manage to get by just working on the hops followed by the apples each year.

You may be able to find work in the fish-processing industry, although the traditional scallop-splitting season from August to beyond Christmas has been drastically curtailed recently by overfishing; casual workers who have turned up at Bicheno have been lucky in recent years to find a week's work. In any event, the craft of splitting scallops is skilled and paid on a piece-rate basis. You may find yourself earning only $2 per hour until you acquire the knack, by which time the season might be over. The bad reports and poor forecasts for the next few years may drive most job-seekers away, so you might find other opportunities in the fish industry. Enquire at CES offices in the main ports — Hobart, Devonport, Bicheno and St Helens — if you have a working visa, otherwise approach the processing factories direct.

Most vacancies in the 'hospitality industry' are in the peak season from December to February. Non-specialists can find work most easily in the East Coast resorts and around the capital. There are also a few jobs in the skiing resorts of Mount Field and Ben Lomond from June to September, but not on the scale of resorts in the Snowy Mountains.

HOBART

ARRIVAL AND DEPARTURE
Air. Hobart's airport is 27km east of the city near Seven Mile Beach. The only bus service to the airport is operated by Tasmanian Redline Coaches (1300-360000); the 30-minute journey costs $6.60. Buses leave the airport shortly after the arrival of flights and all serve the Wrest Point Casino as well as the TRC office at Hobart Transit Centre, 199 Collins St. Services to the airport leave from this depot about an hour before flight departures, and pick up from city

motels, the casino and metro bus stops *en route*. The taxi fare between airport and city is about $22.

Hitch-hiking. It is easy to reach the best spot to hitch north on National Highway 1 (which also leads to the A5 north-west) or east on the A3. From the centre of town go north-east along Liverpool St to the roundabout at the junction of Brooker Avenue (Highway 1) and the Tasman Highway (A3). You should not have to wait too long, particularly if you carry a sign showing the next big town along your route (New Norfolk for the west, Melton Mowbray for the north or Sorell for the east). The proportion of local traffic is high, especially in the evening rush hours, but don't be tempted to walk further out: there are no better hitching spots for miles along either route.

For the lightly travelled A6 south-west, walk to the south-western end of Davey St and catch the traffic as it starts along the Southern Outlet.

CITY TRANSPORT
The Metropolitan Transport Trust (MTT) provides a cheap local bus service in Hobart, Launceston and Burnie. Weekday services are fairly frequent, but are nearly non-existent on Sundays. Bus services operate from 6am to midnight, Monday to Saturday, with a skeleton service on Sundays. For a dollar you can buy the complex Hobart Bus Timetables booklet, full of arcane footnotes such as 'Departure times for Dynnyrne other than for route 51 are approximate only'. Alternatively, call in at the MTT office on Elizabeth St opposite the GPO or dial 132201 for information anytime between 5am and 1am.

Most city services arrive and depart close to the Elizabeth St Mall; on some journeys to the northern suburbs, you have to take bus 100 or 101 (express) to the Glenorchy Interchange at Glenorchy and change to another bus there. A Day Rover ticket costs $3.20 and allows unlimited travel on MTT services at off-peak times (not before 9am nor between 4.30pm and 6pm, Monday–Friday). You buy the ticket from the driver of the first bus you board.

A peak-hour-only ferry sails across the Derwent Estuary between Brooke St Pier in Hobart and the Esplanade in Bellerive. The fare is $1, and Day Rover tickets are not valid on this service. Call 6223 5893 for schedules.

Bicycles can be hired from Peregrine Adventures at Unit 5/13 Beechwood Road, Sandy Bay (6225 0944 or 018-124801).

Taxi fares are $2 plus 80c per kilometre. The three main companies are Silver Top (6223 7711), City Cabs (6234 3633) and Taxi Combined (6234 8444).

ACCOMMODATION
There is little cheap accommodation in the city centre. The Backpackers group has a hostel called Bourkes New Sydney Hotel at 87 Bathurst St (6234 4516). The cost is $11 for a bed in a dorm or $15 in a double. Live entertainment in the bar at weekends attracts some locals as well as inmates.

The most central guest house is the Astor (Private) Hotel at 157 Macquarie St (at the corner of Victoria St; 6234 6611), where bed and breakfast costs $40 single or $50 double. The Tower Motel at 300 Park St (6228 0166), a mile out of town on a main bus route along Argyle St, has facilities for backpackers: the cost is $25 for a single, or $15 each in a twin room.

YHA Hostels. Hobart's main YHA hostel is at Adelphi Court (17 Stoke St, New Town; 6228 4829). To get there take bus 100 to stop 13. Beds in four-bedded rooms cost $12 and twin shares are $17 per person.

The other YHA (6244 2552) is on the other side of the River Derwent. It is in an attractive Victorian building at 52 King St in Bellerive, one of the oldest parts of Hobart. It has beds for $10. You can reach it during rush hours on the ferry from Hobart; walk 200m back along the Esplanade, and King St is on your left. Otherwise take bus 83, 84, 85, 86 or 87 (weekdays only) and get off at stop 19. Do not add to the misery caused to the unfortunate residents of King St, Sandy Bay (on the western shore): numerous travellers turn up there looking for the hostel, which is on the eastern shore.

University of Tasmania Student Residences. During the summer university vacation (December to February), comfortable rooms are let out to travellers. In Hobart, Christ College (6223 5190) costs travellers $25 per night, Jane Franklin Hall (6224 0598) $24 per night and St John Fisher College (6221 7400) the same; these prices include a hearty buffet breakfast.

Camping. The Sandy Bay Caravan Park (6225 1264) on Peel St, 4km south-west of the city centre, charges $7 per person per night for one tent. There are also cabins with *en suite* facilities ($55 for two people) and on-site caravans ($32 for two).

EATING AND DRINKING

The best area for restaurant browsing is North Hobart, especially along the two blocks of Elizabeth St between Burnett and Federal Sts. The best pizzas in town are made at Marti Zucco's. In the same area of Elizabeth St, try Ali Akbar's Lebanese restaurant, Amigo's for Mexican food and Vanidols for southern Asian cuisine; all are BYO. In the city centre, try the Thai Hut at 80 Elizabeth St, the Retro Café on Salamanca Place and Rockefeller's nearby. Mr Wooby's at the back of 65 Salamanca Place is an unlicensed coffee lounge with good food.

Don't miss the seafood, which is uniformly excellent. You can buy take-aways from the floating fish punts at Constitution Dock as well as fresh fish. The Mures Fish Centre — on the waterfront between Victoria and Constitution Docks — is expensive but very good, and has a fairly authentic sushi bar. The Drunken Admiral at 17 Old Wharf also specialises in seafood; sample dishes include chilli prawns and Tasmanian oysters as starters for about $10 and main seafood platters for $17.

Hobart has plenty of top-notch restaurants where you pay dearly to eat well. If you feel hungry in the small hours, head for the 24-hour coffee shop at the Wrest Point Casino. The Casino also has a revolving restaurant — The Point — which charges high prices as you rotate 80 metres above the ground.

At the other end of the spectrum many pubs offer good basic counter meals. For pies and pasties, go to Banjo's on Elizabeth St. If you want to prepare your own picnic or stock up on dried food and portable snacks for a camping trip, YHA members can get a discount of 10% on most foods at Eumarrah Natural Foods at 45 Goulburn St. The Zanskar Wholefood Café at 39 Barrack St offers the same discount on meals and drinks.

Drinking. Most of Hobart's pubs dwell on their nineteenth century past. Although some on the waterfront such as the popular Traveller's Rest at 394 Sandy Bay Road have been tarted up, you can drink in a little history at the Ship, 73 Collins St (built in 1821) or the Custom House, 1 Murray St, at the corner of Waterman's Dock by Salamanca Place. The Dog House Hotel (at the corner of Barrack and Goulburn Sts) and Bourkes New Sydney Hotel mentioned above are recommended as good places to meet other travellers.

It is possible to tour the 156-year-old Cascade Brewery and Woodstock Gardens on Cascade Road, but you have to book ahead (6224 1144) for a place on one of the tours starting at 9.30am or 1pm, and pay a $7 fee.

EXPLORING

Hobart's setting is more beautiful than that of any other state capital except Sydney. It overlooks the broad Derwent River estuary, is surrounded by rugged hills and dominated by the 1270m-high Mount Wellington. The dignified Georgian and Victorian architecture has been carefully preserved, and the overall impression is of a pretty provincial town. The city's proudest modern achievement is Wrest Point, the first casino/resort development in Australia. The rehabilitated waterfront warehouses, whose survival is also owed to tourism, have more charm and add to the attractiveness of the city.

The city centre runs inland from Sullivan's Cove on the western shore of the Derwent River. Most of Hobart's population are on this side of the Derwent, and the suburbs extend south-west (to Sandy Bay, site of the university and the Casino) and north-west through the pleasant New Town area and beyond. The eastern shore is less developed but no less charming.

A fine job has been made of restoring Hobart's Georgian buildings to their former austere elegance. Salamanca Place and the parallel Castray Esplanade (running from Davey St to Princes Park) contain some splendid sandstone warehouses converted to a pleasant mixture of antique shops, galleries and restaurants. Most of the sights are within a 1km radius of the city centre, so are within easy walking distance.

The two main out-of-town attractions are Mount Wellington and the Cadbury chocolate factory. To reach the summit of the former, you will be encouraged to take an organised tour (bookable, like most things in the city, through the Tasmanian Travel and Information Centre). Be warned that tours run to the peak only in clear weather; at other times you may be taken instead to Mount Nelson but not be told until you are under way. An independant alternative is to take the number 48 Fern Tree bus to the foot of the mountain, and walk or hitch the remaining (badly signposted) 11km along Pinnacle Road to the summit.

The chocolate factory is in the north-western suburb of Claremont. Tours of the factory take place Monday to Friday only and must be pre-booked through the Tasmanian Travel and Information Centre (cost $10). The factory can be reached either on a coach trip (for an extra $12), on a Derwent River cruise for $23 (6234 9294) or by city bus: take bus 100 or 101 to the Glenorchy Interchange, then bus 38 or 41.

Battery Point. This spur of land south of the city centre contains one of the finest collections of historic buildings in Australia. There are no signs of the battery of cannons that gave the Point its name in 1818. The oldest structure is the signal station, built in that year, but most of the buildings date from the mid-19th century. The leaflet *Historic Battery Point Trail of Discovery* ($2 from the tourist office) guides you around the highlights, the most charming of which is the ring of 16 cottages known as Arthur's Circus. Only occasional concrete monstrosities, such as the government's Marine Laboratory on the waterfront, diminish the charm of the promontory. A walking tour is organised by the Battery Point Group of the National Trust each Saturday morning; just turn up at the Wishing Well in Franklin Square at 9.30am, and pay $2.50 (which includes morning tea).

Museums. The Tasmanian Museum and Art Gallery complex on Macquarie St (6235 0777) opens daily from 10am to 5pm, admission free. The most interesting features are the museum display on the Tasmanian Aboriginals, the recently restored Commissariat Bond Store (the oldest building in Hobart, built in 1808) and the Gallery's display of works by early colonial artists.

Much of the rest of Hobart's history is housed on Battery Point. The Tasmanian

Maritime Museum at Secheron House traces the island's seafaring past; it opens 1–4.30pm Sunday–Friday and 10am–4.30pm on Saturdays (admission $2). The Van Diemen's Land Memorial Folk Museum at 103 Hampden Road tells the story of the early European settlers, but with more emphasis on the governing classes than their convict charges. It opens 10am–5pm except Sundays (2–5pm) and costs $5, $3.50 for YHA members.

Parks and Zoos. The Royal Tasmanian Botanical Gardens are refreshingly different from those in other state capitals, with excellent roses and herb gardens plus fuchsia and cactus houses. They are just north-east of the city centre at Queens Domain, and can be reached by bus from the city. The gardens are open 8am to 4.45pm daily.

Hobart has no zoo, so you will have to travel further afield if you want to see the island's wildlife. The nearest wildlife centre is Bonorong Park at Brighton, 32km north of Hobart (admission $5).

Shopping. Most shops open from 9am to 6pm, Monday–Friday. Some larger stores and shops in suburban malls stay open until 9pm on Fridays, and additionally on Saturdays from 9am to late. A late-night pharmacy at the corner of Macquarie and Harrington Sts opens 9am–9pm daily. Elizabeth St Mall is the main city-centre shopping street.

Greensleeves Bookshop at 247 Sandy Bay Road (between the city and the University) has the most interesting selection of books in town. The Wilderness Shop is in the Galleria, at 33 Salamanca Place (6234 9370), as is the National Trust Shop (6223 7371) with a range of handmade crafts. Two other galleries and shops that are great for browsing are the Handmark Gallery in Battery Point (44 Hampden Road) and the Huon Pine Shop at 18 Criterion St. The Saturday morning market in Salamanca Place is lively and colourful, but don't expect to find too many bargains among the craft stalls.

To buy the equipment you need for the wilderness, there are some good shops on Elizabeth St: Paddy Pallin at number 76, Country Comfort at 104 and The Jolly Swagman at 107; the first two of these offer 10% discounts to YHA members.

ENTERTAINMENT
Theatre and Music. The big annual event is the Hobart Summer Festival held in late December to January each year, which marks the finish of the famous Sydney to Hobart Yacht Race. Upcoming performances throughout the year are listed in *Press Press*, the *Mercury* and the *Sunday Tasmanian*, and are publicised at the Tasmanian Travel and Information Centre. The Theatre Royal at 29 Campbell St opened in 1837 and has retained its ornate Georgian-style interior and near-perfect acoustics. Call 346266 to find out what's on, but don't be too fussy; the theatre is worth a visit for its historical interest alone. More adventurous productions are staged at the smaller Backspace auditorium. Drama is performed also at the Peacock Theatre on Salamanca Place and at the University Centre in Churchill Avenue on the Sandy Bay Campus (reached by bus 52 to stop 12); dial 6264 1183 for information on forthcoming events.

The University has a Centre for the Arts in a renovated jam factory at Sullivan's Cove on the waterfront near Battery Point. The Centre includes galleries and workshops, and retains some of the antiquated jam-making machinery as museum pieces.

The Dog House Hotel (see *Eating and Drinking* above) has good jazz several nights a week. Good local bands can be seen at Ye Old Red Lion at 129 Macquarie St, Tatt's Hotel at 112 Murray St, Bourkes New Sydney Hotel (as mentioned above) and Round Midnight at 39 Salamanca Place. Touring bands appear at the Derwent Entertainment Centre in Glenorchy City (8km north-west of Hobart).

Cinema. Film buffs from all over Australasia congregate in Hobart each September for its International Film Festival. The event doesn't quite rival Cannes but is nonetheless an interesting showcase, particularly of southern hemisphere movies. For the rest of the year, cinema choice is limited to the West End at 181 Collins St (6234 7288) with seven screens, and the State at 375 Elizabeth St (6234 6318), which shows more arty films.

Nightlife. Try the Wrest Point Casino at 410 Sandy Bay Road (6225 0112), which opens from noon to the early hours.

Sport. Yachting fans congregate in Hobart around New Year for the climax of the Sydney to Hobart Yacht Race, and in February for the Hobart Yacht Regatta. The finishing line is at Constitution Dock. To charter a yacht, ring 6234 9921.

The Domain Tennis Centre is located close to the city on Queens Domain. You can go to the dogs at Hobart Greyhound Racing Club meetings at the Royal Hobart Showground. The Elwick Showground, in the suburb of Glenorchy, is the venue for horseracing and harness racing; check in the *Mercury* for details of meetings. Cricket is played at the Bellerive Oval on Hobart's eastern shore.

THE SOUTH-WEST

The first stretch of the journey south on the A6 from the capital reveals little of the remote and sometimes desolate wilderness in store beyond the end of the Huon Highway. The road splits at the small town of Kingston. About 2km south of Kingston on the Channel Highway are the headquarters of Australia's Antarctic Division, and you can visit the free exhibition between 9am and 4pm, Monday–Friday. Further south alongside the picturesque D'Entrecasteaux Channel, your journey will be enlivened by attractions such as the Model Train World at Huonville and the Winterwood Winery (making wines from fruit and honey) between Woodbridge and Gardners Bay. Just north of Gardners Bay you can go to the Talune Wildlife Park and Koala Gardens (admission $3).

Halfway down the coast from Kingston is the small port of Kettering, where you can catch a ferry to Bruny Island (6238 9201). The ferry operates between about 7.15am and 6.30pm, with nine or ten sailings in each direction daily. If you intend to catch the last boat of the day, arrive a little early, as sailings can be erratic. Timetables are printed in *Tasmanian Travelways* and the Friday edition of the Hobart *Mercury*. The return fare for a car is $11 off-peak and $17 peak; foot passengers and cyclists travel free.

The Oyster Cove Inn overlooking the harbour in Kettering is a pleasant place to wait for the next ferry, and is warmed in winter (and sometimes summer) by a log fire. Another pub worth visiting is the Woodbridge Hotel 5km south of Kettering which has a deserved reputation for good food and a wine list encompassing most wines made in Tasmania.

The North and South parts of Bruny Island are linked by a thin strip of land; on a clear day, stop in the middle to admire the 360-degree views across Isthmus Bay to the west and Adventure Bay to the east. The Bligh Museum in Adventure Bay contains volumes and sketches of the early voyagers to this part of the world including Captains Cook and Bligh. South Bruny Island claims to have the southernmost pub in Australia, as does Dover across on the mainland. To make sure you are able to boast about having drunk in the most southerly, have a drink in both.

The road south-west from Kingston first runs through the orchards of the Huon Valley. Stop off to visit the Apple Museum in the village of Grove to find out much more than you ever wanted to know about the fruit and inspect over 500 varieties of apple. The region's centre is Huonville. Although the town itself is unattractive, the Huon River has some of the best waterside scenery in Australia. If you follow the eastern bank south, you end up in the prettily situated town of Cygnet. Its YHA hostel (03-6295 1551) also functions as a farm and teahouse, with delicious apple cake.

The highway along the western side of the Huon continues south to Geeveston, Dover and Southport. From Geeveston you can make a detour to the Hartz Mountains National Park, 80km south-west of Hobart. The last 15km of the access road is gravel and can be closed due to snowfall. The Park's lakes and crags formed by glacial erosion are considerably more impressive than those of the Harz range in Germany, and have the added bonus of dramatic trails through the rainforest. Dover, overlooking Esperance Bay, is an appealing town and the last real settlement before the wilderness; stock up with petrol and provisions here unless you are prepared to risk the limited and expensive selection at Southport.

The highway proper ends at Southport, but most people who have come this far head west. There are thermal springs 8km along the unsealed B35. Although they tend to be tepid rather than hot, the short walk around them (with the possibility of spotting a platypus) is worth the effort. The Hastings Caves, 3km along, have guided tours through the spectacular rock formations (entrance fee $4 plus $1 to swim in the thermal pools). The B36 road south leads to Lune River, site of the most southerly YHA hostel in Australia (03-6298 3163). It is also one of the most active hostels in the nation: you can hire caving equipment to explore the local glow-worm caves, rent a kayak or a mountain bike, or join a trek into the South West National Park.

Just south of the hostel is Ida Bay, which has a railway line running 6km east to Deep Hole. The line theoretically provides great possibilities for a day's bushwalking around the Southport Lagoon, but the train schedules are not renowned for their reliability. You could find you face a long hike back to Lune River if the last train fails to run. The remainder of route B36 south is suitable only for four-wheel-drive vehicles, ending at Cockle Creek (unsurprisingly, Australia's southernmost township). Should your vehicle break down, you might usefully spend your time sifting through the roadside earth while waiting for assistance; the Lune River area is famous for its gemstones.

The entrance to the South West Walking Track is close to Lune River. It takes bushwalkers through an uninhabited and inhospitable region that is one of the least-explored areas in Australia. The South West National Park is one of only three temperate areas on the UNESCO World Heritage List, and has so far remained virtually untainted by mankind. There are no real roads in the park, but those not confident enough to undergo the strenuous hike can fly into one of the few clearings suitable for light aircraft. One unforgettable feature of this wilderness is the 'false floor' created in places by thick scrub; the closely meshed greenery can be up to 10 metres above ground level. Attempting to walk on this treacherous surface is unwise, as anyone unfortunate enough to fall through has little chance of escape or rescue. Only the most experienced hikers should explore the Park without a guide, although plenty of tours are operated.

The South West National Park is famed for its rainforest which has been made accessible in a few places. The Gordon River Road takes you deep into the interior of Tasmania north of the park. The gateway to the park is at

Maydena where you pay the park entrance fee. After driving a further 15 minutes, turn left on Scotts Peak Road to find the Creepy Crawly Nature Trail. This is along a boardwalk suspended over the rainforest floor and which takes about 20 minutes to complete.

THE SOUTH-EAST

There are arguably more historical relics of early European settlements in this corner of Tasmania than anywhere else in Australia. Visiting the vestiges of a penal settlement is instructive rather than entertaining; but when you've seen enough of man's inhumanity to man, the views and fresh air provide a welcome relief.

Tasman Peninsula. The sea south and east of Hobart is filled with rugged yet beautiful peninsulas and islands, of which the Tasman Peninsula has most to offer in terms of scenery and interest. In addition to Port Arthur (see below), the Peninsula has a variety of natural and man-made attractions. The 90-minute journey along the Arthur Highway runs east from the state capital, then drops down through the Forestier Peninsula to reveal a spectacular view of Eaglehawk Neck, a natural causeway across to the Tasman Peninsula.

This narrow isthmus made the Peninsula a logical choice for the British authorities when setting up a penal settlement. A relatively small force equipped with vicious dogs was installed at the Neck and, although a couple of diehards did get through, the guards successfully prevented any mass escape. The Neck was infamous in early Australia as 'the isthmus between earth and hell'. Nowadays the locals are far more hospitable, and Eaglehawk Neck is a pleasant little place. On the coastline just north of the Neck is a geological formation known as the Tessellated Pavement, vertical shafts of rock sheared off to give a surprisingly uniform geometric pattern, known as 'nature's own footpath'. A few kilometres south of the Neck is a blowhole plus two other coastal phenomena known as the Tasman Arch and the Devil's Kitchen. You can hire a bicycle at Eaglehawk Neck and cycle along road C338 to take in these sights. Take time to enjoy the village of Doo Town, where every house has a name containing the name of the town, including a shack known as 'Doo Nothing'. In nearby Taranna you can pat a Tassie Devil and other native animals at the Tasmanian Devil Park which also features a cider farm with tastings (entrance fee of $5, 30% discount to YHA members).

The road which leads you the long way around the Peninsula via Nubeena to Port Arthur is sealed; a detour via Premaydena to Saltwater River and Lime Bay is not, but is usually passable with care and is well worthwhile. The ruins of the early settlement at Saltwater River are fascinating, and the track down to Lime Bay leads to a pretty cove with clear green water. You can camp near the sea for free. Tasman Peninsula Detours (03-6250 3355) offers half or full-day tours by four-wheel-drive vehicles.

Port Arthur. The main town of the Peninsula lies on a beautiful bay and, with its well manicured lawns, would be unrecognisable to those who knew it in darker days. From 1830 to 1876, it was the headquarters of Tasmania's main penal settlement with 25,000 prisoners. Many of the people sent to Port Arthur could be classed as 'political prisoners', such as the Tolpuddle Martyr and early trade unionist George Lovelace. The penal settlement was designed to show the cruellest face of the British Empire. Most of the original buildings have been destroyed in a succession of bush fires, but a few Victorian remnants are still standing. The town has been somewhat overtaken by the tourist trade, but you can spend a pleasant couple of hours or days wandering among the ruins of the settlement. The visitors' centre is housed in the former lunatic asylum, and offers an audio-visual record of the most notorious penal regime in Australia. Among the other buildings you sense that the British had an altogether unhealthy interest in punishment. For example, the penitentiary was designed to compound the already miserable regime of servitude.

Free tours of the settlement are given by enthusiastic and knowledgeable guides. They depart at regular intervals from the visitors' centre, ending at the Settlement Museum. Entrance costs $7.50. Every evening at the Broad Arrow Tea House, located within the 'historic site' in Port Arthur, the original (1926) film of Marcus Clarke's story *For the Term of His Natural Life* is shown at 7.45pm (October–May); admission $4. This silent version is far more powerful than the tame television mini-series of the same name. The Broad Arrow also has a craft gallery; call 03-6250 2242 for further information and bookings. After the film, anyone capable of suspending disbelief can join a two-hour lantern-lit Ghost Tour (December–April only, $4).

At the mouth of Port Arthur Bay lies the Isle of the Dead, where both convicts and free settlers are buried. While the officers and other free settlers were accorded the respect of a proper burial, convicts were interred seven or eight to a grave with no headstone to mark their existence. There are frequent licensed cruises of the harbour and its environs including a visit to the Isle of the Dead ($6 for the one-hour cruise; $4 for half an hour).

Accommodation in the town is not confined to the 'Old English Tudor Tavern and Motel Complex' as the Fox and Hounds on the Arthur Highway describes itself. The YHA hostel at Port Arthur commands an exceptional view of the ruins (03-6250 2311), and there are also two possible campsites: Garden Point Caravan Park on Stewarts Bay, outside Port Arthur, and another one at Nubeena 13km away.

South of Port Arthur the terrain becomes more rugged. The paved road ends at Remarkable Cave, so-called because of the fascinating formations you can view when the tide is out, and the impressive sight of the Tasman Sea rushing in and out at high tide. A few kilometres farther along a rough track is Cape Raoul, Tasmania's own version of Land's End. Other, tamer attractions on the Peninsula include the Tasmanian Devil Park and the Port Arthur Marine Park, both in the small township of Taranna.

New Norfolk. Most visitors are tempted by the coastline or rugged mountain ranges of southern Tasmania rather than its settlements. But, this town 30km inland has some interesting vestiges of colonialism and a predictable selection of tourist attractions. There is also a jet boat operating on the Derwent River which flows through the town: the 'Devil Jet' runs half-hour trips along the river for $25; dial 03-6261 3460 for details.

The colonial buildings which remain include the Tynwald Mansion on the Willow Bend Estate (named after a twist on the Derwent River) which is now a guest house; the Oast House, now a museum of the Tasman hop industry; and the Old Colony Inn (21 Montagu St; 03-6261 2731) which doubles as a colonial museum (admission $2) and a restaurant serving meals and afternoon teas in the garden in summer. It seems that the only two old buildings which have retained their original purposes are St Matthew's Church in Bathurst St, dating from 1823, and the Bush Inn on Montagu St. This pub, along with several others on the mainland, claims to be the oldest continuously licensed house in Australia. Undoubtedly the best place to eat in New Norfolk — and possibly Tasmania — is Cotswold Cuisine on Lachlan Road (03-6261 2322). The owners cater only for groups of six to 14, and discuss personal preferences for food and wine in advance to produce a specially tailored meal. Before making a definite booking, you should also discuss the price.

A further 40km inland from Hobart is the Mount Field National Park, the first to be established in Tasmania. The Park is particularly popular because of its proximity to the state capital, and has some huge, ancient swamp gum trees. The Russell Falls are close to the entrance, falling 40m with a midway ledge for close-up spectating. In winter, the downwardly-mobile head for the Park to enjoy the skiing.

THE EAST COAST

This part of Tasmania is often referred to as the 'Holiday Coast' or the 'Sun Coast'. But in spite of efforts by the tourist authority to attract visitors and develop resorts, large stretches of the coast are still unspoilt.

Starting from Hobart in the south, the first main settlement on the Tasman Highway is Buckland. This unprepossessing small town is most notable for St John's Church, which has a 14th century stained-glass window painstakingly imported from Europe. Triabunna, the next settlement, has some excellent fish restaurants. The Eastcoaster Resort at Louisville, just north, is a good imitation of a slightly jaded British seaside resort; nearby Orford is livelier. To escape from these resorts, take the ferry from the Eastcoaster Resort across to Maria Island, now a National Park but formerly a penal colony, the first to be established in Tasmania.

Further up the coast, Swansea is a 'proper' town with easy access to beaches. Nine Mile Beach is the nearest, and, while not the island's best, has some beautiful shells and good views of the Freycinet Peninsula (which has a French pronunciation, roughly fray-sin-ay). The Freycinet National Park is very pleasant, with hills and cliffs falling into the ocean. Coles Bay is the only town on the peninsula and the headquarters of the National Park are here. There is a nearby YHA hostel (03-6234 9617; bookings essential) and the area is ideal for a few days of peace and quiet. The walk out to Wine Glass Bay (so-called because of its shape) is recommended, but beware of the Bennet's wallabies that will go to extraordinary lengths to get any food you happen to have about your person. In fine weather, the beach at Wine Glass Bay is among the best in Australia.

The midpoint on the coast is Bicheno, a former whaling port, which has attractions such as a wildlife park and a marine life centre, as well as some good foreshore walks. Easily the most attractive place to stay is the Bicheno YHA (003-751293), only 10 metres from a beach and affording views of some spectacular sunrises and sunsets. At low tide you can wade out to the penguin colony on Diamond Island.

The road north then turns inland, twisting alarmingly through the Elephant Pass to St Marys, and returning to the coast near Scamander. There is a good stretch of beach from here up to St Helens, another 'real' town and a useful centre for exploring the area; the YHA is at 5 Cameron St (003-761661). The crayfish, scallop and abalone catches provide some casual employment, and after a hard day's work you can head for one of the excellent nearby beaches. The Tasman highway inland to Scottsdale and Launceston has some exceptionally good scenery; look out for the village of Wellborough, which looks as though it was shipped intact from rural Spain.

LAUNCESTON

Tasmania's second city and Australia's third oldest has little in common with its craggy Cornish namesake. The Antipodean Launceston is a well-to-do market town that dominates northern central Tasmania. It has numerous colonial buildings, many converted to tourist-related functions. Also, the names are pronounced differently: while Cornwall's version is 'Laun'ston', in Tasmania the middle syllable is pronounced.

The city's chief visual attraction is the dramatic Cataract Gorge a mile outside the city, where the South Esk River cuts deep through the land. The view is especially worthwhile at night when the Gorge is floodlit. By day you can take the long and harrowing chairlift ride across the Gorge for $3. Aspiring daredevils can also go out to Trevallyn State Recreation Area to try out cable hang gliding, which claims to provide the sensation of hang gliding in complete safety. This is one of the few cases in which a 200m trip costing $5 can be considered good value.

Other attractions include the numerous pleasant parks and — for some people — the Casino at Launceston Country Club. Although many colonial buildings have been preserved, Yorktown Square is an unashamedly new (1984) construction of 'cobblestone paths, story-book shop fronts and coach house lamps' housing a predictably twee collection of retailers. The Penny Royal Mill (a renovation of old corn and gunpowder mills) is in a similar vein, but has the amusing bonus of a fleet of ten gunpowder barges that transport visitors along the waterways around the complex.

The city is small enough to explore on foot but the bus terminal is at 112 George St; for public transport information, dial 319911.

Launceston no longer has a permanent YHA hostel, but a temporary hostel operates from December to February and sometimes during other periods as well. For location details and opening times, contact the YHA Tasmania office in Hobart (03-6234 9617); dorm beds should start at $13. During the summer university vacation (December to February), the University of Tasmania student residences are a good bet — travellers pay $25 per night for comfortable rooms at both Leprena and Keslake residences (243917). Other places to try, though more expensive, are Apartments 1930 Style (446953) and the Windmill Hill Tourist Lodge (319337).

Launceston is large enough to support a reasonable variety of restaurants. The best alternatives to the steak/seafood/pizza staples are Woofies housed in the Georgian warehouse Macquarie House in Civic Square, which serves saté, seafood and calorific desserts, the unpretentious Italian BYO restaurant Calibrisella at 56 Wellington St and Food for Thought at 88 St John St, which serves vegetarian food with an Indian influence in the daytime only. The best pubs are both on Brisbane St: the Launceston Hotel, which has a club called Hot Gossip, and the Royal Oak.

In contrast to the mountains south and west, the Midlands around Launceston are scenically uninteresting, especially in drought conditions, which can produce some very un-Tasmanian, parched landscapes. But nearby historic towns such as Oatlands are worth a visit.

THE NORTH-WEST

If your time in Tasmania is limited, get a flavour of the island by sailing or flying to Devonport and heading north-west. The top left-hand corner of Tasmania has the same ingredients of dramatic coastline, rugged mountains, towering forests and undulating pasture (plus logging and hydro-electric projects) that the island possesses in such abundance.

Devonport, population 25,000, is a lively and interesting port. It straddles the Mersey and, as in Liverpool, there is a ferry across the river: from close by the railway station to East Devonport (fare $1). A visit to the Showcase tourist information centre on the corner of Best and Formby Sts (03-6424 0520), which is primarily an arts and crafts exhibition centre, will equip you with the maps and information for a day's tour. You can rent a bicycle to explore the town from Hire A Bike (03-6424 3889). As well as interesting historic buildings, there are some more unusual diversions: the Devonport Brickworks (opposite the Showcase in Best St) will sell you an unfired brick upon which you can inscribe your name. It is then fired and placed in the wall of the brickworks. The Tasmanian Aboriginal Arts Centre is called Tiaggara on Mersey Bluff; admission is $2.

A short way west of Devonport is Ulverstone, a beach resort which is also a good base for exploring inland. You need not be an experienced walker to climb Black Bluff in Leven Canyon, just south of Ulverstone. In order to get there, however, you need to wade through the often icily-cold Leven River. The view from the top of Black Bluff on a clear day makes it worthwhile, across to Cradle Mountain and beyond almost to Lake St Clair.

Tasmania's third largest city is Burnie on the shore of Emu Bay, in an area of farmland. The main industry is paper production, a notorious cause of air pollution. You can take a tour of a pulp and paper mill. Other places of interest include the Pioneer Village Museum on High St (a re-creation of a turn-of-the-century commercial centre), and the Art Gallery on Wilmot St; admission to both is free.

The area around Wynyard has some good beaches, the nearby Rocky Cape National Park, and good trout and sea fishing. Beyond Smithton, the road becomes little more than a track as it approaches Cape Grim, Tasmania's Land's End. The air here is reputed (at least locally) to be the cleanest in the world.

Cradle Mountain and Lake St Clair. This National Park is the most developed in Tasmania, and has become yet more popular with the new highway from Cradle Valley to the West Coast. Its highlights are the 1545m Cradle Mountain, plenty of leisurely strolls on well marked tracks and good fishing for trout in mountain streams. The park ranger's office, on 6492 1133, can supply further information.

The major trail is the 80km Overland Track which takes at least 5 (often 8) days and for which there is a $10 track user fee; it passes Tasmania's highest peak, 1617m Mount Ossa. Most walkers start at the northern end of the trail in Cradle Valley and come out at Lake St Clair. There are extensive visitor facilities at either end including all grades of accommodation. To book a campsite or bunkhouse bed at the recently opened Cradle Valley visitor area, ring 03-6492 1395. Tent sites and some other accommodation at the southern end can be pre-booked by ringing Lakeside St Clair Wilderness Holidays (03-6289 1137); the 16-bed bunkhouse is available only on a first-come, first-served basis.

Like the popular trails in New Zealand there are excellent huts along the track. Walkers who don't want to run the risk of uncomfortable nights if the huts are full (as inevitably happens in the summer holidays) should carry a tent. In any case a tent is advisable in case the weather suddenly turns nasty when you're a long way from a hut. Even when the weather is hot, the stream water is icy cold for washing. As well as having to carry food for up to ten days, you are also expected to carry your own stove as campfires are banned and the hut stoves are not meant for cooking. Although it often seems that every man and his dog walk the Overland Track, it is a reasonably serious undertaking. Campers should be prepared for visits from possums, wombats and wallabies; keep your food safe.

Less hardy souls might be tempted to stay in rustic comfort at the Lemonthyme Lodge on the road between Devonport and the northern trailhead (03-6492 1112), which costs $40 each in a double including breakfast.

Lake St Clair is 18km long and is the deepest freshwater lake in Australia. You can cruise the length of it on *M V Idaclair*; the one-way fare is $12 and you should book in advance on 6489 1137.

THE WEST COAST

The west coasts of Tasmania and New Zealand have strong geographical simi-larities. Both offer steep mountain ranges, fast-flowing rivers, precipitous gorges and inhospitable rain forest. They even have a town called Queenstown as a gateway to the wilderness. Although few would dispute New Zealand's claim to greater grandeur, a visit to the Tasmanian wild west is not without scenic — and human — interest. The vast majority of the western coast of Tasmania is inaccessible and so when people refer to the West Coast they are normally referring to the area around the old mining towns of Zeehan, Strahan and Queenstown.

Queenstown has depended for its livelihood upon mining copper from nearby Mount Lyell for over a century. The mine still functions, but is gradually being developed into a 'living museum' of mining history. The new Mount Owen Track gives an interesting insight into the pioneering days, and provides some spectacular views. The reservoir which will result from a new hydro-electric scheme is to be developed into a resort area, in an unintentional imitation of the setting of Queenstown, New Zealand.

In a public relations exercise to promote the project, the Tasmanian Hydro-electric Commission (HEC) has converted the old Empire Hotel into an infor-mation centre. If you call in, don't expect to find out much about the consequent destruction of the environment or the flooding of important Aboriginal remains discovered in 1990; for that side, consult the Wilderness Society or the Tasmanian Wildlife Commission. The Wildlife Commission will also tell you about the wrecking of the ecology of the King River by waste from the copper mine. (The blasted landscapes were so unusual that they became a tourist attraction in themselves; and some years ago when efforts to plant new trees were made, the city fathers complained that this would harm tourist revenue.) You can see the spot where conservationist David Bellamy was arrested, a few kilometres east of Queenstown at the start of the road to Crotty. The road runs down to Wild Rivers National Park, but is accessible only by four-wheel drive vehicle.

Zeehan is a mining 'ghost town' 60km northwest of Queenstown. In earlier days, it was a community of 10,000 living from a rich vein of silver, lead, and zinc. It reputedly possesses what was once the longest Main St in the southern hemisphere, and a theatre seating over 1000 people that hosted world-famous performers. Close to Queenstown and Zeehan lies Strahan, an old port from where the ore was shipped. Its main purpose nowadays is as a base for tours across the 20km-long Macquarie Harbour to the Gordon River. Half and full-day cruises sail up the river to Gordon Gorge, passing Sarah Island in Macquarie Harbour, a desolate former penal colony. The return journey takes in Hells Gates, the outlet to the ocean. The cost for the half-day tour is $35. Book through the tourist office or direct with Gordon River Cruises on 03-6471 7187. You can also fly by seaplane from the jetty at Strahan up the river for one or four days' canoeing. The day trip costs around $100, and can be booked direct with Wilderness Adventure Camps on 03-6471 7377.

South West National Park is one of the wildest and remotest regions in the world. Small planes from Cambridge Aerodrome in Hobart land at Melaleuca where high-spending tourists take a boat ride on Bathurst Harbour. This area is four days by foot from any settlement.

BASS STRAIT ISLANDS

These offshore islands take isolation and wilderness a stage further. If the Tasmanian bush does not feel remote enough for you, take a trip out to King Island or Flinders Island, off the northwestern and northeastern corners of the mainland respectively. The truly anti-social could visit some of the sparsely populated or uninhabited intervening islands (such as Robbins, Clarke or Cape Barren) *en route* to Flinders Island, or Hunter or Three Hummock Islands between the coast and King Island.

King Island. The 'Roaring Forties' dominate the Bass Strait. These strong westerly winds (so named for the latitude) have driven over 150 ships on to the island. Only half the island has been cleared for farming, the rest being undisturbed native bush with a wide range of wildlife. There are good bushwalking tracks, especially along the unpopulated north coast, and excellent diving in the clear waters with plenty of wrecked ships to explore. In addition, the island has a penguin rookery, a calcified forest and the shimmering Lake Martha Lavinia. Currie, the main settlement, is a working port with an interesting museum tracing the history of seafaring in the Bass Strait. King Island creams and cheeses are especially prized and King Island brie is available throughout Australia.

Flinders Island. This is the largest of the Furneaux Group of islands, and measures about 60km by 30km. The main town on the island is Whitemark, and the airport is nearby. As on King Island, there is still some unspoilt scenery and interesting wildlife. The southernmost part of the island is occupied by Mount Strzelecki National Park, which has good bushwalking trails including a well-signposted track to the 756m summit; the walk should take between two and three hours and is well worthwhile. The Patriarch Wildlife Sanctuary is on the east coast, while on the west is the Wybalenna Historic Site near Emitta, which was the scene of the failed attempt to save the Tasmanian Aboriginals.

One-seventh of Tasmania is given over to National Parks. Although this land is constantly under pressure from mining and logging development interests, Tasmania has a good record on caring for the environment. Pleasant as the cities and towns are, the visitors who get most out of Tasmania are those who relish the wilderness experience, i.e. the sort of people who can cope cheerfully with cold weather laced with frequent downpours. Anyone intending to do any outdoor activities should always carry warm and waterproof clothing and a pair of sturdy shoes, preferably hiking boots. You may find yourself thigh-deep in mud and slush even on less ambitious day walks.

In the highlands it can snow at any time, so warm woollens are essential whatever the time of year. Sufficient food supplies should be taken, although fresh water can usually be found (from melting snow if necessary). A number of areas in National Parks have been designated Fuel Stove Only to prevent forest fires and save trees. Transgressors may be fined up to $5000. Before embarking on any wilderness activity, be sure to complete the Trip Intentions form on the back of the *Welcome to the Wilderness* leaflet available from the Department of Parks. The advice offered on safety in the section *New Zealand: Great Outdoors* holds good for Tasmania, but the island has characteristics that require special attention.

It is foolish to embark upon a visit to the wilderness without extensive preparation and a good map. The Department of Parks, Wildlife & Heritage produces an excellent range of information leaflets on wilderness access, safety, etc. Tasmap, which is a part of the Parks Department, distributes a number of accurate, large-scale maps of National Parks, hiking routes and nature walks. These can be requested in advance by writing to GPO 44A, Hobart 7001, or obtained from its offices at 134 Macquarie St, Hobart (03-6233 3382). Staff at these or any of the many other offices dotted around Tasmania are also willing to issue advice on huts and facilities.

YHA hostels in wilderness areas are another good source of information, especially on arranging transport, making it possible to plan your own adventure in Tasmania. For example the hostel in Deloraine in northern Tasmania (High-view Lodge, 8 Blake St; 003-622996) has a number of treks on offer.

For the less ambitious, there are plenty of half- and full-day tours by four-wheel drive vehicles. Bookings can be made through tourist offices. As a rough guide, a half-day tour might cost $30-$40 and a full day $60-80 including lunch and 'billy tea'. Many operators who run tours by four-wheel drive vehicle, aircraft or raft belong to the Adventure Tours Association of Tasmania; this trade association seeks to ensure high standards of safety.

Scuba diving is also possible in Tasmania, for example in East Wynyard (03-6442 2247) as is rafting, for example on the Franklin River with Peregrine Adventures (Unit 5/13 Beechworth Road, Sandy Bay, Hobart). The best known ski fields are in Mount Field National Park in the south of the state (for cross country) and Ben Lomond National Park in north-eastern Tasmania; the latter is accessible in winter by a steep and slippery road with hairpin bends. Skiing in Tasmania is considerably cheaper than in mainland Australia: a lift ticket at Mount Field costs $10 a day and at Ben Lomond about twice that. Further information on Mount Field (where there is very little public accommodation) is available from the Southern Tasmania Ski Association (GPO Box 1197M, Hobart 7001). To find out about transport, contact the Skibus on 003-340442.

Anglers travel to Tasmania from all over the world to take advantage of the excellent fishing on and around the island. There are game-fishing clubs based in Hobart, Launceston and St Helens, and plenty of sea-angling charter boats in the south and east. Even with just a rod and line you will probably find it easy to catch Australian salmon, whiting and bream from the shore. Since trout were introduced to Tasmania from England in 1864, they have spread to thousands of lakes and streams, making Tasmania prime territory for freshwater fishing. Licence regulations can be checked with the Inland Fisheries Commission at 127 Davey St, Hobart 7000 (03-6223 6622).

Calendar of Events

January	'King of the Derwent' Yacht Race, Hobart
January	Burnie Day and Night Carnival
February (first Wednesday)	**Hobart Cup horserace (public holiday only in Hobart)**
February (second Tuesday)	**Royal Hobart Regatta Day (public holiday only in Hobart)**
February (last weekend)	Launceston Cup horserace
March (first Monday)	**Eight Hour Day**
mid-March	Ross Highland Games
late March	Launceston Festival
March/April	**Easter Tuesday**
April	Tasmanian Canoe Championships
August/September	Circular Head Arts Festival, Smithton
September	Hobart International Film Festival
September/October	Salamanca Arts Festival, Hobart
early October	Launceston Agricultural Show
late October	Royal Hobart Agricultural Show

November (first Monday)	**Recreation Day (holiday only in northern Tasmania)**
late November	Devonport Agricultural Show
December/January	Sydney–Hobart Yacht Race

Public holidays are shown in **bold**.

Adelaide and South Australia

Population of Adelaide: 1,100,000   **Population of SA: 1,450,000**

Residents of the cosmopolitan cities of Melbourne and Sydney tend to regard Adelaide as a backwater, the unexciting capital of a bland, prosperous state, breathing conformity and complacency. Yet Adelaide is heartily recommended by almost everyone who has been there. The city is not nearly as dull as its image. Although it isn't the kind of city — like Sydney or Perth — with which visitors often fall instantly in love, Adelaide has a grace and charm lacking in bigger brasher cities and is certainly a pleasant place to be.

A beautifully planned and sited city, with suburbs on the seashore and the Adelaide Hills rising up to the east, it has a centre that seems more European than others in Australia. The tall traditional lines of the railway station, the State Parliament and Town Hall would not be out of place in a central European capital. Adelaide has the added bonus of being extremely easy to find your way around. As a model for city planners everywhere, the city centre is surrounded on all sides by green parkland. With its biennial arts festival, held in even-numbered years, and a burgeoning range of artistic events throughout the year, Adelaide has a reasonable claim to be the nation's cultural centre. And South Australia is a rich blend of varied coastline, fertile farmland (producing three-fifths of Australia's wine), rugged mountain ranges and seemingly endless stark desert.

The French landed in what is now South Australia in 1792, but found only the desolate Nullarbor Plain north of the Great Australian Bight. The British discovered more benevolent land in the south and plans were laid to settle there. Uniquely for Australia, the new colony was privatised. A South Australian

Company was formed, and parcels of land were sold off to small investors — called 'Capitalists' in the Company's charter — at £1 per acre. Assisted passages were available to those without the means of buying land, so that the new entrepreneurs could hire workers. The whole scheme was designed to be self-supporting and to attract solid, dependable citizens; convicts were specifically excluded. Alone of all the Australian colonies, South Australia was peopled entirely by free settlers, a fact that is still made much of.

The first settlers arrived at Kangaroo Island in 1835 but a larger group arrived on the mainland a year later aboard *HMS Buffalo*. Standing by a gum tree in what is now Glenelg, they proclaimed the area as a new colony and founded the city of Adelaide, named after the wife of William IV. (The gum tree still stands, at the corner of Bagshaw and McFarlane Sts.) They were led by Governor Hindmarsh. His bickering with the Board of Commissioners (who 'owned' the colony) led to the collapse of the South Australian Company 4 years later. Back in the hands of the British government the colony prospered, unfettered by the conflicts between convicts and their warders elsewhere in Australia. The capital benefitted from some remarkably forward-looking town planning. Its first Surveyor-General, Colonel William Light, claimed to have had a vision of how the city should be laid out. He put this into practice and, indeed, the streets of the central area still conform exactly to his plan.

The pattern of migration to South Australia continued to centre upon Adelaide, which today holds three-quarters of the state's population. Most of the rest are within easy reach of the capital, with only a very few venturing into the desert north and west of Port Augusta.

CLIMATE

The often quoted fact that South Australia is the driest state in the driest continent should not lead you to expect unmitigated harshness. Although the northern part of the state is largely inhospitable desert, the areas of interest to most visitors are comfortably benign. Adelaide averages 10 hours a day of sunshine in January, and the low humidity makes the February mean high of 30°C/86°F quite bearable. And despite being 100km nearer the South Pole than Sydney is, Adelaide's geographic location gives it longer, drier summers and shorter, milder winters than the coast of New South Wales. The average winter minimum does not fall below 7°C/45°F, and the winter months of June and July average over 4 hours of sunshine a day. Rainfall in Adelaide is a light 53cm annually, over half of which falls between May and August; at other times of the year you would be unlucky to come away without a suntan. For city weather (and fire ban information), dial 1196.

THE LOCALS

To this day, there is a chauvinistic tendency among the natives to regard themselves as a cut above residents of other states and their rather dubious extraction. In return, South Australians are known disparagingly as 'crow-eaters' by those outside the state, a reference to the alleged dining habits of the early settlers. In many ways, Adelaide deserves its reputation for being conservative, though of course it is big enough to accommodate fringe and radical elements.

The European roots of the settlers are more evident in South Australia than elsewhere in the continent. The state flag, for example, bears the colours of Germany, and Teutonic names are common in the valleys around Adelaide. Immigrants from southeast Europe and the Middle East also assert their national identities. Recent migration has been mainly from Southeast Asia, giving Adelaide an even more cosmopolitan feel (and, incidentally, an excellent selection of restaurants).

Making Friends. In keeping with the relaxed lifestyle which they enjoy, natives of Adelaide and its environs are casual and friendly. If you set out on a specific mission to make friends, you could do worse than to try the pubs and clubs around Hindley St. This area, however, attracts a fair number of eccentrics and miscellaneous oddballs whom you may not care to befriend. It is safer to head across King William St to meet the cleaner-cut clientele at the pubs and restaurants of Rundle St (see *Eating and Drinking*) or to mix with the student fraternity at the University of Adelaide (conveniently located in the north of the city centre) or the would-be yuppies of North Adelaide in their trendy pubs around O'Connell St.

City Layout. In accordance with Colonel Light's vision, the centre of Adelaide is elegantly contained by the four Terraces and measures precisely one square mile. Within this area the streets form a logical grid pattern. The heart of the city is the Hindley St/Rundle Mall area, with King William St — the main central artery — cutting between them.

Outside the centre, geography imposes restrictions on the grid scheme but with the aid of Gregory's street atlas or the RAA Adelaide Tourist Guide map (free from the Travel Centre) you can find most destinations. One 'road' that follows no obvious pattern is Brougham Place (pronounced 'browem'), just north of the city. It comprises three sides of an isosceles triangle plus an additional 'dogleg' from one corner, forming a curious geometric shape. When asking for directions in the centre of town, note that Hindley St is pronounced so as to rhyme with kindly. Gouger St is pronounced 'goojer' and Gilles St as 'guiles'.

ARRIVAL AND DEPARTURE

Air. Adelaide airport is 6km south-west of the city centre, planted firmly in the suburbs, and pilots are adept at dodging the bungalows and shopping malls that clutter the approaches to the runway. The international and domestic terminals are 5 minutes' walk apart. The *Airport Shuttle* departs for the city centre from outside both terminals every half-hour, except at the weekend when it goes hourly; it takes less than half an hour to reach the city centre, and the fare is $4. Because the airport is so close to the centre, a 15-minute taxi ride downtown costs only about $9 and, if shared between two or three, costs less than the bus. There is a well sign-posted official taxi-share scheme for those travelling alone.

The cheapest way to reach the centre is by catching a local bus ($1.40). You should walk along Sir Richard Williams Avenue to the airport gates (10 minutes from the domestic terminal, slightly less from the international terminal). Let yourself out of the gate beside the cattle grid, cross the main road and catch bus 272/273 into the city. Your ticket entitles you to free transfers to other buses, trains or trams within 2 hours.

Reaching the airport from the city is easy. The *Transit* bus departs from a variety of lodgings (including the YMCA and YHA hostels if you book in advance on 8381 5311). Its main pickup point is the Terrace Hotel, which is opposite the railway station/casino. If you're economising, go to bus stop D1 near Light Square and catch bus 276/7 to the end of the Airport Road, then walk to the terminal.

Given its geographical position, it is not surprising that Adelaide is something of an aeronautical hub. Ansett and Australian Airlines have frequent flights to all the state capitals. The main commuter airlines for the state of South Australia are Kendell Airlines (8233 3111) and Lloyd Aviation (8224 7500).

If you want a ticket out of Australia, Adelaide is a possible place from which

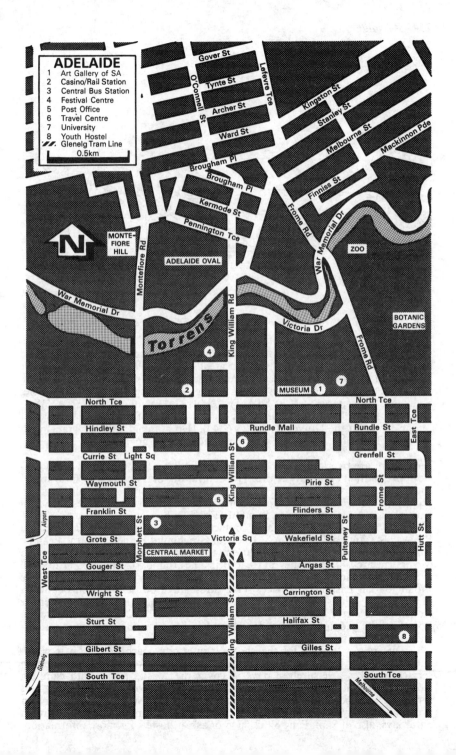

"IF LEAVING THE AIRPORT BY PUBLIC BUS, USE THE GATE BESIDE THE CATTLE GRID".

to depart. Although only two airlines (Qantas and Singapore International) serve the city direct from abroad, there is a great deal of competition among other airlines. In order to get business in Adelaide, carriers such as Cathay Pacific and UTA of France sometimes throw in free connecting flights to Melbourne, Sydney or Singapore. Staff at STA Travel at 235 Rundle St (8223 2426) are clued up about the various options; a second branch of STA is on Level 4 of Union House at the University (8223 6244). (Do not confuse STA Travel with the State Transport Authority, which has the same acronym.)

Bus. There are two long-distance terminals, both on Franklin St in the north-western quadrant of the city centre. The Central Bus Station (used by Greyhound Pioneer Australia) is at 111 Franklin St between Morphett St and Victoria Square (8233 2733), while the Country Bus Terminal for services to South Australia only is across Bowen St at 101 Franklin St.

For information and bookings, contact Dial-a-Coach at Shop 7, Adelaide Railway Station Underpass on 8410 0088. Greyhound Pioneer Australia can be contacted for bookings and information on 132030. Minimum one-way fares to Melbourne are $40, to Sydney $110, to Brisbane around $155 and to Perth $160.

Several companies operate coach services within South Australia. For example Mount Barker Passenger Services serve Strathalbyn on the Fleurieu Peninsula (8391 2977), John's Motor Service goes to Goolwa (8231 5959) and Premier Roadlines to Victor Harbor (8217 0777). Stateliner (8233 2722) serves Whyalla, Port Lincoln and intermediate towns and is linked with Greyhound's inter-state services.

If you are not looking for the cheapest inter-city coach service, it is worth considering the Wayward Bus Touring Company's Adelaide to Melbourne service. It takes a leisurely 3 days to cover the coastal route, with camping stopovers in Beachport, SA and Port Fairy, Vic. Trips cost $135 (10% discount for YHA members) and depart from King William St in Adelaide at 8am every Wednesday. Departures from Melbourne's Performing Arts Centre are on Saturdays, also at 8am. Ring 8232 6646 or ask at hostels for more information.

Train. Long-distance trains serve the Adelaide Rail Passenger Terminal in Keswick, 2km south-west of the city centre (8231 4366, 8217 4086 or 8217 4455). There is a daily overnight service to Melbourne on the *Overland* at 8pm, taking almost 13 hours and costing $42 in an economy seat. The corresponding daytime service, the *Daylink*, is a combined coach/train service, with the same fares, and takes 11 hours. It leaves Adelaide at 6.50am on weekdays and at 7.30am on Saturdays (no Sunday service).

The *Ghan* departs for Alice Springs at 2pm on Thursdays (with an additional winter service on Mondays), arriving 22 hours later for an economy fare of $121. There are five trains weekly to Perth (not Tuesdays or Thursdays), although only the Wednesday and Saturday services on the *Trans-Australian* are straight through; the ones on the *Indian Pacific* from Sydney involve a change at Port Pirie and take an hour longer, arriving in Perth after 41 hours. Whichever day you travel, the trip involves travelling for two nights and a day.

Adelaide has a small network of suburban trains that operate from the railway station on North Terrace, below and concealed by the casino. These trains are operated by the State Transport Authority (STA) and tickets, which must be bought before boarding a train, are interchangeable with other modes of transport: see *City Transport* below. Note, however, that the *Australpass* is not valid on these suburban services.

Driving. The roads of South Australia are suited to those who prefer a gentle spin through the countryside, being adequate but by no means fast. The maximum speed limit in the state is 100km/h, coming down to 60km/h in towns. The minimum driving age is 16.

The blood/alcohol limit in South Australia is 0.08, though holders of learner or provisional licences may not drive with any alcohol in their bloodstream. Random checks are made, especially at night. If convicted, you can expect a $300 fine and 6 months' disqualification from driving. Fines for most other motoring offences are levied on-the-spot. For speeding at 20km/h over the limit or jumping a red traffic light, you could be fined $80; this includes a $5 levy paid to the Criminal Injuries Compensation Fund.

The cheapest alternatives to the major car rental companies are out in the suburbs, but the bus service is sufficiently good to make it easy to reach them. Also, some (such as Action Rent-a-Car) provide a home delivery service.

Try Rent-a-Civic at 670 Port Road, Beverley (8268 1879), which hires small Hondas from $35 per day, including 160km free. You can reach the depot by bus 154–7. Hire-a-Hack is based at the Caltex Service Station, 219 Belair Road (8272 0637) and has cars from $15 per day. Action Rent-a-Car, close to the airport at 280 Burbridge Road (8352 7044), offers a Mazda 121 for about $50 a day all-inclusive. Rentals from these and other cut-price operators are restricted to a radius of 200km from Adelaide.

The Royal Automobile Association of South Australia (RAA) is at 41 Hindmarsh Square (8202 4600). Its free *Tour Planning Map* is adequate for most out-of-town trips, and incidentally contains reasonable maps of the eastern states. It also has an *Outback Motoring* booklet. For the RAA road service, dial 131 111.

Hitch-hiking. Thumbing through the southern part of the state presents no great problems, with a reasonable amount of traffic and few intimidating superhighways. Sprawling Adelaide is sometimes difficult to get out of; the hills begin as the suburbs end. For Melbourne catch bus 161 or 164–166 from bus stop G1 (on the corner of Pulteney and Angas Sts) to the junction of Cross Road, Portrush Road and Mount Barker Road (Highway 1). This is also the recommended route for Sydney. For Port Augusta and the north and west, take bus 224 to where it turns off Port Wakefield Road (Highway 1) into the Salisbury Highway.

Don't be tempted to take the road across the Nullarbor nor the Stuart Highway to Alice Springs without ample supplies of water, food and fortitude. Be prepared for a long wait in Coober Pedy. Traffic is sparse and competition from other hitchers can be considerable. Arranging to share a lift (and expenses) is usually possible by consulting the notice boards at the YHA hostel or the University Union House.

CITY TRANSPORT

Local buses and trains — and the single tram line to Glenelg — are operated by the State Transport Authority (STA), whose enquiry office is at the corner of Currie and King William Sts. There is another office at the railway station. Call 8210 1000 for all local transport information. The excellent *Public Transport Map* is good value at 30c.

Adelaide's bus network has three noteworthy features. The first is the 'Busway', a concrete track from the edge of the city centre to the northeastern suburbs on which specially adapted buses can run at speeds of up to 100km/h. The bus drives on ordinary roads to the start of the busway, but upon joining the track, small side-rollers grip the edges and steer the bus; when it leaves the busway, it reverts to normal running. The system is widely known as the O-bahn, after the original busway in Munich. In the few years it has operated, it has become quite a tourist attraction; a quick ride out to Modbury Interchange and back can be exhilarating.

The second unusual characteristic is that bus numbers may vary depending on whether the bus is running from or to the city. The bus which starts from the city centre and passes the airport, for example, is marked 276 on maps and on the bus itself. But when it turns round at the end of the route, it may bear a different number (272 or 273) if it is travelling through the city centre to a suburb on the other side. If, however, the bus is returning to the centre, it retains the original number (276). This system can be disconcerting at first but has a certain logic once you adapt. A further complication is that services from the city bearing the suffix 'F' for limited-stop or 'X' for express do not set down passengers until they reach the suburbs. One exception to these rules is the Circle Line bus (route 100) which runs around the city about 5km out; it keeps the same number throughout and stops everywhere. This service operates from 7am to 6pm Monday–Friday with no weekend service. Most other buses, trains and trams run from 6am to 11.30pm except on Sundays, when a limited timetable operates from 9am to 10.30pm with long intervals between services.

The third sophistication is the system for validating your ticket. When you board a bus or tram, you buy a ticket from the driver or conductor. The ticket must then be validated in the machine provided (on buses, to the right of the driver). You insert your ticket (the diagram shows which way up), which the machine swallows. After clicking and beeping to itself, the machine expels the ticket, now printed with the price, date and time of expiry. This performance must be repeated if you use the same ticket subsequently when transferring from one vehicle to another. Tickets for suburban trains must be purchased before entering any platforms or trains.

Fares for all modes of transport are calculated on a system of zones. The city and many of the suburbs fall within zone 1, and most suburban destinations fall inside zone 2. Off-peak travel (from 9.01am to 3pm, Monday–Friday) costs $1.40 for one or two zones and $2.20 for all three if you buy your tickets on the bus, but $1.30 and $2 if bought in advance from stations, post offices, newsagents and delicatessens. Fares for travel during rush hours, at nights and weekends are higher.

All but short distance tickets are valid for two hours of unlimited transfers within the appropriate zones. There is no obligation to continue in one direction, so round-trips on a single ticket are permitted within two hours. The $3.80 Daytrip pass allows unlimited travel after 9am, Monday to Friday, and all day at weekends; buy it on the bus or tram, or at the station. You can alternatively buy tickets for ten journeys at a discount of 30% from ticket outlets. If you are caught travelling without a valid ticket, you will be issued with a 'Transit Infringement Notice'; this requires that you pay an 'expiation fee' of $50 within three weeks or face a court hearing.

A sensible feature of the Adelaide transport system is that all bus stops are given a number (clearly shown on the stop itself) which is often quoted by people giving directions; so, for the airport you should get off at stop 15. Alighting from STA buses is performed in the same way as on North American buses. After pushing the buzzer to persuade the driver to stop, stand at the centre door. When the green light illuminates, you need to push the handle; the door doesn't open automatically. Hold the door open for any passengers behind you, to avoid slamming the door in their faces, shopping, toddlers, etc.

Adelaide city centre has a free bus known as the BeeLine, number 99B. Every five minutes during shopping hours, it travels the lkm length of King William St between Victoria Square and the Railway Station/Casino on North Terrace.

A beautiful wood-panelled tram built in 1929 links Victoria Square in the city centre with the seaside resort of Glenelg and is the only survivor from the heyday when Adelaide had 25 trams. The trip takes 30 minutes and is highly recommended.

Taxis. There are ranks at strategic points in the city centre, or you can summon a cab by calling 8223 3333 (Amalgamated), 8211 8888 (Suburban) or 8223 3111 (United Yellow).

Two-passenger pedicabs (bicycle taxis) can be hired by calling 8232 2914 or 8410 0177. They specialise in tours from the city centre for about $20 an hour but are available also for private hire.

Car. Adelaide used to be known as the '15-minute city', on the basis that nowhere in the city was more than a quarter-hour's drive from anywhere else. As the suburbs have spread and traffic has increased, it is more like a 30-minute city, but driving in Adelaide is still quite painless. Most of the roads are wide and fast-moving.

Many city-centre junctions have 'no right-turn' signs that flash during business hours, but which are switched off to permit turns at less busy times. Particular hazards include extra-long 'bendy-buses' used on the Busway, and the Glenelg Tram that won't hesitate to assert its priority. Parking during business hours within the city centre (enclosed by the four Terraces) is tricky. Either leave your car immediately outside this area, where you should be able to park free, or use the Park & Ride facility on the Busway at Klemzig Station or Paradise Interchange; the journey into town takes 15 minutes.

Most petrol stations open 7am–6pm Monday to Friday, 7am–2pm on Saturday. Outside these hours you can use the Shell garage at 111 West Terrace, or head out to Cavan, Darlington or Pooraka to find a 24-hour dispenser.

Cycling. Adelaide offers cyclists as good conditions as can be found in any city: few steep gradients, broad streets with plenty of room for bicycles and nine specially-designated routes through the parks. Cyclists should beware, however, of the tram tracks on the road down to Glenelg.

Considering what a good cycling city Adelaide is, there are few rental shops. Ten-speeds and mountain bikes can be hired from Bike Moves in Unley (8293 2922) which gives a discount to YHA hostellers. Try also Bike and Beach Hire behind the Town Hall in Glenelg (8294 1477).

Accommodation

The *Outback* edition of the free *TNT for Backpackers* magazine includes up-to-the-minute information on hostel accommodation, and is well worth a look if you find yourself struggling to find a bed. The Accommodation Central Agency (8274 1222) offers a free reservations service, but specialises in more expensive hotels and motels. The Government Travel Centre at 18 King William St publishes separate accommodation booklets for city and state, but these don't include hostels or campsites.

Hostels. Adelaide's YHA hostel is in the south of the city centre at 29O Gilles St (8223 6007); it's a 15-minute walk, or you can take bus 171 or 172 from Victoria Square to Hutt St. The hostel is always busy so advance booking is a good idea. It accepts telephone bookings only if you quote your credit card number (so you are charged if you don't turn up). The hostel closes in the morning but posts a notice advising on availability with suggestions on alternative accommodation if the hostel is full. Beds are $11 per night.

The city also boasts several hostels in the VIP Backpackers Resorts chain, one of which is right across the street. At number 263 is the Adelaide Backpackers Hostel (8223 5680) with dorms and double/twin rooms. In winter one part of the hostel is set aside to provide more private facilities for people working in the city. The Backpackers Inn is at 112 Carrington St (8223 6635), in an 1846 building that was originally a pub. Bookings are essential, but assuming you get in you'll be entitled to free apple pie and ice cream every night. Try also East Park Lodge, 341 Angas St (8223 1228) or Cannon St Lodge Backpackers (11 Cannon St; 8410 1218), which is just 50m from the Central Bus Station and has budget dorm beds for $8 per night.

There are plenty of other hostels, including Sunny's (corner of Franklin and Morphett Sts; 8231 2430), which also houses Sunny's Travel (good for tours and budget domestic and international travel); Rucksackers International (257 Gilles St; 8232 0823), which is particularly well equipped to help those travelling around Australia by bike or motorbike (beds from $10); and the YMCA at 76 Flinders St (8223 1611), which accepts both men and women and has good, cheap breakfasts, though it is often full. If you're not bothered about being in the city centre, try Glenelg Backpackers Resort near the beach at 1–7 Moseley St (8376 0007), which has dorm beds from $13 including 'free' breakfast. It was recently voted Australia's number 1 Backpackers Resort.

Hotels and Motels. There are many expensive up-market hotels in the city centre with few low-cost alternatives. The King's Head Hotel at 357 King William St (8212 6657) charges $15–20 per person in a double. The Sportsman's Hotel at 185 Grote St (8231 3250) is fairly convenient and only slightly more expensive than a hostel. You could also try the Afton Private Hotel at 260 South Terrace (8223 3416), but it is often full. Other possibilities include the Austral at 205 Rundle St (8223 4660), which costs $25 for a single, $40 for a double and $60 for a four-bunk room; the Centralia at 65 North Terrace; and the Criterion at 137 King William St.

Student Residences. The University of Adelaide has plenty of college residences that are empty during vacations. The direct approach is best: ring Lincoln (8267 2588), St Ann's (8267 1478), Aquinas (8267 2944) or St Mark's (8267 2211) to check availability. Another place to try if you plan to have an extended stay in Adelaide is the nurses' residence of Queen Elizabeth Hospital, which can sometimes be negotiated for about $80 a week. The Student Housing Office of Adelaide University (8228 5663) can provide a list of lodgings costing from $40 a week.

Holiday Flats. Outside school holidays, you can find fairly cheap rented flats along the Adelaide coastline. Seavista Holiday Suites, 52 Seaview Road, West Beach (8356 3975), on the seafront, cost from $180 a week for two or a minimum of three nights for $90. South Pacific Holiday Flats (16 Colley Terrace, Glenelg; 8294 1352) have self-contained two-person units ranging from $55–65 per day, depending on the time of year. Another to try is Seaside Holiday Apartments (71 Esplanade, Henley Beach South; 8353 1041). Whites Holiday Unit in Glenelg (8341 8300) charges around $30 a night for two with a minimum stay of three nights.

The Town and Country Bed & Breakfast scheme operates through the Government tourist office and has a small choice of properties in its budget category charging around $40 for bed and breakfast.

Camping. The closest caravan site to the city centre is the Adelaide Caravan Park on Bruton St in Hackney (8363 1566); on-site caravans are available from $36 for two people, and cabins with *en suite* facilities from $55 for two. You can pitch a tent for $12 per night at the Marion Tourist Park, 323 Sturt Road, Bedford Park near Flinders University (12km south; 8276 6695) or stay in an on-site cabin or caravan from $33 for two people. Other sites are dotted along the seafront. Pitching a tent in one of Adelaide's many parks will attract unwelcome attention from the authorities, but sleeping out behind a bush has been safely achieved by many travellers, though it can scarcely be recommended as an option.

Eating and Drinking

Adelaide has come a long way from the days (not so long ago) when its main claim to culinary fame was the invention of the infamous 'pie floater', a nondescript meat pie swimming in a bowl of pea soup. The city now has an impressive range of eating places and cuisines in relation to its population. What Adelaide lacks in cheap accommodation, it makes up for with the wide choice of inexpensive eateries. Another pleasure in store for foodies is the Central Market, which has a mouth-watering array of exotic vegetables and delicacies. The market has rather limited hours: Tuesdays 7am–5.30pm, Thursdays 11am–5.30pm, Fridays 7am–9pm, and Saturdays 7am–1pm. If you shop at a bakery, note that the South Australian 'kitchener bun' is a cream-filled pastry.

Despite the increasingly cosmopolitan character of the Adelaide eating scene, Sundays are still a problem. Before resorting to the nearest fast-food chain takeaway, check out the list of restaurants open on Sundays which appears in the free magazine *Dining Adelaide* available from the tourist office. It contains sample menus and prices for about 20 city centre gourmet restaurants and 20 more out of town.

The ratio of BYO to licensed restaurants is not as favourable as it is in Melbourne or Sydney. But over 100 BYO restaurants are included on a list put out by the university radio station 5UV based on its regular restaurant review programme. Also many of the licensed places allow you to bring in wine for a couple of dollars corkage. Many good, cheap places can be found around the Rundle St/Rundle Mall/Hindley St axis; the following is a small selection of the available options.

Rundle St. For lunch, try the Greek specialities at Mezes BYO Restaurant (number 287) or the cheap vegetarian food at the non-smoking Clear Light Café (number 201). Finish up at the Al Fresco Gelateria at 260 for a good selection of coffees, ice creams and sandwiches, which as the name suggests can be consumed outside on pavement tables. A few doors down at 270 Rundle St, Rossini's serves inexpensive Italian food. The licensed Bangkok (at number 217, on the corner of Frome St) has prize-winning Thai food. On the same corner you can also eat bistro-like food at Skips.

Rundle Mall. Most of the restaurants are tucked away in arcades leading off the Mall. They include the Angkor Wat at 28 Regent Arcade, whose food should be Cambodian from its name but is indistinguishable from Thai. Choy Sin on James Place (opposite Myer's store) has a good choice of Cantonese and Szechuan dishes though in rather pretentious (i.e. silver service) surroundings.

Hindley St. Between the pubs, coffee shops and 'adult' bookshops are some splendid restaurants, for example the Melange Bistro-Café at number 21. The strictly BYO Quiet Waters Restaurant (75 Hindley St) opens every night until late for excellent mezes including a vegetarian selection. Shamira, the resident belly dancer, performs on Wednesdays and Saturdays. To splash out, go to the Hindley Parkroyal Hotel at number 65 where Oliphant's Restaurant has an interesting nouvelle Australian menu. Also, in the hotel, the more casual Café Mo offers a snack menu from which you can choose stuffed chicken wings or seafood soup for less than $5.

There are numerous cheap Italian restaurants such as Hindley Pasta Palace at number 100 and Marcellinas at number 273. Jerusalems Lebanese Restaurant at number 131b is cheap and popular. Another non-smoking restaurant is the Peaceful Vegetarian Café at number 167. The teetotal Pancake Kitchen (at 13 Gilbert Place, near the King William St intersection) is always a safe option and is open 24 hours. Just nearby is the cheap and cheerful Penang Coffee House also on Gilbert Place.

Another Adelaide street noted for its eating possibilities is Unley Road which is also known for its antique and junk shops. In numerical order the following restaurants could be considered: The Shah at number 40a (Malaysian), Café 48 at 48 (nouveau), Taco Bill for Mexican food at 50, Sarinah Indonesian Restaurant at 60 with an all-you-can-eat salad bar, La Tombola at 61 (Italian), Cafe Espresso at 66 (ice cream and pasta), La Casalinga at 77 (Italian), Clem's Gourmet Cottage at 94, and further out at 190 Styles which offers interesting dishes in a choice of size, i.e. 'entrees' for $6 and mains for $12.

For one of the most wide-ranging and tasty menus in Adelaide (from Moroccan-style quail to Thai seafood curry) go to Mona Lisa's Bistro at the corner of Hutt and Carrington Sts in the southeast corner of the city centre; food prices are not unreasonable (under $15 for some excellent main courses) though a bottle from the quality wine list will add considerably to the price of your meal. Another well-established city centre restaurant for food lovers is Reilly's at 138 King William St where prices are similar and there are such all-Australian dishes as 'fillet of kangaroo with gum-scented glaze and walnut damper'. At the other end of the spectrum the Arab Steed Hotel on Gilles St offers filling meals for less than $5. Lots of other city pubs serve food. The General Havelock at 162 Hutt St has an innovative menu including Japanese, Thai and German dishes as well as steaks and seafood.

On the northern edge of the city centre a good place for lunch is the café in the State Library on North Terrace (closed Sundays) which has a place for rucksacks to be stored while you eat. North Adelaide has several interesting places to eat, particularly on O'Connell and Melbourne Sts. The Melbourne St Bistro is under the same management as Reilly's and is a more casual and somewhat cheaper place (87a Melbourne St). Zapata's at 42 Melbourne St is an upmarket Mexican restaurant. Rakuba at number 33 O'Connell St (BYO) is the only African restaurant in town; it opens from 5pm to 11.30pm Tuesday-Saturday and shares its premises with an African craft shop. It also hosts musical evenings when everyone is welcome to join in. Vietnamese food is served at the White Crane, 165 O'Connell St (8239 0927). For splashing out and putting on weight, try Mistress Augustine at 145: its trademark is the highly recommended 'Chocolate Slut', the Australian equivalent of the French *assiette de chocolat*.

In addition, there are numerous good seafood restaurants; try King George whiting, the local speciality, at one of the cheap cafés near the fish market on Gouger St.

Each autumn gourmet weekends are held in the wine regions of the Barossa and the Clare, providing a chance to sample the culinary skills of leading Adelaide chefs away from their home territory; see *Further Afield* for details.

DRINKING

Pubs in Adelaide are obliged by law to open from 11am to 8pm daily, and are allowed to open at any time between 5am and midnight. Typically they open 10am to midnight Monday–Saturday. Sunday hours are shorter, generally 11am–8pm. If you're desperate for a late-night or early-morning drink, some pubs around the Central Markets (such as the Woodman's Inn, 235 Grenfell St) open at 5am from Monday to Friday.

Cooper's, the local brewery, takes justifiable pride in its real bottled beer and stout. It is one of the few established breweries in Australia to stick to traditional brewing methods, including wooden barrels and bottle conditioning. 'Cooper's Sparkling Ale' is stronger than average (5.75%) and requires careful pouring (like bottled Guinness) to leave the sediment undisturbed at the bottom of the bottle; don't take it back if it's cloudy. Also try the excellent Aberdeen Scotch Ale and Extra Stout. The South Australian Brewing Co produces less distinguished beers (including West End Bitter, the local fizzy lager), though its Premium Lager and Old Southwark Stout are worth sampling. Bottles can be returned for a deposit of 4c.

The greatest concentration of trendy (and therefore pricey) pubs is in North Adelaide. Places like the Old Lion Hotel at 163 Melbourne St are more like entertainment complexes than local pubs with discos and live bands, though it is worth trying the beers brewed on the premises. Continuing the pub-crawl, try the Kentish Arms (23 Stanley St) with a DIY barbecue and beer garden and entertainment on Sunday afternoons, and the Queen's Head (117 Kermode St). The Dover Castle (47 Archer St) has British-style 'snugs' and plush upholstery, together with incongruous overhead fans.

The Port Dock Brewery Hotel out at Port Adelaide (25 minutes by car from the city centre) has a prize-winning brewery on the premises at 10 Todd St. Beer is pumped to the bar using English brewing machinery. Notable brews include Collector's Pale Ale, Black Diamond Best Bitter and Old Preacher.

Elsewhere there are plenty of pleasant hotels with few of the down-and-out dives found in Melbourne and Sydney. In particular, pubs in the southeast corner of the city centre are rapidly acquiring cult status among drinkers. Try the recently renovated General Havelock at 162 Hutt St with its all day brunches on Sunday or the Earl of Aberdeen at 316 Pulteney St. The Griffin's Head, on Hindmarsh Square at the corner of Grenfell St (8223 7954) has live bands on Sundays in summer. A happy hour in very salubrious surroundings takes place every Friday (4.30–6pm) at the Festival Centre Piano Bar.

Considering the amount of excellent wine produced in South Australia, there is a surprising absence of wine bars serving the local vintages. The biggest selection (over 300 wines) can be found at the casino wine bar. Otherwise, buy from one of the many well-stocked liquor stores and drink at a BYO restaurant, or head out to the wine producing areas. More information about the state's wines can be obtained from the Wine Information Bureau (8365 0500).

For a grand prospect of the city and its spectacularly extensive suburbs, head for the hills. Even the modest elevation of Colonel Light's lookout on Montefiore Hill in North Adelaide — where he had his 'vision' about the city plan — offers a splendid view across the centre to the south. But those with a vehicle should try Mount Lofty Summit, most easily reached by following Greenhill Road up into the hills, where the road to Mount Lofty (and its disused lighthouse) is signposted. Windy Point (near Belair on tourist drive 57) is another good venue for viewing the sprawling city. During the day, you can breeze along Rundle Mall with the bustle and the buskers, up to the Torrens (really only a creek dammed to make an artificial lake) with the joggers, or out to Glenelg on the tram (which reveals a rather genteel English-style resort). Sensibly, planning regulations mean that there are no outstandingly tall buildings in Adelaide, although the price of a cup of coffee on the seventh floor of Myer's department store on Rundle Mall will be repaid on fine days with a clear view of the eastern hills.

Tourism South Australia at 18 King William St issues a brochure for a two-hour walking tour around the city. As well as the predictable historic sights, the centre has some interesting urban embellishments, for example the Flugelman's Balls sculpture in the middle of Rundle Mall: two huge steel spheres which were donated to the city by a local building society. And to celebrate the state's first 150 years, the pavement on the northern side of North Terrace bears the names of 150 famous South Australians. Every Friday you can join a guided walking tour of Rundle Mall and North Terrace starting at 10am, price of $2 (8203 7437).

Adelaide has a reputation as the 'city of churches.' This arose as a result of the many fine places of worship built a century ago — such as the Cathedral of St Xavier in Wakefield St, St Peter's Cathedral on Pennington Terrace and the Pilgrim Church at 12 Flinders St.

Aboriginal culture is more visible in Adelaide than in Sydney or Melbourne and a visit to the Tandanya Aboriginal Cultural Institute on the corner of Grenfell St and East Terrace is recommended (8223 4200). Representatives of various tribes perform music, theatre and dance in the theatre as well as carry out their ancient crafts on the site. The shop sells a good range of traditional artefacts and there is a café. Tandanya is open seven days a week (admission $4, $3 concessions). It is also handy for Rundle St East, well known for its cafés and coffee shops.

Museums. Adelaide has many museums, several of which are operated by the History Trust of South Australia. The Migration Museum at 82 Kintore Avenue (behind the State Library on North Terrace; 8207 7580) concentrates on the history of immigration and settlement of the state of South Australia from early colonial times to the present day. It is housed in a carefully restored former asylum for impoverished women and children. You can glimpse life in a migrant hostel and interact with displays about the lives of the early settlers. A fascinating aspect of the museum is that it mounts special exhibitions on the culture of contemporary migrants like Poles, Vietnamese and Sri Lankans. The museum opens at 10am from Monday to Friday and at 1pm on weekends and public holidays, and closes at 5pm daily. Admission is free, but donations are welcome.

The State History Centre at 59 King William St is the South Australian home to exhibitions from the National Museum in Canberra; phone 8226 8555 to find out what's showing. The building itself is also of note: originally built for the Bank of South Australia in the 1870s, it faced the threat of demolition in 1971, but was thankfully saved after several months of controversy. Opening times are 10am–4pm, Wednesday to Sunday.

The South Australia Maritime Museum (8240 0200) is out at Lipson St in Port Adelaide (bus routes 153–7), and comprises the Bond Store, which is the museum's main gallery, as well as the 1869 lighthouse and two floating vessels. It opens 10am–5pm daily (admission $7). The *HMS Buffalo*, moored on the Torrens at Glenelg, is a reproduction of the ship that brought out South Australia's first governor. The $2.50 entry fee is redeemed only by the other settlers' diaries, which reveal in detail what a ridiculous figure Governor Hindmarsh was.

The most interesting museum of all is arguably the South Australian Museum on North Terrace (8223 8911), an Antipodean cross between London's Natural History and British Museums. One of the most fascinating displays is titled 'Ngurunderi: An Aboriginal Dreaming', which contains a unique collection of *toas*, painted sticks used as totems to represent a place or story. The museum also has excellent collections of Australian natural history specimens and early Pacific cultures, plus displays of Egyptian culture. The museum and shop open daily from 10am to 5pm (free admission). Free tours are available from 2pm on weekends.

Motor enthusiasts will be interested in the National Motor Museum in the picturesque Adelaide Hills town of Birdwood — it's the largest collection of vehicles in Australia, and tells the story of Australian motoring. It is open daily from 9am–5pm (admission $8).

Galleries. The Art Gallery of South Australia on North Terrace has good but conventional collections of Australian, European and Asian art with a regular exhibition programme; dial 8207 7000 for details. To see the work of Australia's leading contemporary artists, visit the Contemporary Art Centre of South Australia at 14 Porter St in Parkside (any bus from 191 to 198 from the city centre, stop 1 or 2; or a pleasant walk through the south parklands). Exhibitions change monthly, and admission is free; call 8272 2682 for details.

The Festival Centre (see below) often has up to three separate exhibitions at once, some related to current performances at the Centre.

Festival Centre. Although a more modest construction than the Sydney Opera House, Adelaide's Festival Centre (8216 8600) serves its purpose well as the cultural heart of the city. It is set in parkland on King William Road above North Terrace. The Festival Centre has three auditoria (the Playhouse, the Space Theatre Cabaret Club and the Festival Theatre), an open-air amphitheatre, a piano bar and the Backstage Bar & Grill.

Parks and Zoos. It is difficult to continue in any one direction in Adelaide for long without encountering a park. Of the many alternatives, the most popular is Elder Park, around the Torrens Lake just up from North Terrace, separating the city centre from North Adelaide. The careful landscaping allows you to relax amid peace and quiet. You can paddle around the lake in a boat hired from the stall next to Jolley's Bistro, by the southeast side of King William Road as it crosses the Torrens. At the eastern end are the historic Botanic Gardens; there are guided tours Tuesday and Friday at 10.30am. The highlight of the Garden is the vast Bicentennial tropical conservatory which contains a number of rainforest trees and other Asian vegetation (admission $2).

Adelaide also has a historic zoo on Frome Road (easily walkable from the Festival Centre, just north of the Botanic Gardens) which is most notable for its collection of bird life and its Nocturnal House. It opens 9.30am to 5pm every day with extended opening on Wednesdays during the summer (admission $6).

If you insist on cuddling a koala, there are several animal sanctuaries in the hills surrounding Adelaide, within about half an hour of the city centre. For example, the Cleland Wildlife Reserve (8339 2444) in the Mount Lofty Ranges (accessible by bus 820) allows visitors to handle the koalas at the morning feeding times. And the Gorge Wildlife Park (8389 2206) in the Adelaide Hills suburb of Cudlee Creek has a large private collection of native animals (admission $4.50). A visit to Cleland can be combined with an enjoyable one-hour bush walk up Waterfall Gully affording magnificent views of the city. The Warrawong Sanctuary (8388 5380), in the distant southern suburb of Mylor, can be visited only by appointment and in the company of one of the guides who take visitors on dawn and sunset nature walks. Another interesting venue for a guided walk is at the St Kilda Mangrove Trail north of Adelaide (8280 8172).

Beaches. Adelaide is favoured with a continuous stretch of accessible sandy beaches, safe from sharks and overeager developers. From anywhere in the city you need only head west to find somewhere to lay your towel on the 32km of wide gently sloping beach. Don't expect the massive breakers of the Indian and Pacific Oceans; the placid waters of Gulf St Vincent are protected from the high seas by the Yorke Peninsula and Kangaroo Island. The same geographical features ensure that the warmth of the ocean is conserved well into autumn, and even a midwinter swim isn't out of the question.

Citizens of Adelaide spend less time discussing the best beaches than their counterparts in Sydney, perhaps because there is little to distinguish one from another. Glenelg is the largest and most interesting resort and has a delightful beach, plus the biggest waterslide in Australia. Largs Bay (north of Port Adelaide) is known for its fish and chip kiosk, though

IF YOU INSIST ON CUDDLING A KOALA...

good tucker is available at most beaches. The only beach officially designated for nude bathing, Maslin Beach, is surrounded by picturesque high ciiffs, but it is a long way south (take suburban train to Port Noarlunga then bus 741).

SHOPPING

Rundle Mall is the main shopping street and is surrounded with more than a dozen small arcades. The most expensive boutiques are to be found along Melbourne St in North Adelaide. The normal shop opening time is 8.30 or 9am, with closing at 5.30 or 6pm from Monday to Friday and at noon on Saturdays. Many city-centre stores open late until 9pm on Fridays, and suburban malls to the same time on Thursdays.

Adelaide has plenty of shops selling equipment for camping and bushwalking expeditions. Two city-centre stockists give a possible 10% discount to hostellers: Flinders Ranges Camping Centre at 108 Gawler Place, and the Scout Shop at 192 Rundle St.

South Australia produces four-fifths of the world's opals (see *Further Afield: Coober Pedy*) and, in terms of choice, Adelaide is the best place to buy them. A large number of jewellers make a good living from selling opals to tourists, including one merchant (Olympic) which has a simulated underground mine at its premises on Rundle Mall. Foreign visitors are able to avoid the 30% sales tax on opals if they present a passport and valid air ticket. A shop worth visiting if only for its name is Faulty Towels on Burbridge Road, which specialises in sub-standard bathroom accessories.

For good quality souvenirs try the Tandanya Aboriginal Cultural Institute mentioned above and the National Trust Heritage Gift Shop in the Southern Cross Arcade off King William St.

Markets. After an hour or two spent checking out the exotic produce and colourful stallholders at the Central Market mentioned in the section on *Eating & Drinking*, you can move on to the Jam Factory Craft Centre at 169 Payneham Road in the inner suburb of St Peters (bus 175 to stop 7) where artisans can be seen at work. If you're looking for something to do on a Sunday, visit the Sunday Market on East Terrace between Rundle and Grenfell Sts where 300 stall-holders converge undercover.

Other markets — such as the Brickworks on South Road at Thebarton, and the Antique Market at 32 Grote St — are more commercialised. The Brickworks is most interesting at weekends when street entertainers are out in force. It also boasts seven 'colonial shops', a miniature golf course and bumper boats, an aquatic form of dodgems. Another popular weekend destination for families is the market at 255 South Road in the distant southern suburb of Reynella.

Books. Bibliophiles are spoilt for choice in Adelaide. On North Terrace, for example, both the University and the State Library have excellent bookshops, the latter particularly good for Australiana. The Europa Bookshop at 16 Pulteney St (near North Terrace) has a fine selection of travel books and maps. The Beaut Little Bookshop in the Victoria Square Arcade specialises (as its name suggests) in Australiana and also has a range of travel books. Several bookshops stay open late, for example Hindley St Books and Cards at 103 Hindley St (open till at least midnight seven days a week), which has second-hand records as well as a good range of books.

Entertainment

The quality, quantity and diversity of entertainment in Adelaide belies the city's reputation for staidness. The best source of details on exhibitions, plays, concerts, etc. is the Thursday edition of Adelaide's daily newspaper, the *Advertiser*. Recorded information on local events can be dialled on 11688, while bookings for major cultural events can be made through the BASS agency on 131 246 (which adds a service charge of $1.80 per ticket). The city sustains several useful free magazines, including *dB*, which is concerned with music and theatre; *The Orb*, nightlife and fashion; and *The Ray*, which covers alternative health and lifestyle. So while the verdant city of Adelaide has no great 'must see' landmarks, there is plenty of culture of every description to enjoy.

Festivals. The prestigious Adelaide Festival runs for 2 weeks around February/March every other year (1998, 2000, and so on). Modelled loosely on the Edinburgh Festival, it attracts theatre, dance and music groups from around the world. As with Edinburgh, there is a Festival 'Fringe' (often referred to simply as 'the Fringe'), which runs over 3 weeks and is based in Adelaide's rejuvenated East End. Although the Fringe does not compare with its Scottish counterpart, it is steadily growing and in 1994 attracted over half a million attendances. For more details contact the Fringe office at 265 Rundle St (PO Box 3242, Adelaide 5000), or ring 08-8231 7760.

Theatre. Some would say that the best performances are staged in the Festival Centre by the State Theatre Company, whose interpretations of anything from Shakespeare to modern Australian drama are consistently good. Most other productions that come to the Festival Centre are mainstream touring shows (some of which originate in London's West End), but the Space Theatre, with cabaret seating and a licensed bar, has a more innovative drama programme. Ticket prices for most performances range from $15 to $35, with students normally qualifying for a discount. Festival Centre events are advertised in the monthly programme, or you can ring 8211 8999 for recorded information. The box office is open from 9.30am to 6pm except Sundays.

The Festival Centre has no monopoly on drama in Adelaide. Commercial theatres include Her Majesty's Theatre on Grote St and the Royalty Theatre at 65 Angas St at the south-east of the city centre. Bookings can be made direct through these theatres or through Dial 'n' Charge BASS. Drama of a more experimental nature can be seen at La Mama Theatre (4 Crawford Lane, off Port Road, Hindmarsh; 8346 4212). It is arguably the most risk-taking amateur theatre in Adelaide but also performs more traditional plays most weeks of the year. Junction Theatre, 5 minutes from the city at the corner of George St and South Road in Thebarton (8443 6200), produces some of the best new South Australian theatre. It's a professional company that entertainingly explores issues of social justice using music and comedy.

Cinema. Several cinemas in or near the centre of Adelaide have interesting repertory programmes, such as the Piccadilly, a beautiful 1930s structure at 181 O'Connell St (8267 1500) and the Chelsea at 275 Kensington Road. The main commercial cinemas in the city centre are Hoyts in the Regent Arcade, off Rundle Mall (8223 2233); the Hindley, at 88 Hindley St (8231 5961); and the Academy in Hindmarsh Square (8223 5000). There are many others out in the suburbs, with drive-ins at Gillies Plains, Elizabeth, West Beach, St Agnes and Marion Twin.

Music. The biggest indoor rock venues are the newly completed Entertainment Centre on Port Road, Hindmarsh, the Apollo Entertainment Centre and the Thebarton Theatre, west of the city centre at 114 Henley Beach Road in Torrensville. Some touring bands play at the open-air Thebarton Oval. Tickets can be bought from branches of The Box Office in many record shops. In addition, there is a surprisingly lively local 'underground' rock scene. Groups such as the Mandelbrot Set, the Always and the Jaynes may not yet have grabbed the world's attention, but they are very popular in Adelaide. Peaches Café & Bistro at 38 Twin St offers live music to accompany dinner on Friday evenings only.

The best city-centre places to see some of the excellent local bands are the Astor in Pulteney St and Le Rox at 9 Light Square (though the latter may be changing its name and style soon due to bad publicity from a drugs bust). Also recommended are the Adelaide University bar, the Tivoli (261 Pirie St), the Exeter Hotel on Rundle St and the Austral Hotel (205 Rundle St). For a good disco in town try the Metro above the Richmond Hotel in Rundle Mall. A little way out of town, try the Arkaba Hotel (or Ark) at 150 Glen Osmond Road, Fullarton.

Free rock concerts are held on summer Sundays (from 4–6pm) at the Festival Centre amphitheatre, and in winter free classical musicians perform in the foyer. On Saturday afternoons there is free jazz on the Centre's Bistro Terrace from 2pm to 5pm. For jazz try the Cargo Club, 213 Hindley St.

The best serious music is performed during the Festival, but at other times consult the *Adelaide Review* for upcoming concerts.

Nightlife. Many of the city's 3000 prostitutes work along Hindley St, Adelaide's rather tame answer to Sydney's Kings Cross. As well as a tacky collection of strip joints and restaurants with topless waitresses, there are nightclubs of varying degrees of respectability. One of the least sleazy is the Rio at 111 Hindley St. If, on the other hand, your idea of a good night out is browsing in bookshops until late, Adelaide is the place to be; see *Shopping* above.

Gambling. The Adelaide Casino was converted from the above-ground part of the railway station on North Terrace as part of ASER, acronym for the inelegantly-titled 'Adelaide Station Environs Redevelopment', a $200 million project which also included the Convention Centre and the Hyatt Regency Hotel. It opens from 10am to 4am, Monday-Thursday and straight through from 10am on Friday to 4pm on Monday. The only days on which you are unable to gamble away your savings are Good Friday and Christmas Day. The conditions for admittance are that you should be over 18 and wearing at least 'smart casual' dress. Entrance is free, as is the *Adelaide Casino Gaming Guide* booklet which is dispensed to the uninitiated. The Australian Poker Championships are held at the casino each October, but an entrance fee of $175 is required.

SPORT

Spectator Sports. The unrivalled event of the year in Adelaide was formerly the Australian Grand Prix held each year in late October or early November. However this major international motor-racing fixture transfers to Melbourne from 1996, presumably to the relief of those Adelaide residents who live in the vicinity of the former circuit, and who used to require passes to reach their homes. On the other hand Adelaide will clearly miss out, if only in terms of the festivities that used to accompany the four-day event, including rock concerts, street parties and vintage car cavalcades.

If you prefer to watch animals, there are three suburban horseracing courses (at Morphettville, Cheltenham and Victoria Park), so one is likely to be running while you're in town. Check the green NewsTab pullout in the *News* for venues and form. Club, interstate and Test cricket is played at the delightful Adelaide Oval just north of the Torrens. South Australians are mad-keen Aussie-rules football fans, and if you want to catch a game, check the sports pages of the *Advertiser*. The South Australia National Football League (Australian rules) Grand Final is held early in October at Football Park in West Lakes. The best teams are the Glenelg Tigers and North Adelaide, known as the Roosters.

Participation. Free maps for joggers can be obtained by calling 8227 4057. Early risers might also wish to join the Sunday morning outings organised by the South Australian Road Runners Association (8212 6115). They meet at the junction of Bundeys Road and Mackinnon Parade, and start the day with a cheap breakfast of coffee and muesli. There is a fun run from the city to Port Adelaide in April, and to the Bay in September; the Festival City Marathon takes place in the cool of August.

Tennis and squash courts are dotted around the city and its suburbs: for city centre tennis dial 8231 4371 or 8276 9229, and for squash 8362 7777. The parkland of Adelaide lends itself to golf, and there are a number of public courses. The nearest to the city is at North Adelaide (8267 2171). Swimming pools might seem superfluous in a city so blessed with beaches as Adelaide, but swimming in the River Torrens has previously been banned due to pollution and the bus or tram ride out to the beaches on a hot day can be daunting. If so, try the Aquatic Centre in North Adelaide (8218 7312). Windsurfers may be hired from various points on the beaches, but beginners will find calmer waters out at the West Lakes, just inland from the coast and south of Port Adelaide. If you're visiting Adelaide in the winter and hanker after winter sports, visit the Mount Thebarton Ice Arena (8352 7977) where an afternoon of skating will cost $5.50 plus $1.20 skate hire, and a toboggan run $3. Skiing is also available. There is excellent horse riding in the Adelaide Hills; consult the *Yellow Pages* under 'Stables'.

THE MEDIA

Newspapers. The leading morning daily is the *Advertiser*, a broadsheet which (as mentioned above) features a pull-out entertainment section on Thursdays called 'Getting Out'. The down-market tabloid is the *News*.

Radio. The headquarters of ABC radio is in Adelaide, and the local ABC AM station is 5AN (891kHz). SA-FM (107MHz) transmits a safe diet of Adult-Oriented Rock, while 5MMM-FM reflects the local 'underground' rock scene. Current chart music can be heard on 5KA, and golden oldies from the 60s and 70s on 5AD (1323kHz AM). The University station, 5UV (531kHz AM), has news and reviews of Adelaide's cultural highlights plus Aboriginal, student and BBC science programmes.

Television. The usual collection of national networks is on offer. ABC is on Channel 2, while Ten is the leading station for sports coverage. If you've acquired a taste for Australian soap operas, remember that the 30-minute time difference between South Australia and the eastern states means you may have to readjust your viewing patterns.

Adelaide could not be described as particularly dangerous. There have been some tales of gratuitous violence — particularly against homosexuals — but nothing on the scale of attacks in European and American cities. Single women might not care to walk alone through the Hindley St area after dark, not least because of the risk of being mistaken for a prostitute. The parks are best avoided late at night.

Drugs. The good soil and benevolent climate of South Australia makes marijuana-growing a popular pastime among the natives, and South Australia has a more liberal attitude towards use of the drug than the other states. Police have discretion to issue an on-the-spot fine to people possessing small amounts of marijuana (up to 100g) or cannabis resin (up to 20g) for personal use, or for growing a small number of plants. It is illegal to possess dope-smoking equipment. Like parking offenses these transgressions are not recorded as criminal convictions. You will be handed an 'Expiation Notice for a Simple Cannabis Offence', which you must pay within 60 days. The offending substance will, of course, be confiscated.

Anyone caught with a larger quantity of marijuana or hard drugs, or who is charged with trafficking, can expect to be treated considerably more harshly. If you get into trouble with drugs or have any legal problems in South Australia, consult the Legal Services Commission of South Australia at 82 Wakefield St (8205 0111, or from outside Adelaide, 008-188 126).

The dialling code for Adelaide is 08. For fire, police or ambulance dial 000.

The main government tourist information office is Tourism South Australia at 18 King William St (between Rundle Mall and North Terrace; 8212 1505; toll-free 008-882092). If you have any specific requests, whether for Greek Orthodox church services or accommodation in a particular vicinity, place yourself in the hands of the staff and their computer. They can provide you with a free print-out of the information you need. There are also offices at 25 Elizabeth St, Melbourne (03-9614 6522), 143 King St, Sydney (02-9232 8388) and 93 William St, Perth (09-481 1268).

Backpackers Information Centre: 314 Gilles St (8232 4747). Holds a range of information on tours, etc., and also hires out camping gear.
American Express: 13 Grenfell St (8212 7099).
Thomas Cook: 45 Grenfell St (8212 3354).
General Post Office: 141 King William St (8216 2222). Open 9am to 5pm, Monday-Friday; a restricted service operates from 7.15am to 6.30pm Monday-Friday, 8.30-noon on Saturdays and 12.30 to 5pm on Sundays.
State Library: North Terrace. Has coin and card phones for after-hours use (closed Mondays).
Medical Treatment: Royal Adelaide Hospital, North Terrace (8223 0230).
Dental Treatment: Royal Dental Hospital, Frome Road (8223 9211).
Disabled Travellers: The tourist office normally stocks a free guide called *Access Adelaide*; further advice is available from the Disability Information and Resource Centre at 195 Gilles St (8223 7522).
Helplines: Life Line — 8212 3444; Poison Information — 8267 7000.

Work

Much of the available non-agricultural casual work in South Australia is within the Adelaide city limits, reflecting the fact that this is where three-quarters of the state's population resides. Hostel notice boards may carry details of factory jobs or you can check in the Wednesday and Saturday editions of the *Advertiser*. Advance copies are available from about 10pm the previous evening. Ignore the short and unhelpful *Casual Work Available* column unless you are enthusiastic about telephone sales. Instead check listings for bar and restaurant staff, labourers and swimming pool cleaners. Apparently jobs delivering junk mail are always available.

Alternatively, you can register with an employment agency. This is especially worthwhile if you have access to a phone. The main Commonwealth Employment Service (CES) office in Adelaide is at 45 Grenfell St (8231 9070) though it is reported to be not altogether encouraging. For example in order to register for office work, you must show that you can type at least 50 words a minute. You may receive a fairer hearing at CES offices in the suburbs or outside the capital, but the amount of work is correspondingly lower. In the grape harvest season, the Adelaide Hills Harvest Service operates from the CES in the suburb of Payneham. Private agencies in Adelaide include Alfred Marks (4/117 King William St; 8231 0999), Manpower (165 Hutt St; 8223 5999) and Drake Personnel (AMP Building, 1 King William St; 8212 4141).

As South Australia is by far the leading producer of wine in Australia, there is scope for grape-picking. The five main vine-growing areas are the Riverland (east of Adelaide), the Barossa and Clare Valleys (north), the Southern Vales (just south of the capital) and Coonawarra in the extreme southeast of the state. Much of the harvesting is mechanised, but the vogue for wines made from handpicked grapes means that demand for pickers is once again increasing. The chances for pickers are reasonable in the Barossa Valley (call in at the CES office in Nuriootpa), but a larger proportion of grapes is grown in the Riverland east of Adelaide. Rather than trailing around from one vineyard to another, install yourself in a town and phone around. If you get really good at hand-picking, you can enter the biennial Grapepicking Championship at the Orlando vineyards near Lyndoch. This competition marks the beginning of the Barossa Vintage Festival in April; should you win, your future as a grape-picker seems assured.

Towns along the Murray River like Renmark, Loxton, Berri, Waikerie and Barmera are flourishing fruit-growing towns. This depends heavily on itinerant workers, of whom there are not enough to keep up with the oranges, melons, etc. There are over a million fruit trees in the Waikerie district alone. If you want work, just ask in the local hotel or caravan park in any of these towns; the 'Snake Pit' bar of the hotel and the campsite in Waikerie where the majority of fruitpickers stay in tents or on-site vans are particularly recommended. In Waikerie the major employer is Lester Twigden who pays a decent hourly rate for rock melon picking in the season (November to March). You will have to have a car or a bicycle to get out to the farms.

The best time to find work in tourism is during the South Australian school holidays (mid-December to the beginning of February), when the seaside resorts all around the coast are at their busiest. The holidays usually run from just before Christmas until the beginning of February.

WINE REGIONS

Many interesting places are accessible from Adelaide for a day trip, although spending a little longer in some of them can be considerably more rewarding. Much of the interest centres on wine, and you might want to equip yourself with the excellent *South Australian Vineyards Map* (on sale at many Adelaide bookshops) before you set off as well as the tourist office's *Wine Country* brochure.

Adelaide Hills. This attractive range of minor mountains southeast of the capital provides an effective bar to the continued urbanisation in that direction. The Adelaide Hills are also known as the Mount Lofty Ranges, after one of the most notable peaks. Mount Barker Road winds up over the hills to reveal a peaceful, central European landscape beyond. The first part of the journey takes you through an area which was devastated by bushfires on Ash Wednesday nearly a decade ago. Over the hills, the major settlement is Hahndorf, which likes to think of itself as an outpost of Bavaria. Indeed, there is a Bavarian Motel on the main road through the town, together with numerous gift shops selling souvenirs with German connotations. Hahndorf is not representative of the area: hamlets such as Stirling, Aldgate, Balhannah and Mount Barker itself are more pleasant, and have some surprisingly good pubs and restaurants catering mainly for city dwellers and well-to-do locals.

The Adelaide Hills are becoming renowned as a centre for excellent cool-climate wines. There are wineries at Bridgewater and Clarendon. The Southern Vales begin at Clarendon, a town largely devoted to tourism.

Southern Vales. The more modest inclines to the south of Adelaide have not proved much of an impediment to sprawling suburbia. The tentacles of high-density housing now extend well into the northern edge of the Southern Vales, to the detriment of this breezy vine-growing region. Whatever the winemakers of Barossa and Clare might say, the Southern Vales produces a lot of good wine. Most of the wineries are conveniently grouped together, permitting easy touring by car or bicycle.

The first Southern Vale winery heading south from Adelaide is Marienberg in the Coromandel Valley, under 20km from the city centre. It is renowned for its female winemaker, Ursula Marie Pridham. Sadly the suburbs have encroached upon the winery to an almost ludicrous extent; all the vineyards have been swallowed up by housing, and all that remains is a small winery and tasting room marooned in suburbia.

The best centre for exploring the Southern Vales is McLaren Vale, the main town in the area. The headquarters of Hardy's is within the town, and there are plenty of other wineries nearby. The Barn Bistro on Main Road (8323 8618) doubles as a modest art gallery and excellent restaurant with an appropriately wide choice of wines. It has the added advantage of being next door to a motel and 500m from the McLaren Vale Hotel at 208 Main Road (08-8383 8208). This cheap and cheerful hotel, next door to Hardy's winery, is renowned for the size of its breakfasts. Together with a bed, they cost $20 single or $30 double.

The McLaren Vale Wine Bushing Festival takes place in late October. It includes tastings of the new wines, concerts, processions and craft fairs. Call 08-8323 8999 for more information.

The Barossa. The 8-by-30 kilometre valley was originally settled by Prussians and Silesians escaping from religious persecution in Europe in 1838. The rolling countryside of the Barossa is punctuated by small settlements whose skylines are highlighted by the spires of prim Lutheran churches. The name was given by Colonel Light, after the site of an English victory over the French in the Spanish Peninsular War, though Barrossa was misspelt to produce the Australian name.

Compared with the relaxed attitude of the Southern Vales and the gentility of Clare (described below), the commercialism of the big Barossa wineries may be a shock. Giants such as Seppelts and Chateau Yaldara charge $3 for winery tours. Some have built 'Public Relations Centres' and promote a range of tourist activities, such as hot air balloon trips for $175 (08-8389 3195). The Barossa produces over 100 million litres of wine each year, over half of South Australia's total, although many of the grapes used are grown outside the district.

In addition to the large wineries, there are many more that are smaller and family-owned, and which still make basket-press red wines in the traditional way and offer 'cellar-door tasting' at no extra cost.

Transport to the Barossa from Adelaide is limited. One simple solution is to join a one-day tour with E & K Mini-Tours (08-8337 8739), which for $18 will take you to several wineries and other highlights. For public transport, the Barossa–Adelaide Passenger Service (085-656258) leaves the Central Bus Depot in Franklin St three times a day on weekdays, twice on Saturdays and once on Sundays. The one-way fare is $5. An alternative is to take one of the regular trains to Gawler (a dormitory town for Adelaide) and hitch for 15km along Barossa Valley Way to Lyndoch and beyond.

Three main towns dominate the Barossa — Angaston, Nuriootpa and Tanunda. They combine rusticity and some garish modernity with the sophistication (of shops and restaurants) that easy access to a big city brings. The Barossa Information Centre is at 66 Murray St, Nuriootpa (085-630600) and can supply a map of the region.

Hiring a bicycle or a moped is a good idea. Bikes can be hired for $10 a day from the Bunkhaus Travellers' Hostel in Nuriootpa (085-622260) or the Zinfandel Tea Rooms at 58 Murray St, Tanunda (085-632822). Elderton Wines (3 Tanunda Road, Nuriootpa; 085-621058), on the banks of the North Para River, is one of the best known wineries, and after touring the vineyards, you can visit the Elderton tasting room, a burgundy cottage in the main street of Nuriootpa.

The long-established Bunkhaus charges $9 for a dorm bed. Tents can be pitched in caravan parks at Lyndoch (085-244262), Tanunda (085-632784) or Nuriootpa (085-621404). The Tanunda Hotel at 51 Murray St (085-632030) is a comfortable and fairly cheap place to stay: a double room with shared facilities costs $44. Another alternative is Barossa House (085-624022), opposite Chateau Dorrien.

Recently a host of cottage-style accommodation has sprung up, all of which is slightly more expensive than these suggestions. The Barossa also boasts the smallest motel in Australia, the Landhaus in Bethany: it accommodates just two people at a time in a restored shepherd's cottage (for more than $130). Zinfandel Tea Rooms in Tanunda (mentioned above) is worth visiting for home-made cream cakes, good sandwiches and German dishes (open 8.30am–6pm).

The week-long Barossa Vintage Festival takes place in odd-numbered years, starting on Easter Monday. It features fairs and a colourful procession between Nuriootpa and Tanunda. On the third weekend of each August, the Barossa Gourmet Weekend enables you to sample some of the state's best wine and food, when the leading chefs of Adelaide are invited to the wineries to produce selections of their fare to accompany Barossa wines at picnics and dinners.

A non-alcoholic treat in the Barossa is to visit the Whispering Wall at Williamstown. The wall holds nearly five billion litres of water inside the Barossa Reservoir. Like similar acoustic phenomena at St Pauls in London and the

Imperial Palace in Beijing, you can whisper into the wall of the dam at one side and be clearly heard at the far end 140m away. The area also has several offbeat museums like the eccentric collection of science and technology exhibits at the Kev Rohrlach Collection between Tanunda and Nuriootpa (admission $5) and the mechanical music museum at Lyndoch (admission $4).

Clare Valley. The Clare Valley wineries are set in more rugged terrain than the Southern Vales or the Barossa, and have more charm; at most places in the Clare, the person who serves you at a tasting is likely to be the winemaker. The wineries cluster around the road north from Adelaide between Auburn and Clare, 120–140km from Adelaide, an easy day-trip. For those without a vehicle, the towns of Watervale and Clare are the best centres as several wineries are within walking or cycling distance of each town. Some recommended wineries include Pikes Polish Hill River Estate, Skillogalee Wines, Tim Adams Wines and the heavily promoted Tim Knappstein Wines in a converted brewery.

The Clare Valley Gourmet Weekend takes place in May each year on the same weekend as the Adelaide Cup. It is regarded by many as a cut above the Barossa's counterpart, and is operated by the Clare Valley Winemakers' Association. The 'weekend of indulgence' commences on Saturday afternoon with a tasting of new vintages in the Clare Town Hall. The $6 admission enables you to try over 150 wines, but be warned that by no means all the new product is ideal for drinking. Amateur wine experts will declaim the virtues of certain wines and insist that they will eventually attain high standards, but some new reds are barbarically acidic and some whites appear unhealthily green. Sunday is gourmet day, when you tour the wineries to taste food as well as old and new vintages. The food costs $6–7 per serving.

Interest in the Clare is not confined entirely to food and wine. Mintaro, a few kilometres east of the main highway, has been listed as a 'heritage town' by the state authorities. It became a ghost town after the reserves of slate were exhausted, and has recently been restored to become a tourist attraction. The Magpie & Stump Hotel dates from 1851–1870, but the most impressive sight is Martindale Hall, a traditional Georgian country house 2km south-east of Mintaro. The mansion was built in 1879 by Englishmen imported especially for the job. Its main claim to fame is as one setting for the film *Picnic at Hanging Rock* (though the rock itself is hundreds of kilometres away in Victoria). The Hall opens at 11am on weekdays and noon at weekends and closes 4pm daily (admission $5). The Hall also doubles as an upmarket guest house, each room equipped with a picturesque four-poster bed and costing $75 per night; this rate includes a country breakfast and free use of the Billiard Room. Call 08-8843 9088 for bookings.

For accommodation with atmosphere, try the Watervale Hotel on the Main North Road in Watervale (08-8843 0109). The back yard sports a small gaol now a garden bar. There are only two double rooms, one with a four-poster and the other with a waterbed. The rate for two of $55 per night includes a splendid breakfast prepared by the gregarious publican and his wife. Just behind the hotel is Crabtree's Watervale Cellars winery, run by Englishman Robert Crabtree. In the town of Clare, try the Clare Hotel/Motel at 244 Main North Road (08-8842 2816), which costs $16 per person for bed only, or $26 with a large breakfast. The cheapest accommodation in the area is at Bungaree Station (08-8842 2677) 12km north of Clare on the Port Augusta Road, where shearers' quarters have been converted to dormitory-style accommodation at $15 per bed per night ($12 for two or more nights). You will need to bring a sleeping bag.

The Tourist Information Centre is in Clare Town Hall at 244 Main North Road (08-8842 2131), and is open 7 days a week.

The River Murray. Residents of New South Wales will tell you that the northern bank of the mighty Murray is best; Victorians claim that they have the most pleasing side of the river; and by the time it reaches South Australia it is wide, slow and superficially unexciting. But hiring a canoe to explore the little-visited Chowilla area of the Murray (on the NSW/SA/Vic border) is a highly recommended get-away-from-it-all experience. The vegetation and wildlife change with each bend of the river and its backwaters. Try Riverland Canoeing Adventures in Loxton North (085-841494) for a complete outfitting service. A double kayak costs from $25 a day.

The area of the Riverland closer to Adelaide is a low-key area with no great thrills for those uninterested in wildlife, but is a good location for lazing or working as a fruit-picker. From the Victorian border the river passes through wine territory, where the grapes for much of Australia's cask wine and cheaper exports are grown. There are some interesting settlements, notably the historic village of Loxton — which has a private hostel at the Riverland Caravan Park (085-847862) — and the town of Berri.

Wine is a better reason to visit Berri than to view the World's Biggest Orange (located here although nearby Waikerie declares itself the citrus capital of Australia). Berri is also a good place to hire a houseboat (see below). After irrigating the vines which go to make half of South Australia's wines, the Murray strikes south, spilling into the lakes and the Coorong before meeting the Gulf at Goolwa. The setting is remarkably similar to the Deep South of the USA, although the climate is more temperate and bearable. Drivers planning to take ordinary vehicles onto the beaches at the mouth of the Murray should note that local owners of four-wheel drive vehicles make good pickings from winching out those stuck in the sand as the tide rolls in.

If you're too lazy (or too rich) to fancy canoeing, a civilised way to mosey along the river is to rent a houseboat. These crafts are more mobile than their counterparts on the Norfolk Broads or in Kashmir, corresponding roughly to Thames barges in terms of their manoeuvrability. The South Australian Government Travel Centre publishes a list of houseboats for hire. Rentals are high — from $300 for a weekend in a two-berth vessel to $1500 for a week in a 4/5 berth vessel. For those who prefer someone else to navigate, two paddle steamers ply the river. Based loosely on Mississippi riverboats, they charge $700–800 for a week's luxury cruise in high season.

Coonawarra and the South-East. The southern region of South Australia close to the Victorian border produces the best red wines in Australia. The 'Terra Rosa' of Coonawarra is a slash of red earth with a limestone base that mimics the Médoc of Bordeaux and supports vines of similar class. Perhaps because of the greater distance from Adelaide these wineries, though open to the public, are not so heavily visited.

A crystal-clear volcanic lake near the town of Mount Gambier undergoes a dramatic colour change from dull grey to deep blue every November and doesn't revert until March. The towns of the area are unexceptional, but there is some attractive pine woodland inland and quiet coves along the shore. The fishing ports of Kingston, Robe and Beachport are pleasant places to stay, not least because of their excellent seafood restaurants.

The long narrow waterway known as the Coorong constitutes a National Park between the mouth of the Murray near Goolwa and Kingston in the south. Yachts and dinghies can be hired near Goolwa (085-553364). Organised tours range from the 'Coorong Pirate Cruise' lasting a few hours (cost $13) to an extended barbecue cruise for $26 hosted by a local character (085-521221). If humorous patter is not to your taste you can exchange chattering people for birds by arranging to camp in the Park. Advice and permits are available from the National Parks and Wildlife Service office in Meningie (34 Princes Highway/ PO Box 105; 085-751200). Flocks of cormorants, pelicans and terns feed along the dunes of this elongated peninsula.

FLEURIEU PENINSULA

The tourist authority's description of this area, about 100km south of the state capital, is 'Holiday Playground', which should prepare you for the resorts of Goolwa and Victor Harbor. There is a great choice of empty beaches along this coast, though after the sheltered waters around Adelaide, you will have to remind yourself that only the Great Southern Ocean lies between this coast and Antarctica. Off-season bathing is regarded with some curiosity by the locals.

These old established resorts are ideal for a few days' rest by the sea, and are only an hour or two by car or bus from Adelaide. (Information on bus services is available from Johnson's Motor Coaches on 08-8231 5959, and Premier Road Lines on 08-8233 2777.) A very interesting day trip to Victor Harbor can be had on the 'Southern Encounter' steam train, run by volunteer enthusiasts, which runs every Sunday between August and November plus May. (No services run in the summer because of the total fire ban in the Adelaide Hills.) The train leaves Keswick station in Adelaide at 9am and arrives 3½ hours later. This gives you only 3½ hours in which to see Victor. The return fare is $34; call SteamRanger Tours on 08-8231 1707 for further details. There is also an occasional local steam service on the Cockle Train between Victor Harbor and Goolwa; the half hour trip costs $10 return. Further opportunities to relive the past are afforded by the horse-drawn tram that trundles along the short causeway between Victor and offshore Granite Island; the 12-minute ride costs $1. The modern way to view this picturesque coast is to ride on the chairlift ($1.75).

Victor Harbor was formerly a whaling station, and was once mooted as the state capital of South Australia. Five kilometres out of town the Urimbirra Wildlife Park is worth visiting (admission $4) for close encounters with Australian wildlife. Be warned that if you splash out 50c or $1 on a bag of feed, only circling sea gulls will be interested; the cheeky kangaroos will prefer the paper bags. The koala feeding (and cuddling) time is 2pm.

Outside January and February there are plenty of self-catering apartments to rent in and around the town, plus a private hostel called Warringa at 16 Flinders Parade (085-521028), which charges YHA members just $8 a night, and an associated guest house that charges $15–20 per person in a double. Details of other accommodation and local attractions can be found in the Visitors Guide published by the Fleurieu Regional Tourist Association (PO Box 430, Goolwa, SA 5214).

KANGAROO ISLAND

'Nature's pleasure island' is the soubriquet of the third largest island off the coast of Australia, which should discourage those who enjoy the big-city life from coming. Kangaroo Island is 150km from end to end, so you should allow at least a couple of days to enjoy its unspoilt habitats.

Kangaroo Island Sealink (7 North Terrace, Penneshaw 5222, Kangaroo Island; 0848-31122; reservations on 131301) is the major carrier to the island, and has up to ten departures from Adelaide a day and the only car ferry. Shuttle buses to and from Adelaide are available. It also offers backpacker specials, such as two-day/one-night self-drive packages including a scenic coach transfer, overnight accommodation and a day tour for $100.

The *Valerie Jane* ferry runs twice daily, seven days a week. With a shuttle bus from Adelaide, the return fare is $76, coming down to $56 without the shuttle.

A two-day/one-night package costs around $115; contact 0848-31233 for details. YHA members are eligible for concessions, and bookings are often essential.

Three airlines fly from Adelaide to the island, taking half an hour. Kendell Airlines (08-8231 9567) and Albatross Airlines (0848-22296) serve Kingscote only; Kendell has stand-by backpackers fares for $38 each way. Air Kangaroo Island (08-8234 4139) serves American River, Penneshaw and Parndana as well as Kingscote; it is owned and operated by Kangaroo Island Sealink and so connects with Sealink tours.

Tours of the island can be good value. Kangaroo Island 4WD Safaris (1800-671 616), for example, offers four-day safaris for $200, leaving from Adelaide. AAA ('Air and Adventure') Tours offers one-day trips to the island from Adelaide for $180, including return flights (08-8281 0530). The Adelaide hostels also arrange tours; try Sunny's (see *Adelaide: Accommodation* above).

Getting around the island can be a problem. The only public transport runs between Kingscote (town and airport), American River and Penneshaw, and advance booking on 0848-22640 is usually necessary. To make the most of your stay, hire a car, scooter, bike or campervan but be prepared for badly corrugated gravel roads. The speed limit in parks and conservation areas is generally 40km/h. You can hire a scooter or a car from Kingscote Hire Cars (0848-22390) or Budget (0848-23133). Scooters and bicycles can be hired from the Penneshaw YHA hostel (0848-31284, or toll-free in South Australia on 1800-018258; bookings essential if you want to stay). Bicycles are also available from the Sorrento Resort in Penneshaw (0848-31028). Hitchers will have better luck in the more densely populated eastern part of the island than in the more beautiful west.

Just as the isolation of the Australian continent has allowed the evolution of many species unique to this part of the world, so Kangaroo Island is one stage further removed and has an even more exclusive range of wildlife. The best site is Flinders Chase National Park, which occupies the western end of the island. It has a great deal of wildlife, including the unique Kangaroo Island kangaroo, which is slimmer and darker than its relatives on the mainland. Other animals to be seen include wallabies, possums, koalas, emus, echidna and (very occasionally) platypus. Koalas are so prolific on the island that the National Parks and Wildlife Service recently proposed a cull, which predictably met with strong opposition. There are also some wild pigs, supposedly descendants of individuals placed there by French explorers to enable victims of the notoriously treacherous coast to survive being shipwrecked. (It is not known if any survivors from the 40 or so wrecks have tucked in.) Memorabilia of Kangaroo Island's shipping past can be seen in the Maritime Room of the Penneshaw Museum.

Seal Bay, halfway along the south coast, is much easier to reach, being only 70km by road from the main towns. This famous Australian sea lion colony — the largest accessible such colony in the world — is home to one-tenth of the species' known numbers. In 1991 several pups were born right on the main beach. Even so, visitors are still allowed on the beach accompanied by a guide and can walk among the bulls, some of whom weigh nearly 400kg.

There is no shortage of beaches on the island though the ones on the battered south coast are more suited to experienced surfers than sea-bathers. Strong currents at Pennington Bay (near American River) should be tackled only by strong swimmers. Inshore fishing is excellent all around the coast, whether from beaches, rocks or boats; bear in mind, however, that no fishing is allowed in National and Conservation Parks. The towns on the island could hardly be described as exciting: number six on the list of nine 'Things to Do in Penneshaw' is 'Visit Condon's Take-Away Food', which offers rooburgers on its menu.

Kangaroo Island is reasonably well supplied with hostel accommodation, though there is no official YHA hostel. In addition to the Penneshaw Hostel

"PIGS WERE LEFT ON THE ISLAND TO FEED SHIPWRECKED SAILORS"

mentioned above, which offers a range of tours and travel services, there is Kingscote Budget Hostel (21 Murray St; 0848-22787) and Nomads Ellson Seaview Lodge (Chapman Terrace, Kingscote; 0848-22030). There is also Linnetts Island Club in American River (0848-33053).

An interesting alternative is the National Parks and Wildlife Service's one-roomed backpackers cottages at Cape Borda and Rocky River in Flinders Chase National Park; the cost is just $10 per person per night. Phone 0848-37235 for booking information.

Otherwise the cheapest accommodation is basic self-catering units, for example Brownlow Units in Kingscote (0848-22293). Often there are reductions of up to a quarter for travelling out-of-season, i.e. April to September. As a rule, the further from the beach, the lower the cost, so that accommodation in Parndana in the interior is cheaper than in the resorts. The main attraction in the middle of the island is the (very) Little Sahara with its white sand dunes surrounded by bush. Try also Casuarina Holiday Units on Ryberg Road in American River (0848-33020) offering a stand-by rate of $25 for two people or $30 per night for three or four (minimum stay of three nights and no linen supplied). If you want to spend a week on the island between June and July it will cost only $150 for up to four people. The owners can also recommend farm cottage accommodation elsewhere on the island, arrange nature tours and hire out canoeing and camping equipment.

You can camp in the National Park, but beware of marauding kangaroos. There are caravan parks at Kingscote, nearby Brownlow, American River and Penneshaw.

The Kangaroo Island Tourist Association can be contacted at PO Box 244, Kingscote 5223 (0848-31185) or at the Information Centre in Kingscote at 37 Dauncey St (0848-22381). A new Information Centre is due to open in Penneshaw.

EYRE PENINSULA

Port Augusta, at the head of the Spencer Gulf, is an industrial town in decline but is also a busy hub for travellers crossing Australia. Few stay for long (although the Wadlata Outback Centre on Flinders Terrace, an 'outback interpretive centre', is worth the $5 admission charge) before heading west or north to Perth or Alice Springs. Those who take the Lincoln Highway southwest along the coast of the Eyre Peninsula discover first a steel town, then a series of sparsely populated beach settlements.

The steel town is Whyalla, South Australia's second city but 30 times smaller than Adelaide. The beaches begin here, and continue sporadically for nearly 300km to Port Lincoln. This city is sandwiched uncomfortably between Coffin Bay and Cape Catastrophe. It is 700km overland from the state capital, but only 300km by air; not surprisingly, there are frequent flights on competing airlines, from Adelaide Sky-Link (08-8234 4877), Whyalla Airlines (toll-free 008-088858), Lincoln Airlines (toll-free 008-018234) and Kendell Airlines (08-8233 3322). Although they are more expensive than the Stateliner coach service, they save you a 10-hour coach journey. Port Lincoln's seafaring activities are increasingly devoted to shark fishing; white pointer sharks breed prolifically around the offshore Dangerous Reef, and there are numerous deep-sea trips for anglers.

After Port Lincoln, the highway turns sharp right and becomes the Flinders Highway. The pattern of beach resorts continues as far as Ceduna, where you rejoin the Eyre Highway to cross the Nullarbor. One of the last attractions on the South Australian part of the trans-Nullarbor highway are the Southern Bight Whales which come into the shores of the Great Australian Bight.

FLINDERS RANGES

Those who choose instead to turn north-east just before Port Augusta find themselves in rough, rugged terrain which will seem familiar to anyone who has travelled through Arizona. The desert gradually rises up to the Flinders Ranges, which continue almost to the Queensland border. Stop off at the township of Quorn if the idea of a train ride on the Pichi Richi steam railway appeals.

Although the mountains of the Flinders are small by global standards, the gorges, canyons and other natural phenomena are truly spectacular and well worth visiting. The highlight, and one of the most accessible areas, is the Wilpena Pound — a massive horseshoe of sheer cliffs — reached by one bus each week from Adelaide. A Stateliner bus departs on Fridays, taking about six hours to reach the Pound, and returns the following Sunday; the cost is $45–50 one way, and bus passes are valid. A double room at the heavily promoted Wilpena Pound Resort (086-480004) costs $80 per night, but the campground outside the Pound charges only $7 for two people. Alternatively you can camp at specific sites within the Pound with a permit from the Ranger (086-480048).

The walk through the Pound and up to St Mary's Peak gives spectacular views of the Elder Range, the (normally dry) Lake Torrens and the rest of the Flinders. There are also a couple of hikes to waterfalls and gorges that are most attractive after some rain. An early morning start into the Pound enables you to appreciate fully the wildlife — kangaroos, emus and all manner of multi-coloured birds — before other people frighten them away from the trails.

A good map of the Pound and its surroundings is published by the Flinders Ranges & Outback Regional Tourist Association (PO Box 41, Port Augusta, SA 5700) for $2 as well as detailed maps of the outback tracks mentioned briefly below for $6; if ordering by post add 50c for postage.

COOBER PEDY

For years this unique settlement on the Stuart Highway was merely a tourist stop along the otherwise featureless journey between Adelaide and Alice Springs. The name is Aboriginal for 'White Man's Burrow', which accurately describes the dwellings of the opal hunters who live here. The only sign that Coober Pedy is a town is the motley collection of shops and motels and a school which peer out above the ground. The inhabitants escape from the unremitting summer heat by residing underground in homes hewn out of the rock. These burrows began when miners arrived to seek their fortunes at the end of World War One, after opals were first discovered in 1915, and have since spread to include such embellishments as an underground church.

For a time, the business of mining opals was superseded by catering for tourists: visitors could step out of an air-conditioned tour bus into an opal mine or dwelling, then re-emerge straight into an air-conditioned motel. Although they were regaled with tales of lucky tourists finding priceless gems, the clear lack of wealth among Aboriginal 'noodlers' (who sift through waste from the mines looking for opals) told another story. Then, in the winter of 1987, more desert was opened up for exploitation; a new seam was discovered and an opal rush began. The settlement of 2500 people (of many various nationalities) has swelled to 4000 by the arrival of prospectors and adventurers; travellers who get to know a local may find that it is worth doing some noodling though chances of success are greater in less exploited places like Mintabie (40km north) and Andamooka. Be careful not to stumble into an abandoned mine shaft concealed by vegetation.

Since the new discoveries, Coober Pedy has become still more popular among visitors, and there are plenty of old-timers who find catering to tourists more profitable than prospecting. Some travellers have also managed to find casual work here; ask at the Lucas Supermarket on Hutchinson St about the possibility of unloading the weekly shipment of goods on a Wednesday night. This bizarre environment has bred a number of unusual local characters. Many of the organised tours take in not only the mines but offbeat places like the residence of 'Crocodile' Harry; his underground house is unfortunately most memorable for the names of his female 'conquests' painted on the roof.

Such social life as there is reinforces the frontier town image, consisting mainly of frequent drunkenness and fighting. If you happen to be here in October during the Gymkhana, the pubs stay open all night. There are several backpackers hostels including the Bedrock Underground Bunkhouse in the Opal Cave Complete on Main St (086-725028) and the underground hostel/motel called the Radeka Dugout (086-725223). The owner of this latter establishment sometimes tries to lure backpackers into listening to his eccentric views on faith-healing, the evils of Catholicism, etc., from which a quick retreat to the pub is advised. When sleeping underground you are advised to choose a bottom bunk to avoid being showered with fragments of flaking rock and also to use earplugs to avoid being disturbed by fellow guests rising to catch the early morning bus. A quieter alternative is the Coober Pedy Budget Motel (086-725163), where a double room costs $25–40. Remember that water, like shade, is in short supply in Coober Pedy, so don't squander it.

The Coober Pedy Tourist Information Centre is in the Council Offices on Hutchinson St (Coober Pedy, SA 5723; 086-725298).

THE OUTBACK

The relatively verdant and populated south-east corner of South Australia does not prepare you for the desolation found in much of the rest of the state. As you travel north or west, the roads become emptier, the landscape more unchanging and the heat haze more hypnotic. Even the most enthusiastic traveller can find that the appeal of arid plain or dry salt lake begins to wane after a few hundred kilometres. You might strike lucky and travel immediately after a rainstorm, which can almost miraculously draw out a sea of colourful plant life including the bizarre state floral emblem, Sturt's desert pea. But otherwise you should be prepared for mile after mile of bleak, dusty earth, punctuated by sleeping or ruined homesteads and sleazy roadhouses.

Although the Stuart Highway to Alice is now sealed, you can easily get bogged in dust if you leave the main road. If you choose to travel one of the Outback 'tracks' like the Oodnadatta or the Birdsville to Queensland through Sturt's Stony Desert, you must make careful preparations. These pass through or near some of the most arid National Parks in the world. Anyone intending to stop in the Witjira, Lake Eyre, Innamincka and Simpson Desert National Parks or Reserves must obtain a National Parks pass for $50 from the Department of Environment and Natural Resources, 60 Elder Terrace, Hawker SA 5434. As for all Outback driving you must make extensive preparations to your vehicle and baggage as facilities along the tracks are so sparse. As routes are rendered impassible by rain, always check with the Northern Roads Hotline (08-11633) before undertaking any outback travel. The *Flinders Ranges & Outback Visitor's Guide* (available from the South Australia Tourism Commission, GPO Box 666, Adelaide 5001) contains extensive notes and warnings on outback travel. It also contains a long list of operators who run four-wheel-drive tours. For recommendations, talk to travellers returning from such adventures. The *Outback* edition of the free magazine *TNT for Backpackers* is a good source of information on Outback tours, travel operators, and so on.

 The South Australian Recreation Institute (304 Henley Beach Road, Underdale, SA 5032; 08-8234 0844) is a good source of information on some of the state's outdoor activities and publishes a number of walking maps and cycling and canoeing guides. The Department of Environment and Natural Resources' Information Centre, located at 77 Grenfell St, Adelaide 5000 (08-8204 1910), has a huge range of information available on everything from National Parks to recycling, and is well worth a visit.

Bushwalking. The 1500km Heysen Trail traverses the state from Cape Jervis to Parachilna Gorge in the Flinders Ranges, via Mount Lofty near Adelaide and the Barossa Valley. Because of fire risk, the Trail is closed between December and April and possibly at other times. It is designed not only for serious long-distance walkers but also for day-trippers who want to expore a short stretch of it. There are numerous huts, hostels, home and farm stays for those who do not wish to carry camping equipment. The route is covered in a series of 11 maps available for $5.50 each from the Recreation Institute.

You might also like to visit the Conservation Centre in Adelaide (120 Wakefield St), which has a range of pamphlets on hiking and wildlife.

Calendar of Events

January	Schutzenfest German Festival, Hahndorf
February	Compass Cup Cow Race, Mount Compass
February	Kangaroo Island Cup Carnival
March	Glendi (festival of Greek culture and food), Adelaide
March	Adelaide Festival of Arts (even-numbered years)
March	Adelaide Festival of Music (odd-numbered years)
Easter	Coober Pedy Opal & Outback Festival
March/April	National Folk Festival, Adelaide

March/April (week following Easter)	Barossa Valley Vintage Festival (odd-numbered years)
May (third Monday)	**Adelaide Cup (horserace), Morphettville**
May (weekend of Adelaide Cup)	Clare Valley Gourmet Weekend
May	Cornish Festival, Yorke Peninsula
June (second Monday)	**Queen's Birthday**
August	Barossa Classic Gourmet Weekend
October	McLaren Wine Bushing Festival
October (second Monday)	**Labor Day**
November	Christmas Pageant, Adelaide
December 30	**Proclamation Day**

Public holidays are shown in **bold**.

Perth and Western Australia

Population of Perth: 1,158,400   **Population of WA: 1,591,100**

Western Australia is a vast and vibrant state with immense variety: the clean and cosmopolitan city of Perth and its pretty port of Fremantle, the fertile south-west and the wild northern regions with their rugged mountains and deserts. More than any other state, WA (as it is invariably known) brings home the immense scale of the Australian continent. It is 20 times bigger than England and six times as large as California. Western Australia is also undeniably isolated: Perth is 2000km and a time zone or two away from the other state capitals. By virtue of its geographical location, you can feel almost as if you are in another country.

Western Australia was claimed for Britain in May 1829, when Sir Charles Howe Fremantle landed at Murray Head (where the High St in Fremantle now ends). In the same year Perth was founded by Captain James Stirling, who modestly named the settlement after a different Scottish city from the one that bears his surname. Perth was an obvious place to settle — sheltered from the Indian Ocean by the Swan River estuary, and surrounded by flat and friendly terrain — but its detachment from the rest of the new continent made early development slow. When gold was discovered a few hundred miles inland around Kalgoorlie late in the 19th century, Perth prospered as the supply port and commercial link for the goldfields.

The state is still one of the world's largest producers of gold, though times are hard in that industry as in every other. Although the state's vast mineral wealth is far from depleted, world recession has marked the end of the economic boom that Perth enjoyed in the 1980s. Some hostels, small tour operators, etc. have been forced to close in the past couple of years. But anxiety about the future is not a Perth trait. Local people are fond of comparing Western Australia to California, and there are certainly strong similarities in climate, lifestyle and wealth. People from the east are not so complimentary and the *Sydney Morning Herald* once called Perth 'Dallas without the intellect'. 'Metro Perth', which takes in Perth, the rejuvenated port of Fremantle and everything in between and around, likes to think of itself as a sophisticated and pulsating metropolis, straddling the Swan River and stretching out to the coast. However it isn't entirely undeserving of its laid-back and country bumpkin image and is no less attractive for that.

That Perth and Fremantle are at last on the world map is due partly to the America's Cup in 1987. When Alan Bond's yacht *Australia II* took the trophy away from the USA for the first time in 137 years, the real prize — as far as Western Australia was concerned — was the chance to stage the competition at Fremantle and the consequent priceless publicity for the state. Visitors to the yacht races were not disappointed by the style of the capital. They found a city that is spacious and well planned, with sweeping freeways, striking modern architecture, sparkling white beaches and splendid parkland.

CLIMATE

Summer visitors are virtually guaranteed fine weather, and even mid-winter can be pleasantly warm. Perth's climate has been called a 'two-strawberry-harvests-a-year climate'. The sun shines for an average 7.8 hours per day around the year. Summer is normally characterized by clear skies and an average high of 30°C/85°F from December to February (which can be uncomfortably hot if, as sometimes happens, the air does not cool significantly at night). Occasional heatwaves can bring temperatures of 40°C or more. On most summer days a climatic peculiarity brings welcome (but sometimes quite chilly) relief from the heat: the 'Fremantle Doctor' is a breeze that blows in from the Indian Ocean between noon and 4pm. March and November are the two best months to visit, especially the latter when the jacaranda are in bloom.

The winter months of June to August manage a balmy mean high of 20°C/70°F, but this is often accompanied by plenty of rain; average rainfall in the wettest month of July is 17cm (more than twice as much as July in London and New York), and there are on average 18 wet days. Over a year, mean rainfall is 87cm, falling on an average of 119 days. For weather reports in the Perth metropolitan area, dial 1196.

The area south of Perth becomes marginally cooler, while much of the rest of the state is desert. The wild flowers for which the state is famed begin to bloom in early September and last till November. The northern extremes have a tropical climate with distinct wet (November–April) and dry (May–October) seasons.

THE LOCALS

Some say that the existing populace of Perth displays an uneasy mix between an expatriate way of thinking — as though their residence in this isolated city is only a temporary aberration — and a cowboy mentality, that they are somehow involved in pioneering the unknown terrain beyond the city limits. Pride in its millionaire-cowboys has been somewhat tempered by the fall of Alan Bond, but a favourite 'sight' remains the exclusive suburb of Dalkeith, where many of the city's millionaires live in flashy houses overlooking the Swan River. It seems that entrepreneurial attributes are still highly prized amongst 'sandgropers', as the people of Western Australia are known. Hard work has resulted for many in a high degree of affluence, but the play is equally hard: leisure time is usually spent in energetic pursuits. One in three Perth residents owns a boat.

Certainly a large percentage of the population could be considered expat: 30% were born in Britain, Italy or Greece. Aboriginals represent a small and mostly invisible minority. If you are interested in their view of Perth you can take a tour with Aboriginal Adventure Tours (344 3163) that will introduce you to the Old Swan Brewery controversy. The city wants to develop the now-deserted site on the river as a tourist complex, ignoring that it is a well documented place of significance for the Nyungah people.

Making Friends. Perth has a young and lively population, dedicated to enjoying themselves. The best way to meet the people of the state capital is to join in with their leisure activities, whether on the beach, jogging in a park or drinking in the current most trendy pub. Sunday afternoon pub sessions in summer are perhaps the best, when you can laze in the garden or courtyard listening to local bands and drinking Swan beer (although Western Australians say you won't make many friends if you stick to Swan Light, only 0.9% alcohol). Or you can join in some of the many organised sporting activities, from walking to windsurfing.

City Layout. Straddling the Swan River and bounded to the west by the Indian Ocean, Perth is a sprawling city with an extensive road network. The city centre is compact and lies just north of the river. Most commercial offices are on St George's Terrace (usually known simply as 'the Terrace'). The main shopping street, Hay St, is one block north, and has its central section laid out as a pedestrian mall. Perth Train Station and the Bus Station are a further two blocks along Wellington St; the station is adjacent to the Forrest Place development, Perth's closest approximation to a city square. Across the railway tracks and accessible by a pedestrian walkway is Northbridge, Perth's cultural and entertainment heart, with the arts complex and many good restaurants. Subiaco, north-west of the city centre, is a sophisticated and picturesque area; the name is often abbreviated to 'Subi'. The suburbs of Perth extend north, south and inland as far as Midland and form a continuous conurbation as far as Fremantle ('Freo') on the coast. The port of Fremantle is 20km from the centre of Perth and is small enough to be covered easily on foot.

ARRIVAL AND DEPARTURE
Air. Perth airport, 21km east of the city centre, is a gateway for services from Europe and Asia. The international and domestic terminals are on opposite sides of the runway and 10km apart by road, making changing flights a tedious and expensive business. In addition, many international flights arrive at or after midnight, when there are no connecting flights.

Transperth operates a daily service to the domestic terminal (routes 200–202, 208 and 209), departing every 40–50 minutes from Stand 39 and from two points on St George's Terrace. The journey costs $2 and takes 40 minutes. Call 132213 for bus information. An alternative is to use the 24-hour Airport Shuttle, which runs between hostels and the domestic ($6) and international ($8) terminals. You can book by ringing 479 4131. Taxis take approximately 20 minutes to get from the city to the domestic terminal, 30 minutes to the international. The fare will be around $15-20 and you should book a few hours in advance.

The market in international air tickets from Perth is lively, with lower fares to Europe than from anywhere else in Australia. Try London Court Travel at

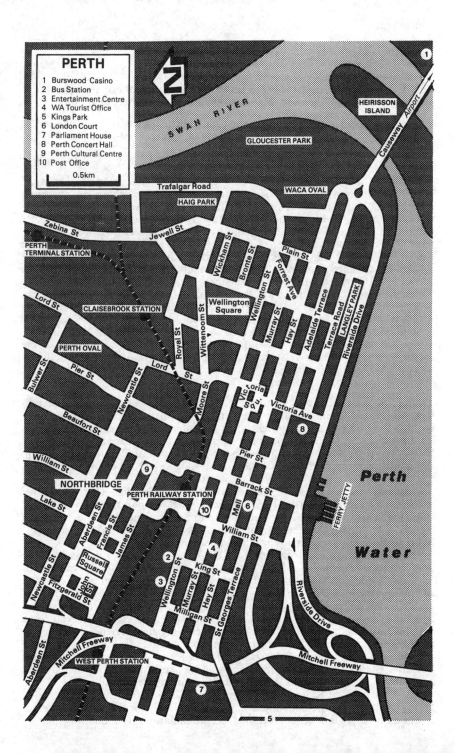

Shop 52 at the St George's Terrace end of London Court (325 6799), or STA, 100 James St, Northbridge (227 7569).

Bus. For services within the state south of Geraldton, the main operator is Westrail (132232). Otherwise the main operators in Perth are as follows:

Greyhound Pioneer: Reservations/information: 132030. Booking office: Wellington St Bus Station (481 7066). Terminal: Westrail Centre, West Pde, East Perth (328 6677).
South West Coachlines: City Busport, The Esplanade (324 2333).

There are daily services from Perth to Adelaide (journey time about 35 hours) and the eastern states. If you are trying to save money on overnight accommodation, it makes sense to catch a bus that departs late in the evening rather than the morning, thus giving you two overnights on board. Daily departures offer a good choice of stopover destinations. The cheapest one-way fares at the time of writing were Greyhound Pioneer's Advance Purchase fares: Adelaide for $95, Melbourne for $122, Canberra/Sydney for $143 and Brisbane for $180. Advance Purchase fares are available on all Greyhound Pioneer services. A 10% discount is offered to backpackers, and 20% to students.

Coaches depart daily to Darwin for around $348 (adult fare). Bus passes can be a very economical way to travel and can include connections to the Pinnacles, Kalbarri, Monkey Mia, Coral Bay and Exmouth.

South West Coachlines serves the area south of Perth, including Rockingham, Donnybrook, Bunbury and Busselton. There are three departures a day to the major centres at 7.45am, 1.30pm and 4.45pm; the one-way fare to Busselton is $25 (YHA discounts available).

Train. The Westrail Travel Centre is on Wellington St; ring 326 2222 or toll-free 008-099150 for information. Westrail runs country services (including some by bus) but you can also buy tickets for the interstate services here. Bookings for long-distance trains are normally compulsory, and cease at 4pm the day before travel. YHA members who book at any Westrail office (i.e. Perth, Fremantle, Albany, Bunbury, Geraldton or Kalgoorlie) are eligible for a 10% discount.

Passenger rail services are sparse in Western Australia. There are three suburban lines around Perth (see *City Transport* below), plus the trans-Nullarbor route to the east and a line from Perth south to Bunbury on which the *Australind* travels. The *Australind* leaves Central Station at 10am and takes just over 2 hours to Bunbury for a fare of around $17 single, $27 day return.

The main services east from Perth are the *Trans-Australian* as far as Adelaide and the *Indian Pacific* via Adelaide to Sydney. The Sydney train leaves Perth at 9pm on Sundays, Mondays and Thursdays, and takes 64 hours; the cheapest sitting-up fare is $220. The *Trans-Australian* departs at 9pm on Wednesdays and Saturdays, arriving in Adelaide 38 hours later. The cheapest regular fare is $165 ($412 with sleeper) but booking 7 days in advance qualifies you for a CAPER fare. The trans-Nullarbor journey is certainly an experience, but whether a fascinating or tedious one depends upon your attitude to train travel. These services, plus the prestige *Prospector* as far as Kalgoorlie, operate from Perth Terminal Station, a clean and modern building 3km south-east of the city and accessible by suburban train from Central Station in a few minutes.

The *Prospector* to Kalgoorlie is reputed to be the fastest train in Australia, taking 7½ hours for the 650km journey. Unfortunately for the budget traveller, it has only first-class air-conditioned accommodation. The one-way fare of around $55 includes a meal. You can get there more cheaply in economy class on the *Indian Pacific* train, or on one of the trans-Nullarbor buses from Perth.

The volunteer-run historic railway association of Western Australia is called the Hotham Valley Tourist Railway (2nd Floor, Commonwealth Bank, 86A Barrack St; 221 4444) and it runs a series of Explorer trains to various destinations no longer served by passenger trains, especially in conjunction with festivals and special events. The price of these day returns is about $25.

Driving. The maximum speed limit in Western Australia is 110km/h, and the minimum speed on freeways is 60km/h. The blood/alcohol limit is 0.08%, though the state government is under heavy pressure from the federal government to reduce this to 0.05%. On some highways you will see white lines painted some distance apart on the roads. These are to aid the aerial police in spotting speeding vehicles. (A good proportion of the state revenue apparently comes from speeding fines so be careful.)

Before attempting to drive to Perth from any other state, ensure your vehicle is in good condition and that you have ample supplies of fuel and water; although the roads through from Adelaide and Darwin are sealed, it is still a long and difficult journey. Most other roads in the Outback of Western Australia are dirt tracks, but some mining companies have built their own roads, and these are often much better than the public highways. Ask locally whether motorists other than employees can use them; some companies issue permits to visitors. In the north of the state, roads are sometimes flooded and impassable for weeks during the wet season (November to April).

To explore the south-west of the state and to do some interesting day trips, a hire car is an asset. One company that rents out older vehicles is Rent-an-Oldie at 789 Wellington St (322 7715). One of the best weekly deals around is offered by Carousel Rent-a-Car at 318 Charles St (328 8999): $257 includes free mileage and insurance. Other companies to try are Terrace Rent-a-Car (118 Terrace Road, City; 008-999595), Bayswater (325 1000 in Perth, 325 3533 in Fremantle) and Swan Car Rentals (368 Guildford Road, Bayswater; 271 4813). Thrifty Rent-a-Car (126 Adelaide Terrace; 325 4700) offers special deals in Western Australia including a YHA discount. For trips further afield, buying a car makes sense. Check the Saturday edition of the *West Australian*, which is packed full of car and van adverts. The registration fee in Western Australia for 6 months is about $110, which includes third party insurance.

Members of foreign motoring associations may use the services of the Royal Automobile Club of Western Australia (RAC), which has its headquarters at 228 Adelaide Terrace, Perth (421 4444). The 24-hour emergency breakdown service can be summoned by calling 325 0333. The RAC publishes a good selection of maps of Western Australia, including an excellent *Perth City and Suburbs* map, which is available at a discount to associate members. All tourists are welcome to call at the RAC's office.

Hitch-hiking. Avoid the temptation to start hitching on one of the short stretches of freeway out of Perth; hitch-hikers are not popular with the local police, who can issue $25 tickets if you stand on the freeway or an approach road. To gain access to the Great Eastern Highway (to Kalgoorlie), take the train to the outer suburb of Midland and then any bus 317 to 323 to a likely looking spot. For the Great Northern Highway north (to Geraldton, Broome and Darwin), take the train to Midland and walk out to the highway. To go south on the Albany Highway or the South Western highway, get the train to Armadale then bus 220, 230 or 235 a little further out to Byford. Given that long-distance journeys from Perth are daunting enough without the added unpredictability of hitch-hiking, you may prefer to arrange a lift in advance through hostel notice boards. To arrange a lift in a truck heading east to Adelaide, visit the Kewdale Hotel at 137 Kewdale Road in the suburb of that name (take bus 341 or 342), which is a favourite haunt of long-distance lorry drivers.

CITY TRANSPORT

All bus, suburban train and ferry services in the Perth area are operated by Transperth. It has information offices at the following locations where you can obtain free timetables and the *Transperth System Map* for $1: City Arcade, Hay St Mall Level; Wellington St Bus Station (adjacent to the train station) and Fremantle Town Hall Arcade. The Perth offices are open from 7.30am to 5.30pm Monday–Friday and 7.30 to 3pm on Saturdays. For telephone information about public transport services, dial 132213.

Not all buses from the city centre arrive at or leave from the Wellington St Bus Station; many serve St George's Terrace, Barrack St or William St, but departure points are clearly indicated on bus schedules. Most bus stops in the suburbs comprise an inconspicuous metre-high orange post and yellow bus stop markings on the road itself.

Perth has the best system of free buses in Australia. The Free Transit Zone is a scheme by which all travel within the inner city (bounded by Kings Park Road, Thomas St, Newcastle St in Northbridge, the Causeway and Barrack St Jetty) is free of charge. Free train travel is also permitted between City West and Claisebrook Road Station. In addition four free City Clipper routes cover the city centre, as far east as Barrack St and west to Milligan St. Pick up the free *Perth Free Transit Zone User Guide* from a Transperth office.

Fares range from 65c to $3.30 depending on the number of zones crossed. For all but the cheapest tickets, you are entitled to free transfers to buses or trains within 2 hours, with no need to continue in the same direction (so round trips are permitted). This transfer facility is so flexible, and the free buses so useful, that the Sightseer unlimited-travel ticket costing $4.60 (or $19.40 for 5 consecutive days) may not be worthwhile unless you plan to travel extensively all day. The Sightseer does, however, have the advantage of giving discounts on a range of attractions. These tickets can be bought from Transperth Information offices. For longer stays, you can buy monthly tickets or 'multiriders', giving ten rides for the price of nine. Multiriders can be purchased from Newspower newsagents throughout Perth or from the City Arcade and Fremantle Transperth offices.

Fremantle can be reached by numerous buses from St George's Terrace, but the suburban trains from Wellington St Train Station are faster. Trains run every 20 minutes during the day with a journey time of 35 minutes. The first train is at 5.45am Monday–Friday, 7.20am Saturday and 8am Sunday, with the last at 11.30pm except on Sundays when trains stop at 7.30pm. There are three other train lines, to Midland, Armadale and Currambine.

You should buy your train ticket before boarding from ticket vending machines located on all train stations (except Leighton and North Fremantle). Alternatively multi riders can be purchased and validated from ticket validating machines at stations. The fine for attempting to avoid payment is up to $100.

Ferries. A 10-minute cruise (costing 65c) across the Swan River from the Barrack St Jetty at the south of the city centre gives fine views of Perth. The ferry will take you to South Perth where the zoo is located just a 5-minute walk from the jetty. A 3-hour cruise takes you to the upper reaches of the Swan River past the Burswood Casino and the 1839 homestead Tranby House. Departures from

Barrack St Jetty take place daily except Saturdays from September to May at 2pm and cost $12. For further information ring the Ferries Office on 425 2651.

Several commercial cruise companies have offices at Barrack St Jetty. Their cruises cost between $40 and $50. One of the most popular is Boat Torque's tour of the Swan River Vineyards departing from Pier 4 (see *Drinking* below). Ferries to Rottnest Island (see *Further Afield*) sail downstream along the Swan River before reaching the ocean beyond Fremantle. The route passes the suburb of Dalkeith, home of the rich and famous (or the once-rich).

Tram. Both Perth and Fremantle have motor vehicles dressed up to resemble trams, but they run on ordinary streets rather than tracks. The Perth Shuttle (367 9404) is a tourist bus that runs around the city (and out to the Burswood Resort Casino) and allows you to complete the circuit, getting on and off as often as you wish, for $9. The Fremantle Tram provides sightseeing tours of the port.

Bicycle. Perth is a Mecca for cyclists. Cycleways abound, and you can ride for long stretches without encountering motorised traffic. The cycleways along the river are particularly attractive, but watch out for pedestrians. Fremantle has a pleasant foreshore cycleway running along the oceanside. Except between 6am–9am and 3pm–6pm on weekdays, you can take your bicycle on suburban trains for a cost of $1.10; at peak times, you have to obtain a permit from Transperth in advance.

Among the hire outfits in Perth are Riverside Cycle Hire at Nedlands Jetty (end of Broadway, Nedlands; 317 1354); Ride Away (275 2320) at the No. 4 Car Park on Riverside Drive (near the Causeway); and East Perth Bicycle Hire (325 6095), who promise to deliver a bicycle to your hotel or hostel within an hour of your call. Make sure any bike you ride is fitted with a bell, as this is a legal requirement in Western Australia.

A company called West Coast Cycle Tours takes small groups on cycling tours of Perth and Fremantle.

Taxis. Perth's taxi drivers have long been renowned among experienced travellers as the most honest and helpful anywhere; for example, it is common for a driver to switch off the meter when approaching an unfamiliar destination to save you paying while he traces the exact address. The standing charge is $1.90 ($2.90 from 6pm to 6am and at weekends) plus 75c per kilometre. If you want to travel outside the city limits (a highly expensive exercise given the extent of the suburbs) you must pay a higher 'country rate' and a 'befouling fee' of $15 if the cab gets dirty.

The wide streets and substantial traffic in Perth make it difficult to flag down taxis in the street, but taxi ranks are scattered liberally throughout the city and in Fremantle. The big hotels have courtesy phones outside. To summon a cab on an ordinary telephone, dial Swan on 322 0111, Black & White on 328 8288 or Green & Gold on 328 3311. In Fremantle, call Swan on 335 3944.

Car. If you have made the journey across the Nullarbor or along Highway 1 from Darwin, you may find the busy roads of Perth difficult to cope with. Freeways extend more deeply into Perth than most other cities, and the tangle of freeways and slip roads west of the city centre can be confusing. However, traffic in the metropolitan area flows fairly freely, and signposting is not at all bad. The roads along the Swan River give breathtaking views.

Despite the good roads, distances in the metropolitan area can be long, and outlying suburbs can be an hour away from the centre during rush hours. To find your way around the sprawl, the RAC map mentioned above is good but you may wish to buy a street atlas: either the ubiquitous *Gregory's* or the *MSD (Metro Street Directory)*.

Some freeways into Perth have a contraflow lane for city-bound buses during the morning rush hour, so outbound drivers should beware. Within the city centre there is a rule forbidding reversing a car during business hours. Note that broad zig-zag white lines on the road indicate a pedestrian crossing ahead.

Downtown street parking is either metered or pay-and-display; the old voucher system of having to buy a voucher in advance from a newsagent is being phased out. The City Council runs a number of car parks costing an average of $1 an hour except in long-term car parks. The Parking Department at 25 Barrack St (265 3184) publishes a free brochure *A Visitor's Guide to Easy Parking in Perth*, which includes a list of all the downtown car parks.

Many petrol stations in Perth are now open 24 hours, so it shouldn't be too hard to find petrol at any time.

Accommodation

If you arrive at Perth airport without a room for the night, the accommodation desk will book a bed for you. The Western Australia Tourist Centre publishes a fairly thorough *Accommodation Listing* each April plus several other specific brochures on pub accommodation, caravan parks, etc. The amount of accommodation in Perth and Fremantle increased dramatically for the America's Cup, and now there are a lot of empty rooms and so special deals are often available.

Hostel Accommodation. The city's three YHA hostels are all in Northbridge and are very busy in the summer. If you plan to visit Perth you should try to book ahead by contacting the YHA office at 236 William St (227 5122) or any YHA hostel in Australia. The largest hostel is Britannia International at 253 William St (328 6121), which is on the airport bus route. Dorm beds start at $14, and it also has a travel agency. Northbridge YHA is at 42–46 Francis St (between Lake and William Sts; 328 7794), and has beds from $13. Cheaper still is Newcastle YHA at 60–62 Newcastle St (east of Pier St Junction; 328 1135), which includes free breakfast in the overnight fee (from $12). There is also a YHA hostel in the beachside area of Scarborough Beach, 15 minutes drive from the city or on bus route 400 (which runs to and from Perth every 20 minutes). It is at Mandarin Gardens, 20–28 Wheatcroft St (341 5431). Cheapest dorm beds are $13, but private rooms and self-contained apartments are also available.

There are also several VIP Backpackers hostels in Perth. Rory's Backpackers is at 194 Brisbane St, north of Northbridge (328 9958), and is in an old colonial house with wide verandahs. East Perth Backpackers (221 1666) is at 195 Hay St East and has beds from $10. Two in Northbridge are City Backpackers (corner Newcastle and Beaufort Sts; 328 7566) and Backpackers International (corner Lake and Aberdeen Sts; 227 9977), which has dorm beds for $10 and beds in twin rooms for $12. Western Beach Lodge is in Scarborough at 6 Westborough St (245 1624). Fremantle has a VIP Backpackers hostel called Ocean View Lodge at 100 Hampton Road (336 2962), which has beds in shared twin rooms for $12, as well as singles and doubles.

One of the best streets for hostel accommodation is Aberdeen St in Northbridge, where you will find Perth Travellers Lodge (numbers 156–158; 328 6667) and Aberdeen Lodge (numbers 79–81; 227 6137). A recommended city hostel is Cheviot Lodge (30 Bulwer St, Northbridge; 227 6817).

The YMCA has an upmarket hostel named Jewell House for women, men and families. It's located in a quiet central city location at 180 Goderich St (325 8488). Basic single rooms start at $20 a night, doubles at $38, triple and family rooms from $45. Weekly rates are also available.

Hotels and Motels. Most of the new hotels built to accommodate visitors to the America's Cup are most definitely upmarket. Two of the cheapest are the Grosvenor Hotel at 339 Hay St (325 3799) and the Grand Central Hotel at 379 Wellington St (325 5638). In Fremantle the Australia Tavern at 4 Edward St (335 2542) is also good value.

Homestays. The organisation Homestay of WA (40 Union Road, Carmel, WA 6076; 293 5347) arranges home and farm accommodation, bed and breakfast or self-catering units. In Fremantle contact Fremantle Homestay at 14 Herbert St (430 4000) where B & B rates start at $25 per person.

Camping. If you are prepared to get up early to avoid the attention of the police, there are several areas of greenery outside the city centre where you could risk pitching a tent. To keep within the law, try the sites at Scarborough, Sorrento or the Fremantle Village & Chalet Centre.

In the rest of the state it is possible to camp provided you either have permission of the landowner or are not within 16km of a caravan or camp site. Fines are occasionally levied, so it is always worth making enquiries before stopping in what you think is the middle of nowhere.

Eating and Drinking

Bill Bailey, an English-born journalist, once said that Perth's cuisine consisted of 'steak, eggs and salad or eggs, steak and salad'. Things have changed since then and Perth now has a fine range of restaurants, and a choice of cuisines covering almost every nationality. If you intend to do much eating out in Perth and Fremantle, invest in the annual *Cheap Eats in Perth*.

If you like Australian burgers, visit Fast Eddy's on the corner of Murray and Milligan Sts. This is probably the best-known burger place in Perth and is open 24 hours a day. On a Friday and Saturday night it can also be quite an experience for viewing 'alternative' parking arrangements, as customers double- and triple-park their vehicles.

About a quarter of Perth's restaurants are Thai, Malaysian, Chinese or Vietnamese. There are numerous Southeast Asian-style food centres in Perth. One of the most popular is the Sunmarket Centre, down an alley off the corner of Murray and Barrack Sts; meals normally range from $5–8. There are new food markets in Northbridge where you can sample food from a number of stalls. For very cheap Malaysian food, try Hawkers Hut at 150 Oxford St, Leederville, which is popular with Southeast Asian students, and Bibik Chan's Satay House at 134b Stirling Highway.

Granary Wholefoods at 37 Barrack St serves brilliant vegetarian lunches for $10 including home-made ice cream.

Northbridge (which is located as the name suggests, just to the north of the horseshoe bridge over the railway at Perth Railway station) contains the highest concentrations of trendy restaurants all vying for the best interior design award (and the worst-dressed staff). There are popular and inexpensive restaurants serving Spanish, Chinese, Indian, French, Lebanese, Italian, Yugoslavian, Greek, Macedonian, Vietnamese, Japanese and Mexican cuisine. Worth mentioning are the Fishy Affair (seafood), 121 James St, Hawker's Paradise (Malaysian), 134 William St, Phuong Huang (Vietnamese), 147 Beaufort St, and Los Gallos

(Mexican), 276 William St. After dinner you can go out to a late night café such as L'Alba at 100 Lake St (which also serves cheap pasta meals) or take advantage of the lively local nightlife.

Perth city centre has many upmarket restaurants with panoramic views; some of the best if you want to splash out are the Room with a View at 18 Esplanade, Hana of Perth (Japanese) on Mill St, and Hilite 33 (French) on Level 33 of the Martin Tower at 44 St George's Terrace; like most revolving restaurants, Hilite offers better views than food.

Fremantle has numerous excellent restaurants and cafés especially along South Terrace. 'Old Papas' has excellent foccacia sandwiches and sweets, and is a place where people go to be seen. The Sail and Anchor pub (see *Drinking*) has good food, both snacks and meals. Among the upmarket places, the most famous are Lombardo's, Sea Shells and Harbour Lights; Sea Shells is the most informal. Kailis Seafood Takeaway (also on the waterfront) is dramatically cheaper, and sells everything from squid 'n' chips to pineapple fritters.

Other areas with good restaurants are West Perth/Subiaco and the suburbs of Claremont, Nedlands and Cottesloe. In Subiaco, the road for restaurant browsing is Rokeby Road, with a Thai restaurant at the corner of Bagot St, Bar Bzar at number 1, El Gringo Mexican at 13 and Little Lebanon at 357. Or have a drink at Oriel's Café where they offer newspapers to patrons.

DRINKING

Basic licensing hours are 9am-11pm from Monday to Saturday, and any six hours on Sundays between 11am and 7pm. Bottle shops are allowed to open 8.30am-8.30pm daily except Sunday. Many pubs have more liberal licences permitting later opening and nightclubs can and do stay open all night. The only drinking hole which has a 24 hour licence is the bar at the Burswood Casino, which is resented by the hotel trade. Furthermore the Casino bar can afford to sell pub-priced drinks, which makes it tough competition.

The Perth/Fremantle area is good territory for real ale drinkers. Perth is the home of the acclaimed Matilda Bay Brewing Co whose range of excellent real ales are available in a number of Perth pubs as well as the eastern states. Its most famous products are Dogbolter (a dark beer) and Redback, which has far more flavour than the average Australian beer. The original pub-brewery in Australia which serves these and other beers is the celebrated pub-brewery the Sail and Anchor at 64 South Terrace, opposite the markets in Fremantle. It brews a Traditional Bitter, Brass Monkey Stout (for those who consider Guinness too light a beer) and Iron Brew (a strong ale of around 7%). Their menu is original though not cheap. A pint of Traditional Bitter and a Cornish pastie will set you back $6. The upstairs Brasserie has good food at restaurant prices with suggestions for which beer to drink with each dish.

Also in Fremantle, His Lordship's Larder Pub and Brewery at the corner of Mouat and Phillimore Sts sells a variety of bitters plus Old Fremantle Stout. The lunch specials here are good value and include a half-pint of your chosen tipple. The Norfolk Hotel at 47 South Terrace has restful decor and newspapers to read. The Brewery Alehouse at 145 Stirling Highway, Nedlands (halfway between Perth and Fremantle) also serves Matilda Bay beers.

The young of Perth are remarkably fickle in their drinking habits and quite spoilt for choice. The places to go at the moment are the Queens at 520 Beaufort St, Highgate, the Brass Monkey on William St in Northbridge and the Lookout Bar at the Observation City resort at Scarborough Beach. Also on the beach is the Ocean Beach Hotel ('OBH') in Cottesloe; obviously these venues are most popular in the summer. A long lasting favourite is the Nedlands Park Hotel (better known as 'Steve's') at 171 Broadway in Nedlands. This is a popular

University pub, with live bands and an excellent garden atmosphere with a do-it-yourself barbecue.

Wine enthusiasts may want to visit some of the wineries near Perth or further afield in the Southwest. Houghton wines are the best known Western Australian wine abroad and the winery on the Swan River can be visited. Boat Torque Cruises (325 6033) runs day-long winery cruises on the Swan which are bibulous affairs; the cost is $45.

Tall buildings have sprouted up in the city centre, so it is difficult to recommend the best candidate for an all-round view. The panorama from the revolving Hilite Restaurant mentioned above is breathtaking, but is strictly for diners: the lift doors open onto the dining area, so surreptitious view-stealing is not feasible. Rather than go up a building, it is better to take free bus 33 to Kings Park which has a commanding position overlooking the river and city and where you can have a barbecue (firewood supplied). The Mount Eliza lookout in Kings Park is a solid metal tower with splendid views, but if you are at all afraid of heights the wide open spaces between the steps to the top could be a bit off-putting.

There are still many reminders of earlier days dotted around Perth, one of the best being the Old Mill just over the Narrows Bridge in South Perth. This flour mill built in 1835 has been restored and contains interesting relics of the pioneer years (open afternoons except Tuesday and Friday). Another notable flour mill is the Dingo Mill just outside Fremantle on the Stirling Highway, whose advertising sign was painted by Alan Bond on one of his first assignments after arriving from Britain; although the mill's name has changed to Great Southern, the sign remains as a stimulus — and warning — to other would-be millionaires.

Fremantle has numerous places of interest, notably the Round House at the west end of the High St. This 12-sided building was originally built in 1831 as a gaol, and later used as a staging post for holding Aboriginals on their involuntary journey to Rottnest Island. It now opens daily from 10am to 5pm to allow visitors to see the cells in which up to 15 prisoners at a time were confined.

Museums and Galleries. Because Perth is such an active sporting city, its museums and galleries are often overlooked. Close to the station in Perth's Cultural Centre is the Art Gallery of Western Australia (328 7233) on James St which opens daily 10am–5pm. It has lively and frequently changing exhibitions mainly of contemporary art. Nearby is the Western Australia Museum on Francis St (328 4411) with an Aboriginal gallery, veteran and vintage cars, meteorites, mammal and wildlife displays. It opens at 10.30am Monday-Thursday, and 1pm Friday-Sunday; closing time is 5pm daily. Admission is free to both of these.

Fremantle has its fair share of museums and galleries. The Arts Centre at 1 Finnerty St is in a renovated lunatic asylum which has a museum wing with informative displays on whaling and pearling as well as a gallery for contemporary Western Australian art and other facilities. (If you're going to be around for some time, you can take advantage of the numerous reasonably priced courses they offer, from paper-making to jewellery crafting.) Two museums will be of interest to lovers of the sea: the Western Australia Maritime Museum in Cliff St and Rolly Tasker's America's Cup Museum, 43 Swan St, North Fremantle with its collection of model yachts from the first America's Cup race in 1851 through to the present day.

Beaches. The ocean beaches have white sand and clear blue water. Going north from Fremantle Harbour, the most popular are Port Beach (near North Fremantle), Cottesloe ('Cott'), the nude beach at Swanbourne, City Beach, Scarborough and Trigg. They are mostly safe, although the heavy breakers at Scarborough (which make surfing there excellent) can be dangerous to the inexperienced; and the rocks near Trigg have a permanent rip current. The ocean beaches can get very crowded, especially as many office workers like to come down to the beach after finishing work. For more details pick up the free *Guide to Perth's Beaches* from the tourist office.

On the river, which suffers no pollution, there are several small beaches which are safe for swimming. Try Crawley, Nedlands or Peppermint Grove on the north bank, and South Perth, Canning Bridge, Como or Applecross on the South Shore. The river is usually a hive of activity: windsurfing, waterskiing and sailing are among the participation sports.

Parks and Zoos. Kings Park is one of the finest in Australia, with panoramic views over the Swan River and city centre. Much of it is still in the native state, with wild flowers abounding in spring: orchids, freesias and 'kangaroo paws', the state emblem. There are special display greenhouses for desert and tropical flora. Ring 321 4801 to find out about guided tours. Look out also for exotic birds such as flocks of black parrots and the colourful green parrot known as 'twenty-eight'.

Closer to the city centre there are some more formal parks: Hyde Park, Stirling Gardens, Perth's botanical gardens located near the city centre, and the Supreme Court Gardens which host outdoor concerts in the summer. Down on the Esplanade the Alan Green Conservatory houses a wide variety of tropical and semi-tropical plants. Queens Park, on the corner of Plain and Hay Sts, has some beautiful lakes and is quite romantic. Lake Monger in Wembley is a lovely lake with wild ducks, black swans and other birdlife.

Perth Zoo consists of 40 acres of exotic and native Australian fauna in naturalistic habitat environments surrounded by landscaped gardens. The zoo is not far from the river in South Perth (20 Labouchere Road; 367 7988) and can easily be reached by ferry from the Barrack St Jetty. Among the highlights are a very successful breeding colony of orang-utans and a display of the rare Australian marsupial the numbat which is threatened with extinction.

SHOPPING

Normal hours are 8.30am-5pm from Monday to Saturday (with late opening to 9pm on Thursdays). Hay St Mall and Forrest Place are the two premier shopping areas. There is a network of underground and covered passages connecting downtown shopping centres (which hardly seems necessary in the Perth climate). The Hay St Mall extends to include Murray St, Barrack St and William St, with numerous arcades branching off. Tourists are steered towards 'Perth's historic centre', a highly-commercialised arcade known as Ye Olde London Court with touristy shops selling souvenirs such as tins of 'Fremantle Doctor', containing only air. Outside the city centre there are lots of American-style suburban malls (as everybody in Perth drives). The suburb with the most classy designer shops is Claremont.

There is a good selection of Aboriginal art and handicraft shops. For example Creative Native at 32 King St sells unusual carved boab nuts and painted emu eggs. The National Trust shop, just along the Terrace at 139 is also interesting. The shop Purely Australian in the Hay St Mall specialises in colourful but not tasteless T-shirts from $12. Many goods are cheaper at one of the out-of-town weekend markets. At the Fremantle Markets, there is a small amount of junk and trash among the good stuff plus a superb range of fruit and vegetables.

There are two markets in Subiaco, the Station St Market which is partly undercover and Subiaco Pavilion at 2 Rokeby Road which features an international food hall. The other markets are further afield, for example the Crescent in Midland which is modelled on a London street market.

The reliably fine weather of Perth adds a certain sparkle to most activities, whether swimming, seeing an outdoor concert or simply strolling around town. Although the heat in summer can sometimes feel excessive, summer is certainly the best time to enjoy the performing arts, as the Festival of Perth takes place in February and March. While lacking the international cachet of the festivals in Adelaide and Sydney, the city puts on an extensive programme of music, theatre and exhibitions, often with outdoor performances (including Australia's only outdoor film festival held in an amphitheatre surrounded by trees on the UWA campus).

Perth's computerised ticketing agency for theatre productions and concerts is BOCS on 484 1133. It's always worth asking about special offers on student tickets as many theatres offer bargain-priced student day-of-performance tickets.

Theatre. The centre of Perth's theatrical world is His Majesty's Theatre, a carefully restored Edwardian building on the corner of King and Hay Sts (322 2929). Ticket prices can be high for the major touring productions it hosts such as imports from New York.

The State Theatre Company of Western Australia is resident at the Subiaco Theatre Centre (180 Hamersley Road, Subiaco) just five minutes from the city centre. The company present an extensive year-round programme in the Centre's two venues, the Hole in the Wall Theatre and the intimate Studio Theatre. Also in Subiaco there is the Regal Theatre (474 Hay St; 381 1557) which hosts commercial theatre attractions and concerts. It is unusual in having a 'crying room' which enables mothers with fractious young children to watch the show through a window without disturbing the rest of the audience.

In the city the Playhouse Theatre at 3 Pier St (325 3500) hosts a variety of drama and dance. The Black Swan Theatre Company, based at the University of Western Australia, is a professional company which is developing an impressive track record with new approaches to classic works as well as nurturing Aboriginal writers. There are three theatres on the University campus, the Octagon, the Dolphin and the New Fortune. The latter is an exact replica of Shakespeare's Fortune Theatre in London; ring 325 3399 for University theatre information. Swy Theatre Company at 55 Murray St (325 8440) presents new Australian and foreign plays.

In Fremantle the Deck Chair theatre company (8A Phillimore St; 336 2372) presents locally inspired and written productions and Spare Parts Puppet Theatre (1 Short St; 335 5044) puts on shows which are of interest not only to children.

Cinema. Drive-in cinemas are extremely popular in the suburbs of Perth, and there are nearly a dozen screens. As well as numerous suburban cinemas, the centre of Perth has many cinema complexes. Details of all films are shown in the *West Australian* or you can ring 0055 14632.

Hoyts Centre, St Martins Arcade, 645 Hay St Mall (325 4992).

Hoyts Cinema City, corner Hay and Barrack Sts (325 2377).

Greater Union Cinecentre, corner Murray and Barrack Sts (325 2844).

"THE THEATRE HAS A CRYING ROOM FOR MOTHERS WITH FRACTIOUS CHILDREN"

Greater Union Town Cinema, 776 Hay St (321 2747).
Lumiere Entertainment Centre, Perth Entertainment Centre, Wellington St (321 1575); now the home of the Film and Television Institute.
Omni — The Big Screen, Railway Parade (481 6481).
Also some excellent inner suburban cinemas that show first releases and quality films are the Astor in Mount Lawley (corner Beaufort and Walcott Sts; 370 1777), the New Oxford in Leederville (corner Vincent and Oxford Sts; 444 4056) and the Windsor in Nedlands (98 Stirling Highway; 386 3554). The beautiful open-air cinema, the Somerville Auditorium on the UWA campus is used mostly during the Perth Festival.

Music. The economics of major-league rock music seem to dictate that Perth often misses out on the world tours of top musicians, simply because it is so far from anywhere.

The Perth Entertainment Centre is on Wellington St close to the city centre, and is a thoroughly modern multi-purpose auditorium and Perth's only real venue for big rock concerts. The relatively small seating capacity of 8000 means that for popular acts it is quite often booked up very early. All ticketing is done through Red Tickets on 484 1222. For information on upcoming performances, look in the *Revue* section of the *West Australian* on Thursdays.

The best places to see local bands are the larger-venue pubs in Northbridge such as the Aberdeen at 84 Aberdeen St and others mentioned under *Drinking.* Other trendy places to try are the Left Bank on Riverside Drive in East Fremantle and the Duck Inn in Subiaco (corner Rowland and Barker Sts). Perth bands to watch out for include Body Motors and the Sunbeams.

You can hear Country music at the Manning Hotel, 27 Manning Road, and Irish folk bands at the lively Irish Club, 61 Townshend Road, Subiaco (381 5213) which is also a good place to go for a drink.

The Concert Hall at 3 St George's Terrace is Perth's principal concert venue and home to the Western Australia Symphony Orchestra. Phone BOCS for ticket information. Free concert performances are presented at the Subiaco Theatre Centre on Sunday afternoons and in the gardens at twilight on Fridays and/or Saturdays during summer.

Nightlife. Perth has many nightclubs especially in Northbridge and in the city centre. In the city try Gobbles at 613 Wellington St and the Limbo Club at 232 William St. Clubs which consider themselves casual but chic include the Exit Nightclub at 187 Stirling St in the city and Havana at 69 Lake St, Northbridge. If you fancy a bop, head for Coronados at 206 Stirling Highway in Claremont, the Shenton Park Hotel at 207 Nicholson Road, Subiaco or various places in Northbridge like the Palladium, the Aberdeen or Network. For the most avant garde music in Perth go to the Berlin Club, 89 Milligan St in Northbridge. Christies nightclub in Fremantle is one of the many which caters to the beautiful yachting fraternity; it gets very crowded on Sundays.

Gambling. The Burswood Island Resort is situated in 275 acres of parkland by the Swan River, between the city and the airport. Although it has a range of restaurants and bars, the main attraction is the Casino; with 142 gambling tables it is one of the largest in the world, and is open 24 hours a day. The dress rules require you to be reasonably smart and you may well have to queue to get in, but you can still spend an interesting evening at the smaller stake tables, where the minimum bet is $2.

SPORT

Spectator Sports. Major sporting events are often ticketed through Red Tickets on 484 1222. Cricket and harness-racing can be seen close to the centre of Perth. The Western Australia Cricket Association ground (more commonly known as the WACA, pronounced 'wacka') is just east of the city centre and is the venue for Test cricket, one-day internationals and Sheffield Shield matches. Just along from the WACA is Gloucester Park (325 8822), the home of the Western Australian Trotting Association which holds meetings most Friday evenings. The highlight of the season is the Benson and Hedges Cup each January. You can also see harness-racing at Richmond Raceway in East Fremantle (339 2535). Horseracing takes place at the Ascot course in summer (the highlight being the Perth Cup on New Year's Day) and Belmont Park in winter, and the greyhounds race at the Cannington Raceway on Albany Highway (458 4600).

Australian Rules Football is played at venues all over Perth every weekend in winter. The only Western Australian team in the premier VFL is the Eagles, who play at the WACA Oval and at Subiaco. If, however, you pick one of the less well-known clubs you will be able to sit on the grassy banks that often form the 'grandstands', enjoy a beer and sunbathe.

The new Superdrome on Stephenson Avenue in Mount Claremont (387 8044) features basketball, gymnastics and water sports.

Participation. Watersports abound in Perth. You can hire windsurfers, waterskis and so on, from various beachside dealers including Surfscene in North Cottesloe (381 2815) and Santosha in Scarborough Beach (341 6843). Surfcats are rented out on the river by several operators on Coode St, South Perth. The Cable Ski Park in Troode St, Spearwood is also good fun: water-skiers are transported around the Park's waterways by means of a cable tow rope. Skis, life jackets and wet suits are all available, as is instruction for beginners. Information on diving, especially around the offshore islands, can be obtained from the Underwater Federation (GPO Box T1789, Perth). *Get Wet News* is the local newspaper for watersport fans.

Elsewhere around Perth the climate makes outdoor sports fun, even for the most indolent of visitors, who feels inclined to resist the keep-fit mentality of west coasters. Perth inhabitants regularly jog along Riverside Walk or in Kings Park where there are also tennis courts. Among the host of other courts around the city, the University of WA has about a dozen, which are busy in term-time but are hired out to visitors during the vacation for $2 per hour. Perth has several golf courses, but for the less able there is a miniature 18-hole Botanic Golf Course at 25 Burns Beach Rd, Wanneroo (405 1475), reached by bus 348 from the Wellington St bus station. The five-acre landscaped course includes waterfalls, ornamental pools and exotic gardens, and a round costs $7.

THE MEDIA

Newspapers. The only morning daily is the *West Australian*, a bulky tabloid with an entertainment pull-out (*Revue*) on Thursdays.

Radio. The ABC networks are 6WF (702 AM), 6WN (810 AM) and ABC-FM, the only 24-hour service in town. The most popular rock stations are 96FM which issues a gig guide and 6PM FM. The Curtin University station is 6NR (927 AM); it broadcasts ethnic programmes in the evening, predominantly in Scandinavian and Baltic languages.

Television. Perth has four TV stations. Viewers in outlying areas of Western Australia can watch satellite transmissions on the Golden West Network (GWN), providing they have the right receiving equipment; many roadhouses and hotels are suitably equipped.

As in most Australian cities, you may encounter the odd brawl usually due to excessive drinking, but it is normally easy to avoid getting involved. Perth is relatively free of crime and there are few areas where you will feel uncomfortable late at night. Jay-walking can incur an on-the-spot fine. For non-urgent calls to the police, dial 222 1111 (2 Adelaide Terrace, Perth) or 335 4555 (Fremantle). Prostitution has been legalised in Western Australia, although brothels are not permitted in residential areas. If Perth could be said to have a red light district it is in Northbridge.

To help you steer clear of the perils of sunburn, smoke-filled restaurants, sexually transmitted diseases, etc. the Western Australian government has produced a *Health Guide for Tourists* which is free from tourist offices. One risk it fails to mention is the habit of the native magpies to attack people, particularly picnickers, during the spring nesting season.

The area code for Perth and Fremantle is 09. In an emergency, dial 000.

The main tourist information bureau is the Western Australian Tourist Centre in Albert Facey House, Forrest Place (483 1111; toll-free throughout Australia 1800-812 808).

Giveaway tourist magazines for Perth and Fremantle include *This Week in ...*, *What's On in ...*, and *Your Guide to ...* The area has a network of electronic information points known as Infowest. These computer terminals are dotted around tourist haunts within the city and out at the airport. At the press of several buttons, you can get a display and print-out of current events, restaurants, entertainment and so on. The drawback is that many machines appear to be permanently out of order, and those that work are often monopolised by addicts of varying degrees of computer literacy. Fremantle has its own telephone information service: Freo-Info, on 335 7652.

British Consulate-General: Prudential Building, 95 St George's Terrace (321 5611).
American Express: 51 William St (233 1177); 177 High St, Fremantle (335 7977).
Thomas Cook: Shop 16, Wesley Centre, 93 William St (321 2896); 119 High St, Fremantle (335 3111).
General Post Office: 3 Forrest Place (326 5211).
Disabled Travellers: ACROD Access Committee — 222 2961.
Medical Treatment: Royal Perth Hospital, Wellington St (325 0101); Fremantle Hospital, Alma St (335 0111).
Women's Information and Referral Exchange (WIRE): 32 St George's Terrace (222 0444).
Helplines: Poison Information — 381 1177; Sexual Assault Centre — 389 3333; State Emergency Service — 277 5333.

In December 1995 the rate of unemployment in Western Australia was one of the lowest in the country. If you are not over-fussy, you should be able to find some way to earn money within a few weeks of arriving. And there are still various agricultural opportunities scattered throughout the state. Unless you have a working holiday visa you should tread warily. Ever since the time of the America's Cup, the Perth immigration authorities have been on the warpath to discourage foreigners from working illegally.

Sources of Work. The main Perth office of the CES (206 Adelaide Terrace) is probably not as useful as the Hospitality office on the first floor of 186 St George's Terrace (322 6155), which handles catering jobs. It is worth having a look at the cards on display in both offices. Also the suburban branches of the CES are smaller and more relaxed, and usually have more time to be helpful. If you can establish a rapport with the staff, your chances of finding work are improved. One of the best centres for casual work in Perth is the Innaloo Job Centre at 384 Scarborough Beach Road (244 1551), which provides a service for employers so that they can lodge requests for labour at any time. These jobs are offered on a first-come, first-served basis, so aim to get to the office before it opens at 7.30am. If you are not immediately successful, it is worth hanging around until mid-morning, as some employers prefer to walk in and take a look at possible recruits. If you still have no luck, at least it's only 20 minutes to the beach for the afternoon.

The *West Australian* is also a good source of jobs, particularly on Wednesday mornings. It is possible to get a copy in the city centre on Tuesday evenings, which is recommended as jobs for building labourers, etc. often commence at 6am and you should call as early as possible. It's also worth looking in the Saturday edition. Few of Perth's pubs and restaurants advertise in the newspaper, so ask in person; the best opportunities for bar and waiting staff are in the city centre, Northbridge and Fremantle areas.

Agriculture. Opportunities in agriculture are concentrated in three areas: the south-east around Donnybrook, the area around Carnarvon north of Perth, and the irrigation project in the far north around Kununurra.

Many travellers continue to fare well in the harvests centred on Donnybrook, Pemberton and Manjimup. Farmers ring the associate YHA hostel in Donnybrook (Brook Lodge, Bridge St; 097-311 520; from $11 per night or $70 per week) throughout the year but especially between November and May, with the peak of the apple harvest falling in the autumn. The manager runs a list system — if you want work you sign the list on arrival and usually your name gets to the top within 3 days. Despite immigration hassles, farmers prefer to hire overseas young people than unreliable drifting Aussies. There is a very friendly hotel in Donnybrook that is a good place to meet farmers (and also to enjoy happy hours and free Sunday barbecues). Pemberton has an official YHA hostel (Pimelea Chalets, Stirling Road; 097-761 153), which also helps guests to find seasonal fruit-picking work at most times of the year. Beds start at $12.

Lemons and grapefruit can be picked around Bindoon (about 80km north of Perth) from November to February, while the orange and mandarin harvests finish in early October. Grapes for Western Australia's excellent wines are picked from February to April in the main wine-producing areas of the Swan Valley near Perth and, further south, Margaret River and Mount Barker, though there are few reports of itinerant pickers being hired for these harvests.

If you are heading north, there are over 100 plantations around the city of Carnarvon, which grow mainly tomatoes and bananas but also peas, cucumbers, pumpkins and other vegetables. The tomato harvest lasts from early August until mid-November, with the month of September being the easiest time to find work. The banana harvest starts in October, but there is casual work available anytime between April and November. The hourly pay is $8 or $9, which is taxed at a lower rate than elsewhere in Australia as Carnarvon is north of the 26th parallel (see the introductory chapter *Work*). Weekly accommodation discounts are offered by the Carnarvon YHA hostel (099-412966) while the Accommodation Centre is about $10 a week cheaper. Be warned that temperatures above 35°C are common in this area. This is such a well known area for casual workers that immigration raids are not unknown. The stretch of coast from Carnarvon to Broome has some prawn fishing opportunities from March to October.

The area around Kununurra in the extreme north of the state *en route* to Darwin is another area where travellers are regularly hired during the first part of The Dry (May to July). If you can't fix up work through the YHA hostel or Kununurra Backpackers (091-681711), ring some of the following farms: Pacific Seeds (091-681172), Desert Seeds (682471), Bloecker (681305), Ord River Coop (682255), Ord River Bananas (681481) and Top Bananas (682418).

The busiest time for agricultural work in the Outback is April to June when the massive wheatfields that cover much of the southern state are seeded. For a job as 'Sheila of all trades' (mainly keeping the male workers supplied with tucker), you might get paid $200–250 a week plus free board and lodging. Several agencies in Perth deal with jobs in Outback areas of the state, primarily station and roadhouse work. Housekeepers and experienced farm hands and bar attendants should try Pollitt's Employment Agency (325 2544).

Mining. Many are tempted by the legendary high wages paid at the mines located in the inhospitable Pilbara region in northern Western Australia. But the employment situation is very tight, with union membership and some experience the usual prerequisites. If you do want to have a go, visit the offices of mining sub-contractors, which are concentrated in or near Mount Newman House at 200 St George's Terrace in Perth. The highest wages of all can be found in the offshore oil and gas industry at Dampier and Karratha, but for this work experience in oil is essential.

Although the gold mines around Kalgoorlie are still thriving, employment possibilities in survey and drilling crews have become more scarce. The accepted way of finding work in Kalgoorlie is to go around or phone all the relevant companies listed in the *Yellow Pages* or on the CES list of mines, drilling, surveying and lab companies. Exploration companies occasionally hire unskilled assistants (known as 'fieldies', 'TAs' or 'offsiders') who are sometimes sent into remote areas (like Leonora at the end of the sealed road heading north) where pay is $500 per week in the hand plus free caravan or motel accommodation. A truck driving licence is essential for this work, which is very easy to get, assuming you can afford the $200 fee for about three lessons and the test (in fact many offsiders don't do any driving). Most people work nearer town and earn about $10 an hour, with weekend work being particularly lucrative.

If your attempts to find work in the field fail, you can usually find a job (at lower pay) in mineral processing plants in Perth such as Analabs (50 Murray Road, Welshpool; 458 7999). The work, which pays about $10 an hour, involves the preparation of rock samples for analysis, a job that is dirty and monotonous.

Tourism. Partly due to the heroic efforts of the Western Australian Tourism Commission, tourism is one of the few expanding industries in the state and employment in tourism has grown faster than most industries in recent years. New charter flights from Europe to Perth have enticed more travellers to begin their vacation in Perth. The resort towns south of Perth are packed with hotels, campsites and cafés, which may be short of staff especially between November and February. In the tourist centres of the north, the tourist season corresponds to The Dry (May to September) and it may be worth enquiring about work in the 'New Gold Coast' around Broome or in Kununurra. A couple of years ago Broome was booming and there was a massive building programme, but that is now over and chances of finding work are not very good.

Obviously in a limited time it is not possible to see much of a state which is as large an area as Western Europe. If you are flying in and out of Perth, you will likely confine your travels to the southwest corner which includes the lovely coast south of Perth plus historic sites and natural features of considerable interest. On the other hand if you are making the journey through the state by land, you must choose between one of the great trans-continental highways, either north towards Darwin or east towards Adelaide.

Western Australia is known as the wildflower state. In many areas, but especially in the Southwest, the rains of winter encourage field upon field of wild flowers to bloom (see *Great Outdoors* below). Whale-watching has also come to the west coast. As many as 4,000 humpback whales travel south along the coast *en route* to Antarctica; the best time to look for them is November.

The YHA in connection with Travelabout 4WD Tours (27 Essex St, Perth; 387 6118) has a programme of adventure tours to the Pinnacles, Monkey Mia, the Southwest, etc. as well as some longer adventures to Alice Springs and the Kimberleys. These cost an average of $65 a day.

If you have no fixed ideas about where to go, you could take an Ansett WA 'mystery flight'; for $99 you book a same-day return ticket to somewhere which is revealed the day before you travel. You might end up in Kalgoorlie, Broome or any one of 13 destinations. You may even decide to view your investment (or gamble) as a cheap one-way flight and conveniently forget to return to Perth. Call Ansett on 323 1111 for more details. Skywest Airlines (478 9999/323 1188) also offers day trips to several destinations (of your choice) but these are much more expensive.

DAY TRIPS FROM PERTH

Travelling in any direction from Perth, including out to sea, brings you to places of interest, though the distances make some of the following day trips fairly strenuous.

Rottnest Island. There is nothing strenuous however about the two-hour ferry trip to Rotto as it is known (unless you suffer from seasickness). This small island about 20km offshore from Perth was famous as an Aboriginal prison between 1838 and 1903. Part of the old Rottnest gaol has become a resort development called the Quad instead of a museum as the Aboriginal lobby wanted.

Visitors go not so much for the history as to enjoy the beaches and the wildlife, by foot or on bicycle, as there are virtually no motorised vehicles. Bicycles can be easily hired from near the ferry jetty, and the 11km-long island can be encircled in three to four hours. You should have no trouble spotting a quokka, a unique member of the wallaby family which an early Dutch explorer mistook for giant rats; hence the name he gave the island in 1696. Neither will the quokkas have trouble spotting you if you have any food they want. The island was made a leisure reserve not long after the turn of the century, and so all wildlife and vegetation are protected. The presiding Rottnest Island Authority (372 9729) enforces the rules, including no campfires on the beach, no spear-fishing and no alcohol on the campsites (this latter to prevent the Perth adolescents who flock here on summer weekends from getting out of hand).

There is plenty of accommodation in case you decide to extend your stay, including tents and cabins for hire at Tentland (292 5033) which is currently engulfed in controversy as Aboriginals are claiming the land which was a mass burial site. The island specialises in self-catering flats and cottages which, like all the island's accommodation, are usually booked up in the school holidays. Daily ferry services operate from Perth's Barrack St Jetty via East St Jetty in Fremantle and also from Hillarys Boat Harbour in the northern suburb of Sorrento which cost a little less than the *Star Flyte* and take two hours. Rottnest Airlines has several flights each day, which give a splendid view of the city and river and cost $25 for a one-way standby ticket.

The Swan Valley. Just half an hour's drive from central Perth and a little past the airport are the 33 commercial wineries of the Swan Valley, many of them established in the mid 19th century. The Swan River flows alongside the historic towns of Guildford and Midland and on through the wineries with the Darling Range in the background to contribute to the picturesqueness. For information about cruises from Perth see the section above *Drinking*.

Many Yugoslavs settled along the banks of the Swan, just as they did in the wine-making Henderson Valley near Auckland. Consult the WA Tourist Centre pamphlet *The Swan Valley Guide* for a map of the region, opening times and descriptions of the wineries or ring the Swan Valley Tourist Bureau on 274 1522. The distances are manageable by bicycle though one drawback is that the Great Northern Highway, which links many of the wineries, is uncomfortably busy for cyclists.

The Heritage Committee has set up a Swan Valley Heritage Trail, designed for motorists, based on the latter part of Captain James Stirling's expedition up the Swan in 1827 and featuring the historical, Aboriginal and natural highlights.

The Beaches. If you want to venture further afield than the city beaches, you can travel north or south and as far as you like to find seaside resorts of varying character. Note that there are virtually no official nudist beaches apart from Warnbro South at Rockingham, which is a half hour's drive or bus ride south of Perth. Rockingham has long since been overtaken by Fremantle as the main port and is now a popular resort. One of the attractions is the short ferry ride from Mersey Point where fairy penguins can be seen on the beaches of Penguin Island in April and September-November (the island is closed May to August).

About the same distance north of Perth is Yanchep National Park with glorious ocean beaches as well as a large lake improbably named Loch McNess (after one Charles McNess who financed its dredging). The limestone caves called Crystal and Yonderup and various wildlife trails provide further interest.

Inland from Perth. The historic towns of the Avon Valley such as Toodyay (even the accepted pronunciation Toojay indicates its sleepiness), Northam and York can be done in a long day-trip by motor car, or if you are heading away from Perth they are worth a detour. These towns are on the Avon River (a major tributary of the Swan) whose fast-flowing waters are the scene of the annual Avon Descent Canoe Race held at the beginning of August. The Avon Valley is well provided with old restored buildings (including the three YHA hostels), local museums and congenial picnic areas. The town of York is Western Australia's oldest inland settlement, and visitors go there to see the well-preserved colonial architecture along the main street and to eat cream teas.

One of the most unexpected sights within range of Perth is the Benedictine settlement at New Norcia 135km north of Perth which was set up in 1846. It has a fine collection of books, artefacts and paintings, some of which were stolen in a daring raid a few years ago and later discovered, damaged, in Sydney Airport. There is a fascinating little museum (open daily 10am-4.30) and an imposing yet comfortable hotel (096-548034) where you can have lunch or stay overnight ($45 a double). The Benedictine Community is still active and you can buy the prize-winning olive oil or honey which they produce.

SOUTH OF PERTH

The *Australind* high speed train takes just two hours to get from Perth to Bunbury, the second largest town in the state (with a population of just 23,000). Alternatively South West Coach Lines (324 2333) departs at 7.45am, 1.30pm and 4.45pm daily from the Transperth Bus Station on Wellington St. The 1.30pm departure serves Margaret River, Donnybrook and other places as well.

The coast south of Perth is the most developed part of the state for holiday-makers, and there should be no difficulty finding accommodation in YHA hostels (all but a handful of the state's 23 hostels are in the Southwest), on campsites or in lodges.

The Coast. Mandurah, Busselton, Dunsborough and Augusta are all charming coastal resorts with plenty of amusements and amenities. The gateway town of Bunbury is a little too commercially prosperous to be an ideal resort whereas Busselton with its famous old two-kilometre wooden jetty and gentrified architecture is very pleasant. Do not drive straight down the coast road without stopping at places like Mandurah to try to catch a crab for dinner or in Yallingup to visit the caves or admire the fierceness of the surf which intimidates all but the most experienced of surfers. The gracious Caves House Hotel in Yallingup is especially recommended if you want to splash out on a night's accommodation ($75 double) and like a game of Scrabble around an open fire in the evening. Alternatively there is a summer YHA hostel here. The Post Office is attached to a general store and café which produces excellent food. Yallingup Caves with their fantastic stalactites were discovered by accident at the turn of the century and can now be toured for $5 ($3 students) assuming you are not likely to succumb to the stifling humidity.

Another beautiful Indian Ocean beach with a restored YHA hostel right on the beach is Quindalup near Dunsborough. The beaches between Perth and Cape Naturaliste are safe for swimming; thereafter care should be taken, though some places like Yallingup have coastal lakes and lagoons suitable for children. The whole coast is also lined with National Parks.

Turning the corner of the coast at Augusta, you can continue east though the road does not begin to follow the coast until you come to Walpole and the picturesquely sited Denmark. There are superb beaches nearby at William Bay and Ocean Beach, as well as a fauna sanctuary on Ocean Beach Road with a range of rare marsupials like the agile, the bettong and the darma (free admission).

Fifty kilometres further along the coastal road, and 400km along the direct route from Perth, is Albany which was established in 1826 and is the oldest settlement in the state (as opposed to York which is the oldest inland settlement). Like so many old coastal towns in the Antipodes, this was a whaling station, which now houses a rather small and uninformative whaling museum. The free Residency Museum on Residency Road is more worthwhile. The coastline around here is spectacular. The strange rock formations, eroded by the pounding seas include Blowholes (usually tame), the Dog Rock, so called because of its resemblance to a sniffing bloodhound (on the road to Middleton Beach) and the Natural Bridge and Gap, which are brilliant on a stormy day when the waves crash 20m up the rock. If conditions are calmer you might consider going out with skipper Les Bail, a friendly sea dog, to look for whales. Your chances are better of seeing kangaroos walking in this area.

Once again the road parts company with the coast and it is necessary to drive 470km before you reach the next coastal resort of Esperance, growing at a surprising rate given its remoteness. In addition to its wonderful seascapes, there is an interesting display in the Municipal Museum about the US Skylab (which burst into flames over Esperance on its descent from orbit). Only 3km from town is the Pink Lake, which in some weather conditions is coloured pink or even purple by the high concentration of salt. In the summer, there are cruises out among the 100 or so islands of the romantically-named Archipelago of the Recherche with its colonies of penguins and seals.

Wineries. In contrast to the mass-production wineries of the Swan Valley, winemakers around Margaret River, a small dairy town 270km south of Perth, are making wines of distinguished quality at rather high prices (although Cape Mentelle's produces cheap reds and whites in 1.5 litre bottles as well as quality wines). The excellent WA Tourist Centre pamphlet called *Vineyards of the South* has detailed maps of the area, with opening times, tastings and other facilities at the 18 wineries open to the public clustered in two areas just off Highway 10. The most famous of the vineyards is Leeuwin Estate (097-576253). It makes wines that thrill the experts and mounts publicity stunts that thrill everyone. One such was importing the entire London Symphony Orchestra to perform on the sloping lawns of the winery (apparently not quite drowning out the kookaburras) for their annual February concert extravaganza; this is Australia's answer to Glyndebourne. The short Leeuwin wine-tasting tour is informative (if a little condescending).

Wine lovers might also like to explore the Mount Barker area, where vineyards are more widely dispersed and the wineries relatively new. Mount Barker is a leisurely three-hour drive away from Margaret River through countryside which by Australian standards is rolling, green and reminiscent of England, especially the apple orchards around Pemberton. But the forests of giant karri trees, from which kangaroos are liable to hop at dusk, leave you in no doubt as to what country you are in.

The South-Western Interior. Several highways from Perth veer away from the coast and take you through forests of Western Australia's answer to the Califor-

"SYMPHONY ORCHESTRAS HAVE TO COMPETE WITH THE KOOKABURRAS"

nian redwood — the karri tree. Karris are a kind of blue gum, which grow tall and straight to magnificent heights. In the early days they were used for street paving and railway sleepers among other things (partly because white ants could make no inroads into the wood) but are now logged more discriminatingly. Karri is an Aboriginal word whose similarity to the Maori word kauri for the equally fine New Zealand conifer, also highly prized as a building hardwood, appears to be accidental.

The trees are especially beautiful in Spring, particularly October when they appear to arise from a sea of colourful wildflowers. If you have a good head for heights, you can even climb the giant Gloucester Tree near Pemberton, thought to be about 300 years old. A platform 61m above the ground is used as a fire lookout but visitors are permitted to climb up for the view. Not far away near Manjimup are four trees of similar age which stand in perfect single file formation. These can be best seen from Graphite Road, about a mile past One-Tree-Bridge.

The Pemberton YHA hostel is in fact 10km out of town and requires a certain fire-building skill if you are to be comfortable in winter; the comments book contains the advice: 'If you arrive in the morning and have a full tank of gas, drive straight on to Albany'. The craft shop in Pemberton featuring mainly wood carvings is superb. The Pemberton Tramway costs $11.50 ($2 YHA discount) though a free walk in the forest is probably more enjoyable.

Some distance east (just north of Albany and Mount Barker) is the Stirling Range National Park with weathered hills rising out of the flat plains. Bluff Knoll and Toolbrunup at 1000m are the only places in the state where snow falls. When the summer heat haze dispels, it is sometimes possible to see the ocean 70km away though you are more likely to see the interesting vegetation close at hand, including many of the primitive grass trees known as black boys (as they grow from what looks like fire-blackened stumps). The splendidly named Porongurup National Park nearby has stark granite domes, lush vegetation and more karri forests.

There are other wonders of nature in southern Western Australia. Pre-eminent among them is Wave Rock near Hyden (340km east of Perth) set among the sweeping wheat and barley 'paddocks' of the central part of the state. Whereas it may have required a little imagination to see the dog in the rock at Albany, it requires no effort to visualise a breaking wave in this giant rock, which is estimated to be 2700 million years old. It is worth exploring the other strangely eroded and ancient rocks in the vicinity, such as the Hippo's Yawn.

Apart from some Aboriginal rock carvings, the man-made wonders of the area pale a little in comparison. But if you are passing through the town of Wagin, self-proclaimed sheep capital of Western Australia, you are obliged to admire the nine-metre tall Giant Merino ram about which the rather modest claim is made: 'it would have to be at or near the top in the all-time world record book of giant rams' (no doubt a gripping publication if it existed).

EAST OF PERTH

The Nullarbor. The Nullarbor Plain is a remarkably desolate area of unrelievedly flat arid scrubland, the kind of landscape for which Australia is famed. The word is often misspelled, so try to remember that it derives from the Latin for no trees 'nul(l) arbor' (and ignore the fact that it is sometimes 'a bore'). Conservationists are trying to have the Nullarbor included on the World Heritage List of unique and precious environments, partly because of the enormous (and accessible) underground river. With luck some amazing sights might meet your eye if you brave the epic crossing by train or coach, such as seeing a dust storm on one side and a rare rainstorm on the other.

Although one might have expected the trans-Canada railway to hold the dubious honour of having the longest straight section of railway in the world, the Nullarbor takes the prize with its 480km stretch. Unlike the railway, the Eyre Highway (Highway 1) touches the coast of the Great Australian Bight at a few places on the South Australian side. The road is now thoroughly civilised with tourist facilities at frequent intervals, so it is not the Outback adventure it once was. Pick up a copy of the booklet *Across Australia* from the Tourist Centre. The map and facilities guide also provides a complete list of accommodation (and recommends pre-booking though this is unnecessary if you carry a tent), bars (with opening hours), food sources (minimal) and petrol stations. If driving at dawn or dusk keep a sharp lookout for wandering kangaroos, wombats, etc. Do not try to carry fruit over the South Australia-Western Australia border. If crossing in winter be prepared for disconcerting jumps in temperature from 5°C to 40°C and winds of up to 100km/h which can cause choking dust clouds.

The Goldfields. One of the last of the great Australian gold rushes brought hundreds of impoverished families to Kalgoorlie and its surroundings in 1893. They pushed wheelbarrows 500km from Perth only to die of thirst as there was no drinking water (a problem that was solved a decade later when a pipeline from the west was opened).

There are abandoned gold mines and gold rush towns throughout Australia and New Zealand. What distinguishes Kalgoorlie is that the gold boom continues or at least has been recently revived because of a rise in the world price of gold. In contrast to the picturesque ghost town of Coolgardie 29km away (the similarity of names can be confusing), Kalgoorlie is surrounded by ugly pits and piles of ore waiting to be processed.

The affluence of former times is reflected in the grand civic buildings which line the streets of both towns. The gambling and womanising are also perpetuated in the two-up games which are so popular and in the brothels along Kalgoorlie's Hay St; both are included on bus tour routes and both are illegal with one exception. The Two-up School on Broad Arrow Road (7km north) is Australia's only legal two-up establishment where visitors are taught the game. It is open only till dark and no alcohol is allowed. (Heavy drinking is an occupational hazard of a visit to Kalgoorlie.) For cheap accommodation try the Piccadilly on Piccadilly St.

You can stick to admiring the relics and recreations of the gold boom days, for example at the Hainault Tourist Gold Mine in Kalgoorlie (where the tour guides are colourful ex-miners) or the statue-cum-drinking fountain dedicated to Paddy Hannan who first struck gold here. Or you can become a latter-day prospector. You can obtain a Miner's Right for $10 from the Mines Department and either head out on your own or join a half-day fossicking tour.

NORTH OF PERTH

As you travel north, Western Australia becomes progressively more rugged, with tin shacks replacing the fine architecture of Perth. The population thins dramatically, as does the number of tourists. Several coach companies make the marathon journey to Darwin, taking two days of straight driving to get to the Northern Territory border and a further 15 hours to Darwin. If you are driving yourself, you will have to get used to dirt roads unless you never deviate from Highway 1. These can usually be travelled comfortably at 50km/h, which is much faster than is the case in the Northern Territory.

Because of the vast distances and the lack of competition (and custom), food and services are pricey, particularly accommodation. Towns are quite likely to have just one charmless motel charging $60 or $70 single, so camping is the only way to accomplish the journey on a budget. Although there are lots of National Parks, few include campsites among their facilities and normally the choice is confined to commercial sites charging $12-$15 per couple. If you do stay at a National Park campsite, the facilities will be well-maintained if basic and the cost will be less than a commercial site, with the ranger coming to collect the fee in the early evening. (As mentioned earlier, free camping is not permitted within 16km of a camping ground, which cuts out most of the coast.) Camaraderie quickly develops among camping travellers of all ages, and advice on pleasant campsites is always shared.

The main consideration for such a trip is the time of year. Although the northern areas can be beautiful in the Wet (December to March), especially the stormy skies, temperatures are too high for most people's comfort, often over 40°C. Although roads follow the high ground, flooding is persistent and can prevent cars and buses proceeding for days at a time. This is also the cyclone season, so most travellers choose the months between May and September. The residents of course endure all the extremes. As mentioned, the government gives a tax break of 20% to everyone who lives above the 26th parallel which is about half way up the state.

The Coastal Route. The first few hundred kilometres are relatively gentle. Even so, the first famous sight you come to, 230km north of Perth, has only recently been made accessible to conventional motor cars, since the road was surfaced. This is the Pinnacles, calcified humps of eroded limestone in Nambung National Park near Cervantes. If necessary you can join a tour from the Cervantes Caravan Park. The Pinnacles is also a popular day-trippers' destination from Perth; tours are offered by the YHA and Moorebus (09-480 5750).

Geraldton is a thriving port and, by Western Australian standards, a major city (population 21,000). Its winters are noticeably warmer than those of Perth, so most people go for the weather. Gourmets on the other hand, go for the huge rock lobsters, prawns, and other seafood which can be bought fresh from the fishermen. North of Geraldton is Kalbarri which, although touristy, has very scenic gorges (cut by the Murchison River) and fascinating geology.

Another long day's drive along the West Coastal Highway brings you to Shark

Bay and Monkey Mia where most people go, not to see the sharks (of which there are many) or the monkeys (of which there are none), but the dolphins. Monkey Mia is said to be the only place in the world where for nine months of the year wild dolphins come in to shore to frolic fearlessly among the legs of bathers. Such a phenomenon could not go undiscovered for long, and what was once a small caravan park owned by a dolphin devotee has now become Monkey Mia Dolphin Resort (099-481320). There is a $5 charge just to park your car and dolphin videos can be viewed. Fish with which to attract and feed the dolphins is sold at the caravan park. The area is ranger-patrolled to protect the dolphins.

Carnarvon is described in the tourist brochures as the tropical gateway to the north, though it is little more than a wide and dusty main street flanked by several shacks. However if you have journeyed this far, you will have come not for the architecture but for the natural landscapes. Near Coral Bay, 238km north, is the breathtaking Ningaloo Marine Park, a 260km stretch of coral that is closer to the coast than any such reef in the world. The tourism authorities intend to promote their coral reef as an undiscovered rival to the Great Barrier reef. If you stop in Carnarvon on your way south, there is a *Dolphin Express* hovercraft which departs daily for Monkey Mia ($35 one way).

Many miles further north is the unmissable semi-Asian sleepy hollow of Broome with the best beach in North West Australia, stretching 22km. This is a developing tourist resort which is distinguished by the oriental influence of the Japanese and Malay pearl divers who began arriving in the 1880s. Despite its modest size, the town has the second largest Chinatown in Australia after Sydney's, along Carnarvon St. Surprisingly there is very little budget accommodation and what there is (e.g. Broome Backpackers at 1877 Crocker Road or Broome Bunkhouse on Carnarvon St) is often full, so a tent is almost essential if you intend to stay more than a day.

For ten days in late August/early September, the colourful Shinju Matsuri Festival or Festival of the Pearl is held to commemorate the valuable gem pearl which brought wealth to this coast. Broome's population of 3,700 swells five or six times for the Festival, so this is probably not the best time to appreciate Broome at its lazy best.

From Broome the Great Northern Highway heads inland, away from the northern peninsulas which are mostly Aboriginal reserves.

The Inland Route. Beginning again in Perth, there is an alternative route which passes through large pastoral properties, fields of wild flowers (spring only), gold ghost towns and rugged mining country. The only really impressive sight is Australia's most massive (but by no means most famous) monolith. Technically Mount Augustus is a monocline (a rock composed of folded strata of boulders and sand whose top inclines to one side). Whether the claim that it is the largest rock in the world (contesting a similar claim made by the Great White Throne rock in Zion National Park in Utah) is difficult to adjudicate. You will find very few Japanese tourists photographing sunsets here, mainly due to its inaccessibility and its less dramatic shape. It is on a track about 300km from either the coastal or the inland highways. Furthermore its immense size is not apparent because of its gentle slopes and scrubby covering. Pinnacles Tours in Perth (09-325 9455) operate one and two week tours starting at $750 and West Coast Safaris (PO Box 467, Exmouth, WA 6707; 099-491 6257) include it as one of their destinations.

The mining region of Western Australia is the Pilbara centred on the oddly-named town of Tom Price. The iron ore is transported mostly by rail to Port Hedland where it is shipped off to Japan. If you are in this area, it is worth taking one of the free tours of the mines put on by the public relations departments of the mining companies; the scale of the machinery used to dismantle entire mountains is a startling sight.

As mentioned the mining companies sometimes build their own access roads alongside the railway tracks which, although unsealed, are faster, straighter and better graded than the state highway. The public is allowed to use these roads, as long as permission is obtained from the Hamersley Iron Ore Company in Karratha or at the Tom Price mine site. A permit lasts for up to a week. There are very few signposts, so watch the milometer carefully to avoid missing a turn-off. Although four-wheel drive vehicles (which can be hired in Port Hedland on the coast) are preferable for exploring the dirt roads of the Hamersley Range National Park, it is possible to visit some of the high points, such as the spectacular gorge and giant ant hills at Wittenoon, in an ordinary vehicle. The geological formations of the Hamersley Range are remarkable for their mineral content and shifting colours. Remember that the temperatures in this part of the world can be brutal.

The inland highway joins the coast at Port Hedland, as it is impossible to cross the totally uninhabited and barely mapped Great Sandy Desert and Gibson Desert. Maps show a dotted route labelled the Canning Stock Route which was surveyed in 1906 but was never successfully established. It did however bring many Aboriginal people in contact with Europeans for the first time, and the history of the Western Desert Puntukunuparna people was written for the first time as a Bicentennial project. The Gunbarrel Highway further south is an actual road, straight as a gun barrel, through the spinifex and sand to Alice Springs via Warburton and Yulara. It can be traversed only by four-wheel-drive vehicles and entry permits for the Aboriginal reserves through which it passes must be obtained in advance (address at the end of this chapter). If you are interested in this route, ask the YHA about its 11-day tour, which costs $650.

Broome marks the beginning of the most rugged and remote region of Western Australia. This area, the Kimberley Plateau, is subject to extremes of rainfall and tropical humidity, so that at least for some of the time the landscapes are not as dry and dusty as they are further south. Unfortunately most of the roads are impassible in the Wet. The Western Australian Tourism Commission publishes a pamphlet on the Gibb River and Kalumburu Road, two unsealed roads which allow you to explore the Kimberley outback. Most visitors remain on the sealed Great Northern Highway from Broome to Kununurra, making only one 16km

"KUNUNURRA IS A GOOD JUMPING-OFF POINT"

detour to visit the crystal clear waters of the mighty Fitzroy River which flows through the spectacular Geikie Gorge National Park.

Kununurra in the top corner of the state is like an oasis on the Ord River and a pleasant jumping-off point for exploring the area, which includes some Aboriginal art. This is still 1000km from Darwin. Massive dams and irrigation projects control the water in this area and are heavily promoted by the tourist authorities. (In fact dams and reservoirs receive enthusiastic billing in many places in Australia, probably as a result of chronic water shortages).

The fantastic rock formations of the Bungle Bungle region are virtually inaccessible without four-wheel drive (and only in season) or the money to pay for a scenic flight. Interestingly, the National Park here recently won an international tourism award for the work it is doing to involve local Aboriginal people and to conserve a fragile ecosystem.

Flora and Fauna. There are about 8000 species of flowering plants in Western Australia plus a host of unique ferns, carnivorous plants, grasses and trees from the wonderful eucalypts of the south to the gnarled baobab trees which flourish in the tropical north (among them an ancient hollowed-out specimen which served as a prison cell in Derby north of Broome). The transformation which a day or two of rain can make to a barren-looking field is astonishing, especially in the drier areas north of Perth, where Sturt's desert pea carpets the land with red and black. The famous carpets of flowers do not last long in any one place. So even in season visitors are not guaranteed to see the spectacular sights illustrated in the *Wildlife Discovery* brochure from the tourist office unless they are very lucky.

A company called Bushwalking Tours (57 Vickery Crescent, Bunbury, WA 6230; 097-214248) conducts gentle half-day hikes around Bunbury south of Perth for $25 which includes a home-cooked picnic lunch. These are intended to introduce visitors to the flora of the area and the owner-guide identifies edible and toxic plants. Further south you can go to Mount Chudalup near Pointe d'Entrecasteaux where there are reputed to be seven species of wild orchid.

In addition to an unusual range of marsupials, Western Australia also has some very interesting birds in such habitats as the salt lakes of Clifton and Preston (20km south of Mandurah), the Archipelago of the Recherche (with seals and penguins as well as sea birds) and the Dryandra Forest near Williams. The Nullarbor is not a place where one would expect to find many birds, however there is a bird observatory 42km south of Cocklebiddy very near the Great Australian Bight. The Eyre Bird Observatory (Cocklebiddy via Norseman, WA 6443; 090-393450) is accessible only by four-wheel drive, so it is necessary to make a booking in advance, either directly or through the YHA, so that the Warden can collect you. You can stay only on a full board basis which costs $39 per night with a YHA discount.

In the north of the state, you should watch out for poisonous snakes such as the yellow whip snake. In the Kimberley region you are almost certain to see crocodiles, deadly sea snakes or water monitors (giant lizards).

Information about National Parks can be obtained from CALM, the Conservation and Land Management Department which has offices throughout the state; in Perth ring 367 0333.

Activities. Bushwalking can be enjoyed in many of the National Parks from the Porongurups and Stirling Ranges in the extreme south to the more forbidding Hamersley Range, which contains the state's highest peaks (up to 1245m). The usual caution with regard to heat exhaustion and dehydration must be exercised. If you are going to walk in scrub, wear sturdy long trousers to fend off attack by the spikes of spinifex which are coated with a natural chemical irritant. Nangar Wilderness Expeditions (PO Box 1209, Victoria Park 6101; 09-458 9738) takes groups of hikers to remote wilderness areas of Western Australia and also on weekend trips to the Southwest.

A few YHA hostels hire out bicycles for $8-$10 a day. The use of a horse will cost considerably more: contact Kookaburra Adventures in Perth (09-474 2526) about their horse-riding expeditions in Yanchep National Park. To learn to scuba dive, contact Barrakuda Dive, 131 William St, Perth (09-321 3724), which provides free transport for backpackers.

Restricted Areas. If you wish to enter one of the many Aboriginal Lands in Western Australia, you must obtain prior permission from the Permits Officer at the Aboriginal Affairs Lands Trust, 35 Havelock St, West Perth (09-483 1222). If you are planning to use the Gunbarrel Highway to Alice, you must also contact the Ngaanyatjarra Council, PO Box 644, Alice Springs, NT 0871 (08-8950 1711).

Calendar of Events

January 1	**Perth Cup, Ascot Racecourse**
January/February or February/March	Festival of Perth
March (first Monday)	**Labour Day**
March (first weekend)	Dairy Festival, Harvey
March (last weekend)	Log Chop and Community Fair, Dwellingup
June (first Monday)	**Foundation Day**
late August/early September	Festival of the Pearl, Broome
late September	Sunshine Festival, Geraldton
September/October	Perth Royal Show
October (first Monday)	**Queen's Birthday**
November (first Saturday)	Boddington Rodeo

Public holidays are shown in **bold**.

The Northern Territory

Population: 160,000   **Capital: Darwin (population 75,000)**

To foreigners and Australians alike, the Northern Territory has traditionally been equated with Ayers Rock, or Uluru — the red rock rising from the red centre of Australia, symbolising the uniqueness of this country. Now Kakadu National Park, famed for its Crocodile Dundee-esque wildlife, not to mention beauty, is starting to challenge the supremacy of the Rock's fame. There is, of course, much more to the Territory: its area is over ten times larger than England and twice the size of Texas, yet with a population equal to a medium-sized town in Europe or North America. Nowhere can you experience more sense of space or eerie silence. Although the Territory has no monopoly on featureless landscapes nor lush jungle, its Outback seems more primeval than that of the other states. Read *Capricornia* by Xavier Herbert, or try to see paintings by Australian artist Brett Bailey, to get a feel of the sheer, continuous emptiness.

Close to Uluru are the Olgas, a range emerging from the stark desert that many find more stunning than the Rock itself. Nearby — always a relative term in the Territory — is the town of Alice Springs. Australia's 'Red Centre' is semi-desert, with hot, dry summers and cold winters. At its heart is Alice Springs, which once epitomised the pioneering spirit of a nation. Now, however, it provides the security of safe suburbia and has what seems to be the highest density of shopping malls in all of Australia.

The northern part of the Territory is known to Australians as the 'Top End'. It is linked to the Centre by the Stuart Highway, widely referred to as 'The Track', the central spine and overland artery that is an essential part of the Territorian consciousness. But the Top End bears little relation to Darwin, the capital of the Territory, has more in common with Singapore than Sydney, and is surrounded by swamps, gorges and more than a few crocodiles. The north is tropical — hot throughout the year with a pronounced wet season, always referred to as 'the Wet', from November to April.

Between the extremes of north and south is the Never Never, immortalised by Jeanine Gunn in her book *We of the Never Never*. Although the term 'Never Never' is sometimes used to describe any Outback location, its precise definition is the region around the town of Katherine. The Barkly Tableland is the eastern centre of the Northern Territory, and is famed as the scene of Australia's last great gold rush. At present the main function of its largest town, Tennant Creek, is to serve travellers on The Track, but recent gold discoveries may trigger another rush.

'Towards Statehood' is the motto of the Northern Territory Government, reflecting the growing self-confidence and desire for greater autonomy. The Northern Territory fell under the jurisdiction of South Australia until 1911, when administration was taken over by the federal authorities; the Territory achieved a measure of self-government only in 1978. One-third of the state's area is Aboriginal land, and the vestiges of native Australian culture are better preserved in the Territory than elsewhere. This is partly because white settlers were markedly less successful in colonising the Territory than other parts of Australia: only in the mid-19th century did the first Europeans travel across the continent from south to north.

The Northern Territory was eventually opened up to establish a direct telegraph link between Australia and Europe, and indeed most of the names of towns and rivers in the Territory are those of the telegraph line's constructors and their friends. The region's great mineral wealth and agricultural potential were first identified at the start of the 20th century. Trade routes were initiated between central Australia and the south, with the help of camels and their drivers imported from Afghanistan. The discovery of gold in the Neve. Never added impetus to the development of the Territory, although the rush itself — like the later one in the Tablelands — was short-lived.

At the same time as the town now known as Alice Springs was in its pioneering days, fishermen and traders were becoming established at the coastal port of Darwin. Today these places have all the trappings of Australian urban life, but just beyond them much of the wilderness is untarnished. One practical aspect of the Territory's remoteness that is of direct concern to travellers is that prices for most things are noticeably higher. Because virtually everything has to be brought in from thousands of kilometres away, goods and services from accommodation in Alice to dinner in Darwin cost more. And the low population density means that many settlements have only one combined hotel/petrol station/restaurant/general store/post office, which usually takes advantage of its local monopoly. When planning your spending, be on the safe side and assume that your cost of living will be at least 25% higher than in the southern states. If you want to save money, visit the Territory during the Wet between November and March/April when visitors are few and prices of many tourist-related services such as car hire and accommodation fall substantially.

THE LOCALS

One in four Territorians is Aboriginal. Many of the native Australians living in the Northern Territory have successfully come to terms with the 20th century without compromising their cultural heritage, although the highly visible alcoholics on the streets of Alice Springs and Darwin show that European settlement has created victims. Adding to the ethnic mix, there are strong Chinese and southeast Asian communities living in the Top End and a number of

Italians around Alice. The European inhabitants fall into two groups: confirmed Territorians who believe fiercely in their home territory, and a large transient population who come to work for a while in mining, industry or tourism before returning to the more comfortable life of the southern states. There is noticeable tension between these established residents and the hard-drinking and rootless bunch of (mainly) male Australians who come to the Territory to try to earn some quick cash. It is said that you need to survive a few 'Wets' before being accepted as a true Territorian.

Making Friends. Visitors to the Northern Territory easily outnumber the locals, so you will hardly be a novelty and should not anticipate receiving much more than basic courtesy from the locals. But conversely there are plenty of fellow travellers in the main centres and it takes little effort to make acquaintances.

GETTING AROUND

Apart from daily bus services between the main towns and expensive flights, there is little public transport in the Northern Territory. In winter, the Territory is half an hour behind the eastern states and 90 minutes ahead of Western Australia. Like Western Australia, the Territory does not implement daylight saving time in summer. Check your watch when you arrive in the Territory before catching an aircraft, bus or train.

Air. Three airports in the Territory can be reached from other states: Alice Springs, Darwin and Yulara (the airport serving Uluru). Only Darwin has services from overseas. Both Darwin and Alice airports have recently been rebuilt and have very modern facilities. The local airline is Air North, which links Darwin, Katherine, Jabiru near Kakadu, Bathurst Island and smaller settlements. Ansett and Australian Airlines flights from the state capitals serve Alice Springs and Darwin; some flights go direct to Yulara.

Bus. The major coach companies run regular services to Alice Springs and Darwin, but don't expect the frequency of services found in south-eastern Australia. Some routes linking Darwin with northern Queensland and Western Australia are interrupted during the wet season from November to May by flooding, sometimes for weeks at a time. Unless you can afford to fly across or are prepared to take the extremely long southerly route via South Australia, you will have to sit it out. Should the bus journey to the coast of Queensland seem too daunting, you need only take the bus as far as Mount Isa to connect with the twice-weekly *Inlander* rail service to Townsville.

If you are travelling on to Perth, it is tempting to imagine yourself crossing direct from Uluru to the west coast — there is even a road shown on the map. In fact no public transport runs along the little-travelled Gunbarrel Highway and the only possibility is to join an Outback tour. Make enquiries at YHA hostels, as the YHA runs occasional trips on this route.

Anyone coming into the Territory by bus (or indeed car) should consider bringing food with them. There are roadhouses every 200km or so, but they are notoriously overpriced.

Train. The idea of a railway line linking the south and north coasts from Adelaide to Darwin has been under discussion for over a century. The compilers of the Thomas Cook timetable have not yet despaired as they include an optimistic footnote on Darwin that 'a line may be constructed at a future date', though probably only for freight. Unless and until it happens, the line north from Adelaide in South Australia terminates at Alice Springs: see *South Australia:*

Train for details of the twice-weekly *Ghan* service. Connections to Melbourne can be made at Adelaide, to Brisbane at Sydney and to Perth at the small junction of Tarcoola where the line from Alice Springs meets the transcontinental railway.

Driving. Three sealed roads lead to the Northern Territory. The busiest is the Stuart Highway ('The Track'), named after the early explorer John McDouall Stuart who successfully crossed from south to north in 1861/2. It runs 3000km up from Adelaide through Coober Pedy, entering the Territory 250km south of Alice Springs and continuing via the towns of Tennant Creek and Katherine to Darwin. A free strip map — *Drive The Stuart* — is available from Northern Territory Government Travel Centres. It covers the whole journey from Adelaide to Darwin, plus spurs to Uluru and Kakadu National Park east of Darwin. If driving The Track south from Darwin, the featurelessness of the landscape is not relieved until the McDonnell Ranges come into view west of Alice. If you plan to do much driving away from The Track, invest in the excellent *Touring Map* of the Territory. Remember that most car rental agreements prohibit driving on unsurfaced roads. For the purposes of car hire, the Northern Territory counts as 'remote' and therefore unlimited distance rates are not available. The standard deal is 100km free per day plus 25c for each additional kilometre.

The Stuart Highway is joined at Three Ways by the Barkly Highway from Mount Isa in Northern Queensland. The Victoria Highway (part of National Highway 1) crosses from northern Western Australia near Kununurra and joins the Stuart at Katherine.

The ironically named Plenty Highway is a shorter route from Queensland to Alice Springs. It is an unsealed route which peters out into a track at the Queensland border but may be passable in the Dry. The shortest journey from Perth to Alice Springs is via the rough Gunbarrel Highway (mentioned above). It is hazardous for inexperienced drivers and unprepared vehicles; most visitors take the long route via Port Augusta and the Eyre Highway across the Nullarbor.

Before attempting any unsealed and lightly travelled route, follow the advice given in the introduction about driving in the Outback. In particular, your vehicle should be fit for the task ahead and in good working order; you should take copious supplies of fuel, food and water; and you should consult local people about your plans. At night, beware of the many animals from kangaroos to cows which stray onto the roads. The chances of having to stare down a buffalo, Mick Dundee style, are remote as most of the buffalo have been shot.

One additional hazard is posed by the massive articulated trucks known as 'road trains'. They haul up to three long trailers with a total length of 50m and a combined weight of 115 tonnes. On narrow stretches of road you should pull over to the shoulder to let them pass; remember that road shoulders are steeper than elsewhere to allow run-off in the Wet. Before attempting to overtake one, make sure you can see clear road for at least one kilometre ahead, as it can take an interminable time to get past. Beware too of 'bulldust' which gathers in hard-to-spot ruts in the road and can send your vehicle out of control as well as engulf it in a cloud of invisibility.

The Automobile Association of the Northern Territory (AANT) is based in the MLC Building at 79–81 Smith St, Darwin (8981 3837) and has a good range of maps and travel information free to members of foreign motoring organisations. You can obtain a free leaflet *Driving in the Territory*, providing a guide to the special requirements for driving in the Northern Territory. The more detailed *Traffic Code Book* is available free from Motor Vehicle Registries or police stations.

A more mundane warning concerns the local driving style. Territorian drivers do not rank among the world's best, and most are unused to traffic. Matters are made worse by the propensity of the locals to drink and drive. The local anti-drink/drive slogan is 'It's too late when you're .08', and indeed if you are caught driving with a blood/alcohol level of 0.08 or over you face automatic disqualification. This is not yet enough to deter some. Speeding offenders are apprehended using mobile radar units.

In the wet season, news of road conditions can be obtained from the Northern Territory Emergency Service on 8984 4455 in Darwin or 8952 3833 in Alice Springs. During the rest of the year, dial 8984 3585 (Darwin) or 8952 7111 (Alice Springs).

Hitch-hiking. The need for careful preparation, and warnings about local drivers, apply equally to hitchers. Take plenty of water and food for long waits and in case a vehicle which does stop for you breaks down and the driver has not made provision for an extra passenger. Try to ensure always that you are dropped off near some form of civilisation (usually a roadhouse) where — if thumbing proves hopeless — you can at least ask for lifts or jump on a bus. Don't expect to have the road to yourself: in high season almost every roadhouse has a hitcher or two, and the notorious settlement of Three Ways is often thick with rival hitch-hikers. When you do get a lift, however, it should be going a fair way. As usual the best way is to fix up a lift in advance by pinning a message up at a freight depot, which often works within a few hours (especially if you are female).

COMMUNICATIONS
Post and Telephone. The Northern Territory has a single area code — 08 — but not all calls are charged at local rates. For example, calls between Alice Springs and Darwin cost almost as much as those to other states. State postal codes begin 08.

Media. If you've enjoyed the variety of television, radio and press elsewhere in Australia, you should narrow your sights in the Northern Territory. Such newspapers and transmissions that exist are surprisingly good considering their limited market. Mainstream television in Darwin is limited to ABC (Channel 6) and the commercial Channel 8 while Alice Springs has only ABC. Darwin is best endowed with radio stations (it has four); in outlying areas you'll be lucky to pick up more than the ABC national programme.

The Territory's main newspapers are the *Northern Territory News* (published daily in Darwin), the four-times-weekly *Centralian Advocate* of Alice Springs and the *Sunday Territorian*.

CRIME AND SAFETY
Most people feel quite safe walking around the towns of the Northern Territory at night. If you are at all anxious you could hire a bike (a good way to get around Alice Springs and Darwin anyway) or take a taxi. You might prefer to avoid hanging around pubs at closing time, as some of the worst-behaved hard-drinking Australian males seem to live in the Territory. You need have little fear, however, of the habitual drunks (both white and Aboriginal) so prevalent in Darwin, who are pathetic rather than malevolent. One exception might occur in Alice Springs where some Aboriginals sleep in the dry bed of the Todd River. If you are crossing on a moonless night you might trip over someone enraged by drink, so carry a torch if possible. In an effort to reduce the level of drunkenness on the city streets, it is an offence to drink liquor out-of-doors within 2km of licensed premises. Perhaps the worst time to be in the Territory is October, when levels of violence escalate during the humid build-up to the Wet, a condition which is sometimes referred to as 'mango madness'.

" *IT IS ILLEGAL TO DRINK WITHIN 2 KM OF LICENSED PREMISES* "

Stories of people losing possessions from hostel or hotel rooms are rare, but with so many travellers passing through it is best to be cautious.

As throughout Australia, you must obtain permission before crossing Aboriginal land; the addresses of the Land Councils are included at the end of this chapter. If you intend to carry alcohol in your vehicle, ask whether this is allowed at the same time as you apply for an entry permit. Any queries about the legalities of drinking and gambling can be answered by the NT Racing, Gaming and Liquor Commission (8981 1955).

Danger issues from a little-suspected source. There are 95 kinds of mosquito in the Northern Territory, some of which are capable of infecting you with some quite nasty diseases. For example there is a fever called Ross River Fever or 'Night Gardener's Disease' which is definitely on the increase and whose symptoms are similar to those of arthritis. Several deaths a month are being attributed to the disease. It is a good idea to take precautions against mosquito bites just as you would in malarial zones.

Flies are not dangerous but they are serious nuisances. Uluru has suffered recently from especially bad plagues of them and people have been resorting to wearing bee-keepers' nets to prevent the sticky flies from heading for the corners of eyes and mouth.

HELP AND INFORMATION

The Northern Territory is better at promoting itself than any other state with the possible exception of Queensland. It produces glossy, informative and up-to-date brochures on a wide range of subjects. The main brochure is the 100-page *Holiday Planner*, which contains a comprehensive list of tours from a city tour of Darwin to a $2000 four-wheel-drive Outback expedition. Furthermore all the Government Tourist Bureaux (in Katherine and Tennant Creek as well as Alice Springs and Darwin) make reservations for accommodation, transport, car hire, etc.

The five out-of-state NT Government Tourist Bureaux are:

Adelaide: 9 Hindley St (08-8212 1133).
Brisbane: 48 Queen St (07-3229 5799).
Melbourne: 415 Bourke St (03-9670 6948).
Perth: 62 St George's Terrace (09-322 4255).
Sydney: corner of Barrack and George Sts (02-9262 3744).

There is the usual range of giveaway tourist literature full of adverts and some useful information. Also try to pick up the Outback edition of the free *TNT for Backpackers* series of booklets, produced by TNT in Sydney; it is often available in hostels. If you are not entitled to the range of free maps available from the AANT (address above), go to the Map Shop in Darwin (Moonta House, 43 Mitchell St) or Alice Springs (21 Gregory Terrace) for a good selection.

WORK

The good news is that rates of pay in the Northern Territory are higher and taxes lower than elsewhere in Australia. The bad news is that employers are few and far between, and when you eventually succeed in finding a job your living costs will be high. Don't place much hope in finding work through the Territory's newspapers, as there are few jobs in the 'Positions Vacant' columns.

Alice Springs is usually the best bet. The tourist trade in both cities, especially during the winter high season (May to October) offers the most opportunities. An advantage of the hospitality industry is that employees are often provided with food and accommodation, alleviating the high cost of living. The Yulara resort (which serves Uluru) often has vacancies as it has no local community from which to draw staff. Although the resort has a long waiting list of job-seekers, many people who register move on before reaching the top of the list. The resort employs (and houses) about 500 people and the average turnover rate for catering and cleaning staff is about 6 weeks.

Darwin is the place where all the Australians deported from Asia end up. Consequently competition for unskilled work is intense. A fair amount of casual employment is available in the dry season, however. The CES's Templine office in Darwin (on the first floor, 40 Cavenagh St: 8946 4866) caters for many transient job seekers. It is especially busy at the beginning of the dry season. Some people sleep outside the building to be the first in the queue when it opens. Although you should get there early and be prepared to remain in the waiting area for hours, some temporary work should arrive if you are patient. Don't be deterred by the hordes of sunbeaten Australians; they may be after the same jobs as you, but you stand a chance if you look 'reliable'. Much of the work revolves around the port (particularly unloading prawn trawlers), so you might decide to bypass the bureaucracy and look around at the quayside for employment. The *Northern Territory News* gives details of ships in port or expected, which could provide clues.

You could always go one better than working at the docks and find work on a prawn trawler any time during the season (mid-April till Christmas). Voyages usually last one or two weeks and payment is a couple of hundred dollars a week. (Deckhands used to be paid a share of the catch; nowadays that is rarely to their advantage, as the waters of the Arafura Sea are now seriously over-fished.) The work is mostly sorting prawns which is tedious but not too tough except that the prawn spines get stuck in your hands. Women are particularly sought after to act as cooks, although you should establish before leaving port the precise nature of your duties.

Women might find the more predictable setting of a shop or an office (for those with word processing skills) more relaxing. The economic expansion in Alice Springs means that shops and offices are often willing to employ transients, especially over the summer; for example the local K-Mart regularly hires travellers at casual rates (higher than normal wages) and you can easily find out when the weekly recruitment takes place. The Alice Springs CES is at the corner of Bath St and Gregory Terrace (8952 7122). Katherine, the largest town between Darwin and Alice Springs, has some job prospects.

The Northern Territory is the place to experience real Outback station life. The cattle farms of Central Australia are almost unimaginably large. Jackaroos and jillaroos are occasionally needed, though inexperienced people should not expect to earn more than about $200 a week.

The Australian Trust for Conservation Volunteers mentioned in the introductory section *Work*, recruits volunteers for projects in the Northern Territory. One recent example was helping with a frog survey in Kakadu National Park; ring the ATCV in Victoria on 03-5332 7490 for details. You might also make enquiries at the Environment Centre at 24 Cavenagh St in Darwin about volunteer possibilities.

DARWIN

For some travellers driving north through the Territory, Darwin assumes almost mystic proportions — the pot of gold at the end of The Track. The city certainly has more to offer than any of the other settlements north of Alice Springs. But due to the time and expense involved in getting to Darwin, it is hard to recommend a visit to the city for its own sake. Most people use it as a base from which to make forays into the wilderness, especially Kakadu. As you approach Darwin and the end of the 2500km-long Stuart Highway, the road suddenly blossoms into an eight-lane racetrack. But then the Highway reaches an ignominious conclusion at a set of traffic lights just outside the city, and the last couple of kilometres into the centre can be deeply anti-climactic. The small downtown is a piece of typical urban Australia transplanted to the tropics. Darwin has something of the feel (yet little of the style) of Key West at the southern tip of Florida, a warm and relaxed but inescapably isolated city.

Darwin's natural harbour was first discovered by Europeans on a visit to the coast by *HMS Beagle* in 1839. It was named after Charles Darwin, the naturalist who had previously sailed on the ship. The Territory's capital was founded in 1869, after four unsuccessful attempts to build at other sites in the area. The first settlements were a response to fears of other European powers creating a foothold in Australia, but after the Northern Territory was annexed to South Australia in 1863 a more serious attempt was made to colonise the area; the Surveyor-General of South Australia and a party of 135 arrived on February 5, 1869. Darwin has had a very rough-and-ready history since then, including one episode (in 1919) where the guns of the Australian Navy were turned on the town to restore order! During the Second World War Darwin was shaken out of its seclusion as it became Australia's frontline against the Japanese, who bombed the city on 59 occasions in the biggest air strike after Pearl Harbour. It is now a cosmopolitan and racially mixed city, with much evidence of new building as a result of Cyclone Tracy which devastated the area on Christmas Eve 1974, killing 66 people in Australia's worst recorded natural disaster.

Climate. Cyclone Tracy was particularly vicious and has been matched only a couple of times in Darwin's history (1897 and 1937), but less destructive cyclones are not uncommon. The threat of summer cyclones (known locally as 'blows') is present from November to April, and you can call a special number (11542) for warnings about them. If you are unfortunate enough to get caught in one, head for the nearest new building; all those constructed since the 1974 disaster are extremely tough and are required by law to have a cyclone shelter.

The months of November to April also constitute the wet season, known in tourist literature as the 'green' season. Darwin is very much a tropical city and visitors should be aware of the debilitating effect the heat and humidity can have, especially when arriving from the drier central areas of Alice Springs and Uluru. Darwin is closer — both geographically and climatically — to Southeast Asia than to other Australian cities; Melbourne is further away than Manila. The city reputedly suffers the highest suicide rate in the world in the month before the onset of the wet season, when humidity is a relentless 95%. From October to December, the Top End is extremely prone to earthquakes.

ARRIVAL AND DEPARTURE

City Layout. The main city centre is on a small peninsula south-west of the rest of the city. The suburbs sprawl out to the north and east, bounded by the coast and the airport. Smith St and Mitchell St both run through the middle of downtown, with the Smith St Mall being the heart of the city centre. It can be confusing to realise that the Stuart Highway (the road to the south) actually runs north out of the city centre. The road curves around to go south a short way out of Darwin.

Air. When the maximum range of aircraft was shorter, Darwin was the first point of entry for most travellers to Australia. Now the only international flights are on Qantas to Singapore, Garuda Indonesia to Bali, another Indonesian airline Merpati to Kupang on the island of Timor (the shortest international flight to Australia), and Royal Brunei to Borneo. Domestic destinations include Adelaide, Brisbane, Canberra, Perth and Sydney, but most are served only once a day or less.

The airport is 8km south of the city centre and has the longest runway in the country. One terminal serves both international and domestic flights. The airport shuttle meets every flight and costs $6 into town. To book a trip out to the airport, ring 8941 1656 or go to the Tram Car next to the Transit Centre (Mitchell and Peel Sts). It is also possible to catch a local bus from the airport into town for 80c: walk out to the Stuart Highway (5 minutes). The journey time is about 15 minutes, and the bus runs the length of Mitchell St where most of the cheap hostels are located. A taxi to town costs about $9 on weekdays, $11 at night and weekends.

Travel agencies in Darwin are more concerned with persuading you to book a tour of the state rather than selling you an onward international flight. One-way flights to Timor are about $200 and to Singapore $340. STA Travel is at Shop T17 in the Smith St Mall (8941 2386).

Bus. The main coach terminal is the Darwin Transit Centre at 69 Mitchell St, which serves Greyhound Pioneer Australia (132030). A regional bus pass is a good idea for exploring the Northern Territory; for example Greyhound Pioneer's *Top End Explorer* costs $145 and permits one-way travel Cairns–Townsville–Three Ways–Darwin; the add-on return fare Three Ways–Alice–Yulara is $150. The *Rock Track* pass for $160 covers Uluru to Kakadu while the *Best of the Outback* for $275 covers Adelaide to Darwin.

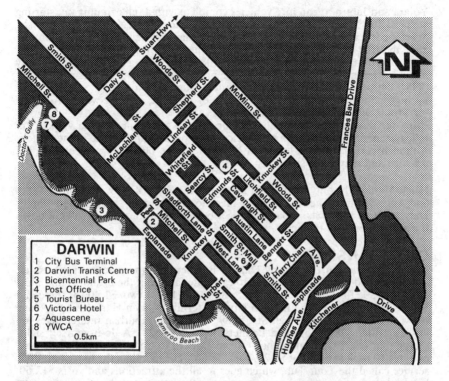

DARWIN
1 City Bus Terminal
2 Darwin Transit Centre
3 Bicentennial Park
4 Post Office
5 Tourist Bureau
6 Victoria Hotel
7 Aquascene
8 YWCA
0.5km

These pass prices compare favourably with the straightforward one-way fares (even with the YHA/VIP discount) — for example, $140 Darwin–Alice Springs (21 hours) and $260 Darwin–Cairns (38 hours).

Boat. Darwin is a gateway port for yachtsmen sailing between Australia and south-east Asia. Most of the hostels have notices advertising shared-expense passages to Bali or Singapore, or you can check the noticeboard behind Darwin Ship Stores at the harbourside. So many world travellers are keen for the experience of a long-distance sailing trip, that even if you are taken on as a crew member, the price will probably be higher than flying.

More locally, Darwin Harbour Ferries (8978 5094) make several daily crossings to Mandorah across on the Cox Peninsula; there are good beaches and a good view of the city. The trip takes about 25 minutes and costs $15 return. The company also runs a 2-hour harbour cruise for $20 on the licensed *Darwin Duchess*. Departures are from Stokes Hill Wharf (at the foot of Kitchener Drive) at 2pm and 5.30 (Wednesday-Sunday).

Driving. As there is so little public transport in the Northern Territory, visitors who want to do some exploring must choose between an organised tour and car hire. Car hire is more expensive than elsewhere in Australia. The cheapest car hire firm is Rent-a-Dent, centrally located at 87 Smith St (8981 1411). Next door at number 89 is Thrifty (8981 8555), which also has campervans and four-wheel-drive Landcruisers from $110 a day plus 25c per kilometre after the first 100km. Territory Rent-a-Car (149 Stuart Highway; 8981 8400) is one of the biggest operators in the state with branches in all the main towns including

Yulara and Jabiru. It can hire vehicles complete with a full camping kit, starting at $750 for 5 days, inclusive of everything except petrol. The *Backpackers' Special* costs $54 a day if you rent for more than 4 days plus 23c per kilometre after the first 100km per day. Hiring a campervan from Brits Rentals (whose head office is in Melbourne; toll-free 008-331454) is a better deal: a 7-day inclusive rental costs about $500. Cheapa Rent-a-Car at 149 Stuart Highway (8981 8400) and at the airport has interesting one-way deals: $500 to Alice Springs, allowing 3 days and a maximum of 1600km, and one-way to Adelaide for $1000, with 6 days and 3200km.

If your travels come to an end in Darwin and you want to sell a vehicle, try to leave enough time to get a good price, after putting up a notice in the hostels. Although cars do change hands in Mitchell St, the police do not condone the practice and may get it stopped.

Hitch-hiking. The only road out of Darwin is the Stuart Highway to Three Ways and Alice Springs. The first sensible place to start hitching is at the junction of Daly and Cavenagh Sts, though taking a bus out past the airport will cut down the amount of local traffic.

CITY TRANSPORT

Bus. Public transport is run by Darwin Bus Service, and comprises 12 routes. A complicated zone system is used to calculate fares, but the upshot is that most fares cost 80c for the first zone (up to 8km), $1.10 for two, $1.40 for three and $1.60 for four zones. The Darwin city bus terminus is on Harry Chan Avenue between Smith and Cavenagh Sts (8989 7513). The suburban interchanges are at Casuarina (8989 8451) and Palmerston (8932 3323). A do-it-yourself sightseeing tour consists of taking bus 4 from Darwin to Casuarina via Fannie Bay, and bus 10 back at a cost of $2.20, considerably cheaper than the tourist minibus service called the Tour Tub, which goes to all the attractions and costs $12.50; between 9am and 6pm you can get on and off when you wish.

Taxis. Dial 8981 8777 to summon a Darwin Radio Taxi. This company also operates 'multi-ride taxis' (12-seater minibuses), which operate as shared taxis, picking up additional passengers *en route* and charging less than the regular taxi fare. Like most things in the Northern Territory, taxis are expensive by Sydney or Perth standards.

Cycling. Darwin has wide streets, few hills and modest traffic, so cycling is a good way to get around. Some of the hostels rent them out or you can visit Pedlar's Pushbike Hire, which operates on Vesty's Beach at weekends and at the corner of Mitchell and Daly Sts. Top End Motorcycle Hire at 57 Mitchell St rents bicycles as well as motorbikes and scooters.

Accommodation

The Northern Territory YHA has a city-centre hostel at 69a Mitchell St (8981 3995), which is very convenient for bus travellers as it is at the entrance to the Transit Centre. Cheapest beds are $12 from October to April, though this goes up to $14 at other times. The YHA also has a travel agency (8981 2560) and money-exchange facilities.

There are three hostels in the VIP Backpackers Resorts chain: Darwin City Lodge is at 151 Mitchell St (8941 1295), Elke's Inner-City Backpackers Lodge at number 112 (8981 8399; beds from $12) and Ivan's Backpackers at 97 (8981 5385). There is a YWCA at 119 Mitchell St (8981 8644), which is cheaper than most Ys: beds in shared rooms are $12, and single rooms are available from $20; both men and women are welcome. A few blocks away from the Transit Centre is the recommended Frogshollow Backpackers (27 Lindsay St; 8941 2600), which is set in a tropical garden. Another one to try is Larrakeyah Lodge at 50 Mitchell St (8981 2933).

When looking for a room, keep in mind that air conditioning and overhead fans can be important considerations in Darwin.

The nearest caravan parks are some way out of town. The closest is the KOA site on McMillans Road in Malak on bus route 12 or the Overlander Van Park on the Stuart Highway in Berrimah (8984 3025).

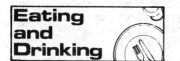

Eating and Drinking

Food options are more limited, and prices higher, than in Australia's other capitals. But you can still eat well and inexpensively in Darwin. Undoubtedly the best value for money is at the Banyan Junction Bazaar in the Darwin Transit Centre where 18 stalls serve various dishes starting at $2.50; you take your own liquor. Lunchtime snacks are available from numerous kiosks in the Smith St Mall: an excellent lunch can be had from the collection of Thai, Lebanese, vegetarian and Mexican counters in an arcade off the Knuckey St end of Smith St. The ritzy Diamond Beach casino on Gilruth Avenue should not be overlooked: it serves cheap three-course lunches and Sunday dinners in the Lorikeet Lounge.

The Lee Dynasty Chinese Restaurant on Cavenagh St has a yum cha menu (i.e. dim sum) at Sunday lunchtimes. For cheap Chinese food try the licensed Jade Gardens in the Smith St Mall, which serves a nine-course meal for $12; and the Noodle House (BYO) at 33 Knuckey St (between Smith and Cavenagh Sts). For vegetarian food, try Simply Foods at 37 Knuckey St. Confetti's at 85 Mitchell St is a trendy café. Pizza addicts can satisfy their craving at Super Pizza (BYO) at the junction of Searcy and Cavenagh Sts in Darwin city centre, or Parap Pizza on Vickers St in the Parap District Centre.

You can sample local delicacies at the Colonial Bar and Grill in the Victoria Hotel in the Mall. Prices are reasonable, for example barramundi or buffalo steaks start around $13. 'Buff and bar' is a Darwin speciality, rather like the American 'surf 'n' turf'. It is possible to buy meat pies made from crocodile, kangaroo, buffalo and barramundi. You can even find witchetty grubs on some menus.

To go upmarket, try Nightcaps Restaurant in the Darwin Motor Inn at 97 Mitchell St. The menu is full of pretentious flourishes but the food is good and not over-priced (about $12 for main courses).

For the best picnic spot in Darwin, see *Shopping*.

Drinking. The bar upstairs at the Vic (as the Victoria Hotel is known) is a good place to go when the heat and humidity get too much; you can sit on a flower-lined balcony drinking beer and watching Darwin's uneventful world go by beneath you. Like most of the city's other pubs, it is not a good place to go if you just feel like a quiet drink: it caters for the people who have made Darwin reputedly the home of the most prolific beer-drinkers in the world. The famous Darwin 'stubby', containing a massive 2.25 litres, is no longer produced in Darwin. The main brewery closed down a few years ago and now the oversized bottles are shipped in from Queensland.

In a vain attempt by the authorities to curb the Territorian thirst, it is illegal to buy alcohol before 10am each day. When ordering, it is usual to specify the beer you want by the colour of the can; thus 'Green' is VB (Victoria Bitter), 'White' is Carlton Draught and 'Yellow' is Castlemaine XXXX.

The Top End Hotel at the corner of Daly and Mitchell Sts has four bars: the Sportsman's Bar, favoured by backpackers; the Frontier Brewery Bar serving beer brewed on the premises (the only boutique brewery in Darwin); the Beachcomber Disco open Wednesday to Sunday (no cover charge); and Matildas Restaurant and Bar.

If you prefer to drink alfresco, you might prefer to become a temporary member of the Rocksitters Club, which meets every Saturday to sit on a rock in the sea at Fannie Bay and drink beer. (By being offshore they appear to circumvent the law against outdoor drinking near licensed premises). Some members are in training for the annual competition in which male contestants are required to drink 18 cans and females nine cans of beer every 24 hours while sitting on the rock. The present endurance record is 12 days.

Few of Darwin's colonial buildings survived Cyclone Tracy. The National Trust (4 Burnett Place, Myilly Point; 8981 2848) produces a good brochure called *Historical Darwin*, which includes all the buildings of Darwin that are of any historical interest. These include the Commonwealth Bank — 'the only example of modern architecture of the 1930s/40s'. It suggests two walking tours, one of the city centre and one of Myilly Point. The Myilly Point Heritage Precinct of four 1939 houses includes the National Trust office and shop, as well as an art gallery and a coffee garden, which are open 7 days a week.

The Museum and Art Gallery of the Northern Territory overlooks picturesque Fannie Bay, and is set in a tropical garden. The Museum has a wonderfully varied collection including an interesting Aboriginal section and a fascinating exhibit of Northern Territory nasties such as crocodiles, snakes and sea snakes. It also houses the Cyclone Tracy Gallery, which includes dramatic film of the storm. The Museum is just out of town on Conacher St, Bullocky Point (8999 8201), reached by bus number 4. It is open 9am–5pm weekdays and 10am–5pm weekends; entrance is free, apart from some special exhibitions. Further north along Gilruth Avenue is the Fannie Bay Gaol, which includes exhibits on the early Northern Territory penal system; it is open daily 10am–5pm, and admission is free. Other places of interest associated with the Museum are Lyons Cottage at the corner of Knuckey St and the Esplanade, formerly the residence of the British Australian Telegraph Company and an early example of Darwin architecture, and the Australian Pearling Exhibition at the Darwin Wharf precinct, which illustrates the history of pearling in northern Australian waters (open 10am–4.30pm weekdays, 10am–5.30pm weekends; $5.50 admission).

The Indo-Pacific Marine at Stokes Hill Wharf (8981 1294) is a marine and ecology centre with a living reef. It is open daily 10am–5pm October to May, and 9am–5pm May to October. Even with an admission fee of $11, it is a lot cheaper than a trip to the Great Barrier Reef, and includes a guided tour.

Aquascene is a tourist attraction that sounds tacky but is in fact fascinating. Thirty years ago a resident started throwing scraps to the fishes in Doctor's Gully, down the hill at the north end of the Esplanade. Now thousands of fish come in each day at high tide for a free meal. Some of the fish are over a metre long and many will take bread from your hand. Unlimited stale bread is included in the admission charge of $4. Feeding times are variable depending on the tide, and are shown in *Northern Territory News* or you can call 8981 7837. There is a $1000 fine for fishing in the surrounding water, so don't get any ideas about catching an easy dinner.

The Festival of Darwin is held in August and the Beercan Regatta in June. The Regatta is a natural consequence of Darwin's beer-drinking reputation; rafts made entirely of empty beercans race around the harbour. From the amount of beer-drinking that surrounds the Regatta, it appears that the participants are preparing the raw materials for the following year's competition. The Royal Darwin Show is in late July and the city's Rodeo (with the inevitable accompaniment of a Country Music Festival) in mid-August.

Parks and Gardens. Darwin has a large tropical Botanic Garden between Gilruth Avenue and the Stuart Highway. Further out, East Point Reserve is a scenic retreat with walking and cycling tracks, and good harbour views. If you are there at twilight, you should see wallabies. The area between the Esplanade and the water became a park with cycle track in 1988 and so is called Bicentennial Park. Few overseas visitors bother to dismount from their bicycles to read the 200 plaques commemorating local notables.

Beaches. Darwin has beaches, though in some places they are little more than tidal mud-flats and mangrove swamps. They run from Lameroo Beach (along the Esplanade) to the 'free' (i.e. nudist) beach at Casuarina. Notices are posted in Darwin city centre, with pictures of scarred victims of attacks by marine stingers, to emphasise the dangers. Even outside the wet season, be on your guard for the occasional crocodile; there have been sightings at Darwin's beaches.

SHOPPING
Darwin City Centre Traders proudly call their patch 'your room-to-move shopping city'. What distinguishes the Smith St Mall from hundreds of similar malls elsewhere in Australia is the lack of crowds. Shopping hours in Darwin city centre are standard: stores open at 9am and close at 5.30pm except on Thursdays (9pm) and Saturdays (1pm). There is free musical entertainment for shoppers in the Smith St Mall most lunchtimes and Saturday mornings when the weekly 'Tropical Market' takes place. The Shopping Centre in the suburb of Casuarina has more liberal hours: 9am to 5.30pm daily (including Sundays) with late opening on Thursdays and Fridays.

One of the best things you can do in Darwin is go down to Mindil Beach on a Thursday evening for the weekly market. It is not so much a venue for shopping as for eating snacks from the Asian food stalls, watching the sunset and lazing around. Provided you get there before the crowds you can set yourself up under a palm tree and have a tropical picnic.

Darwin has several weekend markets. Parap, 3km north of the city, has an open air market at Parap Place from 8am to 1pm on Saturdays. At the northern suburb of Rapid Creek there is a Sunday flea market from 8am to 2pm with a good selection of tropical fruit and vegetables.

Many souvenir shops sell Aboriginal crafts, but the Crafts Council of the Northern Territory Gallery (adjacent to the Darwin Museum and Gallery on Conacher St in Fannie Bay) is best for authentic, high-quality artefacts.

The J R Booktique and Jingili Book Exchange in Central Arcade, 69 Smith St (opposite Woolworths) deals in secondhand books and 'nearly new' clothes. Bookworld is at 30 Smith St Mall, with a branch on the Northern Territory University campus at Casuarina. The District Centre in Parap is not the sort of place you might expect to find an enlightened bookshop, but Educational and Technical Books at 7 Parap Place is a wide-ranging and well-stocked shop. For maps, go to the NT Department of Lands, Planning and Environment, at the Land Information Centre, corner of Cavenagh and Bennett Sts (8999 7032).

Entertainment

It is tempting to suggest that the local drinking habits are due to the absence of anything else to do, but in fact the city is gaining a reputation as a party city. The 'What's On' column of the *Northern Territory News* is surprisingly full. The Darwin Entertainment Centre at 93 Mitchell St (8981 1222) manages a respectable range of concerts, considering the size of Darwin audiences, mostly on Friday and Saturday evenings — recent visitors have included Joe Cocker and Tina Turner. If you show your copy of this book at the box office, you should be entitled to a small ticket discount. Cinema Darwin on Mitchell St (8981 5999) is the city's only commercial cinema, although the Darwin Film Society screens predominantly arty films every fortnight on Tuesday evenings at the Museum Theatrette in Fannie Bay. Call 8981 8424 for forthcoming shows at the small and charming Brown's Mart Theatre at 12 Smith St, home to the Darwin Theatre Company. Comedy shows are staged on Wednesdays at the Atrium Hotel at the corner of Peel St and the Esplanade.

Music. A problem afflicting live music in Darwin is the humidity. This is not so much because the audience and artists feel uncomfortably hot after a few numbers, but because it is difficult to keep instruments correctly tuned. Listening to a barely-competent band struggling vainly to stay in tune is not a pleasant aural experience. Nevertheless, some top-flight performers play at the outdoor Darwin Amphitheatre in the Botanic Gardens, a venue that has hosted AC/DC and Cliff Richard (not on the same bill). A popular pastime at the end of these events is the esky-lid race; ice from the cold boxes is poured onto the slopes, and participants slide down while squatting on the lid of their esky. Alcohol is usually banned, so the locals buy a bottle of Coke, drain some off and top it up with rum.

Folk music thrives at the Top End Folk Club (8988 1301), which meets at the East Point Gun Turret on designated Sunday evenings; admission is $5, and musicians are welcome.

Nightlife. The Victoria Hotel in the Smith St Mall functions as the social centre of Darwin. It has some distinctive features such as a motorised awning that swings to and fro over the upstairs bar to keep drinkers cool, and a juke box that is so loud that you'll hear the pub several blocks before you see it. Every night except Sundays, the Vic offers live music and late opening (until 2am). A visit is worthwhile if only for the spectacle of Australian manhood drinking itself into a stupor.

Fanny's is an all-night disco at 3 Edmund St (cover charge $5–10). At the same address is Squires which is a pub with quieter musical entertainment. The Hot Gossip Entertainment Complex at 21 Cavenagh St is glitzy and expensive, with live bands and a night club.

From June till August, there is a commercial corroboree every Saturday night at the Darwin Travelodge (122 The Esplanade; 8981 5388) costing $12, or $30 including a barbecue.

Casino. The Diamond Beach Hotel Casino is on Gilruth Avenue, overlooking Mindil Beach (on bus routes 4 and 6 from the city). Its cool, glamorous interior is a welcome contrast to some of the city's other nightspots and its gaming tables stay open till 4am. Make sure you are reasonably dressed (no shorts, denims or flip-flops and, to clinch admittance for men, a tie).

Sport. Horseracing takes place year round at Fannie Bay Racecourse on Playford St. Darwin has little other organised sport. There are several swimming pools as a consolation for not being able to swim in the sea due to the risk of box jellyfish (October to May). The best place for sailing and windsurfing is Vestey's Beach at Fannie Bay.

Most spectator sports take place at the Marrara Complex in the northern suburbs. In 1991 it was the venue for the first Arafura Sports Festival for competing athletes from South East Asia, Papua New Guinea and northern Australia, reflecting Darwin's geographical orientation. it is intended that this will become a biennial festival of sport. The Sport Hotline number is 8982 2311.

The Northern Territory Government Tourist Bureau is halfway along Smith St Mall at number 31 (8981 6611). There are two tourist giveaway magazines: the inaccurately titled *This Week in Darwin* (which is monthly) and the *Visitor's Guide*. You can pick up copies from the Tourist Bureau and most hotel receptions.

American Express: c/o Travellers World, 18 Knuckey St (8981 4699).
Medical Treatment: Community Health Centre, Health House, Mitchell St (8981 6155).
Dental Emergencies: 11 Smith St (8981 9149).
Disabled Persons Bureau: Shop 8, Ground Floor, Casuarina Plaza (8920 3213).
Helplines: Alcoholics Anonymous — 8985 4479; Crisis Line (7pm to 7am daily) — 8981 2040; Poison Information — 8927 4777.
Women's Information Service: PO Box 2043, Darwin 5794 (8981 2668).

You could easily blow a thousand dollars visiting the places of interest around Darwin. Try to set aside some money for tours, as there is so much that is worthwhile. Most regional tour operators are listed in the *Holiday Planner* and their brochures are displayed at the Northern Territory Government Tourist Bureau in the Smith St Mall. Although Kakadu is the most popular destination, you might consider the less visited Litchfield Park (Wangi), which is nearer Darwin; it has the scenic Tabletop Range as a backdrop, huge termite mounds, hot springs and waterfalls to compensate for a shortage of crocodiles. This is a feasible destination for people without four-wheel-drive. Day tours for $65 are available from Frogshollow Backpackers in Darwin (see above).

There is a multitude of other tours from which to choose: to the Aboriginal land of Arnhem Land, crocodile-spotting boat trips, hikes, flights and four-wheel-drive expeditions in Kakadu and day trips to swimming holes at Berry Springs and Howard Springs. Many of them involve flying or four-wheel-drive travel, which increases the cost. Some of the hostels put on their own backpackers' tours — for example, Ivan's Backpackers (see *Accommodation*).

One of the biggest tour operators is Adventure Terra Safari, which incorporates Dial-a-Safari, Bushranger Tours and Breakwater Canoe Tours (Cashman Building, 28 The Mall, Darwin; 8941 2899 or toll-free 008-891127). Prices range from $190 for a two-day four-wheel-drive trip to Kakadu to a nine-day canoe trip on the Katherine and Daly River system for $860.

Another long-established tour company is Holiday AKT, formerly known as Australian Kakadu Tours (Shop 19, Star Village, Smith St Mall, Darwin; 8981 5144), which runs an extensive range of tours of the Top End wilderness.

Dangerous Creatures. The local wildlife is worthy of respect, especially crocodiles which achieve huge proportions — up to 7m long and weighing a ton. Since they were made a protected species, numbers have rapidly increased. A pressure group called SCRAM (Saltwater Crocodile Removal Action Movement) lobbies for the right to shoot them. Signs in Kakadu National Park warn that 'swimming is for sharks, barramundi, crocodiles and idiots'. In an attempt to prevent tourists from taking the crocodile warning signs home as souvenirs, the authorities have taken to erecting signs measuring 20 metres square. *Never* swim in an area that you're not sure about, never camp next to an outback river, and never leave remains around from your fishing expedition (see *Health: Perils of the Deep*). Further information is available from the Conservation Commission of the Northern Territory, PO Box 496, Palmerston, NT 0831 (8989 5511). You can take out Crocodile Attack Insurance at branches of the Territory Insurance Office — it pays out $50,000 if you lose a limb.

To learn a number of more obscure facts, visit the Crocodile Farm 40km south from Darwin on the Stuart Highway (just south of the Arnhem Highway turn-off); it opens daily from 9am to 5pm. The 7000 residents include Bert, the largest crocodile in captivity, and a 45-year-old albino. Activity is greatest at public feeding times which are not necessarily daily: call 8988 1450 for details.

Among the other local species, be warned that 14 varieties of Northern Territory snake are potentially lethal. Even so, Graeme Gow, the owner of Reptile World at Humpty Doo (50km south-west of Darwin; 8988 1661) has survived being bitten 84 times in the last 35 years; his charges include 52 different kinds of snake and a score of species of lizard.

As mentioned above, box jellyfish make the ocean waters unswimmable from October to May. The Marine Stinger emergency number is 008-079909. In outback areas, water buffaloes should not be approached too closely, nor should wild pigs or dingoes. And the wetlands in the Top End attract hordes of mosquitoes and flies, so take plenty of insect repellant. Tea tree oil from chemists is helpful if you have been badly bitten.

BATHURST AND MELVILLE ISLANDS

Melville Island is about 80km due north of Darwin, and is the second largest Australian island after Tasmania. Bathurst Island is immediately to its west and almost touches it at several places. The islands are home to the Tiwi people, Aboriginals who have been able to preserve their homeland more successfully than other native Australians. Judging by the cultural dissimilarities between the islanders and mainland Aboriginals, there appears to have been little contact between the two groups. A Catholic Mission was established on Bathurst Island in 1911, and many Aboriginals have been converted to the religion. The islands, though fascinating from an anthropological point of view, are not exceptionally beautiful, and inland the terrain of forest and waterfalls is similar to that around Darwin.

The most common way to reach the islands is with Tiwi Tours (Shop 19, Star Village, Smith St Mall, Darwin; 8981 5115). Trips last one to three days and cost about $200 a day. Each starts with a half-hour flight on Air North to the airport at Pularumpi, the main town on Melville Island. Accommodation is in safari-style tented camps and local guides show participants how to forage for food. For permission to visit independently, apply at least a month in advance to the President of the relevant Tiwi Council: Nguiu Community Government

Council, Nguiu, Bathurst Island via Darwin 0822; or Milikapiti Community Government Council, Milikapiti, Snake Bay via Darwin 0822.

ARNHEM LAND

In contrast to the well travelled wilderness south of Darwin, the land to the east (named after the Dutch town of Arnhem) is mostly still in its virgin state. The Aboriginals have exclusive rights to much of the area. They are expert in moving around these apparently impenetrable rain forests, which are mostly out-of-bounds to outsiders. Arnhem Land Outback Expeditions (PO Box 2523, Darwin; 8948 0648) has three and four day trips costing $200 a day. Most visitors enter by four-wheel-drive from Kakadu to Coopers Creek or fly into the remote airport of Nhulunbuy on the Gove Peninsula, at the northeastern tip of Arnhem Land. Here there is an exclusive golf and fishing lodge. If you have unlimited wealth a better place to go is Seven Spirit Bay on the Coburg Peninsula, a luxury base camp for eco-tours of this pristine wilderness; a 3-day trip costs about $1000.

KAKADU NATIONAL PARK

Few visitors to Darwin miss Kakadu National Park, and few are disappointed. A little time and effort spent investigating the various possibilities is worthwhile. The main topic of conversation among travellers in Darwin seems to be the best way to visit Kakadu.

The edge of its huge area — it is one-quarter the size of Great Britain — lies 150km east of Darwin on the Arnhem Highway, but the main attractions are a further 100km towards Arnhem Land. The park hosts three different habitats: the wetlands and estuaries, home to an astonishing variety of birdlife and other wildlife; the ridgetop area, forested hills rising from the swamps; and the escarpments where much Aboriginal art can be found. Kakadu's principle features are Ubirr (Obiri) Rock and Nourlangie Rock, which have fine examples of Aboriginal rock art going back 30,000 years; Yellow Waters and the South Alligator River, where cruises depart for crocodile and bird-spotting; and Jim Jim Falls and Twin Falls, spectacular waterfalls reached by four-wheel-drive vehicles or boat. There are other attractive creeks, billabongs and 18 developed camping areas, which cost $7 per site; freelance camping is allowed and is free, but you have to get a permit from Park Headquarters near Jabiru (8979 2101). The park entrance fee is $10. Although it is possible to visit the park at its loveliest (and its cheapest) in the Wet, you will be confined to sealed roads and therefore limited in where you can go and probably prevented from walking or camping.

As Kakadu sits on some of the richest uranium and other mineral deposits in Australia, it is remarkable that it is a National Park at all. The area around Jabiru was excluded from the Park (where the only mine, the Ranger Mine, is located), which is suitably distant from the more attractive areas. Jabiru's other claim to fame is a kitsch hotel in the shape of a crocodile. There is still a huge area deceptively called a 'Conservation Area', which is the subject of an ongoing tussle between environmentalists and mining companies.

Arrival and Departure. A Greyhound Pioneer bus leaves the Darwin Transit Centre daily at 7am, arriving at Jabiru at 10.15am and at Cooinda (a hotel/bar campsite) at noon. Hitch-hiking is just possible as far as Jabiru and Cooinda. Once inside the park, hitching is difficult: traffic is light and many of the cars passing through are full. You can, however, get around on the Parklink bus which calls at most points of interest. Individual fares are high, but you can get passes for one, two or three days.

Accommodation. Gagudju Lodge — the Park's YHA hostel — is at Cooinda, on the Yellow Water Billabong (PO Box 696, Jabiru, NT 0886; 8979 0145). Twin rooms are $15 per person, doubles $25 per person; advance bookings are essential. Interstate buses drop people off right at the door. Other affordable accommodation includes the Kakadu Frontier Lodge on Jabiru Drive (8979 2422) and the Kakadu Hostel at Ubirr (8979 2333). There is also the Wildman River Wilderness Lodge half-way between Darwin and Jabiru; details are available from Holiday AKT (see *Further Afield* above).

The most unusual lodgings is the Four Seasons at Jabiru, a futuristic crocodile-shaped hotel known as the 'crocodile motel'. It is luxurious and expensive. At the other end of the price spectrum, you can camp for free at designated sites in the Park.

Tours. Many people settle for the easy but expensive option of taking a tour. A 3-day trip will typically cost around $300 and include a visit to one of the prehistoric rock art sites, a boat tour of Yellow Waters and some crocodile-spotting. To get away from the tourist routes, contact Willis's Walkabouts (12 Carrington St, Millner, Darwin 0810; 8985 2134), a recommended trekking firm that organises unluxurious camping trips in Kakadu (as well the Kimberley and Red Centre) lasting from 3 days to 3 weeks. The longer trips cost about $75 a day, and participants should be fit.

THE NEVER NEVER

The town of Katherine is the main settlement between Alice Springs and Darwin. It is the gateway to the Never Never, an area made doubly famous by Crocodile Dundee's ficticious company 'Never Never Tours' (motto: you'll never survive, and if you do you'll never come back). The town is situated on the Katherine River, the first permanent river on the journey north from Alice Springs, and is where the Victoria Highway from Western Australia meets the Stuart Highway. The river and town are named after one of the daughters of a sponsor of explorer Stuart (he of the Stuart Highway). Katherine is growing fast as a result of the tourist sights in the area and a number of industrial developments.

The main attraction is the Gorge, 32km from town. The Nitmiluk National Park contains a magnificent series of steep-sided gorges separated by rapids, plenty of walking trails and several examples of Aboriginal rock painting. The Cutta Cutta Caves are also close to town.

Accommodation. The backpackers' centre of Katherine is Kookaburra Lodge, part of the VIP Backpackers Resorts chain, on the corner of Lindsay and Third Sts (8971 0257). It offers good hostel accommodation for $13 a night, and also rents bicycles for $10 a day. The YHA hostel is Palm Court Backpackers (corner of Third and Giles Sts; 8972 2722), which charges around $11 for a dorm bed. It also offers several tours.

The Riverview Motel and Caravan Park (8972 1011) is a bit further on, and is only 100m from thermal springs reaching 34°C. Eight kilometres down the road on the banks of the Katherine River is Springvale Homestead (8972 1355), with bunkhouse, camping and van sites available. An Aboriginal corroboree is held here three nights a week, but the ill-effects of packaged tourism are at times glaringly obvious. The Homestead is run by Travel North at 6 Katherine Terrace (8972 1044), which has a wide range of tours available. Low Level Caravan Park also provides excellent facilities for caravans and tent sites from $7. The regional tourist centre is at the corner of Lindsay Avenue and the Stuart Highway (8972 2650), where friendly staff provide free information.

Exploring. Local tours include trips to the Nitmiluk Gorge by boat (ranging from $26 to $68). Cutta Cutta Caves and Edith Falls are also attractive local sites to visit. A night-time crocodile-spotting tour from the Springvale Homestead costs $35 including dinner (the crocodiles in this area are freshies and therefore not dangerous). The highlights of the Gorge, however, can be enjoyed without the help of a travel agency. The ten walks in the Park take you through habitats from swamp and rainforest to plateau, and last from 2 hours to 5 days. If you are here in the Wet, when there is enough water to cover the rapids, the best way to appreciate the Gorge is to hire a canoe and take off yourself. Canoe hire is available from $23. Renting a canoe for a full day ($48) allows you to see much more of the Gorge than the boat tours, and you are provided with all the information that the boat trippers get.

The Barunga Sports and Cultural Festival is a big event at Easter on Aboriginal land 80km south-east of Katherine. Music, art and workshops of Aboriginal culture are on display. Entry permits are not required during the Festival, but are necessary during the rest of the year. See *Great Outdoors: Restricted Areas* for details of how to apply.

Mataranka. Another 20km south-east is Mataranka, with a pleasant campsite and a YHA hostel (Mataranka Homestead; 8975 4544; $13). Just north of the settlement are thermal springs, with a pool so clear that at night you can lie on its bottom two metres underwater, look up and see the stars shining above the palms that surround the pool. During the day you can hike alongside the Waterhouse River or canoe down to the Roper River. *We of the Never Never* was filmed around Mataranka, and an exact replica of the Homestead at Elsey Station (where the story is set) has been built at Mataranka as a tourist attraction/ museum. Tours go from Mataranka out to Elsey Station itself, visiting places mentioned in the book such as 'Red Lily Lagoon', 'Elsey Falls' and 'Flying Fox Creek'. Some include a boat trip along the Roper River fishing for barramundi. The hostel can provide tour information.

The Roper Highway east from Mataranka is surprisingly well surfaced considering it is a road to almost nowhere, eventually petering out into a track to the Collera Mountains. There is hardly ever any traffic, and so it is ideal to travel along just to experience the seemingly endless space and understand the isolation of the tiny missions and stations that you pass.

TENNANT CREEK

Until gold was discovered in the 1930s, the Barkly Tablelands were even less populated than other areas of the Northern Territory. But in the few years of Australia's last gold rush the town of Tennant Creek was created almost literally overnight. The stories of the town's origins are confused, but one popular legend has it that a wagon loaded with building materials and beer for a new hotel broke down miles short of its intended destination, and that rather than transport the contents a hotel was created on the spot.

Tennant Creek is now a town with a population of 3500, and functions to serve travellers on the Track. It is halfway between Katherine and Alice Springs, and close to the important road junction at Three Ways (where the Barkly Highway from Queensland joins the Stuart Highway).

Early mines such as 'The Burnt Shirt' and 'The Dot' can be entered day or night on a range of tours. You can also fossick for gold or watch demonstrations of gold refining at the Government Battery on Peko Road. The town still has gold mines ranking among Australia's richest. The Visitor Information Centre on the corner of Davidson and Patterson Sts (8962 3388) can provide full details on sites of historic interest in the town. If you want to stay for a while, there is a YHA hostel on Leichhardt St (8962 2719) that has beds for $10.

The best-known geographic feature of the region is the Devil's Marbles, a series of precariously balanced granite outcrops on the Stuart Highway 114km south of Tennant Creek. Tours run there from the town daily. Strangely, the smaller weathered outcrops known as the Devil's Pebbles (17km north-west) look much more like marbles than do the rocks to the south.

ALICE SPRINGS

The town now called Alice was founded in 1888 as a site for a railway station on the route of a proposed line through the centre of Australia. The area already had a telegraph station, built in 1871 as part of the transcontinental line to Darwin that put Australia in direct contact with Europe for the first time. Four years after the railway finally arrived in 1929, the town adopted the name of a nearby natural spring; this had earlier been named in honour of Lady Alice Todd, wife of Charles Todd (Postmaster-General of Adelaide at the time). His surname was given to the town's river.

Alice is expanding economically through its role as a tourist gateway for Uluru and the MacDonnell Ranges. It also functions as a support centre for the controversial US intelligence facility at nearby Pine Gap, the biggest American military installation outside the USA. Another technological intrusion is the planned dump for nuclear waste near the town.

Those who have read Nevil Shute's book *A Town Like Alice* might expect a rough-and-ready frontier town atmosphere. In fact it is a prosperous town of 25,000, until recently resembling a suburban building site much more than a pioneering place. 'The Alice' is a disappointment to many travellers, comparing unfavourably with the spectacle of Uluru, the cultural delights of Adelaide, and the beaches and islands of northern Queensland. But Alice is certainly a good place to meet fellow travellers, the Clapham Junction of central Australia.

Climate. Alice averages 9½ hours of sunshine daily. Summer is hot and dusty — temperatures in the 40s are quite typical for February — but the dryness of the air makes it bearable. Summer evenings can be surprisingly cool so take a sweater. Winter days are warm, but the temperature cools off rapidly towards nightfall. The July average minimum is only a few degrees above zero and temperatures often fall below freezing. Travellers from the tropics or the coast may be unprepared for the cold.

Town Layout. The town centre is in the shape of a rectangle, bounded to the west by the Stuart Highway and to the east by the Todd River. Don't waste time looking for a bridge; the Todd 'River' fills with water only once every few years, and a favourite saying is 'you have to see the Todd flow three times before you're a local'. A good map of the town (published by the Regional Tourist Association) is widely available for $1. With Stuart Terrace, Stott Terrace and Sturt Terrace all in the centre of town, it is easy to get confused when asking directions.

Air. Alice Springs' airport is 7km south of the town, off the Stuart Highway. The main connections are with Adelaide and Darwin, plus several daily flights to Yulara (for Uluru) taking only 45 minutes. The Alice Springs Airport Shuttle

Service minibus connects with arriving and departing flights and serves all city centres hotels, motels and hostels; the fare is $6 (8953 0310).

Bus. The bus terminal is at Shop 45, Ford Plaza, Hartley St (8952 7888), which serves Greyhound Pioneer Australia. The standard fare on services to and from Uluru is $55. Prices to Adelaide and Darwin are $156, to Melbourne $214, Sydney and Brisbane $265 and Perth $280.

Train. The railway station (8952 1011) is a 15-minute walk from the western edge of the city. If your luggage is heavy you may prefer to take one of the cabs which meet arriving trains. The *Ghan* departs from Adelaide at 2pm on Monday and Thursday and arrives nearly 23 hours later (12.30pm the following day) in Alice. After a short rest, the return journey leaves Alice at 5.10pm and is scheduled to arrive in Adelaide at 4.30pm the next day, though it is often up to two hours early. The single economy fare is $125. The name derives from the Australian abbreviation for 'Afghan' as the original rail line ran along the route taken by the Afghan camel drivers who opened up central Australia. The Ghan Preservation Society runs restored locomotives on short excursions from Alice 4 days a week; tickets cost $12.

Driving. Members of Australian or foreign motoring organisations can get roadside assistance from the AANT's local contractor, Russ Driver & Co at 58 Sargent St (8952 1087). Centre Car Rentals in the Ford Plaza on Todd St (8952 1405) keeps long hours (7am-11pm daily) and is good value so is Territory Rent-a-Car (corner of Hartley St and Stott Terrace; 8952 9999). The cheapest vehicle available from both companies is a moke. Econo Rent at 85 Todd Mall (8952 9633) advertises 'yesterday's cars at yesterday's prices'. The tourist bureau at Todd Plaza can arrange car hire and issues a list of vehicles and prices, but it does not represent all the companies.

Hitch-hiking. The first possible spot hitching north along the Stuart Highway is at the junction with Wills Terrace. Heading south, the junction of the highway and Stuart Terrace at the foot of Billygoat Hill is feasible, but chances are higher further south at the junction with Ross Highway by Blatherskite Park. Posting a notice at the truck stop 4km north of Alice can result in a long-distance lift. The Todd St YHA hostel has a good lift-sharing notice board.

Local Transport. Alice Springs Bus Service, called Asbus (86-88 Hartley St; 8952 9666), operates four routes around town at infrequent intervals. Timetables are available from the Community Information Centre off Todd Mall next to Westpac. Many travellers hire bicycles, for example from Melanka Bicycle Hire at 94 Todd St which is open seven days a week. For a taxi, call Alice Radio Cabs on 8952 3700 or Alice Springs Taxis on 8952 1877. There is a taxi rank on Gregory Terrace opposite the Council Lawns.

Alice Springs has its own tourist bus called the *Alice Wanderer* (8953 0310), which allows passengers to get on and off at the sites which interest them; a 4-hour ticket costs $10 and a full day $15.

Accommodation

At first glance Alice Springs seems well served with cheap places to stay. But although the average stay is only a night or two, such is the number of backpackers travelling through that many of the best places are often full. You should have few problems finding a room from November to April, and may well get a discount on the prices mentioned below.

The Pioneer YHA hostel is at the corner of Parsons St and Leichhardt Terrace (8952 8855); it is built within a converted open-air movie theatre. Beds in small dorms cost $13. The hostel is very busy and so booking ahead is advisable.

Among the most lively and sociable backpackers' hostels is Toddy's at 41 Gap Road (8952 1322), which has a wide range of room sizes available, including dorms with beds from $10. Other VIP Backpackers Resorts include Alice Lodge, on the east side of the Todd River away from the town centre at 4 Mueller St (8953 1975), which is pleasant and good value; and Ossie's Homestead at 18 Warburton St (8952 2308), which has pet kangaroos by the names of Boomer and Snuggles wandering about the place. Cheapest beds are $12. All of these hostels have pools (of varying sizes) and are air conditioned.

Other backpacker accommodation includes The Lodge at 16 Bath St (8952 3108) and the Melanka Lodge at 94 Todd St (8952 4744; toll-free 008-815 066), which few people rave about; the atmosphere is quite impersonal, the room partitions are thin, and the dormitories can be crowded. The place has been summed up as 'scruffy and noisy'. Beds start at $10.

The Stuart Lodge, run by the YWCA but open to both sexes, is at the corner of Stuart Terrace and Hartley St (8952 1894), and has single rooms for $30 and doubles for $40.

The long-distance buses coming into town will often drop people off at their accommodation.

Camping. The Wintersun Caravan Park (8952 4080), 2km north on the Stuart Highway, has on-site vans for $30 and charges $10 for an unpowered site. The McDonnell Range Tourist Park is 5km south of town near the beginning off the Ross Highway. If you are a tent camper, remember that winter nights can be cold enough to coat your tent in sheet ice.

Eating and Drinking

The Eranova Cafeteria at 72 Todd St has excellent coffee and good sandwiches and lunches. It closes, however, at 4pm (2pm on Saturdays). The Jolly Swagman in the Todd Plaza (opposite Flynn Church) is another good place for lunch. La Casalinga at 105 Gregory Terrace has unexceptional but inexpensive pizzas starting at around $10; it is licenced and opens from 5pm to 1am every night. A less appealing late-night venue is Kentucky Fried Chicken at the junction of Todd St and Stott Terrace (across from the YHA hostel). Toddy's Backpackers (41 Gap Road) has a popular barbecue every night of the week which features kangaroo and is open to non-residents. The excellent ice-cream parlours in Alice are a welcome relief on long, hot summers' days. The Old Telegraph Station Reserve is a good place for a picnic. Electric barbecues are available here, and also along the Todd River.

Drinking. A recent study claimed that the residents of Alice Springs drink two and a half times more than the average Australian. The town's landlords seem to revel in running Outback-style pubs for hard drinkers. Most are rather noisy and rough with linoleum floor and plastic chairs. You can sample lowlife by spending a few evenings in pubs and bars in Alice. Some of the pubs, such as the Old Riverside Hotel, have a bouncer on the door to turn away unsuitably dressed (or looking) men, but plenty of other pubs don't.

The Old Alice Inn in Todd Mall (at the corner of Wills Terrace) has live bands in one of its five bars and nightclub. The Stuart Arms in the Ford Plaza is a lively pub which stays open late.

 Anzac Hill, above Wills Terrace at the north end of the town centre, provides a good view of the town and the MacDonnell Ranges. It is especially good at sunset, when the contrast between the majesty of the mountains and the shabby suburbs is at its most vivid. You can reach the summit by car, or walk up the 'Lions Walk', opposite the corner of Hartley St and Wills Terrace. One of the best sights is the old Telegraph Station, incorporating a small museum, restored by the Conservation Commission. It is 3km north of the town and can be reached by walking north for about 30 minutes beside (or along the dry bed of) the Todd River. The trail almost immediately takes you out of the noise and bustle of the centre and winds past hills until you reach the station and the springs which give the town its name. The Conservation Commission has produced an excellent guide to the buildings; admission is $2.50.

Another interesting glimpse into outback life can be had at the Royal Flying Doctor Service base (8952 1129) near the Stuart Memorial on Stuart Terrace. The $2.50 entrance fee gets you a short film on the activities of the service, a quick tour around the radio room and a visit to the museum next to the souvenir shop. It opens 9am-3.30pm from Monday to Saturday, and (from Easter to October) on Sunday afternoons.

Alice Springs also has an Aviation Museum, in the Connelan Hangar of the former airport on Memorial Drive (8952 4241). It opens 10am-4pm from Monday to Friday, and features the stories of a couple of outback tragedies. The School of the Air (in the broadcasting rather than aeronautical sense) is also worth visiting, as the teaching of children in far-flung settlements by radio is a classic Australian institution. It is on Head St, and opens only 1.30–3.30pm from Monday to Friday during school terms; admission $1.

A walking tour booklet on the town issued by the National Trust (available from the Tourist Office) will take you around most of the remaining old buildings such as the Residency and the Town Gaol.

A new centre on the local Aboriginal culture is named after a professor who championed their cause: the Strehlow Research Centre on Larapinta Drive costs $6. Another recommended outing is to Australia's only date plantation. Admission to Mecca Date Gardens on Palm Circuit south of town is free.

SHOPPING

Most shops open 9am-5.30pm on weekdays with late opening to 9pm on Fridays, and 8.30am-noon on Saturdays; many also open on Sundays. The main shopping area is Todd Mall, which features free lunchtime concerts on Friday. A market is held here every other Sunday. Besides the shops selling endless souvenirs (such as T-shirts bearing the name 'Alice Springs' spelt out in flies), there is a good centre for Aboriginal Artists and Craftsmen at 86-88 Todd St where you can see bark paintings, carvings and musical instruments. The Araluen Arts Centre also has a display of crafts organised by the Crafts Council of the NT. Prices are quite high for handicrafts, but you are welcome to browse. The Alice Springs Peace Group has a shop in Colocag Plaza off Todd St. Bookworm, a buy-sell-or-swap bookshop is also in the Plaza. Almost all the shops in Alice seem to sell the book *A Town like Alice*, which — apart from the title — has little to do with the place, being set in north Queeensland.

Entertainment

For a town in the middle of the bedrock conservatism of the Outback, Alice Springs has a surprising number of 'alternative' events and venues. Reading the posters in shops will tell you what is on, whether a radical folk band, a yoga course, or a political demonstration. The Alice Springs Regional Tourist Association publishes the monthly booklet *Central Australian Visitors' Guide* which gives a good rundown on coming events.

Nightlife. Despite the roughness of some of the pubs, Alice Springs has little outrageous nightlife. Lasseters Casino on Barrett Drive has cocktail bars and a disco in addition to the gambling facilities which are available from 10am to 4am daily. Only respectably dressed people are admitted, with particular attention paid after 7pm. The Old Alice Inn (formerly the Todd Tavern) is a large red-roofed building at the top of Todd Mall. It is a little less fussy about its dress rules. There is live entertainment in the piano bar from 8pm, Thursday-Saturday, and every night at Alice's Disco (sometimes with live bands). The Stuart Arms Tavern, at the junction of Todd Mall and Parsons St, is the main venue for live music, with rock from 9pm to 2am Thursday-Saturday.

Bojangles Bar & Grill at 80 Todd St is a restaurant by day (opening at 11am except Sundays) and a nightclub later on, with live entertainment and dancing until 2am (Wednesday and Sunday) and 6am (Thursday-Saturday nights).

Festivals. The first Monday in May sees a cattle-branding competition followed by the Bangtail Muster, celebrating the traditional end of the cattle-mustering season. There is a collection of satirical floats and a parade, and men on horseback ride symbolically off into the sunset. A few days later, the annual Camel Cup races take place on the track in Blatherskite Park south of the town, commemorating the races held by the Afghan drivers who led the original camel trains in the late 19th century. Many people dress in Arab clothing for the occasion. The event is followed by a big folk concert and campfire in the evening. A Beerfest starts the next morning.

Late September is the time to experience Northern Territory foolishness at its best. As mentioned, the Todd River through the centre of town rarely has any water in it. That hasn't stopped local residents from having a regatta for all classes of boat, just like England's Henley-on-Thames event. The Henley-on-Todd version, which began in 1961 and is held each September, differs only in that the boats have no bottoms and so contestants run down the course holding the sides of the boat. A spotter aircraft patrols the racecourse searching for sharks, and notices are posted which prohibit swimming and diving. There is a surf rescue display and a sea battle in which two warships fight using flour bombs and water cannon. Although the event is becoming increasingly commercialised (most of the 'boats' seem to be sponsored by banks), it is still great fun and, needless to say, a huge amount of beer gets drunk.

As an antidote to such zany antics, you can catch a concert, film or play at the Araluen Arts Centre (8952 5022). Witchetty's Bistro in the Arts Centre hosts a folk club concert every Sunday at 8am. Arty films are shown (but only every other Tuesday) at the Totem Theatre, Anzac Oval, Wills Terrace.

Sport. Horseracing takes place every Saturday at the Alice Springs Turf Club course on South Stuart Highway. In winter there are picnic race meetings in the surrounding townships, culminating in the Alice Springs August races, an event which lasts a week. Australian Rules football is played on winter weekends in Traeger Park, and Rugby League each winter Sunday afternoon at the Anzac

Oval. There are public tennis courts at Traeger Park. Fun runs are organised each Monday at 6pm; call 8952 6967 for the current location. The large Swimming Centre on Speed St is a pleasant place to relax in the heat of the day; it stays open until 7.30pm and costs $1.80.

The Central Australian Tourism Industry Association operates the Visitor Information Centre (corner of Hartley St and Gregory Terrace; 8952 5800) and supplies regional information and maps, and can book accommodation and tours.

Post Office: Hartley St between Parsons St and Gregory Terrace (8952 1020); opening hours are 9am–5pm, Monday to Friday.
Conservation Commission of the NT: corner of Hartley St and Gregory Terrace (8951 5210).
Mapshop: 21 Gregory Terrace.
Medical Treatment: Alice Springs Hospital, corner of Stuart Terrace and Gap Road (8950 2211).
Dental Emergencies: Department of Health Dental Clinic (8952 4766).
Disabled Persons Bureau: Helm House, corner Bath St and Gregory Terrace (8951 5880).
Crisis Line: 8950 2266 (7pm to 7am).

Before heading off to Uluru (which is what most new arrivals in Alice Springs are planning) a few day trips from Alice are worth considering. Chateau Hornsby, central Australia's only winery, is 15km from town, an easy cycle ride south along the Stuart Highway before turning along Petrick Road. Although quite commercial, shows put on here by the Outback raconteur and singer Ted Egan can be amusing (ring 8955 5133 for details).

The main physical attractions are east and west of the town and consist of gorges or 'gaps' in the MacDonnell Ranges. The most impressive is Standley Chasm. The Henbury Meteorite Craters are just off the Stuart Highway south of town, well worth visiting on the way to Uluru or Adelaide.

Just south of Larapinta Drive, 100km west from Alice Springs, is Finke Gorge National Park and Palm Valley. While there are bus tours here, some allow you barely an hour to spend in the Valley. You need much longer to appreciate fully the natural delights of the area, so instead try to get together with two or three others to hire a four-wheel-drive vehicle. Kings Canyon, Australia's modest version of the Grand Canyon, is 323km south-west of Alice. It can be visited on its own or in combination with a trip to Uluru. A new luxury resort, Frontier Lodge, opened in 1991 aiming to become a mini-Yulara.

Tours. As in Darwin you will be faced with many competing promises from tour operators. Uluru is easier to appreciate on your own than Kakadu though you still have to worry about transport and accommodation. To give just one example of the kind of prices involved, camping safaris to Uluru, the Olgas and Kings Canyon cost $285 for 3 days with Sahara Tours (PO Box 3891, Alice Springs, NT 0871; 8953 0881). A 1½-day camping tour to Kings Canyon costs $110, and a four-wheel-drive camping safari to the Red Centre over 5 days $485; all these prices include food and use of camping gear. Another good operator offering tours of a similar kind is Austour (03-9770 2145). Alice Springs Tour Professionals (8953 0666) provides a comprehensive tour booking service for both central Australia and the Top End.

The best known Aboriginal tours are run by Rod Steinert Tours (085-588377, or 1800-679 418 toll-free from Alice Springs). The 'Aboriginal Dreamtime and Bushtucker' day trip operates daily for $67, or $50 if you have your own transport (less YHA discount). The 'Outback Bushman's Dinner' costs $78 by coach or $65 self-drive, and promises the 'true central Australian dining experience', including the dessert known as 'Spotted Dog with Cocky's Joy'.

The National Parks and Reserves run a 'Fun in the Parks' programme, which includes nature walks, slide shows, etc., from April to September for a modest fee of $2.50. Check the *Central Australian Visitors Guide* in the autumn for listings.

ULURU (AYERS ROCK) AND THE OLGAS

The world's most celebrated monolith is almost at the centre of Australia. Uluru is a place of pilgrimage to 300,000 visitors each year, most of whom travel vast distances to see one of the world's natural wonders (and most of whom will get in your photos). A few are disappointed and conclude that the pressures to which they succumbed are an elaborate con trick on the part of the tourist authorities. But the majority decide otherwise after seeing the Rock rising proudly from the empty desert. And if this isn't enough on its own, just 25km to the west are the equally impressive Olgas or Kata Tjuta, which means 'many heads'.

Both sites fall within the Uluru–Kata Tjuta National Park, to which the entrance fee is $10 ($15 from 1997); the entrance ticket is valid for 5 consecutive days after purchase. Despite strenuous objections from the Northern Territory government, the federal government insisted the freehold of the Park be transferred to the traditional Aboriginal owners in 1985. Since then it has been leased back to the National Parks and Wildlife Service. Most of the surrounding land is Aboriginal, and a permit is required to enter it. In addition there are five sacred sites within the Park that are clearly marked and which you should not attempt to enter. Throughout the Park there is a policy of no photography of Aboriginal people or the sacred sites.

Don't imagine that a bus or aircraft scheduled to go to Uluru will drop you at the foot of the Rock. Previously there were tourist facilities around the Rock itself; these were removed when the lodgings and shops were judged to be causing too much ecological and visual damage. The nearest facilities are now in the resort village of Yulara, just north of the Park and 20km by road from the Rock. The area is so popular that Yulara is now the Territory's fourth-largest settlement after Alice Springs, Darwin and Katherine. However much you regret the despoiling of the area by any form of construction, you will be impressed by the amount of thought that has gone into the new resort. The colours blend in with the landscape as effectively as any hotel/campsite/entertainment complex placed in the middle of a desert could hope to, and there are some interesting technological innovations: solar sails that deflect the intense sun and create an artificial breeze around the buildings, and solar panels that heat most of Yulara's water.

Arrival and Departure. Yulara is most easily accessible from Alice Springs, with at least three flights daily (costing over $100). Scheduled bus services from Alice Springs cost around $60 and take over 5 hours to cover the 450km. The Greyhound Pioneer coach leaves Alice at 7.45am and departs Yulara for Alice at 2pm. There are direct flights to Yulara from Sydney, Melbourne, Adelaide and Cairns. Connellan airport is just north of Yulara, with connecting bus services into 'town' costing $8. The Lasseter Highway, the road in from the Stuart Highway at Erldunda, is a fairly easy drive, but you should take care not to be mesmerised by the heat haze and the long stretches of unchanging desert. Beyond Uluru the road to the Olgas is unsealed.

Hitching is difficult on the Stuart Highway north from Adelaide or south from Alice Springs, although possible with persistence. Once on the Erldunda–Yulara road it becomes easier, as nearly everybody is going to Yulara. AAT Kings runs an hourly shuttle between Yulara and the Rock from 10am–3pm ($12 one-way); Sunworth Taxis charge $10 one-way. Alternatively you can join a tour or hitch. Although Greyhound Pioneer buses do go between Yulara and the Rock they are carrying passengers on a tour. Hitching is feasible from Yulara to the Rock but trickier from Yulara to the Olgas. Common sense is needed on the trip to the Olgas: despite the relatively short distance, people have been known to die of heat exhaustion and dehydration.

Visitor Information. The Visitors Centre in Yulara (8956 2144; open 8am to 9pm daily) is a helpful and informative start to a visit to the Park. Slide shows and displays complement the array of printed literature available.

The new Uluru–Kata Tjuta Cultural Centre is a visitor information and display centre developed with the participation of the Anangu (the local Aboriginal people), and is on the road from Yulara to Uluru, on the right just 1km before you get to the Rock itself. It's therefore well placed to allow you to get up to speed on the essential background to Uluru before you visit it. Displays, videos, 'soundscapes' and audio-visual installations are presented with explanations in Pitjantjatjara (a dialect spoken by the Park's traditional owners), English, German, Italian, Japanese and French. The Information Officer at the Centre (8956 3138) can provide information on guided tours, cultural events and ranger activities, including the highly recommended tours around the Rock — the 1½-hour Mala Walk departs at 9am daily from the base of Uluru and is free. All of the businesses at the Cultural Centre are Aboriginally owned.

Opening hours are 7am–6pm from November to March, and 7.30am–5.30pm from April to October.

Accommodation. With a captive market, Yulara prices are high. However on-site caravans become a relatively affordable option if you can get a group of like-minded travellers together; ring 8956 2055 for details. The campground costs $9 per night. The YHA Outback Pioneer Lodge (PO Box 10, Yulara 0872; 8956 2170) has beds costing $18 for the first night, coming down to $10 for the following night(s). Booking ahead is highly recommended, and the central reservations number for the resort is 8956 2737.

Eating and Drinking. Considering the potential for exploitation of hungry and thirsty travellers, food and drink are not as expensive as they might be, though the quality leaves much to be desired. For example, the only fast food outlet in the shopping centre sells indifferent burgers and pizzas. If you want to splash out, the Desert Garden hotel has splendid food considering the distance from 'civilisation'. A cheaper bet is to buy food from the supermarket (more expensive than normal) and cook it on coin-operated electric barbecues.

Safety. Even though the 21st-century comforts of life at Yulara are close at hand, never forget that you are in the middle of one of the most inhospitable deserts known to man. All too frequently visitors perish, usually through dehydration. Make sure you have plenty of liquid, and do not wander off the beaten track.

Uluru. The raw statistics of this lump of rock are that it is 348m high with a base circumference of 9km, covering an area of 33km. It is the world's largest monolith. Its appearance rising suddenly from the stark desert is magical. The Rock is also of great interest to geologists. Whereas most 'Bornhardts' (isolated, exposed rock features in otherwise flat plains) are granite, Uluru is composed of an ancient sedimentary mixture of sand and gravel. Experts believe that only a small proportion of the rock is actually above ground.

It is difficult to get a true picture of the scale of the Rock from a distance as there is nothing to compare it with. Only when you get close to it does its massive size become overwhelming. The most spectacular aspect is the change of colour that sometimes takes place at sunset and sunrise. When this happens, it lasts for only a few minutes but is captured by a thousand cameras. The scenes on the 'sunset strip' west of the rock can be almost comical, with visitors clamouring for the best photographic vantage point, as if waiting for the arrival of an extra-terrestrial being. The colour changes are at their most spectacular after the rare summer thunderstorms; in winter you are most unlikely to see an amazing sunset as the skies are almost always clear.

Most people who go to Uluru feel obliged to climb it, although the Anangu prefer visitors to respect the cultural significance of the Rock by not doing so. Furthermore, of course, the continual stream of people going up and down the same track inflicts lasting physical damage on the Rock. You should ask yourself if you are sufficiently indifferent to these two considerations to allow yourself to follow the crowd and climb up.

Something else to think about is that the views of the surrounding desert from the Rock are considerably less rewarding than the views of the Rock from the desert. The prescribed route for the climb to the top is 1.6km long and takes about 2 hours return. It is steep and strenuous for those unused to climbing, and not recommended if you suffer from vertigo, a heart condition or breathing difficulties. As a result of occasional deaths, commemorated on plaques at the bottom that should give the unfit cause to reconsider, the climb is banned when the temperature reaches 38°C. Wear a brimmed hat to keep the sun off, preferably one that you can attach firmly to your head as it can become windy as you approach the top. Wear sturdy shoes and carry plenty of water: you should drink at least a litre of water per hour. There is a rope for most of the way up, although there is a gap of about 20m on the lower part, left there deliberately by the Rangers on the principle that anyone who can't climb without the rope for this short distance has no business going up the whole way.

In some ways the 3-hour walk around the Rock is more interesting. There are Aboriginal cave paintings (not as spectacular as the ones further north in the Territory) and waterholes. Some areas at the base of the Rock are restricted areas reserved for the Aboriginal community and warning signs should always be respected.

The Olgas. This is a series of dome-shaped sedimentary rocks 20km west of Uluru. Mount Olga (named by Ernest Giles in honour of the Grand Duchess of Russia) towers above the other rocks at a height of 547m, and is considerably taller than Uluru. It is easy to spend a whole day here walking among the domes and through the gorges. Many people consider the Olgas a more spectacular experience than Uluru. They radiate a decidedly eerie atmosphere. The standard tour takes you around the outside and then up into Mount Olga Gorge.

Tours. Those arriving on one of the many tours from Alice Springs will have no problem as everything is taken care of. If you are travelling to Yulara by scheduled bus, ask about the company's Uluru tours. Greyhound Pioneer, for example, do cheap tours around the area, such as a 3-day tour taking in Uluru and Kings Canyon costing $168. You must book and pay for these tours before you arrive at the resort.

Much wildlife resides in the Uluru—Kata Tjuta National Park and around Yulara, including the infamous dingoes, emus and euros (a kind of small kangaroo). There are also 72 species of reptiles, and of the 13 varieties of snake around Uluru, all but five are poisonous. You are much more likely to encounter and be driven to distraction by the swarms of flies that refuse to be swatted away.

A leaflet with brief descriptions of all the National Parks and Reserves in the Northern Territory, called simply *Australia's Northern Territory: A Guide for Visitors* is available from NT Government Tourist Bureaux. It gives information on access and facilities. Campsites are provided in many parks, although facilities are primitive or non-existent; water, if available, may require boiling. It is illegal to camp outside designated areas in the National Parks. In other areas, take care not to camp in a dry river bed (because of the danger from flash floods) or on the bank of a running river (because of the possibility of crocodiles). Before embarking on any adventurous activities, consult the Australian Nature Conservation Agency, whose headquarters in the Territory are at PO Box 1260, Darwin 0800 (8981 5299).

Bushwalking is not recommended in the summer as it is difficult to carry the required amount of water (a litre an hour). The 200km Larapinta Trail running east-west through the MacDonnell Ranges is under construction. So far only a fairly easy 23km section from the Telegraph Station in Alice Springs to Simpsons Gap is open. Much of the rest will be a serious walk with minimal facilities.

If you prefer to join a tour, consult the comprehensive *Holiday Planner* from the tourist office. It lists hundreds of ways of exploring the Territory's great outdoors, from morning canoe trips to full-blown outback adventures, and balloon trips (which are very popular above Alice Springs) to camel rides. It is often possible to get an out-of-season, standby or YHA discount.

One of the more unusual options is to join the 'Outback Mailman' for a day, flying to a succession of remote cattle stations and Aboriginal communities, delivering mail and freight. Chartair in Alice Springs, the airline that runs the service, takes passengers on one of three mail runs lasting up to 7 hours; dial 8952 3977 for further details.

Camels. Central Australia is as much camel country as Egypt or Arabia, and indeed Australia claims to have the only wild camels in the world. The beasts were brought in from west Asia in the 19th century to assist in the development of the inhospitable Centre. While that role has been superseded by motor transport, many camels remain and some are used for treks into the wilderness. The Ross River Homestead (8956 9711), an hour's drive east of Alice Springs, has camels as well as horses you can ride. It also provides campsite and bunkhouse accommodation. Frontier Camel Tours (Frontier Camel Farm, Ross Highway, Alice Springs; 8953 0444) runs a range of camel-based tours; to give one example, a three-day safari into the MacDonnell Ranges wilderness costs around $450, including food and use of camping equipment. Tours are available ranging in length from a few hours to 6 days. Be warned that while no great skill is called for in riding a camel, it can be most uncomfortable until you get used to it.

Restricted Areas. One-third of the Territory is Aboriginal land, and only a few areas (such as around Yulara) may be entered without prior permission. The entrance tickets for Uluru—Kata Tjuta National Park are widely available in Alice, but bear in mind that selling on passes that have not yet expired is illegal. Other areas require a permit, which is normally granted if you apply at least 6 weeks in advance to the Permits Officer at the appropriate address: Northern Land Council, PO Box 39843, Winnellie 0821 (8981 7011) for the Darwin and Katherine region; and Central Land Council, PO Box 3321, Alice Springs 0871 (8952 3800) for Alice Springs and Tennant Creek.

Calendar of Events

late April	Heritage Week, Alice Springs
May (first Monday)	**Labour Day**
early May	Bangtail Muster, Alice Springs
May	Lion's Camel Cup, Alice Springs
May	Gold Rush Festival, Tennant Creek
May	On the Beach Carnival, Darwin
June	Beercan Regatta, Darwin
June (Queen's Birthday)	Barunga Aboriginal Festival, near Katherine
June (Queen's Birthday)	Finke Desert Race (Alice Springs to Finke)
July (first Friday)	**Alice Springs Show Day**
July (second Friday)	**Tennant Creek Show Day**
July (third Friday)	**Katherine Show Day**
July (last Friday)	**Darwin Show Day**
July/August	Barefoot Mud Crab Tying Championships, Darwin
August	Festival of Darwin
August (first Monday)	**Picnic Day**
August (second Sunday)	Merrepen Aboriginal Arts Festival, Daly River
August	Darwin Rodeo
August (last Saturday)	Alice Springs Rodeo
late September	Henley-on-Todd Regatta, Alice Springs
November (last Sunday)	Corkwood Festival (crafts, music, dance), Alice Springs

Public Holidays are shown in **bold**.

Brisbane and Queensland

Population of Brisbane: 1,160,000   **Population of Queensland: 2,830,000**

Queensland's coast meets most people's expectation of paradise. Variations on the theme include the many offshore islands turned holiday playgrounds, the sleepy sugar plantation towns, the travellers' haven of Cairns and the outback wilderness beyond. What makes the coastline exceptional is the immense and fascinating Great Barrier Reef lying off most of the eastern shoreline. Less paradisical — except in name — but still extremely popular, are the unabashedly commercialised resorts around Surfers Paradise on the Gold Coast.

There is much more to Queensland than the coast and its reef: much of the state is uninhabited desert (what the locals like to call the GABA — the Great Australian Bugger All) but there are also excellent farming plains and mountain ranges rich in minerals. Unlike the other states, which tend to be dominated by their capitals, Queensland has a number of important cities in addition to Brisbane. But it is the charms of the coast that attract most visitors, and tourism continues to be the boom industry of Queensland. The state has particular appeal to visitors from the crowded islands of Japan, and indeed many parts of the coastal area have been (controversially) bought up by investors from Tokyo and Osaka.

The capital is anchored firmly near the foot of the state. The first attempt at colonisation began in 1824 when a convict settlement was established near the mouth of the river, for the 'worst class of offenders'. Its swampy, humid location made it ideal for punishment but untenable for any civilised existence. So a year after the first convicts arrived, the site was shifted upstream to the city's present site. It was named after Sir Thomas Brisbane, Governor of New South Wales, which at that time included what is now Queensland. The penal settlement closed in 1839 and the area was thrown open to 'free settlers' three years later. In 1859 the colony of Queensland was separated from New South Wales, and Brisbane established as its capital.

For the next century, the state was regarded by the British and most other Australians as an irrelevant backwater. Although Queenslanders were never ones to apologise for themselves or their state, it took some time for their self-esteem and indeed chauvinism to gather momentum. But today some would say that pride in the state has got out of hand. As visitors from the southern states began to discover the hedonistic delights of the Gold Coast and the Sunshine Coast, Brisbane — the sleepy state capital that lies between these two touristic gems — began to take itself seriously. Like other Australian cities, Brisbane has made a determined effort to project a go-ahead image. It hosted the Commonwealth Games in 1984 and the World Expo in 1988. The new government is making a concerted effort to shed the redneck image the city has had by encouraging the arts. Brisbane is now a curious mix of the crumblingly tropical, the handsomely colonial and the gleamingly modern, embroidered by pleasant parks and the slow, murky Brisbane River. But the condition of the capital is of little concern to the wide spectrum of visitors to Queensland. Most travellers head for the north of the state, a good approximation to a utopia.

CLIMATE

One essential reason for the popularity of Queensland is the glorious climate. Places like Townsville plaster over all their promotional literature '300 days of sunshine a year'. Queensland's weather is sub-tropical in the south of the state and becomes more tropical the further north you go. As with all tropical climates, there is a wet season in summer (October or November to March), much more pronounced in the north than the south. In the north the onset of the wet season is marked by violent thunderstorms. Around Brisbane January is the wettest month and also the cyclone season. Much of inland Queensland around the Charleville area has been devastated by floods in the last few years, and in January 1991 Rockhampton also suffered severe flooding. Other areas are just as likely to suffer drought, so be prepared for extreme conditions.

Although Darwin is much nearer to the equator, Brisbane is the sunniest capital in Australia: it has an average of over 7½ hours of sunshine a day. (So convinced are 'Brissos' — Brisbanites — that they have the best climate in the world, that a radio weather forecaster was once sacked for describing the weather as 'oppressive'.) High humidity in summer is assuaged by sea-breezes, including the 'Barcoo buster' (a westerly wind that cools the southern half of the state). While you're packing the T-shirts and shorts, don't omit to include waterproofs. Tully, halfway up the coast, is the wettest town in Australia, with over 4m of rain each year (four times as much as Brisbane and eight times more than London).

For weather forecasts in Brisbane dial 1196; for marine conditions, 1182; and for cyclone warnings 1190.

THE LOCALS

It has long been fashionable for sophisticates elsewhere in Australia to ridicule the natives of Queensland, describing them as 'banana benders'. They are derided as uncivilised 'Ockers' with regressive politics to match. This latter assertion resulted largely from the antics of Sir Joh Bjelke-Peterson's National Party, which remained in power for 32 years. It was responsible for a great deal of illiberal legislation, such as selling off National Park areas, and repressing the rights of minorities from Aboriginals to gays.

Sir Joh resigned in 1987 in the wake of accusations of corruption, and scandals involving him and his cronies are still coming to light. The National Party lost the state election in 1989. The new Labor government under Premier Wayne Goss has implemented many reforms, not least the abolition of the notorious gerrymander, under which the National Party could win with as little as one-fifth of the vote. Gradually Queensland politics are being steered back into the mainstream but it is a slow process given the attitudes of a significant section of Queensland society, including all those immigrants from other states who were attracted by its conservatism in the first place.

Whatever their political allegiances, most of the state's inhabitants display the national characteristics of being gregarious and laid-back; and many lead an indulgent life of sun, sea and leisure, as is evident from the statistic that Queenslanders have the highest incidence of skin cancer and alcohol-induced brain disease in the world. Ethnic groups are perhaps less visible than in other states, although there is a Chinatown in Brisbane, strong Greek and Italian communities in north Queensland, a contingent of Basques in Trebonne (near Ingham) and numerous Aboriginal settlements.

Making Friends. The sheer number of travellers makes it easy to meet people in Queensland, whether vacationing Australians on the Gold Coast or backpacking travellers on the route between Sydney and Cairns. The bars and hostels in the towns that line the coast are full of like-minded travellers. Most visitors end up signing up for a diving course, yacht cruise or four-wheel-drive expedition, all of which are always very sociable events; see *Great Outdoors* for details.

The natives of Queensland are not yet completely swamped by visitors, and you will meet the locals in one-hotel towns or in the trendier inner suburbs of Brisbane. Better still, join them in one of their favourite pursuits: Queenslanders love gambling and oddball races of all descriptions, and whether you watch the Crayfish Derby in Winton, the lizard races in small towns in the south-west of the state or the heavy-drinking Birdsville horserace, you are sure to meet some colourful characters. It is best to keep off such subjects as politics, feminism and race relations in conversation until you know the sympathies of your new acquaintants. If you happen to be Japanese, you may encounter the unpleasant practice among some of the locals to indulge in 'nip-baiting', yelling insults at Japanese visitors.

Sunmap produces an excellent series of maps of the city and state, which can be bought from most newsagents.

City Layout. The centre of the capital lies in a fold of the Brisbane River, and streets within this area follow the usual grid pattern. A unique feature of the city's street names is that the female gender is used for main streets that run south-west to north-east (Ann, Adelaide, Queen, etc.), while those running perpendicular have male names (Edward, Albert, George, etc.). The heart of the city is the Queen St Mall. The location of King George Square can be confusing as it is in the middle of Albert St, one block north-east of George St.

The waterside is largely given over to swirling freeways, notably the Riverside Expressway running south-east. Across the river is South Brisbane, location of the Queensland Cultural Centre and Expo site. The inner-city suburbs ringing the centre include Fortitude Valley (usually known simply as 'the Valley', and a rough sort of area), Paddington, New Farm and Woolloongabba (called 'Gabba').

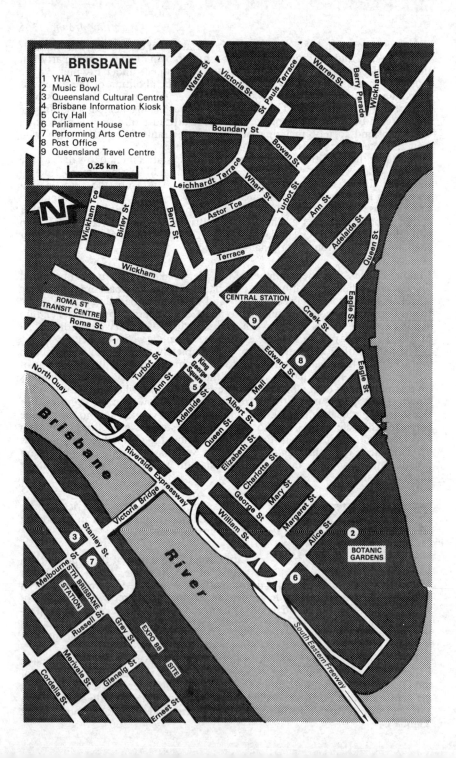

ARRIVAL AND DEPARTURE

Air. Brisbane's domestic terminal has the most modern facilities in Australia. The new international terminal is open 24 hours. The terminals are 12 minutes apart and 10km from the city centre. If you arrive late at night or have an early morning departure, the benches between gates 26 and 38 in the domestic terminal are excellent for sleeping on.

The airport is beyond reach of the city bus and rail services, so the only regular link is provided by CoachTrans Bus Service (3832 1148), which charges $4.50 for the 35-minute journey. The bus runs to the Roma St Transit Centre half-hourly between 5.40am and 8pm. Coachtrans also has direct buses between Brisbane airport and the Gold Coast. The taxi ride from the airport to central Brisbane costs $16.

Brisbane is well connected by international flights: you can travel direct to New Zealand, Europe, North America, Japan, Singapore and Papua New Guinea. Queensland has two other international airports, Cairns and Townsville, but the best bargains in foreign air travel originate in the state capital. The local branch of STA Travel is in Shop 25, 111 Adelaide St (3221 3722).

A busy network of internal flights connects Brisbane, Townsville and Cairns with many other settlements in the state. Small commuter airlines like Flight West (linking Birdsville, Charters Towers, Longreach, etc. with coastal cities) and Sabair (serving Toowoomba) are part of the Ansett network.

Bus. Most long-distance coach companies operate from the Roma St Transit Centre, a big, ugly bus and rail terminal on the north-western edge of the city centre. Telephone numbers for information and reservations are as follows:

Greyhound Pioneer Australia — 132030.
McCafferty's — 1800-076 211.

Competition is fierce to most destinations from Brisbane, so it is well worth shopping around. One particularly useful agency is the Backpackers Travel Centre and Dial-a-Coach office, located on the Balcony Level of the Brisbane Arcade, 160 Queen St Mall (3221 2225). They specialise in budget travel and tours and can handle bus bookin to all major and most minor destinations. They are also the main selling agents for VIP travellers cards.

On the long route up the coast to Cairns, bear in mind that arrival and departure times at intermediate points can be at unsocial hours in the early morning. If you plan to stop off *en route*, check the schedules before you book. Examples of fares to Cairns from the Backpackers Travel Centre include non-stop for $132, or an unlimited stops ticket to use over 6 months for $139.

Brisbane is linked by bus with all the other mainland capitals, and there are numerous daily departures north and south. Express fares to Sydney average $69, to Melbourne $124 and to Adelaide $158. Travellers with bus passes may find that the passes are not valid on some local services, and that a surcharge is payable on routes in remote areas.

Train. Services are operated by Queensland Rail, whose central Travel Centre is at 305 Edward St, Brisbane (3235 1323). Queensland has a more extensive rail network than any other state. Over 10,000km of lines run along the coast and inland, all on narrow-gauge tracks (just over one metre wide) that were laid to cut costs; nowadays the effect is to keep trains' speeds down. There is a network of electric suburban trains around Brisbane, and the 640km stretch between Brisbane and Rockhampton has been electrified.

Seat or sleeper reservations are compulsory on all long-distance trains. Economy-class berths in three-berth compartments cost $30 per night on all

Queensland trains, which includes a pillow, blanket and towel. A first-class berth costs $50 for which you get more bedding as well as more space. Compartments can get chilly between May and October, so it's wise to bring extra clothes or a sleeping bag if travelling second-class.

The only link from outside the state is the line from New South Wales. The XPT service leaves Sydney at 4.24pm daily, arriving at the Roma St Transit Centre at 6.05am the following day. The return trip departs from Brisbane at 07.30am, arriving in Sydney at 9.35pm.

The main long-distance services within Queensland (known as 'Traveltrains') operate from Brisbane north up the coast to Rockhampton, Townsville and Cairns. The *Sunlander* to Cairns departs at 8am every Monday, Thursday and Saturday, arriving at 2.15pm the following day. The economy seat fare is $129. Liquor is sold in the club cars and dining car; meals at reasonable prices are served in the dining car. The other train on this route is the showpiece *Queenslander*, which caters for first-class passengers. The fare is $489 inclusive of all meals and berth. It runs only on Sundays from Brisbane and Tuesdays from Cairns.

The daily *Spirit of Capricorn* to Rockhampton departs Brisbane at 9.40am, arriving 7.05pm (one-way fare $67). The *Spirit of the Outback* with both first and economy-class sleepers, sitting cars, club cars and dining car departs Brisbane at 7pm on Tuesdays and Fridays and travels overnight to Rockhampton and then on to Longreach, arriving 7pm the following day. The return journey departs Longreach on Thursday and Sundays at 7am. The *Spirit of the Tropics*, designed for the budget-conscious and backpackers, travels from Brisbane to Cairns once a week and from Brisbane to Proserpine. This all-sitting-car train boasts a disco car (Club Loco) where passengers can dance the night away.

Other long-distance trains operating in Queensland's Outback include the *Westlander* to Charleville (777km and 16 hours west) and the *Inlander* linking Townsville and Mount Isa; these services are twice-weekly. As with the coastal trains all inland services are air-conditioned and provide sleeping cars and sitting cars with bar and meal service.

Further west is an isolated section of track on which the *Gulflander* operates. This vintage train departs from the isolated settlement of Normanton every Wednesday at 8.30am and travels to Croydon 152km east near the Gulf of Carpentaria, returning to Normanton the next day for a return fare of $64.

A 'Sunshine Rail Pass' gives unlimited economy-class travel on all these routes — plus the extensive suburban network around Brisbane — and costs $267 for 14 days, $309 for 21 days and $388 for 1 month. Sleeping berth fees are additional.

Ordinary one-way tickets allow unlimited stopovers, allowing 14 days to reach the final destination (2 months for a return journey). Breaking the long journey from Brisbane to Cairns is highly recommended and there are several obvious stops: Rockhampton for Yeppoon and Great Keppel Island, Proserpine for the Whitsunday Islands, and Townsville for Magnetic Island. There are also some places that you might prefer to travel straight through, such as Gladstone whose claim to fame is the largest aluminium smelting plant in the southern hemisphere.

When you book your ticket you will need to say where you wish to stop off and for how long, so that the appropriate reservations can be made for you. If you change your mind you can re-book, but a fee may be charged.

Driving. Road surfaces on and near Highway 1 along the coastal strip of Queensland are good, but if you venture far north or west you run into unsealed (and, during the wet season, frequently impassable) roads. The Main Roads Department publishes a useful free guide — *Queensland Road Conditions*. It gives detailed information on road surfaces and work-in-progress, and is updated every 6 months. The state's motoring organisation is the Royal Automobile Club of Queensland (RACQ), whose head office is at 300 St Paul's Terrace, Fortitude Valley (3361 2444). A 24-hour recorded road condition report can be heard by dialling 11655.

The blanket speed limit in Queensland is 100km/h, reduced to 60km/h inside built-up areas. The blood/alcohol limit is 0.05. Queensland motoring law has some unusual features. For example, in an effort to reduce car thefts, it is illegal to leave ignition keys in a vehicle in a public place; when a bus indicates it intends to pull out, you are legally obliged to slow down and give way in a 60km/h zone; making a U-turn at any junction controlled by traffic lights is prohibited unless signs specify otherwise. On-the-spot fines ranging from $80 to $250 are levied for minor offences. When parking, you are legally required to leave at least one metre between your car and vehicles in front and behind.

The rental agreements for most vehicles hired in Queensland specifically exclude the use of unsealed roads. Hire companies based at towns near the fringes of the wilderness rent out four-wheel-drive vehicles, which are not necessarily subject to these restrictions.

Hitch-hiking. Queensland comes closer than any other state to outlawing hitch-hiking. The state traffic code makes it an offence to 'stand on any portion of the road while awaiting a vehicle' or 'inconvenience, obstruct or hinder the free passage of any other pedestrian or vehicle'. This legislation is frequently used as an excuse to hassle hitch-hikers. To keep on the right side of the law, therefore, you should pay particular attention to picking a hitching spot off the main roadway, and keep an eye out for the police. This is not quite as simple as it sounds, as they use a variety of vehicles of which some are identifiable as police cars only when they pull up next to you. If you manage to spot the police before they see you, move away from the roadside, sit on your luggage and try to blend in with the scenery. If they stop, you can expect to be searched for drugs, as 'hitch-hiker', 'hippie' and 'hashish' still seem to be synonymous to some Queensland police.

Women who have happily hitched in the southern states of Australia should think twice before trying in Queensland. Some male drivers have misplaced

"IF YOU SPOT THE POLICE, SIT ON YOUR LUGGAGE AND TRY TO BLEND IN WITH THE SCENERY."

ideas about lone women hitchers, and there have been numerous attacks: not just in isolated areas, but also around the Gold Coast and on the well used Bruce Highway between Brisbane and Cairns. One stretch of this road — from Rockhampton to Mackay — has been the scene of several grisly murders: signs warn 'do not stop'. Hitchers may feel safer approaching lorry drivers at one of the truckers' depots on the Highway.

Leaving Brisbane can pose problems for hitchers. If you're heading south towards the New South Wales border, don't bother to try the South Eastern Freeway from the city centre. Instead, catch bus 191, 199, 501 or 509 to MacGregor. Better still, take a suburban train 35km out to Beenleigh where the Pacific Highway begins in earnest. For the Warrego Highway to Toowoomba and the west, take a train 20km out to Goodna and use a sign to ensure you get a ride beyond Ipswich. The Bruce Highway north is often crowded with competing hitchers: the most sensible place outside the city is 20km north of Brisbane at the start of the Highway proper at Bald Hills, which can be reached on suburban train line 2. Nevertheless, some success has been reported hitching on the main road outside the Brisbane Gardens YHA in Kedron (Chermside bus 172).

Outside the capital, hitching on main routes near the coast is straightforward. If you do have a long wait on the Bruce Highway, it will feel more like an Outback road than a coastal one, as the coast is 35km away. Most interior Queensland roads and the treacherous roads north of Mossman are not conducive to hitching. Some people have successfully hitched rides on yachts along the coast: see *Great Outdoors–Yachting* for suggestions.

CITY TRANSPORT

Bus, suburban train and ferry services are operated by Brisbane City Council. The central information office is on the ground floor of the Brisbane Administration Centre at 69 Ann St, near George St. You can pick up the *Brisbane Public Transport Map*. For public transport information call 131230.

Bus. There are no less than five classes of bus, of which 'City buses' are the ordinary stop-everywhere variety. 'Cityxpress' services pick up only at certain suburban bus stops, then run non-stop to the city centre. 'Rocket' buses operate during rush hours and serve only stops marked with a blue/orange missile symbol. 'Citylimited' is yet another type of limited-stop service, distinguishable by being articulated and air-conditioned. Finally, the Great Circle Line (which has a separate fare structure) serves yellow stops at 800 metre intervals about 7km out from the city centre.

For trips around the city centre, you pay a subsidised fare of 50c. Fares for longer journeys are calculated on the basis of three concentric zones. Transfers are more restricted than in other cities. They can be made only by holders of two- or three-zone tickets, and then only at five specified interchanges to buses travelling in the same direction.

Single journey tickets can be bought from the driver, or from conductors who loiter around bus stops in the city centre with ticket machines; this is to save time in boarding at busy stops. Cheap deals are available at the underground Queen St Bus Station and from newsagents and corner shops showing a blue and yellow 'Fare Deal' sign. Books of ten tickets save 25% on regular prices. An unlimited RoverLink day pass, valid on all ordinary Brisbane buses and city trains, can be bought from bus drivers or at city rail stations for $7.

Train. An excellent suburban rail network, operated by Queensland Railways, fans out from Roma St and Central stations. Ring 131230 for information.

Ferry. Brisbane City Council operates two ferry services across the Brisbane River to Kangaroo Point: one is the launch between the Customs House (on Queen St at the north-east of the city centre) to Holman St on Kangaroo Point, the other from the foot of Edward St to Thornton St. They operate frequently during the day but sparingly in the evenings and weekends. Information on the Brisbane River Ferry Service is available on 131230. There are also riverboat commuter services from Riverside in the city centre to outlying suburbs, which provide a good way of taking a budget-price cruise.

Taxis. Cabs in Queensland are distinguishable both by the sign on the roof and by their number plates, which have white figures on a green background (the reverse of plates on other vehicles). Fares are low: $1.60 standing charge ($2 after 6pm and at weekends) plus 72c per km. To request a taxi in Brisbane by telephone, dial Brisbane Cabs on 3360 0000 or Yellow Cabs on 3391 0191.

Car. Traffic congestion is barely a feature of Brisbane life, with peak hour being exactly that, just 60 minutes. Parking in central Brisbane however can be a problem. Regulations within the Central Traffic Area are strictly enforced by the city authorities; the best plan if you insist upon driving into the centre is to find an off-street lot or a 'parkatarea': this is a special meter where you are permitted to park all day, rather than for just an hour or two. Each meter has two slots; insert your coins in the side facing your vehicle. There are also several car parks including one below the Art Gallery and a bigger one called Expo Car Park in Glenelg. Alternatively, the City Council provides Park and Ride stations at Coronation Drive and in Ann St, Fortitude Valley. Most suburban railway stations have free car parks, so you can invent your own Park and Ride scheme with ease.

City 'transit lanes' can be used by buses, bicycles, taxis and cars carrying more than three people (driver included). But note that bus lanes are strictly for buses. The Gateway Bridge, crossing the river east of the city, is mostly of interest to those bypassing the city between the Gold and Sunshine Coasts. Tolls will be charged on it until the year 2016.

U-Drive Car Rental (3216 0540) is located in Newstead, a few kilometres north-east of the city centre, at 108 Breakfast Creek Road (at the corner of Jordan Terrace). It offers vehicles for hire from $39 per day. You might also try Ace Car Rentals (3252 1088), which charges $28–50 per day, inclusive of kilometres, tax and insurance. YHA members are eligible for a 10% discount from Shoestrings Car Rental (360 Nudgee Road, Hendra; 3268 3334). To hire a campervan, contact Budget at 105 Mary Road (132727) or for four-wheel drive vehicles Allterrain Rentals (Corner of Ann and James Sts, Fortitude Valley; 3257 1101), which offers a 5% discount to YHA members.

Cycling. The volume of traffic and complexity of one-way streets in the city centre, not to mention Brisbane's hilly terrain, makes cycling arduous, but there are havens such as the City Botanic Gardens where special bicycle tracks have been laid out. These have now been extended along the Brisbane River to the suburb of Toowong. The wearing of helmets is compulsory in Queensland.

Brisbane Bicycle Sales and Hire (3229 2433) at 87 Albert St near the Botanical Gardens hires out a range of touring and mountain bikes. You can take your bike on the ferries across the river and on off-peak suburban trains. There are two city bridges that cyclists can use, Victoria Bridge (between Queen St and the Performing Arts Complex) and Story Bridge on Highway 1.

Accommodation

Australia's hospitality industry is at its most developed in Queensland. Much of the state's economic growth has been generated by tourism and consequently there are plenty of luxury hotels, motels, self-catering apartments and backpackers' hostels on offer. There are nearly 30 hostels in the Backpackers Resorts of Australia chain and a host of others. Despite the proliferation of hostels, hostels in the more popular coastal areas are often fully booked. If you're keen to stay in a particular hostel, try to book it. Brisbane has kept pace fairly well with the demand for cheap accommodation and any hostel you find full will direct you to another. If you experience difficulties, the accommodation desk on Level 3 of the Roma St Transit Centre (the coach arrivals hall) should be able to help you find budget accommodation.

YHA Hostels. Both of the city's YHA hostels can be booked through the Queensland YHA office at 154 Roma St (3236 1680). The best bet is the New Brisbane City YHA (3236 1004) at 392 Upper Roma St, 500m west of the Transit Centre. Beds start from $14. The Brisbane Gardens YHA (3857 1245) is at 15 Mitchell St in Kedron, 10km north of the city centre — its cheapest beds are $12 per night. You can reach the hostel by taking bus 172 from Stop 1 outside the Transit Centre.

Other Budget Accommodation. Many hostels charging about $11–12 for a dormitory bed compete for your business with offers of free collection from the Transit Centre, barbecues, etc. Several hostels are full to the brim every night, and so booking ahead is always advisable.

There are several Backpackers Resorts of Australia hostels in Brisbane. The Aussie Way Backpackers at 34 Cricket St (3369 0711) is handy for the Transit Centre, but nonetheless offers a free pick-up service if you need it. It is well known for having a quiet atmosphere. Also quiet (and '*not* a party place') is the Courtney Place Backpackers at 50 Geelong St in East Brisbane (3891 5166); cheapest beds are $12, but a range of single, double and larger rooms are also available. The small Banana Bender Backpackers at 118 Petrie Terrace (3367 1157) is also handy for the Transit Centre. Balmoral House (33 Amelia St, Fortitude Valley; 3252 1397) prides itself on its five-star standards; dormitory beds are $12, but again you can pay more for greater privacy and comfort, up to $48 for a 'river view' apartment.

Of the other hostels in Brisbane, Somewhere to Stay (45 Brighton Road; 3846 2858) is good, and offers free sailing and bikes. Beds start at $11. Free pick-ups are available, or you can catch bus 177 in Adelaide St, which will take you to the West End. Others include The Homestead ('something going on every night', including karaoke and toga parties; 57 Annie St; 3358 3538); and the Sly Fox Hotel right in the city centre (73 Melbourne St; 3844 0022).

Hotels and Guest Houses. The cheapest hotels close to the city centre include the Yale Inner City Inn at 413 Upper Edward St (behind Central Station; 3832 1663) costing $35 for a single and $45 for a double, including breakfast. Prices are lower in the nearby suburbs. Further out in the suburb of Hamilton is another private hotel called the Kingsford Smith (114 Kingsford Smith Drive; 3862 1317), which offers a courtesy pick-up from the airport or city.

Camping. If you are planning to travel much in Queensland it is well worth taking a tent, both to save money (camping can cost as little as $5 in National Parks and State Forests) and for occasions when all other accommodation is fully booked. Don't try to pitch a tent on a spare patch of ground in Brisbane, however, as a local ordinance prohibits camping within a 22km radius of the city centre. Provided you don't want to eat out or go to films in the city every night you can stay in one of the suburban campsites like the Capalaba Campground, 22km from the city.

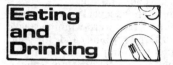

The key to eating well in Brisbane — and the rest of Queensland — is to take advantage of the excellent local produce. Beef, fruit and seafood are the best bets. In particular, mud crabs ('muddies'), prawns and Moreton Bay bugs (a cross between a large prawn and a small lobster, caught near the mouth of the Brisbane River) are usually good value. When combined with ethnic Asian cuisines, the results can be delicious. Most establishments adhere to limited evening opening hours: 6pm to 10pm, Tuesday–Saturday is the norm. For food at any time of the day or night, seek sanctuary at the Pancake Manor; it is situated in a converted church at 18 Charlotte St and never closes. YHA members get a 15% discount.

Almost all the restaurants listed below are BYO; some surprisingly ritzy establishments encourage you to take your own liquor, which helps to keep the bill within reasonable bounds. The glossy brochure *Dining Out: Brisbane* may catch your eye, but it consists mainly of advertisements for plush, expensive restaurants and is of little interest to those seeking plain good value.

Brisbane city centre and Fortitude Valley have a wide variety of perfectly adequate cafés and some good restaurants such as Gekkos (named for the lizards that frequent the place) at 100 Commercial Road serving New Orleans style food. Other good BYOs in this neighbourhood are Giardinettos serving pasta, pizza and cassata at 366 Brunswick St and Al Sahara, a good Lebanese restaurant at 76 Wickham St.

Brisbane's diminutive Chinatown lies on the city side of the Valley, bordered by Brunswick, Ann, Gipps and Duncan Sts; there are numerous Oriental restaurants within and around this block. For a quick lunch in Brisbane, the City Plaza (below City Hall, between Ann and Adelaide Sts) has a good range of takeaway kiosks and outdoor seating. The Cubana, just off the Mall on Albert St is also recommended.

For dinner, it's worth heading out of the city centre to one of the near suburbs. Paddington (2km west of the city) is the trendiest area, though a pale imitation of the Sydney suburb of the same name. Given Terrace is the best street for food: try the Elephant Path Sri Lankan restaurant at number 183 which opens every evening from 6pm. Faces at number 267 is a more expensive venue, but very chic with an open courtyard. The Paddington Palate at 231 Given Terrace also has a garden, but is more of a snacky place. Further along at 283 is Le Scoops, a pavement café specialising in coffees, juices and their own ice creams and sorbets; it stays open into the small hours seven days a week and has live music on Sundays.

The suburb of Red Hill, a little north of Paddington, has some less expensive but equally interesting places. The Nataraja Indian Restaurant at the Red Hill Centre on Musgrave Road has cheap lunch specials and dinner smorgasbords from $15–17. Benjamin's at 195 Musgrave Road has good seafood and vegetarian dishes. Le Figaro at 5 Enoggera Terrace is more upmarket, with an imaginative menu that changes monthly to take account of seasonal availability of produce. Another excellent upmarket restaurant is Le Bronx at 722 Brunswick St, New Farm which serves 'exclusive, innovative French cuisine' costing on average $35 per person plus $1.50 corkage. Cheaper French food is available at the Little Frog, 19 Emlyn St, Coorparoo.

South Brisbane should not be overlooked. Squirrels vegetarian restaurant at the corner of Melbourne and Edmonstone St is cheap and handy for the Queensland Cultural Centre. Out at St Lucia (near the University) Mama's Down Under at 217 Hanken Drive serves cheap but good Italian food. The best Mexican food is at Night of the Iguana, 111 Haig Road, Toowong.

Many pubs serve food especially in New Farm where backpackers congregate at hotels to eat $4 meals and to party. Further out try the award-winning steaks at the Breakfast Creek Hotel (2 Kingsford Smith Drive, Albion) and, for good seafood, Breakfast Creek Wharf. The Aspley Hotel on Gumpie Road in Aspley is an old-fashioned unpretentious Queensland pub with a country atmosphere, cold beer and good tucker.

DRINKING

Licensing hours in Queensland are 10am to 10pm, except on Sundays (11am to 1pm and 5 to 7pm). However new liquor laws are expected which will pave the way for late-night drinking, at bar style restaurants where it will be possible to be served a drink without a meal.

You will not be able to escape the fact that Queensland is beer territory. It is the home of Castlemaine XXXX (pronounced 'four-ex') which has been losing ground to the new Powers Brewery, 35km south of Brisbane. Powers brews a bitter (4.8%) and a light (2.8%). North of Brisbane (inland from Noosa Heads) there is a boutique brewery at Eumundi whose beers are distributed in the capital. (If you're heading north try to stop here on a Saturday when there is a good market.)

Despite the loss of Castlemaine's market share and its acquisition by the New Zealand conglomerate Nathan Lion, its brewery tours are still exceedingly popular and sometimes booked out days in advance, so you should try to book ahead by ringing 3369 3188. The brewery is 2km east of Brisbane city centre at 11 Finchley St in Milton. In view of the liberal quantities of free samples provided at the end of the tour, you should travel to and from the brewery by bus.

If you are a devotee of brewery and distillery tours, take a suburban train south to Beenleigh where you can tour the Beenleigh Rum Distillery for $5.

"YOU SHOULD TRAVEL TO AND FROM THE BREWERY BY TRAIN OR BUS"

Wine is slowly becoming more popular in Queensland, though winery tours around Stanthorpe cannot really compete with the ones around Adelaide or Perth. Look out for Queensland wines such as Robinson's Family Chardonnay and Rumbalara Semillon.

The centre of Brisbane has no particularly exciting pubs, so — as with eating — you should look beyond the downtown area. The trendiest pubs are those with live bands, including the gay hangouts of the Terminus and the Empire Hotel on Brunswick St in Fortitude Valley. Try Dooley's Irish Pub (across the road from the Empire) which has live bands, the Captain Cook Tavern on Anzac Avenue in Kippa-Ring and the Country Club Hotel on Gympie Road in Strathpine.

Some travellers form an immediate and adverse impression of Brisbane as nothing much more than an ungainly country town. Although Queensland writer Robyn Davidson's description of Brisbane in the 1950s as 'a town of never-ending Sundays' is no longer accurate, the climate makes the citizens appear more lethargic than those of the other state capitals. Away from the Queen St Mall, downtown Brisbane can be more deserted than other state capitals outside business hours. But behind the unpromising exterior is a surprising amount of activity and energy, much of it manifested in the many entertainments provided free by the local authority. Sunday afternoons in the parks around the centre are as lively as any European or American city, a direct result of the free activities sponsored by the City Council. For an unusual walking tour of greater Brisbane contact the Moonie Jarl Aboriginal Guides on 3344 2470; their two hour tour ($30) concentrates on the Aboriginal history and culture of the area. The same organisation offers a day trip to unspoiled Bribie Island (about an hour north of Brisbane) that explores Aboriginal sites and explains Aboriginal lore; the cost is $80 including transport.

Three city-centre buildings exemplify the contrasting architectural styles of Brisbane's early planners. The City Hall is solid Victorian, following the same basic design as London's Royal Albert Hall, albeit on a smaller scale. This circular, domed building no longer dominates the city as the highest structure, but still makes an impressive sight at the corner of Albert and Adelaide Sts. On weekdays from 9am to 5pm, you can take a lift to the top for 50c, or just stroll around the sturdy portals. St John's Cathedral on Ann St, on the other hand, was mostly built around 1910 in Gothic Revival Style, but is still waiting forlornly to be completed. To add to this architectural melange, Parliament House at the corner of Alice and George Sts (overlooking the Botanic Gardens) is in the style of the French Renaissance. On days when the state legislature is sitting you may view the unusually abusive debating style of Queensland politicians from the public gallery; call 3406 7111 for details.

Genuine early Queensland architecture comprises villas on wooden stilts (in order to maximise air flow, rather than to avoid flooding). They can be found scattered around the city, but particularly in Paddington. For more information about the many contrasting styles, and on listed buildings, churches and landmarks, ask at the National Trust of Queensland in the Old Government House in George St (3229 1788). This office can also supply details of National Trust properties throughout Australia.

The best views of the city can be had from the top of the Gazebo Ramada Hotel at 345 Wickham Terrace (by Albert and Birley Sts). The view will cost you the price of a drink at the 'Top of the G' cocktail bar, but is well worth it in clear weather. You might also head west to the Mount Coot-tha lookout, for a view of the city that is particularly impressive at night.

You can take in Brisbane from ground level on the Citysights tour (131230). The phony tram makes a circuit of 20 points of interest where you can disembark and catch a later one (between 9am and 4.30pm daily except Saturday) at a cost of $10. You will see, for example, the William Jolly Bridge ('one of the longest single through-arch bridges in the world'), and learn that until 1930 Brisbane residents could set their watches by the copper ball that was dropped from the top of the Old Windmill on Wickham Terrace each working day at 1pm.

South Bank Parklands. The Parklands occupy 16 hectares on the site of the highly successful Expo 88, and include a range of attractions, spread out around the palm-fringed swimming lagoon. As well as souvenir and gift shops, restaurants, cafés and street markets, there is the Gondwana Rainforest Sanctuary and the Insect and Butterfly House, which includes a huge variety of butterflies, cockroaches and spiders ($6.50 for adults, $5 concessions). Next to the Parklands is the huge new Convention and Exhibition Centre.

Queensland Cultural Centre. The State's artistic hub is on the south bank of the river (adjacent to the Expo site and South Brisbane railway station) and indeed has a great deal in common with London's South Bank Centre, both architecturally and artistically. As you cross Victoria Bridge from the city centre, the Museum, Art Gallery and State Library are on your right and the Performing Arts Complex to your left. You can take a tour of the Complex at 12pm, Mondays to Fridays; ring 3840 7500 for details.

There is a variety of places to eat, from the lavish and expensive Fountain Room Restaurant to a couple of cheap cafeterias. Just as at the Sydney Opera House, there are free outdoor performances on Sundays in the plazas and walkways of the Centre; dial 3846 4444 for details. In addition, there are always free exhibitions in the foyer of the Performing Arts Complex.

Museums and Galleries. The Queensland Museum (3840 7555) is part of the Cultural Centre. Its collection is extremely eclectic, from geology through anthropology to technology, and appeals even to those who have no great interest in conventional museums. Of particular interest among the two million exhibits are the world's only surviving German First World War tank, a wall-size cast of most of the world's known tracks of running dinosaurs, the aircraft *Avian Cirrus* (in which Bert Hinkler made the first solo flight from England to Australia in 1928), and the almost Disney-style dinosaur garden, which is popular for picnics. Admission to the Museum is free, although a charge may be made for special exhibitions. It is open from 9am to 5pm every day, except for Anzac Day, when it closes at 1pm, and Christmas Day and Good Friday, when it is closed.

The adjacent Queensland Art Gallery (3840 7303) opens from 10am to 5pm daily. It has a good collection of contemporary Australian art. You can join free guided tours at 11am and noon on weekdays.

The Brisbane City Hall Art Gallery and Museum is on the ground floor of Brisbane City Hall (3225 4355) and opens daily from 10am to 5pm. The permanent exhibits are (understandably) rather parochial, with artefacts and works of art from early colonial days, but they have some unusual touring exhibitions.

There are plenty of specialist museums and galleries in Brisbane, such as Australia's largest toy and doll museum (Pandora's Playthings, 401 Lutwyche Road, Windsor) and Kamaga Aboriginal Arts in the Jagera Arts Centre at 121 Cordelia St, South Brisbane.

Beaches. Brisbane's city centre is 18km inland, so some ground must be covered before arriving at a beach. The nearest good beach is at Redcliffe, 25km north over the Hornibrook Highway Viaduct.

Parks and Zoos. The City Botanic Gardens are arguably central Brisbane's finest asset and among the best-kept gardens in Australia. You can get in at one of the three gates on Alice St (which face Albert, George and Edward Sts) from 8am to dusk daily. Part of the appeal lies in the coolness and freshness, in contrast to the sometimes stifling atmosphere of the Brisbane streets in summer. These gardens are tiny, however, in comparison with the Mount Coot-tha Botanic Gardens west of the suburb of Toowong, 12km from the city. The Gardens open 7am–5pm throughout the year, and you can reach them by bus 39 from the city. The usual features of botanic gardens are supplemented by the Sir Thomas Brisbane Planetarium (the largest in Australia), kookaburra and duck feeding and picnic areas at the nearby J C Slaughter Falls. Nearer to the centre, New Farm Park on Brunswick St has 12,000 rose bushes and — in summer — blooming jacarandas and flamboyant poinciana trees.

The nearest zoo is a long way north in the distant suburb of Kallangur. Much closer is the Lone Pine Koala Sanctuary (3378 1366), which is on Jesmond Road in Fig Tree Pocket — it is 10km south-west of the city, and you can catch bus 518 from the 'koala platform' of the Myer Shopping Centre to get there. You can cuddle a koala anytime from 8am to 4.45pm, and also feed the kangaroos — all in all the Sanctuary has over 80 species of native Australian animals, ranging from green tree frogs to rainbow lorikeets. Adult admission is $12 ($9 for YHA members). The other main koala-cuddling venue in Brisbane is Bunya Park in Eatons Hill (3264 1200).

SHOPPING

Shopping hours have been liberalised over the past few years and now most city and suburban shops stay open until 4pm on Saturdays. Sunday trading in the city centre is from 10am to 4pm at the retailer's discretion. Shops in central Brisbane and the Valley stay open until 9pm on Fridays, and suburban stores have late-night shopping on Thursdays.

Prices for many items, especially dutiable goods, are lower in Queensland. Cigarettes, for example, are about one-sixth cheaper in Queensland than elsewhere in Australia. Brisbane is a good place to buy gear for trips to the bush or the Outback, and several equipment shops give 10% discounts to YHA members: Direct Camping and Outdoor, 142 Albert St; Jim the Backpacker, 138 Wickham St, Fortitude Valley; K2 Base Camp, 140 Wickham St; Mountain Designs, 105 Albert St; and Snowgum, 132 Wickham St.

If you are in the market for souvenirs, try The Proud Australian Souvenir Shop in Pavillion Arcade, Queen St or Queensland Aboriginal Creations, 135 George St. For cheap books visit any one of the many Bookworld outlets. A more discerning selection of books is available at Folio Books, 80 Albert St (corner Mary St) specialising in photography, architecture, graphic design and international writing. The Women's Bookshop at 15 Gladstone Road in Highgate Hill has an extensive collection of new and second-hand books by and about women, together with CDs and cassettes by female artists. It also has a good notice board with what's on in Brisbane for women.

(3223 0444).

The glossy *Brisbane Arts & Entertainment Guide* and the Thursday edition of the *Courier-Mail* are both useful sources of information about events. The mainstream ticket agency is Ticketworld in the Queen St Mall

Theatre. The Performing Arts Complex houses two 2000-seat auditoria — the

Lyric Theatre and the Concert Hall — plus the small Cremorne theatre for more experimental drama. Ticket prices for most shows are in the $15–30 range (usually with modest discounts for students). Apart from the lavish productions at the Performing Arts Complex, there are several mainstream theatres: the Suncorp Theatre in Turbot St (at the foot of the building of the same name; 3221 5177); the Twelfth Night at 4 Cintra Road, Bowen Hills (3252 5122); the Brisbane Arts Theatre at 210 Petrie Terrace (3369 2344); and the Communications House Theatre in Fortitude Valley (131 Barry Parade; 3266 4882) where Brisbane's 'little theatre', the API Theatre Company, performs.

Cinema. The Cultural Centre has no film theatre. The main city-centre venues are the Albert (183 Albert St; 3221 5777), the Forum (160 Albert St; 3221 3255), the George (346 George St; 3221 7866) and Hoyt's Entertainment Centre on Queen St. Cinemas are cheaper on Tuesday nights when a flat rate of $5 or $6 is charged.

Music. Queensland has both a Philharmonic and a Symphony Orchestra, and these perform in the Concert Hall of the Performing Arts Complex. An International Music Festival is held in May every alternate year, which includes every kind of music from Stravinsky to traditional Japanese music to contemporary Australian jazz. Concerts are often held at the Queensland Conservatorium of Music at the south-eastern end of George St (by the Botanic Gardens). Brisbane has an ethnic music and arts centre at 126 Boundary St, West End (3846 2051), which holds cabaret-style multicultural performances in its Café Folkloric on the third Thursday of each month for $9.

While Brisbane's local rock scene is less lively than that of the southern capitals, it is firmly on the map of world tours by megastars. These major league performers play at Brisbane's biggest venue, the Brisbane Entertainment Centre on Melaleuca Drive in the far northern suburb of Boondall (3265 8111), reached by suburban train. Bookings for the Centre should be made through Ticketworld.

The best source of listings for gigs by local bands is the excellent free weekly *Time Off*. The *Blitz* pull-out section of Thursday's *Courier-Mail* is also useful. Several pubs along Edward St have live music at weekends.

The Brisbane Jazz Club is based at 1 Annie St, Kangaroo Point (3391 2006) and has regular bands on Saturdays and Sundays from 8pm. Admission is $7. It also holds an annual four-day jazz carnival over the Labour Day long weekend in May. The Story Bridge Hotel at Kangaroo Point features the 'Up the River Jazz Band' every Sunday afternoon.

Nightlife. There is a sprinkling of night clubs and discos in the centre and the Valley, such as Rumours at 383 Adelaide St, Transformers at 127 Charlotte St, Lexington Queen at 130 Queen St and Mary St at 138 Mary St. The Caxton Hotel in the inner suburb of Petrie Terrace (38 Caxton St; 3369 5544) features a night club, bar and karaoke at the weekend.

Gambling. Brisbane's high-profile new casino is in the former Treasury Building, at the head of the Queen St Mall. It boasts 102 gaming tables and over a thousand gaming machines, and stays open 24 hours.

SPORT
Cricket is played at the Brisbane Cricket Ground on Stanley St south of the city in Woolloongabba; the ground, like the suburb, is known as the 'Gabba'.

The Brisbane Broncos or 'Maroons' are star attractions at Aussie Rules football at Lang Park on Milton Road. The full range of other ball games can be seen in the city. Both codes of rugby are followed (with the Redcliffe Dolphins the best for Rugby Union). The Brisbane Bears represent the state in the Victorian Football League. Basketball is popular; the Brisbane Bullets play at the Entertainment Centre.

Greyhound racing takes place most nights at one of the circuits at Capalaba, the Gabba, Ipswich or Lawton. Horses race at Bundamba and Doomben tracks, and you can see trotting on Saturdays at Albion Park in Breakfast Creek (3262 2577).

The jogging track at the Queen Elizabeth II Sports Complex on Kessels Road in the suburb of Nathan opens from 7.30am to dusk. Admission is $1.50. The Valley Pool, at the junction of East and Wickham Sts in Fortitude Valley northeast of the city centre, is a pleasant pool which is heated in 'winter'.

MEDIA

For up-to-the-minute news, dial 1197 in Brisbane.

Newspapers. Brisbane's quality daily is the *Courier-Mail* (60c). The *Sun* is a tabloid costing 50c from street vendors but available free from the dispensers provided in TAB betting shops in Brisbane. Both papers have a Sunday edition the *Sunday Mail* and the *Sunday Sun*. The sale of soft-porn magazines is restricted, although the Queensland Literature Board of Review has lifted its ban on *Playboy* magazine.

Radio. The local ABC AM station is 4QR on 612. The leading stereo AM station is 4BK on 1296. For better quality sound, tune to Brisbane's answer to BBC Radio 3 (4MBS-FM on 103), ABC-FM on 106 or FM 104 for rock. Brisbane's leading rock station is B105FM. The local community station — 4ZZZ on 102FM — broadcasts a wide range of material, including programmes produced by the women's radio collective MEGAHERS at 5pm on Tuesdays.

The rapid development of Brisbane has attracted a number of petty criminals, but the city is still by no means dangerous. There are some areas where you might not feel comfortable after dark, such as the less affluent parts of South Brisbane, but in general there is no cause for paranoia about attacks by criminals. If you are worried, you can actually hire a police officer for 'special duties': the cost is about $25 per hour (extra on Sundays).

The new government is gradually shedding some of Queensland's more illiberal laws; so, for example, homosexuality has now beem decriminalised, though 'poofter-bashing' among the less savoury elements of society persists. They are also working to repeal the law that prohibits walking more than four-abreast (aimed at preventing demonstrations). It is presumed that there will also be reform of laws governing Aboriginals which, under Joh Bjelke-Petersen, contravened 11 articles of the United Nations Declaration on Human Rights.

Another indication that things are improving in Queensland was the guide to non-discriminatory language circulated among all police officers in the state in 1991 which declared that slang expressions like 'sheila', 'bird', 'gook', 'coon', 'poofter', etc. were to be dropped. The manual also condemns stereotyping expressions such as 'typical yuppie', 'typical Volvo driver' and 'helpful truckie'. Finally there is now talk of legalising brothels as in New South Wales, which might mean a few more red lights would be evident in Kangaroo Point in Brisbane.

One surprising area of resistance to reform is for nude bathing. Although it is widely practised, every so often the police crack down and bathers are subject to fines of $100 or more.

Drugs. Another law that was reformed recently was the Drug Misuse Act which made life imprisonment a mandatory punishment for certain drug offences. Still the police are not as lenient as they are in some other states and vehicles are occasionally stopped and searched by police. A certain amount of illicit drug-taking does, of course, take place, and a large amount of marijuana is grown in the Atherton Tablelands inland from Cairns; but Queensland is one state where it is wise to stick to legitimate pleasures.

The area code for Brisbane is 07. Dial 000 for the emergency services.

The Brisbane Visitors and Convention Bureau is in the City Hall in King George Square (3221 8411), and there is also an information kiosk open daily (except Sundays) in the middle of the Queen St Mall, near Hungry Jacks. Information on Brisbane, Queensland and even northern New South Wales is available from an information booth on Level 2 of the Roma St Transit Centre (3236 2988). The Queensland Government Travel Centre is on the corner of Edward and Adelaide Sts (3221 6111), and can provide a wide range of travel information, as well as a free booking service. Tourist information on Queensland is also available from the 14 regional tourist associations, some of which are listed in the following section.

The addresses of the main Queensland Government Travel Centres outside Queensland are as follows:

Adelaide: 10 Grenfell St (08-8212 2399).
Canberra: 25 Garema Place (06-248 8411).
Melbourne: 257 Collins St (03-9654 3866).
Newcastle (New South Wales): 97 Hunter St (049-262800).
Perth: 55 St George's Terrace (09-325 1600).
Sydney: 75 Castlereagh St (02-9232 1788).

British Consulate-General: Level 26, 1 Eagle St (3236 2575).
American Express: 131 Elizabeth St (3229 2729).
Thomas Cook: Level Q, Myer Centre, corner of Albert and Elizabeth Sts (3221 9749).
Medical Treatment: Royal Brisbane Hospital, Herston Road (3253 8111).
Dental Emergencies: Dentist Emergency Service, 131 Elizabeth St (3221 8957).
Helplines: Alcoholics Anonymous 3229 6566; Life Line 3252 1111.

After having had the highest unemployment rate in Australia for many years, Queensland's economy is growing faster than that of any other state. Hence the employment situation is improving, at least compared with hard hit states like Western Australia and Victoria. Expansion of the hospitality industry seems to know no bounds, while primary industry and agriculture have both encountered problems recently.

Brisbane. Unfortunately reports about the Commonwealth Employment Service (CES) offices in the state vary from 'barely adequate' to 'totally useless'; you are likely to do much better on your own initiative. The Brisbane city CES office is located at 23 Adelaide St, while the inner metropolitan casual office at the corner of Wickham and Gotha Sts in Fortitude Valley might have some unskilled temporary work available. Better still, get hold of an early edition of the Wednesday or Saturday *Courier-Mail* and be first in the morning queue for jobs. You can, of course, approach employers direct for work. There have been reports of good opportunities at the Golden Circle Cannery in the northern Brisbane suburb of Bindha near the suburban train station, especially during the pineapple season (mid-February to early April). Try showing up at the staff canteen early in the morning, and be prepared for some hot, smelly and noisy work. Another possibility is the Campbell Brothers' soap factory on Campbell St in Bowen Hills (3253 6111); wages here are about $10 an hour.

Fruit Picking. Crops ripen earlier in Queensland than elsewhere, and the range of fruit and vegetables is extensive and exotic. Such is the diversity of produce that you could, with luck, find agricultural work throughout the year in the state. Most farmers stipulate previous experience as a requirement for fruit and vegetable harvest vacancies, though inexperienced travellers do often manage to get jobs. Many backpackers' hostels help travellers find work such as the Backpackers Hostel in Innisfail and the City Centre Backpackers in Bundaberg. The possible work available in a region can be deduced from the ten-metre high models of fruits placed by the roadside. For example, the Big Pineapple near Nambour is an indication that the surrounding area (i.e. the Sunshine Coast) is prime territory for work during the pineapple harvest (from January to April). Unfortunately pineapple picking is poorly paid and arduous work.

You could move north for the winter to the citrus fruit region around Mundubbera and Gayndah (inland from Maryborough) from May to September. The apple, peach and plum crops around Stanthorpe near the New South Wales border may see you through the summer and autumn; this is also where most of Queensland's few vineyards are found. In northern Queensland it is possible to find work picking vegetables like capsicums around Ayr and to work in sugar and banana plantations around Innisfail.

Bundaberg (370km north of Brisbane) is a centre for tomato, cucumber and zucchini growing, though recently market prices for these vegetables have been so low that some farmers have been turning their land into golf courses. If you do find work there in October/November, it is likely to be on a contract basis paying $8.50 an hour. (You could also try your luck asking for a job on a golf course.) The Lockyer Valley in the Darling Downs near the town of Gatton has harvests of onions and potatoes lasting from August to November, although problems caused by the increasing saltiness of the soil have been cutting yields. Head for the Tent Hill Caravan Park near Gatton (07-5562 7200) where it is possible to rent a tent for just $22 a week or a caravan for $55 and where the owner knows about local opportunities. Contract jobs, for example with local lettuce growers, will probably pay no more than the minimum hourly wage of $7.80. Potato picking is paid piece work, from $18 a bin. If you start at sunrise it is possible for a dedicated novice to pick six bins by noon, though many travellers find this work too hard to tolerate.

You may do better to head south-east from Brisbane towards the coast, as tomatoes and other vegetables are grown in the Redland Bay area. Other worthwhile prospects include strawberry-picking near the New South Wales border (probably the longest strawberry season anywhere: July–November); tomatoes around Bowen (between Mackay and Townsville) from May to December, with the peak of the harvest in September (though again poor market prices and harvests ruined by the rains have prompted some farmers to plough in their crops); mangoes in the same area in December; and tobacco-picking in the Atherton Tablelands inland from Cairns. The latter season lasts from late September almost until Christmas, but only the biggest farms can support pickers for the full ten or eleven weeks. Most of the plantations are owned by families of Italian immigrants who have not yet shaken off outdated attitudes for employment; women therefore may find themselves confined to inferior work and lower wages. The sugar plantations along the coast, which previously employed thousands, are now largely mechanised, but you may be able to find unskilled work at one of the many processing plants.

The Outback. If you feel you could cope with the difficult and often lonely life on an Outback sheep farm, work is easiest to find in February or March when station managers hire their seasonal helpers. Station work can be found through the Mount Isa CES or the magazine *Queensland Country Life, Land* and other farming journals. Check under the heading *Stock and Land* for shearing team recruitment.

Boats. Life aboard the prawn trawlers whether as a male deckhand or female cook is probably less arduous. They sail out of Cairns, Townsville and remote Karumba on the Gulf of Carpentaria. Try the big companies such as Toros or Raptis, or ask individual boat owners at the quayside. A fair amount of shore-based work is generated by Queensland's fishermen, such as the three fish processing plants in the port of Bundaberg.

Several holiday cruises depart from Cairns to tour the islands en route to Thursday Island, and take on staff to clean, cook and serve the guests. It may be possible in exchange for working long hours on vessels such as the *Atlantic Clipper, Queen of the Isles* and the *Nole Buxton* to earn a passage and have some chances to snorkel and tour the islands. Although this is possible as a one-off, your chances are better if you can stay for a while, in which case a small wage would be paid.

Tourism. Australians and foreigners visit the Gold and Sunshine Coasts around Brisbane in great numbers, while further north the coast and offshore islands are being developed at an alarming rate. As many islands lack a local population from which labour can be drawn, there are employment possibilities; however Queensland is so popular for people of all types that competition will be keen. Anyone who has travelled in Japan or has a smattering of Japanese might try to press their advantage. The tourist season begins in March after the cyclones and lasts until October/November. Be warned that Queensland employers are notorious for laying their staff off at a moment's notice (e.g. when holiday bookings drop).

For island resort work, make initial enquiries at CES offices on the mainland, for example Proserpine, Cannonvale, Mackay or Townsville. You might also try asking Contiki, a large tour operator based in Sydney, which employs large numbers of staff (02-9389 0999).

Marine Volunteers. If you have a background in marine biology or are a scuba diver, it might be worth trying to fix up a position as a volunteer with one of the marine research stations along the coast. The best centre for finding out about any possibilities is the Australian Institute of Marine Science (AIMS) in Townsville (PMB No 3, Townsville Mail Centre, Queensland 4810; 077-789260). It maintains a volunteer programme for qualified scuba divers who have an up-to-date medical certificate to accompany research trips. These last 3 days to three weeks and investigate such phenomena as damage to the Great Barrier Reef. The University of Queensland at St Lucia has a research station on Heron

Island that may be able to provide food and accommodation in exchange for 4 hours of work, though the return ferry fare is $140. Initial enquiries should be sent to the Secretary, Heron Island Research Station, Barrier Reef via Gladstone, Qld 4680 (079-781399). Much further north, the Australian Museum operates a research station on Lizard Island from which researchers study coral reef biology, ecology and geology. Volunteers are required to assist maintenance staff, and opportunities to get involved in field work may arise. In exchange for 4 hours maintenance work per day, volunteers get free accommodation at the Research Station but must pay for their own travel and food (the airfare from Cairns is about $370). Enquiries should be made to the Lizard Island Research Station, PMB 37, Cairns, Qld 4870 (tel/fax 070-603977; e-mail lizard@amss.austmus.oz.au).

While Sydney is undeniably the jewel of New South Wales, Brisbane has no pretensions to be more than the administrative centre of a stunningly varied state. The coast of Queensland has charms unimaginable from the sturdy downtown of Brisbane. Before setting off on the well trodden path to north Queensland, however, you might wish to relax for a few days or find work for a few weeks in the pleasant countryside inland from the capital.

Darling Downs and the 'Golden West'. The region that Queenslanders describe as the Golden West is actually well inside the eastern half of the state. Toowoomba, the centre for the Darling Downs, is only 130km inland from Brisbane. Its numerous parks and gardens and relatively high elevation make it a pleasant place to stay. The Downs are rich agricultural land with fertile black, volcanic soil, and good territory for finding casual farming work. There is also some spectacular scenery in the Golden West, especially along the Great Dividing Range.

THE COAST

The reef and islands set Queensland's coastline apart from ordinary ocean coasts. The Great Barrier Reef, the outer boundary of the continental shelf, is a living organism that is one of the natural wonders of the world. It is a ridge of coral running north-south for 1800km, at a distance of between 15 and 150km from the coast of Queensland. Coral consists of living creatures existing on top of the corpses of their forebears, and is found in many other parts of the world. But only Queensland's coast has sufficient of the right conditions of warm water and gently shelving ocean floor to permit such an extensive reef. The reef has been in existence for at least 10,000 years. Despite increasing threats from man, and a plague of the little understood crown-of-thorns starfish that destroys the reef, it is still growing. You can get a close-up view by joining one of the many tours offered from the mainland, including snorkelling, scuba-diving or riding in a semi-submersible 'submarine'.

In a few places the reef protrudes above sea level to create real coral islands (known as 'cays'), but most of Queensland's islands are formed from sand or rock and lie within the shelter of the reef. From South Stradbroke Island off the Gold Coast to Lizard Island north of Cooktown, the islands range from unspoilt coral outcrops to garish 'resort islands' with new airports to welcome the masses. Most of the islands, unlike the mainland coast, have the added bonus that you can bathe in summer without fear of harm from marine stingers.

There are also many resorts strung along the coast of the mainland, representing — according to your point of view — either opportunities for tremendous fun or gross examples of unmitigated commercial excess. The coast south of the capital is the most obvious candidate for either title.

THE GOLD COAST

The Pacific Highway runs inland for 70km south from Brisbane. If you turn off from it towards the ocean you can find a delightful archipelago of islands, of which North Stradbroke (reached by ferry from Cleveland and Redland Bay) has the most to offer. At Helensvale, you can continue on the Pacific Highway straight to the New South Wales border or turn left for the Gold Coast Highway. Most visitors choose the latter, and the tourist attractions begin almost immediately.

Dreamworld, at Coomera on the highway just north of the Gold Coast, is the largest theme park in Australia with 27 different rides; like Disneyland, your one-price ticket (around $26) buys you unlimited rides. In fact the area is reminiscent in many ways of southern California. The town of Southport marks the top of a 32km stretch of beach where the official motto is 'The Visitor is King'. The Queensland ethos for enterprise is evident everywhere, including less salubrious activities (such as the growing 'escort agency' industry) that enable the Gold Coast to claim to be the place 'where the fun never sets'. The various attractions are undeniably popular: visitors each year outnumber the local residents by ten to one.

Southport is the commercial capital of the Gold Coast: just offshore on the spit at Main Beach is Sea World, the biggest marine park in the southern hemisphere. The strip of beach stretches south in an almost continuous resort development, the most notable being Surfers Paradise. Its Aboriginal name was Oomby Goomby, meaning 'place next to the sea'. Now the place next to the sea has become the Australian equivalent to a Spanish 'Costa' complete with time-share touts. Although the undoubtedly beautiful beaches stretch for miles beyond the built-up areas, swimming is possible only between the coloured flags due to dangerous currents, and these areas of beach are always packed out.

Further south are Mermaid Beach (setting for the University of Technology established by entrepreneur Alan Bond not long before his business demise), Palm Beach and the twin towns of Coolangatta and Tweed Heads. The Queensland/New South Wales border runs right through the centre of this last conurbation, bisecting Boundary St, and the runway of Coolangatta/Gold Coast airport straddles the state border. Just north of the airport is the relatively uncommercialised Currumbin Bird Sanctuary, famous for its lorikeets at feeding time, and facing that is Chocolate Expo, a museum/exhibition/tasting centre devoted to everybody's favourite weakness.

Although the Gold Coast is aimed primarily at big-spending tourists, the Coolangatta YHA on the Gold Coast Highway (230 Coolangatta Road, Bilinga; 07-5536 7644) has dorm beds from $13 per night. It has a swimming pool and a barbecue, and is 3 minutes from the beach. An alternative further south is the Sunset Strip Budget Resort at Coolangatta (199–203 Boundary St; 07-5599 5517), which has shared accommodation from $15 per person per night. And with a range of activities from go-karting to gambling, avocado plantations to zoos, you should never be without something to do if you encounter one of the 78 days in the year when the sun doesn't shine. With a large proportion of young people, you should not be stuck for company either. If the crass commercialism becomes too much, head inland for some good waterholes, waterfalls and views.

THE SUNSHINE COAST

This stretch of coastline has lost the battle with the Gold Coast to become the most popular resort area in Australia, and now seems content to be more refined and picturesque than its rival south of Brisbane. The Sunshine Coast runs from Bribie Island (50km north of the capital) for 80km up to Noosa Heads and has a much more intricate coastline than the Gold Coast, with the beaches indented by craggy headlands, spectacular cliffs and river outlets. Noosa Heads itself is a real beauty spot and is regarded by some as the most chic resort in Australia, with a good surfing beach and some sophisticated hotels and restaurants. Out of season, however, it can be quiet and uninteresting. Noosa has a VIP Backpackers Resort at 9–13 William St (07-5449 8151), which hires out cars and arranges trips to Fraser Island. There are also two Backpackers hostels at Noosa Heads: Koala Beach Resort (44 Noosa Drive; 07-5447 3355) and Backpackers on the Beach (26 Stevens St; 07-5447 4739). Maroochydore, halfway down the coast, has a YHA hostel (07-5443 3151) with dorm beds from $12 per night; the town is a good base to explore the beaches, plantations and mountain hinterland of the Sunshine Coast.

The sugar plantations begin in earnest inland from the Sunshine Coast, and continue north all the way up to Cairns. Some of the cane is used to make Bundaberg rum at the town of the same name. You can take a tour of the distillery if you book in advance. Offshore lies the biggest sand island in the world, the 120km-by-15km Fraser Island. You reach it by vehicular barge or ferry from Hervey Bay or Rainbow Beach, and an admission fee of a couple of dollars is levied by the National Parks and Wildlife Service. Four-wheel-drive transport is necessary to see much of the island. The rewards include swimming in huge freshwater lakes, studying the fascinating wildlife and coloured sandcliffs and relaxing on the accurately named Seventy Five Mile Beach, which runs the whole length of Fraser Island. Moreton Island, further south, is highly commercialised due to its proximity to Brisbane's airport 35km away. For the best beaches on Moreton Island, find a fishing boat prepared to take you to the leeward side of the north end (and arrange to be picked up later).

Hervey Bay has become the focus for whale watching, as schools of humpback whales frequent this area between August and October. Whale-watching trips leave at 7.30am and cost $45.

THE CAPRICORN COAST

If you follow the advice given earlier and break your journey north to Cairns at Rockhampton, you may be unnerved by the sheer quietness of the town. 'Rocky' (or 'Rockvegas' as it is known ironically by some locals) is not the most dynamic metropolis in Queensland, but serves as a good centre to explore the nearby Capricorn Coast — so called because of the Tropic that falls a few kilometres south of Rockhampton. The town itself has more than a dozen National Trust-listed colonial buildings and pleasant riverside parks, but you get the feeling that the most exciting daily event is the train passing on the Brisbane–Cairns line, which runs along the middle of the main street. The YHA hostel is north-east of the centre at 60 MacFarlane St (079-275288); the nightly rate for a dormitory bed is $13.

Buses link Rockhampton with the coastal resort of Yeppoon 44km north-east, including one that leaves from the YHA hostel at 8am and 1.30pm daily. On the other hand hitching out to the ocean is easy. Yeppoon is quiet and relaxed and ideal for a few days' rest. There is pleasant countryside around, plus a zoo (at Emu Park), which you should visit early or late to avoid coach parties. Barrier Reef Backpackers is at 30 Queen St (079-394702), and runs a free shuttle from Rockhampton to Yeppoon.

Great Keppel Island lies offshore, linked to the mainland by a three-times-daily ferry from Rosslyn Bay (just south of Yeppoon) — departures are at 9.15am, 11.30am and 3.30pm. With wide, sandy beaches and several riotous bars and discos, Great Keppel is a favourite destination for young Australians and foreign travellers. There is a good YHA hostel on the island (from $14 per night), which should be pre-booked through the Rockhampton YHA. Otherwise you can stay at the adjacent Keppel Haven, where there are cabins and pre-erected tents. Barrier Reef Backpackers in Yeppoon offers a 3-day package trip to the island for $59.

Another choice of island on this stretch of coast is the coral cay Heron Isla. Unlike many islands it is right on the Great Barrier Reef. Heron Island is accessible by catamaran ($140 return) from Gladstone south of Rockhampton. It is an old resort, and has a University of Queensland research station, which studies, among other things, the island's green and loggerhead turtles. The island is also famed for its good diving and snorkelling, especially clear in October/ November. The cheapest lodge accommodation starts at $100 a day, but you could try to volunteer your services at the research station in exchange for room and board (see *Work* above).

For more information on the Capricorn Coast and its attractions contact its Tourist Organisation (PO Box 166, Yeppoon Qld 4703; 079-394888).

THE WHITSUNDAY ISLANDS

This archipelago of 74 islands was actually discovered by Captain Cook on Whit Monday, 1770. Although none of the islands is on the reef proper, they form a delightful area to explore. Some are ringed with coral formations visible to snorkellers and divers.

The jumping-off point for the Whitsundays from the Bruce Highway and the railway is the small, sleepy town of Proserpine. Regular buses run from here to the lively resort of Airlie Beach, although buses from both the north and south now regularly call into Airlie itself.

One of the best places to stay in Airlie is the recently refurbished Backpackers by the Bay hostel at 12 Hermitage Drive (079-467267), which is on the waterfront and also has its own pool. Beds in small dorms are $12 per night, and booking ahead is advised. Other Backpackers Resorts in Airlie Beach are Beaches (356 Shute Harbour Road; 079-466244), which has its own budget restaurant, and the Whitsunday Village Resort (also on Shute Harbour Road, directly across the road from the bus terminal; 079-466266). There is also a YHA hostel at 394 Shute Harbour Road (079-466312), which has dorm beds from $14 and offers an extensive range of local tours.

Abel Point Marina is about 900m from the edge of town and is the jump-off point for nearly all the day trips and overnight tours to the islands. The average price for a day trip is about $50 — some at that price include lunch, others don't, but all provide snorkelling equipment as a part of the cost. Trips on fully crewed sailing boats taking 3 days and 2 nights are also very popular, and can cope with anywhere from eight to 20 people. You don't have to be part of a group to book. Prices are around $250, including meals, linen and snorkelling gear.

You can visit virtually any of the Whitsundays. There are no longer back-packers resorts on any of the islands, but Hook Island and Long Island do provide some budget accommodation. Water taxi services are available to the seven islands with resorts (Hook, Daydream, Long, South Molle, Lindeman, Hayman and Hamilton) — the average return fare is $22 (more for Hamilton).

If you like the idea of some solitude, it is possible to camp on a deserted island for a night or two with a little advance planning. The cost for doing this will be $3 per person per night. First you need a permit from the Department of Environment and Heritage (467022); then it's up to you to arrange for a boat operator to set you down and pick you up at a pre-arranged time.

NORTH QUEENSLAND

Townsville. The population of 140,000 makes this the second largest city in Queensland. It has some picturesque restored buildings, but the suburban values epitomised by the name 'Townsville' are visible everywhere. In fact the city's name is not as tautological as it sounds, as it was founded by Robert Towns in the mid-19th century as a port to service the region's agriculture. 'Townstown' would have been a worse name.

Townsville is defined by the archet·pal Australian shopping street, Flinders St Mall, a testament to mundanity and materialism. Apart from the 300m pink granite Castle Hill around which the town is built, Townsville and environs are flat. The brown and dull terrain has been enlivened in recent times by an ambitious tree-planting campaign.

The city makes a convenient stopover and has plenty of affordable accommodation. Try the Civic Guest House at 262 Walker St (077-715381), which charges $14 for a dorm bed; the Globetrotters Hostel at 45 Palmer St (077-713242), which is 70m from the Transit Centre and has dorm beds for $12; or Andy's Backpackers (077-212322), which is actually *in* the Transit Centre, and so is ideally placed for coach connections. The YHA have also got a hostel, which goes by the name of Adventurers Resort. It is at 79 Palmer St (077-211522), and has dorm beds for $13.

The Townsville Enterprise information kiosk is in the centre of Flinders St Mall. The railway station is close to the western end of the Mall. Ferries to Magnetic Island and boats to the Reef depart from terminals along Flinders St East. The Transit Centre for buses is on the south bank of Ross Creek, which runs through the city. Buses to Townsville's international airport are frequent, but as it is only 5km west of the city centre you can get a taxi without fear of bankruptcy, or even walk.

Townsville has enough to keep you amused for a day or two. In particular, the students of James Cook University sustain a lively arts and social scene, and the gamblers at the Breakwater Casino provide an interesting spectacle. For decorative buildings and interesting shops, go to Flinders St East. And once the limited attractions of the city begin to wane, you can take the boat across to Magnetic Island.

In order to become more firmly stamped upon the tourist map, Townsville has brought the reef closer in. The Great Barrier Reef Wonderland (077-212411) on Flinders St East, five minutes on foot from the city centre, houses the world's largest living coral reef aquarium, together with imaginative and informative exhibits about the Great Barrier Reef. Visitors can walk underwater through transparent tunnels, and also watch stunning films of life under the sea in the Omnimax Theatre. Joint admission to the Wonderland, the Theatre and the Museum of Tropical Queensland is $28 (though you can ask for a YHA discount).

Some people make Townsville their base for learning to dive, as Mike Ball's Diving Expeditions is one of the biggest dive operations in Australia. Pure Pleasure Cruises (077-213555) runs day trips on a luxury 'wave-piercer' catamaran to the outer reef costing $120 including lunch. For only $5 more there is a special deal for backpackers that includes the reef cruise plus a return trip to Magnetic Island and two free nights' accommodation in Townsville or Magnetic Island. Details from Civic House.

Magnetic Island. Captain Cook was never at a loss for a name, however inappropriate it later turned out to be. This island was so-called because of a fault in *Endeavour*'s compass that was wrongly attributed to a mysterious magnetic force on the island. Magnetic Island is one of the largest and most populated of the islands off the coast of Queensland, and is chiefly attractive for its fine variety of hikes. These include the ascent of Mount Cook, but a number of less strenuous bushwalks are clearly marked by wooden trail signs. Two thousand koalas live on the island so your chances of seeing one in the wild are better here than in most places. You can pick up maps from the Magnetic Island Visitors' Information office, an easy-to-find bright green and orange building at the foot of the quay at Picnic Beach. Staff can give you details of the man-made developments on the island, such as the Oasis Koala Park at Horseshoe Bay and the Marine Gardens Shark World at Nelly Bay. The cheapest place to stay is the Hideaway Budget Resort at 32 Picnic St (077-785110), which has beds for $14 and is a short walk from Picnic Bay Jetty. Wherever you are on the island, beware of the local possums, which take a lively interest in anything that might contain food.

As Magnetic Island is only 8km from the mainland, the ferry ride is fast and cheap. The two ferry services — Magnetic Marine (077-727122) and Westmark (077-211913) — run hourly, with the last ferry at around 6pm on weekdays, later on Saturdays. The return fare is $12. The vehicle barge operates three services daily to Arcadia, but you can hire mini-mokes, scooters or bicycles to explore the island or invest $5.50 in a one-day bus pass.

The remaining 325km stretch from Townsville to Cairns is not devoid of interest, although as the wettest area of Australia its attraction may be obscured by one of the frequent downpours. Inland there is a series of National Parks, including the spectacular waterfalls of Jourama and Wallaman, in the running for being Australia's longest single-drop falls. Offshore, many of the islands are being developed as luxury resorts. One island that is largely undeveloped is Hinchinbrook, accessible by launch from Cardwell, with spectacular mountain scenery and plenty of wildlife including goannas. If you don't want to stay at the low key resort where the boat lands, walk about 45 minutes to a simple campsite on the coast where the pleasure of eating oysters prised from the coastal rocks goes some way to compensating for the belligerent sandflies.

Halfway between Townsville and Cairns is the Tully River where white-water rafting has taken off in a big way. Book a trip in either city, or at the famed Treehouse YHA near Mission Beach (Bingil Bay Road; 070-687137), where dorm beds start at $14, or alternatively you can pitch a tent ($9 per person). Mission Beach is also the jumping-off point for Dunk Island, only 5km offshore and covered with rainforest.

CAIRNS

The capital of Far North Queensland is a traveller's utopia: sunny climate, relaxed tropical atmosphere, cheap places to stay and eat, and an endless variety of activities. But it is a place where visitors entirely swamp locals and where there is unceasing and sometimes bitter competition for the tourist dollar. The Esplanade is now virtually a backpackers' strip and the whole atmosphere is commercial and a far cry from the days when Cairns was a sleepy backwater. Another possible source of disappointment is that the city has no beaches, only mud flats and promenades. The nearest beaches are about 20km away including Buchans Point to the north which is the *de facto* nudist beach (though bear in mind prosecutions for nude bathing occur occasionally).

Cairns is pronounced as a cross between 'cans' and 'kens'. It is a long way from virtually everywhere. The nearest state or national capital is Port Moresby, 750km away in Papua New Guinea. Brisbane, Darwin and Alice Springs are all roughly 2000km away. Although transport links have been improved, the town retains its feeling of splendid isolation. Originally known as Trinity Bay, Cairns battled with the town of Port Douglas further north for supremacy in the far north of Queensland. The choice of Cairns as a railway junction ensured its success, although now the major source of revenue for the town is the tourist trade. What brings many of the visitors is, of course, the Great Barrier Reef; Cairns is one of the points along the coast where the reef is most accessible. But the town is also close to some of the best countryside in Australia, both inland on the Atherton Tablelands and north along the coast.

Climate. Being so far north the town has the typically tropical wet and dry seasons. The Wet (described euphemistically in tourist literature as the 'green' or even 'rainbow' season) lasts from around December until March. If you have planned a southern summer trip to Australia, however, don't be put off a visit to Cairns for fear of the weather. The rain is concentrated in sharp bursts, and Cairns itself enjoys enough sea breezes to keep the humidity down. But don't expect to get very far north from the city during the Wet as many roads are washed out.

ARRIVAL AND DEPARTURE

Air. Cairns airport is just off the Cook Highway, 7km north of the city. In the last decade international services have expanded from one or two per week to a dozen or more, with flights to New Zealand, Singapore, Port Moresby, Tokyo and the west coast of North America. Domestic services are also numerous. The airport shuttlebus (313555) meets all flights and costs $4.

Several agencies specialise in low-cost international flights. Raging Thunder Travel at 105 Lake St (518177/311120) is the Cairns agent for two European student travel companies, Usit Travel and Kilroy Travels, and deals with both international and domestic flights. YHA Travel at 20–24 McLeod St (311705) also operates as a travel agency.

Train. Brisbane-bound trains leave on Monday, Thursday and Saturday at 7.45am amd Tuesday at 8.15am. The station (526249) is on McLeod St at the top of Shield St. The only other train is the weekly freight train inland to Forsayth and a daily service to Kuranda in the Atherton Tablelands. The special Kuranda Scenic Railway is a collection of old-time carriages that stops halfway for a 'photo opportunity' at Barron Falls. The service departs at 9am and costs $23 one-way and $39 return ($33 on non-market days).

Bus. Two companies run services to and from Cairns, and use the terminal at Trinity Wharf: Greyhound Pioneer (132030) and McCafferty's (515899). Lots of local operators cover the region, such as Coral Coaches (317577), which serves Cape Tribulation and Cooktown, and Whitecar Coaches (519533), with services to the Atherton Tablelands, etc. The bus to Kuranda is much cheaper than the Scenic Railway. Note that some services to Cooktown include a boat ride to bypass the worst section of the road.

Predictably there are dozens of backpacker bus tours of the Cairns environs. To give just one example, Tropics Explorer (which offers a range of trips) charges $82 for trips to Cape Tribulation lasting 3 days and 2 nights, led by guides who know their stuff.

Hitch-hiking. Competition hitching south from Cairns is intense, so to be sure of a ride check the lift-share notices at one of the hostels. If you prefer to hitch, you could try thumbing at the beginning of the Bruce Highway by Parramatta Park; get there by walking along Mulgrave Road and Florence St. For a faster start, book ahead for the morning train south from Cairns and invest $4 in the journey as far as Edmonton station which is right on the Bruce Highway. Hitching north is possible though the vast majority of the traffic is tourist traffic: for Port Douglas, Mossman and Kuranda, simply start walking out along Sheridan St which eventually becomes the Cook Highway. The road up to Kuranda branches off to the left a few kilometres out of town, so it's worth using a sign.

CITY TRANSPORT

City Layout. Cairns is a compact town. Although the suburbs sprawl a fair way out, all the best lodgings, attractions and places to eat are within easy walking distance. The centre spreads back from the Esplanade on the seashore to the railway station on McLeod St. The Shield St Mall is the heart of the city.

Public Transport. It is unlikely that you will need to take a public bus as so many hostels have courtesy minibuses into town (even if it's just a 5-minute walk) and to points of interest. Nevertheless a fairly good local bus service links the centre with outlying suburbs. You can pick up maps and timetables from the Information Centre at the corner of Sheridan and Aplin Sts. For information by telephone, call 515732.

Cycling. Cairns has the merits of being flat with wide roads and having little traffic. Bikes may be hired from several hostels or from a shop such as Cairns Cycle Centre, 61 Sheridan St (517135).

Car. The ideal vehicle if you want to drive is a Moke, which can be rented from Cairns Rent-a-Car (137 Lake St; 516077) for $45 a day inclusive, or $52 minimum for a 'serious car'. Peter's Economy Rent-a-Car (36 Water St; 514106) hires out a range of cars, from Daihatsu Miras to Holden Commodores, starting at $45 a day inclusive. Unsealed roads and beaches are out of bounds, in particular Cape Tribulation and the Chillagoe Caves. Other companies include Network Rentals (145 Lake St; 070-316632), which hires out cars and utes.

If you have brought your own vehicle to Cairns and want to leave it for a few days while you go offshore, you can park it at one of the campsites for about $5 a day.

The RACQ emergency breakdown number is 516543.

ACCOMMODATION

Cairns is blessed (or cursed?) with a huge number of backpackers' hostels offering up to 5000 beds in the backpacker price range. Booking ahead is essential for all hostels from June to September, and strongly recommended for the better hostels throughout the year. Expect to pay $12–$16 a night for a dormitory bed or bunk.

One excellent place to stay is the Gone Walkabout Hostel at 274 Draper St, behind the railway station (516160) — this 35-bed house is run by friendly owners who live next door and know the region well. There is also a pool and all of the rooms are air-conditioned. Dormitory beds are $12. Another good place with a pool and air-conditioned rooms is Inn the Tropics at 141–143 Sheridan St (311088). Up Top, Down Under at 164 Spence St (513636) is also recommended; it has small dorms and lots of room.

There are two YHA hostels in Cairns. The biggest is the McLeod St YHA (20–24 McLeod St; 510772), which has 166 beds, starting at $14. The YHA On The Esplanade (93 The Esplanade; 311919) has beds from $15 and together with some of the other hostels on The Esplanade — such as Caravellas and Jimmy's — is somewhat impersonal. Thefts from dormitories are not unknown.

Other places in the Backpackers Resorts chain include the Calypso Inn at 5–9 Digger St (310910), which has beds in small dorms available for $12; Captain Cook Backpackers (204–212 Sheridan St; 516811), where an evening meal is included in the $12 dorm price; Castaway's at 207 Sheridan St (511238); the International Hostel at 67–69 The Esplanade (311545); and Parkview Back-packers at 174 Grafton St (513700).

There are a number of campgrounds close to the city centre, such as the Cairns City Caravan Park. On-site vans cost about $30.

EATING AND DRINKING
Cairns has one of the best deals in Australia in the form of Backpackers' Restaurant in the mall. The price is $5 for all you can pile onto a sizeable plate. You can choose from four or five different main courses plus salad. Drinks are also cheap. With prices so low, the place is packed every night. Other places including discos also have all-you-can-eat-for-$5 offers, for example the Playpens Backpackers Dance Club at the corner of Lake and Hartley Sts. For cheap breakfasts try Rusty's pub on the corner of Sheridan and Spence Sts between 6–9am. Another popular backpackers' restaurant is Brumbys on the corner of Aplin and Grafton Sts. If you're homesick for English food and (more to the point) beer, go to the Cock and Bull, at the corner of Grove and Digger Sts.

Cairns has numerous vegetarian, steak, Chinese and Italian restaurants, most of which are good value. A stroll around the centre, particularly along Grafton St, will turn up plenty. In particular, try Ricardo's at 89 and Milliways at 142 (which calls itself 'The Restaurant at the End of the Universe'). For drinking you have a choice between the bars of swanky hotels or some regular Queensland pubs many of which serve good cheap food.

ENTERTAINMENT
Despite its small population, there is a great deal to do in Cairns: from nightclubs to greyhound racing, and art galleries to zoos. Simply strolling around is also good entertainment, especially on Sunday mornings when the weekly craft and food market takes place in the centre of town. Little remains in Cairns of the early colonial days, but the lack of historic buildings is compensated for by the lively and picturesque waterfront. An evening walk to ogle at the marlin fisher-men's gin palaces is recommended. The Esplanade, which runs north from the small yacht harbour is separated from the sea by a wide strip of parkland, with shaded areas ideal for picnicking.

Cairns manages to attract some decent touring entertainment. A scan through the free weekly entertainment guide *Barfly* reveals which pubs and clubs are hosting live bands, and the longer residents at any of the hostels will know which clubs and discos are in vogue. You can sometimes have a good night out for about $20 at the Canoe Club at the Pier Tavern which features top comedians and other acts. There are four cinemas, including the Coral Drive-in on the Bruce Highway, and a couple of small theatres.

HELP AND INFORMATION
The area code for Cairns and environs is 070. The main information office is the Far North Queensland Promotion Bureau at the corner of Sheridan and Aplin Sts (513588). You will be inundated with free information mostly encour-aging you to sign up for tours. *This Week in Cairns, Port Douglas and the Tropical North* is useful for some what's on information. The free booklet *Welcome to Cairns* carries ads for most of the cruise and tour operators as well as a list of emergency contacts and services.

While Cairns could hardly be described as dangerous, an increasing amount of petty theft and clashes between drunken locals and (probably drunk) travellers have been reported. Do not allow the tropical tranquility to catch you completely off guard.

AROUND CAIRNS

The Islands and Reef. Nowhere else on the coast is so highly organised for trips out to the nearby islands and the reef itself. Cairns has a great number of options, sold direct by boat companies at the harbourside or through hostels and hotels. The main destination is Green Island, on the reef proper just over the horizon from Cairns. Its popularity as a day-trip destination means it possesses many man-made trappings, but the sheer fascination of the reef more than compensates for the crowds and production-line tourism. Remember that rain spoils visibility for snorkellers and divers and that the crossings can be so rough that you will feel ill for the rest of the day.

The cheapest way of reaching Green Island is by launch for $25 return or fast catamaran with the main cruise operator Great Adventures for $35 which includes the use of snorkelling gear. Ropes are extended from the vessel and attached to buoys to give a hand-hold and thus provide reassurance to those unused to swimming so far from the shore. You can choose from other activities, for example scuba diving (for those with a qualification), boom-netting (being dragged along through the water in a net behind a speeding boat) and trips in glass-bottomed boats or semi-submersible craft — the closest most people get to a real submarine. Some travellers strongly recommend a diving course as the best way to see the reef, and indeed learning to dive can cost as little as four times as much as a day trip to the reef. For those with limited time or finances, the cheapest option is to do a half-day's diving course on Green Island which includes instruction and one guided dive.

Other permutations are more expensive such as combining Green Island with Fitzroy Island or Michaelmas Cay; this is a small sandy island full of terns and other birds. Fitzroy has backpacker accommodation for $20 a night with no other facilities apart from the kitchen. If it rains there isn't much to do except walk up to the lighthouse and watch videos in the bar. Lizard Island is much further north and a far more exclusive destination, reputedly one of Prince Charles's favourite spots. Most visitors fly in (90 minutes and $140 from Cairns), and stay in luxurious and expensive accommodation while enjoying the beauty and relative solitude of this part of the reef.

Atherton Tablelands. This plateau, inland from Cairns, is a lush dairy farming area. British visitors often compare it with the West Country of England. The most popular destination in the Tablelands is the small and commercialised town of Kuranda, set in rainforest high above Cairns. Apart from the prettiness of the railway station and its setting, the main attractions are the market days throughout the week, the Tjapukai Aboriginal Dance Theatre and Kuranda's new Skyrail cableway, which allows a 7.5km journey over World Heritage rainforest ($23 one-way, $39 return). Kuranda also has the world's largest butterfly sanctuary.

The quiet and beautifully located Mrs Miller's Kuranda Backpackers Hostel (070-937355) is at 6 Arara St, opposite the Kuranda railway station and the Skyrail terminal. It provides an ideal base for rainforest walks or canoeing on the nearby Barron River. Dorm beds are $13 per night. You might want to consider relaxing in Kuranda for a while, rather than packing everything into a day trip from Cairns.

The Kuranda Scenic Railway between Cairns and Kuranda costs $23 one-way and $39 return ($33 on non-market days) — contact the Queensland Rail Travel

Centre in Cairns for more information (070-526249), or the Kuranda station (070-937225). The trip takes 1½ hours and is included as part of some tours organised by Cairns hostels. The locals travel by Whitecar Coaches, which depart from 51 Spence St in Cairns (070-519533); the trip costs $7.

Other attractions on the Tablelands and the Cairns hinterland include Lake Eacham, a freshwater rain-filled lake surrounded by rainforest; the Curtain Fig Tree, a spectacular example of tree parasitism (a tree becomes draped with, and is eventually killed by, a parasite vine); the Josephine Falls; and the Babinda Boulders. Mrs Miller's Hostel in Kuranda offers a one-day tour of the Tablelands' main sights. White-water rafting, bungy jumping and rap jumping are all available in the region; see *Great Outdoors* below.

North of Cairns. This area is one of beautiful beaches, rainforest stretching down to the sea and spots where Captain Cook had some of his unhappiest experiences (Cape Tribulation, Mount Sorrow, etc). The Cook Highway north to Port Douglas provides excellent coastal scenery, with several lookouts over the most dramatic stretches. After a hundred quiet years, Port Douglas is now a booming tourist destination, with the huge Sheraton Mirage resort charging outlandish prices.

Despite the new buildings, the town has retained much of its quiet and elegant character. It has the flavour of an affluent village set in a well kept park, surrounded by gentle hills offering pleasant coastal walks.

Port O'Call Lodge (070-995422) is part of the YHA, and is a short walk from the beach. Beds in small dorms with ensuite bathrooms are $17, with a free return coach to Cairns included in the price. The Lodge also has its own restaurant, with meals starting at $7. However Port Douglas now boasts a wide range of restaurants, so you shouldn't be stuck for choice.

A range of cruises are available to the offshore Low Isles (which are coral cays) and the Outer Barrier Reef; prices range from $75 to $90.

The sugar-town of Mossman has the beautiful Mossman Gorge to visit. Further north is Daintree and the Daintree Ferry, the barge that takes you across the river for the road to Cape Tribulation. A trip up to Cape Tribulation is one of the most worthwhile things to do in the far north, although you and all your gear will be covered in dirt by the time you get there. The Cape is accessible by tours bookable through any Cairns hostel. In the not-too-distant past the road to the Cape was poor (and little more than a muddy track in places), but now almost all of it is sealed. There is a campground on the Cape and also PK's Jungle Village (part of the VIP Backpackers Resorts chain), which is on the corner of Avalon St and Cape Tribulation Road (070-980040). The Village is right next to Myall Beach, and provides a base for horse-riding, guided bush walks and exploring the Great Barrier Reef.

Not far from the Cape is the Crocodylus Village YHA, at Lot 5, Buchanan Creek Road, Cow Bay (070-989166), which has beds from $14. Two coaches depart daily for the hostel from the McLeod St YHA in Cairns. Activities on offer include night-time guided walks through the rainforest.

The Daintree area is a centre of environmental controversy: the Queensland government has been accused of exploiting the rainforest for commercial logging, damaging the natural environment by the construction of the Bloomfield Track linking the Cape to Bloomfield and causing erosion that threatens parts of the reef. Partly in response to conservation concerns the road was never surfaced and is subject to flooding and mud. Both the rainforest and reef have been added to the World Heritage List of protected habitats, restricting the commercial exploitation of Daintree and enraging the local timbermen who make a living from it. Guided rainforest walks are worthwhile for pointing out or at least telling you about the local animal and plant life, including estuarine crocodiles,

Lumholtz's tree kangaroos and cassowaries; and strangler figs, king orchids and creepers that can grow a metre in a week. You also learn about Aboriginal lore and bush food. It is reassuring to be accompanied by an expert leech-remover. Paul Mason charges $13 for a 4-hour walk, which includes an optional dip in a freezing waterhole. Overnight jungle walks are also available.

Cooktown. If you have a suitable vehicle, you can continue from Bloomfield up to the old gold-mining town of Cooktown (which can also be reached by bus from Cairns by a more circuitous route). In the Gold Rush of the 1880s, it had 41 hotels and 45,000 inhabitants; now it has less than a thousand people, but retains some lovely colonial facades. Cooktown Motor Inn Backpackers ('where a good trip never ends') is at 12 Charlotte St, and has beds in dorms from $12 (070-695357).

CAPE YORK PENINSULA

The first area of Australia to be explored by Europeans is now the continent's last frontier. Virtually all of the massive finger pointing north towards Papua New Guinea has escaped the attention of white settlers. Its unspoilt beauty has been preserved by its extreme isolation. The inland scenery is an almost impenetrable jungle of thick scrub and rainforest, threaded with crocodile-infested creeks. The beaches on both sides of the peninsula are tropical gems and almost invariably deserted. To see these isolated places you will have to join a tour (see *Great Outdoors: Outback Adventures*, below). Much of Cape York is Aboriginal land and thus likely to be preserved as it has been for centuries.

The Cape itself is the most northerly point on the Australian mainland, but many of the islands in the Torres Strait between Queensland and Papua New Guinea are Australian territory. They are the homelands of the Torres Strait Islanders, a race distinct from the Aboriginal groups on the mainland and which has its own unique culture. Turnagain Island is the northernmost Australian possession, just 35km from the mainland of Papua New Guinea.

THE GULF

The shoreline around the Gulf of Carpentaria is mostly saline swampland, changing further from the sea to savannah grassland laced with creeks and dotted with salt pans. Until the Gulf Development Road from the east coast is fully sealed, access is best by air to Karumba or Burketown; the alternative is a difficult road journey. The native fauna is even less hospitable than the terrain, with crocodiles a real threat to those venturing near the water, and poisonous spiders and snakes inland. Some spiders are so big they feed on frogs.

The first Europeans to arrive at the Gulf by land were the transcontinental explorers Robert Burke and William Wills, who reached the area (but, because of the swamps, not quite the sea) in 1861. Their journey is commemorated by place names such as Wills Creek, the 'Burke and Wills Roadhouse' and Burketown. This latter settlement was Nevil Shute's model for the town of Willstown in his novel *A Town Like Alice*. It is a dry, dusty settlement that has never attained the dream of Shute's heroine, Jean Paget, of being 'a town as good as Alice Springs'. However, it is an excellent centre for studying the prolific wildlife in the area, and plenty of organised tours are available.

Karumba is a busy prawn-trawling port with job opportunities for those prepared to spend weeks aboard a trawler for uncertain reward. Inland along the wide Norman River, Normanton is at one end of the *Gulflander* railway line, a charming 'line to nowhere' that was built to transport ore from the old goldmining centre of Croydon, 150km east, to the port at Normanton. Nowadays one service runs each week in each direction, using a monstrously primitive engine hauling antiquated coaches.

INLAND QUEENSLAND

A series of Outback roads heading south from Karumba and ending in Charleville is now called the Matilda Highway. It has various points of interest scattered sparingly along it such as historic pubs (like the Blue Heeler Hotel in Kynuna) and outback museums. The most highly acclaimed of these is the Stockmen's Hall of Fame in Longreach which was one of the main Bicentennial projects. The material it has to work with, i.e. the social history of the men of the bush, is fascinating, even if the building that houses it is a modernist blot on the still, stark landscape. Among many interesting exhibits is a high-tech 'Talking Stockman' reminiscing by a campfire. Admission is $12.

Mount Isa and Western Queensland. Most travellers visit this region of Queensland only through necessity, as it is *en route* from the coast to the Northern Territory. The long-distance buses funnel through Mount Isa and you may be tempted to disembark and take a break for a day or two. Although this town has the world's largest silver-lead mine, its attractions and surroundings would be unlikely to sustain a longer stay. Still, a visit to the Underground Museum or a tour around the Mount Isa mine can be fascinating. The most interesting attraction nearby is Sun Rock (about 40km north, close to the Barkly Highway), which has fine Aboriginal paintings in red ochre. Access is limited; you must apply to the Ranger based at the Old Court House in Mount Isa for permission to visit. The Mount Isa YHA (077-435557) is on Wellington Park Road, opposite the Velodrome, and costs $10 per night.

Channel Country. Only intrepid travellers would wish to visit this desolate region in the south-west of Queensland. It is so-called because of the many channels formed when normally dry creeks overflow after the rare rainfalls. Such is the paucity of precipitation that Lake Yamma Yamma (near Haddon Corner, where South Australia intrudes into Queensland) has been full only twice this century. Highways in the area have recently been improved with the construction of new 'beef roads' for transporting cattle in the region, but are prone to be impassable in the unlikely event of a rainstorm; a more likely problem is that your vehicle will get bogged in the red dust. The region is most notable for relics of the pioneer past.

The state borders of Queensland, South Australia and New South Wales meet at Cameron Corner. About 100km north is the Dig Tree, where Burke and Wills died on their journey back from the Gulf of Carpentaria. The legend surrounding this sad event is gripping because so improbable. The Dig Tree is so-called because when the two explorers returned from their epic four-month expedition to the Gulf, they expected to find a relief party waiting, as arranged, at the solitary tree. But the party had moved off the day before, leaving a message pinned to the tree reading 'dig 40 feet west'. Burke and Wills did so and found some supplies, then carefully reburied the remainder so that Aboriginals would not find them. They then set off in search of the relief party, but headed in the wrong direction. Meanwhile the relief party decided to check one last time but, on finding the supplies apparently undisturbed, they abandoned Burke and Wills for good. The unfortunate explorers eventually returned to the Dig Tree, where they starved to death. A monument has been erected to their memory, and numerous four-wheel drive tourists visit the gnarled old tree.

Those properly equipped can cross the nearby border into South Australia and head north then west to Birdsville. Less well prepared travellers can fly direct from Brisbane and several other points, as many do for the annual race meeting each September. The town (usual population 100) is at the top of the cattle track that bears its name, which runs 486km south to Marree in South Australia. For decades cattle were driven along the Birdsville Track to the former railhead at Marree, for onward transportation to the south and east. Birdsville is still an important cattle town (although new roads mean that the journey along the Track is no longer necessary) and lies on the edge of the bleak Simpson Desert. Its isolation does not deter the thousands of visitors to the Birdsville Races. Beer is imported by road train to the town's only pub, the Royal Hotel on Main St (011 and ask for Birdsville 15). Accommodation is in extremely short supply, so many racegoers sleep under trucks or beneath their light aircraft.

Beaches. Queensland's endless beaches are not only appealing to look at, they are almost unbearably tempting to swim from. Most slope gently down to the warm ocean, protected from the roughest seas by the reef. Despite the occasional shark, swimming is usually safe anywhere on the coast during the winter and spring months from June to November (although you should not bathe near river mouths in the north due to the risk of crocodile attacks). During the rest of the year, however, swimming from the northern part of the coast is risky. Signs warning of danger from marine stingers are posted along the coast from Mackay northwards. Although they may overstate the period during which these creatures pose a threat, to be on the safe side the warnings should be heeded. It is frustrating to happen upon a deserted beach yet not be able to cool off in the sea, but save your swimming gear for the islands. Beaches on most of the offshore islands are free of marine stingers throughout the year, and you can swim, snorkel or dive quite safely. A few of the islands close to the shore (such as Magnetic Island) suffer from the menace, although stinger nets are strung across some of the popular beaches. Always take local advice before you take the plunge. For emergency treatment advice for sea wasps dial the toll-free Marine Stingers Line on 008-015160.

Diving. To select from the many competing schools, ask newly qualified divers (of whom there are many) to assess which appears to be not only the best value but also has decent safety standards. The PADI (Professional Association of Diving Instructors) is a good indication. Most courses last for five days, and the cheapest cost around $250. One of the longest established and best known schools is Mike Ball Watersports in Townsville (077-723022). Prices are somewhat higher than those charged by many dive schools in Cairns and nearby islands, but the teaching is better. Normally three days are spent learning the technique in a swimming pool, followed by two days (or a day and a night) on the reef. Unless you are abjectly useless (e.g. afraid of the water), you will almost certainly earn a certificate as a qualified diver. Most people are content with snorkelling and the equipment is easy to borrow or rent.

Sailing. Yachting enthusiasts from all over the world travel to Queensland to take advantage of the excellent sailing made possible by the many harbours dotted along the coast, the beautiful shore, and islands with safe anchorages and predictable weather. Plenty of bareboat yachts are available for charter, and Airlie Beach, Bowen, Townsville and Cairns are popular bases. One of the largest charter companies is Whitsunday Rent-a-Yacht, based at Shute Harbour (reservations on 1800-075111). Costs are high, but are obviously more manageable if shared by a large group; daily rates for eight-berth yachts range from

$400 to $560. If you require a skipper and crew the costs escalate astronomically. Instead of chartering a yacht, you could either sail as a paying passenger or try to charm a yachtsman and hitch a lift. The best places to get a free ride are Townsville, Shute Harbour and Bowen.

Rafting. White-water rafting trips are available from Cairns and Townsville to the Tully River. Raging Thunder Travel in Cairns (518177), for example, charges about $122 for a full-day trip to the Tully River and $65 for half a day on the Barron River nearer town. Kayaking is also possible, and even more ambitious trips combining rafting and ballooning.

Cycling. The journey north from Brisbane along the Bruce Highway benefits from a tailwind, but is not as enjoyable as it might appear from a glance at a map. The road is busy and rarely runs right along the coast. Look for interesting detours taking you further from the sea but using more pleasant roads; the inland route from Brisbane to Rockhampton via Gayndah and Biloela is quiet and scenic and, while not well surfaced, is a pleasant ride. The next section north from Rockhampton to Mackay is desolate with only a couple of roadhouses and a few small townships on the 350km stretch of road. North of Mackay the traffic eases, but you may soon tire of rattling over the numerous railway crossings that link the sugar cane plantations. The tarmac stops at Daintree, and an all-terrain bike is essential for any further progress. The run up to the Tablelands west of Cairns can be an enjoyable ride, doubly so on the steep descent.

If you prefer not to battle against the headwinds all the way back to Brisbane, your bicycle can accompany you by bus or train. The cost of transporting a bike from Cairns to Brisbane is $12.60 by train, or $10 with most coach companies (if dismantled).

Blue heeler dogs, favoured by cattlemen, seem particularly vicious in Queensland; watch out for the one halfway between Mossman and Wonga Beach that is not averse to biting passing cyclists.

Outback Adventures. There are large tracts of Queensland where inexperienced travellers should not venture independently, but you may rest assured that plenty of tour operators are willing to sell you a place on a package trip. Each company is licensed by the state government, but some expect more active participation from their clients than others. While the established organisation Australian Pacific Tours (107 Draper St, Portsmith, Cairns; 070-311155/519299) may be too conventional for your tastes, you might prefer their well planned tours to the one offered by one contractor who — after his expedition had to be rescued from Cape York — accused the participants of being a 'bunch of wimps'. As with diving schools, ask other travellers for their recommendations of the various tours on offer. Often the cheapest and most enjoyable tours are those organised by local hostels, but they are also the quickest to fill up.

Most overland tours north of Cairns take the coastal route to Cooktown, then strike inland skirting an Aboriginal Reserve to Lakefield National Park, the biggest in Queensland and with outstanding flora and fauna. The journey up to the tip of Cape York then becomes really rough, with narrow bush tracks and repeated difficult crossings of creeks. Wilderness Challenges (070-556504) run safaris to Cape York; expect to pay at least $1000 for a 10–15 day trip.

Bungy-jumping is well established in Queensland from the Gold Coast to north of Cairns. The famous New Zealand bungy-jump entrepreneur, A J Hackett, has his operation at a 44m tower in the rainforest at Smithfield in the Barron Gorge, 15 minutes from Cairns (070-311119). It is in a lovely location and so worth visiting even as a spectator. The jump can be combined with a half-day or full-day rafting trip on the Barron River which costs respectively $129 or $179.

The newest adventure activity to come to Queensland is rap-jumping which consists of abseiling (or rappelling, hence the name) while facing forwards. This takes place on several cliff faces in Barron Gorge near Kuranda and can be booked in Cairns (070-321606). The same company has introduced the activity to Magnetic Island and hopes to expand to various locations. The price varies with the height of the jump, so that ten jumps up to 45m cost $50 while three jumps up to nearly 100m cost $79.

Restricted Areas. There are two military reserves on the coast of Queensland — Wide Bay near Gympie, and Shoalwater Bay north of Rockhampton — where entry is prohibited. In addition, numerous areas in far north Queensland, including some islands, are Aboriginal Reserves — for many of these approval in writing is required from the Aboriginal Affairs Department before you can visit them.

Calendar of Events

January	World Series Cricket, Brisbane
February	Redcliffe Yacht Classic
March	Queensland Eisteddfod, Ipswich
March/April	Easter Cup, Brisbane
March/April	Brisbane to Gladstone Yacht Race
May (first Monday)	**Labour Day**
June	Mount Isa Show
June	Magnetic Island Rediscovery
August	Mount Isa Rodeo
August	Cooee-calling Championships, Cooee Bay
August	National Agricultural Show, Brisbane
August (third Wednesday)	**Brisbane Exhibition Day (public holiday in Brisbane)**
September	Birdsville Races
September	Redland Strawberry Festival, Cleveland
September	Winfield Cup Grand Final (Rugby League), Brisbane
late Sept/early October	Warana Spring Festival, Brisbane

Public holidays are shown in **bold**.

NEW ZEALAND

New Zealand is so far from everywhere else that it was one of the last places on the planet to be settled by man. Despite the coming of the jet age, much of New Zealand remains isolated in ways that will strike the recent arrival from Europe, North America or even Australia immediately. The content of some New Zealanders' lives seems to have changed very little since their forebears arrived (mostly from Great Britain) in the 19th century. Farmers still muster their sheep with dogs and rural mailmen still know everyone on their routes by name. Of course many of these clichés are being overtaken by modernisation and progress, and the unspoiled rural idyll is becoming a romantic fiction perpetuated in the many tourist complexes devoted to New Zealand farm life. The increasing sophistication of New Zealand has both positive aspects and disadvantages for the visitor who will find less novelty but more comfort.

While the village atmosphere is less strong than it was 20 years ago, it still exists. Visitors will find themselves the object of much friendly interest and curiosity that they would be unlikely to find in Maryland, Munich or Melbourne. This unfeigned interest and concern for visitors is one feature that makes New Zealand uniquely attractive, and which has prompted some writers to call it 'the last utopia'. Such plaudits should be sufficient to attract large numbers of tourists. But New Zealand's remoteness is a serious impediment to potential visitors.

Fortunately New Zealand has its spectacular topography as a trump card. Volcanoes, glaciers, fiords and rivers have to be outstanding to justify an investment of hundreds or thousands of pounds or dollars, but no visitor could be disappointed with the natural wonders of New Zealand. One of the most fascinating aspects of its sharp and rugged contours is that many have been altered by volcanic activity in recent times and will soon change again. New Zealand's geology, like its history, is youthful, full of potential, and quite unlike anything in Europe.

After having been one of the world's fastest-growing tourist destinations, visitor numbers began to drop slightly at the beginning of the 1990s. Still, nearly a million tourists arrive in this country of just over three million every year. Investment in tourism has been vigorous and on the whole beneficial. Facilities from luxury hotels to campsites, from public relations offices to local museums, from ski resorts to bungy-jumping centres are expanding in number and improving amenities. Like any country that is so heavily dependent on tourism, there may come a time when New Zealand will be considered 'spoiled' by crass developments and crowds. But that day is a long way off, and the visitor in the 1990s will be amazed and delighted by just how little the pressures of modern society have impinged on the landscapes and psyche of New Zealand.

CLIMATE

New Zealand's climate may come as a shock if you have been travelling in the hot, dry areas of Australia and are expecting its neighbour's weather to be similar. Rainfall is terrifically high on the west coast of the South Island, where some of the country's foremost attractions are located. An entry in the visitor's book of a mountain hut on the Routeburn Track reads, 'In New Zealand you don't tan — you rust'. The New Zealand Tourist & Publicity Department plays down the fact that visitors have to be lucky to see Mount Cook or Mount Taranaki out of cloud, or to see Milford Sound in the sunshine. Their evasive descriptions of the weather — for example, 'the west-facing coasts are relatively exposed and therefore good for surfing' — hardly do justice to the inconvenience to walkers and sightseers caused by frequent torrential downpours. Many places receive over 200 inches/500cm of rainfall (ten times more than London).

Heavy rains can be dangerous as well as merely irritating. It is not uncommon for bridges to be washed out on South Island roads, preventing traffic from getting through for anything up to a fortnight. The local airport might also be under a metre of water. After negotiating a main road like Arthur's Pass in such conditions, it is not unusual to emerge on the eastern side of the country to find dry weather. The eastern coastal areas of both islands, where the vast majority of the population lives, are generally much drier with some areas even suffering summer droughts. Auckland has precipitation on about 12 days in the winter months and 6 days a month in the summer, while the corresponding figures for Christchurch are 6 and 5.

Fluctuations of temperature between areas are not as pronounced as differences in precipitation, though the mountainous interiors of both islands usually receive enough snow from June onwards to support a vigorous ski industry. Except in the mountains, temperatures throughout New Zealand are moderate, though obviously warmer in the Bay of Islands than in Dunedin, which is 11 degrees further from the equator. When transferred to the northern hemisphere the corresponding latitudes would be Crete and Bordeaux or Los Angeles and Seattle.

The average maximum summer temperature for Auckland is 23°C/74°F, while Christchurch is a couple of degrees cooler. Winter maximums in the two cities hover around 15°C/59°F and 11°C/52°F, respectively. There are occasional heat waves in December/January, but air-conditioning is uncommon, unless you are using the term — as New Zealanders do — to refer to heating as well as cooling. Generally summer temperatures — especially in the North Island — are sufficiently balmy for men to don shorts and knee socks (known as 'walk shorts' and 'walk socks') before going off to work.

Another inescapable climatic feature is wind. Although windy Wellington takes the prize, Auckland and Christchurch often become blustery too. There can also be gales in the mountains. Calm conditions are rare and the air always has a fresh quality.

THE PEOPLE

It is often noted that New Zealanders seem to make a habit of inviting strangers into their homes and sharing the addresses of their friends and relations. Even people involved in the tourist industry seem to take a more personal than commercial interest in visitors' welfare; directories of accommodation will often include a line, 'your hosts: Bob and Betty Tuckwell'. Their refreshing generosity and hospitality no doubt derive from a not-too-distant time in the country's history when travel was extremely difficult and settlers would not hesitate to call on other farmers either from necessity (flooded rivers, blocked roads) or for company, which has always been in short supply. The population of New Zealand is just 3.2 million in a country whose area is greater than Britain's.

Almost all of the post-Maori settlers have come from the United Kingdom, either in this generation or in the previous three or four. New Zealand was much more reluctant than Australia in the 1960s to accept waves of immigration from southern Europe and more recently from south-east Asia. This means that New Zealand lacks not only the Italian delicatessens of Melbourne and the Vietnamese restaurants of Sydney, but also the cosmopolitan character that a multi-ethnic society creates. The one exception is the relatively large population of Pacific Islanders, mainly people from Samoa, Tonga, the Cook Islands and other New Zealand protectorates. Although they represent only 2.7% of the total population of New Zealand, Auckland is the largest Polynesian city in the world.

An enjoyable pastime for visitors is to try to isolate cultural differences between the north and the south. It could be said by British observers that a journey south from Picton is comparable to travelling north from Watford, and the Scottish influence is felt from Dunedin south.

Much of the population participates in outdoor activities, often to the exclusion of other interests. They tramp (i.e. hike), sail, ski and dive. They are also amazingly innovative when it comes to exploring their remarkable country and have invented or at least adapted a host of sports and vehicles. The most famous is bungy-jumping, but there is now surf-rafting, blackwater rafting, water sledging, sky-cat flying, and so on. They have even invented one or two bizarre indoor activities, such as the famous 'bar-fly hopping' in a pub in Napier, which involves bouncing off a trampoline and trying to attach yourself high on a wall with velcro. You can't fault New Zealanders on imagination, which perhaps they've had to develop for want of other excitements.

MAKING FRIENDS

The New Zealand approach to foreign visitors is less guarded and formal and more openly patriotic than the British, for example. They sometimes refer to their country as 'Godzone' (God's Own) and assume that foreigners will agree with them that New Zealand combines most of the attributes of an ideal country (many nationalities are guilty of this but perhaps with less justification). This chauvinism extends to male/female relationships. Although many New Zealand males like to think of themselves as less boorish than their Australian counter-parts, many are unaware of their ingrained sexism. For example, you may be hard-pressed to find a New Zealand man in a pub able to accept graciously a drink from a woman.

They are soft-spoken (except in a pub near closing time), and are so unhurried in their reactions that in conversation you sometimes wonder for a minute whether they have heard you. On a personal level the majority are unpretentious and modest, to the extent that one guide book warns the unsuspecting visitor not to give a New Zealander anything with a designer label visible.

A certain amount of parochialism pertains at all levels of society and many New Zealanders exhibit a breathtakingly narrow range of interests. An unhealthily intimate knowledge of sheep-rearing is almost universal. However, the claim that when they are not discussing the price of lamb they are discussing the rugby results is grossly unfair. You will meet plenty of New Zealanders who are informed on a wide range of topics from the impact of their country's anti-nuclear foreign policy to the ethics of planting pine trees instead of the slower-growing native trees like rimu and kauri. The high proportion of New Zealanders who have travelled extensively abroad further mitigates the rural insularity often encountered.

Though on the one hand many young New Zealanders consider an 'Overseas Experience' or 'OE' to be obligatory, they (like Australians) also tend to be dismissive of Britain and British culture. There is a certain amount of inverse snobbery in the Antipodean habit of denigrating the old country for its supposed obsession with class backgrounds and for its lethargy. But individual British travellers will be welcomed as warmly as the ubiquitous Canadians, Scandinavians and Germans. New Zealanders cannot risk being too enthusiastic about Australians, as they feel almost as culturally threatened by them as Canadians do by Americans. Also Australians abroad do seem to assume some of the arrogance associated with travelling Americans (e.g. they can be overheard complaining in loud voices about New Zealand's backwardness) and so they may deserve some of the abuse heaped upon them by the locals.

Language. North Americans find New Zealanders quaintly English because of their terminology ('bangers' for sausages, 'petrol' for gas, 'knickers' for women's underpants, and so on). But there are also many colourful words and expressions unfamiliar to the British ear. For example, a 'dairy' (pronounced dearie) is a corner shop, a 'bach' (pronounced batch) is a modest weekend cottage in the North Island, a 'crib' is ditto in the South Island, 'jandals' are flip-flops, and so on. Many expressions heard in New Zealand are also in common Australian usage, such as 'chook' for chicken, 'paddock' for field, 'bludger' for sponger, etc. But don't assume that all Aussie expressions will be understood: if you ask a New Zealander what he has in his 'Esky' he will probably return a blank stare. In New Zealand parlance that useful object, the insulated drinks cooler, is called a 'chillybin' or in cruder contexts, a 'piss bin'.

A number of Maori words have entered the language of English-speaking New Zealanders such as *hangi* for earth-oven, *marae* for a Maori meeting-house and enclosure, *pakeha* as a non-derogatory term for white person (the original Maori word meant pale-skinned, while the word 'Maori' means ordinary), and so on. See below for more details about the Maori language.

Some visitors have remarked that every vowel uttered by a New Zealander sounds the same: a kind of 'uh' — what phoneticists call the 'schwa' — like the vowel sound in the word th*e*. 'Fish and chips' thus becomes 'fush und chups'.

American readers will be especially interested in an amusing little book called *A Personal Kiwi–Yankee Dictionary* by Louis S Leland Jr, on sale in airport bookshops and elsewhere.

THE MAORI PEOPLE

Seafaring Polynesians with a relatively advanced culture landed their giant canoes on the shores of New Zealand as long as 1000 years ago. Whereas Aboriginals represent a mere 1.5% of Australia's population, the Maori people comprise over 12% of New Zealanders and are very much in evidence. Most of them remained on the North Island as in former times their limited food supplies would not permit them to survive the harsher South Island winter. Even today only one in 16 Maoris lives in the South Island. Maori place names — not too difficult to pronounce but hard to remember — are much more common in the North than the South. If you walk into a North Island pub, chances are there will be a high proportion of Maori people who are quite likely to be evenly dispersed among the Pakeha (European) drinkers. The level of integration is a pleasant surprise after Australia. Mixed marriages have been commonplace from the beginning and it is sometimes claimed that there are no full-blooded Maori people left. Most white New Zealanders whose families were among the early settlers have at least one Maori ancestor. This is cause for pride rather than shame, and Maori culture has achieved a certain amount of respect both in New Zealand and internationally.

According to the official line as typified in the government tourist literature, integration of the Maori into New Zealand society is total: 'today both Maori and Pakeha are a united population, sharing the same legal rights and enjoying a harmony experienced in few other countries'. This version does not take into account the vociferous minority who maintain that the land deals between European settlers and the Maori people in the 19th century were unfair and should be renegotiated. The Treaty of Waitangi, which gives its name to New Zealand's national day (February 6), was signed in 1840 but has never been ratified by the British or New Zealand governments. If it were to be ratified (which, politically, is out of the question) the Maori would come into possession of a great deal more land than they hold at present. The sympathy of white New Zealanders with the Maori cause usually stops short of condoning the return of land which may have been farmed by Europeans for 100 years.

The government reserves certain places in parliament and the civil service for the Maori, and has actively tried to foster the culture and language with the eventual aim of making New Zealand a bilingual country. In fact all Maori people speak English (often with a particularly strong New Zealand accent) and many speak no Maori at all. But with government assistance there is now a flourishing Maori-run network of kindergartens called *kohanga reo*, where pre-school children learn the Maori language, history and mythology.

Maori culture (known as Maoritanga) is more accessible to the visitor than Aboriginal culture. Maori legends are commonly quoted and usually involve mountains falling out with one another or making unsuitable marriages. Much of New Zealand's best literature such as Keri Hulme's *Bone People* and Maurice Shadbolt's books draw upon elements of Pacific mythology. This richly storied system of belief did not prevent the Maori from accepting the white man's religion (with certain adaptations) quickly, and interesting architectural hybrids resulted.

The Maori Collection at the Auckland Museum provides a good introduction. Rotorua, in the centre of the north island, is the heavily promoted centre of Maori tourism. It is difficult to see Maori dances, music and rituals outside the commercial context of Rotorua and places like it. But if you do stay long enough in a New Zealand town to get to know some local Maori people, you may be honoured with an invitation to a hangi, a Maori feast. Many maraes do welcome visits from interested parties, though formal ceremonies (which entail the traditional *hongi* greeting of pressed noses) are rare. Maori handicrafts are easier to find as carvings from wood, bone, shell and jade are sold in souvenir shops throughout the country.

IMMIGRATION

Most nationalities, including British, Irish, Australian, Canadian and US visitors, require only a passport to enter New Zealand. It must be valid for at least 3 months beyond your intended departure from New Zealand. Arriving British and Australian tourists are usually granted a stay of 6 months, whereas North Americans and most European nationalities are allowed 3 months.

Upon arrival, you may be asked to show a return or onward ticket and enough money to fund your stay; if you look sufficiently respectable, the immigration officers are unlikely to challenge you. The amount considered appropriate is

NZ$1000 for each month of your proposed stay. If you can show a form called *Sponsoring a Visitor* that has been completed and sent to you by a New Zealand resident promising to provide accommodation and support, you need only NZ$400 for each month. Foreign nationals admitted as tourists are not allowed to work, though there are special provisions for working holidaymakers (see *Work* below).

All visitors may apply for permission to extend their stay to a maximum of 12 months. Applications can be lodged locally with the Immigration section of the Department of Labour (addresses in local telephone directories). Britons planning to spend a lot of time in New Zealand should note that they are allowed to stay for only 12 out of every 24 months.

For more complete information on immigration requirements, contact the New Zealand Immigration Service, New Zealand House, 80 Haymarket, London SW1Y 4TE (0171-973 0366). The *Guide for Visiting New Zealand* is for those who intend to stay temporarily and covers the topic of casual work. A separate self-assessment guide is for those who are considering emigration, and explains the points system that is now in operation. The current fee for processing an application for residence is about £300. American citizens should contact the New Zealand Embassy at 37 Observatory Circle, NW Washington DC 20008.

CUSTOMS

You will be issued on the flight with 'Passenger Arrival Papers' (a combined immigration/quarantine/customs form). All incoming aircraft (except those arriving from directly across the Tasman), are sprayed on arrival by the Department of Agriculture. Upon landing there will be an announcement pleading with you to remain seated, as the fumigators will refuse to board the aircraft if people are standing.

New Zealand is very serious about protecting its agriculture from imported nasties and it is an offence not to declare agricultural products at entry. All arriving travellers must complete an Agriculture Quarantine form, declaring the potentially harmful contents of their luggage, including food of any kind. Many seemingly innocuous items such as a tin of sardines, shelled nuts, coffee beans and straw hats must be inspected for pests and diseases and treated if necessary. More exotic items such as bird's nest soup, jumping beans and dead bees are completely prohibited.

In addition to all animal, plant and other food products, you are required to declare any 'used tents, sporting equipment or other camping equipment' and also bicycles. If you confess that you have visited a farm or forest in the 30 days preceding your arrival in New Zealand, you may be asked to subject your footwear to disinfectant spray. Large 'amnesty bins' are provided at international airports, urging you to dump your illegal imports before reaching Customs.

Goods and Currency. The standard duty-free allowances are 200 cigarettes or 250 grams of tobacco, 4.5 litres (six bottles) of wine or beer and 1.125 litres (40 fl oz) of spirits. Only passengers over the age of 17 are entitled to the allowance.

There is no limit on the amount of New Zealand or foreign currency allowed in or out. You are supposed to declare gifts if their combined value exceeds NZ$500. For complete details of the regulations, request the leaflet *New Zealand Customs Guide for Travellers* from the Collector of Customs, Private Bag, Wellington.

New Zealand Customs dogs must be among the fittest in the world as they do their sniffing while walking on-the-spot on baggage conveyor belts.

Departure Tax. Leaving New Zealand the departure tax is $20.

Travellers whose intention is to earn money in the Antipodes have traditionally tended to work in Australia rather than New Zealand, partly because wages are higher in Australia, and because New Zealand has previously not offered a working holiday visa to British travellers. A more pressing reason has emerged in the early 1990s, i.e. the disastrous state of New Zealand's economy with the recession causing shops and businesses to close on a massive scale and unemployment to rise above 10%. Still, there are always some opportunities for those who persevere. Australian citizens are at liberty to take up employment at any time and US and Canadian students can apply for a temporary work permit (see below).

Working Holiday Visas. This recently introduced annual scheme allows 2000 UK citizens aged 18–30 years to have a 12-month working holiday in New Zealand. The current fee is £60, and applicants need to produce evidence of a return travel ticket and at least NZ$4200 for living expenses. Offers of employment in New Zealand are not required. Further information is available from New Zealand House, Haymarket, London SW1Y 4TE (0171-973 0366).

Working Visas. Anyone who has contacts in New Zealand and can obtain a firm offer of employment before leaving the UK can apply for a temporary work visa (the current fee is £60). Your New Zealand sponsor should be prepared to prove to the Immigration Service that it is necessary to hire a foreigner rather than an unemployed New Zealander.

Young people on *bona fide* holidays who want to do casual work can apply inside New Zealand to one of the seven Immigration Service offices (Auckland, Manukau, Hamilton, Palmerston North, Wellington, Christchurch and Dunedin) for a work permit (as opposed to the work visa described above). Applicants must have a written offer of work. The fee for processing an application for a work permit is $117. As long as local residents will not be disadvantaged, there is a chance that a work permit will be granted for the specific job and period. There is of course no guarantee that any application, however genuine, will be approved. In fact the percentage being approved has been steadily decreasing since 1988, mainly because of the increase in the number of complaints from unemployed locals.

If you are a genuine working holidaymaker, flitting from job to job as you travel, the work permit system is tiresome, anxiety-inducing and expensive. Many travellers have chosen to dispense with it. It is reported that New Zealand employers are less concerned to see a work permit than a tax number. Eight-digit numbers from the Inland Revenue Department can be applied for from post offices. In Auckland the IRD office is in Takapuna (09-486 1511). The basic rate of tax is 24% with no tax-free allowances.

As in Australia, the immigration authorities have begun to take a keener interest in people working without permission and there are frequent cases of immigration swoops on fruit farms, especially in the Bay of Plenty and Nelson areas, followed by deportations. Travellers will have to decide for themselves, after discreetly talking to locals, whether their case is strong enough to convince the authorities to issue a work permit and, if not, whether they are prepared to take the risk of working illicitly.

American students are eligible to apply for a six-month work permit from CIEE (205 East 42nd St, New York, NY 10017) to work between May and October; the processing fee is US$96. The Canadian Universities Travel Service (Travel CUTS) administers a similar work abroad scheme for Canadian students with departures in early May and mid-August. All visas expire at the end of October. The registration fee is C$200, and participants must have at least C$1000. Despite the gloom and doom about the New Zealand recession, most students have little difficulty in finding temporary jobs in catering, retailing, farming, etc. The point of allowing foreigners to work only during the New Zealand winter is to avoid competition with New Zealand students seeking holiday jobs in summer.

Several work opportunities in New Zealand for school-leavers are organised through GAP; enquiries to the GAP office, 44 Queen's Road, Reading, Berks RG1 4BB.

The minimum wage in New Zealand for people over 20 years of age was $245 in 1991; many jobs pay considerably more than that. An experienced data-processor employed through a temp agency in Wellington or Auckland would expect to be paid about $12.50 an hour, though office work is difficult to get without a work permit.

FRUIT PICKING

The climate of New Zealand lends itself to fruit-growing of many kinds including citrus fruits and kiwifruit. You may find picking work by reading the notices in YHA hostels or by approaching farmers directly, possibly after getting their names and addresses from the owners of small country stores. There is also a growing trade in fruits and vegetables from roadside stalls and directly from the farmers' properties, so you should keep your eyes open while travelling along country roads where you might even see signs posted 'Pickers Wanted' as happens in Kerikeri in the far north. Just turning up in town and asking around is a good bet for work while the season is on. Below are some general guidelines as to what areas to head for in the appropriate seasons. Motueka, the bay of Plenty and Kerikeri are favourites among travellers.

Most farmers offer some kind of accommodation which is useful in a climate as rainy as New Zealand's. Farmers often provide fresh fruit and vegetables, milk and sometimes lamb. Some farmers are so keen to recruit pickers that they circulate notices around YHA hostels, for example 'Orchard Work Available January to March; apply Tauranga YHA Hostel'. Other farmers visit the local hostel early in the morning and round up their daily requirement of pickers. It is always worth asking the hostel warden if he or she knows of any possibilities, once you have distinguished yourself by carrying out your hostel duty with alacrity and cheerfulness.

The demand for workers during the apple harvest between February and April is very great in the Nelson/Motueka area. Packers are also needed at the processing works in Stoke just outside Nelson. The union is strong here and has succeeded in making it obligatory for farmers to provide accommodation other than just a campsite. The negotiated rate of pay is about $23 per bin; the average picker fills three to four bins a day, though star pickers manage between six and eight.

Another excellent area for finding work is the Bay of Plenty where most of New Zealand's kiwifruit is grown. The harvest traditionally commences on May 1, though it is wise to arrive a week or two earlier than this. The fruit must be picked carefully by hand and placed in a large canvas bag worn like an apron.

An expert picker can pick 1300kg in a day at the peak of the harvest which lasts for about 6 weeks altogether. Rates of pay (either by the bucket or by the hour — called 'award rate' as in Australia) are relatively high for this crop. Because students are not available at this time, there have in the past been serious labour shortages, just as for the apple and pear harvests in the North Island in March/ April. However it should be noted that because of the crisis in the fruit-growing industry, many growers have resorted to doing casual labour themselves especially in the packhouses which in 1991 were inundated with local applicants.

The semi-tropical north of the country, which specialises in citrus growing, is another favourite. There are several big packing sheds which employ a large number of casual workers in November/December. Kiwifruit production is also important in this region, though a recent decline in the world market meant that some casual workers have been hired to strip vines for pig feed as the fruit couldn't be sold; the packaging was worth more than the fruit. Hideaway Lodge in Kerikeri (see Bay of Islands below) is a good place to find out about agricultural jobs of all kinds, from strawberry-picking in December to kiwifruit pruning in July.

FARMS

The system of working on organic farms in exchange for board and lodging is well advanced in New Zealand. Anyone interested in working on the land should join WWOOF (Willing Workers on Organic Farms, PO Box 10-037, Palmerston North, North Island; 06-355 3555). For a fee of £5/US$7/NZ$10 the organisers (Andrew and Jane Strange) will send you a fix-it-yourself list of about 100 farms and smallholdings which welcome volunteers in exchange for food and accommodation.

Much of New Zealand resembles a great big dairy and sheep farm, though in order to find work it is usually necessary to have some relevant skills or experience in milking, mustering, etc. Wages on sheep stations are not high, perhaps $250 a week in addition to room and board. The Saturday edition of the *New Zealand Herald* and the *Waikato Times* of Hamilton are recommended for experienced people looking for work on the land.

THE TOURIST INDUSTRY

Tourism employs large numbers of people, not all of whom can be supplied locally. This is perhaps most noticeable in the year-round resort of Queenstown in the South Island. Many young people, from both New Zealand and overseas, congregate in this attractively situated town to find work in the many motels, restaurants, etc. Job offers can be seen on the notice board of the YHA hostel or on the central town notice board in the pedestrian mall. A good place to get to know the transient working population is Eichardts pub. Waiting and barten-ding staff are usually paid about $8 an hour which is not supplemented with tips as there is virtually no tradition of tipping in New Zealand.

Adventure travel is booming and you might get taken on by a camping tour operator or a yachtas a cook; if you're a skier, you should try one of the ski resorts. The main ski resorts in the Southern Alps are Coronet Peak and the Remarkables, serviced by Queenstown. Of course Queenstown's year-round popularity with young travellers means that there are often more people looking for work than there are jobs, so it might be advisable to try more out-of-the-way tourist areas. You often stand a better chance of finding work in remote underpopulated places on the tourist trail (of which there are many in New Zealand).

Fishing. Oyster-shelling work is readily available in the North Island between

April and December, especially at the end of the season during the Christmas rush. Look up *Fisheries* in the Yellow Pages in Whangarei or Kerikeri. The pay is a decent $8 an hour and you may even be given a gumboot allowance.

The New Zealand dollar, occasionally referred to as the 'kiwi', is much weaker than the Australian dollar. At the time of writing the exchange rates were NZ$2.39 — £1 and NZ$1.56 — US$1.

Notes and Coins. The denominations of notes in circulation are $5, $10, $20, $50 and $100. Despite extravagant protests from some quarters, the picture of the Queen was replaced on all but the $20 note in 1992. The new $5 note bears a picture of the mountaineer Edmund Hillary; the suffragette Kate Sheppard, appears on the $10 note, Apirana Ngata, a Maori politician, on the $50 and the physicist Lord Ernest Rutherford on the $100. A more serious threat than the deletion of the Queen to New Zealand's self-image is posed by the Reserve Bank's suggestion that eventually there may be a common currency in New Zealand and Australia (provided Australia is willing to amalgamate its economy with a weaker one).

The following coins are in circulation: 5c, 10c, 20c, 50c, $1 and $2. The NZ 10c and 20c coins appear identical in size to their Australian counterparts.

Banks. Each international airport has a bank immediately outside the customs hall, which is open for passengers arriving on international flights.

The five major banks are the National Bank of New Zealand, Bank of New Zealand, ANZ, Postbank and Westpac. Because Westpac is one of Australia's major banks, many travellers mistakenly assume that they can easily have money transferred between the two countries through Westpac, but they are completely separate institutions.

Opening hours are from 8.30 or 9am to 4.30pm Monday to Friday except Tuesday when many open half an hour later. Most banks now charge 25c for every transaction on top of whatever fee is levied for changing travellers' cheques. A modest stamp duty of 5c per cheque must be paid at all banks.

If you open an account, be warned that there is no cheque guarantee card, which makes cashing cheques other than in branches of your own bank impossible. The most versatile bank is probably Postbank, although despite the name banking facilities are not available at all post offices. If you are staying put and earning money, you can open a high-interest term account (minimum 4 weeks) with a building society.

Credit Cards. Plastic money has penetrated surprisingly far, and many little businesses in the 'wop wops' (New Zealand expression for the back-of-beyond) accept Bankcard/Access/MasterCard and Visa. Take-away pizza joints as well as more established restaurants and stores often accept credit cards. You can draw cash up to your credit limit on Visa at branches of the National Bank and ANZ Bank, and on Access through Westpac.

Note that although the National Bank is associated with Lloyds Bank (even using the same black horse logo), Access cards are not accepted.

Tipping. There used to be signs posted in the arrivals hall of Auckland Airport exhorting foreigners not to tip. The practice is still virtually unknown in New Zealand. Service charges are not added to restaurant meals nor are credit card users given a chance to add a gratuity on the sales voucher.

Sales Tax. A goods and service tax (GST) of 12.5% is applied to almost every item. As in Britain, it is incorporated into the advertised price of merchandise rather than added at the till. Some services are advertised minus GST however this fact is usually clearly signposted.

TELEPHONES
The first New Zealand telephone engineer perhaps had an unusual sense of humour, as the New Zealand telephone dial is unlike any other. The dial face is the only one in the world to be numbered clockwise. Although the dialling motion remains the same (i.e. clockwise) it is disorienting to have the distance between 9 and the stop much shorter than the distance between 1 and the stop.

Public Telephones. Much of the quaintness of New Zealand's telephone system has disappeared with the complete overhaul of the system by New Zealand Telecom. If you have any difficulty calling a number, try ringing the NZ Number Update Help Desk (free of charge) on 0155.

Local calls cost 20c a minute. Phonecards can be bought in denominations of $5, $10, $20 or $50 from many retail outlets. Modern card phones predominate in the big cities now. At the other end of the technological spectrum, New Zealand still has a few of the old payphones with a button on the front labelled A and another on the right-hand side labelled B. If you come across one of these, the correct procedure for local calls is to insert two 10c coins, dial the number, wait for a reply and then push button A to connect the call. If no one answers, push button B, hang up and your money will be returned. The last manual switchboard operator was made redundant in 1991 (she had been an operator on Great Barrier Island for 55 years), the end of an era in which it was not impossible for foreign visitors to have a call put through by a kind-hearted operator even when they lacked the correct change.

Overseas Calls. International subscriber dialling (ISD) phones are widespread, and overseas calls are most easily made using a phonecard. The number for international directory enquiries is 0172 and the foreign operator access code for collect or charge card calls is 0170.

The minimum call length to North America and Britain is one minute, which costs $4. The trickiest part is finding a suitable time to phone when your friends and family will be neither asleep nor out at work. The UK is 11 to 13 hours behind New Zealand (depending on daylight savings) and so mid-morning is often the best time to catch your nearest and dearest the previous evening. Morning is also suitable if you are dialling the US: when it is 11am in Auckland, it is about 3pm the previous day in Los Angeles and 6pm in New York.

Toll Calls. Local calls within the 'toll-free calling area,' shown at the front of directories, are free of charge from private phones. Charges for long distance calls using Telecom within New Zealand are clearly set out at the beginning of all New Zealand telephone directories. The ten charging steps depend on distance, and four call rates depend on time. For example a three-minute call from Christchurch to Auckland costs about $5 in the peak (8am-noon Monday-Saturday), $3.50 in the early morning (6am-8am) and evening (6pm-10.30pm), and $1.75 in the cheap time (10.30pm-6am daily). If calling from a private house and you want to pay for the call, simply ask the operator (010) for 'price required service' before placing the call. The operator will then ring back a minute or so later with the cost. Alternatively you can dial a special code which will result in the call being specially featured on the next bill: dial 013 in place of 0 for an STD call (i.e. within New Zealand) or dial 016 instead of 00 for an ISD (i.e. international) call.

Long-distance calls are cheapest on Telecom's new rival, Clear Communications. You can access the network from a private phone by dialling 050 before the area code and number.

Directory Enquiries. The National Directory Assistance Service is available on 018. New Zealand has just five area codes: Auckland and Northland 09, Waikato and Bay of Plenty 07, Hawke's Bay and southern North Island 06, Wellington 04 and the whole of the South Island 03. Numbers prefixed 025 are for mobile phones; those beginning 0800 are free calls.

POST
The New Zealand Post Office has a storied past. Originally it used means as various as Maori runners, pigeongrammes and postmen-cum-mountaineers reputed to have carried items such as children's bicycles over mountain ranges at Christmas time. Apparently in 1842 it took mail 127 days to get from Auckland to Wellington and was frequently routed through Sydney to speed up delivery. Today the rural mailman maintains this colourful tradition by undertaking far more deliveries than just the mail, depending on his or her initiative. Rural mailmen are not employees of the post office but contracted freelancers, and so it is not uncommon for the mailman to deliver newspapers (without stopping his vehicle), milk, bread, library books, spare parts, bales of wool and anything else needed to be taken in or out of town. Many country addresses consist merely of a Rural Delivery number (e.g. RD 6) which might include dozens of farms. Unless the mailman knows everyone by name, the post cannot easily be delivered. A few mail runs to outlying areas accept paying passengers, and occasionally the mail truck doubles as a local bus (as is the case along the Wanganui River). Such trips are very worthwhile if you get the chance. Sorting is still done manually and there are virtually no post codes in New Zealand. Many government departments and other organisations collect their post daily from the post office so addresses often consist merely of the name of the body, the words 'Private Bag', then the city. (Letters posted within New Zealand addressed to a government minister do not require a stamp.)

Post offices (or 'post shops' as they are officially known) normally open 9am-5pm Monday to Friday. An ordinary letter or post card within New Zealand costs 45c standard or 80c Fast Post (the terminology replaces 'air mail') which is recommended for urgent letters to all but the nearest destinations. The 1996 rates for overseas air mail were: $1 for postcards and aerogrammes to any destination (Europe, North America or Australia) and for medium size letters (up to 200g), $1.80 to Europe, $1.50 to North America and $1 to Australia. Air mail correspondence often arrives at its overseas destination in less than a week. Surface mail takes 6–10 weeks depending on the sailing dates, which are listed at post offices. To ship home unwanted items, you can use either surface post ($14.50 for a kilogram sent to Britain) or, as in Australia, surface air lifted (SAL) which costs $19 for the first kilogram and should take less than three weeks.

Telegrams. In conjunction with the Synet Communications company, New Zealand Post operates a telegram service. Synet telegrams are most easily sent from post shops, though you can also phone them through on freephone 0800-800 012. Within New Zealand a same-day service to cities is available if the telegram is lodged before 11.50am on weekdays. Telegrams lodged after noon or those going to smaller towns will be deliverd the morning of the next working day. International telegrams are usually delivered within 24 hours.

Telegrams of up to 100 words cost $14.50 within New Zealand. Overseas telegrams cost $25 for 25 words or less and $1 for each additional word. As is usual, the address is charged as words. With these high prices, you might prefer to send a fax, which will cost about $6 for the first page sent overseas plus the cost of the telephone call.

THE MEDIA

Programme information for both television and radio is given in the daily press. The *TV Guide* gives adequate details of the week's viewing, but the *Listener* ($1.80, published by the Broadcasting Corporation of New Zealand) is more comprehensive and informative. It provides schedules and frequency information for all television and radio stations including the independents. In addition it has a useful *Arts Diary* covering the whole country.

Radio. British visitors may be delighted to learn that the BBC World Service is available on FM in much of New Zealand.

The Broadcasting Corporation of New Zealand (BCNZ) operates most of New Zealand's radio stations. Like so much in New Zealand it is in dire financial difficulties. For example the National Programme, which broadcast to the nation on the AM network, went off the air in mid-1991. The National Programme was the home of news and commentary, Maori programming (which is no longer on television), parliamentary reports, sports and jazz.

The 'Concert Programme' on FM is networked throughout the country. At one time it broadcast every moment of every debate in Parliament but this was abandoned in favour of mostly classical music. (A recent suggestion that the government should introduce a quota of 20% New Zealand music has not gained much support.) The Concert Programme carries a 15-minute news and commentary programme from the BBC at 11pm.

If and when the National Programme returns to the airwaves, it will probably resume its old suffix YA; 1YA in Auckland, 2YA in Wellington, 3YA in Christchurch, and 4YA in Dunedin. The same identification procedure is used for the FM Concert Programme and for the limited network of 'Stereo Hit Radio ZM FM'. Commercial radio stations use the suffix ZB with the same numerical prefixes: 1 for Auckland, 2 for Wellington, etc. Local commercial stations which have been increasing rapidly can be recognised by the number of the nearest big city and the first letter of their name in place of the B, so for example Wanganui's radio station becomes 2ZW.

Television: Two national channels are operated by Television New Zealand (TVNZ). The private TV3, launched in November 1989, went rapidly into receivership but was still on-air in 1996. TV One aims to be a little more highbrow with more public service programmes, documentaries, British imports, etc.; TV Two is more populist, with the usual diet of sport, soap operas and American imports, and TV3 lies between the two. Homesick visitors from Britain will be glad to hear that TVNZ carries ITV's *News at 10* and the BBC's *Newsnight*.

A recent change in licensing policy has enabled regional television to be revived and, not surprisingly, it was the South Island which took advantage of the change first. Canterbury Television (CTV) was launched in 1991 with Nelson scheduled to follow, though it is difficult to imagine how such small audiences (the total population of the South Island is well under a million) can support their own television stations. But as one newspaper editorial put it, 'Parochialism is alive and well in New Zealand and so there is every chance regional television will be successful'.

Relatively few programmes are made in New Zealand, and what drama programmes there are are often accused of being too worthy. One of the longest-running and most popular series is called *Mud and Glory* and is based on the All Blacks rugby team. There is now talk of trying to launch an indigenous soap though it would be difficult to compete with the raft of popular Australian productions in this genre. Sky TV is available in most regions, offering three channels for news, sport and films. It shows the BBC's *Six O'Clock News* first thing in the morning. Access to satellite TV costs about $15 a week.

All stations have almost as much advertising as US television, i.e. about every eight minutes after 5pm.

Newspapers. The New Zealand press is more like that of Australia and the USA than Britain, with most people reading a local rather than a national paper. Each city has a morning paper: the *New Zealand Herald* in Auckland, *Dominion Times* in Wellington, *Waikato Times* in Hamilton, *Christchurch Press* and *Otago Times* in Dunedin. Reading one of the two Sunday papers — The *Dominion Sunday Times* from Wellington and the *Sunday Star* from Auckland - is not as entrenched an institution as it is in Britain but these come as close to national newspapers as any.

It is certainly worth buying a few of the papers during your stay to gain an insight into local concerns. The Friday or Saturday editions are useful for their entertainment sections. Saturday editions usually have the most pages, with supplements and long lists of classified advertisements. New Zealand newspapers are more independent than Australian ones, though Rupert Murdoch has shown interest.

Newspapers cost 60c ($1.20 for Sunday editions) and are usually purchased from dispensing boxes on city street corners which operate on the honour system. It is customary for hotels and motels to deliver a complimentary newspaper, along with a pint of milk, to your room.

The Library of the British High Commission in Wellington has a good selection of British newspapers and periodicals; those in the British Consulate-General in Auckland are three weeks out of date. Because of the large number of British expatriates, the *Observer* and *Sunday Times* are sold in major city newsagents. The results of British football matches are published in most daily papers throughout New Zealand and also in backpackers' newspapers; you can, of course, get them sooner by tuning to the BBC World Service.

Getting Around

Information on travel options in New Zealand is so widely available that you should not have too much difficulty getting from A to B. The people who run your accommodation or any Visitor Information Centre assistant will be pleased to advise on the options. Although there seems to be a wealth of operators of coach and airlines, in fact many of these are integrated with one another rather than in competition and so they will be more forthcoming on interconnecting services than you might expect.

AIR

The two main domestic airline groups are Air New Zealand National and Ansett New Zealand. Despite being in competition with one another, their basic fare structures and special deals are very similar, though marketed under different promotional names which can be confusing. For example both offer a 30% or 40% discount on a few seats on certain flights: Air NZ National calls these Thrifty fares while Ansett calls them Good Buy fares. The advantage of shopping around is that when one airline has sold all its bargain seats, another may have a few left. A good travel agent like STA (see *Help & Information* below) is a useful ally in the search for the cheapest available fare.

Undiscounted air fares are high in New Zealand despite the relatively short distances between centres of interest. For example current one-way economy fares are Auckland-Christchurch $314, Auckland-Wellington $232 and Christchurch-Queenstown $252. Ansett offers a wider range of discounts and tends to be the one which sparks off price wars. For example to counteract a downturn in business in the early 1990s, Ansett introduced a 'return free' offer which meant you could fly Auckland-Christchurch-Auckland for the price of the economy one-way fare of $314. (The catch was that you could stay only a maximum of seven days and you had to book a week in advance.) Ansett has special fares for overseas travellers, giving discounts of 20% on one-way trips and 30% on return fares. These can be bought before arrival in New Zealand (whereupon you save a further 12.5% on GST) or from any Ansett NZ office in New Zealand. With this 'See New Zealand' discount, the one-way fare Auckland-Wellington is $162, Wellington-Christchurch $301, and Auckland-Christchurch $220.

Air NZ National's network is larger than Ansett's, incorporating the regional airlines Eagle Air on the North Island, Nelson Air on the South and Mount Cook Airlines which specialises in tourist routes; these are collectively referred to as Air NZ Link. Ansett NZ is partnered with Tranzair commuter lines serving Blenheim, Nelson and Whangarei, with Bell-Air which serves the Bay of Plenty and with Waterwings Airways serving Queenstown, Te Anau and Milford. Almost all destinations are served at least daily (with occasional Saturday exceptions). Peak-time services — especially on Monday mornings and Friday evenings - get booked up early, as do flights which use small aircraft such as 18-seater Bandeirantes and Piper Chieftains. Therefore, if you plan to fly to smaller centres, try to design your itinerary carefully and reserve seats as far in advance as possible; this can be done prior to your arrival through travel agents and airline offices abroad, although you probably won't be offered the cheapest deals.

Holders of an International Student Card whose travel plans are not urgent might consider travelling standby and getting a 50% discount. About 45 minutes before take-off, register at the Domestic Ticketing Counter of any airport. About 10 minutes before departure, you will be told whether or not there are seats (there usually are). For anyone who relishes last-minute surprises on a grand scale, Ansett offer $99 Mystery Flights which are day returns to an unknown destination. As in Australia, these provide an economical way to fly. The only way to go from Auckland is south, so you could get a cheap flight to Wellington or Christchurch and throw away the return half.

In addition to student stand-bys, there are so many kinds of discounted fare — on return flights booked in advance, late-purchase one-way flights, off-peak travel, and so on — it is worth phoning or trudging around to travel agents and airline offices to compare prices. The information and reservation numbers in Auckland for Air NZ National is 09-793 510 and for Ansett NZ the toll-free number is 09-307 6950. Airline telephone numbers in the other cities are provided in the appropriate sections.

Inter-Island Flights. The Cook Strait Sky ferry shuttles between Wellington and Picton about six times a day and Wellington to Blenheim a couple of times daily. The cost for the 30-minute flight is $59, about twice as much as the ferry (described below). If you book at least four days in advance, the fare drops to $49. The toll-free reservations number within New Zealand is 0800-655455; in Wellington dial 388 8380 or in Picton 573 7888. Flights are timed to link up with coaches and trains to Christchurch and Nelson. The Aerodrome in Picton is just next to State Highway 1, so is convenient for those intending to hitch-hike south. For those going into Picton there is a shuttle bus to cover the 5km distance for $4.

There are also many small local airlines from Southern Air (which serves Stewart Island in the extreme south) to Great Barrier Airlines serving Northland and the islands. Some are independent of the big airlines. They may also offer student and other concessions, so always enquire rather than assume your informant is giving you the most advantageous information.

Airports. Facilities range from a hut which is opened only once or twice a day to coincide with the arrival and departure of flights, to fully fledged (if still somewhat inadequate) international airports in Auckland, Christchurch and Wellington. Air New Zealand and Ansett NZ each has its own domestic terminal at these airports, so you have to change terminal if you change airline. Details of transport arrangements between the city and airport for Auckland, Christchurch and Wellington are given under the *Arrival and Departure* heading for each city.

Baggage. Luggage limits are now according to volume, so that neither of your two pieces can exceed total dimensions of 158cm (i.e. when you add together length, width and height). On Air NZ each piece must not weigh over 25kg and on Ansett the maximum allowed weight per item is 30kg. There are boxes at check-in to test the dimensions of cabin baggage (which is supposed to weigh under 5kg), but these are not used as fastidiously as in Australia.

Air Passes. Both airline networks have air passes of interest to people who want to cover the country in a short time. Ansett NZ's Airpass comes in the form of coupons which must be used within 60 days: four coupons (equals four flights) costs $523, 5 for $633, 6 for $732, 7 for $820 and 8 for $877. Mount Cook Airline operates a separate air pass called the Kiwi Air Pass which allows you one return trip on all Mount Cook routes (which serve the Bay of Islands,

Auckland, Rotorua, Taupo, Wellington, Christchurch, Mount Cook, Queens-town, Dunedin and Milford Sound). All travel must be completed within 30 days. The price is $899, which also includes discounts on Mount Cook's scenic flights. The Kiwi Air Pass must be purchased before arrival in New Zealand.

BUS

The three major lines are Mount Cook, Newmans and InterCity. Mount Cook Landlines operates only in the South Island, and Newmans only in the North. (If you see a Mount Cook coach in the North Island, it will be a tour bus.) InterCity, formerly the New Zealand Railways Road Service, operates on both islands. A number of smaller companies operate along local or limited routes. As in the case of aviation, many are partially owned by or integrated with the big companies so that the bus passes described below are accepted on most of them. Most timetables operate on a Sunday to Friday basis with limited services on Saturdays. As in Australia, timetables use the 12-hour rather than 24-hour clock. All coaches in New Zealand are obliged by law to be non-smoking.

Some sample fares are: Auckland-Rotorua $41, Rotorua-Wellington $72, Auckland-Wellington $89, Christchurch-Picton $55, Nelson-Queenstown $152 and Christchurch-Dunedin $51. (Refer to the section on *Cheap Deals* below which describes how to find discounted fares.) Try to buy tickets in advance from bus depots or agencies, when it is easier to prove your eligibility for any discounts. The national reservation numbers are Mount Cook 0800-800737; Newmans 0800-733500; and InterCity 03-379 9020. It is usually possible to buy a full-fare ticket from the driver, though this can be a clumsy and long-winded procedure. Bicycles are charged an extra $10 whatever the distance travelled.

Buses tend to be relatively antiquated but comfortable and reliable enough. Some are divided into passenger and freight sections, with the front for around 25 passengers and the rear devoted to cargo. The front seats of many long-distance buses are fitted with safety belts, although few passengers use them. Some routes are patronised mainly by tourists and on these routes coaches seem almost like tour buses, complete with sheepskin-covered seats. For example, on the scheduled trip along the west coast of the South Island, the driver will probably make several photo stops and may also provide a freelance commentary on the countryside. You therefore run the risk of catching a bus driven by someone much more interested in irrigation systems, power stations or birdlife than you are. But on the whole their local information is entertaining, and you are spared the catalogue of passenger rules which oppress the long-distance coach traveller in Australia.

Journey times are pleasingly short compared with Australia: Auckland-Wellington 9 hours, Auckland-Bay of Islands 5 hours, Auckland-Gisborne 9 hours, Picton-Christchurch 5 hours, Picton-Nelson 2 hours, Christchurch-Dunedin 5 hours, and Christchurch-Queenstown 7 hours.

Cheap Deals. Nobody needs to pay full fare on long journeys, as a discount of 30% on journeys costing more than $20 is offered for a number of reasons and you would have to be fairly unlucky or ill-informed to pay full fare. YHA members qualify on all the major operators, as do ISIC holders. Off-peak and advance purchase discounts can be even higher.

Travel Passes. All three operators have their own passes for overseas visitors. InterCity's Travelpass permits travel on its trains and inter-island ferry as well as its bus network (and is not significantly more expensive). Neither the Newmans nor the Mount Cook bus pass is valid for the ferry. To redeem this disadvantage, they both offer a free one-way flight across the Cook Strait but you will still have to pay for a flight or ferry crossing in the other direction unles you arrive in New Zealand on one island and plan to fly out of the other.

The Mount Cook Landlines pass is called the Kiwi Coach Pass. It is valid not only on Mount Cook and Newmans services but on some InterCity, Kiwi Experience and Grayline sightseeing services as well. It can be bought after arrival in New Zealand provided you can show a passport and overseas air ticket. The pass is valid for a certain number of days of travel within a prescribed period. Current fares are: $345 for 7 days of travel in 11, $399 for 10 days within 16, $449 for 15 days within 23, $659 for 25 days within 35 and $735 for 33 days within 45.

Newmans Flexi Pass is valid on some local services (in the Bay of Islands, Hawke's Bay region and the area west of Nelson) as well as Newmans and Mount Cook. Its distinguishing feature is that it can be bought as a one-island or a two-island pass. Prices for the nationwide pass are as follows: $364 for 7 days, $420 for 10 days, $495 for 15 days, $580 for 20 days, $675 for 25 days and $750 for 30 days. For the one-island pass you save 10% on the short holidays and less than 5% on the 25 and 30 day passes.

Finally Intercity's Travelpass is valid on trains, the Cook Strait ferry and InterCity coaches. Like the Mount Cook Kiwi Pass, your time is limited by the terms of the pass. The cost is $379 for 8 days of travel within 14 days, $469 for 15 days of travel in 22 and $629 for 22 days of travel in 31. As an alternative to buying a travel pass, it might turn out to be cheaper to buy a YHA card which entitles you to 50% discounts on all InterCity services. The card costs $75 for 14 days of travel and $99 for 28 days.

InterCity in conjuction with Kiwi Experience (see below) offers a Backpacker's Pass which is valid for three months and consists of a certain number of vouchers, more than one of which may be necessary for any journey. For example bus and ferry journeys take one voucher, train journeys take two vouchers and Kiwi Experience trips take roughly one voucher for each day of the trip. The current prices are $309 for ten vouchers, $414 for 15 vouchers and $519 for 20 vouchers. Kiwi Experience now offers a New Zealand Pass which allows you to travel on its entire network within three months for $420. They also have single-island passes which cost $176 for the North Island and $255 for the South Island.

As a basis for comparison, the cost of buying ordinary tickets separately to cover the major centres (i.e. Auckland–Rotorua–Wellington–Picton–Christchurch–Franz Josef–Queenstown and back to Auckland) would cost about $600 excluding the ferry crossings or $430 with a 30% discount. Pass holders should reserve seats in advance, as they are not given priority when competing for space immediately before departure.

Backpackers' Buses. As in Australia, the last few years have seen the introduction of many new backpackers' coach services which combine public transport with tours designed specifically for budget-minded young travellers. Typically you travel in a group of about 18 on an adapted bus and make frequent stops for sporting as well as sightseeing purposes. For one of these backroad trips, you might expect to pay between $20 and $30 a day plus food and accommodation.

The best known is Kiwi Experience (36 Customs St, PO Box 1553, Auckland; 09-366 1665) whose bus passes are mentioned above. It covers both islands and has a choice of routes: Auckland to Wellington in two or four days ($65 and $115 respectively), Nelson to Queenstown in six days ($128), and Queenstown to Christchurch in three days ($77). The trips are flexible enough to allow you to drop off one bus and rejoin the next one, which is an advantage if you want a change of company as well as a stopover. Kiwi Experience has three departures a week in the summer. In order to guarantee that the next bus will pick you up, you must confirm a seat at least 48 hours in advance. Kiwi Experience has linked up with Intercity to offer a Backpackers' Pass (described above).

Other backpackers' buses include the West Coast Express (Nelson to Queenstown) and Back Road Tours (2/5 Malvern Road, Auckland 3; 09-765 631) which operates the East Cape Fun Bus and the Northcape Shuttle; both are described in the North Island regional chapter. Backpackers' buses can sometimes be cheaper as well as more fun; the West Coast Express was recently advertised for $99 whereas the Mount Cook bus fare for the same route was $152, or $106 with a 30% discount.

TRAIN

InterCity publishes a *National Timetable* which can be requested from InterCity Marketing (PO Box 12440, Wellington) or picked up upon arrival. It includes schedules (but not fares) for the eight train routes and the network of buses which InterCity operates. Rail services were drastically reduced in the 1980s, though two routes were restored in 1992: Auckland to Rotorua and Auckland to Tauranga.

Staff cuts are still being made, which may account for InterCity's continuing reputation for incompetence. While most visitors have nothing but praise for the rail service, problems do arise and it is not unknown for rail passengers (even on the premier Auckland to Wellington *Silver Fern* service) to be transferred onto coaches with no offer of compensation and no attempt to inform waiting friends and relatives of the delay.

In egalitarian New Zealand, there is only one class of travel. Rail journeys which take as long as the equivalent bus rides tend to cost about the same as the coach, but are somewhat more if they are faster than the bus. Sample one-way fares (which are not included in the *National Timetable*) are $110 for the *Silver Fern* (Auckland-Wellington), $60 *TranzAlpine Express* (Christchurch-Greymouth), $50 *Southerner Express* (Christchurch-Dunedin) and $55 on the *Coastal Pacific* (Picton-Christchurch). Other places served by trains are Napier (on the *Bay Express* from Wellington) and Invercargill (on the *Southerner Express* from Christchurch and Dunedin). Tickets may be bought in advance from stations or travel agencies, which is highly recommended during school holidays. The central bookings office is on Beach Road, Auckland (09-792 500). If you board a train without a valid ticket, you are liable for a 'service charge' of a few dollars in addition to the cost of the ticket.

Because tourists are the principal market, all the routes in New Zealand not only have names but a marketing atmosphere reminiscent of the modern-day *Orient Express*. Of course this has advantages: for example in the upgrading of passenger services, buffet cars were introduced on all trains. The *Silver Fern* attempts to simulate air travel by providing a free meal and several of the express trains offer steward service at your seat. The overnight service between Auckland and Wellington called the *Northerner* is not as glamorous and is therefore cheaper. It doesn't have sleeping accommodation; it has a buffet, albeit teetotal. The *Silver Fern* takes just over 10 hours to cover the 685km distance, while the *Northerner* takes about half an hour longer. Both run Sunday to Friday only.

Cheap Deals. As on buses, the standard discount is 30%. It can be obtained in various ways. ISIC holders and YHA members should request a student saver. Other travellers may also get a 30% or even 40% discount on certain off-peak journeys if they book in advance. (The earlier you book the better your chance of getting a saver fare.) As with the bus deals, the discount is available only on one-way journeys costing more than $20. Day returns also cost 30% less than the full return fare.

For information on a travel pass which includes the railways, see the section above on InterCity's Travelpass and on the YHA Travelcard.

FERRY

Unless you fly, you will have to take an InterCity ferry across the scenic Cook Strait. Two passenger vessels link Wellington in the North with Picton on the South Island. The newer and more luxurious ship is the *Arahura* (from a Maori word meaning 'Pathway to the Dawn' - in fact dawn sailings are available only from the Picton end, and not on Mondays) and the *Aratika*. The entertainment feature of which they are proud is the bank of poker machines, as these are not yet allowed to operate on New Zealand territory.

The 85km journey takes 3 hours and 20 minutes. There are normally four sailings daily in each direction, though at certain times of the year (usually March), the timetable is reduced when one of the vessels is withdrawn for its annual survey.

Wellington to Picton	*Picton to Wellington*
8am Wednesday–Sunday	5.40am daily except Monday
10am daily	12 noon Wednesday–Sunday
4pm daily	2.20pm daily
6.40pm daily except Sunday	7.45pm daily except Monday
	10.20pm Monday only

The cost of the crossing depends on season, falling from $33 in the high season (between early December and mid-February) to $27 the rest of the year (apart from school holidays in March, May and August). Day returns cost exactly the same as the single, so if you want to do someone a favour or try to make a small profit, you can buy a day return instead of a single and give or sell the return half to a traveller at the other side. There are no student/YHA discounts on the ferries. Cars cost $106 in low season and $140 in high season, while bicycles cost $16.

The toll-free information and booking number for the Interislander service is 0800-658 999. The local numbers are as follows: Wellington 04-498 3999 or 04-725 3990, Auckland 09-792 500 and Christchurch 03-728 299.

New Zealand Rail is hoping to introduce a high-speed catamaran by 1994 (similar to the new service between mainland Australia and Tasmania) which will reduce the journey to one and a half hours.

CITY TRANSPORT

There are few surprises, except that bus fares in some cities are reduced in off-peak hours from Monday to Friday, and taxis can't be flagged down as they don't cruise (and remember don't tip). As in the UK, local authorities have been deregulating their bus services resulting in the loss of some services. In some towns such as Wanganui, buses have actually been replaced by taxis since the latter offered more competitive prices.

Bicycles are fairly well provided for. There are sometimes specially assigned traffic signals for cyclists, some of which require you to push a button to persuade the lights to change in your favour. Pedestrians will find that most traffic signals provide a button to push; a 'walk' sign and a loud buzz indicates when it is safe to cross. Although the traffic may be so light that only the most cautious think it necessary to wait for the signal, pedestrians can be issued with a 'notice for failing to adhere to regulations' (fee $35).

DRIVING

Adequate as the bus and train services are, many people prefer to have the use of their own transport. Campsites, both official and ad hoc, are often difficult to reach by public transport, as are other inexpensive kinds of accommodation like motorcamps and lodges. If you shop around, renting a car can be one of New Zealand's bargains. Often travellers club together to hire a car or van, or else a car-owner will put up a notice in the local YHA hostel offering a lift in exchange for petrol money, which makes the bargain even more attractive.

Driving in New Zealand is dangerous. On average, two New Zealanders die each day in road accidents. In 1991 the World Health Organisation declared New Zealand the third worst nation after Venezuela and Portugal, though the government is making a concerted effort to crack down on the main offending groups (e.g. young drinking males). If a group of New Zealanders gets together, the topic of conversation will quite often be 'my last prang'. City drivers, both men and women, are definitely fast and often aggressive. In the country, the greatest hazard is people driving at 30km/h on roads which are suitable for three times that speed. Despite the appalling statistics, most visitors find New Zealand country driving a pleasure, with uncluttered roads and changing scenery. (It is probably because of the absence of heavy traffic that motorists are tempted to ignore speed limits and become careless.)

Road System. Most of the state highways have only two lanes, though there is sometimes one paved shoulder on to which slower vehicles move to allow cars to pass. Quite a few country roads are dirt or gravel (in New Zealand parlance, 'not tar-sealed').

The term 'motorway' is applied loosely, because of a bureaucratic oddity whereby new motorways receive preference for funds from central government. So when cities like Wanganui, New Plymouth and Dunedin needed a new bridge or bypass, the local council simply called the resulting two-lane road a motorway. The only 'real' freeways are short stretches radiating from the four largest cities. Although you are meant to overtake only in the outside lane on motorways, New Zealand drivers very commonly overtake on the inside.

Driving conventions are similar to those in the UK (e.g. driving is on the left), but New Zealand has few roundabouts; those that exist are signposted in laughable detail. Junctions are badly designed and road geometry can be confusing. Often there is little warning of junctions between busy roads and it is possible to be caught out by traffic coming from an unexpected direction. Treat all main road junctions, especially in open country, with great care. At crossroads controlled by traffic lights, left-turning traffic must give way to oncoming vehicles intending to turn right.

Rules of the Road. Driving is on the left. The speed limit on the open road in good conditions is 100km/h. On city and town streets the limit is 50km/h. Laws are enforced by traffic officers, who function independently of the police. These Ministry of Transport law enforcers drive black and white cars marked 'Traffic Safety Service'. Speeding motorists are prime targets, though in a small town it is easy to avoid trouble as everyone knows which day of the week to expect the officer's visit.

Alcohol. For motorists under 21 years, the blood/alcohol limit is zero. Older drivers are restricted to 0.08%, which is the same legal maximum as in Britain. The maximum penalty is a $1500 fine and six months in prison.

Routes and Maps. A free map showing main roads is available from Visitor

Information offices throughout New Zealand. But if you plan to cover much of the country it is probably wise to invest in a road atlas, preferably the one published by the AA, which costs $19.95 and is reasonably good. The New Zealand Automobile Association has a reciprocal agreement with international motoring organisations including the British AA, RAC and the American AA, so if you are a member take your card to get a discount on books and maps, obtain free route information and use the ferry booking service (see *Before You Go*). The principal AA offices are at 342 Lambton Quay (PO Box 1794), Wellington (04-473 8738), 99 Albert St, Auckland and 210 Hereford St, Christchurch. If you aren't a member in your home country, you can take out a special visitor's membership in New Zealand at a reduced rate.

Road Signs. National state highways are numbered 1 to 8 and are indicated on signs (and some maps) by white numbers inside a red shield. Secondary route numbers of provincial highways 10 to 99 are marked in white on a blue shield. Signposting ranges between the less than adequate and the utterly abysmal. The Automobile Association is responsible for destination signs, which are infrequent. If you do spot a yellow fingerpointer sign in the distance, it is just as likely to be pointing you towards the local bowling green as to the next big town. Look out for such amusing signs as 'Feed Moose' or 'Peerless Sheep Nuts', both advertisements for animal feeds.

Although the New Zealand road authorities have begun to introduce international warning signs and symbols, you will still see some of the old signs which spelled every instruction out in plain English, both on signs and on the road, for example 'Beware Wandering Stock'. Few need any explanation, except perhaps 'free turn' which appears at junctions controlled by lights and means you can turn left at any time with care. 'No exit' is used in the sense of 'no through road' (except at entrances to car parks, etc., when it means 'no exit').

A sign which might puzzle you is a red circle enclosing the letters LSZ for 'Limited Speed Zone'. This means that the motorist must be prepared to slow down to accommodate other traffic, animals, etc. Extra persuasion may be applied in the form of 'judder bars', i.e. humps in the road designed to slow traffic.

The sequence of traffic signals is red-green-amber-red. Beware of jumping red lights in Auckland where several automatic cameras have been installed (look for the sign 'Red Light Camera Ahead'). When a light changes to red as you approach it, don't assume you'll have time while stationary to consult a map, tune the radio or light a cigarette; the sequence is often fast.

Fuel. 'Super' (96 octane, corresponding to 4-star) costs around $1 per litre ($4.50 per Imperial gallon, $3.50 per US gallon), with 'regular' (91 octane, 2-star) a few cents cheaper. Unleaded is six to eight cents cheaper and diesel is about 25% cheaper. Because of the natural gas supplies in the North Island, New Zealand has been in the forefront of developing alternatives to petrol. When world oil prices peaked, a synthetic petrol plant was built at New Plymouth which is once again fully operational after a period of idleness when world oil prices were low. Many petrol stations advertise CNG (Compressed Natural Gas) or LPG (Liquid Petroleum Gas). These can only be used in engines which have been specially adapted, and although much cheaper than petrol they are also less efficient unless perfectly tuned. CNG is not available on the South Island.

Filling stations can be surprisingly far apart, especially in the South Island. Before embarking upon a long journey (e.g. Te Anau to Milford Sound, a round trip of 250km without any petrol stations), make sure your tank is full. The same advice applies to weekend trips anywhere, although many stations are now open seven days a week.

Car Hire. Renting a vehicle is expensive in New Zealand. You must be at least 21 to hire a car. Hertz, Avis and Budget operate desks at airports, but charges are high. Other agencies, such as such as Thrifty or Southern Cross, set up office in caravans just outside the airport doors.

As an indication of how important backpackers' tourism is, both Avis and Budget offer 'Backpacker Specials', e.g. $499 per week (plus GST) with Budget and $249 inclusive for three days with Avis. These specials are still much more expensive than the prices offered by small independent operators (some of whom call themselves 'boutique' rental firms). A few places hire out scooters and mopeds as well, starting at $25 a day.

Competition among car hire firms is intense, and it is always cheaper to find your own way into town and then shop around for a discount rent-a-car outfit; you can usually pick up promotional leaflets in city tourist offices. Offers such as '$32 a day unlimited distance' or '$20 a day plus 2c a kilometre' will catch your eye, but be sure to read the small print. Often the unlimited rates apply only to rentals lasting for a minimum period (which may be as much as 21 days) or may apply only if you intend to remain inside the city in which you hire the car. Collision damage insurance (at least $9 a day) will be added, with GST of 12.5% applied on the whole deal. Some companies impose a surcharge on drivers under 25.

The head offices of the big companies are based in Auckland:

Avis, 17 Nelson St; 09-525 1982 or toll-free 0800-655 111.
Hertz, 93 Hobson St; 09-304 0989.
Budget, 83 Beach Road (PO Box 4418); 09-309 6737.

Lesser known and cheaper companies with branches in more than one New Zealand city include:

Avon Rent-a-Car, corner of Tuam and Antigua Sts, Christchurch; 03-793 822.
Economy Rental Cars, 215 Kirkbride Road, Mangere, Auckland; 09-275 3777.
Letz Rent-a-Car, 51-53 Shortland St, Auckland; 09-778 902; also at 200 Yaldhurst Rd, Christchurch; tel: 03-379 6880. This company rents out scooters in Dunedin and Queenstown.
Percy Rent-a-Car, 154 Durham St, Christchurch; 03-379 3466; also at 219 Hobson St (PO Box 5364), Auckland; 09-303 1122.
Rhodes Rent-a-Car, 338 Riccarton Road (PO Box 6053); 03-348 8219. South Island only.
Southern Cross, 0800-650700 toll-free.
Rent-a-Wreck, PO Box 38809, Wellington; 0800-653227 toll-free.

You could advertise for people to share the expense of hiring a car on hostel notice boards, etc. Also see the section on *Hitching* below for a contact address to fix up shared travel expenses.

Relocation Deals. Because there are so many one-way rentals along certain routes, for example Auckland to Wellington, Picton to Christchurch and Queenstown to Christchurch, you can often get a good deal returning a car to its place of origin. Budget Rent-a-Car in Wellington for example might offer a good car for $25 with 700 free kilometres and a maximum of 24 hours to deliver it to their Auckland depot. Similarly, a canny traveller disembarking from the Picton ferry in the holiday season can negotiate a favourable rate for the trip to Christchurch (which rivals the train fare), then pick up a few hitch-hikers willing to share expenses.

One company which has recently been advertising these relocation deals is Southern Cross in Christchurch (03-794 547).

Campervans. Hiring a campervan is so popular in New Zealand that it may seem on some roads that 90% of vehicles are Maui 'Campas' or Daihatsu 'Travelhomes'. The average size is considerably smaller than the average American RV (recreational vehicle) though six-berth deluxe vans are available. Prices include unlimited mileage, and vary significantly depending on size and season. A two-berth model in the off-season will cost about $84 a day, and $136 in the summer, whereas a six-berth luxury vehicle will cost $129 a day in the winter and $220 or thereabouts in the peak season. Some of the cheap car rental firms offer campervans — for example, Scotties in Auckland (see *Auckland* section) were offering family campervans from $50 a day plus 20c a kilometre or $70 a day unlimited mileage for a minimum hire of 3 days, while Kiwi Car Rent-a-Wreck, also in Auckland, has campervans from $30 a day plus GST and insurance out of season.

Campervans usually consume about 12.5 litres of petrol or diesel per 100km (or 18mpg). As with hired cars, mandatory insurance of about $13 a day is extra. Most companies impose a minimum hire period of 3 days or, more commonly, 1 week. Compare terms, as some companies will allow you to pick up (or 'uplift' in their jargon) in Auckland and drop off the vehicle in Christchurch or vice versa for no extra cost. Others throw in the ferry crossing free of charge, or ask you to drop your car in Wellington and pick up another one in Picton. If you plan to take a vehicle across the Cook Strait in the summer months, book a ferry crossing in advance.

Some of the main companies have agents in the UK (see *Before You Go*). Once in New Zealand, campervan hire addresses are:

Adventure Rental Vehicles Ltd, PO Box 43235, Mangere, Auckland; 09-256 0255.
Budget, PO Box 73126, Auckland International Airport; 09-275 7139.
Maui, Richard Pearse Drive, Mangere, Auckland; 09-275 3013; also at 533–540 Memorial Avenue, Christchurch; 03-358 4159.

Buying a Car. High imoport tariffs have been removed, bringing the pricesof imported cars down to what they are in the UK. Mazdas and Toyotas are the most popular models at present. Nevertheless there is still a high proportion of lovingly maintained old vehicles still on the road. (At least half the cars on the road are more than five years old.) Indeed, large profits could be made by any visitor to New Zealand who knows about veteran British cars. Some of the more pristine Morris Minors, Standard 10s or Rover 90s, still in everyday use in New Zealand, could be shipped back and sold to collectors.

But travellers who merely want to buy a car to see them through a few months will have to invest substantially. The most basic new cars cost around $20,000, and most secondhand prices are high: a ten-year-old Mini can set you back $7000, a 20-year-old Holden $1500. As cars have a good resale value, you could reasonably expect to recoup a good proportion of your outlay at the end of your stay. Some car dealers offer guaranteed buy-back rates to travellers, for instance Wheels in Christchurch (see page 483). For others consult the New Zealand Guaranteed Buy-Back Vehicle Association (825 Dominion Road, Auckland; 09-696 587).

The documentation involved in buying or selling a car is similar to that required in Britain. Road tax is known as 'registration'; together with licensing it costs $185. The mechanical test is a 'warrant of fitness' or WOF, renewable every six months at a cost of $12–15 (this is the seller's responsibility).

Insurance. New Zealand has a novel 'no-fault' compensation scheme, whereby accident victims are recompensed by the government regardless of who caused the accident. As a result motor insurance is not compulsory. But insuring your vehicle is recommended; comprehensive cover costs about $600 per annum. The AA of New Zealand recommends its own AA Insurance Ltd.

HITCH-HIKING

It is difficult to imagine a country more favourable to the hitch-hiker than New Zealand. Most distances are manageable, large cities are few, crime is low and the locals are hospitable. Furthermore motorways are rare; hitching on them is the one infringement for which the Ministry of Transport officers are liable to stop and lecture you. You may run into some competition from other hitch-hikers, mainly German, Canadian, American and Australian, though surprisingly not much from New Zealanders or British travellers. (A middle-aged couple in Rotorua who picked up 4,500 hitch-hikers over a period of seven years reported that only a few dozen were Kiwis and Poms.)

Competition is likely to be stiff leaving the ferry linking the North and South Islands. To avoid having to join the queue of hitch-hikers leaving Picton or Wellington, try advertising your desire for a lift during the ferry crossing by pinning a notice to the back of your seat or to your luggage, and by getting into conversation with motorists.

The road along the west coast of the South Island has the reputation among hitchers for being impossible. But if you do get a lift south from Fox Glacier or heading north from Wanaka, chances are the vehicle will be going the whole distance (265km) and so it is worth trying, especially if you make an early start. If you hitch on a Sunday you are asking for interminably long waits. Some experienced hitchers recommend walking a few kilometres out of town to persuade drivers you have earned a lift.

To pre-arrange a lift on a shared-expenses basis, contact the Travel Share Centre (Ground Floor, 18 Heather St, Parnell, Auckland; 09-773 027) which keeps a register of drivers looking for passengers and vice versa.

Accommodation

No visitor to New Zealand need ever worry about finding accommodation. Comfort and congeniality at a reasonable price are easy to find, from the humblest mountain hut or hostel to the most genteel guest house. Even four- and five-star hotels cost less than their counterparts elsewhere. Claims about the warm welcome you will receive from the owner or manager of whatever accommodation you choose are not exaggerated and it is not at all unusual for hosts to offer to collect you from an airport or station.

Campsites are a popular option even for those who don't have a tent or caravan, and motels are ubiquitous. It is easy to obtain information about all kinds of accommodation either during your trip or after you arrive in New Zealand. The New Zealand tourist office publishes a *Where to Stay* guide with 1400 listings in all categories. Jasons Travel Publications (PO Box 9390, Newmarket, Auckland; 09-520 6155) publishes several accommodation guides that may be of interest to visitors planning extensive travels, i.e. *Jasons Holiday and Leisure Accommodation* ($5.95), which includes hostels, campsites, bed and breakfasts, tourist flats and so on, and *Jasons Motels & Motor Lodges* ($9.95), which lists more than 1600 properties offering more upmarket accommodation. Although heavily dependent on advertising, these books do give one-line entries to non-advertisers and are therefore reasonably comprehensive. There are also several specialist associations (for bed and breakfasts, pubs offering accommodation, etc.) that can send you lists of their members (addresses included below). Establishments listed in these various directories (including Jasons) may have a supply to give to clients.

For many kinds of accommodation there may be a small surcharge if you stay only one night. If you are travelling out-of-season, ask about reductions. In the high season (Christmas to early February), some accommodation will inevitably be fully booked. But the European experience, of trudging miserably between booked-up pensions and being greeted with indifferent shrugs, is very rare. It is far more likely that the staff will direct you to a more promising hostelry.

YHA Hostels. As elsewhere, you are expected to be a member of a national YHA (and hence the International Youth Hostels Federation) before you stay at an official YHA hostel. If you haven't already joined the YHA you can buy an international guest card, valid for 1 year, at a cost of $24, or in six instalments at a cost of $4 per night.

YHA hostels are located not only along the traveller's familiar circuit, but in some out-of-the-way locations like Okarito and Akaroa on the South Island and Opoutere (a wonderful hostel) and Great Barrier Island in the North. The *NZ Hostelling Handbook* can be obtained from YHA shops abroad or from New Zealand hostels or hostel offices. Naturally it contains far more detail about the facilities offered at the 53 year-round hostels and five seasonal ones than does the New Zealand material in Volume II of the *International Youth Hostelling Handbook*.

Write to the YHA of New Zealand National Office ahead of time (PO Box 436, Christchurch; 03-379 9970) for a free leaflet called 'The Good Bed Guide', a condensed version of the *Handbook*.

An advantage of YHA membership is that members are entitled to a wide range of discounts on such things as coach, rail and air travel and various outdoor activities.

Hostel prices range from $9 to $19 with an average of about $15. Most have twin or family rooms that cost slightly more than dormitory accommodation. As these are limited in number they may be booked up in advance. Not all hostels accept payment by credit card. Many hostels feature an impressive array of facilities from laundries to cycle rental. Quite a few operate shops selling whatever the managers have the energy to market, from postcards to individual cupfuls of rice. Others act as agents for specialist local tours from white-water rafting trips in Queenstown to glowworm-viewing expeditions in Franz Josef. The notice boards of YHA hostels are always worth studying for offers of lifts, ideas for unusual excursions, equipment for sale, local or hostel events such as barbecues, etc.

As in Australia the main hostels are often full, especially in December and January, so if you know your dates in advance it is advisable to book. This can be done through the National Reservation Centre, YHANZ, PO Box 68-149, Auckland (09-309 1802; fax 09-373 5083); you can make payment by credit card (include Visa or Mastercard number, expiry date and name as it appears on the card). Auckland, Wellington and Christchurch hostels can also be booked via the Internet (web page http://yha.org.nz/yha). Alternatively your local YHA can make a reservation using the computerised IBN worldwide booking system. The alternative is simply to risk leaving it until a day or two in advance. Hostel managers will ring their counterparts on your behalf to fix up a booking, collect the fee and issue a receipt to be presented at the relevant hostel. Occasionally you may be charged for the telephone call.

Smoking is banned in every hostel, except in a few that have a designated (and highly polluted) smokers' lounge. Hostels are open 24 hours.

Budget Accommodation. Surprisingly, other forms of accommodation cost little more than YHA hostels and sometimes undercut them. For example, many private hostels, tourist lodges, and caravan parks known as motor camps offer beds for less than $15 without the accompanying YHA ethos. If you intend to use this level of accommodation, take a sleeping bag or equivalent; bedding is not usually supplied, though sheets and blankets are sometimes available for hire. Cooking facilities, on the other hand, are invariably supplied free of charge.

The source of addresses that most people use is the free booklet *BBH Backpacker Accommodation*, which is available from Budget Backpacker Hostels NZ Ltd (Foley Towers, 208 Kilmore St, Christchurch; or Rainbow Lodge, 99 Titiraupenga St, Taupo). It lists nearly 200 hostels and lodges charging between $10 and $20 for their cheapest beds, from Kaitaia in the far north to Stewart Island at the extreme south of New Zealand. An unusual (and useful) feature of the booklet is that it provides subjective 'BPP ratings' for the various lodgings, from 91% ('very good') for Arcadia Lodge in Russell ('a home for free spirits for 60 years') to 42% for the Golden Cross Hotel in Waihi. As these ratings are based on backpacking clients' assessments, they are fairly trustworthy.

Rival leaflets include *The Backpackers Bible*, available from Backpackers Marketing, 34 Auckland St, Picton (03-573 6598), and *New Zealand Backpacker Lodges* ('the little red book'), published by the Backpackers Association, PO 5475, Auckland.

Holiday parks are of interest not only to campers; they also have a choice of cabins, flats, motel units and on-site caravans. Typical prices are $30 for a basic two-person cabin, $38 for a tourist cabin (with kitchen facilities but no bedding), and about $33 for an on-site caravan, again for two people. Privately run parks may offer bunkroom accommodation in a lodge for even less than YHA hostels, though facilities in such places can be basic. A directory is published each October by the Camp & Cabin Association of New Zealand (PO Box 394, Paraparaumu; 04-298 3283) listing over 240 motorcamps throughout the country.

Camping. Roadside campsites in New Zealand are excellent and numerous, and once again kitchens, hot showers and sometimes TV lounges are provided. If you are preparing your own meals you'll have to carry your own utensils including saucepan. Also, carry warm bedding as extra blankets are not usually available. A tent pitch costs $7 or $8 per person. If you are planning to camp in New Zealand, be sure that your equipment can withstand torrential downpours. (You should be able to pick up a second-hand tent locally for about $30.) It is also common practice to camp anywhere along the road, though it is forbidden in rest areas. Even glossy campervan brochures advocate choosing your own sure-to-be-idyllic camping spot.

Each regional authority manages countryside parks in its area where camping is often allowed but sometimes only with pre-arranged permission (as in the case of parks run by the Auckland Regional Authority). This kind of camping is considerably less luxurious than the roadside variety. Although pit toilets are provided at all designated campsites, there may be no ready supply of drinking water, so always check before heading into the bush. There are usually restrictions on camping along the well known walking tracks so a tent may become a liability. Huts are usually located at appropriate intervals along tracks, where bunks, gas rings and toilets are provided for the hut fee of $8 or $12 depending on facilities. Pitching a tent beside a hut (where allowed) costs $4 per person.

Hotels. When New Zealanders refer to 'hotels' they normally mean bars, whereas the term 'private hotel' means a hotel without a bar. As in Australia, all premises that have a licence to sell alcohol must also provide accommodation. Many hotels fulfil the letter of the law by keeping one or two token unmaintained rooms, while others are attempting to rehabilitate the image of the country pub.

Of the most upmarket hotels in New Zealand, many belong to the THC group (Tourist Hotel Corporation, formerly a government enterprise). At the other end of the spectrum, New Zealand is one of the few countries in which hotels sometimes offer dormitory accommodation. For example, an old-fashioned wood-frame hotel in the centre of Christchurch (the Hereford) offers relatively cheap dorm beds, while the famous 'Formerly the Blackball Hilton' (not connected to Hilton International) in the South Island village of Blackball charges a similar price for bunk accommodation.

Motels. New Zealand seems to have as many motels as the USA, but without the neon signs. A double room usually costs between $60 and $80 with a surcharge of about $15 for each extra person. They always come equipped with bed linen and are serviced daily.

One surprising feature is that they are usually equipped with kitchens. While motels around the world are congratulating themselves for having just installed tea-making machines, New Zealand motel rooms come equipped with corkscrews and whisks as well as all the basic crockery and cooking utensils (though don't expect anything as exotic as a garlic press). These 'motel flats' as they are known often have a separate bedroom and are designed for families, though they do very well for small groups of friends too; these are normally not serviced. There are also serviced units in most motels which provide conventional non-catering motel accommodation.

Guest Houses. Most guest houses charge about the same as motels, but as they often have a more interesting atmosphere (e.g. colonial architecture, pleasant gardens) and the price includes breakfast, many travellers prefer them to motels. Some owners take such a maternal interest in their clients that it is not unknown for young travellers to have their clothes ironed for them. Surprisingly, guest houses in Auckland are not noticeably more expensive than elsewhere. You can obtain the leaflet *Bed & Breakfast Hotels*, published by the Travel Hotels/Motels Federation, which lists 30 bed and breakfasts well distributed over both islands, by writing direct to the Federation at 52 Armagh St, Christchurch. The brochure is revised annually and published in October. Alternatively you can purchase the *New Zealand Bed & Breakfast Book* by J & J Thomas for £9.95 (including air mail postage, from the Moonshine Press, PO Box 41022, Eastbourne, New Zealand).

Home and Farm Stays. No country could be better suited to the concept of farm holidays than New Zealand. While it is possible to attend a regulation sheep-shearing or demonstration of mustering at specially created tourist centres, it is more enjoyable to see, and even participate in, the genuine thing. Try any of the following organisations:

New Zealand Farm Holidays Ltd, PO Box 256, Silverdale, Auckland (09-307 2024 or 09-426 5430). Dinner, bed and breakfast from $78 per person.
Rural Tours, 92 Victoria St, PO Box 228, Cambridge (07-827 8055). 250 homes in 60 locations. Dinner, bed and breakfast for $96 per person.

Farmhouse & Country Home Holidays, PO Box 31-250, Auckland 9 (09-410 8280/8601).

Farmstay Ltd, PO Box 263, Warkworth (09-422 0590). 300 properties throughout New Zealand offering dinner, bed and breakfast for $90.

Hospitality Plus, The New Zealand Home & Farmstay Co Ltd, PO Box 56-175, Auckland 3 (09-810 9175).

New Zealand Home Hospitality Ltd, PO Box 309, Nelson (03-548 2424).

New Zealand Host Homes Ltd, PO Box 60, Russell (0885-28030).

Rural Holidays New Zealand, PO Box 2155, Christchurch (03-366 1919).

Others are listed in NZTD's *Outdoor Holidays* booklet.

Most operate a voucher system aimed at affluent travellers and do not send out lists of farms to contact, but will be happy to fix up a farm stay at short notice once you are in New Zealand. It is not unusual to be told the hosts' hobbies (e.g. spinning, antique guns), so you can choose someone compatible. Your stay is usually on a full board basis, though some listed above also arrange bed and breakfast only. The cost for full board can be at least $100 per person per day — bed and breakfast deals are a lot cheaper (e.g. from $60 per person per day with Rural Holidays New Zealand).

If this seems too extravagant and you are willing to earn your keep, contact Willing Workers on Organic Farms as described on page 387. Alternatively, join an international home-hosting organisation like Servas as mentioned on page 24. Not surprisingly the New Zealand host network is excellent.

At one time gourmets had to resign themselves to the prospect of a culinarily grim few weeks if planning a trip to New Zealand, just as they might if visiting Russia or Romania. But it is now possible to eat well, often extremely well, for bargain prices. A taste of what is in store can be had by eating on an Air New Zealand flight as the catering standards of the national carrier are renownedly high. Also New Zealand's wine industry has made extraordinary advances in the past five years and it may be partly because of the creation of a wine culture that food in restaurants has improved so dramatically.

Outside the cities you will also encounter some infuriatingly conservative eating habits in both restaurants and private homes (especially in the South Island), where menus may still be based on 'meat and two veg' plus perhaps a salad whose most exotic ingredient is pickled beetroot. When asked for salad dressing, waitresses have been known to look quizzical and ask for elucidation of the concept. New Zealanders are the greatest consumers of meat in the world and meat-eaters should not miss sampling a New Zealand meat pie or steak while touring the country. Vegetarians will find it tough going outside Auckland, Wellington and Christchurch. When a whole sheep can be bought for as little as $20 and good meat retails in supermarkets for $3 a pound, there is not much demand for lentils.

Seafood, fruit and vegetables as well as meat are usually of the highest quality. Finally New Zealand has caught on to the current fashion of serving lamb which is slightly pink and refraining from frying all fish (including clams) in batter. As in Australia, hogget refers to one year old lamb.

The dairy products are superb, and relatively inexpensive. New Zealand is now producing more than the once-ubiquitous cheddar and it is possible to find home-produced Brie and Camembert. Look for Ferndale Abbey cheeses in delicatessens, assuming, that is, you can find a delicatessen (as opposed to a 'superette' or corner food store). The ice cream sold at corner stores, however, is of good quality.

RESTAURANTS

The number of ethnic restaurants and restaurants offering more adventurous cuisine has been steadily increasing. Safe and dull family restaurants still prevail in small out of the way towns, where the modest prices go some way to compensating for the predictable cuisine. Tuesday evening in a typical town like Wanganui (which has a population about twice that of Stratford-upon-Avon) can be dire. You should be able to find a Chinese restaurant, though the brown sauce on the table will be of the HP variety rather than soy sauce. A typical menu would be steak, chips and salad, possibly from a serve-yourself salad bar, for about $16 including a beer. Many pubs sell food of this ilk, and quantities are so generous that no one could deny they are good value. And of course you can always find a fish and chip shop where the locals go for their 'greasies'.

However city eating can be a delight, and even the most innovative menus using superb ingredients will not cost more than $50. The problem of Sunday eating remains, however, and even restaurants in fashionable cosmopolitan areas like Auckland's Parnell are often closed. Outside the more sophisticated centres, you will find that even classy restaurants close at 9pm, perhaps a legacy of a farming culture where people have to be up extremely early.

The service is generally of a typically New Zealand standard, which is to say genuinely helpful and unpretentious. This is not to say that you won't come across an example of the kind of upmarket and precious city restaurant described by J B Priestley as 'making a half-hearted pretence not to be in New Zealand but in some more exotic place ... with two or three solemn young men who looked as if an inspector from Michelin might arrive at any moment.' This is no longer so laughable as some food writers claim that the best New Zealand restaurants would merit a Michelin star if they were to be visited by that elite body of inspectors.

As in Australia, the word 'entree' refers to the starter rather than the main course. In the main resorts more pretentious licensed restaurants sometimes charge outrageous prices (e.g. $50 for a main course) on the assumption that Japanese tourists will pay whatever is asked, though normally you can be assured of good value. A surcharge of $2 or so may be levied at weekends and on public holidays to cover higher staff wages.

Bring-Your-Own Restaurants. Not only does taking your own 'grog' keep the price relatively low but BYO establishments are often more fun and informal. There is a legal maximum corkage fee, though about a third of BYOs charge nothing for corkage. A few licensed (i.e. non-BYO) restaurants also allow customers to bring their own beverages, however they may charge as much for corkage as they like, and have been known to charge according to the price of the wine. Always enquire beforehand.

Snacks. Pies are universally available and cost between $1.50 and $2. Normally you help yourself from a glass case after having chosen meat (mince) or bacon and egg. 'Dairies' are found in all neighbourhoods and sell pies, filled rolls and other snack foods. They may be the only source of nourishment you will find open late at night or on Sundays. Another worthwhile snack food available at most dairies is ice cream. New Zealanders consume almost as much ice cream as the voracious Russians, and the quality and value is excellent. A single scoop costs about $1. Watch for roadside fruit stalls in country areas. Many operate on the honour system.

Fish and chip shops are numerous and the quality is reasonable. Shark is sometimes sold but euphemistically as 'lemon fish' or 'flake'. You can't be sure that you are eating fish from New Zealand waters; because so much of the catch is exported they have recently had to start importing frozen fish from Argentina.

Tipping. The tradition of no-tipping in New Zealand is still going strong. There are no hidden extras on most restaurant bills; the price printed on the menu is what you pay. (A handful of restaurant menus show prices exclusive of GST but this is very rare.) Food service is prompt and courteous and, because nothing is to be gained by favouring the wealthy-looking customers, completely egalitarian.

SPECIALITIES
The influence of Maori food can still be seen. Some fish shops, for example, sell 'paua patties' which are green-coloured abalone burgers. Also watch out for pipis (similar to cockles) and the prized toheroas (like clams) which are made into soup, though the season is very short. Upmarket restaurants serve whitebait fritters, more like delicate omelettes, flavoured with the tiny transparent fish which go by the name whitebait. The striking green-lipped mussels can be bought fresh or pickled. New Zealand scallops are superb. Smoked eel is a treat for gourmets; confusingly, the Maori word for eel is 'tuna'. In the months of April and May you can find muttonbirds in some shops and restaurants. Muttonbird is a type of shearwater, larger than a seagull, and with a high fat content which was a useful component in the early Maori diet before the introduction of mammals for food. It is an acquired taste.

There are also a number of exotic fruits and vegetables which are especially noticeable in the greengrocer shops of Auckland where the Pacific Island community is so large. Tamarillos are red and have a slightly soapy tart taste which is pleasant as long as the fruit has ripened, but avoid eating the bitter edges. Feijoa is a green lemon-shaped fruit combining the flavour of kiwi fruit, passion fruit and bubblegum which can become addictive. Horned melon is a strange-looking thing which tastes fine.

People from the far south maintain that Bluff oysters from Foveaux Strait are the best in the world, though the oysters have recently been hit by disease. The season runs from March to August, and starts with a local festival. If you notice some oyster shells while strolling along a beach, remember that it is against the law to prize any off for your dinner. A further regulation prohibits the selling of trout, even though the lakes and streams abound with the fish. So, unless you or a friend (or the staff of a restaurant where you happen to be dining) catches a trout, you will not have a chance to sample the national fish.

The traditional Maori method of cooking is in a hangi or ground pit. Vegetables, especially the Maori staple kumara (sweet potato), and fish are wrapped in flax leaves and lowered into a rock-lined pit, whereupon boiling water is poured over them and the earth replaced so that the food steams over a period of several hours. This is not often done these days except for special Maori feasts. There are commercial hangi evenings at a few hotels in Rotorua where the traditional fare is supplemented with European imports like lamb and venison. These evenings are pricey and appeal principally to tourists on coach tours.

DRINKING

New Zealand's drinking habits are left over from an earlier time when all public drinking was crammed into the hour between 5 and 6pm. While the cities have their fair share of trendy drinking spots, the public bars in many hotels (i.e. pubs) are joyless establishments with virtually no seating. The practice of standing is a remnant of the time when pubs were so crowded for the 6 o'clock swill — which ended only in 1967 — that there was no room for chairs and tables. Even in hotels that claim on their signs to have incorporated 'novel innovations, cultural amenities and modern facilities', there will probably be tacky plastic upholstery and a radio badly tuned to the local country music station. As closing time approaches, pubs tend to become rowdy, often with one table of men engaged in juvenile drinking contests. You have to choose between the public bar, where working men go to play pool or darts, and the lounge bar full of besuited businessmen where prices are half as much again. But pubs are not usually hostile places, even to women travelling alone. You might attract some curious stares, but usually you will be served with courtesy. And some are not altogether gloomy. A few hotels in country areas have well maintained gardens, where you can enjoy draught beer and crayfish.

All hotels have a bottle sales counter where you can buy cans and bottles of beer as well as a depressingly limited selection of wines, at prices somewhat higher than in a city bottle shop.

Licensing Laws. New legislation liberalising the sale of alcohol has made some significant improvements to the life of the drinker, though there is still a strong Temperance Alliance. Wine is now sold in supermarkets and grocery stores; note though that many wine shops do not sell beer.

It has also become possible for pubs to apply for a 24-hour licence (excluding Sundays) and to date about 15 places in the country have successfully done so. But a nation's drinking habits cannot be changed overnight and one of the first all-night sessions at a hotel in a small town near Invercargill closed at 1.30am. Even the places with 24-hour licences have to close at 3am on Sundays. All pubs and taverns are closed on Sundays, unless they also serve food. Sunday drinking is however allowed at clubs, nightclubs and entertainment venues, plus restaurants and cafés which serve meals and you may even come across a café where it is possible to buy a drink without a meal. There is no active campaign to introduce alcohol sales on Sunday, though winemakers are applying pressure to be allowed to make off-sales from their vineyards on a Sunday.

Most pubs continue to maintain the traditional opening hours of 11am to 10pm with an extra hour on Thursday, Friday and Saturday. Drinking up time is usually about half an hour, though most pubs display a sign 'No jugs served after 9.45'. Private clubs, mainly drinking clubs masquerading as sports clubs, can serve alcohol until 1am or even 3am to people who are also dining, though most close well before midnight through lack of custom.

Other laws which might affect travellers are that the minimum drinking age is still 20 unless accompanied by an 'adult' relative (including spouse) in which case it is 18.

Local authorities are in charge of licensing, and entire suburbs of Auckland, Christchurch and Wellington are dry, in a snobbish attempt to keep out unsavoury elements.

Beer. The differences among New Zealand beers are more marked than those between Australian lager-type beers. Although lagers are certainly popular — Rheineck and the prize-winning Steinlager are the best known — many New Zealanders drink draught beer which approximates to British bitter.

Two giant brewers own almost all the pubs in New Zealand: Dominion Breweries and Lion. Dominion's DB (Draught Bitter) is a very ordinary but adequate beer containing 4% alcohol. Dominion also promotes a premium beer called Kiwi Lager which is tasty, strong (8%) and costs over $2.50 for a third of a litre. A litre bottle of DB costs about the same. DB Export Dry, in the style of Japanese dry beers, is tasty and popular.

Lion Brown has the pale colour and inoffensive flavour of British keg beer; Lion Red is sweet and malty. Lion's premium bottled beer is McGavin's, a pleasant ale. Other names occasionally crop up on beertaps such as Leopard (brewed in Hastings) and Speights, an old Dunedin brewery; both are now owned by the two giants. Also look for Monteith's, a good draught beer.

Although brewing has not kept up with wine-making in New Zealand the number of boutique breweries has been increasing. Mac's began brewing at Stoke near Nelson in the early 1980s and produces an interesting range of bottled beers from Mac's Real Ale to Black Mac, a dark and delicious brew. Aucklanders prefer a bottled beer from Henderson called Stockan's Trad Dark which is cheaper thann Black Mac.

Measures. For a country so small New Zealand has a bewildering variety of beer measures. Just after you think you have mastered the sizes, you find a completely different terminology being used in a different region. For example many South Island pubs continue to think of their beer glasses in the old sizes based on ounces: 3oz (rare and found only in a few pubs on the west coast), 5oz, 7oz, half pint or 'handle' and 12oz.

In fact the glasses are in metric units so what is called a '12' actually contains 360ml, closer to 13 ounces. The same range of glasses is available on the North Island but the metric numbers are used, so you ask for a 'three-sixty' (which is one of the most common sizes), a 'two-eighty' and so on. The terms 'pint' and 'half pint' are still acceptable though the amounts they signify are not standard. A pint will get you anything from just under 500ml to just over 600ml.

It is cheaper and easier to buy beer by the jug. The standard jug contains one litre and costs $4, though 2 litre jugs are also available. Usually you will be given 7oz glasses with a jug.

Cans of beer from off-licences are 440ml and start at $1.30. The price of a case of 24, known as a 'two dozen lot', starts at about $25. A flagon, formerly a half-gallon or 'half-g' and now 2.25 litres, is what many drinkers take home with them from the bottle store.

Whisky and other spirits are sold in pubs, though are seldom drunk as hotels continue to act as beer emporia primarily. A nip will cost about $1.50. Gin and tonic drinkers will be interested to learn that gin is cheap; a bottle costs about $13.

Wine. New Zealand produces some excellent wines which win international awards, many of which are not significantly more expensive than Australian wines in Australia. There are also some that are downright filthy. (New Zealand may not have any poisonous snakes but it does have Corbans Velluto Rosso, a combination of jam and lighter fluid). Often the cheap wines are sickly sweet, though quite a few good wines cost less than $10 and some decent ones, like Mission Winery's white burgundy, cost about $6.50.

Although wine consumption is still a long way behind Australia, it is creeping up in New Zealand and so the situation is gradually improving. Half the wine sold in New Zealand is in casks. But even as the standard of table wine improves to satisfy a more sophisticated home market, the hefty government tax on wine means that New Zealand wine drinking will never be able to match the pleasures of Australian wine drinking. The duty on imported wines is even steeper and so the few Australian wines for sale are no cheaper than the home-produced ones.

The two giant wine-makers are Montana and Cooks, whose wines are readily available in most British supermarkets. Despite the Anglo-Saxon names, some of New Zealand's best and oldest winemakers are of Mediterranean extraction, especially Yugoslav, such as Babich and Selak. New Zealand's cool climate favours the production of white wines. especially sauvignon blanc and chardonnay. There are also some very creditable chablis-style wines. Look out for Delegats' sauvignon, Hunter's sauvignon and chardonnay, Nobilo's gewurtztraminer, Babich's Irongate chardonnay and Te Mata Estate's wines cabernet and chardonnay. Red wines do not flourish so well in New Zealand's climate though some cabernet sauvignons are worth trying, for example those of the Matua Valley vineyard. An increasing number of vineyards are now open to the public for tasting and buying and some have good restaurants attached to them.

Kiwifruit wine, a favourite with Japanese tourists, has a pleasant, not overly sweet fruit taste and makes a novel gift. It is slightly cheaper than grape wine, possibly because the locals tend to turn up their noses at it.

Unfortunately New Zealand has jumped on the wine-cooler bandwagon and Corbans and Montana produce mixtures of wine (40%) and fruit juice. In fact New Zealand fruit juices are delicious even though most of them seem to be apple-based, and are best drunk neat. The small cartons cost about $1.

It is easy to be rude about the nightlife and the artistic provincialism of New Zealand. But considering that its total population is only the same as the city of Madrid, it is hardly surprising that it cannot offer a large choice of theatres, rock groups and so on. In fact for its size, the entertainment and artistic achievements are remarkably varied and occasionally sophisticated.

Tickets for major productions and events can be booked though the BASS Agency which has outlets in various suburbs of Auckland plus Hamilton, Tauranga, Rotorua, Wellington and Christchurch. The main number in Auckland is 09-307 5000. Expect to pay a $5 transaction fee. Concert and theatre prices are usually in the $30–35 bracket with concessions.

The Arts. Despite its geographical isolation, New Zealand was for a long time culturally swamped by the mother country. Recently however it has produced a creditable number of indigenous artists and performers. Almost all have felt that it was necessary to spend time in Europe, particularly London, and much talent has inevitably been lost. The much larger potential audience of Australia is a constant temptation for creative New Zealanders. Some of the lost talent has been replaced by emigrés who value the chance to make their mark in a fledgling culture.

All the cities have established theatres which perform everything from Shakespeare to Alan Ayckbourn, with a preponderance of the latter. The National Orchestra and several ballet and opera companies tour the country between mid-February and November, often scheduling their major productions for the end of the season.

Cinema. A few New Zealand-made films have made an international impact — most recently *Once Were Warriors*. One earlier box office success was the film *The Dog's (Tail) Tale*, a cartoon film based on the popular Footrot Flats cartoon strip about a canny sheep dog. This may not have won any prizes at the Cannes Film Festival but was very amusing all the same. There is usually a reasonable choice of films at city cinemas, all of which cost $9 with some special $5 or $6 deals on Monday evenings and for all matinees. Drive-in cinemas were prohibited for decades but in 1987 the government decided that they were not such a threat to community life and ordinary cinemas after all — yet another piece of evidence to support the claim that New Zealand is at least 20 years behind the rest of the world.

The censor's classification of films is a complicated business: G means General Exhibition, GY is the same but recommended as suitable for those 13 and over, GA is more suitable for adults, R16 or R18 films are restricted to people over those ages and RP13 or RP16 are approved for people over those ages or under if they are accompanied by an adult. The censors are kind enough to spell out possible objections, such as 'Language may offend', 'Some scenes may disturb' or even 'Explicit sexual content may offend'. The allocation of an 'R' for Restricted can be enforced by law whereas 'G' classifications are merely recommendations.

Popular Music. The only New Zealand bands to have achieved international recognition are Split Enz, Crowded House and to a lesser extent The Chills. Most bands leave for Australia or America as soon as they achieve national success.

A reasonable number of international stars like M C Hammer and Lisa Stansfield tour, usually in November/December, and New Zealanders travel long distances and pay high prices (at least $50) to see them. The cities have their fair share of rock venues and folk and jazz clubs, all with a decided tendency towards traditional music, plus a growing number of nightclubs. Some cosmopolitan visitors claim that advertisements for these clubs which read 'Live and Raging' are a trifle optimistic.

Museums and Galleries. The standard of exhibits is normally high, even in small local or regional museums, though you won't find many Old Masters on display. Many New Zealand artists, both Maori and Pakeha, exhibit their work at galleries throughout the country. Admission is normally free, but quite a few historic houses charge an entry fee. The New Zealand Historic Places Trust (PO Box 2629, Wellington) administers about 40 properties from farm buildings to historic missions, water mills to stately homes. It publishes a free brochure of all its properties and opening times.

SPORT

'Rugby, Racing and Beer' is a popular pub sing-along, praising the merits of New Zealand's purported favourite pursuits. Cricket and sailing are also capable of inciting a high level of national fervour. There is almost no professional sport played in New Zealand. The cricket season runs from November to April, tennis from September to April, and soccer from May to September. Baseball is surprisingly popular, but more as a participation sport.

Sports stars are esteemed as national deities (especially in rugby and cricket) and the amount of media coverage during important matches is staggering. It is noticeable, however, that when these gods lose, there is a virtual news blackout especially on National Radio and especially when New Zealand is playing against the Poms.

Rugby. Now that South Africa has been readmitted into the international league of sporting nations, New Zealand's national sport is set to recover from the reverses it suffered during the decades when the All Blacks (the national Rugby Union team) maintained controversial links with South Africa. Match attendance declined noticeably after the Springbok tour of 1981 which divided the country and led to serious civil disturbances, but is now likely to soar once again. Although deplored by purists, rugby has introduced cheerleaders, music and other American-style entertainments. The season lasts from May or June until September and tickets range from $8 to $30. The premier Rugby League club prize is the Tusk Cup.

Horse Racing. Racing takes place around the year and is another national obsession. All but the smallest towns have their own well groomed floodlit race tracks which may host only one or two meetings a year, either trotting or flat racing. Successful horses, jockeys, trainers and breeders become household names in New Zealand for example Maree Linden who became the first female jockey to participate in the Melbourne Cup in 1987. There is also a large network of over 400 betting agencies licensed by the nationwide Totalisator Agency Board (TAB) which accept bets on Australian races as well as native ones. Although Sunday racing was legalised in 1989, punters cannot bet through the TAB on Sunday races.

Trotting or harness racing is nearly as popular as flat racing (or 'the gallops') having grown out of informal roadside contests among the settlers who brought horses with them. The foremost prize is the Lion Brown Interdominion Championship, in which Australian and New Zealand pacers and trotters compete. This race is held during the first fortnight in March, and the stakes total more than a million dollars. To study form, consult *The Turf Digest* ($2). All racing and trotting radio broadcasts are on the Racing Network, which links the ZB stations and a number of others.

Dog Trials. Apparently the introduction of sheep dog trials in New Zealand predates those in Britain, having started in Wanaka in 1867 as compared to Bala, Wales in 1873. Rural competitions where farmers show off the sheep-mustering skills of their top animals are still popular and are worth seeing, especially if you happen to have missed seeing their Scottish and West Country counterparts on BBC2's *One Man and his Dog*. Because of the enormous size and ruggedness of stations, New Zealand has bred a special tough dog called a 'huntaway' whose loud bark shoos the sheep away and makes it possible for the heading dogs to take over. Demonstrations for tourists in a number of places, especially around Rotorua and Queenstown.

Tourists are also invited to sheep-shearing demonstrations. The annual championships take place in Masterton near Wellington every year in March and the whole nation follows the 'Golden Shears' contest.

If you are lucky, your visit will coincide with a rural show day, which is often the annual social highlight for country and small town locals. The Agricultural & Pastoral Society organises many fairs around the country where prize stock and produce are displayed, handicrafts are exhibited and lighthearted entertainments are arranged.

GAMBLING

A nation of racing fans is a nation of gamblers, and recent statistics indicate that New Zealand surpasses not only Australia but the rest of the world. Because of this national tendency, gambling is strictly controlled. For example slot machines (not including traditional one arm bandits) were only legalised in 1987, and only in approved premises. Football pools are still illegal, though this may well change in the next few years.

'Housie' or bingo is very popular. To confirm this just check under the heading 'Housie' in any newspaper's classified section. Many pubs and clubs have a Housie night at least once a week, usually Wednesday or Thursday. A card costs from $6 to $7 and entitles you to play 40 games.

When the second national lottery, Instant Kiwi, was introduced in 1990, sales for the original Lotto dropped briefly but were soon back to record highs. Nearly two-thirds of New Zealanders buy at least one Lotto ticket every month and over a third buy Instant Kiwi. Tickets may be purchased at participating dairies, shops and country post offices. A minimum four entries costs $3 while the maximum ten (per card) costs $6.50. For Lotto you have to wait until the winning numbers are read out on prime time Saturday evening television, whereas Instant Kiwi is indeed instant as it consists of a card you scratch off. Proceeds go to a collection of charities including one to help compulsive gamblers.

If you enjoy shopping in Harrod's or Bloomingdales, you may find New Zealand's shopping facilities a little provincial (and a lot more friendly). You also may be initially struck by the Britishness of the big names, including Woolworths and Boots. Most shop fronts are functional at best and dowdy at worst, even in downtown Auckland. Shopping centres are depressingly similar and the range of products on sale very repetitive. The largest chain of department stores is called Farmers, whose unimaginative appearance some travellers have compared unfavourably with that of Eastern European shops before democratisation. (Like so many retail businesses in New Zealand, Farmers have been experiencing financial difficulties to the point where in 1991 they had to close down their flagship store in central Auckland and turn it into a furniture showroom.)

Trendy areas lined with boutiques and cafés are few and far between. In cities there is less centralisation than in other countries and many suburbanites are content to shop locally. Each residential area has its own shops, its own butcher, baker, second-hand shop, etc. Look for Central Mission Goodwill Stores and Opportunity Shops for cheap secondhand goods. The large cities have second-hand bookshops which is lucky as new books from overseas are expensive. If you are shipping an expensive item out of the country, ask about GST exemptions; though many disclaim any knowledge of this, it does exist. Many shops geared to the tourist trade will arrange to ship goods; expect to pay about $12 for an item weighing one kilogram, and don't worry about its non-arrival until about three months after purchase. Duty-free shops are neither as numerous nor as cheap as they are in Australia.

Normal shopping hours are 9am (occasionally 9.30am) to 5.30pm Monday to Thursday and 9am to 9pm on Fridays. The expectation among shop employees of a 5-day week is prevalent but slowly weakening, as some downtown and suburban shops now open on Saturday mornings or occasionally until 4pm.

Trading on Sundays and on statutory public holidays is largely prohibited though 1991 saw the introduction of Sunday trading in some branches of the big supermarket chains Foodtown and New World, thereby taking business away from the corner dairy, which was once the only source of essential foodstuffs on Sundays.

A few items which you might want to buy but would have trouble specifying are 'jandals' (the Kiwi word for flip-flops) and 'Snowtex' (for tissues/Kleenex).

Smoking is becoming relatively more expensive than it used to be with a standard brand pack costing over $4.50 now (about 75% of which is tax). Imported rolling tobacco (e.g. Old Holborn) is a bargain at around $7 for 50 grams. The major brand of rolling papers (30c) is Zig Zag; there are two varieties of which the blue packets are the lighter.

Souvenirs. The most common mementoes bought by tourists are greenstone or paua jewellery, sheepskin and woollen products or outdoor gear. Some of the signs and advertisements for retailers of such souvenirs are in Japanese, and their prices reflect this affluent big-spending market. Greenstone is a kind of jade peculiar to New Zealand, found only between two rivers on the South Island near Hokitika (where there is a greenstone factory open to the public). Although the supply of this semi-precious stone is dwindling, prices are not prohibitive. Many stones are fashioned into Maori 'tiki', an ornate figure which is said to represent an embryo and hence the source of life. These carvings are understandably expensive so if you see a cheap one for sale it is undoubtedly a mass-produced imitation. The shells of paua (the Maori word for abalone) are vivid blue-green and are made into cheap jewellery; a pair of earrings, for example might cost $15. There is the predictable range of tacky souvenirs such as key rings and bottle openers adorned with greenstone or paua.

New Zealand is a paradise for crafts people and there are interesting little workshops scattered all over the country but especially on the Coromandel Peninsula and around Nelson. Of the 4,000 registered craftsmen and women, a large number specialise in ceramics which has been strongly influenced by classical Japanese ceramics.

Woollen jumpers, socks and blankets are not remarkably cheap despite the overabundance of wool. Designer pullovers and hand-knits are popular and pricey. Knitting unusual jumpers is a thriving cottage industry. One material which you may come across is 'slink', the very soft skin of newborn lambs.

New Zealand-made tramping boots, tents, sleeping bags, fishing rods, wetsuits, etc. are generally of very high quality, and the prices reflect this. Hallmark and Macpac Wilderness make good quality camping gear while Line Seven and Dorlon make sailing gear. Canterbury Clothing is famous for its rugby shirts, and Swanndri for its woollen bush shirts and jackets ranging in price from $100 to $150. (If you hear a New Zealander talk about his or her 'Swanni', you will now know what they mean.)

If you have some New Zealand currency left over when flying out of the country, you should not have too much trouble spending it at Auckland Airport. Especially recommended are tins of peeled lamb tongues, sure to impress, and a bargain at about $3. Auckland must have one of the few airports where departing tourists are encouraged to buy a side of lamb (which costs about $50, about seven times more than the farmer receives). Remember that all passengers on flights via the USA must clear US Customs, in which case your frozen meat or seafood would have to be declared, inspected and possibly confiscated.

If you want a preview of New Zealand specialities (including kiwifruit toothpaste) before you leave Britain, visit Kiwifruits at 25 Bedfordbury, London WC2N 4DA (0171-240 1423), which carries a good range of New Zealand wines and Canterbury Clothing, while its outlet at 6 Royal Opera Arcade behind New Zealand House stocks New Zealand books, carvings and other souvenirs.

Photography. Top name film costs from $6.50 for a 24-exposure 135 or 110 cartridge. Developing costs $10-$15 in cities where there is competition.

Electrical Goods. New Zealand appliances operate on 230 volts at 50 Hertz which are compatible with the UK electrical supply but not with the American or Canadian one. New Zealand has a peculiar angled plug and it is difficult to find an adaptor.

Those who are prepared to throw themselves enthusiastically into the enjoyment of outdoor pursuits are those who find a trip to New Zealand most satisfying. The mountains and glaciers keep the skiers, climbers and hikers happy while the rivers and beaches provide entertainment for fishermen, divers and windsurfers. And between the mountains and the sea, people cycle, raft, watch birds, ride, explore caves, hunt and canoe — every adventure holiday in the book, it seems, with the possible exception of air sports.

Many New Zealanders consider their Great Outdoors to be the country's greatest resource, as fish are to Iceland or coffee is to Brazil. As they cannot export it (except in glossy calenders and *Beautiful New Zealand* magazines), they promote it heavily to foreign visitors, and the complete novice or anti-athlete is not neglected. Every local tourist office displays an impressive array of brochures to persuade you to don a wet suit, mount a bicycle or hire a mountain guide. The booklet *Outdoor Action Holidays*, revised annually by the Department of Tourism, is a valuable source of information; for each sport and activity a list of operators is given with an indication of prices.

National Parks. New Zealand has a long tradition of preserving its wilderness, partly in response to a Maori chief who gave three sacred peaks on the North Island to the nation in 1887 on the condition that they could not be settled and spoiled. They were then incorporated into Tongariro National Park, one of the four National Parks on the North Island. The mountain range on the South Island is almost continuous National Park, though divided into nine designated parks, from the mammoth Fiordland National Park in the south to the coastal Abel Tasman National Park in the north. They are vigorously maintained by the government and improvements for the benefit of visitors are constantly being carried out. The newest National Park, Kahwangi, was created in 1995. Some new walking tracks have been opened to take pressure off the most heavily used tracks, such as the Milford and the Routeburn. There are also three Maritime Parks (Bay of Islands, Hauraki Gulf around Auckland and Marlborough Sounds) and 21 Forest Parks, all of which are administered by the Department of Conservation.

National Parks are well provided with information centres that offer advice to people wanting to explore and often act also as miniature museums with interesting displays of anything from the geological history of the area to accounts of early hero-explorers and local characters. The staff seem uniformly knowledgeable and courteous and willingly try to answer questions ranging from 'why is glacier ice coloured blue?' to 'will I need my raingear today?' or 'are there any places where camping is forbidden?'. If you are attempting any route that is out of the ordinary, always discuss your plans with a park ranger (officially called 'Conservation Officers') and register your intentions in as much detail as possible.

Some National Parks run a semi-educational summer programme involving guided walks, films and demonstrations. Summer programmes are organised fairly late in the year so schedules come out close to the beginning of the season. Information about National Parks, etc. can be obtained from the New Zealand Tourism Board, PO Box 95, Wellington, or by calling in at any of the Department of Conservation Visitor Centres.

There is no fee for admission to National or Maritime Parks, though there is a fee for overnight stays. Tickets costing $4 must be bought in advance from Department of Conservation offices, information centres and other outlets. Depending on the category of the hut, overnight stays cost one, two or three tickets and camping next to a hut costs one ticket. An annual hut pass costs $60. In very remote areas, there are simple shelters with no facilities that fall into Category 4 and are free. Anyone wanting to spend one or more nights in a Park should obtain the brochure *Backcountry Huts*.

Wildlife. Until the Maori arrived, New Zealand was completely devoid of mammals, with the exception of a rare breed of bat. Apparently moas, giant emu-like birds whose skeletons and fossilised eggs can be admired in many museums, served the purpose of cattle by grazing the land, until they were wiped out by the early moa-hunting Maori. A few unique species of bird have survived, though many were destroyed by settlers and by introduced animals (particularly rats) which found these flightless birds easy prey. The most famous flightless bird has become New Zealand's national symbol (but not Air New Zealand's); the kiwi is difficult to spot in the bush as it is a nocturnal bird. But several zoos and 'kiwi houses' scattered around the country make it easy to admire this surprisingly small creature. One of the most endangered is the kakapo; only 47 of these flightless nocturnal parrots are believed to survive on a few coastal islands including Great Barrier Island and are the subject of a concerted effort by conservation experts.

Nowadays there are rigorously enforced laws protecting the native fauna (and also vegetation) and equally energetic attempts to keep the number of non-indigenous animals like deer, rabbits, wallabies and opossums under control. (It has been estimated that there are even more opposums in the country than there are sheep.) Many of these species are such pests that they must be constantly culled. Deer hunting is encouraged for this reason and licences may easily be obtained from park rangers.

For those who simply want to observe the wildlife, there are many nature reserves and feeding grounds. Whale-spotting has become very popular from Kaikoura north of Christchurch. Hector dolphins favour Akaroa Harbour. The prehistoric-looking lizard called tuatara is protected on a couple of offshore islands such as Poor Knights in the Hauraki Gulf or Stephens and Trio Islands in the Marlborough Sounds. But they are also on view to a wider public in Auckland Zoo and the Invercargill tuatarium. There are colonies of penguin and albatross on the Otago Peninsula near Dunedin. White heron gather on the west coast near Okarito and gannets breed at Cape Kidnappers on Hawkes Bay. One bird you will have no trouble seeing is the kea, a charmless dull-coloured parrot with red underwings and a discordant cry, an unlovable answer to Australia's kookaburra. The kea likes human habitations, especially rubbish bins, and will peck at almost anything from (unoccupied) hiking boots to sheep.

TRAMPING

Hiking, always known as tramping, is New Zealand's national pastime, and every visitor should make an effort to penetrate the country's bush on foot. Visitor information centres often distribute leaflets describing simple strolls and strenuous treks which can be made from the centre. For example from the North Egmont Visitor Centre you can make a 20-minute circuit past some typical North Island vegetation or begin a four-day circuit of Mount Egmont, with several choices in between which are all well signposted.

Even Britons who have never tackled Mount Snowdon and Americans who have never strayed from the Midwestern prairies find themselves tempted by the idea of a relatively serious mountain walk while in New Zealand. For whatever reason, the Milford Track has become so famous, especially among American city-slickers, that many people book months in advance. But there are dozens of other tracks on both islands which may not be household names but are equally scenic.

One of the Department of Conservation's most ambitious projects is to establish a network of interlinking tracks from the North Cape to Bluff in the South, though this has had to be put on hold for the present due to the expense and difficulty of persuading unsympathetic landowners to allow the public access.

Tramps are designated according to difficulty: 'walks' are simple enough for children and are usually maintained by regional parks authorities; 'tracks' are easy-to-follow paths though they can be steep and strenuous; 'routes' can be difficult to follow and therefore appeal to experienced hill walkers who can navigate by compass.

Many visitors of average fitness elect to do a two to four day tramp along a clearly marked track supplied with huts. *Tramping in New Zealand* (Lonely Planet, $19.95) describes in detail 40 tramps ranging from mild to strenuous and is useful for choosing a suitable trek. One of your prime considerations may be the amount of pedestrian traffic you wish to encounter. Tracks like the Heaphy and the Abel Tasman coastal walk in the South Island were so heavily used this past season that the park authorities are considering putting up 'Full' signs at the beginning.

Access to the starting point of some walks is sometimes a little tricky, though enterprising locals usually operate a minibus or motor boat specifically for trekkers. It is also not uncommon to meet someone on the trail who has arranged for a car to be waiting for him or her at the other end and who will offer a lift.

Tramping huts are usually simple solidly built structures, similar in atmosphere to YHA hostels but without male-female segregation. Hut beds cannot be reserved beforehand, and so there is sometimes an undignified scramble for beds along the popular routes at the popular times. The tourist literature often advises trampers to carry a tent in case huts are full, but this is of little use when camping is prohibited. It is amazing how many bodies can be crammed into a hut after the bunks have been taken, and trampers will not be turned out into the cold unless there is a less crowded hut within easy range. On the main tracks resident wardens can help with any problems, though their main task is to maintain the hut and surrounding trails and collect the hut fee. If there is no warden there may be an honesty box.

In all cases you must be self-sufficient in food, though gas rings and running water are normally provided. Unless you opt for one of the pampered escorted walks on the Routeburn or the Milford tracks (over $600 for the three-day walk) you will have to carry all your food as well as carrying out your rubbish so try to avoid an excess of tins. If you fancy the luxury of freeze-dried lamb dinners, you should purchase a camping saucepan before setting off. But for walks of a couple of days, it is perfectly feasible to dine on cold food such as muesli, dried milk, tinned fish, bread (preferably pumpernickel or rye if you can find them), cheese, dried fruit, 'scroggin' (a New Zealand concoction of fruit, nuts and seeds specifically for tramping), etc. You can also take some packet soups which can be boiled up in a borrowed billy. It is a little trickier borrowing dishes and utensils, so you should carry your own.

Equipment and Safety. Despite the absence of dangerous creatures, much emphasis is placed on outdoor safety. Alarming posters published by the New Zealand Mountain Safety Council show innocent hikers wading waist-deep in freezing water a few hours after having enjoyed a picnic in the same place. In fact sudden changes of weather, very common in maritime climates, account for the bulk of the problems. Long dry spells are rare but, if you are lucky enough to encounter one, keep your eye on the graphs that show risk of forest fire and be very careful with any flame.

In addition to your provisions — enough to last the walk plus emergency rations in case you become weather-bound — you must have a warm sleeping bag as bedding is not supplied and even summer nights can become extremely cold in the unheated huts. A worn-in pair of boots is a definite asset, though some people do attempt the simpler tracks in plimsolls, which soon become inadequate in bad weather.

Warm and waterproof gear is essential. Even if you feel like an idiot packing a woollen hat, gloves, long johns and rain gear in the middle of summer, you should not walk without these items. Snowfalls are not particularly rare on passes and saddles in summer, though you are more likely to be bombarded by torrential rainfall and piercing winds. The New Zealand Mountain Safety Council publishes a pamphlet on hypothermia, a condition that should be guarded against at all costs. Another of their useful leaflets is called *Heading for the Bush*, which explains how to cope with wilderness dangers such as swollen river crossings and how to attract the attention of rescue parties. These are mainly relevant to the off-the-beaten-track routes, which should not be attempted by the inexperienced. A large number of companies conduct escorted hikes in remote terrain, which cost from $150 for 2 days to nearly $3000 for 3 weeks.

If you haven't brought your own equipment and don't have a New Zealand friend from whom you can borrow it, you should scan hostel notice boards for second-hand tents, rain gear, and so on, which you can in turn sell at the end of your travels. An alternative is to buy it from a shop that has a buy-back policy such as the Sports Bazaar in Auckland (538 Karangahape Road; 09-309 6444).

WATER SPORTS

Jetboating. Most of the rivers of New Zealand are so fast and turbulent that a special boat had to be invented to cope with them. The jet boat, developed about 25 years ago, operates by sucking water in and jetting it out the back with such force that the craft is propelled forward. It can travel upstream, through rapids and in just a few inches of water. Although it is fast, the sensation is not much different from riding in an ordinary outboard motor powered boat. A typical trip would last an hour and cost between $40 and $70. Often you will have to wait for a full complement of tourists to assemble before the trip can take place. In a few places it is possible to hire a jet boat and drive it yourself on lakes and gentle rivers.

Rafting. Adventurous travellers are more attracted to the idea of white water rafting. Rafting operators can be found in about ten towns on both islands, offering trips which last from a few hours to a week. Sometimes access to the starting point has to be by helicopter. Queenstown is the capital of rafting and few who visit can resist the temptations laid so enticingly before them by the competing operators.

Prices start at $75 for a morning on the Wairoa River (two hours drive from Auckland and therefore popular) to $800 for a five-day camping expedition in the backcountry of the South Island. Rivers are graded internationally on a scale of one to six, and several companies take novices through grade five rapids. Rafters are given a wetsuit, a paddle and half an hour of instruction, and usually a picnic or barbecue at the end of the run.

New Zealanders seem able not only to perfect sports that are well known, but to invent new ones. For example many visitors to the Waitomo Caves now take advantage of the opportunity to go 'blackwater rafting', which consists of rushing through pitch-dark caves on a rubber dinghy (see the section on *Waitomo* below). Surf-rafting is also available which involves going to sea on a motorised raft while wearing a wetsuit and life jacket.

Bungy-jumping. Even more popular is the sport of 'bungy-jumping'. While ten years ago jumping off high places with thick elastic bands around your ankles was the preserve of members of 'Dangerous Sports Societies', it is now available to everyone. The New Zealander A J Hackett turned this activity into a commercial success near Queenstown in the mid 1980s and now operators have sprung up all over the Antipodes. In 1991 A J Hackett opened his first European venue, a cliff in Normandy. You can't fail but hear about all the possible locations for doing a death-defying leap as you travel around New Zealand, from a high building in central Auckland to deep in the bush. In some cases you can elect to enter the water, though most people just skim it. Jumps usually cost not much less than $100 which includes a certificate of your achievement and possibly also a photograph. Although most companies observe strict safety measures, there are cases in which the length of the bungy has been slightly misjudged and the jumper hits the water unexpectedly and gets hurt. Remove all jewellery and contact lenses in case you do go under.

Fishing. New Zealand has a reputation for having some of the best fishing in the world, both for wealthy tourists in pursuit of big game like marlin or for more humble rod fishermen. The locals are so confident that their fishing is unsurpassable that recently some hotel proprietors on Lake Taupo (famed for its trout) were promising free accommodation to any fisherman who failed to catch a fish. But not all reports of fishing are as favourable, especially among game fishermen who are catching fewer and fewer marlin and shark in the once-fecund waters of the Bay of Islands, the Coromandel and the Bay of Plenty. Commercial Japanese fishing fleets are blamed for the depletion. As big game charter boats cost anything from $500 a day, this will come as a disappointment to only a few.

There is no closed season for fly fishing, though most South Island fishing trips take place between October and May. A guide in remote areas will cost about $300 for two anglers including transport. Rods and waders can be hired though you are encouraged to bring your own. The sport is monitored by the many branches of the Acclimatisation Society (headed by the aptly named Tony Drinkwater) which issue licences for trout and salmon fishing valid throughout New Zealand, though all government tourist offices can arrange a one-month permit for visitors. Special permits are needed for Rotorua and Taupo, while no permit is needed for game fishing. Trout weighing up to 10lb are fished on a catch-and-release system. River fishing is done with a dry fly cast at a fish already spotted. The less challenging 'harling' (trolling) and fishing from motor boats is also available. For a long list of fishing guides and outfitters, see the tourist brochure *Outdoor Holidays*.

Other Activities. Canoeing, windsurfing, surfing and scuba diving all flourish in various places. Not to mention more obscure activities such as parapenting, a cross between hang gliding and parachuting which you can learn in the Port Hills of Christchurch, near Queenstown and other places where conditions permit. The much more sedate sport of golf is exceedingly popular and many of the courses are wonderfully scenic. A round of golf shouldn't cost much more than $10.

As New Zealand lacks a reef, the bombed Greenpeace flagship *The Rainbow Warrior* was sunk off the North Island coast at Matauri Bay, for the benefit of divers. The water is said to be clearest in April whereas in spring plankton obscures the fish. New Zealand is also a nation of yachtsmen, and sailboats may be chartered in resort areas such as the Bay of Islands. Cruising yacht captains should remember to fill in the Ministry of Transport's 'ten-minute form' and hand it in at any police station, informing the authorities of their intentions; this is to help Search and Rescue in case of an emergency. Sometimes the best surfing beaches are accessible only by crossing private land; always ask the farmer's permission and be sure to close gates and refrain from littering.

SKIING
Alpine skiing is booming in New Zealand and the industry is aiming for a million skier visits per season. Commercial and club ski fields equipped with a range of lifts, ski hire facilities, etc., are opening and expanding all the time, so that there are now 24 in total. The season lasts from June until October, though artificial snow makes it possible for some fields to remain open until November.

Skiing in the South Island is centred on Queenstown, Wanaka, Mount Cook, Mount Hutt and Tekapo and in the North Island at the ski villages of Whakapapa and Turoa on Mount Ruapehu and also on Mount Taranaki. Most skiers prefer the drier conditions and more reliable snowfalls of South Island skiing, though heavy investment in snow-making equipment is improving conditions and increasing the length of the season throughout the country. Furthermore South Island skiing is marred by the danger of avalanches. Because there are so few roads into the mountains, heli-skiing (where skiers are flown to mountain tops) is popular even though it costs from $350 a day.

CYCLING
New Zealand, like the Netherlands, is considered an ideal cycling country, though the terrain could hardly be more different. The scarcity of traffic together with the magnificent scenery persuade many that cycle touring is an excellent way to travel around New Zealand, which is true, until it rains and the famous nor'wester wind begins to blow in your face. Another problem is that away from the main roads (which are often quieter than a British B-road) you will have to contend with gravel. Helmets are compulsory.

To rent a bicycle in Auckland, contact Bicycle Tour Services (09-276 5218), which hires out a range of touring bicycles and equipment. Mountain and touring bikes are available for $70 a week. For $25 the company provides a week's detailed itinerary for independent cyclists with accommodation arrangements including farms where you can stay on a work-for-keep basis.

Alternatively, buy a bicycle and sell it at the end of your trip. Often 'bike for sale' notices can be found in the city hostels or other backpacker venues. Expect to pay $500–600 for a fully equipped touring bicycle in top condition. Bicycle insurance is expensive in New Zealand (and sometimes unobtainable) so it might be better to invest in a state-of-the-art lock and use it carefully.

Cyclists who get fed up during the rainy periods often manage to hitch with their bikes. Buses usually carry bikes for an extra $10 if they have space in their holds. Most will insist that you remove the panniers, cover the chain and sometimes even take the pedals off.

One company that organises cycling tours on both islands is New Zealand Pedaltours (PO Box 37-575, Parnell, Auckland; 09-302 0968). It offers 32 departure dates per summer and nine routes. Naturally the trips are expensive as everything short of good weather is provided — a fully equipped bicycle, a guide, all meals and accommodation (hotels or campsites) and a support van to carry luggage and help out with repairs. The company also offers a trip-planning service for those who prefer to travel independently. Cycles can be hired or purchased on a buy-back scheme. New Zealand Pedaltours also sells two hand-books for cyclists: *Cycle Touring in the North Island* ($14) and its companion volume for the South Island ($7); air mail postage is an additional $12. These guides include information on accommodation and shopping facilities as well as terrain and routes. AA maps are useful, so take your card if you're a member. The Bicycle Association of New Zealand can be contacted at PO Box 2454, Wellington.

Another company organising cycling tours is Flying Kiwi Wilderness and Cycling Expeditions (Deer Park Road, Koromiko, RD3, Blenheim; 03-573 8126), which offers original and slightly eccentric tours of both islands; see the section on *The Great Outdoors* in each chapter for more details.

It is possible to hire cycles for a day in places such as Rotorua, Queenstown and Wanaka as well as the big cities. You should expect to pay at least $10 a day for an ordinary bicycle and $12 to $15 for a mountain or racing bicycle. The Penny Farthing Cycle Shops, with branches in the three major cities, have a few bicycles for hire. If you are very keen and enjoy group events you can participate in the annual circumnavigation of Lake Taupo (about 160km) in November and various other fun rides.

Health

New Zealand has a well deserved reputation for its pristine water, clear air and absence of dangerous fauna. It promotes itself as safe, clean and benign, with crystal clear water and air. The freedom from poisonous reptiles and insects (with one minor exception) comes as a wonderful relief after the perils of the Australian Outback or oceanside. It has also taken some progressive anti-smoking measures, for example banning smoking on all public buses.

However dangers do lurk in New Zealand, especially if you intend to do any 'tramping', i.e. hill-walking. The vagaries of the weather have already been noted in *Climate*. Rain, wind and cold can have dire consequences for under-prepared trampers. Details are provided in *Great Outdoors*, above. Also, streams and rivers may not be as clean as they once were due to the high numbers of trampers.

Traces of the unpleasant parasite giardia (well known to most trans-Asia travellers) in have been found in places including the Abel Tasman National Park and the Routeburn Track. This is due to carelessness in disposing of human waste. Trampers should also exercise caution when taking drinking water downstream from a sheep station.

Medical Treatment. New Zealand's social services provide free prescriptions and free treatment in public hospitals. As mentioned on page 11, UK passport holders are entitled to these services free of charge, though they must pay for consultations with a doctor and for some medicines. If you do have to seek medical attention, ask if you should claim a refund from the doctor or from the local health office.

Furthermore, there is a unique and enlightened scheme whereby the government pays compensation for personal injuries sustained in any accident which takes place in New Zealand no matter who is to blame. This precludes the possibility of litigation. Payments cover medical expenses but not loss of earnings outside New Zealand. Full details appear in the leaflet *Visiting New Zealand* from the Accident Compensation Corporation, PO Box 242, Wellington.

If your hotel or hostel cannot recommend a clinic or a doctor, then consult the list of doctors at the beginning of the local telephone directory. The emergency telephone number in large cities is 111.

Pharmaceutical products obtained without a prescription are pricey. Chemist shops are open 9am-5.30pm Monday to Friday with some staying open until 9pm on Fridays. Emergency contacts are posted on most chemists' doors at closing time.

Optical services are also expensive, with a decent pair of spectacles costing about $200. Dispensing opticians are called 'optometrists'.

HEALTH HAZARDS

Creatures. New Zealand is absurdly proud that its shores are snake-free. The discovery of a dead snake in Te Anau in 1991 made national headlines. Many animals were brought to New Zealand by white settlers, for example the opossum which has done irreparable damage to the native forests, but no one introduced snakes. There are also no venomous spiders or insects with the single exception of the katipo, a large spider which favours beach habitats. But it is not particularly common and its bite is rarely fatal. Even the local version of the yeti, the Great Hairy Moehau of Maori mythology is said to be shy and gentle (and is the subject of repeated searches by the Blue Mountain eccentric Rex Gilroy who believes that it may still exist in remote Fiordland).

The wildlife, however, is not entirely benign. Swimmers should be aware that mako sharks (which are not especially dangerous) occasionally come in near the shore. And jellyfish swarms occasionally make swimming unpleasant (as opposed to dangerous). Sandflies proliferate in many areas and are a terrible nuisance, just as they are in coastal parts of Australia. Two recommended repellents are called 'Dimp' (a cream) and Repel (a spray) which are both relatively effective if applied at frequent intervals. If you are badly bitten Histofax cream relieves the itching.

Wasps have been a recurring problem on the west coast of the South Island, driving tourists out of their campsites and diminishing the food supply of native birds. The problem became so serious that a wasp parasite was introduced in the South Island to control the swarms of pests. Anyone with an allergy who plans to go into the bush should carry appropriate medication. A less desirable parasite infests some of the lakes on the South Island. The rash which results from contact with the snail-borne parasite is known as 'duck itch'. Warning signs are usually posted in affected swimming areas.

Acts of God. While getting off lightly on the flora and fauna front, New Zealand fares less well in terms of natural disasters. Erupting volcanoes, avalanches, floods, tornadoes and earthquakes take a regular toll of life and property. Australian slang for their neighbour is 'the quaky island' or the 'shaky isles'. Leaflets published by the New Zealand Ministry of Civil Defence on these dangers advise what action to take in an emergency.

New Zealand is seismologically very active. The fault line running the entire length of both islands actually bisects Wellington, which makes the capital particularly subject to earth tremors. No part of New Zealand is considered free from earthquake danger, though the risk varies greatly. For example Nelson is liable to have a quake every 16 years, whereas Auckland can expect one every 260 years. All buildings in the country must be constructed so as to withstand disturbances of the earth. If you have the misfortune to be caught in an earthquake, resist the temptation to run outside. It is safer to stand in a doorway or shelter under a strong piece of furniture. The back page of all New Zealand telephone directories provides emergency advice.

Although periodic flooding in cities is unlikely to cause anything more than inconvenience, flooding in the great outdoors can be more serious. It is not uncommon for river levels to rise dramatically making crossings which were previously quite safe impossible. Trampers frequently find themselves stranded when streams and rivers suddenly swell.

The volcanoes of the North Island (Ruapehu, Tongariro, Ngauruhoe) are dormant and most unlikely to erupt in the forseeable future. However there is a great deal of thermal activity in the area which can be dangerous. Most people enjoy the sight of bubbling mud pools from the safety of boardwalks built in commercial thermal areas, however not all such areas are fenced off and charge admission. If you hike in Tongariro National Park, be careful of stepping through the crust into boiling mud as happened a few years ago to a foreign tramper near Ketetahi Springs, causing second degree burns.

New Zealand is also subject to occasional freak storms, cyclones and dangerous rip tides and undertows. See *Australia: Health* for advice on how to cope.

AIDS. The number of reported cases (less than 500) is low by American and European standards. Condom machines are quite widespread in hotels, though condoms are very expensive. In a chemist's shop you pay $17 for 12.

Crime and Safety

New Zealand enjoys a reputation for safety. It is far from nuclear threats — applications to emigrate rose substantially following the Chernobyl disaster — and and it has a mostly sane, law-abiding populace. The country's wholesomeness and safety extend to its city streets where crime, by world standards, is very low. The New Zealand version of the television programme *Crimewatch* had many of Clive James's viewers in the northern hemisphere helpless with laughter at the triviality of the crimes under investigation ('anyone who has seen this van from which a sheepskin rug was stolen on the evening of March 6th ...').

Police drive white cars with red and blue lights. They are barely in evidence on town and city streets. Unless you drive especially recklessly they will pay no attention, as a separate traffic department deals with road offenders.

Crime does exist, however, and is increasing at what New Zealanders consider an alarming rate. The New Zealand tourism authorities are worried that their country's safe image is being threatened. The disappearance of a Swedish couple who were tramping on the Coromandel Peninsula was the highest profile crime in a decade. A massive police operation over two years culminated in the arrest of a man who was convicted of raping and murdering them. This incident had the effect of galvanising New Zealanders into doing everything in their power to make tourists feel welcome and secure.

Tourists are a favourite target of thieves throughout the world and New Zealand is no exception, even if it does happen infrequently enough to make headlines. Usually the main targets are wealthy tourists, however there have been several reported cases of theft from backpackers' hostels. If your hostel gives you a key to your room, use it. Exercise a reasonable amount of caution, especially in remote sightseeing spots where tourists park. You might also think twice before camping alone in the middle of nowhere, though of course this is perfectly safe most of the time. Posters displayed at the ferry terminals in Wellington and Picton warn of the possibility of losing your rucksack on the ferry, so keep yours with you if possible. If you are unfortunate enough to lose one, pester the Railways Corporation for compensation, as they have been paying out lump sums of $1000.

An even more alarming trend was reported in the South Island of travellers perpetrating crimes, such as one who stole a moneybelt from a fellow hosteller, another who stole the car of a local after accepting a lift and still another who mugged a native who had offered a bed for the night. This kind of thing soon sours relations between travellers and locals.

Gangs are common in New Zealand, especially the Mongrel Mob whose large gatherings (for conventions or heavy rock concerts) are well publicised and are unlikely to affect travellers. However local gangs of street kids, often runaway teenagers, are a problem for late-night city strollers in certain streets such as Cuba Mall in Wellington. Serious problems are unlikely to arise unless you hassle them.

Drugs. Cannabis thrives in the New Zealand climate and is widely grown and consumed. The strain grown is said to be among the most potent in the world. The police periodically find large plantings amongst maize crops or forests, though they trace and destroy only a fraction of the total. The most recent big haul by helicopter (from which a detective fell and was killed) was from the Whangarei district, justifying Northland's reputation as the cannabis capital of the country. The drug enforcement authorities concentrate on prosecuting pushers and growers, though ordinary possession incurs a minimum fine of $100 up to $1,000 or a year's imprisonment or both. The Minister of Police wants to introduce on-the-spot fines for possession. A fairly strong and respectable lobby is calling for the legalisation of cannabis, on the grounds that enforcement is a waste of taxpayers' money and police time, and also that the drug search warrant powers have eroded civil rights. Most hitch-hikers will be offered a joint at some stage. A peculiarly New Zealand term for marijuana is 'electric puha'. Hard drugs are not as grave a problem as they are in Europe and North America.

The New Zealand government tourist organisation is the Visitor Information Network. It runs 23 Visitor Information Centres around the country, with some notable omissions (such as Christchurch) where tourism information is handled by the regional Canterbury Tourism Council. Overseas, the New Zealand Tourism Department is a commercial organisation which energetically publicises and promotes New Zealand tourism. The figures are impressive: until the Gulf War and world recession threw a spanner into the works, the number of overseas visitors was increasing by over 15% annually; numbers from the UK doubled between 1986 and 1991. For addresses, see page 23.

Useful additions to the range of information available to visitors are the free backpackers' newspapers available from hostels, etc. Both *Kiwi Backpacker* (36 Custom St, Auckland) and *New Zealand Backpackers News* (50 Somme St, St Albans, Christchurch) carry editorial material and advertisements of interest to young travellers, and provide a valuable supplement to the giveaway papers distributed by local tourist offices which contain useful information on regional events and performances.

In places without a Visitor Information Centre, you may find a local Public Relations Offices (PRO), one of whose tasks is to provide visitor information; relevant addresses are given in the appropriate sections of this book. Another source of information on local sights is the series of 17 regional *Jasons Passport Maps*, funded by advertisers and given away free at information centres.

The New Zealand Automobile Association has already been mentioned as a useful source of road maps, itineraries and motoring information. It also publish accommodation guides. Local district maps are free of charge, however a small charge is made for country maps. Literature is available only to members of affiliated motoring organisations.

For information on New Zealand maps contact the InfoMap Centre, Department of Survey and Land Information, Private Bag 903, Upper Hutt, New Zealand (04-527 7019). The InfoMap series includes a wide range of maps, from street maps to maps of walking tracks, and are available from most New Zealand map retailers and all DSLI offices (look under 'Land Information' in the *Yellow Pages*).

For a catalogue of New Zealand maps, write to the Infomap Centre, Private Bag, Upper Hutt, New Zealand (which is part of the Department of Survey and Land Information). Indicate whether you are interested in touring maps, regional park maps, topographical maps or walking track maps. The Infomap retail outlet is in Wellington at 103 Thorndon Quay.

Mothers travelling with children may make use of 'Plunket Rooms', located throughout New Zealand. The Plunket Society was formed at the beginning of the century to provide prenatal and postnatal advice and care. Their rooms are located centrally in most towns and have first class loos which women travellers may wish to visit.

Emergencies. To summon help by telephone, dial 111 in cities. Elsewhere call the operator (by dialling 010) or dial the toll-free emergency number posted in public call boxes.

If you are venturing into the wilderness, always register your route intentions with rangers or contacts who can alert Search and Rescue workers if you fail to return.

In the case of financial emergencies, see the section *Emergency Cash* on page 54 to find out about how to arrange for money to be transferred from home.

Consulates. The British High Commission is on the ninth and tenth floors of the Reserve Bank Building behind Parliament at the corner of The Terrace and Bowen Stt in Wellington (04-472 6049). There are also Consulates-General in Auckland (151 Queen St) and in Christchurch (The Dome, Regent Theatre Building, Cathedral Square). The American Embassy is at 29 Fitzherbert Terrace, Thorndon, Wellington.

Students. To book anything from a hired campervan to a whale-watching trip, visit the International Travellers Centre in Auckland (First Floor, 10 High St). Student Travel Services (NZ) Ltd (09-309 9723) and STA Travel (09-309 9995) are associates who specialise in student and young people's travel. Addresses in Christchurch, Dunedin and Wellington are given in the city chapters. Visitors holding an ISIC card are eligible for a range of domestic travel discounts and some discounts in theatres and cinemas.

PUBLIC HOLIDAYS

Six of the ten statutory holidays have fixed dates. These are Christmas, Boxing Day, New Year's Day, January 2, Waitangi Day on February 6 (to celebrate the signing of a treaty with the Maori people in 1840) and Anzac Day on April 25 (to commemorate the battle of Gallipoli where 88% of New Zealand troops died). Good Friday and Easter Monday change from year to year as does the Queen's Birthday (the first Monday in June) and Labour Day (the fourth Monday in October).

In addition each of the regions has an Anniversary Day, often commemorating the day the first ships arrived with their European settlers. Auckland's Anniversary is celebrated not only in the city but also in a region extending from the north of the country to Taupo. It is almost impossible to predict when some of these are going to be held, as they are decided each year and seem to have no standard formula.

NORTH ISLAND

Cape Reinga
Ninety Mile Beach
Mangonui
Kaitaia
Kerikeri
Bay of Islands
Paihia
Russell
Whangarei
Dargaville
GREAT BARRIER ISLAND
Kawau Island
Warkworth
Hauraki Gulf
Coromandel
AUCKLAND
Whitianga
Coromandel Peninsula
Manukau Harbour
Thames
Waihi
White Island
Mt Maunganui
TASMAN SEA
Tauranga
East Cape
Hamilton
Bay of Plenty
Lake Rotorua
Waitomo
ROTORUA
Mt Tarawera
Lake Taupo
Taupo
4
Gisborne
New Plymouth
Lake Waikaremoana
Poverty Bay
Turangi
2
Mt Ruapehu
3
Mt Taranaki
Ohakune
1
Hawke Bay
Pipiriki
Napier
Cape Kidnappers
Hastings
Wanganui
Palmerston North
1 Whanganui National Park
2 Egmont National Park
Otaki
3 Tongariro National Park
Paraparaumu
Castlepoint
4 Urewera National Park
Porirua
Masterton
WELLINGTON
Picton
Cook Strait
100 km
SOUTH ISLAND

The North Island

Population of Auckland: 910,000   **Population of Wellington: 350,000**

The North Island is far more densely populated than the South, containing nearly three-quarters of the country's total population. In addition to the capital Wellington and the largest city Auckland, six other cities have more than 50,000 people, which by New Zealand tandards is very populous indeed.

Whereas the most sensational geographical phenomena of the South Island are due to glaciation, the remarkable feature of the North is its volcanic history. The most impressive mountains of the North Island such as Mount Taranaki and Mount Ruapehu were formed as symmetrical cones by erupting volcanoes, and much of the surrounding land was enriched by the lava flows. Some volcanoes like Ngauruhoe are still active, though you are more likely to be swallowed up by an earthquake than buried in lava, as the possibility of full-scale eruptions is very remote.

Elsewhere on the North Island the scenery encompasses tame pastoral scenes, majestic tropical beaches and even a few barren near-deserts. Each of the two bulges of land halfway down the Island — the Taranaki Peninsula in the west and the East Coast Province — has its individual character and various attractions. There is a choice of routes from Auckland to Wellington but the boiling mud and geysers in the centre are not to be missed.

AUCKLAND

Some say that Auckland is Sydney for beginners. The harbourside location, complete with overcrowded bridge, justifies a comparison to some extent, but there are many differences. Though Auckland boasts of its sophistication, it has a long way to go before it can match Sydney's cultural life, restaurants and markets. Not that Auckland wants to emulate a city whose brash competitiveness and self-importance are well known. Auckland is proud of its low-rise skyline and of the fact that the best views of its city and harbour are to be had from the grass-covered hills rather than from the tops of 300-metre towers. Auckland is content with its achievements, which may be modest in comparison to those of Sydney but dramatic when compared to the rest of New Zealand. With nearly a third of the country's population concentrated in Greater Auckland, it is obvious that the city can offer more of everything to the international visitor.

What radical breakthroughs there are in New Zealand are more than likely to take place in Auckland. For example, shops and pubs tend to stay open later (first Saturday shopping and now Sunday shopping were pioneered in the fashionable suburb of Parnell) and night club acts are liable to be more risqué in Auckland than anywhere else in the country. This has the not necessarily desirable result of making Auckland more like other world cities, with the attendant problems of crime and commercialism, not to mention the predictability of modern urban life.

Yet Auckland has gone only some way down the road of progress. The city centre boasts many fine old buildings and green spaces that have been protected from the worst excesses of commercial development. Even the many American-style shopping arcades off Queen St do not manage to be convincing, perhaps because of the less-than-chic window-dressing and sign writing.

Great efforts have also been made to preserve and beautify the harbour and its surrounding buildings. The price to be paid for such renovations is that restored buildings such as the Old Customs House and the Auckland Ferry Building are now glorified shopping centres, but they are a definite visual asset, especially when viewed from the harbour. Even the wharves and warehouses behind the station look quite spruce.

Auckland's setting is also distinguished by the volcanic hills scattered around the city. In fact there is evidence of about 60 volcanoes inside the city limits. The trip to the top of one of these hills, such as Mount Eden or Mount Victoria on the North Shore, is worthwhile for an overview of the sprawling city — an Auckland poet has called it 'a series of easy sleazy villages' — and for the sudden rural ambience created by the sheep and cattle that graze in these reserves (called 'domains' in New Zealand). Even the Auckland Domain on which the Museum now stands is an ancient volcano. It is odd — but typical of New Zealand — to see the sign 'Wandering Stock' just minutes after leaving a fast city road.

CLIMATE

Auckland's weather in summer is mostly genial, and hot days send everyone to the North Shore beaches. The blistering heat of an Australian summer's day is rare, partly due to the moderating influence of the water that virtually surrounds Auckland. There is quite often a stiff breeze that creates attractive shifting skies and keeps down the humidity, but can also chill the air. The winters are normally mild (around 13°C) but fairly rainy, with July as the wettest month with an average of 21 days of precipitation.

The rest of the island follows a similar pattern, with an average rainfall of 135cm a year, though the eastern areas are somewhat drier. The southern parts of the island are several degrees cooler than Auckland, while Northland, the narrow peninsula stretching north of Auckland to the same latitude as Sydney, is semi-tropical and winters remain pleasantly mild. Unfortunately, this is also the wettest part of the North Island.

THE LOCALS

Although the population of the city is creeping towards one million, it retains a small-town atmosphere. A shop assistant in Sydney would be unlikely to initiate a friendly conversation with a foreign visitor about his or her proposed itinerary, yet this is not uncommon in Auckland where many residents have not yet lost the habits of hospitality. On the other hand, unpretentiousness and modesty are under threat in any big city. Auckland has not been immune to the pressures of yuppiedom and one-upmanship, which may manifest themselves as discourtesy on the roads or in conversation.

A large proportion of Auckland's population was not born in the city. Greater Auckland has been growing rapidly, both in population and in area, sprawling over an area twice that of London. Among the many newcomers is a large contingent of Samoans, Fijians, Tongans, Cook Islanders, etc., making Auckland the largest Polynesian city in the world. Their influence is most noticeable in those residential suburbs where there is a high proportion of rented accommodation. Although large numbers of Maori people live in the city, and the number is increasing, their profile is relatively low. In the downtown district, Karangahape Road (sometimes referred to simply as 'K Road') is the Polynesian area.

 **City Layout.** Because Auckland incorporates a number of hills and waterways, streets do not keep to a grid pattern, and it is not always easy to get your bearings. Even locating the sea is not a safe means of navigating as the Manukau Harbour to the south-west and the Waitemata Harbour to the north are only a few kilometres apart and could be confused by a newcomer gazing down from the top of Mount Eden. But it is usually possible to locate the cluster of downtown buildings as they are the only buildings more than a storey high.

ARRIVAL AND DEPARTURE

Air. Auckland International Airport is 23km south of the city in the suburb of Mangere. If you arrive in daylight, you will have the sensation of landing on water as your aircraft banks over Manukau Harbour on which the airport is situated.

The airport has a McDonalds, a TAB betting shop and other 'amenities' as well as more important additions such as a tourist information centre, a bank of courtesy phones for booking accommodation (including many hostels), and shops selling books, postcards and souvenirs in the arrivals-cum-transit lounge. Similarly, those departing from Auckland International Airport can spend their remaining dollars on Maori mementoes, kiwifruit wine, New Zealand cheddar, etc. in the departure lounge shops. If you are leaving the country, keep $20 aside for the departure tax that you must pay at check-in.

There are three separate terminals, one for international flights, one for Air New Zealand domestic services and one for Ansett New Zealand. The terminals are connected by a complimentary shuttle bus; even with luggage you should manage the 800m walk in 10 minutes.

The journey into town takes about 40 minutes. The cheapest way is to use Johnston's Airporter, the bus service that runs every 20 minutes to the Downtown Airline Terminal, dropping off passengers at hotels and hostels *en route*. The basic one-way fare is $10, although if YHA members remember to show their card they can pay just $6. Tickets may be purchased from the driver if you have not been able to buy them from the relevant counter at either end in advance.

Several other shuttle services cost a little more but take you door to door.

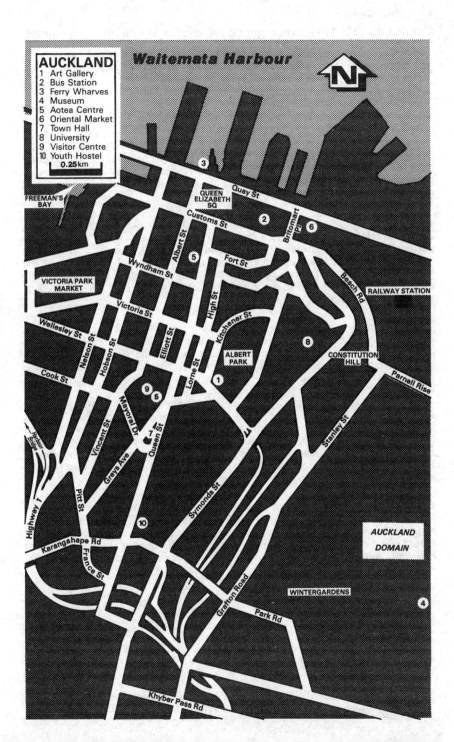

Shuttle Link (275 1234) is one option, and charges $14 for one person or $20 for two.

Taxi ranks are outside both international and domestic terminals. The fare to the city centre is about $35, with a surcharge after 10pm and at weekends. The Auckland Taxi Co-op (300 3000) operates a taxi share scheme that brings the price down to $10–12 per person.

Most airlines have their offices within a short distance of the Downtown Airline Terminal. Air New Zealand is on Quay St (379 7515). Ansett New Zealand is at 75 Queen St or 50 Grafton Road (302 2146). For cheap flights out of New Zealand try STA Travel at 10 High St (309 9995) or 29 Princes St.

Because of a recent expansion of fast water transport to islands in the Hauraki Gulf, several small commuter airlines and charter companies have disappeared from the scene. To fly to Great Barrier Island or the Bay of Islands, contact Great Barrier Airlines (275 9120).

Bus. The Downtown Airline Terminal at 86 Quay St (357 6606; next to the Travelodge Hotel) also acts as a depot for Newmans (0800-777 707) and its partner Northliner Express (307 5873). Intercity also has an office there. The Terminal is open daily 7am–6pm during the summer, and 8am–5pm in the winter. You can also leave luggage there ($2 for a half day, $4 for the whole day). InterCity (357 8400) uses the railway station as its depot and sells tickets from an office inside the station.

Train. The railway station (enquiries and bookings 0800-802 802) is on Beach Road, a street that, despite its name, does not run along the waterfront. Few city buses pass the station, so you may have to walk the 10 minutes from the city bus station or from the bottom of Symonds St. Pedestrians (unlike cars, which must make a detour) can reach the station by heading straight down Constitution Hill.

Like all railway stations in New Zealand, Auckland's rarely bustles; however its travel office is open from 7.45am to 5.30pm weekdays and 9am to noon weekends to advise. The two main departures each day are the *Silver Fern* at 8.30am and the *Northerner* at 8pm (arriving in Wellington at 6.40pm and 6.40am respectively). The left luggage office operates free of charge to InterCity clients. Because there is so little action at the station for much of the day, don't expect a row of taxis to be waiting for your arrival.

Driving. Comparison shopping among car hire firms is especially worthwhile. Promotional leaflets are widely available at information offices, hostels, etc. Most of the small rental firms offer to deliver the car to you free of charge. Note that it may be possible to negotiate a better rate than the ones originally quoted especially out of season. Here are a few of the cheaper local agencies:

Ace Tourist Rentals, 39 The Strand, Parnell (303 3112).
Adventure Campervans (256 0255). Campervan hire.
Best Value Rental Cars (275 6890).
Dizzy Duck, 1 Grosvenor St, Grey Lynn (377 8088).
Henderson Rental Cars, 34–38 Valley Road, Henderson (838 8089). Specialises in trucks and 4WD vehicles.
Kiwi Car Rentals, 430 Queen St (358 0188). Also hires out bicycles.
North Harbour Rental Cars (444 7795).
Russell's Rental Cars, 32A Tirimoana Road, Te Atutu South (836 3309). YHA members get a 10% discount.
Scotties Rentals, 33 Valley Road, Mount Eden (630 2625; toll-free 0800-736825). Run by a couple in Auckland and their brother in Christchurch. One-way rentals

available, with free airport pick-up. Also offer a buy-back and lease option for longer term visitors. Vehicles include stationwagons, and vans equipped with camping gear. Readers of this guide should get 10% off if they quote discount authority no. VW96KS.

Prospective car buyers should attend the Saturday car market at Newmarket on the Khyber Pass Road (at Broadway) early in the morning (before 10am). Or ask at Auto Court at 95 Ponsonby Road. Ask around for car dealers which offer a guaranteed buy-back deal; for example the Georgia Hostel (see *Accommodation*) can advise.

The AA is at 99 Albert St (377 4660).

Hitch-hiking. Because of its massive sprawl, Auckland is more awkward than other cities to hitch from. Nevertheless you can try to hitch south from almost the centre of town. From the top of Queen St, go over Grafton Bridge and walk down the steps to the motorway. For better prospects, invest in a bus to the end of the motorway, i.e. Albany if you are heading north or Papakura if you are heading south. The Greenlane roundabout is a favoured hitching spot for southbound travellers. But bear in mind that the locals will look kindly upon hitchers, so if you're down to your last $16 (i.e. the airport tax) and you're about to leave the country, you'll probably be able to hitch to the airport.

CITY TRANSPORT

Bus. The Auckland Regional Council (ARC) operates most city and suburban buses. Weekend evenings are a problem as all city buses stop at 5pm on Saturdays and Sundays. One alternative (apart from ringing for a taxi) is to ring one of the shuttle buses mentioned above in the context of transport from the airport. Under public transport deregulation changes that came into effect in 1991, a few late-night and weekend services are offered by taxi and private mini-bus companies in the outer suburbs.

The bus information kiosk is at Bus Place, 131 Hobson St. For information by phone ring Buz-a-Bus on 366 6400 (7am–9.30pm). Many buses originate at the Downtown Bus Terminal near Britomart Place which is near the harbour, just off Customs St East. Buses from outside the city centre will be marked either 'Downtown' or 'Midtown' depending on whether they terminate at the Downtown Bus Terminal or at the corner of Victoria and Queen Sts (i.e. Midtown). This corner has a large number of bus stops, plus plenty of friendly Aucklanders willing to advise travellers.

A few of the buses you might need are:

635, 645 and 655 to Parnell via the Domain (from platform 3 in the Downtown Bus Terminal).
005 to the Victoria Park Market.
302 to One Tree Hill (from Victoria St E).
274/275 from Customs St E for Mount Eden (for gardens, views and several good hostels)

The road along the harbour is called Tamaki Drive which takes you to the famous Kelly Tarlton Aquarium; take any bus beginning 72–76 from platform 1 in the Bus Terminal.

An inner city shuttle bus called the 'Street Car' runs along Queen St every ten minutes connecting the Ferry Building and the K Road. It is primarily a shoppers' bus and operates on weekdays between 7am and 6pm and Saturdays 8am-3pm; the fare is 40c.

Fares are calculated according to a system of zones. Inner-city rides are 40c, but fares outside start at $1 and increase to $6.60. The ARC offers a day pass called 'Busabout' which costs $8 and is valid on all city routes and at any time after 9am on weekdays. This is more flexible, and hence better value, than the $7 tourist Explorer Bus. This double-decker, operated by United Airlines, makes its circuit once an hour (10am-4pm only) from the Downtown Airline Terminal to the bungy-jumping spot at Freemans Bay (see *Sport* below) and on to Mission Bay, Kelly Tarlton's, Auckland Museum and Parnell.

Car. Parking restrictions operate between 8am and 6pm on weekdays except Fridays and late-shopping nights when the restrictions extend until 9pm. Finding a parking place is normally not a problem, but you are allowed to park only on the left side of the road, i.e. not facing oncoming traffic. Car parks can be found at the following city locations (among others): Britomart Place beside the bus terminal, Victoria St E and High St (near the university), the Civic Centre on Mayoral Drive, and the corner of Customs St W and Hobson St. Charges in car park buildings and downtown meters average about 50c for half an hour, though there are some bargains if you are willing to walk a little. For example the car park at the new Chinese Markets on Quay St charges $1 a day.

Traffic does not usually get snarled up, except on the kilometre-long Harbour Bridge. When the bridge was opened in 1959 it had only four lanes which soon proved inadequate. A Japanese engineering firm later attached four more lanes to the bridge which are universally known as the Nippon Clip-ons. But even eight lanes are not enough for the 90,000 vehicles which now cross daily. The Auckland Regional Council has approved the building of a tunnel (instead of a second bridge or a monorail suspended from the present bridge) though this will not be completed for some time.

Taxis. Call Auckland Taxi Co-op on 300 3000, Alert Taxis on 309 2000 or Eastern Taxis on 527 7077. Do not try to hail a cab downtown; find the nearest taxi rank.

Cycling. Although you need to cycle a long way to get out of the city and into the countryside, a bicycle is a useful way to reach points of interest within the city. The Regional Council publishes a free leaflet with a 50km cycle tour of the city and isthmus, which you can pick up at the Auckland Visitor Centre.

You can hire bikes from any of the following: Pennyfarthings (corner Khyber Pass Road and Symonds St; 792 524), Georgia Backpackers Hostel (see below), Backpackers Bicycle Hire (430 Queen St; 358 0188), which advertises ten-speeds at $10 a day, Pedal Pushers (360 0512) or Bicycle Tour Services (22 Walmsley Road, Orahuhu; 276 5218).

Cycles are forbidden on the Harbour Bridge, so take a boat instead; the fare for bikes is $1, but no charge is made at weekends.

Ferries. A trip on the Waitemata Harbour should not be missed. The shortest trip is the one to Devonport on the North Shore, a service used by commuters who wish to avoid the bridge as well as by joy-riders. North Shore Ferries (303 3319) operates this 15 minute service every half hour during the rush hours Monday to Friday (6.15-9.15am and 3-6.30pm) and hourly during the day: on the hour if departing from the Downtown Ferry Building in the city and on the half hour returning from Devonport. The fare is $3.50 single, $6 return. The historic ferry *MV Kestrel* operates as a floating party on Friday and Saturday evenings with traditional jazz and bar facilities from 7am for $10.

Ferries also serve the islands in the harbour such as Rangitoto, Waiheke and Great Barrier Island. These trips are dealt with in the section *Further Afield*.

If you plan to arrive at Auckland airport in the high season or late at night, it might be worth booking your budget accommodation ahead. A number of hostels have courtesy phones at the information desk in the airport and will advise on transport or even provide their own courtesy shuttle. You may also see a booth for hostel touts. The competition is fierce, and worth exploiting for discounts and special deals. Although there is a choice of affordable accommodation downtown, some travellers find the city centre a bit scruffy and dead compared to Parnell, Ponsonby, Mount Eden, etc.

YHA Hostels. There are two Auckland hostels, one in the city and one in Parnell. The City Hostel is at the corner of City Road and Liverpool St (309 2802), not far from Queen St and next to the Sheraton. Overnight fees are relatively high, but the hostel has most things that backpackers might need, including a complete travel booking service for buses, trains and ferries. The Parnell Hostel is at 2 Churton St (379 3731) and is a bit cheaper.

Private Hostels. There are many hostels in addition to those run by the YHA, and like the YHA hostels many of these run an ancillary travel service and advise on car hire, public transport, and so on. One hostel held in high regard is Georgia Parkside Backpackers, 189 Park Road, Grafton (309 8999), at the south-west corner of Auckland's Domain. Its cheapest dorm beds are $12, although you need to stay for more than three nights to get this rate. Another popular hostel is City Garden Lodge (25 St Georges Bay Road; 302 0880), which starts at $16/17 for small dorms. Nearby are Lantana Lodge (60 St Georges Bay Road; 373 4546), which has similar rates, and Leadbetter Lodge at number 17 (0800-506 888), which has dorm beds from $11. Ponsonby Backpackers at 2 Franklin Road, Ponsonby (360 1311) charges similar prices.

There are a couple of highly rated hostels near the centre in Queen St, under the same management. Kiwi Hilton Backpackers at number 430 (358 3999) has dorm beds from $9.50, and Aotea Square Backpackers at number 295 (303 3350) has beds in its spacious dorms for $10. Both hostels also offer good value car and campervan rentals. Another good one is International Backpackers at 8 Maunsell Avenue (358 4584), which benefits from having a quiet and peaceful location. Dorm beds are $14. Berlin Lodge (formerly Mount Eden Backpackers) is at 5a Oaklands Road, Mount Eden (638 6545), and has dorm beds at the same price, as well as a range of smaller rooms.

Downtown Backpackers is at 6 Constitution Hill (303 4768) and has prices in line with the other hostels; it also has a policy of accepting only passport-carrying foreigners, which you may or may not regard as a good thing. Ideally located for the centre is Auckland Central Backpackers (9 Fort St; 358 4877), which is cheap, busy and well equipped.

If the above places are all full, some more you can try include Eden Lodge, 22 View Road, Mount Eden (630 0174) and the long-established Ivanhoe Lodge, 14 Shirley Road, Grey Lynn (846 2800). Another alternative is the YWCA at 10 Carlton Gore Road (377 8763).

Guest Houses and Hotels. As usual there is a sizeable leap in price from hostel-style accommodation to the bed and breakfasts and guest houses. One exception is the Grande Vue Tourist Hotel (303 3017) at the corner of Princes St and Eden Crescent, which has relatively low prices. Another cheap one is Freeman's Bed & Breakfast at 65 Wellington St (376 5046) near the Victoria Park Market, which has four self-catering apartments costing $85 for one or two people, and

$12 for each additional person, as well as friendly B & B accommodation for $45 single, $65 double and $83 triple. Another good B & B is Aachen House, 39 Market Road, Remuera (520 2329), which charges $65 single, $90 double, although a recent change of management may mean that these prices will change. The most conveniently located hotel, though not a B & B, is the Kiwi International at 411 Queen St (379 6487), which has singles and doubles/twins (with shared facilities) for $39 and $49, respectively, and 'bunkroom' beds at $20 per person.

Other B & B choices are the Bavaria Bed & Breakfast Hotel (83 Valley Road, Mount Eden; 638 9641), which has single and double/twin rooms for $69 and $99, respectively; the Ascot Parnell (36 St Stephens Avenue, Parnell; 309 9012), whose rates are $78.50 single and $117 double/twin; and Aspen Lodge at 62 Emily Place (379 6698).

To be near the airport for some reason, you might choose the Skylodge International Motel (144 McKenzie Road, Mangere; 275 1005), which has a budget hostel, or the Auckland Airport Skyway Lodge (30 Kirkbride Road, Mangere; 275 4443), which has a range of accommodation, starting at $17 per night.

Camping. There are a number of motorcamps and caravan parks in and around Auckland. Meadowcourt Motel near the airport (630 Great South Road, Manukau; 278 5612) has plenty of space for tents ($7 per person). The North Shore Caravan Park (419 1320) is 5km north of the bridge and has a large number of on-site caravans and cabins. Finally the Tui Glen Motor Camp in the scenic wine-growing area of Henderson west of Auckland (3 Edmonton Road; 836 8978) has budget units available for $35 double in addition to caravan and tent sites.

Eating and Drinking

Auckland is by far the most cosmopolitan city in New Zealand and therefore has the best range of restaurants and food shops. As Aucklanders have gradually overcome their suspicion of foreign cuisine, ethnic restaurants representing a broad range of nationalities have sprung up. It may be that they are a little behind the fashions and trends (for example Middle Eastern food is extremely popular and Thai food is just catching on) but there is plenty of choice and there are some delightful and original restaurants scattered throughout the city. Odd combinations of cuisine such as Russian and Middle Eastern (at Le'Haim) or Mexican and Filipino (at Papagayo) are reminiscent of some of the unusual gastronomic bedfellows to be found in Sydney. An Auckland by-law stipulates that all restaurants must provide a genuine smoke-free zone.

For Auckland's version of the international food hall, try the Chinese Market on Quay St which has about 14 stalls selling main dishes for about $5 each. Similarly the Plaza Shopping Centre at 128 Queen St has ten different ethnic food stalls serving only during shopping hours.

The company which publishes the ubiquitous *Tourist Times* giveaway also distributes a free *Dining Guide* newspaper which covers 140 restaurants and cafés (which have paid to be included). The published menus should whet your appetite and give a specific idea of prices. Most first courses cost $6-$10, main courses $15-$20 and desserts about $8. The Auckland Visitor Centre also have printed lists of restaurants but with no indication of menus or cuisine.

Probably the best street for browsing for restaurants is the Ponsonby Road. Interesting restaurants are scattered along its entire length. There are a number of BYO restaurants featuring modern New Zealand cuisine (e.g. rack of lamb in a lemon thyme sauce, seafood with chillis, ginger and lemon grass) and a range of ethnic restaurants. Here is a selection in numerical order: at 29 Ponsonby

Road there is a Korean barbecue restaurant called Nihonkaku; at 42A, Sawadee serves Thai food; at 43, Wheelers serves contemporary food; similarly the Bronze Goat at 108 and Oblio's at 110 have innovative dishes like chicken livers with cherries or home smoked mussels; at 222, the Cotton Club is a Cajun restaurant with live jazz; Prego at number 226 is Italian, Spanish 260 at that number serves Spanish dishes in two sizes ($9.50 or $18); Alhambra at 283 has live music to accompany its eclectic menu and Dr Livingstone I Presume at number 286 supplies marshmallows for toasting to accompany its interesting menu.

Parnell is the most upmarket area of town, but it has some affordable cafés and ethnic restaurants as well as fine established restaurants. Firmly in the latter category is La Trattoria at 259 Parnell Road which, like many Parnell restaurants, has an outdoor eating area. The many Italian eateries include the eccentric Valerios (number 311) and the more straightforward Zigolini's (number 421). Pizzerias include Gino's Portofino at 156 and the associated Portobello at 131. Parnell has plenty of cafés where you can stop just for a cappuccino. There are trendy California-style bar-grills like Veranda (number 279) and Rick's (mentioned below in the section on *Music*). Among the ethnic cuisines available, try Bananas at number 317 which has a selection from almost every South Asian country, Pars Tandoori for an upmarket Indian restaurant and Papagayo at number 333 mentioned above for its surprising combination of Mexican, Spanish and Filipino food. If you've become hooked on nouvelle Antipodean, try Feel for Food at number 251 or Memphis at number 100. As the premier shopping street of Auckland, Parnell Road also has good food shopping: try Fraser's Place, a delicatessen with upstairs café at number 116, or the Gourmet Cookshop at 390.

A quite different atmosphere exists on the Karangahape Road, an area which some have seen as a (very) watered-down version of Sydney's Kings Cross. If there is a South Pacific area of Auckland this is it, though don't expect to find restaurants representing this cuisine. Here the bars are rougher and the restaurants not quite so well scrubbed though you can find trendy places charging lower prices than restaurants in more desirable neighbourhoods. The El Inca restaurant can be found at number 335 where South American food is served and live music is sometimes provided. Vesuvio at number 309 also provides live music at weekends. Clowns at number 469 has original and unusual dishes (BYO or licensed; minimum charge per head $20); it is closed on Sundays and Mondays. Shesh Besh at number 98 is a reasonably priced Israeli restaurant. Yamato at number 183 serves Japanese dishes more cheaply than those served at Auckland's downtown Japanese restaurants.

Naturally the city centre also has good cafés and restaurants. For example the Mexican Café (upstairs at 67 Victoria St W) was voted ethnic restaurant of the year in 1991. Despite being licensed rather than BYO it is not expensive (main courses average $14); to save on the price of cocktails go to the happy hour between 5 and 7pm. Another choice for Mexican food fans is Panchos at 18 Elliott St. Further along Elliott St at number 39 is Le'Haim Mediterranean Café which unexpectedly specialises in Russian food: a meal of smoked salmon blinis with caviare and sour cream plus a shot of vodka will cost $16.50. Around the corner is the Middle East Café at 23A Wellesley St, which specialises in four dishes, chawarma, vegetarian falafel, sis kebab and salads, where a tasty lunch would cost $7.50 and a one-plate dinner $12.

Just a few minutes away is High St (running parallel to Queen St) where you might be tempted by the cheap vegetarian food at Badgers (number 47) or at Simple Cottage (number 50). Around the corner in Vulcan Lane try the Kerouac Deli for lunch. Continuing away from the waterfront, High St turns into Lorne St where another wholefood café called Domino's serves cheap food, while carnivores can indulge in the excellent steaks served at Tony's (number 32).

There is an unlicensed 24-hour café on Customs St E. Queen St itself is packed full of restaurants. Among the best are Baan Thai at 456 and Caravanserai at 430.

Indian restaurants are few, but one you might like to try is the upmarket Maharajah appropriately located on Khyber Pass Road at number 19; it is open Tuesday-Saturday from 6pm, and is BYO. In fact there are several good Asian restaurants along this road, for example two Thai restaurants at 473 and 477 (Sri Siam and Chao Phraya), and a Szechuan restaurant the Great Wok of China at number 404. Perhaps the most authentic Chinese food in Auckland is available from the Hong Kong Kitchen, 5-7 Albert St downtown.

If you are staying at a hostel in one of the suburbs like Mount Eden it won't be necessary to go into town for dinner. Ask the people in your hostel for recommendations. Further afield are the numerous restaurants in Mission Bay, a picturesque seaside community along Tamaki Drive, such as Hammerhead Restaurant at number 19. Devonport also offers good eating, especially on Victoria Road; try Something Fishy at 71 or Portofino at 26.

Chinese take-aways are generally of good quality, much better than their English counterparts. These are scattered liberally around the city and prices are low. Some will even deliver to your door, for example Dial-a-Chinese on 792 702. Fish and chip shops are also easy to find. Finally, for breakfast at any time of the day or night, go to the City Café at the corner of Customs St E and Queen St, open 24 hours.

DRINKING
The good news is that a few Auckland bars have taken advantage of the new 24-hour licence. The bad news it that these are both in posh hotels, the Regent on Albert St and the Pan Pacific on Mayoral Drive. Still, opening hours are generally loosening up and so you shouldn't find yourself being kicked out at 10.30pm on a Friday night wherever you choose to socialise.

If you want to talk about your travels with like-minded people go for a drink at the Backpackers Pub on the corner of Hobson and Victoria Sts (in the Downtown City Hostel). If you want to meet Auckland students, go to the Kiwi, a basic pub on Symonds St which often gets packed.

A more interesting selection of drinks can be found at the Shakespeare Tavern at 62 Albert St (on the corner of Wyndham St) which has the distinction of housing one of New Zealand's boutique breweries. A range of ales, stouts and lagers are brewed on the premises including Sir Toby Belch's Ginger Beer (low-alcohol) and the very potent King Lear Old Ale (original gravity of 7.5%). The other hotel which serves these brews is the Strand Tavern at the bottom of Parnell Rise. Another wonderful pub in Parnell is the Nags Head on the St Georges Bay Road which has six draught beers and a good atmosphere. Watch for pubs advertising Stockan beers (brewed in Henderson). Guinness drinkers should head for the harbourside suburb of Herne Bay where there is a pub which sells a good approximation of the real thing.

One of the best wine selections in Auckland can be found at Hancocks near the Victoria Park Markets (Corner Sale and Wellesley Sts). Much of New Zealand's wine is grown not far from Auckland in the Henderson region and a tour of the vineyards can make an enjoyable day trip. If you are more interested in beer, ring Lion Breweries on 377 8840 to see if a tour can be arranged.

Exploring

Auckland's downtown overlooks the picturesque Waitemata Harbour where yachts career over the surface and ferries wend their way to the offshore islands or to the North Shore where many fairly affluent Aucklanders choose to reside. The North Shore also has shops, museums and beaches of interest to visitors who can choose between the ferry or the Auckland Harbour Bridge to get there. Cruises on the harbour are a popular form of entertainment, and have become more so now that Pacifica have introduced their high speed *Wave Piercer* hovercraft and Fullers have fast catamaran services to the islands.

After many years of boasting an 11-storey office building as its tallest skyscraper, Auckland now has the Pacific Tower on Albert St which was opened in 1991 and has 41 storeys. You might also want to visit the observation deck of the BNZ Tower at 125 Queen St for a view over the city's magnificent setting.

Most tourist handout maps cover only the downtown area, so if you want to visit the interesting North Shore suburb of Devonport or other suburbs, you will have to purchase a detailed map with street index, such as the ones produced by Minimaps. (Note that the one called *Auckland City* includes the eastern suburbs, which are of limited interest to visitors, but not the North Shore. A separate map covers Devonport, Takapuna, etc. while the *Metromap* covers central Auckland in more detail.) The AA publish a useful map in colour of Downtown Auckland, which clearly shows the amount of green space, as well as many landmarks. Queen St running down from the Karangahape Road to Customs St near the waterfront is Auckland's main shopping street.

The Auckland Visitor Centre in Aotea Square (off Queen St) has a leaflet called *Heritage Trail*, which allows you to guide yourself on a two-hour walking tour. Taking yourself on a walking tour of the inner suburb of Parnell is also recommended.

Museums and Galleries. Although the excellent Auckland Museum is called the War Memorial Museum, military memorabilia comprise only a part of the collection. There are superb Maori and Polynesian exhibits, including a meeting house and war canoe. Some of the Museum's holdings, such as burial chests, still hold spiritual significance for certain Maori tribes who are lobbying to have them returned, so the collection is unlikely to increase. Admission is free. There are tours around the Maoritanga hall at 10.30am and 12.45pm daily. The Pounamu Maori Cultural Group puts on performances of music and dance in the Museum auditorium at 11.30am and 1.45pm which last half an hour and cost $6.50. Among the other exhibits is one devoted to paintings of early Auckland, while another shows Auckland from its geological beginnings to the present. The Museum is open from 10am to 5pm daily (309 0443) and admission is free. Catch a Parnell bus (635/655) from platform 3 of the bus terminal.

A new open-air museum that will feature Auckland's Maori past is scheduled to be built on the volcanic cone of Mount Mangere (*en route* to the Airport).

The Auckland City Art Gallery is in the corner of Albert Park where Wellesley St intersects with Kitchener St (792 069). Although it has some Old Masters, it specialises in New Zealand art both colonial and contemporary. One entire room is devoted to paintings in which the Maori people feature. The building itself is in an elaborate mock-French style favoured by the Victorians. The Gallery is open daily 10am–4.30pm and offers free guided tours at midday Monday to Friday and 2pm on Sundays. There is an admission charge for some prestigious special exhibitions. The Gallery has also opened a contemporary art wing — known as the New Gallery — based in a building across the road (307 7700).

There are of course many other specialist museums and art collections in Auckland. At any one time you should be able to choose from about 25 special exhibitions, ranging from a display of artists-against-mining of the Coromandel Peninsula to an exhibition of horseracing greats. One of the best museums in Auckland is the Museum of Transport, Technology and Social History (846 7020), usually referred to as MOTAT, which houses collections covering trams, rail, steam, road transport and aviation, as well as a Victorian village and a 1920s shopping street. It is on two sites (linked most of the way by tram) on Great North Road and Motions/Meola Roads, Western Springs. Admission is $8, with 25% off for YHA cardholders. Take bus 045 (Pt Chevalier) from Customs St.

Other permanent museums include the Naval Museum on Spring St in Devonport (open 10am–4.30pm), the National Racing Museum at Ellerslie Racecourse (open racedays only, unless arrangements for a group visit are made; 524 4069) and Kinder House at the corner of Ayr St and Parnell Road. The latter contains photos and paintings of early Auckland by Rev. John Kinder, and charges admission of $1. It is open 11–3pm except Sundays. The new Hobson Wharf National New Zealand Maritime Museum is in downtown Auckland (358 1019).

The New Zealand Historic Places Trust has opened several Victorian properties to the public, including Ewelme in Parnell, once owned by a clergyman with the glorious name of Vicesimus Lush. Locations and opening hours are readily available from the Auckland Visitor Centre.

Parks and Zoos. The largest park is the 200-acre Domain, whose volcanic hill is crowned by the War Memorial Museum. As you stroll up the hill from downtown, watch for confused-looking ducks trying to cross Domain Drive to the duck pond. Be warned also that if the wind is blowing unfavourably, the odours from the margarine factory on the south side of the park can be unpleasant. The Wintergardens below the Museum contain some exotic plants; the green-houses are open from 10am–4pm. If you continue past the Museum and down the other side you are on your way to Parnell.

WATCH OUT FOR FLOCKS OF DUCKS CROSSING DOMAIN DRIVE IN AUCKLAND.

The other big hills scattered around Greater Auckland are also domains (i.e. city parks). There are some remains of a Maori fort at the top of Mount Eden (bus 274/5 from Customs St East) and pleasant Eden Gardens is nearby (admission $2 in an honesty box). An observatory at the bottom of the instantly recognisable One Tree Hill (bus 302 from Victoria St East) is open to the public on Tuesday and sometimes Thursday evenings in summer. On clear nights you can look through the telescopes (admission $4 or $6), but there are displays and events whatever the weather; ring 656 945 for details.

The Botanical Gardens are 27km from the city centre and are virtually inaccessible by public transport but might be worth stopping to see if you are driving south on the motorway or to the airport. The Gardens are located at 102 Hill Road in Manurewa (266 7158) and are open 9am-5pm; free admission. Another distant attraction you are unlikely to see is the Rainbow's End Adventure Park (262 2030) off the Southern Motorway.

Auckland has a zoo of international stature where most native New Zealand fauna can be seen. It is located in Western Springs near MOTAT to which it is connected by an electric tram. The zoo is trying to breed endangered species like the flightless kakapo and the prehistoric tuatara; the latter provide very little entertainment to zoo-goers as it seems that the way they have survived for so many millenia is by never moving. The nocturnal house is a better bet, as that is where you can see kiwis. Admission is $8.50 (378 7487 or 378 1620). Take bus 045 from Customs St E to Western Springs.

Pursuing the wildlife theme, Auckland has an extraordinary aquarium which almost gives visitors the impression that they are under the sea. It is named after its late founder Kelly Tarlton who opened his underwater world in 1985. Despite the crowds and the steep admission charge of $9, it is fun to move alongside giant sharks, winged stingrays, etc. just on the other side of the acrylic tunnel. The moray eels, kingfish and a few other species are fed by divers at 2pm. The tourist literature makes it sound almost as big as Disneyworld, whereas the circular tunnel would in fact fit into an average school classroom. In case you feel you have not got your money's worth, there are changing exhibitions and films about Tarlton's wreck diving around New Zealand's shores. It is open 9am-9pm (528 0603) and is accessible by any bus heading out along Tamaki Drive, i.e. numbers starting 72, 73 74, 75 or 76.

SHOPPING

If the sheepskin and greenstone emporia along Queen St do not thrill you, the Victoria Park Market, a ten-minute walk away on Victoria St W, might hold more appeal. Handicrafts, fashionable clothing and jewellery, farmers' produce, etc. are all on display. Perhaps to prevent it from turning into a flea market, second-hand goods may not be sold. You can also buy food and snacks (including good quality ice cream) and listen to musicians and buskers. It is open daily from 9am (10am on Sundays) and closes at 7pm. There is a separate weekend market in the car park with lots of casual traders trying to entice you to buy from their $25 racks.

The newest market in Auckland is the Chinese Market on Quay St past the city Bus Station. It has nearly 150 stalls, which feature artificial plants, New Zealand football jerseys, African crafts and many other objects which have nothing to do with the Orient. Although it is worth a visit, be prepared for a somewhat plastic touristy atmosphere. For the complete antithesis you can venture out to the southern suburb of Otara (Newbury Road, off East Tamaki Road) where there is a colourful Polynesian flea market on Saturday mornings.

Specialist craft shops abound both downtown and in the glamorous shopping districts of Parnell, Remuera and Ponsonby. There is an extensive craft market on the third Sunday of the month (10am-4pm) in the Old Mission House in Mission Bay (out Tamaki Drive) and on some Saturdays a craft fair is held in the Holy Trinity Church in Devonport (near the ferry wharf). Shoppers might like to visit Devonport which has a high proportion of twee shops.

The 1980s in Auckland saw an epidemic of upmarket shopping centres. The Customhouse is a renovated building from the 1880s, housing cafés and tourist shops, a junior version of The Rocks in Sydney. There is an epidemic of such centres: the Queen's Arcade is just across the road and the restored Ferry

Building is yet another upmarket shopping complex. Duty-free shopping is available nearby at the downtown terminal (Quay and Albert Sts). Expansion of such facilities has been brought to a halt by the current recession which has hit Auckland especially hard (resulting in some heavily discounted prices in an effort to move stock at any price). The closure of the six-storey Farmers Trading Company department store on Hobson St leaves the city centre without a major department store. Like so many cities in the western world, people tend to shop for ordinary items in their local suburb, leaving the downtown area to tourists. The waterfront area of Auckland has gone so upmarket that even the Central Post Office has been chased away and may be turned into a casino. If you need something specific like a watch-repairer or stationery shop, you will either have to ask a local to steer you towards one, or traipse in and out of the numerous arcades off Queen St. On Queen St between Marmion and Waverley Sts is Real Groovy Records and its associate Groovy Threads, where you can stock up on 1960s music and buy what used to be called fab gear.

Most shops close at noon on Saturdays. The exceptions are Parnell (where shops stay open 10am-4pm on Saturdays and Sundays) and some downtown shopping centres such as the Customhouse and the Ferry Building which are open seven days a week.

The shop at the War Memorial Museum is worth a browse as it carries good quality artefacts, greeting cards, etc. Similarly the Conservation Centre on the corner of the Karangahape Road and Liverpool St sells gifts made of natural timbers, etc. The Greenpeace Shop is at 16 High St. For New Age clothing, try Stranded in Aotearoa at 119 Symonds St. Wheeler's Bookshop near the Remuera post office specialises in New Zealand books and cards. The Broadsheet Bookshop at 476 Mount Eden Road and the Women's Bookshop at 228 Dominion Road carry feminist books.

If you are planning any outdoor expeditions in New Zealand and haven't brought your own equipment, you might consider buying second-hand gear and then selling it at the end of your trip. The Sports Bazaar on the K Road (number 538) has a large stock of second-hand tents, sleeping bags, boots and packs which they will buy back from you. Many travellers find that this is cheaper than renting. The Secondhand Sports Shop at 14 Upper Queen St might be worth checking out as well. Tisdalls at 176 Queen St specialises in upmarket tramping gear, though it tries to cater for less committed outdoor types too. The YHA office and shop is at 36 Customs St at the corner of Gore St (794 224).

Every suburb has its own shopping area and these are worth visiting if only for their evocation of neighbourhood shopping a couple of decades ago (though with some Polynesian adaptations). Beside a typical Antipodean bakery specialising in pink-iced buns, you will find a Polynesian greengrocer selling all manner of unrecognisable fruits and vegetables. Even the most staid-looking suburban shopping area probably has a Pacific Island emporium selling cheap and cheerful basketware, toys, housewares, etc. There is a good one in Three Kings.

Entertainment

The *New Zealand Herald* carries extensive entertainment listings. The tourist giveaways are also useful in this respect, for example the small-format *Great Time Guide* and the *Tourist Times* newspaper both list sports and cultural events, as well as including information on forthcoming exhibitions. Look out also for the *Metro Magazine*.

At long last Auckland has a proper arts centre. The Aotea Centre opened in September 1990 to much acclaim with Kiri Te Kanawa singing at the opening ceremony, fulfilling a promise she had made many years ago to inaugurate New

Zealand's first purpose-built opera house. Although there have been complaints about inadequate acoustics, the Aotea Centre is a big improvement on Auckland's other cultural venue, the Town Hall. The Centre is located in Aotea Square near the corner of Queen and Wellesley Sts. In front of it is the Visitor Centre where you can pick up a quarterly *Aotea Centre Events Guide* to tell you what operas, ballets, plays (both mainstream and experimental) are coming to Auckland. Alternatively ring 309 2678 for recorded information, 307 5050 for general information about the Centre or 307 5040 to enquire about tickets. Tickets for most shows are distributed through BASS (307 5000) which charges a $5 transaction fee in addition to the ticket price of around $35. (For some shows, students can get $20 standby tickets half an hour before curtain time.) There is a booking office at the corner of Queen and Victoria Sts (366 0541) or ring The Corner on 303 3206. All the facilities in the Aotea Centre seem to be sponsored, from the Air New Zealand foyer to the Chase lounge bar. Best of all is the doorway sponsored by a retail company and called, in all seriousness, Farmers Entrance. The Centre mounts (sponsored) exhibitions and puts on free foyer entertainment such as puppet shows; free summer lunchtime concerts (mostly jazz) are held Tuesday to Friday at 12.30pm.

The concert hall and theatre in the nearby Town Hall are still used for second-string concerts and other entertainments.

Music. As mentioned in the section on eating, a number of restaurants attract customers with live music. Similarly bars often put on evening entertainment both at the weekends and during the week when business is slower. Surprisingly, Saturday afternoons are a popular time for live entertainment, ever since the Alexandra Tavern in Parnell began this trend in the mid-1970s. The main venue for international name bands is the Western Springs Stadium with a capacity of 60,000. For the benefit of complaining locals, the City Council limits the number of summer rock concerts to six. The other main concert location is the Mount Smart Stadium.

The most prestigious venue is the Gluepot, in the Ponsonby Club Hotel (corner of Jervois and Ponsonby Roads). There are two other venues in the hotel which feature less well known acts. Another of Auckland's better known venues is Rocks in the Attic in the Imperial Arcade at 44 Queen St. Ricks Blue Falcon Restaurant and Club at 27 Falcon St in Parnell has live music every night except Tuesday, while in its sister venue, Rick's Café American in the Victoria Park Market, you can listen to music to accompany your goat curry or pan-fried sardines on Sundays and Mondays only.

Jazz can be heard at a number of hotels at weekends including the Strand Tavern (mentioned in *Drinking*), and the associated Birdcage Tavern at 133 Franklin Road (which runs off the Ponsonby Road). The main jazz club is the Cotton Club at 222 Ponsonby Road (Wednesday to Saturday from 8pm). The Inner City Blues & Folk Club is held on Mondays from 10pm at Java Jive. An annual folk festival is held in late January at Oratia, outside the city limits on the road to the Waitakere hills.

If you want to hear some classical music without paying the $35 required to see the New Zealand Symphony Orchestra or Auckland Philharmonia at the Aotea Centre or Town Hall, then try the School of Music's free lunchtime concerts given by students at the university; the theatre is at 6 Symonds St.

Theatre. The theatrical life of Auckland is far from moribund. The established Mercury Theatre on France St (303 3869) favours a safe programme (Broadway hits, Gilbert & Sullivan, popular farces, etc.) but has a second stage upstairs called The Gods where more experimental plays can be seen. (The motorway bisects France St, so you should be aware that the Mercury is at the Karangahape Road end.) Student standby tickets are often available for Mercury productions.

The main auditorium in the Aotea Centre is the ASB theatre, which seats 2250 people. The much smaller Herald Theatre has a more innovative programme. One of the losses to the theatre scene is His Majesty's Theatre which used to be Auckland's West End clone; although a fierce battle was waged to save the Victorian horseshoe theatre building, it was torn down a few years ago and the site is now just a hole in Queen St.

In summer try to attend an outdoor performance. Free performances of Shakespeare plays etc. are put on in the University grounds each January/February; remember to take a blanket or a cushion. Good plays are often mounted at the University of Auckland's Maidment Arts Centre during term, so make enquiries (793 685). Sunday evenings are taken over by United Theatrespots, spontaneous events which involve audience participation.

Cinema. There is usually no shortage of films in Auckland, though many cinemas are located in distant suburban shopping centres. To find out what's showing at the Mid-City Cinema Centre (four screens on Queen St), ring 302 0277 or 309 7445, though they don't take phone bookings. Also on Queen St is another cinema complex, the St James Theatre (303 3264). Tickets cost $4.95 for any film starting before 5pm.

The best art cinemas are the Capitol Theatre, the lovely renovated building at 610 Dominion Road in Balmoral (630 0634), and the Devonport Cinema at 56 Victoria Road, Devonport (445 4470); both feature exotic ice creams. Ask about Tuesday discounts. You can also find interesting reruns at the Hollywood in Avondale (20 St Georges Road; 828 8393). Classic movies of the past are screened at 4pm on weekends; they even have a Wurlitzer organ played to accompany silent films. Its sister cinema is the Classic at 321 Queen St, which shows continuous adult movies.

SPORT

The *Great Time Guide*, distributed free of charge through a number of downtown and airport outlets, carries a diary of forthcoming sports events, almost all of which seem to be racing (either cars or horses). The two main tracks for flat racing are at Ellerslie and Avondale, whereas most trotting club meetings are at the Alexandra Park Raceway in Epsom, which has a happy hour from 5pm. Sample prices for admission to Ellerslie are $15 for the stands (where dress standards are enforced), $7 on the lawn and free in the infield. It has pleasant gardens which are open 8am-7pm, as well as the museum of racing mentioned above. Cricket and rugby are played at recently refurbished Eden Park.

Whether you want to participate or merely be an observer, you will want to pay a visit to Bungee Bats at the bottom of Halsey St (just west of downtown). Jumps into the harbour from about $85 take place between 11am and 6pm; bookings can be made on 303 0030. You can choose whether or not you want to enter the water.

Another New Zealand invention for adventurous types is available near Auckland. Sky-cat flying is like hang gliding but requires less skill. This takes place on weekends at Takapuna Beach on the North Shore and costs $20 to $30 for half an hour; ring 528 7594 for details.

Sporting types might enjoy joining a Ross Adventure, which consists of a half-day tour of Devonport and environs by bicycle and sea kayak. These half-day trips start at 7.30am and 1pm and cost $65. One of the highlights is the view from the top of Mount Victoria (and the fast cycle ride down the mountain). Dedicated joggers will gravitate to the Domain (provided they are not discouraged by the contours) whereas hill-walkers might be interested in doing the four-hour coast-to-coast walk through Auckland. Not many countries can be traversed in a few hours but New Zealand narrows to just a few kilometres at Auckland, and an official 13km walk has been designed which links the domains (parks) of Auckland and starts (or finishes) downtown. A leaflet and map describing the walk can be obtained from the Auckland Visitor Centre. As you are never far from a city road, it is possible to curtail the walk at any point and catch a bus.

Water sports lovers will take themselves off to one of Auckland's many beaches, such as Mission Bay, St Heliers Bay and Judges Bay, all accessible from Tamaki Drive, where you can swim or windsurf. To find out prices for hiring a windsurfer, ring 520 4585 or 528 5277. There are many excellent underpopulated beaches on the north shore, especially in Takapuna. Cheltenham Beach in Devonport is within walking distance of the ferry wharf.

You can hire a tennis court and equipment at the City Courts on Stanley St (733 623) or have a work-out at the YMCA on Pitt St (303 2068). There is also a 50km cycle track in and around Auckland, which leads from the Museum to the waterfront and follows the shoreline as far as the Savage Memorial, which affords sweeping views of the harbour.

Several companies charter yachts either to sail yourself or with crew, for example Rainbow Yacht Charters on Symonds St (308 9419). You can take a two-day sailing course at the Rainbow Sailing Club at Pier 2, Westhaven Marina (just under the Harbour Bridge; 780 719) which costs $270. Most people are content just to watch the sailboats in Waitemata Harbour. If you happen to be around on Auckland's Anniversary Day in January, watch the races at what is billed as the largest one-day regatta in the world.

THE MEDIA

Newspapers. Newspaper publishing in Auckland is in a sorry state with the *Auckland Star* and the much more recent *Auckland Sun* having bitten the dust in the past year or two. There is still a choice of Sunday papers: the *Star, Times* or *News*. The Saturday edition of the *Herald*, has about 100 pages, most of which are solid advertising. Most newspapers are sold from honesty boxes.

The travellers' free newspaper *Kiwi Backpacker* is published monthly from the same address as the YHA office at 36 Custom St (777 049). Its British editor recently encountered immigration difficulties and was facing possible deportation, so it was not certain the paper would survive. A selection of overseas newspapers (including the British quality Sundays) is kept in the newspaper reading room in the basement of the Auckland Public Library on Lorne St, and British dailies are available at the UK Consulate-General at 151 Queen St.

Radio. In contrast to print journalism, broadcasting seems to be flourishing. Auckland has no less than 17 radio stations. The minor stations usually specialise, for example one of the new FM stations is devoted entirely to country and western music, and Radio Rhema is a Christian station.

Radio Pacific (702AM), a 24-hour talk station, has been named the Most Outstanding Station in Australia and New Zealand in the past, and is very influential in Auckland. The other main talk-back station is 1ZB on 1080kHz. Of the music stations, Radio 97FM plays classic hits, while Radio 91FM and Radio 89FM play top 40 rock. The university radio station BFM broadcasts on 95FM and plays alternative tracks and new releases. Listen to their *Entertainment Guide* at 6pm on Fridays. The Maori station is called Aotearoa Radio and is broadcast on 603AM. The Concert Programme is available on 92.6FM and the BBC World Service on 91.8FM. For commercial-infested phone-ins, tune in to 1ZB on 1080AM.

Because of a much publicised rise in crime in the early 1990s (sex assaults increased 12% and murders by 25%), the laissez-faire attitude of many people in the tourist industry is disappearing. You will be encouraged to lock your valuables and your doors and to take care walking downtown alone at night. These are the precautions you would expect to have to take in any city and it is up to you to decide whether you can afford to make an exception in Auckland. Muggings are still extremely uncommon.

Some residents have become unnecessarily alarmist and consider their city to be a very dangerous place. South Auckland is regarded by middle class Pakeha residents as the most dangerous area, and some Aucklanders claim that they would not visit the southern districts of Mangere and Otara except in a car with locked doors.

A certain amount of red light activity can be seen on Karangahape Road and on Fort St downtown.

The Central Police Station is on Vincent St (794 240). The Rape Crisis number is 764 404.

The STD code for Auckland is 09. For fire, police or ambulance dial 111.

Auckland Visitor Centre: Aotea Square, 299 Queen St or PO Box 5561 (366 6888). Open weekdays 8.30am–5.30pm, and weekends 9am-4pm.
British Consulate-General: 17th Floor, 151 Queen St (303 2971/3). Open 9am-5pm from Monday to Friday.
American Express: 95 Queen St (798 243). Also 67 Symonds St (793 441).
Thomas Cook: 96 Queen St (772 666). Open Monday to Friday 8.30am-5pm and Saturdays 9am-1pm. Also corner of Customs St E and Queen St (797 799).
Department of Conservation Centre: Corner Karangahape Rd and Liverpool St (307 9279).
Automobile Association: Corner Albert and Victoria Sts (774 660).
Student Travel Centre: 10 High St (309 9723).
Post Office: Mail Service Centre, 167-191 Victoria St W (792 200).
Medical Services: Auckland Hospital, Park Road, Grafton City (797 440).
Medical Emergencies: 122 Remuera Road (524 5943).
Emergency Chemist: 60 Broadway, Newmarket (520 6634).
Auckland City Creche: ATI Building, Wellesley St (773 570).
Disability Resource Centre: 658 069.

DAY TRIPS FROM AUCKLAND

From Auckland it is easy to explore a variety of interesting landscapes and attractions. The Auckland Regional Council publishes a series of leaflets called *Day Trips* available from the Visitor Centre though these are aimed mainly at residents. For those who wish to join a small group tour, there are several good ones to choose from including Bush and Beach Ltd (PO Box 40-047, Greenhithe, Auckland; 473 0189) whose imaginative full day natural history tours cost about $95 and That Other Tour (PO Box 56-306, Auckland 10; 366 3523) whose prices are similar. Another day trip operator is Awesome Adventures on 404 6409. But it is also very easy to visit many of the places of interest under one's own steam.

Hauraki Gulf. Several companies can take you sailing on the Gulf for one or more days. Capt'n Hook's Sailin' Safaris (480 7659) charge $100 for a 24-hour trip (including meals and cabin plus sailing tuition. This sounds better value than the 8am-4.30pm cruise with Cruzing Yacht Charters (025-939 369) which costs $60 not including food.

Beyond the Waitemata Harbour, several islands are dotted around the Hauraki Gulf which are accessible by public transport and are of interest to day-trippers. The most unusual is Rangitoto whose volcanic cone is clearly visible from downtown Auckland. Rangitoto last erupted in about 1750, the most recently active of Auckland's volcanoes. It is most remarkable to see vegetation struggling to survive, especially the unusual miniature kidney ferns, amidst the bizarre jumble of black lava rocks.

An easy track leads to the 259m summit, having been built by prisoners in the 1930s. Wear sturdy footwear as the crushed lava can be hard on the feet, not to mention unpleasantly hot on a sunny day. There are splendid views from the top, of Auckland on one side and the islands of the Gulf on the other. The island is well organised for visitors with all the points of interest well signposted, such as a gull breeding colony and lava caves.

Ferries leave several times a day from the ferry docks in Auckland and arrive at Rangitoto Wharf about 45 minutes later. Sinclairs Ferries (025-927 337) have recently joined Fullers (774 074) on the Rangitoto route and charge half as much ($8 return instead of $16). With Sinclairs there is an additional Department of Conservation fee of $1.50. Sinclairs ferries leave from opposite Princess Wharf at 9am, 1pm and 2.45pm. From the wharf you can walk to the summit (4km) in about an hour and then down to the only other wharf at Islington Bay, or you can follow the edge of the island and avoid the central hill. Whichever you choose keep your eye on the time as you should not miss the last ferry back (5.30pm in summer; 4pm in winter). The estimated timings on the signboards are unreliable, grossly generous for some stretches, and very tight on others.

Attached to Rangitoto by a causeway is the island of Motutapu whose verdant cover provides a complete contrast with the barren volcano. Motutapu is one large farm administered by the Department of Conservation; however visitors are welcome to walk across the paddocks, swim at the beaches and admire the harbour views. Ross Adventures (see *Sport* above) have recently obtained permission from the DOC to take daytrippers on mountain bikes around Motutapu. Unlike Rangitoto, Motutapu has a campsite. Prior arrangements should be made with the Ranger who is also in charge of Rangitoto (727 674).

The much larger island of Waiheke has a permanent population of about 5000, many of whom commute into Auckland on Fullers new catamaran service, the *Quickcat Express*. This service takes 35 minutes and departs from Pier 2 at the ferry docks in Auckland five times a day (7.50am, 10am, 2pm, 4pm and 5.30pm with some weekend variations); ring Fullers Gulf Ferries (393 918 or 771 771). The fare is $21 return. Alternative transport is provided by the *Pacifica Wave Piercer* (366 1421) which charges $19 return on weekdays and $14 on weekends, and by the Subritzky Shipping Line (534 5663) from Half Moon Bay (about 20km from downtown Auckland) which is primarily a vehicular and freight line. All sailings are subject to weather.

The island's buses meet all arriving ferries to take day-trippers to the sandy beaches on the northern side which are sheltered and safe: Oneroa has a choice of water sport facilities and a private hostel, Hekerua House (728 371) while Onetangi has a bird reserve and a YHA hostel beside the beach (728 971). The latter sometimes arranges special promotions to persuade hostellers to spend a couple of days on Waiheke; it will be easy to find out about this in your Auckland hostel.

The great barrier to overdevelopment by tourism on Great Barrier Island used to be that it took at least five hours to get there by sea. But in the last couple of years both Fullers and Pacifica have introduced fast transport to cover the 80km distance and some people even go there for day-trips. Fullers' *Jet Raider* takes one hour and 45 minutes ($45 day return, $89 period return). Pacifica's *Sea Flight* takes longer as it goes via Waiheke every Tuesday, Thursday, Friday and Sunday and costs $40 for a single or day return and $80 for a period return. Cheaper and slower transport is available on Gulf Trans (734 036). You can of course also fly with Great Barrier Islands (275 9120) which does the trip in 25 minutes twice a day. Once on the island you can get around by bus; a day-tripper's coach ticket costs $15 and will get you back from the last harbour stop (Port Fitzroy) and then return to Tryphena where you catch the boat back to Auckland.

For the time being the Barrier, as it is known, remains relatively unspoiled. Rugged bush covers most of the island, which houses several rare birds and a variety of native flora. There are enough residents (about 1000) to provide reasonable amenities. But people do not go to Great Barrier for the night life or high culture; they go for the tramping, surfing, scuba diving, crayfishing and crayfish eating. Many of its little harbours, especially Whangaparapara, are favourite destinations for South Pacific yachtsmen. As most of the island's residents — many of them having come to the island to lead an alternative lifestyle — appear to be dedicated sportsmen, it is not difficult to hire equipment and difficult not to get local advice on where the best places are to try out a sport. The east coast beaches are excellent for surfing whereas the west coast is tamer.

Other islands in the Hauraki Gulf include Kawau Island (two ferries daily from Warkworth; 425 8006), famous for its governor's mansion overlooking the water. Tiritiri Matangi Island, has been made a reserve for endangered species, especially rare birds. Little Barrier Island has the largest remaining native forest in New Zealand and pristine wetlands which protect many unusual native animals. For permission to visit these zoological sanctuaries and information about access, contact the Department of Conservation (address in *Help and Information*).

Hibiscus Coast. The habit of tourism boards around the world is to assign glamorous names to sections of coast, and the shoreline north of Auckland has not escaped the trend. The Hibiscus Coast stretches about 26km from Silverdale to Puhoi, an interesting little town — with a good and very crowded pub — originally settled by Bohemians (i.e. people from the central European province of Bohemia, rather than people of unconventional morals). Orewa is quite a large seaside resort, complete with shopping centres, entertainment arcades and golf course. Waiwera, a few kilometres further north, is perhaps more interesting as it has hot springs and thermal pools, traditionally of therapeutic benefit. It is possible to bathe in the pools surrounded by the hibiscus bushes that provide the excuse for the coast's name. This area is billed as a winter resort though it is at its best in the summer. Not far away, the Wenderholm Park administered by the Auckland Regional Council has lovely beaches and bush walks. To get to this coast by public transport catch bus number 895W from platform 5A in the Downtown Bus Terminal, which goes to Wenderholm between October and April, but only as far as Waiwera the rest of the year.

Waitakere Ranges. This is a remarkably rugged area, whose highest peaks (up to 500m) are easily visible from the city and within half an hour's drive of downtown. There are 250km of walking tracks, ranging from five-minute strolls suitable for grandmothers in high heels, to overnight expeditions for well equipped hiking parties. There are many objects of interest from large kauri trees (some with a circumference of 7m) to Fairy Falls, a steep cascade of water that gathers in a pool surrounded by sheer semi-circular walls.

In addition to the pleasures of walking through virgin bush are added the pleasures of the ocean. You can get to the cliff-lined west coast via many walking tracks but by only four roads, which branch off from Scenic Drive. The beaches at the end of these roads at Whatipu, Karekare, Piha and Anawhata are all very picturesque — particularly Piha, guarded as it is by the 100m-high Lion Rock just offshore, which can be climbed in about half an hour. If you go swimming or surfing at any of these beaches, look for patrolled areas, as rips and currents can be dangerous.

The Arataki Visitor Centre (817 7134) on Scenic Drive is open 7 days a week from 9am to 5pm. A short nature trail from the Centre leads you past many native trees and plants, all helpfully labelled. The Information Officers can advise on suitable walks, issue permits for the campsites and inform you of any special events. Anyone who plans to spend some time in the Waitakere Ranges should purchase the *Walking and Tramping Tracks* map available from Arataki or the Regional Parks Information Centre at the downtown ferry buildings (09-366 2166), which is where you must also book overnight accommodation.

Several other Regional Parks within easy range of Auckland also offer enjoyable tramping possibilities. A variety of backpack campsites and vehicle-based sites are available throughout the Regional Park network. Facilities are basic and fees are about $6. You can pick up a leaflet at the Regional Parks Information Centre.

Henderson Valley. Hedonists may prefer to tour picturesque valley vineyards rather than rugged hills. A large number of New Zealand's major vineyards are located within half an hour of downtown Auckland in the Henderson Valley, north of the Waitakeres. The Yugoslav influence on wine-making in the district is enormous, and the majority of wineries are now or once were run by people with Serbo-Croat names. The names Corban's, Babich and Delegats will be familiar to anyone who has browsed in a New Zealand wine shop, and these vineyards are all within about 5km of each other. Follow a route along Lincoln Road to Taupaki and Kumeu. Some of New Zealand's best wine is made by the Matua Valley Winery in Waikoukou Road, Waimauku a little further north.

The Winemakers of West Auckland (528 4388) publish a leaflet which describes the wineries, and gives instructions for finding them. Most are open Monday through Saturday and offer tastings. Even without private transport you can visit a few of them on foot after reaching the Valley by bus.

NORTHLAND

The 345km peninsula stretching north of Auckland is not much more than 100km wide at its broadest point, so beaches are never far away in Northland. Although the scale of Ninety Mile Beach (actually only 64 miles long) at the far north of the island is not quite typical, both shores of the peninsula have some wild and battered stretches of coast as well as sandy coves lined with semitropical trees and flowers. The main roads don't follow the coasts very closely so it is always worth venturing down a dirt track to see what you can discover. If only the latitude were closer to the equator, this could be a holiday destination to rival the Seychelles or Barbados, though with over 2,000 hours of sunshine each year and the highest average temperatures in New Zealand, the climate is at least as attractive as the Mediterranean or Florida. In any case this is an area superbly suited to a week or month of lounging and relaxation. In addition to six YHA hostels there is a plethora of other hostel, camping and bed and breakfast accommodation. If you drive north on Highway 1, try to take in the Waiomio Caves south of Kawakawa or the Abby Caves near Whangarei Falls, both of which are refreshingly undeveloped. The latter can be explored on a two-hour take-a-torch tour; ring 09-437 0609 for details.

Northland offers plenty of short and long walks, to which any YHA hostel or local tourist office will direct you. Although this part of New Zealand is not particularly mountainous, there are plenty of one day climbs which afford sweeping views. For example Mount Manaia just across the bay from Whangarei is a rigorous two-hour climb. As is so often the case in New Zealand, artificial aids — in this case wire handrails — have been installed to make the climb possible for anyone. What is not usual for New Zealand is that the view from the top takes in an oil refinery.

Bay of Islands. The most popular resort area of Northland is the Bay of Islands, 240km north of Auckland, which includes the adjacent towns of Paihia and Russell plus Kerikeri 23km further north. In addition to the glorious ocean scenery and opportunities to try water sports (especially game fishing), there are many places of historical interest including New Zealand's oldest stone building (the mission house in Kerikeri), the oldest wooden building (Kemp House in Kerikeri), the oldest church and the hotel with the oldest licence (both in Russell) and the Treaty House in Waitangi where Maori chiefs ceded their land to Queen Victoria in 1840. There is a recently constructed walkway through mangrove forest (populated by strange clicking crabs) from Opua to Paihia, which takes a leisurely 3 hours, and then Russell is only a short ferry ride away, so the attractions are not widely dispersed. The Bay of Islands is one of New Zealand's three Maritime Parks. The Department of Conservation's Bay of Islands Maritime and Historic Park Visitor Centre is on The Strand in Russell (09-403 7685), and is open daily. For tourist information and bookings try Bradley's Booking Office on Russell Wharf (403 7596) and Bay of Islands Sports Fishing on The Strand (403 7008).

Access to the Bay is easy, both for car-owning Aucklanders (which means that the resorts can be crowded at weekends) and for travellers who have the choice of bus services operated by Northliner Express (part of the Newmans network), InterCity or the Mini Bus Company (which appear in the InterCity timetable) all for about $40.

The obvious way to see the Bay of Islands is by boat. Try to befriend a local yachtsman (for example at the important yacht harbour at Opua) to take you for a sail or join a group chartering a yacht for a day or more. One of the best charter operators for experienced sailors is Great Escape Budget Yacht Charters in Kerikeri (09-407 8920), which charges just $70 per day per boat. Gungha Cruises (Rd 1, Kerikeri; 0800-478 900) offer day-long trips around the Bay of Islands for $60. A company called Coastal Kayakers can take you on a seven-hour kayak trip from Paihia through mangroves at a reasonable cost of $55 (plus there are backpackers' discounts). Details are available from the Paihia Public Relations Office (09-402 7426).

Otherwise you can join one of the several cruises offered by the ubiquitous Fullers company. Their original and most famous cruise is called the 'cream trip' (because it was originally patronised by dairy farmers). It costs $45 for a 5½-hour trip, departing daily (in summer) from Paihia at 10am. Other choices include a four-hour trip to Cape Brett to sail through Hole-in-the-Rock, a natural bridge in the rock (if the sea is calm enough); the cost is just a little less than the Cream Trip.

Some say that nearby Tauranga Bay has the most beautiful beach in the country. Coopers Beach near Mangonui has a popular beach campsite, though if you are prepared to walk a few miles past the 'Camping Prohibited' signs, it is possible to camp undisturbed. Some beaches that are owned by Maori councils charge admission at the access road.

The area around Kerikeri is covered with orchards of kiwifruit and oranges. Travellers will soon notice signs, especially in Hideaway Lodge (Wiroa Road; 09-407 9773), advertising the availability of casual work, picking or packing fruit, virtually throughout the year. The main season for citrus picking is late September to early December, the kiwifruit harvest starts in late April. Beds at Hideaway Lodge start at $12 in a dorm.

Cape Reinga. Those who find the idea of visiting John O'Groats appealing will certainly want to visit the northernmost point in New Zealand, the lonely lighthouse on a storm-battered cape. (Just as Ninety Mile Beach is shorter than advertised, so Cape Reinga is not in fact the most northerly point; North Cape is a few kilometres closer to the equator, however it is inaccessible by road and so is ignored.)

The Maori name Reinga means 'place of leaping', not because it was a favourite suicide spot but because it was believed to be the gateway through which spirits departed to their homeland. Anyone who has read of the similar belief held by Pacific Islanders as described by Arthur Grimble in *Pattern of Islands* will be relieved to hear that Cape Reinga and Spirits Bay are not nearly as spooky and dangerous. However in certain conditions swimming can be perilous, as the meeting of the Tasman Sea to the west and the Pacific Ocean can result in unpredictable currents and turbulence.

Although it is easy to drive up to the Cape and back again along the road through the middle of the peninsula, most people prefer to join a full-day tour by bus or four-wheel drive vehicle so that they can travel along Ninety Mile Beach. The tides determine whether you travel the beach route on the way up or back. Individual motorists are discouraged from attempting the drive as it requires skilled driving and knowledge of the area because of tides and soft sand. There is even some quicksand on the Te Paki Stream flanked by giant yellow sand dunes which are fun to ski down barefoot.

Rather feebly, the tourist literature describes the drive along Ninety Mile Beach as 'one of the world's most exciting beach bus routes' (though it is not clear what competition they have in mind). No doubt they will be inspired to greater heights by the arrival in 1992 of a 15-passenger land yacht which it is estimated will be able to travel at up to 100km/h on a good day (and zero km/h for 25% of the time). In the meantime, Mike's Cape Reinga Bus Tours (09-408 2826) are well known among backpackers as are Sand Safaris (27 South Road; 09-408 1778), both in Kaitaia. One possibility is to camp overnight at the Cape, an option available with King's Adventures who provide sleeping accommodation on their bus. Otherwise you stop at the top for just an hour or so. All these tours can be booked though the Kaitaia YHA hostel at 160 Commerce St (09-408 1840). If you are not on a tour, there is free camping with toilet facilities at Tapotupotu Bay about 3km before Cape Reinga.

Another hostel where you can get good information about interesting trips in the Far North is Main St Hostel, 235 Commerce St, Kaitaia (09-408 1275) which is run by Maori people and organises swimming, snorkelling and fishing day trips for $30 and visits to a local marae for $15.

The West Coast. The western side of the Northland peninsula is less developed than the east partly because of the notorious rip tides which make swimming dangerous. But the area is very beautiful. The special attraction north of Dargaville is the Waipoua Forest of kauri trees where many magnificent trees escaped the ravages of 19th century exploitation. Highway 12 (unsealed) passes through the forest for about 17km and many specimens can be seen right next to the road, such as the amazing one over 50m high, 13m in circumference and 1,200 years old. The Kauri and Pioneer Museum in the village of Matakohe (on the road back to Auckland) has exhibits of the colourful gum which was widely exported at the turn of the century to be used in varnishes and polished ornaments. The nearest YHA hostel to the forest is Opononi, a tiny seaside holiday town overlooking Hokianga Harbour, where there are some strangely sculpted and always-changing sand dunes, some of which are seven metres high. Look for blackberries to pick in February, and enquire at the hostel about local hangis (Maori feasts).

COROMANDEL PENINSULA

At first glance this rugged and mountainous peninsula, about an hour and a half's drive south and then east of Auckland, appears to be of interest only to holidaymakers eager to enjoy the beaches and trampers looking for unspoiled wilderness. But it has been heavily exploited by lumbermen, miners and fishermen ever since the first white entrepreneurs arrived. The great forests of kauri trees were ruthlessly logged for the shipbuilding industry though some regenerating kauri stands (and some original ones) can be seen among the dense forests. The peninsula is littered with abandoned mining relics, especially of the gold boom in the 1870s. Now that exploitation of the wilderness is no longer accepted as inevitable, recent attempts to revive the goldfields and prospect for other minerals have met with stiff opposition from environmentalists and those concerned with safeguarding the prosperity of the tourist industry.

The numerous beaches, many of them empty even in summer, are not only lovely for swimming, but are wonderful places to collect shells. The little seaside village of Hahei is famed for its pink-tinged beach, coloured by powdered shells. On some beaches you may also find fragments of gems such as agate and jasper. Nearby Cathedral Cove has some weird and wonderful rock formations but be prepared for a stiff 45-minute walk from the car park. Hot Water Beach is aptly named as the water that is just a little way below the surface is very hot indeed; at mid to low tide you can excavate a bath for yourself if you are so inclined.

Whitianga is a bustling tourist resort, especially popular with deep sea fishermen. A controversial marina, large enough to accommodate 350 boats, has been completed, so Whitianga will become even more crowded in future. It is already one of the more developed Coromandel towns with a large choice of motor camps and motels. There are two YHA hostels on the peninsula — one at Opoutere and an associate hostel at Coromandel — and also some good backpackers: in Coromandel Tui Lodge at 600 Whangapoua Road (07-866 8237) and the Backpackers Bed Barn on Rings Road (07-866 8327) both have dorm beds from $13, and Paradise Backpackers on Adlor Hill Road in Port Charles (07-866 6922) has beds from $15. Thames, at the base of the peninsula, is a good place to stay and has an interesting mineralogical museum (open 11am–3pm). Try the Dickson Holiday Park in town (07-868 7308) or Sunkist Lodge (506 Brown St; 07-868 8808; beds from $13), both of which are ticket agents for Peninsula Buses. Another lovely resort is Pauanui, also on the ocean side of the peninsula.

The village of Coromandel with a population of less than 3000 has many attractive colonial buildings left over from the prosperous times of the gold rush. Although its name (which derives from the first British ship to use the harbour in 1810) has lent itself to the peninsula, other larger towns like Whitianga and Thames are more popular centres of tourism. Just north of the town there is a miniature railway ($6).

Access to the peninsula is fairly straightforward. InterCity's Peninsula Buses have a daily service from Whitianga to Auckland, some of which go via Tairua and others of which take the longer, more scenic, route via Coromandel. Note that when people say it takes an hour and a half to get to Coromandel they mean to Thames at the base of the peninsula. The roads get much slower after this point and buses take at least 3 hours to get from downtown Auckland to Whitianga. If you want a six-day off-the-beaten-track backpackers' tour, try Kiwi Magic Tours (57 Harrisfield Drive, Tauranga; 07-544 3328).

The road that hugs the western side of the peninsula is unsealed beyond Colville, but it is possible to drive out to the tip at Cape Colville (Fletcher Bay). Unfortunately there is no road right around the end so it is necessary to backtrack 30km down to Coromandel before you can cross to the other side and down to Whitianga. The alternative cross-peninsula road is rugged mountain road 309, which is unsealed and is said to be the road along which most of the peninsula's illegal marijuana is grown.

There are many miles of walking track on the Coromandel Peninsula, which are somewhat more challenging than a walk through Auckland but are nevertheless perfectly suitable for the amateur. The peninsula's state forest covers a large area of hills, which rise to 835m. Although the area was heavily logged, many trees and flowers have regenerated. Some of the abandoned lumber operations and mines are sufficiently defunct to be almost picturesque. The walks in this forest can be a little daunting for the unfit, however they are well marked between huts and should not present difficulties. The Kauaeranga River runs deep into the forest and is a popular destination for trampers. You can arrange to be dropped off and picked up at the end of the trail by Peninsula Buses; enquire at Thames Information Centre (Queen St; 07-868 7284), open daily 9am–5pm. Further information about the Coromandel can also be obtained from here.

CENTRAL NORTH ISLAND

If the North Island can be imagined as a giant sea creature swimming through the Tasman Sea — as indeed the Maoris did think of it — the two 'flippers' on either side and everything in between constitute the central region. Maori legends give interesting accounts of the formation of the various mountains, valleys and lakes scattered around the centre of the island. Falling within this region are the North Island's foremost tourist attractions of Rotorua with its thermal activity and Maori industry, and Waitomo with its glow-worms. Few visitors to New Zealand will miss either of these though there are many other places of interest. The original three National Parks of the North Island are evenly spaced along a line bisecting the island horizontally. If you are travelling between Auckland and Wellington you will have to consider your route carefully, unless you are privileged to have enough time to explore both sides of the island.

THE EAST COAST

Much of the coastline south of the Coromandel Peninsula is equally rugged and beautiful, though the inland areas are more densely populated and agriculturally productive. Highway 2 follows the coast of the aptly named Bay of Plenty, continuing around the outstandingly scenic East Cape to the inaptly named Poverty Bay (things have changed since Captain Cook named it in 1769) and on to the resort town of Napier overlooking Hawke Bay, before turning inland towards Wellington. Although this area is popular with New Zealand tourists, it involves a sizeable detour for overseas visitors hurrying down to the South

Island and so is often overlooked. Apart from its scenic attractions, the Maori influences are particularly strong and interesting in this part of New Zealand, especially in the relatively isolated East Cape where over a quarter of the land is owned by Maori councils. The backpackers' East Cape Fun Bus (Backroad Tours, 2/5 Malvern Road, Auckland 3; 09-864 400) has contacts with several Maori maraes, one of which provides overnight accommodation.

Bay of Plenty. Although orchards and fields are not in themselves a prime tourist draw, they make a pleasant backdrop to the beaches and oceanscapes of the Bay of Plenty. In addition it is gratifying to indulge in freshly picked kiwifruit, and the occasionally delicious wines which are made from the excess crop can be sampled at wineries in Tauranga, the largest town on the bay, and also at nearby Te Puke. Te Puke (not pronounced as it looks but Poo-kee) is said to be the kiwifruit capital of the world and two tourist complexes prove it: Kiwifruit Country on the main road from Whakatane devotes itself to the life and times of the Chinese Gooseberry. It includes a 12m-high slice of kiwifruit, which constitutes the world's most pointless lookout — it gives a good view only of the car park. Nearby Longridge Park 'covers every aspect of New Zealand rural life' (in case you missed seeing sheep). Ask at the Te Puke Public Relations Office (07-573 9172) about the $7 tour of kiwifruit farms and packing operations. As mentioned in the introductory section on *Work*, this is a favourite destination for casual workers during the harvest which lasts about six weeks from the beginning of May. May is also when the Kiwifruit Festival is held where there are fruit weigh-ins and other exciting events. This area is also a good place to try unusual native fruits like tamarillos (which look like tomatoes) and feijoas.

Tauranga's harbour is completely protected by Matakana Island, and has become one of the foremost shipping ports in the country mostly for pulp and paper. Despite recent industrial accretions, it remains a pleasant holiday resort with one of those recreated colonial villages at Tauranga Historic Village on Seventeenth Avenue (07-383 337).

Even more pleasant is Mount Maunganui, situated at the harbour entrance and now easily accessibly via the new harbour bridge. A full range of water sports is available on Ocean Beach which stretches for several miles along the coast. Alternatively it is possible to climb Mount Maunganui (232m) in an hour and a half. The summit affords fine views over the city harbour and islands of the Bay. Many miles out to sea is White Island, a particularly active volcano which has foiled several attempts to mine it. You can see steam pouring from the craters from several coastal lookouts. This whole area is one of the most seismologically volatile in the country; the town of Edgecumbe about 90km south of Tauranga suffered the worst damage in the most recent earthquake of 1987.

A regular coach service between Auckland and Tauranga is operated by Newmans, InterCity, Supa Travel and Call-a-Bus, a trip that takes around 3½ hours. There is also a daily rail service from Auckland. For further information on the Bay of Plenty area, contact the Tauranga Visitor Information Centre on The Strand (07-578 8103).

Hawke's Bay. The next large bay, past the lightly populated East Cape, is Hawke Bay (but note the province is called Hawke's Bay). Those without much time or without private transport will opt for the direct inland route along Highway 2, which bypasses the Cape, and thereby saves over 200km. However the long drive on Highway 35 around the coast of the Cape is spectacular. The coast is too sparsely populated to support any public transport.

Whichever road you choose, you will arrive at Gisborne, a large and prosperous town on Poverty Bay, with pleasant beaches within walking distance of the town. Its claim to be the most easterly city in the world (i.e. closest to the international dateline, which is about 900km away) will not necessarily enhance a visit, but will give you something unusual to put on your postcards.

It is a further 216km to Napier. The town had to be completely rebuilt after an earthquake in 1931 that killed 256 people, the worst natural disaster in New Zealand's history. There is little evidence of the catastrophe now, though much of the land on which modern Napier stands was under the sea before the earthquake. The Art Deco architecture that dominated the rebuilding of the town in the 1930s is noteworthy and enthuasiasts can join an Art Deco guided walk of the town at 2pm on Wednesdays, Saturdays and Sundays (daily from 26 December to the end of February) for $7 from the Art Deco Shop on Tennyson St. Self-guided walking maps are available for $1.50. It is remarkable how many places around the North Island are of very recent creation, emphasising how geologically young and capricious New Zealand is. The Hawke's Bay Museum on Herschell St includes a fascinating audio-visual presentation on 'The Great Hawke's Bay Earthquake'.

Napier is New Zealand's closest approximation to Blackpool or Coney Island, with many seaside attractions along the Marine Parade including Marineland and an aquarium, illuminated fountains, paddle boats and a kiwi house (with a live talk daily at 1pm).

At the bottom of the arc of Hawke Bay is Cape Kidnappers, famed for its colony of gannets. The gannet is an attractive bird (roughly the size of a goose) that is virtually unafraid of humans. Those interested in seeing the birds should take a shuttle bus to the end of the road at Clifton Beach; Kiwi Shuttle charges $15 return for the 25km trip from Napier. You then walk for a couple of hours along the sandy beaches to the cape. This walk can be undertaken only at low tide and is worthwhile only between late October and April when the birds are in residence (the chicks are born in December). Alternatively you can take a tour with Gannet Beach Adventures (06-875 0898), Unimog Adventure Tours (06-835 4446), Quadventures (06-836 6652) or Gannet Safaris (06-875 0511).

Hawke's Bay is another wine-making district of New Zealand and there are 24 wineries in the *Hawke's Bay Wineries Guide* leaflet, most of which are open to the public. One of the most developed for tourists also makes excellent wines, the Mission Winery on Church Road, Taradale (a suburb of Napier). There are also two cideries in the vicinity: St Andrews Estate in Havelock North (06-877 6441) and Plumpton Park Estate (06-834 4643). It would be easy to organise your own winery tour by bicycle; cycles can be hired from Napier Cycle World (104 Carlyle St) and Bike Torque (120 Carlyle St).

All travel information about the province of Hawke's Bay, including tide times for the trip to Cape Kidnappers, is available from the Napier Visitor Information Centre, Marine Parade (06-834 4161) or Hastings Visitor Information Centre, Russell St (06-878 0510).

ROTORUA

The town of Rotorua (population 67,000) attracts tourists on many counts. Best known for its hot springs, geysers and other geothermal features, it also has many aspects of Maori culture on show, a place for viewing kiwis, and two complexes (the Agrodome and Rainbow Farm) featuring slick shows about sheep farming. Its picturesque location on Lake Rotorua clinches its irresistibility for most visitors to New Zealand. With all this, it is inevitable that tour buses swamp the place, especially as Rotorua is a popular destination for day-trippers from Auckland. Sky gondolas and luge rides are also among the list of tourist attractions. Any place that can persuade the Japanese Tour Bureau to set aside more than a day on its itinerary (when the average Japanese worker gets only 8 days of holiday in the year) must be special.

Do not allow this apparently relentless onslaught of tourism to put you off. Besides, there are advantages to the commercial development — for example, the restaurants are more interesting than they are in other New Zealand towns of comparable size and are probably preferable to the over-priced imitation Maori hangis (meals cooked in the ground) featured by several big hotels. On the other hand, there are also more authentic alternatives to the hotel-hosted Maori concerts and hangis in the town. Rotorua's attractions are so unusual that it is worth tolerating some commercialism. There are plenty of ways to avoid the tour buses, by renting a bicycle or even by joining a tour. An adventurous day trip that you can join locally and is recommended by many backpackers is Carey's Capers (07-347 8035). The tour hits the highlights of the thermal and scenic attractions in the area and is good fun; the cost is $55 for a long day.

Thermal Activity. A large area of the North Island from Mount Ruapehu to White Island in the Bay of Plenty, encompassing Rotorua and Taupo, is full of strange volcanic features. One of Rotorua's most memorable aspects is the unmistakable stench of sulphur and the hissing and steaming of bores in public places. Until the late 1980s almost every Rotorua home had its own bore for domestic heating, however these were (controversially) closed down so as not to dissipate the pressure behind the tourist geysers. A further threat to Rotorua's unique resources is that there is apparently a market for Rotorua mud in exclusive beauty salons in Australia, though so far the depletion has not become noticeable.

Although the whole region has geothermal activity, many areas have been fenced off and made safe for tourists; admission is charged at some of them. The dramatic features are thoroughly tamed with pathways laid down between bubbling mud and boiling whirlpools, and have acquired cute names like Devil's Cauldron and Champagne Pool. It is not impossible to see steaming hot springs and mud pools in their natural state; however this requires a commitment to tramping and an element of risk. Every year there are numerous scaldings and an occasional death even inside the commercial thermal sites if a visitor strays off the path. So it is best to heed all those signs, tiresome as they become, reminding visitors to keep to the paths. As well as providing health cures for rheumatic and arthritic patients, hot springs have proved dangerous throughout Rotorua's history. The Postmaster Baths, so named in 1892, were reputed to suppress the taste for alcohol. But as recently as 1950, the pool was bulldozed after a number of drunken bathers drowned in it.

Of the thermal areas in the vicinity of Rotorua, Whakarewarewa (or Whaka as it is conveniently shortened) is the most heavily visited as it is so close to town (about 3.5km) and also because it features the Maori Arts & Crafts Institute near the main entrance. The admission charge is $10.50. Whaka can be reached on foot, by bike or by the shuttle bus that operates from the tourist office at the corner of Fenton and Haupapa Sts (open 8am–5.30pm daily; 07-348 5179) and charges between $7 and $10 return. Whaka's foremost attraction is the Pohutu Geyser, which once again has been spouting up to 30m into the air.

The next nearest thermal area is Hell's Gate 15km around the east side of Lake Rotorua (admission $10.50). After visiting in the 1880s George Bernard Shaw claimed he would have gladly paid *not* to see the infernal sights at Hell's Gate. The most distant thermal centre is Orakei Korako, 75km south. Waimangu boasts the world's largest boiling lake whereas Orakei features silica terraces. Read the tourist literature and decide which of the sites most appeals to you; if you choose to visit more than one you run the risk of overdosing on mud. These thermal sites are most impressive in winter when steam rises everywhere.

Many Rotorua hotels and even hostels (including the YHA hostel on the corner of Eruera and Hinemara Sts; 07-347 6810) have their own thermally heated pools or jacuzzis. Hostels with their own spas include Funky Green Voyager at 4 Union St (07-346 1754); Totorua Central Backpackers at 10 Pukuatua St (07-349 3285); Cactus Jack Downtown Backpackers at 54 Haupapa St (07-348 3121); and Backpackers Rotorua at 105 Amohau St (07-348 7654) — all of these have dorm beds from $13-14. For $7.50 you can visit the complex of mineral pools at the Polynesian Pools in the Government Gardens, open 8am to 11pm daily (07-348 1328).

Maori Culture. The Maori Arts & Crafts Institute at Whaka provides a good introduction to Maori culture with its meeting house within the *pa* (fortified area). This is the venue for the daily lunch-time concert of Maori music (summer only). Elsewhere on the site, you can see carvers, weavers and other crafts people at work. The main Maori settlement in Rotorua was originally on the lake, a little west of the present town. Ohinemutu (which is poignantly translated as 'the girl cut off from the world') has an ornate neo-Tudor Maori church, built in 1910. Wandering around the church's graveyard, it is interesting to see how many members of the Maori Expeditionary Battalion died in European wars. There is also a statue of Queen Victoria, incongruously under a Maori canopy, and a magnificent meeting house where Maori concerts take place at 8pm nightly. These are possibly more authentic and less expensive than the other more heavily promoted ones; ring the Tamatekapua Meeting House (07-348 4894) for details of forthcoming events.

Performances of song and dance are also mounted in several of the main hotels (like the Travelodge in Eruera St) as well as in the Civic Theatre Building on Haupapa St. The latter costs $10 and includes a commentary between dances. One can't help but suspect that the traditional dances to celebrate marriages, battles, etc. have been somewhat diluted and tailored for the benefit of tourist audiences.

Scenic Attractions. If you decide to rent a car to explore the region try Rent-a-Dent on 07-349 1919. One of the best ways to see the area is to hire a bicycle for a day or two. Cycles can be hired from several of the hostels mentioned above, including the YHA hostel and Cactus Jack's.

With a copy of a sightseeing map (e.g. *Rotorua: Gateway to Geyserland* costing 80c) you can plan your route. An obvious choice is to circumnavigate Lake Rotorua, about 45km. The minor road that hugs the northern edge of the lake is especially beautiful. There are plenty of attractions en route, though some of them, like the hedge maze at Fairbank or the peacocks at Hamurana Springs, are simply gimmicks to attract tourists into their souvenir shops and tea rooms. The small island in the middle of the lake Mokoia has been cleared of rats in order to turn it into a conservation area for New Zealand fauna, which makes it an interesting destination. You can also bathe in a thermal pool. Fishermen will be interested in the statistic that there is a 97% chance of catching a trout on Lake Rotorua.

The 'agricultural stage shows' at the Agrodome (on the west side of the lake) and Rainbow Springs (5km north on the Auckland Highway) are worth seeing if you have not seen sheep dogs at work elsewhere. There are shows at 9.15am, 11am and 2.30pm at the Agrodome and 10.30am, 1pm and 2.30pm at Rainbow Springs. Next to Rainbow Springs on Fairy Springs Road are skyline rides in cable cars, chairlifts or just in a harness and 1km luge rides (luges are like go-karts) — there are two tracks; one for beginners and one for experts. More adventurous activities are a little further afield: the River Rats Rafting Company (07-347 6049) can take you not only white-water rafting on the Rangitaiki River east of Rotorua for $45–$55 but also water sledging, which involves riding down the rapids on a sledge for $78, plus a barbecue lunch (ask for a YHA discount).

Tarawera. The Pink and White Terraces at Mount Tarawera were once considered among the world's most outstanding tourist attractions. Early descriptions of the terraces, which stood about 20km south of Rotorua, make them sound marvellous, and indeed photographs that survive in the Rotorua Art and History Museum (now housed in the Bath-House in the Government Gardens) corroborate this. But in 1886 Mount Tarawera erupted so violently that the explosion was felt in Auckland and heard in Christchurch. Along with about 150 Maori who lived on the slopes of Tarawera, the famous terraces were engulfed forever.

The eruption created a new thermal valley, Waimangu, and buried Te Wairoa Village, which is now an attraction known as the Buried Village. Launches cruise on tranquil Lake Tarawera, which filled in the giant crater. You can also land on Mount Tarewera by helicopter or travel by four-wheel-drive vehicle to the summit. The tourist authorities have been considering the possibility of recreating the terraces in a different place, at Wairakei (a geothermal power station just north of Taupo), ever since the chemical process that turned the terraces pink was discovered in 1986, but this would be an exceedingly expensive procedure.

AROUND TAUPO

Lake Taupo. An hour south of Rotorua is yet another place of pilgrimage for tourists. Perhaps because of the proximity of the internationally famous Huka Lodge, Taupo has become a rather exclusive resort with expensive restaurants, hotels and late-night bars and nightclubs. There are also more moderately priced restaurants, however, and the usual selection of American-style junk food outlets. There are also several backpacker hostels, including Rainbow Lodge at 99 Titiraupenga St (07-378 5754), Sunset Lodge at 5 Tremain Avenue (07-378 5962), Burkes Backpackers at 69 Spa Road (07-378 9292) and Berkenhoff Lodge at 75 Scannell Street (07-378 4909). All of these have dorm beds for $13. There is also relatively affordable accommodation available in motorcamps, motels, inns and campsites.

The town of Taupo is set on Lake Taupo, famous for its oversized trout (average 2kg) and for its great depth, which has not yet been successfully measured. The lake is considerably larger than Rotorua, and a car rather than a bicycle is the preferred vehicle for covering the 165km distance of its circumference. There are also daily sailing trips on the lake costing $20 (07-378 8444). There are campsites, boat jetties and swimming spots off Highway 1 heading south. The western side of the lake is less accessible but has some magnificent coloured cliffs called Karangahape and more hot pools at Tokaanu. The Craters of the Moon thermal area has been especially active in recent years. Walter's Tours in Taupo take backpackers around the lake on day trips. Taupo's Visitor Information Centre is at 13 Tongariro St (07-378 9000).

Tongariro. Tongariro National Park, which was granted World Heritage status in 1991, is roughly half way between Auckland and Wellington. It incorporates the highest peaks of the North Island, all active volcanoes, now pleasure grounds for sightseers as well as naturalists, skiers and trampers. The Whakapapa Visitor Centre (07-892 3729) is situated in Whakapapa Village (on State Highway 48) and can provide information on activities, accommodation, the weather, and so on, and will guide you towards the most interesting geological formations such as lava monoliths and ash-covered deserts.

Hostels, motels and camping grounds can be found in Whakapapa Village, Ohakune, Turangi at the southern end of Lake Taupo and in the community called National Park at the junction of Highways 4 and 47. Both Howards Lodge (07-892 2827) and Ski Haus are on Carrol St and are good sources of information and transport for exploring the park. Be sure to have warm clothes as Tongariro is an alpine area and weather conditions can be extreme, even during the summer months.

Many travellers choose to walk the Tongariro Crossing, a one-day traverse between Mount Tongariro and Mount Ngauruhoe. This track starts from the Mangatepopo Valley at the base of Ngauruhoe, crosses over large flat craters, past the Red Crater, Emerald Lakes, lava flows and the Blue Lake and descends past the Ketetahi Hot Springs to finish. While you may view these springs from the track, bathing is not permitted at present as they are on private land. This is a full-day trip and you will need good boots, warm and wet weather clothing and plenty of food and water. In the summer there is transport available from both Whakapapa Village and National Park to enable you to do this trek. For those wanting to do a shorter walk there are several tracks taking from 15 minutes to 5–6 hours to walk starting from Whakapapa Village.

WAITOMO

Prior to travelling around the North Island, many people have never thought of glow-worms as an obvious tourist attraction. But after ticking Rotorua off their list, most visitors head for the caves at Waitomo, renowned as a favourite habitat for glow-worms.

Waitomo is now accessible by InterCity bus from Rotorua on tourist excursions only, departing Rotorua at 9.30am and returning at 2.30 which allows only one hour at the caves. Hitching is tricky though possible. The caves are 8km west of Highway 3 and are not near any town amenities. When you are leaving you can catch a local minibus in the early morning which goes as far as Te Kuiti on the main road.

In addition to the fancy Tourist Hotel Corporation hotel there is Juno Farm Accommodation (08-138 7649) whose main activity is organising horse trekking ($25 for two hours) but who offer various kinds of accommodation for $12. The farm is about one and a half kilometres before the caves. Otherwise you can walk a kilometre beyond the caves and pay $8 for a bed in a very basic dormitory hostel patronised mainly by cavers called the Tomo Group Hut where a bunk costs $8.

Some of the caves have been especially adapted for mass tourism: spotlights show the insects and a short guided boat ride takes tourists into the blackness to see the glowing worms, which transform the roof of the cave into miniature heavens. Post cards can be purchased in the shop which describe the life cycle of the glow-worm, though for some reason they have not yet begun to market greenstone or paua shell worms. Tours of the Glow-worm Grotto depart every hour on the hour between 9am and 4pm with extra tours at 4.30 and 5.30pm in summer. There is a hefty entrance fee of $11.50. Tours of the other tourist caves Ruakuri and Aranui (which feature odd limestone formations) are less popular, and somewhat cheaper.

The museum of caving in Waitomo (free admission; 08-138 6219) is excellent, providing a vividly illustrated history of the region's exploration. It is also the centre for booking some of the exciting new cave activities in Waitomo. Black-water rafting is recommended by almost everyone who tries it. This involves wearing a wet suit and crash helmet with miner's light and floating through the caves on an inflated inner tube. You can get on and off to lark about on rocky ledges in the caves and go over five-metre waterfalls (for which some training is provided). Be prepared to feel very cold by the end of this three-hour adventure; the cost is about $50. You should try to book ahead as demand is great and numbers are limited. There are also caving and abseiling trips for beginners which you can enquire about at the museum.

The above-ground environs can be explored on horse back (see Juno Farm above) and you can do your John Wayne imitation by tying your horse up outside the local pub. Waitomo's Roadside Bar is a pleasant enough watering-hole and a good place to meet cavers, some of whom work as guides in the caves. This, together with a post office and shop, constitutes Waitomo, so it makes a pleasant contrast with the bustling commerce of Rotorua.

It is worth noting that Waitomo does not have a monopoly on all the glow-worms of New Zealand. They thrive wherever there are damp conditions with enough airborne insect life to feed on. Although they won't be as numerous in other places, it is fun to stumble across the pinpricks of light yourself. Locals can often direct you to a good viewing place.

THE TARANAKI

The capital of this western province is New Plymouth, once known for its parks but now associated with the offshore natural gas fields and for its synthetic petrol plant.

Mount Egmont/Taranaki. The predominantly dairying province of Taranaki, which occupies the western bulge of the North Island, is dominated by a symmetrically formed volcanic peak. Until recently maps labelled this 2517m mountain Egmont, but in deference to Maori protests it is now officially also called Mount Taranaki, a compromise that many New Zealanders consider symptomatic of their government's indecisiveness.

Whichever name you choose to call it, it is a magnificent mountain. But like the mountains of the South Island that attract visitors from far and wide, you have to be lucky to see it on a clear day. Some maintain that the best chance of seeing the conical peak is from an aircraft, as it often pokes through the clouds that obscure it completely from landlubbers. The romantic Maori explanation for the persistent cloud and mists is that Taranaki is weeping for his lost love Pihanga (wife of Mount Tongariro); tacky post cards portraying the myth are widely available in the region, but provide little consolation for failing to see the mountain itself.

There are three approach roads from Highway 3, each ending at some visitor amenities. There are several 'on demand' shuttle bus services operating, but otherwise you will have to rely on the good nature of motoring tourists if you do not have your own transport. From the much less heavily used coastal road, a huge number of minor roads radiate in towards the mountain to serve the farms and Maori settlements in this area. The round trip from New Plymouth around the mountain via the coast is 180km, though there is a smaller circle that cuts a third off this distance. Unless it is a clear day, there is not much point in approaching the mountain at close range, though the displays at the North Egmont Visitor Centre about the geology and unique plant life are interesting. The park is known for its flag trees, which have come to resemble pennants because of the constancy of the prevailing winds.

From the North Egmont Centre there are colour-coded walks of various lengths. For the more adventurous it is possible either to circumnavigate the volcano — a 4-day hut-to-hut walk that requires no experience — or to climb it. Although the ascent of the peak is accomplished by large numbers of people, bear in mind that more people have died on Mount Taranaki than on any other New Zealand mountain either due to a sudden change in weather or because of slipping over a bluff. The main route leaves from the North Egmont Visitors' Centre (and café) and follows a private road to the steps. When the steps run out you have to scramble over scoria and then up a lava flow to the summit. To improve your chances of seeing the view before the mid-day clouds descend, it is possible to stay in the camphouse at the Visitors' Centre. Take warm clothes as even in mid-summer it can be snowing at the top. Novices are advised to join one of the guided climbs organised by local alpine clubs. From the summit it is possible to see the other great mountains of the North Island — Ruapehu, Ngauruhoe and Tongariro — which serves to emphasise how small a place New Zealand is.

WHANGANUI RIVER

While the genteel town of Wanganui (population 40,000) retains its original spelling, the river on which is it sited and the National Park upstream are now officially spelled with a 'Wh', the preferred Maori spelling. The town is the starting point for the trip up the lovely Whanganui River to Pipiriki, where the park headquarters are located. If you do have some time in Wanganui visit the interesting museum, which has a good Maori and settlers' collection (admission $2). People with kids will want to visit the best children's playground in the country. The town centre has recently been renovated and revitalised, greatly improving the town's visual appeal.

The picturesque Riverside Inn at 2 Plymouth St (06-347 2529) is an associate YHA hostel. Cheapest beds are $15 per person, or B & B costs $45 for a single, $60 for a double. The hostel also arranges sightseeing and river trips. Also good is Tamara Backpackers at 24 Somme Parade (347 6300), which has beds in small dorms from $13.

The rural mailman welcomes visitors on his daily rounds along the 80km road up to Pipiriki and back, and this makes a very good day trip. Don Adams will collect you from your lodgings at about 7.30am and bring you back in the mid-afternoon, all for a modest $25. The early morning start often means that you see the valley at its most beautiful with the mist clinging to the river. Frequent stops are made to visit old mills, fossilised walls, and so on, and the mailman is a fund of local legends and gossip. On the opposite (and roadless) side of the river you can see several farms that depend on private aerial pulleys to convey themselves and their produce across the river gorge to town.

River trips were once a popular holiday for urban New Zealanders but these have now been reduced to day cruises in the summer. The preferred method nowadays of getting on to the river is in a jet boat, a method of propulsion invented in New Zealand (and, according to the now-retired Editor of the *Oxford English Dictionary Supplement*, himself a native of Wanganui, first used in 1964). While the road leaves the river at Pipiriki, jet boats penetrate further upriver. Trips will leave with a minimum of four people willing to pay $30 each. Jet Boat Tours (06-385 4128) charges $60 per person for a four-hour trip. One of the main attractions is the 'Drop Scene', where some people are able to persuade themselves that the river is flowing uphill.

Anyone interested in the trip upriver should obtain the Department of Conservation's leaflet about the river road from the Wanganui Visitor Information Centre at 101 Guyton St (06-345 3286). A leisurely 6-day trip on the Whanganui River for $500 can be booked with Baldwin Adventure Tours (06-343 6346), which also hires out two-person Canadian canoes for $35 a day and kayaks for $25 a day. It also has weekend trips on motorised river vehicles for just $75, which includes an overnight camp-out.

From Wanganui it is a fast 2½-hour drive to Wellington 200km due south. There are frequent coach services with InterCity and Newmans.

WELLINGTON

The Wellington authorities have chosen to promote their city as one of the great harbourside cities of the world, comparable to San Francisco and Hong Kong. The setting is indeed magnificent, with steep hills descending to the spacious harbour. But Wellington is a tiny city by world standards (with a population of just 150,000, though there are over 350,000 in the region), and if it were not for the cluster of high-rise buildings downtown, it would more closely resemble an English seaside town than a great modern capital city.

Some people maintain that of New Zealand's major cities, Wellington is the most genuinely New Zealand in character, having shaken off the colonial past. In the pursuit of progress, it has been rather ruthless with its old buildings, and many charming old wooden buildings downtown have been replaced by concrete and glass. However this trend may have finally been halted both by recession and by a City Council policy of encouraging restoration. So for example in 1991 one of the landmark buildings on the waterfront, the Odlins Building, was saved from demolition. However ambitious new building projects are not a thing of the past. Approval has been given to construct a 30-storey modernistic tower on the corner of Johnston and Waring Taylor Sts, which is due for completion in 1996. Work continues on upgrading the harbourfront, which may acquire the snappy name 'The Quays' to replace the clumsy-sounding 'Lambton Harbour Revelopment Project'.

Considering how susceptible Wellington is to earth tremors, it is surprising that there are any old buildings left at all. Wellington is situated on 4 active faultlines. Scientists predict that a major earthquake is virtually inevitable in the next century, though it is not known whether it will be more or less severe than the last major quake of 1855. Before disembarking from your aircraft, train, coach or ferry, read the introductory section on what to do during an earthquake. In some parts of the city there are height restrictions of 30m (about six storeys), partly because of earthquake danger and also to avoid interrupting views of the harbour.

CLIMATE
Wellington is notorious for being the windiest capital city in the world. A visitor might unwittingly come to the conclusion that the people of Wellington suffer from some dreadful genetic defect that causes them to walk at an incline. In fact, the winds that give Chicago the name 'Windy City' are no more than breezes when compared to the stiff southerlies into which you may find yourself leaning in Wellington. On some days the gales are so strong that only Captains (rather than First Officers) of Air New Zealand aircraft are permitted to land at the city's airport. The southerlies wreak havoc with hairdos and umbrellas. To escape the wind, you will either have to stay indoors until it blows over (usually no more than 3 days), leave town by crossing over to the South Island or travel inland where the Tararua Ranges afford some protection. Wellington gets just as many hours of sunshine as the much balmier Bay of Islands though it gets significantly more rain too.

THE LOCALS
The rivalry between Auckland and Wellington is rather more subdued than that between Sydney and Melbourne, though it certainly exists. For example

"*VISITORS MIGHT THINK THAT WELLINGTONIANS SUFFER FROM SOME EXOTIC DISEASE.*"

occasional campaigns to attract tourists from Auckland to Wellington meet with mirth and scepticism. Wellington became the capital in 1865 after Auckland had been the seat of colonial government for 25 years. Nowadays Wellington is full of politicians, civil servants and a large professional class that is perhaps a little disapproving of the business ethics and commercial energy associated with Auckland. Wellingtonians take themselves and their culture rather seriously. The difference can even be seen in the free newspapers published in both cities. Whereas Auckland's *Tourist Times* carries pages of advertisements and accompanying editorial on souvenir shopping, the *Capital Times* of Wellington and (especially) *Great Events* devote the majority of their pages to reviews of art exhibitions and opera productions; Wellington is proud of its role as New Zealand's city of culture and hosts a biennial arts festival. There are no American-style amusement parks in the region, but rather restored colonial cottages, antique shops and art galleries.

For such a small city Wellington is surprisingly cosmopolitan, with a good range of ethnic restaurants. Like most white-collar bureaucratic towns, it is also prosperous. Less affluent people tend to live in inland commuter towns like Lower and Upper Hutt, while the rich survey the city from houses on the hillside. Some houses are built on such steep hills that residents have installed private cable cars with which to winch themselves to their front doors.

Making Friends. The Wellington City Information Centre keeps detailed information about clubs and associations, many of which welcome visitors, from the Backgammon Club to El Club Espanol y Latino Americano de Wellington.

City Layout. The geography of Wellington has forced the population to settle along the two narrow valleys that are traced by Highway 1 to the west coast and Highway 2 to Upper Hutt, and the downtown area is therefore rather elongated. Note that the main shopping street Lambton Quay is not on the water despite its name; in fact it was an actual quay until the great earthquake of 1855, which raised more land out of the harbour and so pushed Lambton Quay back.

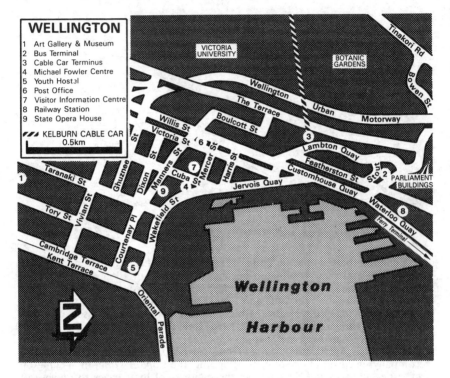

WELLINGTON

1   Art Gallery & Museum
2   Bus Terminal
3   Cable Car Terminus
4   Michael Fowler Centre
5   Youth Hostal
6   Post Office
7   Visitor Information Centre
8   Railway Station
9   State Opera House

KELBURN CABLE CAR
0.5km

ARRIVAL AND DEPARTURE

Air. Wellington International Airport is located in Rongotai on an exposed promontory just 8km south of the city centre. The domestic terminal is by far the busiest in the country, as many flights between towns on the two islands are routed through Wellington. It continues to be the butt of many complaints (even Prince Philip was once goaded into being rude about it) and a strict curfew (even for Ansett's Whisper jets) compounds the problem of frequent delays.

The international terminal — which has flights to and from Brisbane, Sydney and Melbourne — is situated between the Air New Zealand and Ansett NZ terminals. If you are leaving the country from Wellington, you must pay a departure tax of $20.

The bus service into town is privately run by Tranzit Coachlines (387 2018). Services operate every 20 minutes from the airport and from Bunny St (near the railway station) between 7am and 7pm and half-hourly outside those times between 6am and 9.30pm. Weekend services are reduced to half-hourly between 8am and 12.30 on Saturdays and noon to 8pm on Sundays. Tranzit buses from downtown call at several stops on Lambton Quay, Willis St, etc., which are clearly marked with a red logo. In the reverse direction, buses will stop almost anywhere you request along the route. The one-way fare is $4.50. A slightly more expensive door-to-door service is provided by Super Shuttle's minibuses (389 8787), while the taxi fare is about $15. For a cut price trip, you must walk 1km from the airport entrance along Calabar Road, right on Broadway to Miramar Junction where you can catch city bus number 3, 25 or E24.

The Skyferry to Picton (the cheapest air link between the two islands) may be contacted at any time on 388 8380. It is based in Air New Zealand's domestic terminal at Wellington Airport (see *New Zealand: Getting Around*).

Flight information can be obtained by dialling 388 9900. Ansett NZ's office is at the corner of Hunter St and Customhouse Quay (471 1146; toll-free 0800-800 146) while Air New Zealand is at 139 Vivian St (385 9911) and also the corner of Featherston and Grey Sts. For flights out of New Zealand try the downtown Adventure Travel Shop (Grand Arcade, Willis St; 473 1787) or STA Travel (233 Cuba St; 385 0561).

Bus. InterCity services stop on the Waterloo Quay side of the railway station (near platform 9). The booking office for coach and rail travel (498 3190) is open from 7am to 7.30pm Monday to Saturday and 8.15am to 7.30pm on Sundays. Newmans Coachlines' main depot is at the Interisland Ferry Terminal (385 1149). There is a morning and evening departure for Auckland and daily services to Palmerston North, Napier and New Plymouth.

Train. Wellington Railway Station is more bustling than those in Auckland and Christchurch as Wellington is served by Cityrail's fast commuter trains along the Hutt Valley (and beyond to Masterton) and along the Kapiti Coast to Paraparaumu. Some of these suburban runs are worth doing for their own sakes; for example the scenic trip to Porirua is a gem of a journey. The station is at the top of Customhouse Quay, where tickets may be bought between 7.30am and 5.30pm (from 7.30am to noon on weekends); telephone 472 5399 for information.

Driving. There is less choice of car hire firms in Wellington than in Auckland or Christchurch and so cheap deals are harder to come by. Try Thrifty at 16 Fifeshire Avenue (384 6711) or Southern Cross, 3 Kent Terrace (385 1596). The main international firms — i.e. Budget at 81 Ghuznee St (385 9085), Hertz at 166 Taranaki St (384 3809) and Avis at 25 Dixon St (385 0266) — all have outlets at the airport and ferry terminals. If you're making straight for Auckland, ask about relocation deals (see introductory section *Getting Around: Driving*).

The AA is at 342–4 Lambton Quay (473 8738).

Hitch-hiking. As there is only one corridor out of Wellington which serves the city's suburbs as well as further destinations, it is difficult to get a long distance lift from anywhere close to the city. For Highway 1 north to Auckland you should invest a few dollars in the train. The first good point is Porirua; when you leave the station, walk up to the right of the tracks to the traffic lights at the end of the motorway. A better point is a few stops further on at Paremata, where there is a roundabout on Highway 1 immediately outside the station. If this is crowded with other hitchers, take the train to Paekakariki or to its terminus at Paraparaumu which has a handy set of lights just across the road from the station.

You may find hitching advice posted on the notice board at the Wellington YHA hostel or at private hostels.

Ferry. Information regarding the ferry service to the South Island may be found in the introductory section *Getting Around: Ferry*. For up-to-date times and prices, ring the railway station on 498 3190. A shuttle bus runs between platform 9 of the railway station and the ferry terminal; it is a two kilometre walk if you are feeling energetic.

There is also a local ferry service to the mouth of Wellington harbour. East by West Ferries (499 1273) sails from Queen's Wharf in Wellington and arrives at Days Bay 20 minutes later, which provides easy access to the pleasant seaside town of Eastbourne. The price is $11 return.

CITY TRANSPORT

Bus. The two main city bus terminals are at the railway station and at Courtenay Place. You can obtain the free *Wellington City Bus Route Guide*, which carries detailed information about routes and times, from these and other outlets. Ring the Busline on 385 9955 for all city bus information. With the recent deregulation of public transport, it is likely that many routes and times will change over the next year or two.

Buses run from about 6am until 11.30pm during the week. Fares vary according to the distance travelled, ranging from $1 to $2.90. If you are planning to make a number of journeys, buy a ten-trip ticket from one of the city bus terminals, which will save you a fifth over the cash fare.

There are a number of worthwhile deals available. The *Downtowner* costs $3 and allows five trips within the central business district (between the station and Courtenay Place) including the cable car. It is aimed at shoppers and is valid from 9am–3pm Monday to Friday.

The *Daytripper* which costs $6.50 allows you unlimited travel on the Wellington bus network for one day as long as you begin your travel after 9am on weekdays. The *Bus Route Guide* sets out a suggested *Daytripper* itinerary which takes in the scenic waterfront drive along Oriental Parade, the drive up Mount Victoria, the Botanic Gardens by cable car and several other places of interest.

The frequency of many services is severely reduced at weekends, and some routes are discontinued completely, for instance the trip up Mount Victoria and the marine drive along Evans Bay Parade. So try to plan your itinerary for a weekday.

If you are interested in taking a bus tour, enquire at the City Information Centre about the daily tours run by Wellington City Transport; these depart daily at 2pm and cost $21. The long established rival is Wally Hammond's Sightseeing Tours (472 0869) which cost $20 for 2½ hours.

Cable Car. Like San Francisco, Wellington has a restored cable car (originally built in 1899) which runs from Lambton Quay opposite Grey St, up the Kelburn Hill to the eastern entrance of the Botanic Gardens. The trip lasts just four minutes and costs $1 on weekends and $1.50 on weekdays. After admiring the sweeping views over the harbour and perhaps stopping for some refreshments at the tea house, most people turn north and walk through the Gardens though the opposite direction brings you to the Victoria University of Wellington.

Car. The Wellington Urban Motorway takes traffic right into the city centre, keeping delays to a minimum. Also Wellington has a good record vis-à-vis drinking and driving; during a recent police campaign 10,752 drivers were tested and only 19 were over the limit (compared to 163 out of 9,000 in Auckland).

Parking, however, can pose problems. Anyone who is going to have the use of a car in Wellington for any length of time should pick up the *Parking Guide* leaflet from the Information Centre. In order to cure the locals of their haphazard parking habits, the city council has taken steps to police Friday evening and Saturday parking, and fines have been doubled. There is a $10 fine for allowing your meter to expire and $40 for parking on double yellow lines. The council has just installed 900 new meters which accept 20c, 50c and $1 coins. Car parks are located on Victoria St, under the posh James Cook Hotel on The Terrace, in the Williams Building at the corner of Boulcott St and Gilmer Terrace, in the James Smith's Council Car Park in Wakefield St behind the State Opera House, in the Lombard Parking Building in Lombard St and in the Clifton Terrace car park. Many of these are pay and display, so have plenty of change. An enormous new underground car park is planned for under the New Midland Park Tower and is scheduled to be opened in 1993.

Taxis. Taxi ranks are located outside the railway station, on Whitmore St (between Lambton Quay and Featherston St), outside Deka in Dixon St, in Bond St and at the corner of Willis and Aro Sts. To phone a cab, dial 385 9888 for Wellington Co-op Taxis or 389 3023 for Capital City Cabs. Since deregulation in 1991, it has been much easier to find an empty cab.

Cycling. Between the strong winds and steep hills, Wellington is far from being a cyclist's paradise, though a gentle trip around Marine Drive can be enjoyable and there are annual races in the city that are increasingly popular with mountain bikers. To find out about hiring a bicycle try Bicycles Unlimited at 65 Courtenay Place (385 1233), which has mountain bikes for $25 a day and road bikes for $15 a day, including helmet and lock, or phone 474 0578 weekdays 8am–8pm.

Hostels and Budget Accommodation. There is enough choice of good budget accommodation and a fast enough turnover of visitors (most people tend not to linger in Wellington) that you do not usually need to worry about not having a roof over your head. However, the numbers of independent travellers coming through the city are increasing and booking ahead often turns out to be a good idea, particularly during the summer. The competition among hostels is not as cut-throat as it is in Auckland so there aren't many sweeteners like free pick-ups, etc.

New Zealand's newest YHA hostel is the Port Nicholson in downtown Wellington which, like the new Auckland City hostel, is rather an upmarket place charging $18 in a four-person room with *en suite* bathroom and $22 for a double. It is located on the corner of Wakefield St and Cambridge Terrace (801 7280) near Courtenay Place (where all buses from the railway station arrive) and a host of good theatres, restaurants, etc.

The two most centrally located hostels are Rosemere Backpackers Hotel at 6 MacDonald Crescent near the corner of Willis and Dixon Sts (384 3041), which has beds from $13, and Trekkers Hotel at 213 Cuba St (385 3580), which offers good clean backpacker accommodation ($17 for a bunk, $19 per person in a twin) in a slightly seedy area. Trekkers also has its own travel shop, café, bar and restaurant. Downtown Wellington Backpackers (473 8482) is handily located opposite the railway station, and has over 180 beds, the cheapest of which are $16.

Maple Lodge is a private hostel in Mount Victoria at 52 Ellice St (385 3771), just before the tunnel begins. Take bus 2 and stop at the Basin Reserve. Dormitory beds are $15 (4 beds per dorm), singles $18, and doubles $16 per person. Weekly discounts are available. The hostel is non-smoking, quiet and clean. Also on Mount Victoria is the Beethoven House Hotel, an offbeat kind of place that will appeal more to classical music fans (as Beethoven is played from 7am) than to smokers (as smoking is banned). It stays open around the clock, so that if you arrive at 10.45pm on the last ferry from Picton, you don't have to worry, though it is better if you can phone or write ahead. Take bus 2 or 5 to Brougham St and walk along to number 89 (384 2226). If you enjoy being the centre of attention try to make your visit to the Beethoven coincide with your birthday, as the somewhat eccentric manager makes a point of celebrating as many birthdays as possible. Breakfasts are free, and it is a good source of information on job possibilities. Cheapest beds are $15.

Another possibility in the budget category is also on Brougham St. Although Rowena's City Lodge at number 115 (385 7872, reservations 0800-801414) looks like a mental asylum, it is highly popular and offers dormitory accommodation for $14, as well as singles, doubles and twins. It has the unusual feature of a picnic and barbecue area complete with appropriate provisions if required. There are also tent sites available for $9 per person.

If you're really down on your luck, the Emergency Night Shelter for homeless men is at 304 Taranaki St (385 9546).

Guest Houses and Hotels. In a more expensive bracket is the Terrace Travel Hotel at 291 The Terrace (382 9506), which charges from $40 single and $55–75 double, though it also has budget rooms for $20. If you are looking for more luxury, try Tinakori Lodge, the restored home of an early New Zealand Prime Minister. It is at 182 Tinakori Road (473 3478) in the historic area of Thorndon near the ferry terminal. Single bed and (lavish) breakfast costs $66, double $77 and triple $88. Another family-run bed and breakfast with character is the Victoria at 58 Pirie St, Mount Victoria (385 8512), which charges $40 single and $60 twin.

Camping. Although there are plenty of campsites along the Kapiti Coast north of Wellington, there are not many within easy reach of Wellington city. Hutt Park Holiday Village (95 Hutt Park Rd, Moera, Lower Hutt; 568 5913), which is 15 minutes' drive from the ferry port, is the closest. It has motel units and tourist cabins from $32–40 for two, as well as backpacker units and tent and caravan sites.

Eating and Drinking

Few of the clichés about eating out in New Zealand hold true in Wellington. The range of good restaurants and cafés is very impressive for a city of its size. Increasingly, restaurants are staying open past 10pm and many are also open on Sundays. Old established conventional restaurants like Plimmer's House and Kasey's have been replaced with Thai restaurants and fashionable coffee bars. Furthermore the distribution of restaurants around Courtenay Place and Willis St is so dense that you can usually find a congenial spot simply by wandering around (unless it is Sunday). The southern part of the downtown area has better pickings than the northern part which is mainly given over to highrise government and commercial buildings (i.e. Lambton Quay, Customhouse Quay, Featherston St).

The most interesting street for restaurants is Cuba St incorporating the pedestrian Cuba Mall between Ghuznee and Dixon Sts. As well as a number of Chinese restaurants (which normally stay open seven days a week), there is plenty of variety: from Konditorei Aida at number 181, an Austrian cake shop, to Monsoon at number 124 in the Mall which is Burmese. Also try one of the two Thai restaurants, Sala Thai at number 134 or Thiayathep at number 36, or Havana Midnight Expresso at number 178 which stays open till 2am. Café Istanbul serves Turkish food at number 156 and Cuba Cuba at number 179 concentrates on vegetarian dishes.

If a stroll along the kilometre length of Cuba St does not succeed, turn into Manners St where you will find the Ruby Chinese Restaurant at number 141 which advertises an 11-course set menu for $17, and the theatre upstairs in the Regent Centre where most main dishes cost about $13-$16. Locals often recommend the popular Mexican Cantina at 19 Edward St (near the Manners Mall) though it closes early (10pm) and does not take reservations, so you may have to queue.

If you are getting tired of innovative menus, try the steak and eggs at the Green Parrot at 16 Taranaki St which stays open late. Seafood restaurants tend to be located in fashionable harbourside locations and are therefore pricey. The Shorebird at 301 Evans Bay Parade specialises in fish which is not overpriced: the main fish of the day costs $18.50 which includes a bowl of fish chowder and a salad plate.

As throughout New Zealand there is a preponderance of Asian cuisines such as is offered by Toko Baru, an Indonesian restaurant at 146 Featherston St which stays open until 1am (last orders at 10.30pm) and Siouws at 41 Vivian St, a Malaysian curry and grill house. If you are having trouble finding anything open on a Sunday evening, head for Chevy's Licensed Café (97 Dixon St) which sells burgers and tacos from 11.30am-1am throughout the week or the Aro St Café (BYO), a little out of the city centre (90 Aro St), which has exotic food and live music Thursday to Sunday. Kahlo's, which opened in 1990 at 103 Willis St, aims to be like a public living room where you can go to drink coffee while writing a letter or reading a newspaper; it has a cheap and simple menu.

The Wakefield market, offering a range of fresh food and other goods, is at the corner of Jervois Quay and Taranaki St, open Friday 11am-8pm and weekends 10am-5pm. If you are self-catering and have your own transport, you should stop at some of the roadside stalls along the Kapiti Coast near Otaki (about an hour north of Wellington) where abundant fresh fruit, berries and vegetables are sold.

DRINKING

Wellington is not as well endowed with pubs as it is with restaurants; while there are over 300 restaurants, there are less than 50 licensed hotels. The restaurant district is also the best for pubs and discos. Try the Romney Arms Tavern on Plimmers Lane for food and music, and Greta Point Tavern on Evans Bay Parade which closes at 10.30pm (9pm on Sundays). So far there are three hotels with all-night licences: the Bond St Inn, the Lord Nelson Tavern and the posh Plaza International Hotel at 148 Wakefield St. At popular downtown pubs like the Featherston on Featherston St, you can buy wine by the glass and beer by the pint.

Wine lovers may want to take a trip to Martinborough, 80km east of Wellington, where an increasing number of good wines are being produced.

It takes about 40 minutes to walk from the station to the art gallery (longer into a headwind) and so it is worth mastering the public transport system. A more pleasant walk follows Oriental Bay south of the city centre where you can stop to swim on a hot day or admire the view and the affluent residences overlooking the harbour. Wellington has done a great deal to enhance its natural attractions, both in terms of quality of culture and the surroundings in which performances can be enjoyed (see *Entertainment*, below). The city is often compared to an amphitheatre, as it rises in a semi-circular bowl around the harbour. Some of the best views of the city can be had from the harbour itself, so if you take the Cook Strait ferry or the East by West ferry mentioned above, be sure to admire the views of the approaching or receding city.

Excellent panoramas may also be enjoyed from the top of Mount Victoria (bus number 20, Monday to Friday only), where the lookout is 200m above sea level. Ask for the special leaflet at the bus terminal about the Mount Victoria trip and the walks you can do from the summit. Although the Botanic Gardens at the top of the cable are not so elevated, they are easier to get to than Mount Victoria and afford an impressive sweep.

Buildings of Interest. It is fun to join one of the free tours of the Parliament Buildings, which are at the north end of The Terrace. J B Priestley once compared the House of Representatives to a 'cosy City Council chamber brought up to date with microphones', and the seat of New Zealand's government retains a small-town air of informality. The times of tours depend on when the House is sitting, but usually they take place every hour in the mid-morning plus a couple more after lunch; ring 471 9457 for details. All tours include the Beehive, the easy-to-spot administrative building where the Prime Minister has his office.

If Parliament is in session, try to turn up just before 2pm to see the opening ceremony. Watching a debate in Parliament House can be most entertaining, not least because of the colourful personal abuse exchanged between government and opposition. And when they are not insulting their opponents, New Zealand MPs seem to spend their time in Parliament reading newspapers or catching up on correspondence; each member has a generous supply of stationery. If you want to see life-sized puppet caricatures of prominent politicians from New Zealand's equivalent of *Spitting Image*, have a lunchtime drink at the Back Bencher Pub in Molesworth St.

Other buildings of note include the timber Gothic church of Old St Paul's in Mulgrave St near the station (where concerts are sometimes put on; 473 6722), and a restored craftsman's cottage from 1858 called the Colonial Cottage Museum at 68 Nairn St. It is open 10am–4pm Monday to Friday and 1–4.30pm on weekends (384 9122). Admission is $3, $2 for students. The New Zealand Historic Places Trust is housed in a gracious Edwardian building, Antrim House, 63 Boulcott St (472 4341).

Museum and Galleries. The Museum of New Zealand on Buckle St (385 9609) houses a good collection of Maori and colonial artefacts and is expanding its Pacific collections. It also includes the Academy of Fine Arts, which exhibits both national and international artists. Normally the Museum is open from 9am to 5pm daily (free admission), but at the time of writing it is closed to the public prior to the Museum's relocation in a new, specially built waterfront building from 1998. The City Gallery in Civic Square (801 3021) is a centre for both New Zealand and international contemporary visual arts, including painting, photography, sculpture, film and video, design and architecture. It is open 11am–5pm daily, and on Thursdays until 8pm for a range of special events.

Except for the Maritime Museum on Queen's Wharf (472 8904; admission by donation) and the restored home of the author Katherine Mansfield at 25 Tinakori Road (473 7268; admission $4), most of the museums are scattered around the Wellington region rather than in the city itself, for example the Settlers' Museum in Petone, the pioneer Cobblestone Museum in Greytown, the Tramway Museum in Paekakariki, and so on. Bibliophiles will enjoy browsing in the superb collection of rare books and manuscripts including a copy of the Treaty of Waitangi and a log book of one of Captain Cook's voyages, in the Gallery of the National Library in Molesworth St (474 3000).

Parks and Zoos. The Botanic Gardens at the top of the cable car are pleasant without being thrilling. The roses in the Lady Norwood Garden are at their best in mid-November. The Wellington Observatory is inside the Gardens and, as in Auckland, is open to the public on Tuesday evenings provided the night is clear. The new Education and Environment Centre in the Gardens has interesting displays about horticulture and the environment (open 9am–4pm and weekends 10am–4pm).

You can go for a bush walk along the 8km of trails at the Otari Native Plant Reserve (take bus 14 to Wilton Road). To see native fauna instead of flora, visit the Wellington Zoo in Newtown, which has the regulation nocturnal house for kiwis. The zoo is open 9.30am–5pm daily; take bus 10 to Newtown Park.

SHOPPING

The main shopping stretch between the station and Courtenay Place along Lambton Quay and Willis St is styled (at least by the tourist office) the Golden Mile. The biggest downtown department store is Kirkcaldies. Cuba Mall has some unusual shops including Cubacade Antiques and Curios.

For pottery try Earthworks Pottery in the AA Centre at the end of Lambton Quay or the Potter's Shop in the Kirkcaldies Building on Johnson St which is run as a cooperative. The National Library bookshop has reproduction prints, maps and engravings as well as cards. If you want to buy a modern map of New Zealand go to Infomap's shop in Heaphy House, 103-115 Thorndon Quay.

Browse in Tala's South Pacific Centre at 106 Victoria St for Maori and South Pacific crafts, books and tapes. Two second-hand bookshops you might try are Arty Bee's at 172 Cuba St and the Courtenay Book Exchange at 66A Courtenay Place. Trade Aid Shops in the Cuba Mall and several other locations sell quality handicrafts from the developing world.

One of the best markets for finding non-tacky gifts (as well as food) is the Wakefield Market mentioned above. It is open Fridays to Sundays only.

Entertainment

There is no lack of theatre, music and art in Wellington, and the city has spent lavishly over the past decade on buildings to house the arts. It may be on the brink of spending a great deal more ($270 million to be exact) on a new Museum of New Zealand on the waterfront, though this is some years off (assuming the project does go ahead).

The main concert hall is the architecturally striking Michael Fowler Centre (named after a dynamic mayor) which seats 2500. Even if you can't attend a concert, pop in to see the abstract wall hangings which represent Wellington in ten different aspects (including windy). Much of the interior is of rimu, a much-prized native timber, which gives the auditorium very live acoustics. The Centre is on Wakefield St at the top of Cuba St (472 3088). When booking a seat bear in mind that viewing is limited from the front rows. The MFC is part of the new Civic Centre which houses the new library on Victoria St, art gallery, information centre and children's museum. It is built round Civic Square which is designed to provide a restful atmosphere and a contrast to all the high rise building in this area.

In addition to the weekend issues of the two Wellington dailies, the *Dominion* and the *Evening Post*, the free magazine *Great Events* (produced by the Greater Wellington Promotion Council) has review articles on plays, concerts, sporting events, etc. and the *Capital Times* also has what's on listings. The BASS booking agency is in the State Opera House (385 0832). An international Festival of the Arts is held in March of even-numbered years.

Wellington has its fair share of outdoor entertainment. For details of events, ring the Public Relations Office (801 4000) or for information on the 'Summer City Festival' (December to March), ring the Parks and Recreation Department

(499 4444). (The amount of busking in Wellington may diminish if a local Council proposal to charge a fee to buskers is put into effect.)

Music. In addition to classical concerts, the Michael Fowler Centre in Wakefield St hosts concerts by visiting artists performing music of all kinds; ring the ticket office (471 1573) for details of the MFC's programme and also the Town Hall. Other concerts, including opera, are staged in the nearby State Opera House in Manners St (385 0832). This booking office also handles tickets for performances at the nearby Circa Theatre. Free concerts are put on at Broadcasting House in Bowen St (opposite the British High Commission) and also on Thursday lunchtimes in the university School of Music (471 5369). A local Maori cultural group rehearses in the Marae near the station; ring 472 1626 to see if it is possible to attend.

For tickets to see major rock and folk concerts, ask at Colin Morris Records, 44 Willis St (473 5196). Quite a few pubs and restaurants have live entertainment, most of which are listed in the *Evening Post* and on numerous billboards scattered throughout the city. Try the BYO As You Like It Café at 32/34 Riddiford St, Newtown (389 3983) where musicians perform at weekends. For folk music contact the Wellington Folk Centre (10 Holland St) on 485 0617 and listen to the recorded message. If you happen to be in Wellington for the Queen's Birthday Weekend (early June) you can go to the National Folk Festival at St Patrick's College in Kilbirnie.

Theatre. Wellington supports four professional theatre companies as well as several amateur ones. The Downstage Theatre Company usually performs interesting plays in the playhouse at the corner of Courtenay Place and Cambridge Terrace (384 9639). Student tickets booked in advance cost $20 for a downstairs seat and $15 in the gallery. Taki Rua Theatre at 12 Alpha St (384 4571) puts on a range of productions written by both Maori and non-Maori writers, with an emphasis on bicultural and Maori themes. The Circa Theatre on the corner of Taranaki and Cable Sts (801 7992) is an innovative and well established co-operative. The Wellington Repertory Theatre in Dixon St and the Stagecraft Theatre in Upper Cuba Mall are also worth checking; students are regularly given a discount.

The main downtown cinema complex is the Regent Centre in Manners Mall (472 5182). As in the rest of New Zealand, films that begin before 5am are half-price. The City Cinema at the City Gallery (see above) is open every night for screenings of art-house films.

SPORT

The calendar in the *Capital Times* includes sporting events, not all of which are likely to interest the visitor, such as netball tournaments or under-15 water polo championships. Horseracing takes place regularly at Trentham in Upper Hutt and night trotting is at Hutt Park. Rugby Union is played at Athletic Park (take the Island Bay route 1 bus) while cricket and soccer are played at Basin Reserve. Tickets to major events at Athletic Park cost approximately $20 in the covered seats and $15 in the uncovered seats. Enquire about tickets at the Wellington Rugby Union (472 2151). Wellington City Transport puts on special buses when there are important matches. An international motor race is held on Wellington's streets and waterfront on the first weekend of December.

The City Information Centre can advise people in search of exercise, especially those who are content with walking. There is an aquatic centre at Kilbirnie Park (through the Mount Victoria tunnel) with saunas, exercise classes, and so on. The Freyberg Swimming Pool (384 3107) on Oriental Parade is open daily from

6am to 9pm. Those who prefer to brave the sea can walk along the harbour to the beaches on Oriental Bay where downtown workers swim in their lunchtimes or travel further afield to Worser and Scorching Bays. The bays along this coast are full of yachts, especially at weekends. If you want to hire a windsurfer, ring 472 3306.

Wellington is the perfect city to take up kite-flying. Check local papers for kite flying demonstrations staged by the New Zealand Kitefliers' Association.

THE MEDIA

Newspapers. The *Dominion* newspaper has a reputation for even-handed and reliable coverage of political and business news, and is the closest New Zealand has to a national newspaper, closely rivalled by the *New Zealand Herald*. (It is the paper which took on the British Government by publishing excerpts from the banned book *Spycatcher*.) The *Evening Post* is more downmarket and has a considerably higher circulation.

Foreign newspapers may be read at the Public Library every day including Sunday afternoons. The new library was opened in November 1991 in Victoria St as part of the new civic centre development housing the Michael Fowler Centre, new art gallery, information centre and cafés. Alternatively, you can read home newspapers at your embassy (see *Help and Information*).

Radio. On the AM dial, tune to 567 for 2YA, 657 for 2YC, 1035 for 2ZB and 783 for 2YB. ZM-91 (nicknamed Hitradio) can be found on 90.9FM and is worth listening to for its frequent gig guides, as is 93.5FM. The Concert Programme is on 92.5MHz. The commercial 24-hour radio station Radio Windy specialises in classic rock and broadcasts on 94.1FM. The newest radio station is MORE FM on 98.9 and 100FM, while Fox FM is on 91.7.

It is possible to tour the TV-NZ complex at Avalon in Lower Hutt at 2pm on weekdays. Ring 236 8168 for details.

Wellington seems to have escaped the recent increase in armed crime which Auckland and Christchurch have been experiencing. However gangs of disaffected youths do roam around Cuba St and late night strollers can be hassled; provided you don't hassle them back there should be no problem, though there have been a few muggings on Cuba St and Vivian St. Massage parlours and associated activities may be found in the Ghuznee and Vivian St area. The Central Police Station is on the corner of Victoria and Harris Sts.

The area code for Wellington is 04. For fire, police or ambulance dial 111.

City Visitor Information Centre: Civic Administration Building, corner Wakefield and Victoria Sts (801 4000). Open seven days a week 9am–5pm.

British High Commission: 44 Hill St (472 6049).*US Embassy:* 29 Fitzherbert Terrace, Thorndon (472 2068).

American Express: c/o Century 21 Travel, 203 Lambton Quay (473 1221).

Thomas Cook: Greenock House, Lambton Quay (473 6267).

Automobile Association: 342 Lambton Quay (473 8738).

STA Travel: 233 Cuba St (385 0561).

Post Office: 43 Manners St (473 5922). Post restante services.

Medical Services: Wellington Public Hospital (385 5999).
Free Ambulance: 472 2999.
Emergency Dentist: 472 7072.
Emergency Chemist: 59 Cambridge Terrace (385 8810).
Gay Switchboard: 472 8609.

DAY TRIPS FROM WELLINGTON

The environs of Wellington are not as immediately appealing as those of Auckland, Christchurch or Dunedin, and are certainly less well known. However it is possible to spend an enjoyable few days exploring the region by car and on foot. There is a host of good beaches both on the relatively densely populated west coast and on the more distant and remote east coast. From Eastbourne (accessible by city ferry or bus 81) there is a four-hour round trip coastal walk you can do to Pencarrow Head that affords great harbour views. There is a blue penguin nesting-ground here.

Freshwater swimming in rivers and lakes is popular and pleasant picnic spots can usually be found nearby. There are several ranges of hills for hiking (though the weather at altitude is often shockingly windy and wet). There are also wildlife sanctuaries, historic buildings and the inevitable craft centres to visit. Some of these attractions are a little too far from Wellington to be visited comfortably on a day trip, however appropriate detours can be made when travelling to or from the city.

Several unsealed roads lead to bays at the southern tip of the North Island — for example, popular Makara Beach, about half an hour's drive from the city. Although it can become crowded on fine days, the throngs are easily left behind by walking a short distance. Owhiro Bay is even nearer the city, at the end of bus route 1 or 4. A one-hour walk brings you to the volcanic feature known as Red Rocks and a few kilometres beyond is a seal colony, which can be seen in winter only. Similarly on the eastern side of the harbour, scenic drives followed by stiff walks take you to a variety of headlands, all with vantage points for different views of the city.

The West Coast. Most weekending Wellingtonians head up Highway 1 to the so-called Kapiti Coast, a series of beaches about 50km north of the capital that enjoy excellent weather. The city suburban rail link terminates at Paraparaumu, which is the heart of the Kapiti Coast. The coast is sheltered by picturesque Kapiti Island 5km offshore, which — like so many small offshore islands in New Zealand — has been turned into a bird sanctuary. It can be visited, but first you will need a permit from the Department of Conservation (PO Box 5086, 2nd Floor, Bowen State Building, Bowen Street, Wellington; 04-472 5821), which also distributes a very informative leaflet about the reserve. Call 0900-52748 to book for Kapiti. Three commercial launches take people to the island.

Further north on this coast is a very fine Maori church at Otaki (75km from Wellington). Many Maori adopted Christianity very soon after it was introduced to them, and Rangiatea church was completed in 1850. There are also old Maori mission buildings in Otaki as well as an interesting local museum and an 1830s whaler's cottage. A Heritage Trail has been set up that guides visitors to a number of historic sites with the aid of a map and brochure.

Beaches such as Raumati, Peka Peka and Waikanae are safe and extensive enough to absorb the crowds easily. It is also worth leaving the main coastal road to climb into the hills, which afford excellent views. If you are fortunate enough to be in the area on an exceptionally clear day, it is possible to see the

South Island in one direction and Mount Egmont in the other. Advice on accommodation, special events etc. is available from the Kapiti Coast Promotion Council, PO Box 263, Paraparaumu (04-298 8993).

The Wairarapa Region. As the average New Zealander's threshold of tolerance for crowds is lower than that of most nationalities, some Wellingtonians have forsaken busy Highway 1 and the popular coastal beaches for the more secluded hinterland. On the eastern side of the Tararua Range (hills rising to over 1500m, locally famed for their almost unremitting rain and wind) is a pleasant rural valley dubbed the Wairarapa. It has a number of attractions, in particular the Mount Bruce National Wildlife Centre north of Masterton where some of New Zealand's endangered species are bred. Naturally it features a nocturnal complex, a craft shop and easy bush walks. It is open daily.

South-east of Masterton there are several wineries around Martinborough (a town whose streets are in the pattern of a Union Jack) though they are not so geared up for tourist visits as those of Hawke's Bay or the Henderson Valley. Although there are no backpackers' hostels in this area, there are charming B & Bs and campsites. The first week of March sees that most quintessential of New Zealand festivals in Masterton, the international sheep-shearing Golden Shears competition.

A further hour's drive east allows you to follow one of the unsealed roads down to the Pacific Ocean. Riversdale, where a number of holiday homes have been built, is the main resort. In a heroic attempt to entertain visitors to this coast, the locals organise special events such as frog-races, sand-castle-building competitions and obstacle races for tractors. A drive of 50km north brings you to Castlepoint, which every March hosts a horse race on the beach. There is another charming country race track at Tauherenikau near Featherston. There are buses to the Wairarapa from Wellington, but only on weekdays. For further information contact the Tourism Wairarapa Visitor Centre, PO Box 814, Masterton (06-378 7373).

The Great Outdoors Anywhere on the North Island, whether near the cities or on far-flung offshore islands, you will find enticements to swim, hike, fish and sail. The four National Parks of Egmont, Whanganui, Tongariro and Urewera all offer tramps and climbs of varying difficulty, but many are well suited to the novice. For example, every summer (weather permitting) thousands of day-trippers climb to the summit of Mount Taranaki, the second highest peak after Ruapehu. From one end of the island to the other, there are also numerous state forests, some covering vast areas. The New Zealand Department of Conservation (PO Box 10-420, Wellington; 471 0726) can send a range of leaflets on the North Island's National Parks and related topics, or you can approach one of the many regional Conservancy offices.

The North Island also excels at water sports, with its hundreds of miles of ocean beach, some sheltered enough for safe bathing and snorkelling, others attractive to surfers. Although not quite as well established as on the South Island, white-water rafting has become popular on a number of rivers, namely the Mohaka in Hawke's Bay, the Motu, Wairoa and Rangitaiki Rivers in the Bay of Plenty and the very similarly named Rangitikei south of Lake Taupo. A list of North Island rafting tour operators can be found in the tourist department's *Outdoor Holidays* booklet or try Riverland Outback Adventures, RD2, Napier (06-834 9756).

Flying Kiwi Wilderness and Cycling Expeditions (Deer Park Road, Koromiko,

RD3, Blenheim; 03-573 8126) are well known for their extensive and eccentric tours of the South Island (see *The South Island: The Great Outdoors*), but they now cover the North Island too. The *Northern Wanderer* tour, for example, takes in Auckland, Coromandel, the Bay of Plenty, Rotorua, Urewera, Napier and Wellington, and costs $450 for 8 days (food extra).

TRAMPING

The long-distance tracks of the North Island are not as well known as South Island tramps like the Milford and Routeburn Tracks, and therefore are often less densely populated. A further advantage of trekking in the North is that the season is longer, and most paths can be tackled in November and in April, months that are usually impossible in Fiordland.

Some might claim that the North Island treks are less spectacular, though this would be hotly disputed by many experienced locals and visitors. Certainly some of the best walking is not amidst high mountains but rather along coastal cliffs (for example, near both Auckland and Wellington) or around lakes such as Taupo and the exquisite Lake Waikaremoana. It takes about 4 days to encircle the latter, though this achievement is somewhat diminished by the knowledge that a road runs for a good distance (although of course motorists are less likely to notice the orchids and kakabeak trees, some of which can be found only in the Urewera National Park as it has the largest area of untouched forest in the country).

SKIING

The main ski fields of the North Island are as far away from the centres of population as it is possible to be: Whakapapa Village, the centre for skiing on Mount Ruapehu is 350km from Auckland and 335km from Wellington. As mentioned in the *Introduction*, snow-making machines have reduced the inconvenience caused by the vagaries of the weather. An even less likely disaster is that the ski mountains, which are active volcanoes, might erupt, though claims are made for a super-efficient early warning system. Perhaps the only realistic danger is that you will come into contact with an 'Auckland bomber', a skier who skis recklessly fast and terrifies less confident skiers.

When the conditions are right, the skiing on Ruapehu is excellent. Turoa together with the larger Whakapapa are the two commercial skifields, with all the appropriate amenities for both beginners and advanced skiers. Beyond the groomed trails there are usually empty and often exciting slopes. The nearest YHA hostel is at Ohakune, on the south side of Mount Ruapehu and 18km from Turoa Ski Field. Turoa has seven ski lifts including the only lift in New Zealand which serves a glacier. Transport is available from the hostel on Clyde St (06-585 8724). During the season (July to October) Ohakune becomes a lively little town with about 15 restaurants and plenty of accommodation.

The second skiing area on the North Island is the southern slopes of another volcano, Mount Taranaki. Access to the Maunganui Ski Field is from Stratford where there is limited budget accommodation, except at Stratford Holiday Park on Page St (06-765 6440).

The South Island

Population of South Island: 862,000   **Population of Christchurch: 302,700**

Some say that the further south you travel from Auckland, the further you travel into the past, ending at a fisherman's house on Stewart Island with no electricity, motor car or telephone. South Islanders are frequently characterised as being sleepy and reluctant to accept change. While slightly resenting this reputation, they are at the same time proud of their unhurried, uncompetitive way of life and have no wish to emulate what they perceive to be the fast living of the North Island. They realise that the west coast of their island is geographically and scenically unique and they would not trade it for all the artificial petrol factories and 'flash buildings' of the North Island, often referred to as the 'Mainland'. There is always strong opposition to proposals for hydroelectric developments as the South Island's environment suffers while the North Island's economy benefits. But there are also strong pressures to welcome investment that will create local employment and provide an economic boost.

Christchurch continues to promote itself as 'the most English city outside England'. But the colonial influences soon fade once you leave the big city, with the notable exception of the dignified city of Dunedin, which betrays its strongly Scottish heritage. Much of the South Island is farming country, some of it rich and productive, much of it suitable only for running sheep. The society is fundamentally rural with all the advantages and disadvantages that entails. But of more immediate interest to the visitor is the wilderness, especially the Alps, which extend for most of the island's length.

CLIMATE

Christchurch residents are contemptuous of the ignorance of North Islanders who assume that the South Island has a climate not unlike that of Antarctica.

In fact, the east coast of the South Island is often hot and dry in the summer, and droughts are not uncommon on the coastal plains and hill ranges north of Christchurch.

Between 2 and 3 inches of rain falls on Christchurch each month of the year, so there is no season when you can be sure of escaping one of the torrential downpours that periodically overtax the drainage system and render umbrellas useless. Still, the total precipitation is a fraction of what it is on the west coast as the Southern Alps force the clouds to drop most of their water in the west. The temperatures in Christchurch are moderate with very pleasant highs of around 25°C in the summer and crisp temperatures in the winter, usually staying above freezing but occasionally slipping below, at which times snow can fall.

Like the cities of the North Island, Christchurch is subject to strong winds at any season, which the locals recognise for their various properties. For example the north-westerlies bring dry heat that can be extreme in summer, while the southerlies bring rain and cold. On the other hand, it can become so still, especially in winter, that the smoke from household fireplaces hangs in the air creating unacceptable levels of smog.

The northern part of the island has the best weather, with Blenheim and Nelson vying for the title of 'Sunniest City in the South'. Both have an average of about 6½ hours of sunshine a day throughout the year. The west coast is mild but exceedingly wet; the quantity of rain that falls in some coastal and mountain areas, not to mention Stewart Island in the extreme south, is staggering. So don't plan to travel around the South Island without some superior rain gear. All the rain does of course account for the glorious lushness of the vegetation.

CHRISTCHURCH

Christchurch is the administrative and cultural capital with a population of less than a third of a million. It is a civilised city, if a little staid, with a spacious centre, neo-Gothic stone buildings and an air of calm confidence that some would call smugness. They have a tradition of preserving their historic buildings and green spaces, though recently have embarked on large-scale plans for redevelopment that are shamelessly aimed at increasing tourism and have aroused a great deal of hostility from some of the natives. Luxury hotels, upmarket shopping precincts and even now a tramway have been built while Cathedral Square is threatened with plans to 'do it up'. The city is exceedingly popular with Japanese honeymooners and as a result of this peculiar interest, a ten-day Festival of Romance was introduced in 1992 over St Valentine's Day. Although favoured by the mayor Vicki 'Turn-a-Fast-One' Buck, it fills many of the inhabitants with chagrin as they consider such measures to be undignified and are beginning to wonder whether they live in a toy town. Perhaps it is inevitable that Christchurch's fustiness and eccentricity would be replaced by late twentieth-century entrepreneurialism.

This sort of crass investment seems a long way from two decades ago when, after a visit to Christchurch, the author J B Priestley wrote that Christchurch looks 'as if it might have been lent to New Zealand by the Anglican church — at its best'. Most of the main streets are named after Anglican diocese, both English (Durham, Hereford, Worcester, etc.) and colonial (Barbadoes, Montreal, Colombo). Punting takes place on the River Avon, uniformed school boys can be seen cycling home and a red double-decker bus takes tourists on city tours. But Christchurch is not Singapore or Dallas; it is still unmistakably a New Zealand city where walking paths on the outskirts may be closed for several weeks in the spring for lambing and pubs are closed on Sundays, streets have Maori names like Papanui and shops that sell sheepskins seem to outnumber

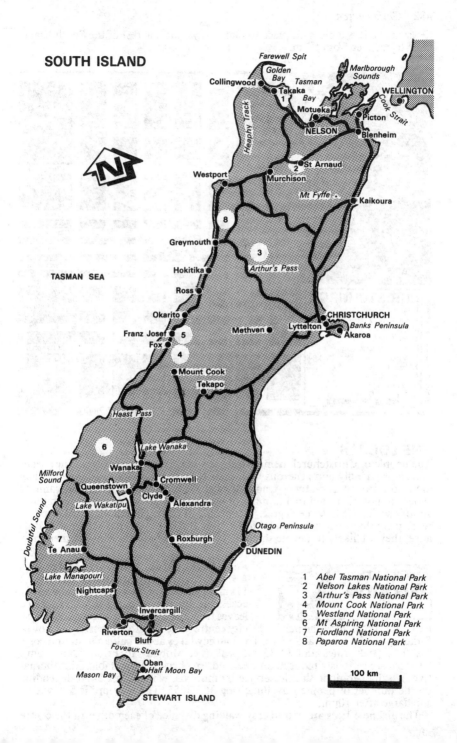

SOUTH ISLAND

Farewell Spit
Golden Bay
Collingwood • Takaka
1
Motueka
NELSON
Tasman Bay
Marlborough Sounds
WELLINGTON
Cook Strait
Picton
Blenheim

Heaphy Track

Westport
2 St Arnaud
Murchison
Mt Fyffe
Kaikoura

8

Greymouth
3
Arthur's Pass

Hokitika

Ross

Okarito
Franz Josef 5
Fox
4
Methven
CHRISTCHURCH
Lyttelton Banks Peninsula
Akaroa

TASMAN SEA

Mount Cook
Tekapo

Haast Pass

6
Lake Wanaka
Wanaka
Queenstown
Lake Wakatipu
Milford Sound
Doubtful Sound
Cromwell
Clyde
Alexandra

Otago Peninsula

7 Te Anau
Roxburgh
DUNEDIN
Lake Manapouri
Nightcaps

Invercargill
Riverton
Bluff
Foveaux Strait
Oban
Half Moon Bay
Mason Bay
STEWART ISLAND

1 Abel Tasman National Park
2 Nelson Lakes National Park
3 Arthur's Pass National Park
4 Mount Cook National Park
5 Westland National Park
6 Mt Aspiring National Park
7 Fiordland National Park
8 Paparoa National Park

100 km

newsagents. It is a pleasant place to plan forays into the rest of the South Island ... or to recover from them.

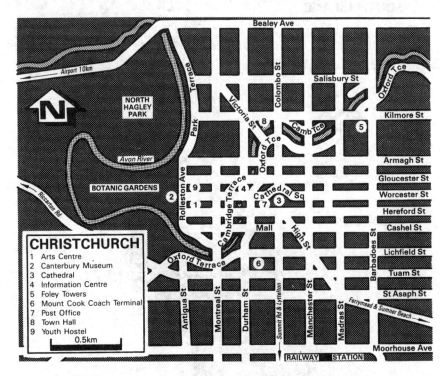

CHRISTCHURCH

1 Arts Centre
2 Canterbury Museum
3 Cathedral
4 Information Centre
5 Foley Towers
6 Mount Cook Coach Terminal
7 Post Office
8 Town Hall
9 Youth Hostel

0.5km

THE LOCALS

The people of Christchurch demonstrate few big city characteristics. They seem almost as friendly and generous with their time as other South Islanders. They are also fairly conservative. A host of rules — for example jeans and running shoes are not permitted in a number of hotels and clubs — tends to inhibit and stultify social life to some degree. The people of Christchurch may strike you as more prim than spontaneous and fun-loving. But once you make their acquaintance, they are likely to devote themselves unstintingly to showing off their city.

ARRIVAL AND DEPARTURE

Air. Christchurch International Airport is 11km north-west of the city centre and easily accessible by public bus 24L. The service leaves from the airport terminals about every half hour. If catching the bus in the city centre go to the stop opposite the Tower Building at 65 Cathedral Square. The journey takes about half an hour and costs $2.70 at peak times and $1.35 off-peak (i.e. Monday to Friday 9am–4pm). Services are seriously reduced on weekends so check the timetable. The alternative is a door-to-door shuttle service by minibus, which costs $4–6 depending on the number of people travelling; ring 365 5655. The taxi fare is $15 with a surcharge after 10pm.

The airline offices are within easy walking distance of each other in the centre of the city. Air New Zealand is at 702 Colombo St (379 5200), while Mount Cook is at 91 Worcester St (348 2099) and Ansett NZ is at the corner of Worcester St and Oxford Terrace (379 1300). Students should check with STA at 223 High St (379 9098) to arrange onward air travel. Other travel agencies that offer discounted international fares include the Adventure Travel Shop, 77 Cashel St (379 7134) and Greg Miller Travel, Upper Level, Merivale Mall, 189 Papanui Road (355 9019).

If you are leaving New Zealand from Christchurch, you must pay a departure tax of $20.

Bus. There is no single coach depot in Christchurch, though timetables and bookings for the two major companies can be made at various travel agencies such as the YHA Travel Centre at the corner of Gloucester and Manchester Sts (379 9970), Trailblazers at 86 Worcester St and the agencies mentioned above, as well as at the Visitors Centre (see below).

Mount Cook Landline is the main coach operator on the South Island. Its terminal is at 40 Lichfield St, between Durham and Colombo Sts (348 2099). The two other ticketing offices in Christchurch are at 91 Worcester St and 47 Riccarton Road, just past Hagley Park. The toll-free reservations number is 0800-800737.

InterCity Coachlines has daily coach departures to Queenstown (via Mount Cook), to Dunedin and to Picton. The InterCity coach for Queenstown departs at 8am and arrives at 5.45pm while the Dunedin services depart at 9.15am and 1.15pm arriving 6½ hours later.

Many private minibus services run daily between Christchurch and Greymouth via Arthur's Pass; call 0800-800847 for schedules.

Train. The railway station is in Addington Road, and the Super Shuttle provides a connection to the city centre, costing about $3. The ticket office opens at 7am every day of the week, closing at 5.30pm on weekdays, 1.15pm on Saturdays and 9.15am on Sundays (opening again on Sundays for an hour from noon).

The three daily train departures all take place in the early morning while the arrivals are all between 6pm and 7.30pm. The train for Picton leaves at 7.30am, for Dunedin and Invercargill at 8.30am daily (plus an extra Friday night service leaving at 5.15pm) and for Greymouth on the West Coast via Arthur's Pass at 9am. For schedule information call 0800-802802. Students, backpackers and YHA members are entitled to discounts of 20–30%.

Driving. Entering and leaving Christchurch by road is fairly straightforward, although many city centre roads are one-way. The intense competition among car hire firms in Christchurch results in a large choice of reasonably priced hire deals. Here is a selection of the smaller firms:

Avon Rent-a-Car, corner of Tuam and Antigua Sts (379 3822).
Pegasus Rental Cars, 127 Peterborough St (365 1100).
Renny Rent-a-Car, 156 Tuam St (366 6790).
Rhodes Rent-a-Car, 501A Blenheim Road (348 8219). Also hires four-wheel-drive vehicles and has an office in Dunedin (779 950). YHA members get 10% discount.
Southern Cross Rental, 105 Victoria St (379 4547). Ask about relocation deals if you are heading for Picton.
U-Save Rent-a-Car, 112 Hazeldean Road (379 3492).

Christchurch is reputed to be a good place to buy second-hand cars, partly because the climate isn't conducive to rust, and also because quite a few travellers decide to sell their cars after touring the South Island. Check in the Christchurch *Press* for the times of car auctions, and go ahead of time to check the cars over.

A car dealership that promises to buy back cars from travellers is Wheels at 20 Manchester St (366 4855). The AA is at 210 Hereford St.

Hitch-hiking. Christchurch Transport Ltd's free booklet *Explore Christchurch* describes how hitch-hikers can use the city's bus routes to get out to the best hitching spots. The Bus Kiosk (see below) will also be able to provide advice.

CITY TRANSPORT

Bus. The city's public transport system is focused on Cathedral Square, with bus routes heading off in all directions. For information on routes and timetables contact the Businfo line on 366 8855. An Explore Pass, providing a full day's travel on the 'Big Red Bus' services, costs $5 — you can buy one from Big Red Bus drivers, the Bus Kiosk in Cathedral Square or from Christchurch City Council service centres. The Kiosk is also the place to go with bus-related queries.

Also based on Cathedral Square is the Tramway, which goes in a loop taking in Worcester St, Rolleston Avenue and Armagh St.

Car. Parking problems are rare in Christchurch. There are several parking buildings in the centre of town, for example on the corner of Manchester and Gloucester Sts, on Lichfield St and on Oxford Terrace across from the Information Centre. There is metered street parking throughout the downtown area. The meters allow from half an hour to four hours, though you will require 10c or 20c coins no matter what the maximum permitted time is. Twenty cents buys anything from 10 to 40 minutes, depending on how prime the location is. Meter regulations are in force from 9am to 5pm Monday to Thursday, 9am–8pm on Fridays and 9am–1pm on Saturdays.

Taxis. Call Gold Band on 379 5795 or Blue Star on 379 9799.

Cycling. Christchurch encourages cycling both with its untaxing terrain and its special traffic provisions for cyclists, including a pleasant cycle track through Hagley Park. Bicycles cannot be ridden nor parked in the Cashel St pedestrian mall, nor even wheeled through the Botanic Gardens.

Bicycles may be hired from Rent-a-Cycle, 141 Gloucester St and from the travel centre Trailblazers at 86 Worcester St (366 6033).

Water Transport. Whereas in Oxford and Cambridge you can hire your own punt to pole yourself along the Rivers Cherwell or Cam, in Christchurch you must allow someone else to do the punting. The Punting-on-the-Avon Company (corner of Worcester St and Oxford Terrace; 379 9629) takes you out on rides lasting 20 or 30 minutes which cost respectively $10 or $12 per person.

Canoes, paddle boats and rowing boats may be hired between 9.30am and 6pm daily from the Antigua Boatsheds, 2 Cambridge Terrace (366 5885). The cost is $4 per hour per person. One hour allows you to paddle through the Botanical Gardens and back.

Away from the city centre, there are ferries which leave from Lyttelton Wharf bound for Quail Island (a 30-minute trip) or across the harbour to Diamond Harbour (15 minutes). The one-way adult fare for the latter trip is $3.60. There are about ten sailings a day during the week, and six at weekends.

Accommodation

Jasons Holiday and Leisure Accommodation lists over 50 hostels, lodges, motorcamps and guest houses in Christchurch, so there is plenty of choice. Even some of the downtown hotels offer cheap backpacker accommodation. For example, the centrally located, bright yellow wood-framed Hereford Private Hotel at 36 Hereford St (379 9536) has dormitory accommodation from $15 (although it may be full in the high season). Single rooms cost $25 and doubles $35. The Ambassadors at 19 Manchester St (366 7808) has similar accommodation at similar prices. Stonehurst Lodge at 241 Gloucester St (379 4620) also offers backpacker accommodation.

Hostels. There are two IYHF hostels: one is in the city centre, the other about two miles north-east of Cathedral Square. The Rolleston House YHA hostel at 5 Worcester St (377 9013) could not be more ideally located, as it is opposite both the Museum on the edge of the Botanic Gardens and the Art Centre. The hostel, which is in an old building formerly a university residence, charges $16 (366 6564).

The suburban hostel is called Cora Wilding after the founder of the New Zealand YHA movement, and is in a lovely setting. It often has beds when the downtown hostel is full. To get there take bus 10 from behind the Cathedral in Worcester St and after a ten-minute ride get off at Tweed St. It is in a very pleasant neighbourhood for cyclists, and can also be reached on foot in less than half an hour by walking alongside the River Avon past Swanns Bridge and left into Evelyn Couzins St. The castle-like hostel is at number 9 (389 9199).

A mini-chain of hostels called Pavlova Backpackers has become very popular among South Island travellers. The Christchurch one is right in Cathedral Square at number 50 (366 5158) and charges $13.50 which includes a free slice of pavlova. Its main rival is Foley Towers (formerly Avon View) at 208 Kilmore St (366 9720), which is non-smoking. The manager is responsible for the admirable leaflet on budget accommodation throughout New Zealand.

Charlie Brown's at 268 Madras St (379 8429) was advertising the lowest prices in New Zealand at the time of writing: $8 in a dorm, $20 for two people in a double. Other backpackers' hostels include Bealey Road Hostel (70 Bealey Road; 366 6760), Aarangi Backpackers (15 Riccarton Road; 348 3584) and the small non-smoking, non-drinking hostel called Dreamland (50 Perth St; 366 3206).

Guest Houses. Gracious old Christchurch homes offering bed and breakfast might make a welcome change from hostels. Two which charge only $25 are at 141 Opawa Road (365 3718) between the airport and town, and 7 Selwyn St (332 8141) in the direction of the Cashmere Hills.

Camping. Several motor camps are located in the vicinity of the Addington Racecourse about 3km from the centre; try the Showground Motor Camp just 3km from the city centre (Whiteleigh Avenue; 338 9770), which charges from $26 for two people in a unit, Amber Park (308 Blenheim Road; 348 3327) or Riccarton Park Motor Camp (19 Main South Road; 348 5690). Another good one is Meadow Park Holiday Park at 39 Meadow St off Papanui Road (352 9176), which charges $30 for two in a standard cabin and $18 for two people pitching a tent. If you don't mind being further from central Christchurch try Pineacres Motor Park near Kaiapoi (327 5022) or South New Brighton Camping Ground (388 9844) not far from the beach. A few intrepid souls have been known to pitch their tents in Hagley Park as discreetly as possible.

Eating and Drinking

There are nearly 100 Bring-Your-Own grog restaurants in Christchurch, compared to less than five in the late 1970s. They run the whole gamut of upmarket to humble, conservative to innovative with a reasonably broad range of ethnic cuisines from Greek to Indonesian.

Recommendations for cheap eateries often find their way onto hostel notice boards, so keep your eyes open. The giveaway monthly *Christchurch Tourist Times* includes several pages of restaurant reviews and recommendations (unfortunately not always impartial as the paper is funded by advertising). Also consult the free *South Island Restaurant Review* for ideas.

Dux de Lux in the Arts Centre is a long established gourmet vegetarian restaurant in an excellent location, the Arts Centre, on the corner of Montreal and Hereford Sts. It now has a brewery on the premises whose brews can be tasted either in the Brewery Bar which serves tapas (especially seafood snacks) or the Tavern Bar which has live music Monday to Saturday, though the complex is open seven days a week from 10am till midnight. Queues at the cafeteria-style counter can be long at lunchtimes and bookings for the dining room are often necessary in the evening. There is plenty of outdoor seating.

Another good vegetarian restaurant is the Main St Café at the corner of Colombo and Salisbury Sts which has pleasant wood-panelled decor and is open seven days a week; main courses cost about $17. In fact this area of Colombo St just north of Victoria Square and the river is recommended for restaurant browsing. Nearby, Spagalimis is a basic pizzeria at 55 Victoria St where a good one or two person pizza can be bought for $8.50. It functions both as a licensed restaurant and as a popular take-away. There are several worthwhile Mexican restaurants including the Mexican Cantina at the corner of Worcester and Manchester Sts which, like its counterpart in Wellington, closes at 10pm. Also try the Mexican Café in the Guthrey Centre.

While wandering around central Christchurch, you will have no trouble finding tasty snack food during the day. In recent years ethnic food vans and stalls have operated in Cathedral Square despite opposition from local traders. Nearby Middle Eastern takeaways will sell you falafels - spicy deep-fried chickpea rissoles served with salad and pitta bread - for about $5 which you can eat in the Square on a sunny day. Then you can amble through the Chancery Arcade to buy a frozen yoghurt. The Saturday and Sunday market in the Arts Centre includes ethnic food stalls which will sell you a cheap and interesting plate of Brazilian bean stew or Ukrainian dumplings. If you want to splurge on some out-of-this-world desserts visit Strawberry Fayre at 114 Peterborough St.

The Oxford Victualling Co by the river is open seven days a week for traditional roast meals at low prices. The upstairs bar serves counter lunches (e.g. sandwiches) and is patronised mainly by shoppers. The other native cuisine of New Zealand, the Maori hangi, can sometimes be sampled at the National Marae (address below in *Exploring*) where hangis cost $25 a head; ring 388 7685 for details.

Since the Greek bandleader at the Mykonos Taverna (112a Lichfield St) returned to Greece, the restaurant at that address has become Mood Indigo aimed at 'the more mature customer'; they offer a set menu for $30 (winter special), which includes accompaniment by a jazz trio.

DRINKING

With the passing of the Sale of Liquor Act in 1990 there is a much wider choice of late-night drinking place than there was a few years ago. Pubs like Dux de Lux, the Coachman Inn at 144 Gloucester St and The Park at Nancy's (described below) stay open till midnight or 1am from Thursday to Saturday at least. However there are still lots of licensed premises which stick to the old closing times of 10pm on week nights and 11pm at weekends due to lack of late-night custom.

Warner's Hotel in Cathedral Square (adjoining Pavlova Backpackers Hostel) is popular with travellers because of its central location, the availability of draught Guinness in both bars and live Irish music. Another Christchurch institution is The Park at Nancy's (1 Riccarton Road at Deans Avenue) which, at 140 years old, is the oldest hotel in the city. Although it now has a fancy restaurant overlooking Hagley Park and an appealing supper menu with items like filled potato skins and nachos for $5, it retains the old public bar which is for locals. Another pub you might try is Hats, formerly the rough King George Hotel but recently bought by the Polytechnic student union (Hats stands for Happily Acquainted Tertiary Students). It is at the corner of Madras and St Asaph Sts.

There are some picturesque drinking holes in Lyttelton and Governor's Bay which are impracticable to visit in the evenings. Stonehurst Lodge (mentioned in *Accommodation* above) organises 'country pub crawls' which leave Christchurch at 5.30pm three nights a week and end up in the bar of the Stonehurst. The cost is $20.

Occasionally you can find the west coast brew Monteith's (now owned by Dominion Breweries) on tap in Christchurch pubs. To find out if you can tour the old Christchurch Brewery ring 379 4940. Most hotels including Nancy's and Warners Hotel have a bottle store; the one at Nancy's is part of the Neighbourhood Liquor chain. The cheapest off-licence is the Imperial bottle store on the corner of Barbadoes and St Asaph Sts, followed by Wilson & Neil on Hereford St at Fitzgerald Avenue. All of these are good places to stock up on supplies for a BYO restaurant.

Although the bulk of New Zealand wine is made around Auckland, there are a few wineries around Christchurch. The oldest commercial vineyard in the area is St Helena Estate, a 20 minute drive north of the city. It is possible to taste and buy between 10am and 5pm Monday to Saturday.

Because the city of Christchurch is so flat, the Cathedral spire can be seen from most quarters and provides a useful landmark. The Avon (which is named after a river in Scotland rather than the one running through Shakespeare's birthplace) winds gently through the enormous Hagley Park and Botanic Gardens. The central streets are basically on a grid pattern with the exception of Oxford Terrace and Cambridge Terrace which flank the river. Colombo St is the longest straight street in the country, if you don't count the short interruption made by Cathedral Square. In addition to the green strips alongside the two riverside terraces, there are many parks, gardens and leafy squares like the new Victoria Square around the city.

Guided walks leave from the kiosk in Cathedral Square (daily except winter) at 10am and 2pm; the two-hour tour costs $8. The Information Centre has a brochure *The City Walk Guide* which you can follow on your own.

The two blocks of Worcester St between Cathedral Square and Hagley Park are being torn up at present to put down tramlines and unimposing Worcester St is to be turned into a boulevard. This is a small-scale revival of the trams which once ran from the city to New Brighton, but the distance is so short - walkable in less than ten minutes - as to be of merely touristic appeal. If you are staying for only a day or two the tourist handout map should suffice. If you want more detail buy the official bus route map for $2 which includes a street index and extends to the suburbs.

In addition to the city centre, the other areas of Christchurch which reward exploration are Lyttelton Harbour, the beaches (such as Sumner and Brighton) and the Port Hills beyond the posh suburb of Cashmere. These are described in the section below on *Day Trips*. Do not be confused by numerous references on signs to Canterbury, the region of which Christchurch is the capital.

In the summer, Cathedral Square provides plenty of free entertainment.

Jugglers, clowns and musicians find the square ideal for busking and many performers participate in the Summer Times Festival (early January to late February) when performances take place over the lunch hour. Festival events are also held in the Arts Centre Quadrangle and in North Hagley Park.

One of Christchurch's unique forms of entertainment is still going strong. The Wizard of Christchurch amuses a tolerant audience every day (August-May) at 1pm outside the Cathedral with orations on topics as diverse as media bias and the inferiority of women. He associates himself with many local campaigns and a plaque in his honour will be mounted on the old-fashioned telephone box in the Worcester Boulevard which he was instrumental in preserving. Despite his eccentricities he commands much local respect and finds his way into all the official promotional literature. Cathedral Square is the New Zealand equivalent of 'Speaker's Corner' and the Wizard has to compete with Bible-bashers and many others.

Museums and Galleries. The Canterbury Museum is especially recommended for its reconstruction of a colonial street, including a pub, gun-maker and provision store. The natural history sections are also most interesting, especially if you have not seen a giant moa skeleton elsewhere in your travels. The Museum is located on the edge of the Botanic Gardens and is open every day of the year from 10am to 4.30pm. Admission is free.

The Museum's Antarctic exhibition was so popular that it has been expanded into its own centre in Orchard Road which includes an 'Antarctic Experience' for visitors. Whether or not you will have to wear the woollen hiking gear you have been saving up for Fiordland remains to be seen. But even the non-hands-on exhibitions in the Museum are interesting, about the history and exploration of Antarctica including the sledges, fur apparel and meagre entertainments which accompanied Scott, Shackleton, etc. on their expeditions.

The principal art museum is the Robert McDougall Art Gallery next door to the Museum in the Botanic Gardens, with the same opening hours except Sunday when it is open 2–4.30pm only. The Gallery has more Maori artefacts than the Museum whose collection is not on display for conservation reasons. The CSA (Canterbury Society of Arts) is a commercial gallery at 66 Gloucester St which exhibits contemporary New Zealand arts and crafts in six galleries and is open seven days a week. For Maori handicrafts, visit the Nga-Hau-E-Wha National Marae (250 Pages Road; take bus 5N) where you can admire Maori carvings on the building itself as well as pieces carved by a resident craftsman. Guided tours cost $5.

The Cathedral was built in 1864 and is of limited architectural interest, though you can have a free guided tour if you like (daily except Sunday at 11am). On a clear day, it might be worth paying $1 to climb the 133 steps of the tower to try to glimpse the distant Alps.

The transport and technology museum at Ferrymead will interest even those who are not train-spotters. In addition to the vintage cars, steam locomotives and restored tram cars, there are displays on everything from old washing machines to mechanical musical instruments to old fire engines. It is open 10am–4.30pm daily and admission is $7 (384 1970). Catch the Sumner bus numbered 3J or 3K. In summer some of these call at the park entrance; otherwise there is a bit of a hike from the bus stop. A rail link to Ferrymead, using the Lyttelton rail line, has been proposed by a tourist promotion group but has so far come to nothing.

If you are at all interested in aviation history you will want to visit the Royal New Zealand Air Force Museum at Wigram Aerodrome which opened about five year ago and is reputed to be the best aviation museum in the Antipodes. Take bus 25.

Parks and Zoos. One of Christchurch's nicknames is 'Garden City of the Plains' so you will not be surprised to find plenty of green space in the city. The long-established Botanic Gardens behind the Museum provide a pleasant venue for strolling or reading on a sunny bench. British visitors will be less interested in the rose garden than in the display of New Zealand native plants. Greenhouses specialise variously in desert plants, ferns, orchids and tropical plants.

The old zoo and aquarium at 155 Beach Road (bus 19M; admission $3) has been somewhat eclipsed by the Orana Wildlife Park on Mcleans Island Road beyond the airport (359 7109). As the park operates like a safari park, you must join a bus tour. The South Island's first Kiwi House is open 10am–5pm and the lions are fed at 2.30pm. The park entrance fee is $12 per adult.

A small area of native bush has been preserved close to the city. Dean's Bush is easily accessible by bicycle, buses 8, 21 and 24, or on foot through Hagley Park and along Kilmarnock St. It contains many fine rimu, white pine and tea trees, as well as Canterbury's oldest building (1843), which was originally a homestead and is now a museum.

SHOPPING

The central pedestrian mall has all the stores you would expect plus one or two unusual ones. More interesting shops can be found in the redevelopment of Colombo St north of Kilmore St, a ritzy shopping and restaurant area. Ballantynes Department Store, accessible from the City Mall, is fairly expensive; DIC across the road and the Farmers Trading Company on Gloucester St are both cheaper. Routine shopping is even cheaper outside the city centre, for example at the Riccarton Mall. The Central Mission Goodwill Store (Armagh and Manchester Sts) and the Save the Children Fund charity shop (Bells Arcade between Cashel and Lichfield Sts) sell second-hand clothes and other items. There are several Army Surplus stores; the best one is at 77 Manchester St.

There is a shortage of dairies and grocery shops in the central business district of Christchurch, so if you want to buy some provisions ask a local for directions.

The outdoor market held in the quad of the Arts Centre on weekends (10am–4pm) has many interesting stalls selling arts and crafts, including jewellery, pottery and other portable and affordable items. In fact the Arts Centre provides permanent studio space for potters, sculptors, candle and toy makers, leather workers, etc. Craft shops remain open throughout the week. The Riki Rangi Maori Carving Centre in the Arts Centre complex sells distinctive and expensive wood and bone artefacts. A shop called Hands at 5 Normans Road (off the Papanui Road) carries all the materials and equipment for spinning and weaving and does an international mail order business.

Browsers in downtown Christchurch will be struck by the number of souvenir and sheepskin shops, whose names all seem to incorporate the word 'Nature'. One you might try is the environmentally friendly Wild Places in Shades Arcade. The city centre is fairly deserted on Saturdays though a few shops (mainly catering for tourists) are open. Saturday shoppers should head for the beach suburb of Brighton where most shops stay open until 9pm on Saturdays. The Robert McDougall Art Gallery has a shop selling books, reproductions and local crafts, open daily.

Scorpio Books at 138 Oxford Terrace is the most interesting bookshop in town and a good source of information on 'alternative' events. GP Books at 147 Hereford St has a good stock of maps and guides. Kate Sheppard's Women's Bookshop is at 145 Manchester St.

New and second-hand sports goods can be found at Recycled Recreation, 81 Manchester St near St Asaph St and at Secondhand Camping, 167 High St.

Duty-free shopping is available at the corner of Colombo and Gloucester Sts to those flying out of New Zealand from Christchurch.

Entertainment

The Arts Centre, housed in the gracious buildings of the original university, is the focus of the city's cultural life. The complex encompasses the Court Theatre where mainstream plays are performed plus three others devoted to art films, dance and experimental theatre. Concerts and recitals are held in the Great Hall at lunchtimes on Fridays and possibly other times as well; these usually cost about $6. Films organised by the Canterbury Film Society are shown in the Clockwork Theatrette on Tuesdays and Sundays. The James Hay Theatre is the opera venue if you happen to be in town when the Canterbury Opera Company or a touring company is performing.

There are other theatrical options in the city: try the Theatre Royal at 145 Gloucester St (379 5147) or the Repertory Theatre at 146 Kilmore St (379 8866). Tickets usually cost about $25, though student stand-bys are sometimes available for $15. If you have a student card, it is always worth enquiring about discounts before buying a ticket at any of the city's cinemas, e.g. the Academy, Midcity, Hollywood, Hoyts, Metro and Regent on the Square.

The main music venue both for the symphony orchestra and big name popular artists is the Town Hall on Kilmore St, across the river from Victoria Square. The box office at the Town Hall sells tickets to other concerts and productions as well. If in doubt ask at the Visitor Information Centre.

Music. In addition to the serious music alluded to above, Christchurch does have a choice of rock venues some of which levy cover charges. Pubs which often have music include Warners Tavern on Cathedral Square for Irish music, Nancy's at Nancy's Corner (Riccarton Road and Deans Avenue), Dux de Lux and the Bush Inn Hotel at 364 Riccarton Road (348 7175). Coyotes and Azure are both in the centre. The public bar of the latter is called the Ilam bar which is patronised by university students and the dress standard is casual.

There are a few nightclubs, where dress standards are enforced. If interested try the Firehouse on Colombo St, the Palladium on Gloucester St opposite the Library, The Rattlesnake in the City Mall or The Edge on Hereford St.

SPORT

The daily *Press* gives details on local sporting events from race meetings at Riccarton Racecourse or Addington Raceway to cricket matches at Lancaster Park. During championship race meetings, special city buses take punters from the city to the racecourse. There is a TAB office on Gloucester St just east of Cathedral Square.

If you would like to take some exercise yourself, Hagley Park is perfect for joggers, the River Avon good for rowing, the Estuary and Ellesmere Lake (a shallow body of water south of the city) suitable for windsurfing not to mention birdwatching, and to the east there are many beaches for swimming and surfing. The *Visitor's Guide* distributed free of charge by the Information Centre gives a thorough rundown of participatory sports for visitors. The outdoor Centennial Pool on Armagh St (668 917) is open weekdays 8am-2pm and 5-6pm, while the main indoor pool is at Queen Elizabeth II Park in North Beach. There are several new walks in the hills overlooking the harbour and Banks Peninsula described in *Further Afield* below.

THE MEDIA

Newspapers. The *Press* is a respectable morning paper whose masthead bears a strong resemblance to that of the London *Times*. The other paper, the evening *Star*, publishes only Saturday and Wednesday editions.

Radio and Television. The BCNZ National Programme is carried by 3YA on 675AM while the Concert Programme (3YC) is on 963AM and 89.7FM. The local independent station is 3ZB (1098AM) and 3ZM (91.3FM) is the 'stereo hit radio' station of Christchurch, often relaying the ZM network from Wellington. Its newest rival is affiliated with the MORE FM station also in Wellington. The university station broadcasts on 91.8FM, while the commercial Radio Avon is on 93FM. Christchurch launched its own regional television station in 1991 amidst gloomy predictions that the potential audience numbers could not sustain it.

Christchurch is being forced to reassess its self-image after a spate of armed hold-ups (which are most unlikely to affect visitors) and arson attacks on pubs. Furthermore hostels have had to start issuing keys and posting warnings after several backpackers had their luggage and valuables stolen from hostels, possibly by other travellers. But for the most part the worst that will happen is that your pint of milk disappears from the hostel fridge.

It is probably unwise to wander around Hagley Park or the city centre alone at night, but nowhere else could be described as a no-go area. Avoid rough pubs like the Foresters Tavern (on Oxford Terrace near Manchester St) where gang fights are not unusual.

The police station is at the corner of Cambridge Terrace and Hereford St (379 3999) and the free Legal Advice Centre is at 203 Gloucester St.

The STD code for Christchurch, as for the entire South Island, is 03. For fire, police or ambulance dial 111.

Christchurch/Canterbury Visitor Centre: 75 Worcester St, at the corner of Oxford Terrace (379 9629). Open Monday–Friday 8.30am–5pm, and weekends and holidays 8.30am–4pm.

Automobile Association (Canterbury) Inc: 210 Hereford St (379 1280).

Post Office: Cathedral Square (353 1899). Other post offices are less crowded — for example, at the corner of High and Tuam Sts.

Medical Services: Papanui Medical Centre, 438 Papanui Road (352 9053), and after-hours service at Christchurch Emergency Medical Services, Bealey Avenue (365 7777).

British High Commission: Christchurch Trade Office, The Dome, Regent Theatre Building, Cathedral Square (379 6100).

Public Library: Gloucester St near Avon River (379 6914).

American Express: 78 Worcester St (0800-801 122).

Thomas Cook: corner of Armagh and Colombo Sts (379 6600).

STA Travel: 223 High St (379 9098).

Department of Conservation: Private Bag, Christchurch (379 9758).

DAY TRIPS FROM CHRISTCHURCH

Once the modest pleasures of the city have been exhausted, there are places outside Christchurch that deserve a visit. Scenic walks just outside the city give you a view of the area and you can see just how flat the Canterbury Plain is. One of the most enjoyable destinations — preferably for more than a day — and one that is remarkably unspoiled considering its proximity to the city is the Banks Peninsula (see below). If your time is very limited and you want a glimpse of South Island scenery you might take advantage of the day return fare ($74) on the *TranzAlpine Express* through Arthur's Pass to Greymouth. Travelling up and back to Kaikoura for a day is probably not worthwhile, as the coastal scenery isn't all that varied and you would miss out on the wildlife pleasures of Kaikoura described below.

Lyttelton. The port of Lyttelton, 11km east of the city centre, is perhaps a little like Fremantle must have been a decade or so ago before yuppies transformed it. To get there take a Lyttelton bus (28G/H) that follows the road tunnel to the harbour. If you have a car, a more scenic route, 8km longer, winds its way through the delightful Port Hills, which divide the city from the harbour, via Sumner and Evans Pass. The Port Hills have also fallen victim to the mania for expensive development and a multi-million dollar gondola cableway from the Mount Cavendish Reserve to Lyttelton Road should soon be opened. If you eschew all this glitz, there is a walking track that affords marvellous views: the Mount Pleasant Bluffs track starts from near Mount Cavendish and goes up to Evans Pass, a round-trip hike of a couple of hours. A shorter 1-hour walk can also be done along the Motu-Kauti-Rahi Track.

Lyttelton with its hitherto unpretentious atmosphere may begin to go the same way as Fremantle, but is still relatively un-tarted up and an area full of character. The setting is picturesque with Victorian streets rising steeply from the water and old houses, most of which have not been over-renovated. The pubs are typical seamen's pubs as Lyttelton is an international harbour, and cafés like Chans Café serve steak and chips for $10. There are various cruises around the harbour including one in an old tug.

Beaches. There are many lovely beaches within easy reach of Christchurch, such as the charmingly named Taylor's Mistake, which is always a few degrees warmer than the city. Scarborough Beach at Sumner and New Brighton Beach are favourites among surfers, whereas the beach on Corsair Bay on the Lyttelton side is better for bathers. Although only 10km from Christchurch, Sumner has some interesting wilderness, and an away-from-it-all atmosphere as well as a good beach. In the early days a Christchurch tram served these beach communities, but nowadays you'll have to get there by car or bus.

Banks Peninsula. Despite its proximity to Christchurch the Banks Peninsula has a feeling of remoteness. Some of the roads over the 850m hills seem like goat tracks to the uninitiated and are signposted as unsuitable for caravans. There is also a summit walk from the Port Levy Saddle to Hill Top from which you can survey the peninsula, which is criss-crossed with streams and deeply indented with bays and inlets. The walk takes 4 hours and water should be carried.

The main town on Banks Peninsula is Akaroa, about 80km from Christchurch. It is a pleasant town stretched along the waterfront, with a lighthouse (which was in active service for the guidance of shipping as recently as 1976), a herb farm (open daily) where a craft market is held on the first Saturday of the month, a charming museum with relics of the local Maori people, whalers, etc., and an old established newspaper called the *Akaroa Mail*. It also boasts a superb fish and chip shop where you can buy marinated green-lipped mussels and paua patties.

Akaroa is very proud of its French heritage as it was here that a shipful of French settlers landed in 1840 just days after Britain had laid claim to the area. In fact the French influence survives only in a few street names and in the imported vegetation (such as fennel) that now grows wild in the nearby valleys. For those who have more than a day to spend, there is plenty of accommodation in Akaroa, which is a popular resort, including two hostels. The YHA hostel is

Mount Vernon Lodge (304 7180), an uphill 1½km-walk from the post office bus stop. Chez La Mer is a private backpackers' hostel on Rue Lavaud (304 7024). Some farms offer accommodation, including Onuku sheep farm 6km from town, which operates as a hostel (304 7612).

Cruising in the harbour is especially worthwhile between November and April when you might see a school of Hector's dolphins. The hostels will be able to advise, or ring Akaroa Harbour Cruises (304 7641) to confirm that they are continuing their daily 1.30pm cruises.

To get to Akaroa from Christchurch, catch the Akaroa Shuttle, which departs from outside the Information Centre on Worcester St opposite Noahs Hotel at 10.30am and 5pm on weekdays and noon only at weekends. Departure times from the Akaroa Post Office are 8.20am and 3.20pm Monday–Friday and 10.30am Saturday and Sunday. The journey lasts just under 2 hours and costs $14 single and $24 return. If you want to book a seat in advance ring 304 7421 in Akaroa. Private coach tours are available for seeing towns on the Peninsula beyond Akaroa.

NORTH OF CHRISTCHURCH

State Highway 1 between Picton and Christchurch is especially scenic north of Kaikoura where it traces the magnificent coast, but with a range of hills always in sight. It is a good road with few hazards and not much traffic, but drive carefully around the mountainous bends and through the tunnels — one of these has such a sharp curve in it that articulated lorries cannot get through without reversing in the middle.

If you wish to linger in the far north of the island, Sounds Air (388 2594) flies from Picton to Kenepuru Sound on Marlborough Sound for $78.

Kaikoura. The resort town of Kaikoura, about halfway along this road, has become the whale-watching capital of the Antipodes. In the last century it was an important whaling station and if you visit Fyffe House, a restored whaler's cottage, notice the whale vertebrae that have been incorporated into the foundations of the house.

Two competing companies run whale-watching trips and swim-with-dolphin trips. New Zealand Nature Watch (90 Esplanade; 319 5662) is the pakeha company, which has a scientific emphasis, while Kaikoura Tours (Railway Station, PO Box 89; 319 5045 or freephone 0800-655121) is run by Maori people from the marae. Although the local Maori have filed a claim under the Treaty of Waitangi for the exclusive rights to these waters, there seems to be a degree of cooperation between these companies — for example, if one spots a whale, it will radio this information to the other.

The 3-hour trips to watch whales cost about $75 and take place in a 10 or 12-person speed boat (Naiad) equipped with two very powerful outboards. It is likely that bigger, less exciting boats will be introduced due to the popularity of these trips. Of course there is no guarantee that the sperm whales will put in an appearance, though the chances are good, especially between April and August. The tours use hydrophones to listen for the whales' clicking and to measure their depth. Depending on luck and the time of year, you may also see dolphins, seals and albatross.

The 2-hour dolphin trips are cheaper ($50) and involve entering the water wearing a wet suit and snorkelling gear. It is not unusual to have the chance to sport with several hundred Dusky dolphins who don't mind being approached within a metre or two. Most tour participants consider this ample reward for enduring the cold of being underwater for up to 2 hours. Hector's dolphins may also be spotted, though they are more rare and are in fact endangered. These trips have become so popular that it is virtually essential to book in advance during the holiday season.

Kaikoura is also justly famed for its surf and for its enormous crayfish, which can be bought from roadside stalls for about $18; supplies have usually run out by mid-afternoon. Restaurant menus also include them in season. If you are driving from the north, perhaps you could buy a bottle of one of the excellent wines made in Marlborough to accompany your crayfish. The beach has rock pools to explore, paua shells to collect and sea birds to admire. To see seals sunning themselves on the rocks follow the 5km shoreline track. Surfers from Christchurch flock to Kaikoura, especially on summer weekends.

The YHA hostel is at the southern end of The Esplanade (319 5931). Kaikoura Backpackers Hostel (Whitehouse, 146 The Esplanade; 319 5916) seems to be run a little like a prep school but provides adequate accommodation including a new spa pool, and information on local highlights. Beds start at $13 with self-contained units going for $40 per couple. There are several pubs but the New Commercial Hotel on Brighton St is the only one to have a garden, complete with do-it-yourself barbecues. A couple of miles inland the Mount Fyffe State Forest has several signposted bush walks, including a fairly strenuous one to the 1600m summit of Mount Fyffe.

Arthur's Pass. Highway 73 through Arthur's Pass is the most scenic way to cross the island, especially in summer when the flowering rata trees cover the hillsides around Otira with scarlet. The road can be a challenge in good conditions (caravans are not allowed over Otira Gorge), but downright frightening in heavy rains, which cause trees and boulders to tumble down the vertical mountains onto the road. Occasionally, the Pass has to be closed to traffic, especially in the winter when snow and ice add to the difficulties. The rail journey is spectacular and more relaxing, taking nearly 3 hours to complete the 140km journey.

The township of Arthur's Pass has some accommodation (including a YHA hostel, 0516-89230), the Visitor's Information Centre for the surrounding National Park (0516-89211) and ski equipment hire shops for the winter season June to September. It is an excellent starting point for tramps, including a 6-day trip to Lewis Pass. There is a good choice of huts, so simply obtain a map of the area and plan a walk.

Nelson and the North-West. The north-west corner of the South Island encompasses lakes and mountains but is particularly appreciated for its hot weather and its coastline dotted with lovely beaches and small resort towns. Access to Nelson is by Highway 6 from Blenheim on the east coast or Westport on the West Coast; both routes are covered by Mount Cook Landlines (548 8369). There are also daily bus services to Collingwood, a pleasant town on Golden Bay at the end of the surfaced road, which is the nearest village to the beginning of the Heaphy Track 30km south.

Nelson is a laid-back town which has gained an immense amount of popularity among travellers in recent years. The Public Relations Office at the corner of Halifax and Trafalgar Sts (548 2303/4) has all the necessary information on local attractions, car hire firms, handicraft centres and accommodation. Nelson now has at least ten hostels, many of which are often full. Among the best known are Pavlova Backpackers at the corner of Trafalgar and Bridge Sts (548 9001), Tasman Towers at 10 Weka St (548 9750) and Bumbles at 8 Bridge St (548 2771). Nelson and nearby Motueka are well known for a high concentration of creative and alternative artists and craftsmen, so there are many studios of weavers, potters, jewellers, glassblowers, etc. in the region open to the public. It is also a place which attracts lots of working holidaymakers because of the opportunities for casual work picking apples or tobacco, especially between February and May (see introductory section on *Work* for further details).

The large sweeps of Tasman Bay, on which Nelson is situated, and Golden Bay, 100km to the west, have many safe sheltered beaches and accompanying campsites. As it is not difficult to find isolated beaches, especially at the western end of Highway 60 which ends in the fishing village of Collingwood, you may not be tempted by the 'most complete holiday park in Australasia', Tahuna Beach Park near Nelson, which boasts one thousand caravan sites, a camp supermarket, skating rink and 'baby's powder room', not to mention sewage dump points.

In some ways this coast is New Zealand's nearest equivalent to the Gold Coast of Queensland, as it has some large beach developments, as well as a large population of retired people and sun-loving holidaymakers. But it is on a considerably more restful scale than the Gold Coast, with beautiful unspoiled scenery predominating over tacky commercialism. The long lizard tongue of land at the extremity of Golden Bay is Farewell Spit, a wonderful place for anyone interested in birds. Collingwood Safaris (PO Box 15, Collingwood; 524 8257) are permitted to drive out onto the spit to admire the Arctic waders, which migrate to Siberia in the autumn. Walkers are not allowed into the reserve and must stop 4km from the vehicle track. There is also that uniquely New Zealand tour, accompanying the postman on his rural mail run, a five-hour trip which costs $25.

The Nelson Lakes National Park is one of the seven National Parks on the South Island, and is often overlooked in favour of the more spectacular fiords, glaciers and high peaks further south. The township of St Arnaud, a few kilometres east of Highway 6 and 100km south of Nelson, is where the park's Visitor Centre is located (521 1806), plus a petrol station, a shop and a private hostel called the Yellow House. St Arnaud is at the head of Lake Rotoiti (pronounced Row-tow-ee-tee), which is one of the park's two main lakes together with Lake Rotoroa meaning 'large waters' (not to be confused with Rotorua which means 'second lake'). Camping, swimming, boating, tramping and skiing (August/September) are the primary attractions. There is an efficient network of transport between Nelson and St Arnaud or Murchison offered by Nelson Lakes Transport (521 1858) and Wadsworth Motors; the former also has minibus services to the beginning of tracks in the park such as Rainbow Valley and Matakitaki.

The other National Park in the region is Abel Tasman with headquarters at 1 Commercial St, Takaka (525 8026). The Abel Tasman trek (which is described in *Great Outdoors*) begins or ends in the tiny coastal settlement of Totaranui. There are several local transport options for reaching the beginning of the track which includes a leg on a water taxi, namely Skyline Travel in Nelson (548 0285) which operates only from 1st November to 31st March, and Abel Tasman National Park Enterprises near Motueka (528 7801) which now run to Takaka and Totaranui all year round. A more unusual way of exploring this coast than by walking is to join a sea kayaking trip; see *Great Outdoors*.

When strolling along the sandy beaches look for colourful shells, living shellfish, birds and insects, though be careful picking up driftwood on beaches as this is where the poisonous katipo spider lives. If you fail to see any fat bush worms, short-eared bats or oystercatchers, then you may have to derive your wildlife thrills from visiting one of the several 'tame eel' colonies in the area, namely at Moutere halfway between Nelson and Motueka, and Kotinga near Takaka.

When it is time to leave the Northwest, you might wish to consider joining the backpacker bus Westcoast Express (bookable through Tasman Towers and other hostels) which takes six days to reach Queenstown and costs $99. It has become so popular that the company now runs four buses on the route. A local has recently set up a hitching agency, which arranges shared-expense lifts to

Christchurch and down the West Coast for a fee of $4. Look up H Bachard in the phone book to see if he is still doing this.

MOUNT COOK AND THE GLACIERS

Although on a map the townships of Fox Glacier and Mount Cook are separated by a mere 35km, the fastest land connection takes nearly nine hours, about twice the time it takes to drive the 330km from Christchurch to Mount Cook. So it is perhaps a little misleading to group these two tourist magnets together as many visitors cannot manage to see both unless they have a lot of time, can afford to fly or are capable of advanced mountaineering. However the glaciers and the mountains are all manifestations of the remarkable geology of the Southern Alps which have been described as an economic nuisance but a geographical masterpiece.

Mount Cook. At the end of 1991, the highest peak in the Southern Alps suffered a massive avalanche. The slide of much of its snowcap changed the shape of the mountain noticeably. Nevertheless, at 3,764m (12,431ft), Mount Cook is to New Zealand what the Grand Canyon is to the States and Ayers Rock to Australia, and is possibly its most heavily visited scenic wonder. Yet even here commercialism has been kept at bay, and it is easy to leave behind the coachloads of honeymooning Japanese - apparently Mount Cook is one of the most popular destinations for newly-weds whose overweening ambition is to take one of the aggressively marketed 'flightseeing' trips. This type of visitor normally stays at the grand (and expensive) Hermitage Hotel which opened in 1884 and dominates the place. Budget travellers are more likely to stay at the modern YHA hostel (627 0820) or at the Glentanner Motorcamp at the head of Lake Pukaki, 24km from Mount Cook village (627 0855).

With a little exertion, you can hike away from the village of Mount Cook and within an hour or two you will have certainly gained some solitude and possibly some superb views. The good views are irritatingly unpredictable and the weather cooperates on no more than half the days in the year. Often a large measure of patience is required before the clouds finally permit an unimpeded view of the peaks and so it is fortunate for many of the Japanese newly-weds that they have each other to distract them from their disappointment. Surprisingly, the chances of having fine weather are better in the winter. So if you are determined to admire Aorangi the cloud piercer (the Maori name for the mountain whose ownership they now claim), be prepared to spend a few days in the vicinity. The Tourist Corporation attempts to console disappointed visitors by reminding them that without the high precipitation the glaciers such as the 29km Tasman Glacier behind Mount Cook would soon disappear.

The same degree of chance affects scenic flights, which are able to take off only 50% of the time. Mount Cook Line offers the largest range from their 30-minute flight over the Tasman Glacier for $139 to the hour-long 'Grand Circle' which includes a ski-plane landing on a glacier snowfield for $275.

The Glaciers. Franz Josef and Fox Glaciers are the most easily reached and arguably the most spectacular glaciers, especially as they come so remarkably close to sea level; however there are 58 others in Westland National Park alone. If you have been disappointed by the grimy appearance of glaciers in other parts of the world (such as the Alps and Rockies) the Franz Josef and Fox are delightfully pristine. Their most remarkable feature is the speed at which they travel — recently as much as 40cm per day, i.e. 1km in less than 2 years — which is caused by the steepness of their long descents (11km and 13km, respectively) and the mighty quantity of snow that falls at the top. At the time of writing the advances of these two glaciers are particularly spectacular, and indications are that this will continue for several years, making now an excellent time to see these natural wonders.

The two glaciers are 25km apart and each has sprouted a township complete with post office, shops, accommodation, pubs and tourist facilities. Both also have National Park visitor centres where informative displays are mounted, questions are answered and brochures describing local walks and activities are distributed. Although it is possible in both cases to view the glacier from the car parks, it is more rewarding to approach or even climb onto the glacier on foot. Alpine Guides (Westland) Ltd (Hobnail Coffee Shop, Fox Glacier; 03-751 0825) runs a range of trips for casual hikers, keen mountaineers and rich folks who want to see the scenery from a helicopter, although which trips they can offer at any one time is dictated by the changeable conditions on Fox Glacier. The standard guided glacier walk lasts for 4 hours (departing 9.30am and 2pm) and costs $34, which includes the hire of hobnail boots and alpenstock. The guide cuts steps out of the ice where necessary. The pace set on these walks is usually more suitable for a fit hiker than a day-tripper, although the aim is to set a pace that the 'average' tourist can handle. Glacier walks should not be undertaken independently.

Alpine Guides also have trips that combine helicopter rides to and from the glacier with 2½ hours exploring the ice formations on the glacier itself; the price of this half-day excursion is $155 (minimum of three people). More ambitious overnight trips and ice climbs are described in *Great Outdoors*.

An alternative independent walk is to Robert's Point, which is situated beside the Franz Josef Glacier affording good views of the blue and deeply crevassed surface of the glacier. The three-hour walk through dripping temperate rainforest is not overly strenuous, though the slippery stream crossings can become a little tricky and, as throughout New Zealand, people who suffer from vertigo might not enjoy the swing bridges and rockface ladders. If you are lucky you may hear a booming crash as chunks of ice break off from the glacier. But over the past centuries, the glaciers have been generally receding and the approach road to the car park at Fox follows the gouged out valley, now littered with enormous boulders and mounds of rubble indiscriminately dumped by the glacier, which has retreated over 3km since Captain Cook visited in 1770. Interesting geological formations abound, such as sculpted rocks known as *roches moutonnées*; but those who think they have seen enough sheep for a lifetime need not worry: *moutonnées* here does not mean 'sheep-shaped' but rather 'wig-like'.

THE WEST COAST

As if these geological phenomena were not enough, there are some amazing rock formations just offshore at Punakaiki less than 200km north of the Glacier. The Pancake Rocks are enormous striated stacks of rock which millenia ago were hurled down from the top of the cliffs into the sea. Even more impressive and fascinating to watch is the way the surf pounds into the caverns and tunnels along the coast spouting up when you don't expect it. If you stay in a tent or cabin at the pleasant Punakaiki Motor Camp (731 1894) you can walk down to the boarded walkway at high tide for the spectacular and noisy show (which is especially exciting at night).

Punakaiki is part of the relatively new Paparoa National Park which has some good day walks through the rainforest vegetation (though sign-posting is minimal). The park Visitor Centre is at Punakaiki (731 1895) where you can get maps and information. An interesting walk (which can be done in a long day) follows the Croesus Track from Barrytown south of Punakaiki to the odd little community of Blackball. If you stay at the famous Formerly the Blackball Hilton (732 4705), a once dilapidated country hotel which has been brought into the modern era with backpacker rooms for $15–17 and a licensed bar, you can try your hand at goldpanning in nearby Blackball Creek. If you want to meet the friendly locals, have a drink at the Working Men's Club down the road from the Hilton.

The West Coast has an interesting mixture of people: some have their roots there, others are newcomers including alternative types. Newcomers sometimes find the social life somewhat cliquey though the pubs are often classics of their kind (try the pub in Barrytown north of Greymouth which has music at weekends). Many pay scant attention to closing time.

The gold rush of the 1860s and 1870s has left some traces of historical interest. For example the Ross Historic Goldfields Walk near the coast north of the Glaciers follows the network of water races and abandoned tailings for 3km and provides an interesting introduction to the brief mining boom. A few places like Westport, Hokitika and Greymouth survived the depletion of gold supplies, but most faded away. A few kilometres south of Greymouth is Shantytown, a replica mining town complete with church, doctor's surgery, working sawmill, and a gold-panning claim on which you can try your luck. For a glimpse of the industrial history of the northern west coast there is an enjoyable 10km walk from Ngakawau north of Westport which follows a coal mine railway (closed in 1958) though tunnels and across gorges.

It is also worth visiting a genuine ghost town, such as Okarito, which now has a handful of tumble-down houses set along a windswept shore, a shop which opens for a few hours on Saturday, a YHA hostel without electricity and an atmosphere of desolation. (Apparently this combination appeals to the Booker Prize-winning novelist Keri Hulme, who has chosen to live here.) As the tiny museum on the wharf indicates, there were once dozens of hotels to supply the hard-drinking miners.

Okarito Lagoon is a reserve for the white heron or kotuku. Although you need a permit to enter the sanctuary, you can sometimes see the birds from the road. Further along the coast south of the Glaciers is a seal colony at Gillespies Beach. As you go along the tiny road from the highway to the beach, keep checking over your shoulder for a view of Mount Cook and Mount Tasman. If you have time, stop at Lake Matheson on your right which is renowned for its capacity to mirror the high peaks. Even if the mountains are not visible, the one-hour walk around the lake's reedy banks is very peaceful and pleasant.

QUEENSTOWN AND FIORDLAND

If you have seen just one glossy New Zealand magazine, chances are that the photos of mountains, lakes and fiords were taken in the south-west corner of the South Island. Even visitors who have begun to feel that they have had a surfeit of magnificent scenery still make the trip to Queenstown and beyond. Only callous cynics remain indifferent to the sublime landscapes of Fiordland.

Fiordland National Park runs into Mount Aspiring National Park to cover a vast area of the country, pockets of which have yet to be explored. Roads are few and the ones that exist are often of relatively recent construction. Although motoring or flying allows the visitor to appreciate the scenic attractions to a certain extent, this is an area which should be enjoyed on foot or on water. For more details of the famous walking tracks in the area, of opportunities for skiing between June and October and of rafting expeditions based on Queenstown, see *Great Outdoors* below. The Fiordland Travel Agency in Queenstown (Steamer Wharf, PO Box 94; 442 7500 or toll-free 0800-656501) has a complete range of tours but is not of much use to the independent traveller.

Queenstown. There is no doubt that this is the most touristy place in New Zealand. With a permanent population of only 3,300, it is swamped both summer and winter with thousands of tourists. Even though long-stay residents use the pejorative-sounding word 'loopy' to refer to tourists, their hostility does not run deep and many will be only too glad to point you towards their favourite trip or drinking hole.

Queenstown is New Zealand's boldest attempt at an international resort. From having been a sleepy picturesque lakeside village not so many years ago, its appetite for development nowadays seems rapacious. Hotels and time-share complexes are being built even faster than they are in Portugal's Algarve, and mini-golf courses and alpine slides are frantically being opened to amuse the ever-increasing numbers of easily-bored tourists. The downtown streets are lined with signs which clamour for the tourist dollar. Queenstown traders are alone in the country for being allowed to open seven days a week, 24 hours a day; the usual shopping hours are 9am-5.30pm and 7.30-9pm except on weekends when the shops close for the afternoon.

Not many visitors can withstand completely the pressure to participate in at least one of Queenstown's attractions. In fact there's not much point in coming unless you do. One of the most obvious is to take the gondola up the hill ($9) to see the view and to watch other tourists eating overpriced lamb in the Skyline Restaurant. It is perfectly possible to walk up the 450m hill starting on Kent St and proceeding amidst exotic trees, though it is a steep two-hour climb on a hot day. (Tickets for the cable car trip down the hill are rarely checked.)

The *TSS Earnslaw* is an 80 year old working steamer which chugs out onto Lake Wakatipu several times a day. The Maori legend attached to Lake Wakatipu is interesting: the wicked giant who abducted a beautiful princess was set alight by the hero-rescuer. As his body melted a giant depression formed in the earth and soon filled with water (Wakatipu means 'the hollow of the giant'). Only his thumping heart survives, said to account for the phenomenon of the level of the huge lake rising and falling 8cm every quarter of an hour. Obviously the tour organisers are not convinced that the scenery alone will entertain as the trip leaving at 2pm stops at the Mount Nicholas Sheep Station for the usual demonstration of sheep dogs and shearers at work, and then on the return journey there is a sing-along which seems to appeal greatly to the over-60s. This three-hour afternoon excursion takes place daily and costs $32; there are other trips available in the mornings and evenings where the point seems to be to eat and drink. The rival trip is the Walter Peak Tour on a luxury catamaran for $36.50.

But despite the inescapable commercialism and inflated prices, Queenstown is a pleasant town to spend a few days preparing for (or recovering from) a foray into the wilderness. The development has not been indiscriminate, for example the strip of park between the lake and the Esplanade has been preserved intact with trees carefully pruned so as not to impede the lovely view. One of the real advantages is the wide choice of eating and drinking establishments, which keep reasonably late hours. Highlights include the deservedly popular pizzeria 'The Cow' in Cow Lane (about $16 a head), a Mexican restaurant called Saguaro's in Beach St, the innovative Pot-au-Feu on Camp St near the Mall (where it might be a good idea to book) and a coffee shop with tasty cheap food called Gourmet Express, the Cardrona Café in the Mall which serves wholefoods; all are BYO.

There are a number of pubs, the best known of which is Eichardt's Hotel around the corner from the Steamer Wharf, where it is not difficult to meet people. Many of these, on both sides of the bar, will be travellers who have decided to spend more than a few days in Queenstown. Watch for happy hours between 5 and 7pm especially in the winter ski season.

As always, the YHA hostel is a good place to decide which tours or tramps to sign up for; less predictably it is a good place to eat with the kitchen producing cheap and delicious curries, pasta and vegetarian dishes for less than $8. The obliging management will store baggage and offer advice, though much can be learned simply by studying their notice board and chatting to people in your dormitory. It is essential to book a bed in the summer and also during the ski season. Among the large choice of other budget accommodation, Bumbles (442 6298) on the Esplanade (nearer town than the YHA hostel) and the Pinewood at 48 Hamilton Road (442 9470) are most often recommended. The newest hostel is the Backpacker's Hilton between the lake and Beach St (442 7180) above a bistro restaurant. The Queenstown Accommodation Agency at 30 Shotover St (442 7518) charges no commission for putting you in touch with one of the lodgings registered with them. The so-called Queenstown Information Centre on the corner of Shotover and Camp Sts (442 8238) is really just the retail outlet for Danes Shotover Rafts and its affiliated tour operators.

On the basis that 'a million people can't be wrong' you may want to visit another of Queenstown's top attractions: the 'only live stage show in the world to portray the beef and dairy industry' held daily at the Cattledrome about six kilometres north of town, at 9.30am and 2.30pm. This is 'your chance to see, smell and touch a live beast'.

There is a welter of excursions which can be made from Queenstown. One of the most interesting is to Skipper's Canyon, where the road is so tortuous that rental car insurance becomes void and the elements so brutal that telephone wires are made of much thicker wire than normal. This was a thriving community during the gold rush and now thrives once again as a centre for bungy jumpers from the 70m high Skippers Canyon Bridge. Another former gold-mining town is Arrowtown which has been restored. It is a 20-minute drive north of Queenstown, and is accessible only by hitching or on the Double Decker sightseeing tour which departs from the top of the Mall at 10am and 2pm and allows a one hour stop and costs $24 return.

Milford and the Fiords. The south-west coast of the island is among the most dramatic in the world. Even the names evince an atmosphere of daring exploration and brushes with death such as Resolution Island, Preservation Inlet or Doubtful Sound, or on a more mundane level, of foul weather, in names like Dark Cloud Range and Wet Jacket Arm. Although these deep inlets are called 'sounds' a more exact description is fiord.

Milford Sound is the most northerly of these fiords, and its fame relative to the other 14 fiords probably has more to do with its accessibility than its intrinsic superiority. Unless you are a yachtsman, you will not be able to make a comparison as the area of Fiordland (4725 square miles) has very few roads. Only one other fiord, Doubtful Sound, can be approached by road (which includes the steepest road in New Zealand), though to reach this road you must first cross Lake Manapouri by boat. Even Milford could not be reached by motor car until 1954 when the Homer Tunnel was completed.

But the drive from Queenstown still takes about five hours, as there is no direct road, but rather a 291km loop via Te Anau (pronounced Te-an-ow). This makes the day trip from Queenstown a very long day of driving. InterCity's tour departs 8am and returns at 8.30pm and costs $107, while Fiordland Travel's trip departs 7.15am and costs $118. Kiwi Discovery at 37 Camp St have cheaper day returns costing $59 which depart at 7.30am. Apparently hire cars are very often damaged on this road by drivers paying more attention to the scenery than the bends in the road. It is possible to travel from Queenstown to Milford in a relatively straight line, but for this trip you will need a stout pair of boots, a stock of provisions and a reasonable level of fitness (see description of the *Routeburn Track* below).

Of course many visitors avail themselves of the countless scenic flights which converge on Milford at midday when the tranquil bay becomes like a wasp's nest which has been disturbed. At least the angry humming of those 65 to 70 small airplanes distracts you from the silent humming of the sandflies which are a torment here like everywhere else in Fiordland. Mount Cook Line runs flights from Queenstown varying from one and a half hours at $173 (including a brief landing at Milford Sound) to four hours including a cruise on the Sound ($244). There are also short flights from Milford starting at $45 for 10 minutes. One-way flights from Milford to Queenstown are bookable only after arrival in Milford, and often the flights are full; the fare is $146. Bear in mind that cancellations due to weather are commonplace. Even when the planes do take off, the turbulence can be alarming to all but fearless flyers.

Although the boat cruises on the Sound are basically old-fogey cruises, they are worth doing. In the first place they whisk you out of the range of sandflies and in the second they take you amidst some of the most spectacular scenery anywhere. The boats, often accompanied by dolphins, take about an hour to reach the Tasman Sea at the mouth of the fiord before they turn back. Because the rock faces rise vertically from the 300-metre deep water, the launch can approach very close to the fiord walls, so that spectators are often drenched by the incessant run-off. It is usually possible to see seals (though next to impossible to photograph them successfully), and to see the improbable vegetation clinging to the sheer rock with clear evidence of past avalanches. So much rain falls on this coast (20 feet per year), that the cliffs are almost constantly dripping with water. Yet there are only two permanent waterfalls: Bowen Falls near the wharf and Stirling Falls which is among the highest sheer drops in the world (equivalent to 50 storeys). The commentary is informative and lively even if the jokes can become a little forced ('Stirling Falls, so-called because it pounds down, to coin a phrase, which makes cents,' etc.) and the assumption that everyone will recognise elephant and lion shapes in the rock formations is somewhat optimistic. The guides have worked so hard at inventing a spiel to cheer up those depressed by rainy weather that they seem positively disappointed on a sunny day.

There are two rival tours: the Red Boats run by the Tourist Hotel Corporation and the Milford Haven launch run by the Fiordland Travel Company. Both cost $35 for about one and a half hours and leave several times a day. (Try to avoid the early afternoon sailing which is the one taken by all the day trippers arriving in Twin Otters.) Considering that this is one of New Zealand's foremost attractions, there are precious few facilities locally. However there is Milford Lodge (249 8071), set back a kilometre or so from the water, which offers mountain hut-style accommodation. It operates from November until April and costs $17 per person.

Fiordland has many other charming settlements in which to base yourself for sport and relaxation. Te Anau is more convenient than Queenstown for access to Fiordland; the park headquarters are on the edge of the tame and pleasant Lake Te Anau near the road to Manapouri (249 7921). Wanaka is another very popular resort town, especially for people who want to break the journey between Fox Glacier and Fiordland. There are YHA hostels in both Te Anau (249 7847) and Wanaka (443 7403) both of which have a wide choice of other accommodation, restaurants and services.

DUNEDIN AND THE SOUTH

Looking at a globe, the southern tip of the South Island looks as though it should have been one of the last places on earth to be settled. In fact there were Maori moa-hunters in the region in the 13th century. European settlers arrived much later; the small town of Riverton, a few miles beyond Invercargill on the southern tip, is thought to be the oldest European settlement in New Zealand as it was an important sealing and whaling post in the late 18th century.

Unlike the wild frontier atmosphere of Fiordland, south-east New Zealand has a feeling of solidity and rootedness, just like the stone-built towns of Scotland on which it was modelled; as the word 'stalwart' was originally a Scottish dialect word it is a particularly apt description for Dunedin and many other southern towns. It is not difficult to hear a Scottish intonation and slightly rolled r's in the local speech even now. Otago province has always regarded itself as fiercely independent.

One of the best reasons for spending time in this part of the world is for the wildlife. The Dunedin Visitor Centre now distributes two main brochures, *Focus on Dunedin* and *Dunedin at a Glance*.

Dunedin. For such a remote and small city (population 120,000), Dunedin has a distinguished history and vigorous civic life, principally because the oldest university in New Zealand, the University of Otago, has been located here since 1869. Early prosperity based on the discovery of gold in Otago meant that there was enough wealth to endow a university and build impressive buildings, both public and private, most of which can be admired today. Notice especially the railway station, the University's clock tower and various churches.

Dunedin's strong Scottish heritage is evident in the city's name, which is the Gaelic form of Edinburgh, and the city abounds in street names lifted directly from the Scottish capital, which should amuse visitors who know Edinburgh well. The heritage of the province is described vividly at the Otago Settlers Museum at 31 Queens Gardens, near the railway station (open weekdays 10am–5pm, weekends and public holidays 1–5pm; admission $4). Obviously the people of Dunedin are an energetic lot; when the first two settlers' ships landed at Dunedin, they tied up outside what is now the main post office on Princes St. The intervening land has all been reclaimed. The Otago Museum (477 2372) on Great King St (near Albany St) is also interesting with good natural history, Maori and Polynesian collections, as well as a hands-on science centre and a craft gallery and shop. Another place of interest is Olveston, a grand Edwardian home filled with treasures gathered in Europe and the Orient at the beginning of this century. It is at 42 Royal Terrace (477 3320); the tour (which takes place five times a day) costs $10.

There are plenty of things to do in addition to the city's cultural delights — for example, tours of the Cadbury Chocolate Factory at 280 Cumberland St (474 1126). Waiting lists for this tour are long, so be sure to book with the Visitor Centre or directly in advance; the factory is closed December to February. A tour of the small and historic Speight's Brewery (477 9480) is also worthwhile and is even recommended by the alcohol-free YHA. Samples are plentiful but not free as the daily tour costs $5.

The Visitor Centre is part of the Municipal Chambers on the north-eastern side of the easy-to-recognise Octagon (474 3300).

There are several good look-outs for a panorama of the city. If you are restricted to foot or bicycle go no further than the Northern Cemetery near the pleasant botanical gardens and aviary. Those in vehicles can drive up to the Centennial Memorial on Signal Hill, but make sure the brakes are in good order as the descent is very steep. Baldwin St is said to be the steepest street in the world.

Dunedin's YHA hostel is a little over a kilometre from the Octagon at 77 Stafford St (474 1919). There are also several backpackers' hostels; these include Penguin Palace Backpackers on Queens Gardens (479 2175); the highly rated Elm Lodge (74 Elm Row; 474 1872); Manor House (28 Manor Place; 477 0484); and The Chalet at No 296 on the High St (479 2075). Dorm beds in all of these are around $13–14, except in The Chalet, which starts at $15. There is a large student contingent of 8000 centred around the imposing Victorian university, and so out-of-term you might find an empty room. If you don't mind being away from town, there are several motorcamps, particularly Tahuna Park Seaside Camp near St Kilda Beach (Victoria Road; 455 4690), which charges $15 per person in a cabin the first night and $13 thereafter.

All city buses depart from the Octagon, including the privately run Ritchies airport bus which takes about 45 minutes to cover the 29km distance (cost $9). This airport service leaves the city about an hour before scheduled flight departures (477 9238). City bus services are run by several companies, and a comprehensive route and timetable booklet is available free of charge. Be sure to get the latest information from the Dunedin Visitor Centre.

Otago Peninsula. Several of the principal attractions of the region are on the Otago Peninsula, a projection of land on the south side of Dunedin Harbour which can be seen in a very scenic round trip of about 70km. The most unusual attraction is the colony of royal albatrosses at the end of the peninsula. Elsewhere in the world these impressive birds can be viewed only by dedicated ornithologists and sailors, but in this case there is a breeding colony just a few miles from a city. You have to be unusually unlucky not to see one of these enormous birds (with wingspans sometimes exceeding three metres) swooping overhead. The Albatross Centre (478 0498/9) is open year round though the colony itself is closed during the breeding season (late September to late November). Admission costs $15–25 and advance bookings should be made with the Dunedin Visitor Centre.

Also at Taiaroa Head is a community of rare yellow-eyed penguins. The nesting sites are on private land owned by the conservationist Howard McGrouther; admission costs $20. The birds usually make an appearance in the late afternoon/ early evening. Seals also favour this headland and can be seen at any time. Most people arrive on tours, for example the deluxe one offered by Twilight Tours/ Wild South Ltd (PO Box 963; 476 1443) which visits both the albatross and the penguins. The cost of this nine-hour tour is $48 ($40 to YHA members), the proceeds of which go to help the project.

The man-made attractions on the peninsula are perhaps less thrilling: the gardens and pottery at Glenfalloch and the Victorian castle at Larnach, built by an eccentric in 1871 and reputed to be the only castle in Australasia (admission $10). If you want to spend more than a day on the peninsula, a good place to stay is the Larnach Castle Lodge (476 1302) where there are affordable bunk rooms in the old stables as well as singles and doubles.

Dunedin City Transport buses do not serve the peninsula, but Otago Road Services go part way. Otherwise you will have to hire a car (try Top Car Rentals on 477 6677), a bicycle (the YHA hostel and Penguin Palace hire out mountain bikes), try to hitch or join a tour — many are available through the Visitor Centre. Other backpackers' tours costing between $25 and $40 are run out of the YHA hostel and Elm Lodge.

The conventional local tour company is called Newton's Tours (105 Melbourne St) which offers four tours daily, one to the historic buildings of the city, the second to Larnach Castle and the other two taking in the Peninsula's wildlife. A special backpackers' fare of $12 allows you to travel along all three of these routes but does not include admission fees.

Another way to see the peninsula is from the harbour. *Southern Spirit* is a large yacht that takes people into the harbour for fishing — the salmon fishing in this area is gaining an international reputation — and wildlife viewing. Monarch Wildlife Cruises (corner of Wharf and Fryatt Sts; 477 4276) operates the 16m wooden motor vessel *Monarch* all year to Taiaroa Head, where the albatross — as well as several other species of bird and also fur seals — can sometimes be seen from the water. The tours also include time ashore to see the albatross or yellow-eyed penguins. The cruise costs $45, with $6 off for YHA members. For a description of the new waterborne activity of surf-rafting see *Great Outdoors* below.

If you are worried that the penguins, seals and sea birds on the Otago Peninsula are being pestered by too many visitors, you might prefer to travel an hour north to Moeraki, where you can see not only the famous rounded giant boulders but join a two-hour boat tour in an inflatable *Naiad* (the same vessel as is used for the whale-watching at Kaikoura) to look for yellow-eyed penguins, Hector's dolphins and spoonbills. Further details from Moeraki Nature Tours (RD 2, Palmerston; 439 4864).

About 90 minutes south of Dunedin and half way to Invercargill is another worth-while conservation project where you can see penguins, fur seals, sea elephants, cave wetas, glow-worms, etc. Catlins Wildlife Trackers south of Owaka provide a two or three-day package including farm accommodation and meals, guided walks and boat rides, and the loan of binoculars, snorkelling gear and torches.

Invercargill. The southernmost town in the country is usually visited only because it is en route to Stewart Island. The Visitor Information Centre (82 Dee St; 218 6091) does its best to persuade you to admire the 'fine old brick city water tower' and to tour the aluminium smelter at Tiwai Point. But only two destinations hold much appeal: the 'Roaring Forties Experience' at the Southland Museum about the subantarctic island protectorates of New Zealand; and the tuatarium, where you can see prehistoric-looking reptiles. Tuatara is a Maori word meaning 'spine on the back' and the creature is like a miniature dinosaur. The only other remarkable feature of Invercargill is the number of street names which are Scottish monosyl-lables: Tay, Earn, Lowe, Bond, Don, Doon, Forth, Spey, and so on.

The Rest of Southland. The obvious prosperity of Invercargill derives from the rich agriculture of the region, acknowledged in one of the city's monuments, a revolving blade of grass. Sights to be seen in other towns in Otago and Southland include things like the memorial to the first refrigerated shipment of lamb to be sent to Britain in 1882. Some places achieve local fame because they host stud ram sales. None of this will be of much interest to non-locals.

Further inland is a rich fruit-growing belt where apricots, peaches, cherries and strawberries can be bought at wayside stalls, or blossoms admired, depending on the season. This area around Alexandra, Clyde and Roxburgh is a useful desti-nation for people looking for casual fruit-picking work. One crossroads to head for is Fruitlands, much more plausibly named than another southern town called Nightcaps.

Stewart Island. The third-largest island in the unequal archipelago of New Zealand is Stewart Island, called Rakiura by the Maori which means glowing skies. The island is only 65km long and about 40km wide at its extremities (about the size of Tenerife). But Stewart Island is not the Tenerife of the South Tasman Sea. With high rainfall levels, a resident population of no more than 500, and a total of 20km of roads, it can hardly provide the facilities associated with tourist paradises. Until very recently there was no electrical supply and households relied on generators and wood-burning stoves.

Despite the primitive facilities, or perhaps because of them, many New Zealanders and foreigners make the long trek to this southern outpost, and it can't just be to get away from the sheep. The principal attraction is the wildlife. The island was declared a nature reserve in 1903 and, although some animals such as deer and possums were introduced, the damage they have done to the vegetation and native animal life has not been as extreme as it has been elsewhere in New Zealand. Kiwis are more numerous than anywhere else in the country (the birds, in contrast to the people) and Mason Bay, a 14km sweep of beach on the west side of the island, is one of the easiest places to spot a kiwi.

Mason Bay, however, like the rest of Stewart Island, is accessible only on foot or by water. It is almost comical that the Automobile Association's road atlas should devote most of its final page to Stewart Island, showing the four or five streets around Oban (the only settlement on the island) and the rest as red dotted lines to denote footpaths. Walking on Stewart Island is not to be undertaken lightly. Almost all of the tracks are rated 'strenuous' as they climb and descend constantly, with slippery mud underfoot rain or shine (and it usually does both dozens of times in a day). The further you get away from Oban, the more confident you should be of your abilities in the bush. The Department of Conservation in Oban maintains the very simple huts (which are free) and the tracks, some of which have wooden walkways over the most boggy sections. But you will have to reconcile yourself to hours of squelching and frequent spills on the steep sections or on stretches with picturesque names like Chocolate Swamp. Check with the DOC Visitor Centre on Main St (219 1130) for maps and advice.

Launch trips are also available from several local characters to otherwise inaccessible beaches, small offshore islands and perfect fishing spots. One of these islands is called Mutton Bird Island, after the bird prized by the Maori and still hunted by descendants of the original inhabitants of the island. No one else is allowed to kill them.

There is no YHA hostel but several private homes offer hostel-style accommodation for about $10; ring 219 1065, 219 1230 or 219 1425 for possibilities. It is to be hoped that the new complex on Halfmoon Bay called Shearwater Inn ($26 per person) is not the beginning of a trend to develop the island. Dining facilities are still limited. Even milk and bread may be unavailable from the general store unless you have ordered in advance. The best bet is to try to buy some of the fish brought in daily by the local fishermen. (Apart from tourism, fishing is the only source of livelihood on the island.) If you are planning to do some tramping, try to bring supplies with you to the island.

You can reach Stewart Island by air or by sea. Southern Air flies daily (weather permitting) taking 18 minutes to travel from Invercargill to Oban. The standard return fare is $135, though there are ways of getting there for less. For example pairs travelling together are entitled to a $17 discount each. But best of all students and YHA members can travel for half the full fare. Day returns are popular but there are no discounts. To make advance bookings contact Southern Air, PO Box 860, Invercargill (218 9129 or toll-free 0800-658876).

The ferry takes over two hours to cross the 32km distance of Foveaux Strait, reputed to be one of the roughest stretches of water in the world. The ferry is operated by Stewart Island Charter Services Ltd (PO Box 24, Halfmoon Bay). Sailings from the fishing and oystering community of Bluff, the most southerly town on the New Zealand mainland, are at 9am and from Stewart Island at 2pm daily in January, Monday to Friday in February, and Monday, Wednesday and Friday the rest of the year. The fare is $35 single, $70 return with a 33% discount for YHA members or students who show up at the dock for standby accommodation. Local fishermen sometimes take passengers for less than the price of a ferry ticket; look for adverts in the Invercargill YHA hostel. If you are a committed hitch-hiker, you can go down to the docks in Bluff and see if any of the fishing vessels is willing to give you a lift. Even if you don't succeed, perhaps you'll have the chance to sample a few of the famous Bluff oysters available between March and August (though their numbers have been severely reduced by a parasite over the past few seasons).

The Great Outdoors

Just as every Dutch town boasts of its nearby windmills and bulb fields, all South Island towns with unmemorable names like Omarama claim to be set in the midst of unsurpassed scenery and to be ideal bases for boating, fishing, tramping, skiing, and so on. Just in case this isn't sufficient, they usually try to find something else with which to entice you, such as 'farm safaris', horse and wagon rides, potters' studios and the inevitable sheep shearing. In most cases these little-known townships are telling the truth: the opportunities for exploring the unspoiled natural world are remarkably various throughout most of the island.

It is not hard to find out about the various possibilities for tramping, rafting, skiing, etc. when you're in Christchurch but it may be more difficult to decide where to spend your money. Agencies like the YHA Travel Centre, STA at 223 High St and Trailblazers at 86 Worcester St will inundate you with brochures and information.

Flying Kiwi Wilderness and Cycling Expeditions (Deer Park Road, Koromiko, RD3, Blenheim; 03-573 8126) offers extensive and eccentric tours of the South Island. The route starts in Picton, continues to Christchurch, Tekapo, Queenstown, Milford, Lake Manapouri, Fox and Franz Josef Glaciers, Nelson Lakes National Park, Nelson and back to Picton. One of the features of the tour is that sporting equipment is carried, principally five mountain bikes and a five-person canoe. This hippy-inspired trip takes 17 days to see most of the main sights on the island and combines camping accommodation in out-of-the-way locations with sleeping on the converted bus. The cost is $950 plus around $7 per day for food. An extended 24-day version is also on offer for $1200.

TRAMPING

The majority of Kiwi visitors as well as those from overseas choose to do at least some bushwalking. In addition to the wonderful views, other incentives to bestir oneself are the exotic vegetation (giant tree ferns, the largest buttercup in the world known as the Mount Cook lily, etc.) and the birdlife (including the charming fantail which can frequently be seen fluttering in the branches of trees). Travellers who have planned to do some fairly serious walking from the outset will have brought their hiking boots, sleeping bags and heavy duty rain gear. It is possible to hire boots and packs in Christchurch, Te Anau, Queenstown, Mount Cook, etc. though relying on a pair of boots that you have not worn in yourself is risky. Those without equipment will probably content themselves with one of the less demanding tracks or with a day walk, wearing a comfortable pair of sturdy running shoes.

The Department of Conservation's National Parks Service publishes leaflets which provide enough route and hut information for the average walker. Of course specialist guide books are likely to enhance your pleasure, such as *Tramping in New Zealand* published by Lonely Planet or the *AA Book of New Zealand Walkways*. Unless you are very confident and experienced, you should select your walk carefully; the relevant sources of information will rate them from mild to strenuous to help you choose accordingly. If you have a local friend prepared to escort you, you probably don't have to worry. Otherwise you might prefer to choose from among the more popular tracks, despite the crowds (most of them overseas tourists), as they are well provided with huts and signposts to

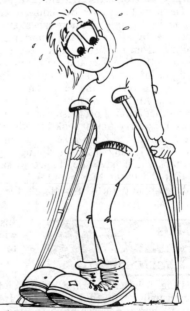

"RELYING ON A PAIR OF HIRED HIKING BOOTS CAN BE RISKY!"

minimise dangers from erratic weather which causes flash floods, blizzards, etc. Another possibility is to join a group though this is absurdly expensive in many cases (see below). You are supposed to register your intentions with the Department of Conservation if you intend to do anything out of the ordinary on your own; if you do sign up, be sure to de-register as otherwise you will waste police time.

Most of the tracks are well maintained with wooden walkways placed over slippery sections, for example, and huts located in strategic locations (see the introductory section on the *Great Outdoors* for hut information). Hostels both YHA and private are a fund of information on transport to tracks. Generally, the more difficult the access to the starting and finishing points, the less crowded a track is likely to be.

Milford Track. The most popular of all is the Milford Track, which is so famous that it seems to have become a household name with a great many slightly overweight Americans. Magnificent as the four-day walk from the end of Lake Te Anau to Milford Sound undoubtedly is, many prefer a less heavily used track. It is necessary to book ahead because of limited hut capacity and at certain times of the year this must be done three or four months in advance. With the Milford (as with several other tracks) you must choose between a guided walk with a commercial company or a 'freedom walk'. The cost of joining a guided party on the Milford is over $1,100, which entitles you to stay in a more luxurious standard of hut and includes all meals. Bookings should be made with the Tourist Hotel Corporation in Te Anau (Box 185; 249 7411).

Independent walkers must pay a track fee of $153 which includes the launch trip from Te Anau Downs to Glade Wharf at the end of the lake, a launch from Sandfly Point (aptly named) at the end of the walk to Milford and hut accommodation. This must also be booked ahead, as only 40 independent walkers are allowed to set off each day in the season (November to mid-April). Occasionally there are last-minute places, especially as the season approaches its end around Easter. Bookings must be made with the Department of Conservation, PO Box 29, Te Anau (249 7921).

Routeburn Track. The widely accepted runner-up to the Milford is the Routeburn Track which is unquestionably beautiful and un-pre-bookable (unless you choose to go on a $800 guided trip with Routeburn Walk Ltd, PO Box 568, Queenstown; 442 8200). But there is really no reason why a person of average fitness who has a supply of warm clothes and a warm sleeping bag should not do this walk independently. The three-day walk (which can be completed in one day by supermen/women) can be done in either direction, though most people start out in Queenstown and end on the Milford Road about 30km from Milford. The total distance covered is 39km as compared to the Milford at 54km.

There are two ways of reaching the starting point. One is to catch the Magic Bus (442 7880) which leaves Queenstown at 8.30am and arrives at the start of the walk about 10.30am. It is preferable to take the Glenorchy Holiday Park shared taxi from 56 Shotover St in Queenstown at 6pm (summer months only), spend the night in the lodge or camping at Glenorchy which is 48km along the north shore of Lake Wakatipu, and then proceed to the walk the following morning at 8.30am (total price $32). The advantage of this plan is that the village of Glenorchy is in an extremely beautiful location (with a good pub), and also that you begin the walk earlier than the rest and therefore can lay claim to a bunk at the Routeburn Falls hut. The huts are often so crowded that people end up sleeping on the kitchen floor, but no one is turned away. When you emerge at the other end you can either hitch or wait for the morning Mount

Cook and InterCity buses on to Milford. If you don't emerge onto the road until the afternoon you will have to take the bus away from the fiords to Te Anau.

The Glenorchy taxi-cum-minibus also transports hikers to the beginning of the Rees-Dart walk (another magnificent though more strenuous walk north of Glenorchy) and the Greenstone-Caples walk which intersects the Routeburn so that the two can be done consecutively. A new track was opened a few years ago called the Kepler which is a four-day loop. Transport from Te Anau is straightforward and the changing vegetation and scenery from rainforest to mountains are recommended.

Abel Tasman Track. If hiking up and down mountains and risking three solid days of rain does not appeal, an alternative is the Abel Tasman trek by the shores of Tasman Bay. The 27km coastal walk, which takes most people between two and three days, is mostly along tidal beaches, so check the tide tables posted in the huts. The track does not always follow the beach and a few steep trails require cautious footing. Most people complete this walk comfortably in plimsolls, and so the $570 fee for having a guide and equipment seems excessive. It has become so popular that huts are often jam-packed. Carrying a tent might make the experience more comfortable but it won't be any cheaper. All walkers on the track must obtain a Facilities Use Pass from the Department of Conservation which costs the same whether you camp or sleep in the huts. There is an alternative inland walk in the Abel Tasman National Park with the same starting and finishing points (i.e. Wainui Bay and Marahau) but which is far less crowded.

As this is the sunshine belt of the South Island you are much more likely to have hot weather here, and walking is not confined to the summer season. Abel Tasman National Park Enterprises (528 7801), run by a local called John Wilson, operates a launch service along the coastal length of the walk (Kaiteriteri to Totaranui takes over three hours) which connects with a bus from Motueka (launch price $35, discounts for YHA members). As it makes several stops *en route* it is possible to do just part of the coastal track. The rival bus company is Skyline Travel (548 0285) which operates daily from November to March.

Also in the north-west of the island, the Wangapeka Track (5 to 6 days) and Heaphy Track (4 to 5 days) are more strenuous and also trickier to get to. Heavy rainfall occasionally damages the track and bridges so you should be prepared to ford fast-flowing rivers with the aid of a rope. Both tracks are popular with Kiwis, especially the Heaphy, which was almost as hotly contested by conservationists and developers a few years ago as the Franklin River in Tasmania. Now there is a new controversy, whether or not to allow mountain bikes on the trail. The Department of Conservation has decided to allow a trial period to see what effect it has on the environment and on other trail users.

Mountaineering. Anyone who is tempted to do (or learn about) mountaineering is well catered for in the alpine areas of the South Island. There are courses and routes for complete beginners and for experienced mountaineers. For example Alpine Guides in Mount Cook Village (PO Box 20, Mount Cook; 562 1834) offer climbing courses and guided trips over the Copland Track which connects Mount Cook and Westland National Parks. The high pass is 2150m and so requires the use of crampons, ropes and ice axes. Alpine Recreation Ltd (PO Box 75, Lake Tekapo) run four-day climbing courses in Mount Cook National Park.

Alpine Guides (Westland) Ltd, which is mentioned above in the section on the Glaciers, can airlift you to a high mountain hut from which you ascend to 6,000m and return the same day; the cost is $265. They have recently started one-day introductory ice climbing and abseiling courses on Fox Glacier for $115.

SKIING

There are quite a few fully-serviced ski areas in the South Island, mostly around Queenstown and in the region of Arthur's Pass. Facilities in the commercial fields have increased rapidly, and there are plenty of slopes suitable for both novices and experienced skiers.

Wealthy skiers still rely to a large extent on helicopters to convey them to the tops of mountains and glaciers and in some ski areas this is the only option (e.g. Mount Cook). There are also heli-skiing operators in Fox Glacier, Tekapo, Wanaka and Queenstown. Heli-skiing down virgin mountain sides is primarily of interest to strong experienced skiers who can afford to spend about $400 for a day's skiing.

The Queenstown Area. There are two ski fields near Queenstown: Coronet Peak (18km along the road to Arrowtown) and the Remarkables Ski Area which opened in 1985 in the jauntily-named mountain range (28km east of Queenstown). New snow-making machinery at Coronet Peak came into operation during 1991, extending the season (mid-June to October) and stabilising conditions. The Mount Cook Company continues to invest heavily in the Queenstown ski industry and owns and operates both ski areas. Both ski fields have several chair lifts, plus Coronet Peak has T-bars and other lifts. There are of course all the other facilities expected at ski resorts including lights at Coronet Peak to allow night skiing and the only licensed restaurant in a New Zealand ski area. There is a single ticketing system for both areas, and shuttle bus and lift passes are interchangeable. Lift passes per adult cost $45 and the return trip on the shuttle bus is $18. It is easy to find out about transport and equipment hire in Queenstown, for example at Kiwi Discovery, 37 Camp St (442 7340).

Although the Remarkables has a few routes for advanced skiers, it is best for beginners, with 75 instructors in the ski school. Three-day introductory ski courses can be done for as little as $150 which is excellent value by world skiing standards. They even guarantee that any beginner will be able to ski after one day of lessons. Instruction costs about $25 for a half day and $40 for a full day. One feature of the Remarkables Ski Area is that there is a high level, cross-country ski trail and instruction is available if required.

If you do not want a package, ski equipment hire will cost about $25 a day. It is usually a little trickier booking accommodation on your own during the one-week Queenstown Winter Carnival which has recently been moved forward a week to start on the middle Saturday in July. This annual event involves such unlikely diversions as dog races on the slopes at Coronet Peak and jelly wrestling as well as ordinary ski competitions. The Remarkables area hosts a less flamboyant, more family-oriented, festival during the first week of September (school holidays). Even outside the festival periods Queenstown has a lively atmosphere geared to skiers, with many bars showing videos of the day's skiing, before the disco music is struck up. A few nightspots such as the Penthouse upstairs from Eichardts Hotel stay open until 3am. Consult the local *Mountain Scene* paper for information about pub entertainments.

Other Ski Fields. Snow conditions are also fairly reliable at the more distant ski areas at Cardrona (1½ hours north) and Treble Cone (although bad weather closes down all skiing in the area from time to time). There are shuttle services from Queenstown, however the main access point is Wanaka. Treble Cone is 29km from Wanaka around the southern end of Lake Wanaka and Cardrona is about the same distance due south.

Mount Hutt (not to be confused with Lower Hutt near Wellington) is about an hour's drive west of Christchurch. Accommodation, restaurants and shops are all located in the nearest town of Methven which is a half-hour's drive from the lifts along a toll access road. There are several buses a day to the ski field. The ski season is longer here than elsewhere in New Zealand (early June to mid-October).

Lake Tekapo is another possible venue for skiers. You can cross-country ski on Two Thumbs Range or downhill ski at Round Hill (for beginners) and Mount Dobson (for intermediate skiers). Information on equipment hire and transport is available from the YHA hostel in Lake Tekapo (05056-857).

There are many other centres of alpine activities in the South Island many of which are run by ski clubs and are cheap, friendly and uncommercialised. One such is Mount Robert Snow Field in the Nelson Lakes National Park which is a two-hour walk from the car park. Equipment can be hired in St Arnaud (521 1850) and more information can be had from the Nelson Ski Club (PO Box 344, Nelson). There are several club fields near Arthur's Pass such as the Temple Basin Skifield which is run by the Christchurch Ski Club, Mount Olympus, Mount Cheesman and Craigieburn.

RAFTING

Every article about rafting on the rivers of the South Island goes on about adrenalin rushes and heart-stopping moments of fear. Yet the New Zealand Professional Rafters Association claim that the most dangerous thing about rafting is the drive to the river. So anyone in search of thrills without danger may want to sign up with one of the many competing rafting companies.

As with skiing, Queenstown is the rafting capital of the South Island. The two main rivers are the Shotover (claimed to have once had the second highest concentration of gold of any river in the world) and the Kawarau. On the scale of one (a river fit for swans to glide on) to six (unraftable by all but a few), the Shotover is graded 4 to 5 and the Kawarau is graded 3 to 4. Prices for the 4½ hour Shotover trip vary considerably according to company and season, typically about $90 and possibly more in winter. The Kawaura is an easier (and shorter) expedition, though with four sets of rapids, and costs about $65 year round. The launching points are usually reached by minibus, though there is expensive helicopter access as well.

As wet suits are worn, rafting can take place around the year. The recommended age limits are 13 and 60, and on some a good level of fitness is expected of the participants. All the companies provide transport, wetsuits, foot gear, helmets and life jackets, plus usually some social event at the end such as a picnic, barbecue or sauna. As well as straight rafting trips, several companies offer a six or seven-hour multi-activity package including the bungy jump from Skippers Canyon Bridge, a jetboat ride and a rafting trip; the inclusive price is just less than $200 (or $110 if you skip the bungy-jump). Some operators are beginning to experiment with different kinds of boat; for example a river guide called Eric Billoud has introduced 'funyaks' which are inflatable kayaks to the Kawarau River.

Any travel agency or hostel in Queenstown will steer you towards a rafting trip or combined adventure. The following is a selection of Queenstown rafters:

Danes Shotover Rafts, Queenstown Information Centre, corner Shotover and Camp Sts, PO Box 230; 442 7318.
Kawarau Raft Expeditions, 37 Shotover St, PO Box 266; 442 9792.
Kiwi Discovery, 37 Camp St; 442 7340.
Makin' Waves, Shotover St; 442 8636. The newest rafting company in Queenstown was offering raft trips on the Shotover for $69.

Rafting takes place on many other South Island rivers from the Motueka River in the north to the Taieri River in Otago. Many involve an overnight stay and some are accessible only by helicopter.

An innovative variation of the theme of rafting is surf rafting, i.e. going into the open sea in an inflatable raft. The main location for this activity is Dunedin where it costs $38 for a half hour trip (less YHA discount).

From Motueka you can paddle yourself along the coast in a sea kayak either as part of a guided group or independently. Ocean River Adventures (Sandy Bay Road, Marahau, RD2, Motueka; 527 8266) organise one, two and four day guided sea kayaking trips for $65, $185 and $270, which includes all camping, fishing and snorkelling equipment. This is a good way of exploring the coastline without having to compete for limited hut space along the Coastal Track. Ocean River Adventures also hires out single kayaks for $30 a day and double ones for $55. You would need at least four days to visit the seal colony on Tonga Island. The company continues to provide whitewater raft trips in the Buller Gorge.

FISHING

The merest glance at a map of the South Island reveals the large extent to which the island is covered with a network of lakes, rivers and tributaries. Almost all claim to be prime venues for trout fishing, from Stewart Island (where the season is best in April) to the Motueka River in the north. Fishing lodges abound and often hotel proprietors will be glad to advise on local opportunities. Guiding services are available in all areas and start at $40 an hour/$200 a day. Some of the swankier operations fly their clients into remote wilderness areas and then transport them by jetboat. But it is perfectly feasible to catch a fish after renting tackle and a boat (motorised or dinghy) and spending a peaceful few hours trolling or stationary on Lake Wakatipu, Te Anau, Wanaka, Tekapo, etc.

Trout weighing 2kg are commonplace and some are as large as 5kg. Remember that you will have to obtain a tourist licence and obey the local regulations; enquire at any fishing equipment shop about catch and size restrictions, the dates of the season, etc. (The usual rule is that any fish less than 35cm must be thrown back.) As though to be consistent with their names, rainbow trout will bite gaudy lures whereas brown trout prefer more sober colours.

Vacation Work also publish:

	Paperback	Hardback
The Directory of Summer Jobs Abroad	£7.99	£12.99
The Directory of Summer Jobs in Britain	£7.99	£12.99
The Teenager's Vacation Guide to Work, Study & Adventure	£6.95	£9.95
Work Your Way Around the World	£9.95	£15.95
Working in Tourism — The UK, Europe & Beyond	£9.99	£15.99
Working on Cruise Ships	£7.99	£12.99
Working with the Environment	£9.99	£15.99
Teaching English Abroad	£9.95	£15.95
The Au Pair & Nanny's Guide to Working Abroad	£8.95	£14.95
Working in Ski Resorts — Europe & North America	£8.95	£14.95
Kibbutz Volunteer	£7.99	£12.99
The Directory of Jobs & Careers Abroad	£9.95	£15.95
The International Directory of Voluntary Work	£8.95	£14.95
The Directory of Work & Study in Developing Countries	£7.95	£10.95
Live & Work in France	£8.95	£14.95
Live & Work in the USA & Canada	£8.95	£14.95
Live & Work in Australia & New Zealand	£8.95	£14.95
Live & Work in Scandinavia	£8.95	£14.95
Live & Work in Germany	£8.95	£11.95
Live & Work in Belgium, The Netherlands & Luxembourg	£8.95	£11.95
Live & Work in Spain & Portugal	£8.95	£11.95
Live & Work in Italy	£7.95	£10.95
Travellers Survival Kit Cuba	£9.99	–
Travellers Survival Kit: Russia & the Republics	£9.95	–
Travellers Survival Kit: Western Europe	£8.95	–
Travellers Survival Kit: Eastern Europe	£9.95	–
Travellers Survival Kit: South America	£12.95	–
Travellers Survival Kit: Central America	£8.95	–
Travellers Survival Kit: USA & Canada	£9.95	–
Travellers Survival Kit to the East	£6.95	–
Travellers Survival Kit: Lebanon	£7.99	–
Hitch-hikers' Manual Britain	£3.95	–
Europe — Manual for Hitch-hikers	£4.95	–

Distributors of:

Summer Jobs USA	£9.99	–
Internships (On-the-Job Training Opportunities in the USA)	£15.99	–
Sports Scholarships in the USA	£12.99	–
The Directory of College Accommodations USA	£5.95	–
Emplois d'Ete en France	£7.99	–
Making It in Japan	£8.95	–

Vacation Work Publications, 9 Park End Street, Oxford OX1 1HJ
(Tel 01865-241978. Fax 01865-790885)